T0202956

Lecture Notes in Computer Science 12188

More information about this series at http://www.springer.com/series/7409

Margherita Antona · Constantine Stephanidis (Eds.)

Universal Access in Human-Computer Interaction

Design Approaches and Supporting Technologies

14th International Conference, UAHCI 2020
Held as Part of the 22nd HCI International Conference, HCII 2020
Copenhagen, Denmark, July 19–24, 2020
Proceedings, Part I

 Springer

Editors
Margherita Antona
Foundation for Research
and Technology – Hellas (FORTH)
Heraklion, Crete, Greece

Constantine Stephanidis
University of Crete and Foundation
for Research and Technology – Hellas
(FORTH)
Heraklion, Crete, Greece

ISSN 0302-9743   ISSN 1611-3349 (electronic)
Lecture Notes in Computer Science
ISBN 978-3-030-49281-6   ISBN 978-3-030-49282-3 (eBook)
https://doi.org/10.1007/978-3-030-49282-3

LNCS Sublibrary: SL3 – Information Systems and Applications, incl. Internet/Web, and HCI

This Springer imprint is published by the registered company Springer Nature Switzerland AG
The registered company address is: Gewerbestrasse 11, 6330 Cham, Switzerland

Foreword

The 22nd International Conference on Human-Computer Interaction, HCI International 2020 (HCII 2020), was planned to be held at the AC Bella Sky Hotel and Bella Center, Copenhagen, Denmark, during July 19–24, 2020. Due to the COVID-19 coronavirus pandemic and the resolution of the Danish government not to allow events larger than 500 people to be hosted until September 1, 2020, HCII 2020 had to be held virtually. It incorporated the 21 thematic areas and affiliated conferences listed on the following page.

A total of 6,326 individuals from academia, research institutes, industry, and governmental agencies from 97 countries submitted contributions, and 1,439 papers and 238 posters were included in the conference proceedings. These contributions address the latest research and development efforts and highlight the human aspects of design and use of computing systems. The contributions thoroughly cover the entire field of human-computer interaction, addressing major advances in knowledge and effective use of computers in a variety of application areas. The volumes constituting the full set of the conference proceedings are listed in the following pages.

The HCI International (HCII) conference also offers the option of "late-breaking work" which applies both for papers and posters and the corresponding volume(s) of the proceedings will be published just after the conference. Full papers will be included in the "HCII 2020 - Late Breaking Papers" volume of the proceedings to be published in the Springer LNCS series, while poster extended abstracts will be included as short papers in the "HCII 2020 - Late Breaking Posters" volume to be published in the Springer CCIS series.

I would like to thank the program board chairs and the members of the program boards of all thematic areas and affiliated conferences for their contribution to the highest scientific quality and the overall success of the HCI International 2020 conference.

This conference would not have been possible without the continuous and unwavering support and advice of the founder, Conference General Chair Emeritus and Conference Scientific Advisor Prof. Gavriel Salvendy. For his outstanding efforts, I would like to express my appreciation to the communications chair and editor of HCI International News, Dr. Abbas Moallem.

July 2020

Constantine Stephanidis

Foreword

HCI International 2020 Thematic Areas and Affiliated Conferences

Thematic areas:

- HCI 2020: Human-Computer Interaction
- HIMI 2020: Human Interface and the Management of Information

Affiliated conferences:

- EPCE: 17th International Conference on Engineering Psychology and Cognitive Ergonomics
- UAHCI: 14th International Conference on Universal Access in Human-Computer Interaction
- VAMR: 12th International Conference on Virtual, Augmented and Mixed Reality
- CCD: 12th International Conference on Cross-Cultural Design
- SCSM: 12th International Conference on Social Computing and Social Media
- AC: 14th International Conference on Augmented Cognition
- DHM: 11th International Conference on Digital Human Modeling and Applications in Health, Safety, Ergonomics and Risk Management
- DUXU: 9th International Conference on Design, User Experience and Usability
- DAPI: 8th International Conference on Distributed, Ambient and Pervasive Interactions
- HCIBGO: 7th International Conference on HCI in Business, Government and Organizations
- LCT: 7th International Conference on Learning and Collaboration Technologies
- ITAP: 6th International Conference on Human Aspects of IT for the Aged Population
- HCI-CPT: Second International Conference on HCI for Cybersecurity, Privacy and Trust
- HCI-Games: Second International Conference on HCI in Games
- MobiTAS: Second International Conference on HCI in Mobility, Transport and Automotive Systems
- AIS: Second International Conference on Adaptive Instructional Systems
- C&C: 8th International Conference on Culture and Computing
- MOBILE: First International Conference on Design, Operation and Evaluation of Mobile Communications
- AI-HCI: First International Conference on Artificial Intelligence in HCI

Conference Proceedings Volumes Full List

http://2020.hci.international/proceedings

14th International Conference on Universal Access in Human-Computer Interaction (UAHCI 2020)

Program Board Chairs: **Margherita Antona, Foundation for Research and Technology – Hellas (FORTH), Greece, and Constantine Stephanidis, University of Crete and Foundation for Research and Technology – Hellas (FORTH), Greece**

- João Barroso, Portugal
- Rodrigo Bonacin, Brazil
- Ingo Bosse, Germany
- Laura Burzagli, Italy
- Pedro J. S. Cardoso, Portugal
- Carlos Duarte, Portugal
- Pier Luigi Emiliani, Italy
- Vagner Figueredo de Santana, Brazil
- Andrina Granic, Croatia
- Gian Maria Greco, Spain
- Simeon Keates, UK
- Georgios Kouroupetroglou, Greece
- Patrick M. Langdon, UK
- Barbara Leporini, Italy
- I. Scott MacKenzie, Canada
- John Magee, USA
- Jorge Martín-Gutiérrez, Spain
- Troy McDaniel, USA
- Silvia Mirri, Italy
- Stavroula Ntoa, Greece
- Federica Pallavicini, Italy
- Ana Isabel Paraguay, Brazil
- Hugo Paredes, Portugal
- Enrico Pontelli, USA
- João M. F. Rodrigues, Portugal
- Frode Eika Sandnes, Norway
- Volker Sorge, UK
- Hiroki Takada, Japan
- Kevin C. Tseng, Taiwan
- Gerhard Weber, Germany

The full list with the Program Board Chairs and the members of the Program Boards of all thematic areas and affiliated conferences is available online at:

http://www.hci.international/board-members-2020.php

HCI International 2021

The 23rd International Conference on Human-Computer Interaction, HCI International 2021 (HCII 2021), will be held jointly with the affiliated conferences in Washington DC, USA, at the Washington Hilton Hotel, July 24–29, 2021. It will cover a broad spectrum of themes related to Human-Computer Interaction (HCI), including theoretical issues, methods, tools, processes, and case studies in HCI design, as well as novel interaction techniques, interfaces, and applications. The proceedings will be published by Springer. More information will be available on the conference website: http://2021.hci.international/.

General Chair
Prof. Constantine Stephanidis
University of Crete and ICS-FORTH
Heraklion, Crete, Greece
Email: general_chair@hcii2021.org

http://2021.hci.international/

Contents – Part I

Robots in Universal Access

Contents – Part II

Universal Access to Learning and Education

Intelligent Assistive Environments

Design for All Theory, Methods and Practice

Universal Design of ICT: A Historical Journey from Specialized Adaptations Towards Designing for Diversity

Miriam E. N. Begnum[1,2](✉)

[1] NAV Norwegian Labour and Welfare Administration, Department of Design,
Sannergt. 2, 0557 Oslo, Norway
miriam@begnum.no
[2] NTNU, Department of Design, Teknologiveien 22, 2815 Gjøvik, Norway

Abstract. Over the last decades, the field of computer science has moved from specialized adaptations and add-on assistive technologies, toward universal solutions catering to a diverse set of user needs. Two paradigm shifts have arguably occurred on this journey: 1) a shift in disability perspective (from a medical model to a psychosocial and situated model) and 2) a shift from reactive accessibility efforts to proactive inclusive design efforts. In addition, we have changed our perception of the end-user (from 'Mr. Average' to situated individuals), have expanded our disciplinary epistemologies (from positivist objective knowledge to critical and empathic qualitative insights), and changed the way we build digital solutions (from plan-based with little user contact to iterative with high user contact). This article tells the story of this journey, and how these shifts have all influenced the way we think today. We argue that different ways of thinking about and arguing for universal design today are not necessary confrontations – but can be seen as evolvements over time to complement the different societal systems in which we are designing.

Keywords: Universal design · Disability model · Design for all best practice

1 Introduction

Universal design (UD) of Information and Communication Technology (ICT) is today interdisciplinary and multifaceted, with different types of regulations, standards, principles, processes and disciplinary practices that have matured and changed over time. Given the interdisciplinarity, practitioners in the field of UD of ICT hold different schools-of-thoughts and disciplinary points-of-view. Further, we practice under heterogenous national systems with different UD regulations, within different sectors and markets. As such, it can be hard for young researchers and practitioners struggle to identify the common guidelines for UD of ICT; agreed upon recommendations towards 'good practice'. By highlighting key paradigm shifts from the past, the current rationale and values of the UD of ICT movement becomes clearer.

This historical outlook also provides a platform for discussing some of the apparent current confrontations in the field. When designing digital solutions, most agree the ability to utilize a variety of design approaches is beneficial in order to match a diverse

M. Antona and C. Stephanidis (Eds.): HCII 2020, LNCS 12188, pp. 3–18, 2020.
https://doi.org/10.1007/978-3-030-49282-3_1

set of aims and constraints. However, diverging perspectives on an epistemological level is somewhat more confusing and polarizing. At the end of the paper, we therefore reflect on some of the challenges we face today when designing digital solutions to fit a diverse set of user needs. In relation to the different approaches and terminologies in use, we ask: Could these all be viewed as part of the Universal Design movements? And what important next contributions are needed on the continued journey towards designing for diversity?

2   Research Approach

The research approach applied in this paper, is an unstructured literature survey, qualitatively summarizing evidence on a topic to provide an overview [1]. In terms of extensiveness, the review was ended based on a feeling of literature command relative to its scope and length [2]. Chronologic and thematic structures are combined to tell a story of the theoretical history of a field; similar to that of a framework review [2]. From this 'theoretical base', we reflect and propose viewpoints for future discussions.

3   An Inclusive World: Universal Solutions for Diverse Users

3.1   Shifting Disability Perspectives

Modern parents are likely to stand in the principal's office, demanding their special needs child get the best education possible. The idea that we should hide away our children with disabilities due to shame, is absurd. Whether it is acceptable or not to exclude persons with disabilities (PwD), is similarly argued to be a product of a cultural perception – for example that disability represents a divine punishment or that disability means less capable [3]. Different models for defining 'disability' co-exist in our culture (see Table 1) and though often not reflected upon, the way we think about and understand disability and diversity, affect how we behave, the societal rules we accept and whether we recognize inclusion or exclusion.

Disability as an Act of God, Illness or Victimhood. *Moral (or religious) model*, under which a disability is viewed as a self-inflicted (or divine) punishment [4, 5] is an outdated view on disability. However, some may still think of a disability as a test of faith or a God-given opportunity for character development [6]. Another somewhat outdated way to thinking about disability, is of disability as a 'disease' or an individual abnormality. This understanding of disability as a person's negative deviation from normal human bodily function is called the "medical model" [5]. In 1980, the World Health Organization (WHO) reflected this model: *"a disability is any restriction or lack (resulting from an impairment) of ability to perform an activity in the manner or within the range considered normal for a human being"* [7].

The medical model is also called the *illness model*, as it seeks to correct (treat, reduce or repair) any 'abnormal' bodily functions. It has two other key offshoots models. First, the *rehabilitation* model believes that with adequate effort on the part of the person with the disability, the disability itself can be overcome [8]. WHO split disabilities into the categories: temporary or permanent, reversible or irreversible, and progressive or regressive. The rehabilitation model is critiqued for not taking permanent disabilities into account. We see this view in arguments over e.g. diabetes reversion. Second, the *expert (or professional) model* takes the view that a professional (typically a medical expert) should identify a disability and create a plan for treatment or assistance [9]. A person with a disability is in this view assumed to benefit from any intervention to correct or minimize his/her 'deficiency'.

All three models originated in the 18th centuries [10]. They place the source of the problem within a single impaired person and as such solutions are found by focusing on the individual [5]. From this follows that if a design does not fit you due to a disability, it is your deviation from 'normal' that is wrong and must be corrected – not the design itself.

Finally, among the older models on disability, we find the (still widespread) *charity (or tragedy) model* [4]. This view arose in the 19th century, differentiating disabled people from other disadvantaged community groups and categorizing them as aged, sick, insane or defectives, and deserving of charity. Today, this model is critiqued for depicting disabled persons as victims, deserving of pity and aid [9].

Disability as Multifaceted. The above described individual models faced pushback from PwD [11] as well as from the nursing profession [8]. Disability movements state individuals themselves are fully capable of making decisions about their life. This is reflected in the *empowerment model*, which holds that disabled persons have the most insights into their own disabilities, and thusly the ones that should be in charge of any treatment plan (with professional expert as advisors or service providers). This viewpoint seeks to provide the individual with autonomy, power, choice and control; and opposes the expert and charity models.

We now view disability as something more complex and multifaceted [8]. The medical model is somewhat modified in the *spectrum model*, where disability is defined along a scale of 'normal' function. The label 'disability' and its seriousness are derived from functional ability threshold levels (we start to talk about mild, moderate or severe disabilities).

Other disability models are also taken up, for example related to social security schemes. The *legitimacy model* recognizes that disability can be defined in many ways, thus stipulates any individual rights should be based on personal needs for assistance and adaptations [9]. The *economic model* approaches disability from an economic analysis viewpoint, and defines a disability based on a person's ability to work, and the degree to which economical and productive conditions are affected [6]. It is mostly used by policy makers to assess distribution of benefits [5]. The challenge is one of creating societal systems that support individuals in a cost-effective manner, promoting equity with incentives and subsidies while decreasing stigma [5].

Disability as Contextual. In the 70s and 80s, the *social model* is promoted by disability movements, as a response to the medical model. This is also called the *barrier model*. The social model was articulated in 1976 [10]. It argues that society creates disabilities through a lack of awareness and concern about those who may require some modifications to live full, productive lives [8]. In this model, disability is a complex collection of conditions, many of which are socially created [9]. Disability is now an exclusion experience and a socially constructed phenomenon – in contrast to previous models that place the responsibility of 'overcoming the disability' on the individual. From this view follows that if a design does not fit you, it is not *you* that is 'wrong', but the design.

If disabilities are mainly socially created, it is a societal responsibility to remove attitudes that exclude from participation – instead of placing the responsibility of "overcoming" the disability on the individual. If society has created physical and social barriers, it must take responsibility for tearing these down. The social model is as such linked to the *(human) right-based model*, which focuses on how disabilities should not affect a person's opportunities for participating in the society, nor the access to products, goods and services [4]. This model gained traction in the 1980s, and political discourses led to a range of laws embracing the rights of PwD [9].

The critique of the social model is not acknowledging that the society cannot accommodate or adapt for *all* lacking abilities in *all* contexts [4]. However, 'softer' versions of the social model appear. The *social adapted model* acknowledges that individual disabilities may somewhat limit equal participation in a non-disabled community, but still upholds that disabilities are overall mainly socially created [4, 9].

A nurse with a disability is credited for developing the *interface model*, stating that a disability exists at the meeting point between a medical diagnosis and the environmental [8]. Under this model, the role of the nurse is altered to support the preferences of PwD, while offering treatment. This is in line with the views of the empowerment model and merges the social and medical models [4].

The *biopsychosocial model* focuses explicitly on the interaction between a person and the contextual factors. As such, it draws on the interface model developed by the nurse profession but emphasizes the environment – not treatment. Disability is viewed as connected to both bodily functions (physical and mental) and social factors (possibilities for participation in a specific context and environment). In 2002, the WHO's International Classification of Functioning, Disability and Health (ICF) was updated to reflect the biopsychosocial model instead of the medical [14]. This was a paradigm shift, impacting the role and responsibility of designers.

The *(Nordic) gap (or relational) model* of disability is similar to the interface and social adapted models in promoting social inclusion for people with disability in the community by looking at people–environment interaction [12, 13]. It emerged in the early 2000s and overlaps with the biopsychosocial model in viewing disability as contextually created. The gap model states disabilities are appearing if there is a gap between a person's abilities and the expectations of the social, digital, cognitive or physical environments or interactions. The role of the designer or developer under this model is to minimize and prevent gaps from occurring. This means the aims, needs, emotions, abilities, cultures etc. of the users must be identified and taken into account.

Disability as Embodied Experience. In rejecting the medical model view of disability as something 'abnormal' with the body (to be fixed), in favor of viewing disability as contextual (barriers being problems to be solved), disability is normalized. Looking at varying abilities as part of normal human traits leads to the conclusion that bodies (including brains) are of equal value regardless of being labeled as 'disabled' or not.

The *identity (or affirmative) model* shares the social model's understanding of disability as socially constructed, but extends it with viewing disability as an aspect of who a person is [6]. This identity is viewed as positive; as a marker of membership in a minority identity, much like gender or race – and not as a tragedy for an individual [6]. Critical disability theorist is criticizing the "ableist understandings of disability" and not valuing atypical embodiments [15]. This is a direct reaction to the still common charity view, and is related to Disability Pride movements [9].

The identity model is extended in the *cultural model* [6]. While the medical model and the social model emphasize one factors each – body or context – the cultural model include a wider range of factors. The cultural approach focuses on how different notions of disability operate in the context of a specific culture.

Table 1. Overview of Disability Models

Disability Models
Moral: A disability is a self-inflicted or divine punishment.
Medical: A disability is a negative deviation from normal human bodily function.
Rehabilitation: Treatment to overcome the disability.
Expert: An expert identifies the disability and plan treatment to correct deficiency.
Charity: A disability is a personal, undeserved tragedy; deserving aid and sympathy.
Empowerment: The disabled person should be in charge of treatment or assistance.
Spectrum: A disability is defined along a range of seriousness based on ability.
Economic: A disability is defined by (in)ability to work and productive conditions.
Legitimacy: Disabilities can be defined in many ways; base rights on personal needs.
Social: Disabilities are mainly socially created, thus societal responsibility to remove.
Right-based: Disabilities should not affect opportunities for participation in society.
Social adapted: Individual disability may limit, but societal responsibility to reduce.
Interface: Support the preferences of persons with disability, while offering treatment
Gap: Disability is contextually created; the gap between person and situated context.
Biopsychosocial: Disability defined by interaction between person and context.
Identity: Disability is a part of personal identity.
Marked: Disabled and their families is a large and influential customer base.
Cultural: Disability operate in the context of a specific culture.
Limit: All humans are faced with limits.

The *marked model* combines a minority rights with a consumerist model, that looks at personal identity [9]. The marked model view PwD and their families and friends as a large and influential customer base with consumer power. In contrast, the *limit model* seeks to avoid categorizations such as 'disabled', 'abled' or 'normal'. It emphasizes that all humans face individual limits (no humans can fly, not all can climb a mountain, some cannot walk) and focuses on embodied experiences and commonalities between people across typical categories. The limit model deviates from social and identity models by taking the stance that not all limits are 'normal' or 'good' – and recognizing that some people want to overcome certain of their limits [6].

Summary. There is a paradigm shift in the 2000s, where we move from:

- An official WHO definition of disability as a 'wrong' within the individual.
- The default notion that PwD needs treatment and are less capable.
- Making individuals responsible for fixing their disability issues.

   To:

- An official WHO definition of disability as 'limitations' in contextual interactions.
- The default notion that disabilities should not affect opportunities for participation.
- Making society responsible for creating inclusive contexts.

3.2   From Reactive to Proactive Accessibility Efforts

For coming generations, it may be hard to envision a world without phones, texts, e-books, remote controls or speech technologies. Early versions of all these innovations were created as technological adaptations for PwD. It appears PwD are not only inventors of groundbreaking technologies, but also early technology adopters. Many was designed by end-users themselves or for close acquaintances. For example, Captain Fraser lost his sight in WW1 and got tired of learning Braille, so he led the team that innovated LPs and released the first talking book in 1935 [16]. Chat rooms were developed by two deaf researchers as a long-distance phone alternative for deaf people in 1964, and text messaging was developed in 1972 by Cerf, who was hard-of-hearing and wanted easy communication with his wife and friends [17]. Pellegrino Turri invented the typewriter for his blind friend in 1808 [3].

Moving through 1970–1990, the personal computer is making its presence known. We get the mouse, keyboard, icons, windows, applications and dialogue boxes. As before, adaptations are created for persons with different needs. Assistive technologies (AT) are built, such as screen readers and screen magnifiers for users with visual impairments, key-guards and switch systems for persons with motor impairments. Stakeholders such as the National Federation of the Blind and the Trace Center collaborates with tech-giants such as IBM and Microsoft [17] to research and create specialized adaptations. For example, Thatcher was inspired by his blind professor to pioneer the screen reader – which was released by IBM in 1986 [18]. However, accessibility adaptations are lagging behind mainstream innovations, as Stephanidis [19] expresses: *"Each generation of technology (...) caused a new 'generation' of accessibility problems to blind users"*. The accessibility efforts become increasingly reactive.

In 1990, the Americans with Disability Act is legislated and in 1998, Section 508 requires information technology is made accessible to people with disabilities. Stakeholders, including the Trace Center, now promotes a more proactive approach to accessibility – moving away from third-party add-ons to provide out-of-the-box accessibility at no extra cost to users [20]. We start thinking about accessibility as something to be designed from the start. Standards and guidelines to support technical accessibility are developed. The WCAG criteria is particularly impactful; WCAG 1.0 in 1999, evolving to version 2.0 in 2008, and 2.1 in 2018 [21]. The move from reactive accessibility efforts to proactive inclusive design efforts is also a paradigm shift. In embedding accessibility into mainstream solutions, we move towards UD.

Summary. There is a paradigm shift in the late 90s, where we move:

- From specialized design as 'add-on' in a reactive accessibility approach.
- To a proactive accessibility approach focused on technical standards.

3.3   From Mr. Average to Situated Individuals

The discipline Human Computer Interaction is born in the early 80s, merging engineering with psychology and human factors [22]. Focus is on creating interfaces that are easy to understand and use, and during the 80s guidelines such as Shneiderman's direct manipulation of objects (1982) and golden rules of interface design (1986), Norman's gulfs of execution and evaluation (also 1986) and Nielsen usability heuristics and heuristic evaluation (1990) was developed [23]. Initially, this development was focused on 'Mr. Average' – a user that is male, white, western, middle class, educated, English speaking, able-bodied, young, tech-savvy, healthy and cis [24].

With the increase in digital solutions, we start worry about novice users with low digital competence. With this realization, we start to broaden our user focus. Initial focus was on access to computer technology. On a global level we started to understand that poverty leads to disability, and that disability leads to poverty. On a societal level, public spaces were used to promote digital competence. However, research found it was not so easy to reach non-digital users. Digital divides are often more complex than simply physical access. Some influential factors on usage uptake was found to be culture, race and socio-economic background. We realize people with different cultures, ages and genders might have different preferences and desires.

We discuss whether the system should automatically adapt to the user, or if the user should be able to adapt the system; we talk about multi-modality and the option to choose input and output devices according to your preferences. The aim to create use adaptations to cater to a diversity of needs is supported by the technological advancements. Through dialogue independence, the software system is separated from the user interface, enabling the flexibility to move towards catering to diverse users within one solution. With the new accessibility regulations, users with disabilities are added to the expanded focus. Age, digital literacy, capabilities and culture perspectives are now thought of aspects of marginalized user groups in danger of exclusion.

Another major shift is when moving to the contextual disability models – such as the gap, the social and the biopsychosocial models. Now, we start thinking about contextual needs – expanding UD to cover non-disabled users. We slowly start to view our users as situated individuals, with their own unique experiences and needs that may put they at risk for exclusion in a particular contextual setting.

Summary. We move from thinking mostly about 'Mr. Average' (a white, western, young male) to thinking about different user groups (elderly, disabled, non-western) – and from this move towards thinking about our users as uniquely situated individuals in their particular contexts of use and with their subjective embodied experiences.

3.4   Increased User Contact and Changed Methodology

As digital solutions became more widespread, we needed a design approach that could provide early user feedback. There was a move from mainly doing late large-scale usability testing in plan-based development, to agile and iterative process models. Further, user (human) centered design (UCD) increases its uptake.

The developer and designer initially worked at a distance from the user, often with a task-based focus on user needs. The designer observed, designed, improved and acted as the expert. User needs specification could be expressed through use cases; and systems designed using UML models. Interfaces could be user tested in labs.

If viewing the professional designer or developer as the main expert within a typical (post-)positivist epistemology, it makes sense to get the expert to articulate objective, static, generalizable insights, and specify precise criteria to make sure the correct solution is built, in the correct way [25]. In such a frame of mind, the preferred methods would be quantitative – such as summative user testing and usability metrics benchmarking, eye tracking, surveys, marked research, statistical analysis, expert analysis, task analysis and so forth.

However, as the agile world opens up and cross-disciplinary negotiations start, it makes more sense to view the practitioner as an interpreter within both critical and constructivist paradigms; facilitating dialogue and reach a compromise between varying stakeholder. UCD is founded on user needs and focused on understanding the user in contexts of use, and advocates involving or testing with users early on. Identifying solutions that fit stakeholders' needs within the defined constraints (which may change over time) fit well with the agile process of continuous updating the goal based on new insights and circumstances.

UCD emphasizes understanding users and their requirements, conducting iterative prototyping and evaluation, and are typically quite task focused. UCD approaches with minimal user contact are most common in agile projects [26]. Here, lean data collection makes sense; and using methods such as direct user feedback, guerilla testing, workshops, web analytics etc.

More political stances by the designer or developer – such as participatory design (PD) was introduced as early as in the 70s – but did not gain the same popularity as UCD. Viewing technology as non-neutral and co-constructive, PD seeks to empower the end-user, and focuses on power dynamics [27]. User involvement and ethical design is also important [28]. PD advocates viewing user input and practical experience as alternative expert interpretations and argues users and stakeholders should be equal partners. As design thinking approaches becomes popular, co-creation becomes more mainstream. Both PD and design thinking apply critical design perspectives. Design thinking does not seek to empower end users – but rather support divergent ideas. Still, both approaches promote methodological approaches that builds relationships with end-users.

UD is adopted in 2006 by the UN Convention on the right of PwD, and defined as: *"the design of services, products, environment and systems so that they may be used, accessed and understood by all people, to the greatest extent possible"* [29]. Note that the terms are no longer specifically focused on disabled users – but is rather "for all". UD is cleverly branded as 'good design', hereby countering resistance from designers who feel accessible design would hamper creative processes and increase costs [15].

With accessibility regulations of ICT and new ways of defining disability, we move from specialized "add on" accessibility to accessibility compliance with specified standard. However, adhering to technical accessibility standards does not automatically ensure inclusive experiences and usability in real life [30, 31]. This is not typically reflected in regulations, which tend to refer to measurable standards – and not qualitative benchmarks. For example, though UD recognizes the necessity of ATs extending design, testing AT compatibility in real-life is not an emphasized procedure. Increasingly, we have started to talk about checking both 'technical' and 'usable' accessibility in order to emphasize this point.

As emphasizing accessibility compliance to technical standards becomes a popular strategy for meeting diverse user needs in computer science, we sense a troubling simplification of UD concept. Shneiderman [32] theorizes universal access is not sufficient to ensure universal usability due to the complexity of computing services. I believe the issue is also related to changed development process models. In a user-centered, innovative and experimental agile team, accessibility checklists does not work well as a one-time quality inspection step – particularly not when completed towards the end of a project [33].

In order to make sure more than the average user was considered, educational information on diverse needs are built to help the designer understand diverse user needs. Initially, personas and other mapping tools are used to aid the designer in doing UD by communicate the needs of user groups with disabilities. Using these tools, we move towards more specified guidelines on who and what should be considered. This helps key user groups and diversity needs to not be forgotten, however, does not guarantee that all important perspectives, are included.

As the developer and designer must focus on interactions in the contexts of use, checklists and guidelines become too limited to cater to these diverse and contextual needs. Additionally, personas and other mapping tools are criticized for stereotyping the users. Several activists argue that basing UD standards on human statistics reinforced norms of race, gender, and ability [15]. There is now a tension between what is called 'representative thinking' versus involvement of real people in the process.

There is also discussions of costs, both of user centeredness and of UD. We start hearing the argument that one for all solution prove difficult in some cases, because requirements for one group could be exclusive to one another – just as the social model was critiqued [34]. However, the impossibility to really design for everyone could be viewed as inherent to design, rather than a characteristic of UD [35].

Perhaps to counter this argument, pro-UD arguments often fit a marked model on disability; framing disability as a part of consumers identities similarly to other personal aspects. In this model, one would argue for UD based on the economic benefits of a larger marked. Tapping into edge-case needs to trigger innovation is also argued for based on economic opportunity. Looking back, we can see how specialized developments for disabled users has transformed mainstream use of technology. This supports the argument of the innovative power in edge-case approaches.

Edge-case design is also promoted within inclusive design. Inclusive design is both advocating for specialized design approach (designing for distinct users with specific needs), and for focusing on user diversity and (avoiding) design exclusion causes. It is a user-centered approach, advocating collaborative design and user involvement. With regards to specialized design, focus is on disabled users, in particular perceptual, cognitive and physical disabilities, but also on non-disabled users under suboptimal conditions of use. The idea of edge-case design as inclusive approach, is that if you design solutions that fit the edges of user needs, your solution will also fit the average.

We see that the UD principles on flexibility aligns well with tech trends such as need for responsive design with rapid development and heterogeneity of mobile devices. Context of use becomes increasingly important, as technology becomes pervasive. Generally, there seems to be a slow shift from relying on quantitative data and expert inspections, to appreciating situated insights and co-creation. By moving in this direction, we start valuing in-depth understanding as a tool for design – more than the idea of objectivity and generalizations of user needs.

Summary. Related to the way we approach the design and development of digital solutions, we have changed:

- From an emphasis on user facts, to an emphasis on user empathy.
- From late and elaborate user testing, to early and lean user feedback.
- From generalized and stereotyped needs, to diversity aspects and contextual needs.
- From low user contact, to workshops, co-creation and user involvement.
- From neutral views on technology, towards value-based and critical design.
- From accessibility and AT focus, towards lived experiences.

4   Discussion

Combined with the bio-psychosocial model, modern legislation on UD of ICT reflects socio-economic, democratic and ethical reasons for ensuring all citizens are able to use solutions. UD can be viewed as a concept and political strategy that has evolved from social and rights-based disability models; focusing on disabling barriers and enabling environments [12]. Establishment of legislation and guidelines is a significant step toward ensuring UD; however, this alone does not guarantee successful change and implementation. The story told in this article emphasizes cultural changes in our societies, which has broadened and changed the disciplinary field. A significant paradigm shift in the understanding of disabilities, from a medical model to a contextual model, was not the only one. There was a coinciding shift from add-on accessibility to UD. Together, these shifts introduced radical changes to the way we look at disability, and thus the role of the designer/developer in creating digital solutions.

Can the different approaches and terms in use be viewed as part of the UD movement? The term 'universal design' is today used interchangeably with terms such as 'universal access', 'design for all' (DfA) and 'inclusive design'. We find different practical design approaches applied. The question then is; do they represent the same movement and community? To this I would answer; Yes.

I hypothesize the co-existence of different terms is partly due to different legislation in different countries using different terms, more than regional differences in how we approach UD. However, if you study the approaches as reported in literature, you see differences. UD historically focused on the end result, and how to measure this. This may be why the 7 design principles for UD are quite similar to a checklist. The word 'universal' in UD may be interpreted as referring to a set of principles that are stable, timeless and value free. But UD is neither of these things.

UD as an approach is not contradicting the recognition of accessibility as "good design" for disabled users. Today, accessibility is usually regarded as a precondition for UD. However, the notion that UD is presented as an improved alternative to accessible design – where focus is on meeting prescribed requirements for use by people with disabilities – is a miscommunication. UD was supposed to extend accessible design (see Fig. 1) [36]. Nor is it correct that UD is contrasting adaptable design (enabling individual modifications to a standard design) [15]. AT compatibility and supporting the flexibility to personalize and adapt the system are highly relevant for ensuring technological variety. UD draws on flexibility – which is expressed in UD principle 2 "flexibility in use" [36–38].

Both these miscommunications are problematic, as a) accessibility versus UD has been blurred, and b) the room for flexible adaptation according to needs appeared too small to be practical. But as UD sought to extend accessibility and adaptivity, there is no inherent conflict between inclusive design and UD approaches.

Standards and guidelines are regarded as practical and fit requirements specification approaches, but not as a replacement for direct user testing or user involvement. Looking at where we are today on UD in the computer science, I believe most would agree that a best practice approach for UD uses early direct user contact [39]. Further, many agree with active involvement of end-users in co-creative workshops and the importance of user empathy [39]. As such, I believe we are collectively moving away from (only doing) a checklist-approach and towards adhering to the inclusive design approaches. However, we sense a gap between those that adhere to generalizable standards to reflect user needs (representing user groups through stereotyped check-lists), and those that argue for active user involvement and empowerment.

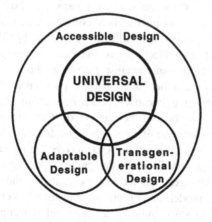

Fig. 1. Relationship between accessible, adaptable, transgenerational, and universal design [36].

Design approaches within UD movements have been expanding [15]. I argue that newer approaches such as inclusive design could be regarded as more mature or updated versions of UD. Compared to the UD literature, inclusive design more explicitly focused on edge cases, exclusion cases, and apply more critical design perspectives – and turning away from the traditional values of objectivity. We see that the inclusive design dimensions (compared to the design principles in UD) read more like guidelines for the design practice; 1. Recognize diversity and uniqueness, 2. Inclusive process and tools, and 3. Consider the broader context and impact of the design.

It is argued that UD is as of yet not in harmony with critical disability theory and disability acceptance; for example, that UD holds hidden values [40]. To this I would respond; we are on our way. Design approaches increasingly hold values from critical and participatory design. Still, our design approaches vary, and are influenced by the resources at hand and the constraints we operate under [41, 42].

It is true that the UD movement historically has not focused much on perspectives such as classism, sizeism, homophobia, transphobia and gender expressions. Now, we seem to move towards designing for as diverse a range of people as possible and merging of UD with diversity movements; regarding users as individuals; with unique and situated needs. In this move, there appears to be an increasing overlap between (dis)ability movements, feminism, anti-racism and other political movements. For example, the limit model of 2009 overlaps with intersectionality views.

Intersectionality suggests that people have unique experiences based on the combination of their identities, and that these can be oppressive multiple times (for example as a non-white, non-cis, disabled single mother) [43]. Further, that it is impossible to understand discrimination and oppression by considering one singular identity. I also see the identity model increasingly reflected in the way we speak, as we are moving away from labels such as 'an autistic person', 'a blind person', 'a poor person'. Instead, we now recognize that any challenges are a part of us, and say a person 'with fatigue', 'with autism', 'who is blind', 'with low income', and so forth.

It is argued that most of us are still on a journey – both in our personal and professional capacity [43]. As an international community, we are living or designing in quite different societal systems, with different cultures and politically correct stances, different regulations and legal mechanisms and different populations. D'souza [44] argues UD may come under functionalist paradigm (because it caters to utility), pragmatic (because it is instrumental in nature), positivistic (because it strives for universal principles), normative (because it prescribes certain rules) and critical theorist paradigms (because it gives voice to the oppressed). I argue this fluency provides an advantage to the UD community. Different arguments for UD, strategies for promoting UD and methodologies for implementing UD may be fitting based on the organizational or societal system we are living or designing within, and over time.

While our context changes, the technology changes, the political environment changes, and our process models and organizational structures changes, the UD of ICT movement have started to value building a deeper relationship with users, avoiding stereotyping or guessing their needs and seeking to understand real lived exclusion experiences and contextual needs. The 'user sensitive inclusive design' approach may thus be indicative of the direction of UD approaches today – merging ID with empathic design traditions and PD [45, 46]. Different approaches to UD of ICT are part of the same story towards the ultimate goal of solutions that fits as many as possible of their users, and that are experienced as inclusive.

What are the next steps on the journey forward? With an increasing recognition of the individual lived experiences of users, intersectionality perspectives may inspire critical design perspectives and participatory design approaches that focus on power dynamics [43, 47]. Intersectionality is focused on individuality, and though the notion of designing for all fits with designing for lived experiences (and e.g. the limit model on disabilities), it is arguably hard to design for individuals within a checklist-based approach to UD [48]. The latest model-based tools (from the inclusive design movement) merge the support of generalized specification based on statistics on user needs with the mapping of individual lived experiences [49]. Looking ahead, more tools facilitating collecting the insights of situated, embodied, individual experiences could be beneficial, to fit different situations and individual design preferences. It is also argued that more diversity guidelines are needed in the design of the design tools themselves, to fit the diversity of users and designers to be involved [50]. Further, including marginalized users and being sensitive to their needs means the design process and methods must also be inclusive. Here, we still face some challenges in making the UD process inclusive. For example, related to co-creative workshop-techniques, these currently largely depend only on visual design methods and visual communications – and are as such excluding persons with visual impairments.

5 Conclusion

In this paper we have outlined some of the different stances related to universal design (UD) in the field of computer science. This is a story of a journey from specialized adaptations, via accessibility checklists and generalized summaries of marginalized users, towards designing for a diverse set of situated and individual user needs. We ask, related to the perceived diverging disability perspectives, terminologies and methodological approaches in use; Can all the different approaches and terms in use be viewed as part of the UD movement? And what important next contributions are needed on the continued journey towards designing for diversity? We argue that the article overviews how over time, culture and policies change, and new technologies emerge –potentially creating new barriers or possibilities for inclusion. Reflecting these changes, methodological approaches and tools are created and updated to advance the disciplinary practice. We further show how one set of guidelines seldom replace the old radically, rather, they usually update the original, extend the original, provide alternatives to the original or merge with the original. As such, I argue that different arguments and stances that have evolved over time, though diverging, belong to the same movement. Further, that the richness of views and approaches within the UD community could be viewed as a collective strength rather than as a divider.

References

1. Robinson, P., Lowe, J.: Literature reviews vs systematic reviews. Australian and New Zealand J. Public Health **39**(2), 103 (2015)
2. Merriam, S.B.: Qualitative Research, A Guide to Design and Implementation. 2nd edn, Wiley, San Francisco (2009). Jossey-Bass, A Wiley Imprint
3. Lazar, J., Goldstein, D., Taylor, A.: Ensuring Digital Accessibility through Process and Policy. Morgan Kaufmann, Burlington (2015). Elsevier
4. Begnum, M.E.N.: Views on Universal Design and Disabilities among Norwegian Experts on Universal Design of ICT, in Norsk konferanse for organisasjoners bruk av IT (NOKOBIT). Open Journal Systems: Bergen, Norway (2016)
5. Rialland, A.: Models of Disability: keys to perspectives (2001)
6. Retief, M., Letšosa, R.: Models of disability: a brief overview. HTS Teologiese Stud./ Theolog. Stud. **74**(1), 8 (2018)
7. WHO, International Classification of Impairments, Disabilities, and Handicaps, World Health Organization (1980)
8. Smeltzer, S.C.: Improving the health and wellness of persons with disabilities: a call to action too important for nursing to ignore. Nurs. Outlook **55**(4), 189–195.e2 (2007)
9. Langtree, I.: Models of Disability: Types and Definitions. revised 2019 (2010)
10. Durell, S.: How the social model of disability evolved (2014). https://www.nursingtimes.net/roles/learning-disability-nurses/how-the-social-model-of-disability-evolved-09-12-2014/. Accessed 31 Jan 2020
11. United States Public Health Service: The Surgeon General's Call to Action to Improve the Health andWellness of Persons with Disabilities. (2005) II, Understanding Disability. Office of the Surgeon General (US); Office on Disability, Rockville (MD). https://www.ncbi.nlm.nih.gov/books/NBK44671/
12. Lid, I.M.: Developing the theoretical content in universal design. Scandinavian J. Disabil. Res. **15**(3), 203–215 (2014)
13. Lid, I.M.: Universal design and disability: an interdisciplinary perspective. Disabil. Rehabil. **36**(16), 1344–1349 (2014)
14. ICF: Towards a common language for functioning, disability and health. WHO/EIP/GPE/CAS/01.3. The International Classification of Functioning. World Health Organization, Geneva. (2002). WHO: http://www.who.int/classifications/icf/training/icfbeginnersguide.pdf
15. Hamraie, A.: Universal design and the problem of "post-disability". Ideol. Des. Culture **8**(3), 285–309 (2016)
16. The History Press: How the talking book was born (2020). https://www.thehistorypress.co.uk/articles/how-the-talking-book-was-born/. Accessed 19 May 2020
17. Kouba, B.J., Newberry, B.: Assistive technology's past, present and future. In: Seok, S., Meyen, E.L., Boeventura, (eds.) Handbook of Research on Human Cognition and Assistive Technology: Design, Accessibility and Transdisciplinary Perspectives, IGI Global, US (2010)
18. Sapega, M.: Remembering Jim Thatcher, Accessibility Pioneer (2019). Accessed 28 Jan 2020
19. Stephanidis, C.: User interfaces for all: new perspectives into human-computer interaction. In: Stephanidis, C., Salvendy, G. (ed.) User Interfaces for All - Concepts, Methods, and Tools. Human Factors and Ergonomics, 1 edn. Chapter 1, Lawrence Erlbaum Associates, Mahwah (2001)

20. Vanderheiden, G.C.: A journey through early augmentative communication and computer access. J. Rehabil. Res. Dev. **39**(6), 39–53 (2002)
21. W3C, Web Content Accessibility Guidelines (WCAG) 2.1. 2018, W3C (World Web Web Consortium). https://www.w3.org/TR/WCAG21/
22. Carroll, J.M.: Human computer interaction - brief intro. In: Soegaard, M., Dam, R.F. (eds.) The Encyclopedia of Human-Computer Interaction, 2nd edn., The Interaction Design Foundation: Aarhus, Denmark (2014)
23. Myers, B.A.: A brief history of human computer interaction technology. Interactions **5**(2), 44–54 (2001)
24. Abascal, J., Azevedo, L.: Fundamentals of inclusive HCI design. In: Stephanidis, C. (ed.) UAHCI 2007. LNCS, vol. 4554, pp. 3–9. Springer, Heidelberg (2007). https://doi.org/10.1007/978-3-540-73279-2_1
25. Dahlbom, B. and L. Mathiassen, Computers in Context: The Philosophy and Practice of System Design. 1st edn, Wiley-Blackwell, Oxford (1993)
26. Begnum, M.E.N., Thorkildsen, T.: Comparing user-centred practices in agile versus non-agile development. In: Norsk konferanse for organisasjoners bruk av IT (NOKOBIT), Ålesund, Norway (2015)
27. Muller, M.J., Kuhn, S.: Participatory design. Commun. ACM **36**(4), 24–28 (1993)
28. Kensing, F., Blomberg, J.: Participatory Design: Issues and Concerns. Comput. Support. Coop. Work **7**, 167–185 (1998)
29. UN, Convention on the Rights of Persons with Disabilities (CRPD) (2006). https://www.un.org/disabilities/documents/convention/convoptprot-e.pdf
30. Fuglerud, K.S., Sloan, D.: The link between inclusive design and innovation: some key elements. In: Kurosu, M. (ed.) HCI 2013. LNCS, vol. 8004, pp. 41–50. Springer, Heidelberg (2013). https://doi.org/10.1007/978-3-642-39232-0_5
31. Silva, J.L., Silva, J.C.: Graphical user interface redefinition addressing users' diversity. In: Bogdan, C., Kuusinen, K., Lárusdóttir, M.K., Palanque, P., Winckler, M. (eds.) HCSE 2018. LNCS, vol. 11262, pp. 319–326. Springer, Cham (2019). https://doi.org/10.1007/978-3-030-05909-5_20
32. Shneiderman, B.: Universal usability. Commun. ACM **43**(5), 84–91 (2000)
33. Harder, S.K., Begnum, M.E.N.: Promoting and obstructing factors for successful universal design, in Norsk konferanse for organisasjoners bruk av IT (NOKOBIT), Open Journal Systems, Bergen, Norway (2016)
34. Bianchin, M., Heylighen, A.: Fair by design. Addressing the paradox of inclusive design approaches. Des. J. **20**(sup1), 3162–3170 (2017)
35. Heylighen, A.: About the nature of design in universal design. Disabil. Rehabil. **36**(16), 1360–1368 (2014)
36. Story, M.F.: Maximizing usability: the principles of universal design. Assist. Technol. **10**(1), 4–12 (1998)
37. Connell, B.R., et al.: The principles of universal design (1997). Accessed 28 Jan 2020
38. Rossetti, R.: The Seven Principles of Universal Design. Action Magazine (2006)
39. Begnum, M.E.N.: Universal design approaches among Norwegian experts. In: Antona, M., Stephanidis, C. (eds.) Universal Access in Human–Computer Interaction. Design and Development Approaches and Methods, UAHCI 2017. LNCS, vol. 10277, pp. 3–20. Springer, Cham (2017). https://doi.org/10.1007/978-3-319-58706-6_1
40. Winance, M.: Universal design and the challenge of diversity: reflections on the principles of UD, based on empirical research of people's mobility. Disabil. Rehabil. **36**(16), 1334–1343 (2014)
41. Hjartnes, Ø.N., Begnum, M.E.N.: Challenges in agile universal design of ICT. In: NordDesign 2018. Linköping, Sweden: NordDESIGN Series (2018)

42. Begnum, M.E.N.: Methodology for universal design of ITs; epistemologies among norwegian experts. In: Miesenberger, K., Bühler, C., Penaz, P. (eds.) ICCHP 2016. LNCS, vol. 9758, pp. 121–128. Springer, Cham (2016). https://doi.org/10.1007/978-3-319-41264-1_17

43. Erete, S., Israni, A., Dillahunt, T.: An intersectional approach to designing in the margins. Interactions **25**(3), 66–69 (2018)

44. D'souza, N.: Is universal design a critical theory. In: Keates, S., Clarkson, J., Langdon, P., Robinson, P. (eds.) Designing a More Inclusive World. Springer, London (2004). https://doi.org/10.1007/978-0-85729-372-5_1

45. Newell, A.F., Gregor, P.: User sensitive inclusive design in search of a new paradigm. In: CUU 2000, Arlington, ACM (2000)

46. Newell, A.F., et al.: User-sensitive inclusive design. Univ. Access Inf. Soc. **10**, 235–243 (2011)

47. Schlesinger, A., Edwards, W.K., Grinter, R.E.: Intersectional HCI: engaging identity through gender, race, and class. In: Proceedings of the 2017 CHI Conference on Human Factors in Computing Systems. Association for Computing Machinery, Denver, pp. 5412–5427 (2017)

48. Treviranus, J.: The value of the statistically insignificant. In: EDUCAUSE Review, New Horizons (2014)

49. Inclusive Design Research Centre: The Inclusive Design Guide. https://guide.inclusivedesign.ca/. Accessed 31 Jan 2020

50. Choi, Y.S., et al.: Are "universal design resources" designed for designers? In: ASSETS 2006: Proceedings of the 8th International ACM SIGACCESS Conference on Computers and Accessibility, USA, ACM (2006)

From Accessible Interfaces to Useful and Adapted Interactions

Laura Burzagli[✉] and Pier Luigi Emiliani

Consiglio Nazionale delle Ricerche, Istituto di Fisica Applicata "Nello Carrara",
Via Madonna del Piano, 10, 50019 Sesto Fiorentino, FI, Italy
L.Burzagli@ifac.cnr.it

Abstract. Ambient intelligence (AmI) is presently considered an important technological development able to support people in all environments (home, office, school, hospital, city). The paper aims to show that: i) the present state of technology already offers the possibility of implementing useful and usable support applications; ii) however its usefulness could be enhanced, increasing impact on all people, with particular reference to people who have some limitations of activities (e.g. older people), if deployed in a carefully planned way; iii) a way off from present limitations may be an artificial intelligence control of the environment itself and of the services made available in it. It is also shown that accessibility is a fundamental prerequisite, but the real problems are the usefulness and usability of available environments and applications. The discussion will be made with reference to an implemented experimental application to support feeding. Its interesting features and remaining limitations are used to support the above statements.

Keywords: Ambient intelligence · Artificial intelligence · Interaction

1 Introduction

Traditionally, HCI dealt with access to information and interpersonal communication (e.g. using computers, tablets, and mobile telephones). In the past, the equipment were normally available with a predefined interface. Therefore, the approach to grant accessibility was the adaptation of the standard interface to allow use by all people. Due to the Design for All movement [1] these adaptations are now available by default in the operating systems of all computer-based systems. For example, screen readers, the normal access systems for blind people, are now widely available and an audio interaction is often provided too.

More recently, the implementation of intelligent objects and their interconnection in integrated systems led to the emergence of ambient intelligent (AmI) environments (smart home, smart office, smart school, smart hospital, smart city) [2]. These are supposed to support people in their activities and favor human contacts. Additional levels of complexity in interactions are generated by these technological developments, due to the complexity of activities to be carried out in the AmI environments.

It is important to consider that in an environment where complex activities are carried out, the starting question is not how to use the available technology, but what

M. Antona and C. Stephanidis (Eds.): HCII 2020, LNCS 12188, pp. 19–32, 2020.
https://doi.org/10.1007/978-3-030-49282-3_2

are the activities that people need to carry out, what functionalities are necessary to support people, what is the information to be exchanged with the environment and why this information must be transferred.

These problems were considered in an intelligent kitchen for the implementation of an experimental application to support people in a fundamental activity as feeding [3]. The purposes of the work were:

- To identify, structure and integrate a set of services able to guarantee the foreseen support
- To show that a useful and usable application can be set up using available technology
- To point out that limitations are present and most of them can be addressed with the support of intelligence (artificial and/or human) in the system.

A summary of the learned lessons is presented in the following.

2 Ambient Intelligence – Scenarios, Definitions, Interactions and Services

Let us now start considering a scenario, showing how an AmI kitchen could support people. Mary starts asking "What shall I eat today?". The kitchen, knowing that Mary is diabetic, controls what she ate in the previous days and tells her: "According to your agenda tomorrow you will have a meeting. It will be difficult for you to have the food completely under control. Therefore, I advise you to eat X and Y". "Do I have at home all the ingredients to prepare X and Y?" "You have everything to prepare X, but for Y you used most of the ingredient Z yesterday". "Let me look in the fridge, how much is available". She starts moving, but she is blind and the kitchen tells her:" Be careful, one of the drawers of the pantry is opened. You could stumble on it". She knows the layout of the room and she is able to close the drawer. The ingredient is not enough, but the kitchen tells her:" Do not worry, I will call the market and they will add Z to the deliver today".

John has already chosen the dishes. The recipes are available, but he does not know how to cook the food (his wife is visiting her sister). Therefore, the recipes are segmented in elementary operations (find a pot, cut the ingredient W in small slices, put it in the pot and so on). A film shows him the details. Possible superposition about steps are suggested (e.g. warm the oil while you cut W). Obviously, the gas cooker and the oven know the temperature and time necessary for cooking the dish. However, John remembers that his friend Jane suggested the addition of an ingredient to improve the taste. He asks the kitchen to call Jane.

George is preparing his dinner. He has some manipulation problems and care must be used in the selection of tools. The kitchen tells him not to use the knife he has picked up and gives precise instructions about the tool to use, the way to handle the onion that he is supposed to cut and so on.

Frances has prepared all dishes and she thinks that everything is ok. However, she likes to have everything under control. From time to time she switches off the oven and tastes the dish, changing, when necessary, the cooking program. However, the kitchen feels that she is becoming bored. It asks her if she wants to explore Facebook or to speak with a friend. Tim is at home and could be available.

With the implemented application this scenario does not come true, but useful functionalities are offered and how to proceed to improve it can be inferred.

2.1 Definitions

Unfortunately, there is not a unique definition of intelligent environments. They can be characterized at different levels of complexity of their contents, interfaces and possible use.

At the first level, environments where intelligent objects, i.e. objects containing and controlled by computers, are available, can be considered. They offer enhanced functionalities aimed to favor people in their everyday activities in the kitchen. Considering, for example, microwave ovens, in addition to the normal functionality of heating food, they offer additional functionalities as a grill and/or are sold with accessories that allow steaming. Therefore, they are supposed to support any necessary cooking need. They also offer automatic procedures. For example, it is possible to put in them frosted food and they, as a function of weight, are able to defrost it automatically.

At the second level, environments where the intelligent objects are interconnected may be considered. For example, the oven can be connected with the mobile telephone of the owner, so that s/he can start cooking when s/he likes and be informed of the situation.

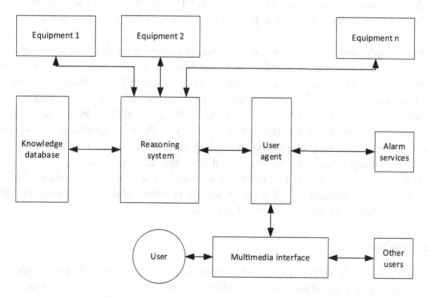

Fig. 1. Block diagram of an AmI environment

Finally, really intelligent environments are emerging, where interconnected computer-based objects are under control of a control unit. This is supposed to evolve to be an intelligent control unit, able to offer people support for their needs, as sketched in Fig. 1. The system is also supposed to control the security of the kitchen (alarm services) and to constitute the node of a social system (other users), but these aspects will not be considered in the paper.

However, as it will detailed in the following, from the user perspective the crucial point to be discussed, is not how the environment is set up and organized or how she will be able access it, but what is the real support that this is able to offer in some of the activities that are essential for living.

2.2 Interactions

The emergence of intelligent objects and their integration in intelligent environments obviously has an impact on their interfaces and the ways of interacting with them. Continuing with the example of the microwave oven, the "simple" versions had normally an interface made of two dials, one to set the temperature and the other to set the time, and an on/off switch. New intelligent versions have a control panel with more than 10 buttons and some dials, whose combination is necessary to program the different options of the system. They have more functionalities, but they require additional abilities from the users. This implies that accessibility is not anymore only a problem of being able to use the interface elements, but to understand the functionalities of the object and the combinations of controls to use them. The starting point is: how an intelligent equipment is supposed to help people? The complexity of the problem again increases when several interconnected objects must be used to obtain the requested result.

In principle, two possibilities are available to interact with the AmI environment. The first is to construct an interface with the objects and the functionalities of the environment on a computer-based system as a tablet. Using this approach, the accessibility problem is reduced to the problem of accessing the tablet and the interaction is organized as an exchange of messages (video, audio, gesture). This is the approach in the implementation of the described prototype, where the main emphasis was on the investigation of the support needed in feeding (i.e. decide what to eat, control the availability of ingredients, acquire them and cook the selected dishes).

The second possibility is to implement an interface with the environment able to allow a "natural" interaction as the one in the above sketched scenario. However, this was not considered in the implemented application.

2.3 Services

AmI is a set of technologies for the implementation of environments where people are living. Living is a multifaced process, which requires complex activities. A detailed analysis is necessary in all living environments leading to:

- The identification of activities to be carried out
- The identification of the functionalities to be made available as a function of the available technology and the abilities of the user(s)

- The design of services (harmonized combinations of functionalities) to support people
- The identification of the necessary interactions (information to be conveyed to people and to be obtained from them) in an accessible form.

Any implemented service must deal with the complexity of the real living situation and be able to adapt itself to different people, to possible variations of their personal situation, due, for example, to age or pathological or traumatic events, and to the context.

Adaptation means not only the modification of the interface to make the service accessible, but mainly the modification of the service itself, because different people may prefer or need to carry out the same activity in a different way or to exchange different types of information, as, for example, in the case of older people with minor lacks of mental abilities.

Fortunately, the first step of the above procedure has already an agreed upon solution. A classification of the activities necessary for living has been produced by the World Health Organization (WHO) and reported in the ICF document (International Classification of Functioning, Disability and Health) [4]. The document has been internationally agreed upon and is presented as an open document, where the single activities can be segmented in additional sub-activities as far as necessary.

3   The Kitchen and Feeding Activities

Let us now briefly consider the main services to be implemented to allow an easy execution of tasks necessary for feeding, pointing out the information that must be made available to the user and to the system (interaction) and the potential role of the reasoning system.

Reference is made to the implemented application where a tablet is used as an input-output system [5]. Some services offered by this application are considered to point out: (i) the main functionalities to be made available to construct an environment able to favor feeding; (ii) limitations of the system to be satisfied by a system as the one sketched in Fig. 1.

People sign in the application with their profile (see menu in Fig. 2).

3.1   Support in the Management of Recipes

Choice of the Recipe

A starting point of the activities necessary for feeding is to know what to eat, i.e. the selection of recipes, adapted to the habits of the user. Possible choices are shown in the menu (Cookbook) in Fig. 2. The following alternatives are made available: name of the recipe or name of an ingredient in the list of ingredients or in the title of the recipe (Search option), and type of course (Starters, First courses, Second courses, Side dishes, Desserts). This is obviously not exhaustive, but a starting point for grasping the complexity of the problem.

Recipes are organized in a database and access to widely available internet sites can be offered. When the recipe is searched on the network, the possible roles of the reasoning system could be:

- The selection, among the different available versions of the recipe for a dish, of the one that is more suitable knowing preferences and habits of the person using the system;
- The restructuring of the description according to the model scheme used in the system.

Fig. 2. Options in the recipe's selection and start of execution

In the implemented system, recipes contain some information to advice if dishes are not suitable for people who are diabetic or suffer of the coeliac disease. However, this part should evolve to be able to reason, on the basis of the knowledge of the medical situation of the user, the diet in the preceding days, and the agenda of the following days, to suggest a possible diet, which takes also into account what the user has available at home and her possibility to acquire new food.

Different levels of complexity need to be considered for planning the future development of the system, taking also into account that, normally, in feeding, the starting point is not the selection of a recipe, i.e. of a single dish, but the planning of meals. The choice of a meal depends on several factors, some of which are listed:

- Type of meal. What meal? Breakfast, lunch or dinner?
- Availability of ingredients
- Nutritional value

- Possible nutritional problems
- People to be fed: a person or the family? In the second case, a mediation is necessary between tastes and needs of all involved people
- Possible guests (information available about their tastes and previous meals?).

Adaptation of the Recipe

Then, it must be considered that the selection of a recipe from a cookbook does not imply the direct implementation as described, but some modifications are possible, for example in the ingredient list and in the number of people to be fed. The personalization of the recipe implies the need of memorizing the modified recipe in a personal diary.

It is also important to memorize this information in a structured form to be considered in a future in (semi)automatic decision procedures. Therefore, an electronic notebook is made available, able to memorize variations in the recipes and possible comments. The diary is made of four sections:

- Recipes (dishes already prepared)
- Recipes under preparation
- Shopping list
- Preferred dishes.

Clicking on a dish, information about it is presented (right part of Fig. 2) with:

- A picture of the dish
- Some general information (number of people, difficulty and time necessary for preparation)
- The list of ingredients with the quantities necessary for the selected number of people. Faces near the ingredients have the following meaning: green – the ingredient is available in the pantry; orange – the ingredient is partially available; red – the ingredient is not available.

Clicking the "modify ingredients" button it is possible to add or delete an ingredient and/or to change its quantity according to the tastes of the user. If the number of people to be fed is changed the quantity of ingredients is recalculated.

Using the "Add to the shopping list" option, access to the available shopping lists is possible. They are created through the analysis of the recipes and are made of three columns: the name of the ingredient, the quantity necessary for the preparation of the recipe and what is available in the pantry (Fig. 3). The possibility is offered to create a shopping list with the lacking ingredient or to add it to a preexisting list.

It is possible to modify the list telling to the system to leave in it only what is necessary for the selected recipe (button – Take only what is necessary), to add items, and to decide the quantity to be bought. Then it is possible to go to the shop, i.e. to an in-line shop.

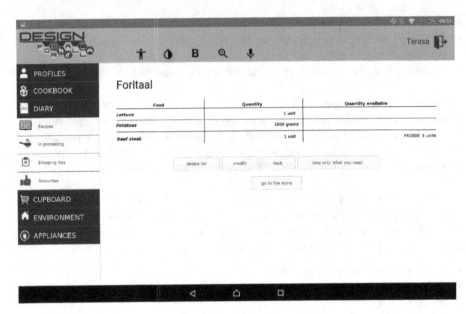

Fig. 3. Shopping list

Instructions for the Preparation of the Dish

Clicking the button "Put in process" the preparation instructions are offered, in free text format. Some operations are presented in red to show that they could present some difficulties because e.g. the user has some minor manipulation problems (any user has a personal profile, where abilities, preferences etc. are listed).

Preparation instructions segmented in steps can be required. In this case, the above description is subdivided in elementary steps that are presented individually to the user for execution.

3.2 The Pantry and the Shopping List

The management of the ingredients can be considered at two interconnected levels:

- The control of what is available (pantry);
- The compilation of the list of what must be bought (shopping list).

In the implemented application, three levels of the pantry have been considered:

- For food which do not need to be chilled (the shelf);
- For food that need to be chilled (the fridge);
- For food that need to be frozen (the refrigerator).

As a consequence, it is necessary to have and make available to the person in the kitchen information about the availability of needed ingredients, the total quantity and the form in which they are available (for example part is in the fridge and part in the refrigerator).

When choosing a recipe and filling the shopping list, it is also necessary to consider that e.g. a frozen ingredient cannot be used immediately, but need some time to be unfrozen and/or that additional activities need to be listed (e.g. need of washing vegetables). The different forms of possible availability of the necessary ingredients has an impact on the representation in the data base and may increase the complexity for the users. A too detailed list (e.g. fresh tomatoes in the fridge, peeled tomatoes in cans or tomato sauce) may cause confusion in some users, while a too simplified list may reduce the opportunities. This is an adaptation to be delegated to the intelligence in the system.

Another import element for the management of the pantry is the expiration date of the single items. For example, a near expiration date can be an important selection criterion for the consumption of a specific food. The main problem is that the possibility of implementing an efficient service from this perspective clearly depends on the availability of a technology able to record data directly on the products, at least the weight and the expiration date, and to communicate them automatically to the AmI system.

3.3   Preparation of the Dish and Management of the Appliances

As already mentioned, the recipe, when available with all corrections and personalization necessary to match it to the individual users, is organized in a sequence of steps to be carried out to prepare the dish. In addition, the application must also list the necessary tools for checking their availability. The steps are presented to the users showing them the actions to be carried with a level of detail matched to the individual needs.

Moreover, normally is necessary to cook several dishes together when a complete meal is supposed to be prepared. The system should be able to optimize the sequence of actions to carry out according to different criteria. One criterion may be the optimization of time, i.e. the minimization of the time for the preparation of the entire meal. However, other criteria might be valid, e.g. the efficient use of the available tools, limited in any home environment. These optimizations are normally carried out by the user, but could be also taken over by the home system, which should also be able to suggest the steps of the recipes to be carried out in parallel, when time, ingredients and tools are available.

The above-considered activities require the use of appliances. The use of the oven, for example, requires many decisions for selecting the type of cooking, the duration, the starting time. The automatic or distant management of all cooking parameters as well as the interaction with the single steps of the cooking procedure do not present difficulties any more from a technological perspective. When a recipe is chosen and the oven is necessary, the AmI system can manage its complete functionalities. An interface is made available to have information about the programmed activity and to modify it if necessary (see Fig. 4).

If something is wrong with the equipment, this can be communicated to the users or external calls to the assistance organization can be issued.

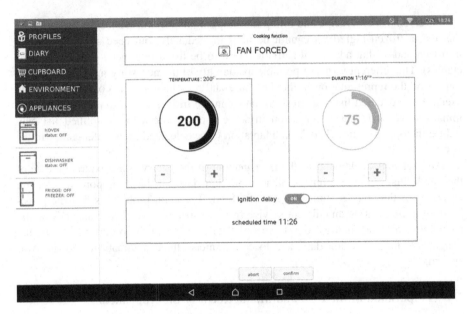

Fig. 4. Control of the oven

3.4 Preparing a Meal – Optimization of the Procedure

As a first example of possible advanced functionalities that could be built in the system, a procedure to optimize the preparation of a meal was implemented in the application.

As already mentioned, in the system database the recipes are made available in two different ways:

- An explanatory version, with the recipe described in natural language
- A "step-by-step" version, where the recipe is structured as a sequence of operations necessary to cook the dish, with additional information for each step, e.g. the time necessary to carry it out.

This breakdown led to the creation of a new 'entity' within the recipe database, called *step,* which has become the backbone of the optimization process for the recipe implementation and is enhanced by the identification of dependencies among the various tasks.

The organization of the procedure in elementary steps, particularly when two preparations concur to the same dish, is very useful from a logical perspective, and the execution of the steps may be optimized, for example from the perspective of necessary time, if a careful analysis is carried out. For example, if the chosen dish is pasta with a tomato sauce, one can remember that it takes about fifteen minutes for the water to reach the boiling point. Therefore, it could be convenient to execute the tasks of filling the pot with water and putting it on the fire at the beginning. Then, while waiting for the water to boil up, one can execute the tasks necessary for the preparation of the sauce. Then, while the pasta is cooking (about 10 min), the cheese can be grated, if one likes it.

Alternatively, the use of necessary equipment (for example pots) could be optimized. In future real implementation of the application, a careful analysis of all aspects for which optimization could be useful should be made and a corresponding optimization algorithm developed.

Presently, an algorithm has been developed able to take one or more cooking recipes into input, and produce as an output an orderly series of tasks, which allows the user to cook the selected dishes, optimizing their preparation time. In order to achieve the optimization, the steps of the recipes are recombined recursively, constructing a structured procedure to guide the user. Obviously, the importance of the optimization procedure increases if an entire meal must be prepared. The introduction of intelligence in the system could allow the organization of meals with any combination of dishes and for any number of people, considering any optimization criterion.

4 Accessibility and Adaptations (from the Interface with Equipment to the Interaction with the Entire Environment)

In the implemented experimental application, four categories of adaptations have been considered in order to accommodate moderate low vision problems, moderate dexterity problems, moderate cognitive problems, presence of diseases for which a diet is fundamental, as the coeliac disease and diabetes.

Two levels of adaptation to the user were considered and tested. The first is the adaptation of the application interface used for the presentation of the information. In the operating systems of the available equipment (e.g. tablets) accessibility support are available: for example, for people with reduced visual abilities the contrast foreground/background and the colors may be changed, fonts may be enlarged, parts of the screen zoomed and audio interactions may be offered. Alternatively, people can be helped in the management of home appliances using vocal messages. These features may be activated on the equipment when switched on and retained for the entire session or may be activated by the user when necessary. This is accomplished using icons in the interface (see icons at the top of Fig. 2).

The second level of adaptation is more general and possible only when a complete user profile is available. From the health perspective, if, for example, a recipe includes an ingredient at risk, as gluten for people with the coeliac disease, this is pointed out with a warning in the recipe description and, using a suitable data structure and targeted decision criteria, an alternative ingredient is suggested. This can be obviously made for any disease for which the diet is important. As already pointed out this should and will hopefully considered in the future by intelligence in the system able to analyze the recipes, to consider information about the users and to produce accordingly recommendations, using information widely available on the network.

From the security perspective, the adaptation is extended to the level of implementation of the recipe. The application is able to point out difficulties and risks connected to the use of single tools or the performance of specific actions. With the list of necessary tools contextually shown with the recipe, just from the beginning possible problems e.g. for people with reduction of manipulation abilities can be identified, suggesting alternatives when possible. Obviously, this has an impact on the necessary granularity for the description of the recipe.

In case of cognitive problems, critical steps can be pointed out and detailed instructions made available. For example, if the difficulty is due to problems in measuring the time necessary for the different steps of food preparation (e.g. cook for an hour) the system is able to plan alarms. Alternatively, if the problem is the management of the pantry, the shopping function may be carried out automatically by the application, on the basis of the chosen recipes and what is available at home. Moreover, the granularity of the task can be adapted to the abilities of the user. Therefore, for any critical situation a suitable adaptation can be proposed by an expert able to match the available information and the flexibility of the AmI environment to any specific problem. At the moment these adaptations are supported by information explicitly made available in the recipes, but it should evolve into a recommendation system managed by intelligence in the system.

5   Implementation of the Prototype - Technical Outlines

The section is not supposed to describe in details the technical implementation of the prototype, but to support the statement that useful applications can be implemented with available technology, open to future improvements, e.g. with the contribution of Artificial Intelligence.

The prototype is based on a hybrid application developed in the Apache Cordova framework. It is implemented using CSS3 and HTML for the rendering functions and JavaScript for the logic components. Tools specific for every supported platform (e.g. Android, iOS) allow the compilation of the application in the selected software environment. The JavaScript code, HTML tag sets e the CSS3 style sheets are managed by the specific WebKit, the software component driving the layout for the page rendering on a web browser. Moreover, the use of a specific hardware as a GPS or a video camera or other components of the system, e.g. the accessibility components, is made possible by the standard APIs. The interface has a set of commands common to all platforms and is able to map them on the specific instruction set of every single platform.

For accessibility some facilities are implemented with the installation of a specific plugin, for example for the management of the speech API in CORDOVA (text-to-speech and speech-to-text) (org.apache.cordova.speech.speechrecognition and cordova-plugin-tts). For the inversion of the color and the magnification of portions of the screen a specific plugin has been developed (it.cnr.ifac.eilab.securesettings).

A particular attention has been devoted to the speech technology, in order to test technological possibilities and its real impact. In Android, experiments have been carried out to verify the possibility of using the TextToSpeech and SpeechToText functionalities, i.e. the possibility of reproducing as speech a character string and to produce a text string starting from an audio signal. The implementation of the TextToSpeech functionalities are available in the operating system through the class android.speech.tts.TextToSpeech. On the contrary, the functionality SpeechToText is not a native feature of the operating system, but it is possible to use it accessing, with the 'Intent' mechanism, another application available in the device and implemented as 'Activity'. In the present case, it is only necessary to look for the Activity that implements the 'Intent': RecognizerIntent.ACTION_RECOGNIZE_SPEECH. An application that makes it available, normally used by the software developers, is Google Voice Search.

In order to test the feasibility of the speech interfaces, two applications have been developed. In the first case the native Android functionalities TextToSpeech e SpeechToText have been integrated. Then MultimediaMedia, and TestCordova have been used, implemented using the Cordova framework. The functionalities to be tested have been implemented using two plugins: com.wordsbaking.cordova.tts 0.2.1 "TTS" e org.apache.cordova.speech.speechrecognition 0.1.0 "SpeechRecognition".

Both in the application using the native Android functionalities and in the one implemented in Cordova the recognition in Italian language was possible. The only limitation is that voice interaction can be used only if the system is connected to Internet. In Android the offline voice recognition is possible (input alternative to the keyboard), but Google does not make it available for third party applications. In any case, the carried-out experiments guarantee the technological possibility of using and input and output voice interface.

A first evaluation carried out by experts confirmed the validity of the application design [6]. A further step for the creation of a product from this prototype is the performance of tests with users in different contexts of use. From this perspective, an additional option which could guarantee a higher level of usability is the presence of suitable sensors or command and processing abilities able to recognize the need of using speech (for example the user cannot use the hands because they are wet). Another interesting aspect to be tested is whether the voice should be used as an independent interface or as an integrated component of a graphical and voice interface. These aspects suggest some elements of future developments of the application.

6 Conclusions

As a result of the preliminary evaluation carried out with the implemented application, it is confirmed that:

- The AmI environment is mature enough to allow support of people in crucial activities for independent living
- An ambient interface is necessary for interactions (bi-directional exchange of information) adapted to allow the easy use of available functionalities by all users and in all specific situations
- Large space is available for increasing usefulness and usability of the application
- Artificial Intelligent may produce a crucial improvement.

References

1. Emiliani, P.L., et al.: Design for all for eInclusion. In: Emiliani, P.L., Burzagli, L., et al. (eds.) Assistive Technology from Adapted Equipment to Inclusive Environments. Assistive Technology Research Series, vol. 25, pp. 815–820. IOS, Amsterdam (2009)
2. Ducatel, K., Burgelman, J.-C., Scapolo, F., Bogdanowicz, M.: Baseline scenarios for Ambient Intelligence in 2010. IPTS Working Paper (2000)
3. Burzagli, L., et al.: The FOOD project: interacting with distributed intelligence in the kitchen environment. In: Stephanidis, C., Antona, M. (eds.) UAHCI 2014. LNCS, vol. 8515, pp. 463–474. Springer, Cham (2014). https://doi.org/10.1007/978-3-319-07446-7_45
4. WHO - ICF: International Classification of Functioning, Disability and Health. World Health Organization, Geneva (2001)
5. Burzagli, L., Baronti, P., Billi, M., Emiliani, P.L., Gori, F.: Complete specifications of ICT services in an AAL environment. In: Cavallo, F., Marletta, V., Monteriù, A., Siciliano, P. (eds.) ForItAAL 2016. LNEE, vol. 426, pp. 51–60. Springer, Cham (2017). https://doi.org/10.1007/978-3-319-54283-6_4
6. Burzagli, L., Gaggioli, A.: Evaluation method for an app involving kitchen activities. In: Cudd, P., de Witte, L. (eds.) Assistive Technology from Harnessing the Power of Technology to Improve Lives. Studies in Health Technology and Informatics Series, vol. 242, pp. 204–207. IOS, Amsterdam (2017)

Integrated Assistive Auxiliary System - Developing Low Cost Assistive Technology to Provide Computational Accessibility for Disabled People

Paulo André da Rocha Perris[✉] and Fernando da Fonseca de Souza

Centro de Informática – Universidade Federal de Pernambuco – UFPE,
Av. Jornalista Anibal Fernandes, s/n, Cidade Universitária (Campus Recife),
50.740-560 Recife, PE, Brazil
{parp, fdfd}@cin.ufpe.edu.br

Abstract. Assistive technology has evolved over the years with fantastic technological innovations. However, the literature shows that they are not always accessible academically and financially to whom it should really help. This paper shows the redesign of a conventional mouse for the use of people with specific needs, more directly, quadriplegia, low cost and parts that are easy to find in specialized stores, here called assistive auxiliary hardware - AAH. It also shows the development of auxiliary assistive software - AAS, which together with AAH, form the Integrated Assistive Auxiliary System - IAAS, of patent belonging to the Federal Institute of Bahia - IFBA, but free for researchers from all over the world to use in their research.

Keywords: Computational resources · Low mobility · Quadriplegia · Assistive technology · Innovation

1 Introduction

Assistive technology over the years contributes to the rehabilitation of people with disabilities (PWD) by providing accessibility to places and resources to facilitate their day-to-day life. Among these resources are the computational ones, which aim to update the knowledge of these people and enable them to graduate or professional qualification, through the accessibility devices and the distance education environments [1–3].

Several initiatives have been created to support accessibility, including responsive design, from Assistive Technology (AT), which helps web environments to fit the media and user profiles that access them, providing an increase in usability. All basic navigation mechanisms (icons, buttons, search, lists, segmented controls, actions tabs, modal views, navigation bar, tab bar, and toolbar) are set for both desktops and mobile devices [2].

Educational technologies, developed for Distance Education, provide a number of opportunities for a more effective learning process [4]. From the evolution of these technologies, each person, with or without deficiencies, can become a student, capable

M. Antona and C. Stephanidis (Eds.): HCII 2020, LNCS 12188, pp. 33–47, 2020.
https://doi.org/10.1007/978-3-030-49282-3_3

of qualifying individually and having her own responsibilities in the educational process, as well as controlling the goal that he wishes to achieve [5, 6].

The reason for using our scenario in distance education environments is that it assists our methodological object, in the activities to be carried out, delimiting and covering the entire technological scope (testing and validation software, pointing device, assistive auxiliary software) that was used and developed by researchers to prove their theses [7].

2 Related Articles

In the scope of assistive software development, many researchers seek to develop applications that aim to test assistive pointing devices as an alternative, as an alternative to Fitts software [8]. Others are concerned with the calibration of the device, for greater precision in its positioning [9], but few develop software that works together with pointing devices and promotes complete accessibility to computational resources for PWD.

Analyzing the papers found in a systematic mapping, we observed that not all technologies (hardware or software) are available for free or free for development by the academic community.

The technologies analyzed in this topic, aim to assist people with severe motor mobility limitations. However, there are particularities existing in their compositions, development, modes of use and applicability that will be improved or discarded in this paper, as they are pointed out as weaknesses or ineffective in their own.

The vast majority of software developed in AT are due to the usability of the devices and frontal detectors on the user's face (webcam, Kinect, infrared sensors, wii remote). This fact makes natural locations difficult for any device to develop its pointer usability, since the variance of light and the distance from the user to the front sensors, directly influence its performance [10].

All pointing devices covered are frontal. Three use glasses as support for the sensors and have data communication sensors on the top of the monitor, to detect the face (eyes and mouth). The focus of the devices is always on the user's face (eyes, nose, mouth).

The difficulties encountered by the researchers in reading the papers found were as follows:

1. Control of brightness, of the environment for a perfect reading of the movements by the cameras;
2. A limit distance, for a perfect reading of movements and gestures by the camera or sensors;
3. Control of multiple objects that will fit the image detected by the camera (analysis of the pointing object and disposal of secondary objects);
4. When used on mobile devices (smartphones, tablets) high energy use, considerably lowering its autonomy; and
5. Obstacles that come in front of the sensors that capture the user's movements and gestures.

The devices found in the literature, offered prices ranging from $40 to $86 dollars [10–12]. Device calibration or device assistance software ranges from $1,699 to $45,900 [9, 13]. For many researchers, this is pointed out as a factor of extreme difficulty for the continuous research in the area of AT.

All of these facts bring up the research question: can there be a solution in assistive technology, of low cost and that is efficient?

3 Methodology

3.1 Pointing Device

From the database found in the systematic mapping papers, we found solutions to the problems pointed out by other researchers in their respective papers and developed the assistive auxiliary hardware - AAH.

AAH was developed with the same mechanical functionalities as a conventional mouse, but cleaner and directed to the problem of accessibility for people with specific needs, specifically, quadriplegia. The AAH is positioned on the headrest of the user's wheelchair and captures the movements of the head through the led and the optical sensor. It captures the user's head movements, similar to using the mouse on a mousepad, where in this case, the user's head is the AAH mousepad.

The AAH (Fig. 1) consists of an LED, two resistors (51 Ω and 51 K), two capacitors (100nF and 10mF), a button (normally open state), an M16183 integrated circuit (optical sensor), a magnification prism lens for focus and a USB cable to power the device. All the necessary components are easily found in specialized stores and their cost does not exceed 9 dollars (Fig. 2).

Two prototypes, with the same configuration, were developed for the execution of controlled experiments in the laboratory (Fig. 3). The led, which will indicate the movements of the user's head and facilitate the reading of the AAH optical sensor (Fig. 4), will be in the position of the user's occipital bone.

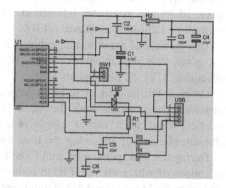

Fig. 1. First AAH prototype   **Fig. 2.** Electronic scheme for making the AAH

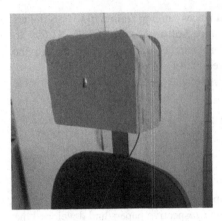

Fig. 3. First prototype simulating the head-rest of a wheelchair.

Fig. 4. Led pointing head reading location.

3.2 Hardware Efficiency Test

To assess the effectiveness of the AAH device we use FittsStudy, software developed to conduct and analyze studies pointing to established international and academic standards based on ISO 9241-9 [14].

The tests took place in a quiet room, with only the participant and the researcher. Two forms of interaction were used in the experimental object.

- Conventional mouse
- AAH

Sixteen research subjects (also called participants) without motor impairment were selected. No participant with quadriplegia was selected, so as not to generate a high expectation in the usability of the device, and in case of failure, discouragement to proceed with the following tests [11]. All were recruited among students of the discipline of human computer interaction, from the Federal Institute of Science and Technology Education of Bahia - IFBA, Irecê Campus.

This number of experimental subjects is sufficient to perform tests following Fitts law, given that similar surveys used: 12 participants [15], 9 participants [16], 16 participants [17], 12 participants [18].

Defining the number of research subjects based on similar research is a recommendation, as it avoids both the small number of research subjects that have no statistical significance, and an excessive number that can introduce noise due to the difficulty of carefully following the tests with all of them [7].

During the tests, performed with FittsStudy software, the screens were shown with indications of where the AAH hand should be (Fig. 5). In the unidirectional test, the participant could stop the AAH at any point in the rectangle. When this happened, the participant pressed his head back, in the headrest of the wheelchair, indicating a click, the signal changed to the other rectangle, the participant pressed the mouse pointer on that other rectangle and pressed his head again, in headrest of the wheelchair. The exact point (x, y) of each position has been recorded, each positioning pair will establish a distance.

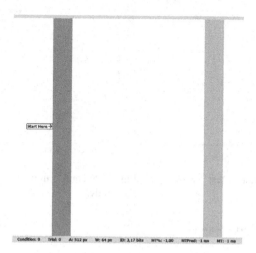

Fig. 5. Unidirecional Test in FittsStudy Software

3.3 Metrics

Considering the difficulty index (DI) of a task and the time in which it is performed, if the DI (bits) is divided by the time (s), the information transfer rate between the human being and the computer in bits/s. According to [7], this is a provocative idea, because it is based purely on an analogy, not based on human psychomotor behavior. Despite this, the transfer rate measurement has been widely used to analyze and compare pointing devices (such as the mouse), represented by the formula:

$$T_t = \frac{DI}{T_m}$$

Being T_t - throughput in bits/s, T_m - movement time in seconds and the DI - effective bit rate in bits. The conventional mouse was chosen as the gold standard because its transfer rate is well known: values from 3.7 bits/s to 4.9 bits/s.

3.4 Hardware Validation Result

The first tests using AAH, resulted in values very close to those of the conventional mouse (diagonal line), enabling AAH to be used in computational activities involving PWD.

In the first series of tests (univariate Fig. 6), the results were quite diverse and not so uniform, as the participants were making their first use of AAH. In the following three tests (univariate Fig. 7, bivariate Figs. 8 and 9), carried out on different days, to avoid fatigue of the participants, the results were more uniform and many closer to the values of the conventional mouse.

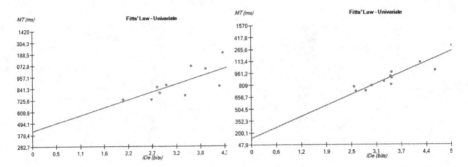

Fig. 6. First univariate test result in FittsStudy.

Fig. 7. Second univariate test result in FittsStudy.

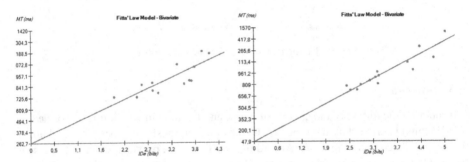

Fig. 8. First test result bivariate in FittsStudy.

Fig. 9. Second test result bivariate in FittsStudy.

3.5 Assistive Auxiliary Software

With the approval of the AAH, it was observed the need for software that would assist in the computational activities that would be proposed to the students. An analysis was made of all the needs that the user would have to access the computational resources available, to perform basic activities on a computer.

Important points were addressed for the development of the software, among them, the independence of the PWD in choosing which applications should be available to him. The possibility of exchanging applications was also a point noted by the researchers. Interviews with students of the HCI discipline and a wheelchair user with C6 spinal cord injury, being the main consultant and evaluator of the set (hardware and software) developed in this research.

The assistive auxiliary software - AAS, works by monitoring all the actions of the AAH, mainly, the duration of its click, which when pressed for a few seconds (3 no more than 5), opens a window bringing the main programs to the user, being able to be reconfigured at any time by the PWD itself. The AAS was developed following the HCI rules (large icons, easy to observe and very intuitive), as shown in the Fig. 10.

Fig. 10. AAS menu with add application (1), Applications added (2), Slot empty (3)

With the creation of AAH and AAS, the Integrated Assistive Assistive System - IAAS was developed, which aims to provide access to PWD to computational resources in the performance of specific activities.

In order to prove the effectiveness of the IAAS, the research participants were asked to carry out the activities: access the browser, type in a specific website address, access the distance education environment, watch a video lesson, answer a thematic exercise in the environment and end your session.

To measure the effectiveness of the IAAS, the execution times of the participants who performed the activities were computed. Errors found during activities were also scored. And at the end, a questionnaire was issued scoring the level of user satisfaction with the IAAS and possible improvements in it.

4   Activities and Results

4.1   Statistics

Statistical results from two accessibility testing sessions and activity resolution by 16 participants proved the effectiveness of the joint use of AAH and AAS (IAAS). Such a prove is based on the P-Value found that presented statistical results of 28.2% (significant value) in a confidence interval of 95% (Fig. 11) [19].

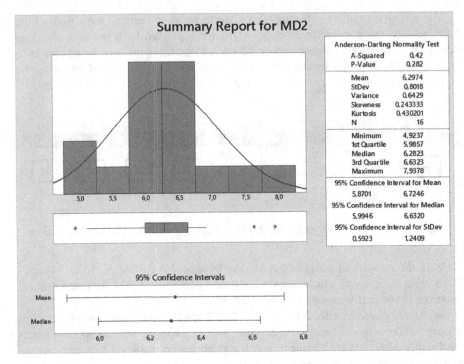

Fig. 11. Minitab Summary Report obtaining p-value of 0.282 over a 95% confidence interval.

4.2 Usability and Evolution

Only for two of the test users, it was not possible to observe the usability evolution with IAAS (user 3 and user 8) (Fig. 12). They Users in an interview, claimed tiredness and discomfort in relation to the routine of activities proposed with the IAAS. They claimed not to be very willing to do the activities.

For the User 6 of the test, however, it was possible to observe a marked evolution, He started with data transmission values below a conventional mouse on the first day of testing, being only the eighth on the first day, becoming the third on the second day of testing.

Users 4 and 15 already beginning the activity with data transmission values higher than the use of a conventional mouse, they continued to evolve in the usability of AAH on the second day of testing. We attribute this to your experience in better controlling your head movements, keeping your focus on the experiment and your motivation to develop new technologies.

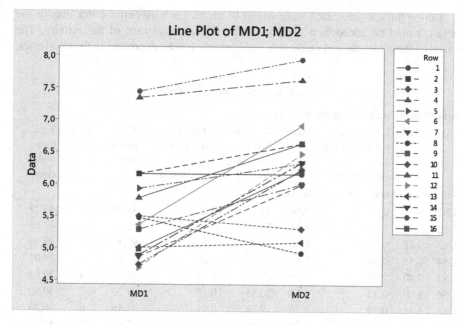

Fig. 12. Minitab Line Plot over usability evaluation.

4.3 Low Cost

The value of the material to build the AAH (LED, two resistors - 51 Ω and 51 K; two capacitors - 100nF and 10mF; one button - normally open state; an integrated circuit - optical sensor - M16183; a magnifying prism lens for focus; and a USB cable to power the device) is just $ 9. For its turn, the AAS is free through its Creative Commons License, and can be accessed and employed by any researcher, but not patented, because the copyright of the software belongs to its developers from the Federal Institute of Science and Technology Education of Bahia - IFBA.

4.4 Practical Activity in a Real Environment

To measure the efficiency of the IAAS, it was proposed to all users, to perform activities in an e-learning environment. The activity consisted of logging on to e-learning, finding the course module, watching a video on a proposed topic, answering a questionnaire with multiple options on the topic shown in the video, sending your answers by e-learning, finishing leaving the platform.

During the activities, each stage would be timed. Each user error (click outside the target), would be added as a penalty, 0.30 s in their total time of the activity. The results of these two days of qualitative experiments, can be expressed in the two tables.

Table 1. First day of activities.

Scoreboard of activities on the first day

User	Login	Locate the module in the web environment	Movie	Read and answer the exercise	Submit the activity in the web environment	Total without errors	Errors	Total time with errors
US1	6,22	2,23	8,60	24,33	0,11	41,49	6	43,29
US2	5,41	1,47	8,21	26,51	0,15	41,75	18	47,15
US3	9,18	0,55	8,50	28,01	0,15	46,39	12	49,99
US4	6,55	0,24	8,16	22,15	0,13	37,23	6	39,03
US5	7,49	1,01	8,20	21,19	0,24	38,13	6	39,93
US6	8,02	0,33	8,15	20,55	0,15	37,20	12	40,80
US7	6,48	0,29	8,20	19,38	0,11	34,46	6	36,26
US8	11,02	0,41	8,33	24,55	0,13	44,44	24	51,64
US9	6,50	0,27	8,10	26,17	0,14	41,18	30	50,18
US10	5,32	0,57	8,22	29,52	0,12	43,75	0	43,75
US11	6,53	1,12	8,22	20,49	0,12	36,48	6	38,28
US12	8,06	0,52	8,17	26,43	0,15	43,33	24	50,53
US13	10,08	1,03	8,13	23,51	0,14	42,89	12	46,49
US14	5,44	0,45	8,09	21,16	0,10	35,24	6	37,04
US15	8,30	0,55	8,16	24,50	0,12	41,63	18	47,03
US16	5,59	0,51	8,20	28,17	0,14	42,61	0	42,61

All participants were amazed at the additional time penalties for errors in their activities. They claimed that they did not imagine that small mistakes could add so much end time.

Participants were asked if they had made fewer mistakes, they would have finished their activities in a better time. All were unanimous in saying that it was. Even with this assertion, participants were not imposed any new rules on errors on the second day of testing.

Table 2. Second day of activities.

Scoreboard of activities on the second day

User	Login	Locate the module in the web environment	Movie	Read and answer the exercise	Submit the activity in the web environment	Total without errors	Error	Total time with errors
USR1	0,55	1,26	12,05	26,12	0,08	40,06	2	40,66
USR2	0,24	1,13	12,04	28,01	0,12	41,54	3	42,44
USR3	0,21	1,03	12,05	26,15	0,12	39,56	3	40,46
USR4	0,37	0,26	12,03	26,19	0,10	38,95	2	39,55
USR5	0,22	1,24	12,05	27,55	0,16	41,22	3	42,12
USR6	0,31	0,55	12,04	26,38	0,12	39,4	5	40,90
USR7	0,20	0,47	12,03	25,17	0,11	37,98	2	38,58
USR8	0,19	0,35	12,04	27,52	0,09	40,19	8	42,59
USR9	0,21	0,51	12,05	29,43	0,12	42,32	6	44,12
USR10	0,26	0,43	12,08	29,50	0,11	42,38	2	42,98
USR11	0,19	0,59	12,05	25,17	0,12	38,12	1	38,42
USR12	0,28	0,47	12,05	29,19	0,11	42,1	2	42,70
USR13	0,23	1,00	12,06	26,33	0,12	39,74	3	40,64
USR14	0,28	0,48	12,03	25,08	0,10	37,97	6	39,77
USR15	0,22	1,02	12,05	27,03	0,09	40,41	3	41,31
USR16	0,27	1,06	12,09	29,04	0,11	42,57	0	42,57

The result of the second day of activities, it was possible to notice, that some of the characteristics of the browser chosen for the tests, such as saving login and password. All those who had problems with long logins and passwords, resolved by just clicking the OK button to log in, without the need to type again using the virtual keyboard and IAAS.

Table 1 shows the result of the comparative analysis of the activities performed by the participants, making it evident that the participants US8 and US9 had a greater increase in time for having made more errors (Tables 2 and 3).

Table 3. Relationship between normal time and time with penalties.

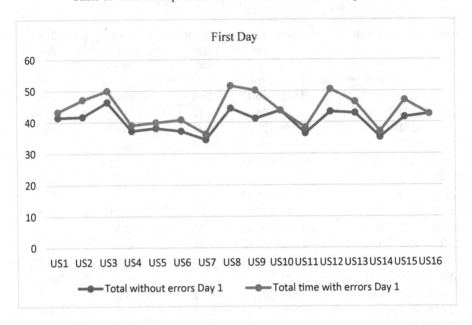

On the second day of activities, all participants were unwittingly careful not to make errors or make the fewest errors possible. Asked about the care not to make errors, they replied that they would not like to have extra time for penalties. It was observed with this, that the time of carrying out the activities increased naturally (Table 4).

Table 4. Relationship between normal time and time with penalties in second day.

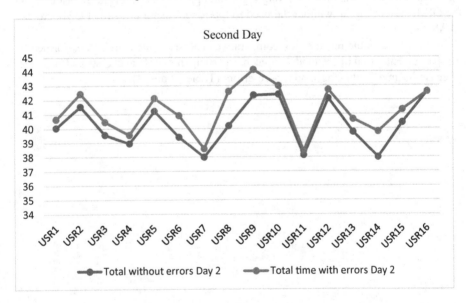

The difference between the number of errors on the first day of activities and the second day of activities is graphically visible (Table 5), showing only participant 10 making more errors on the second day than on the first.

Table 5. Comparison number of errors.

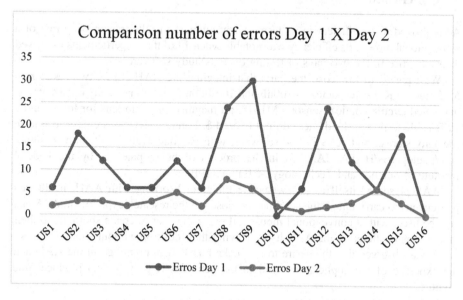

Frame 1 - Comparison number of errors.

Table 6. Analysis of final times with errors from the activities of days 1 and 2.

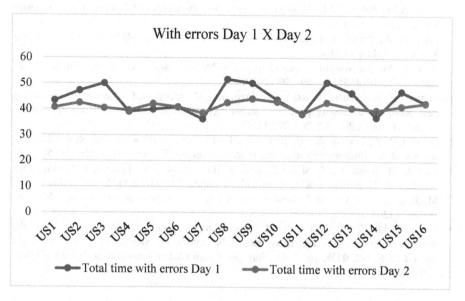

After a comparative analysis of the times with errors from the first day with the second day of activities, we noticed that 12 of the 16 participants improved or maintained the times when the activities were performed (Table 6).

5 Conclusion

AAH proved to be efficient in its tests, when compared to the transmission rate of a conventional mouse. Its efficiency was notable when 14 of the 16 participants improved their expertise in the two days of testing on FittsStudy software.

With regard to low cost, the parts that integrate the AAH (LED, two resistors – 51 Ω and 51 K; two capacitors - 100nF and 10mF; one button - normally open state; an integrated circuit - optical sensor - M16183; a magnifying prism lens for focus; and a USB cable to power the device) do not exceed $ 9 and all devices are easy to find in specialty stores., and AAS is free software, with its code available at: https://github. com/pauloperris/HASA. IAAS is in the process of being patented by the Federal Institute of Science and Technology of Bahia - IFBA.

AAS presented itself as a new mouse function. Working with AAH, it allowed participants to carry out all the activities proposed in the research experiment. AAS can also be used, with a conventional mouse, allowing the user to create shortcuts to their favorite applications on the AAS itself, leaving their desktop without shortcut icons.

It was observed that the desire to not make mistakes in pointing out the AAH and the expertise of the applications used in the activities (e.g.: browser) produce time savings.

References

1. Cook, A.M., Polgar, J.M.: Assistive Technologies: Principles and Practice. Elsevier Health Sciences, St. Louis (2014)
2. Cook, A.M., Polgar, J.M.: Essentials of Assistive Technologies-E-Book. Elsevier Health Sciences, St. Louis (2014)
3. Kurt, S.: Moving toward a universally accessible web: web accessibility and education. Assistive Technol. 31(4), 199–208 (2019)
4. Martins, P., Rodrigues, H., Rocha, T., Francisco, M., Morgado, L.: Accessible options for deaf people in e-learning platforms: technology solutions for sign language translation. Procedia Comput. Sci. 67, 263–272 (2015)
5. Alsobhi, A.Y., Nawaz, K., Harjinder, R.: DAEL framework: a new adaptive e-learning framework for students with dyslexia. Procedia Comput. Sci. 51, 1947–1956 (2015)
6. Laabidi, M., Jemni, M., Ayed, L.J.B., Brahim, H.B., Jemaa, A.B.: Learning technologies for people with disabilities. J. King Saud Univ.-Comput. Inf. Sci. 26(1), 29–45 (2014)
7. Mackenzie, I.S.: Human-Computer Interaction. An Empirical Perspective. Elsevier, Waltham (2013)
8. Bandeira, I.S., Zucatelli, F.H.G.: A human-computer interface and an analysis on the drawing of curves with a face tracker mouse. In: Antona, M., Stephanidis, C. (eds.) UAHCI 2016. LNCS, vol. 9738, pp. 3–14. Springer, Cham (2016). https://doi.org/10.1007/978-3-319-40244-4_1

9. Biswas, P., Langdon, P.: Multimodal intelligent eye-gaze tracking system. Int. J. Hum.-Comput. Interact. **31**(4), 277–294 (2015)
10. Azmi, A., Nawaf, A.M., Majed, A.S.: The wiimote with SAPI: creating an accessible low-cost, human computer interface for the physically disabled. IJCSNS Int. J. Comput. Sci. Netw. Secur. **9**(12), 63–68 (2009)
11. Rodrigues, A.S., et al.: Evaluation of the use of eye and head movements for mouse-like functions by using IOM device. In: International Conference on Universal Access in Human-Computer Interaction, pp. 81–91 (2016)
12. Martins, J., Rodrigues, J.M.F., Martins, J.A.C.: Low-cost natural interface based on head movements. Procedia Comput. Sci. **67**, 312–321 (2015)
13. Kurauchi, A., Feng, W., Morimoto, C., Betke, M.: HMAGIC: head movement and gaze input cascaded pointing. In: Proceedings of the 8th ACM International Conference on PErvasive Technologies Related to Assistive Environments, pp. 1–4 (2015)
14. I. ISO: Ergonomics of human-system interaction - Part 411 – evaluation methods for the design of physical input devices, iso/ts 9241–411:2012. International Organization for Standardization, p. 411 (2012)
15. MacKenzie, I.S., Kauppinen, T., Silfverberg, M.: Accuracy measures for evaluating computer pointing devices. In: Proceedings of the SIGCHI Conference on Human Factors in Computing Systems, pp. 9–16 (2001)
16. Yousefi, B., Huo, X., Veledar, E., Ghovanloo, M.: Quantitative and comparative assessment of learning in a tongue-operated computer input device. IEEE Trans. Inf. Technol. Biomed. **15**(5), 747–757 (2011)
17. Zhang, X., MacKenzie, I.S.: Evaluating eye tracking with ISO 9241 - Part 9. In: Jacko, J.A. (ed.) HCI 2007. LNCS, vol. 4552, pp. 779–788. Springer, Heidelberg (2007). https://doi.org/10.1007/978-3-540-73110-8_85
18. Jose, M.A., Deus, R.L.: Human-computer interface controlled by the lip. IEEE J. Biomed. Health Inform. **19**(1), 302–308 (2014)
19. Soukoreff, R.W., MacKenzie, I.S.: Towards a standard for pointing device evaluation, perspectives on 27 years of Fitts' law research in HCI. Int. J. Hum.-Comput. Stud. **61**(6), 751–789 (2004)
20. Fitts, P.M.: The information capacity of the human motor system in controlling the amplitude of movement. J. Exp. Psychol. **47**, 381 (1954)
21. Krapic, L., Lenac, K., Ljubic, S.: Integrating blink click interaction into a head tracking system: implementation and usability issues. Univ. Access Inf. Soc. **14**(2), 247–264 (2015)
22. Cuaresma, J., MacKenzie, I.S.: FittsFace: exploring navigation and selection methods for facial tracking. In: Antona, M., Stephanidis, C. (eds.) UAHCI 2017. LNCS, vol. 10278, pp. 403–416. Springer, Cham (2017). https://doi.org/10.1007/978-3-319-58703-5_30

Co-creating Persona Scenarios with Diverse Users Enriching Inclusive Design

Kristin Skeide Fuglerud[1]([⊠]) , Trenton Schulz[1] ,
Astri Letnes Janson[2] , and Anne Moen[3]

[1] Norsk Regnesentral, Postboks 114 Blindern, 0314 Oslo, Norway
Kristin.Skeide.Fuglerud@nr.no
[2] Division of Diagnostics and Technology, Akershus University Hospital,
Oslo, Norway
[3] Institute of Health and Society, University of Oslo, Oslo, Norway

Abstract. In this article, we will examine personas as methodological approach and review some critiques about how its use may omit or stereotype users with disabilities or even restrict user involvement. We review previous persona creation methods and compare it to our approach where we involve diverse users directly in the personas creation process, to ensure more grounded personas. This approach has recently been refined in a project where we are building a tool aiming to give citizens more control over their health information. We discuss our experiences and offer some experience based guidelines for using our method.

Keywords: Co-design · Participatory design · Universal design · Inclusive design · People with disabilities · Health information management · Patient engagement

1 Introduction

The concept of personas have been around for over 20 years [1]. Personas are "fictitious, specific, concrete representations of target users" and are used to keep people in mind throughout the design cycle. Success stories are reported [1, 2], but each team has documented different ways of using personas. Common claims are that personas help visualize a typical user, support empathy, and bring designers closer to understand the users they will be designing for. The premise is that understanding at least one typical user should result in a better product or service than designing for a general user whose abilities may change depending on the preferences of the designer.

Experts that have experience with using personas assert that some of the most important benefits are that (1) personas supports audience focus through challenging assumptions, prevention of self-referential design, and (2) that personas help in prioritizing product requirements and product audience [3]. It is recommended that personas are generated from aggregated user research, combining input from many users into a narrative form [4]. Personas can be built on both qualitative and quantitative data, such as interviews, focus groups, questionnaires and demographics. Because humans are naturally good at modelling other people, personas can be more engaging and

© Springer Nature Switzerland AG 2020
M. Antona and C. Stephanidis (Eds.): HCII 2020, LNCS 12188, pp. 48–59, 2020.
https://doi.org/10.1007/978-3-030-49282-3_4

memorable than many other representations of user research [5]. When personas are based on data from activities involving users it can be a way of giving users "voice" or a say in a project similar to user centered or participatory design [6]. Users, however, do not normally participate in the persona creation process itself.

If personas are used to stand in for the typical user, how will they function for the atypical user? That is, how well can personas stand in for or "replace" persons with disabilities, especially if the persona creation process normally excludes the users? How can we set up co-creation processes that ensure participation of people with disabilities and foster a deeper understanding by attending to and including the needs of persons with different disabilities?

In this article, we will examine the use of personas for design purposes (Sect. 2) and focus on a method for co-creating personas that also include disabilities (Sect. 3). Then, we look at some common critiques to the personas approach (Sect. 4). This will be used to compare to the method we recently used in a project where we are building a tool for giving citizens more control over their health information (Sect. 5). We end with a discussion of this method and guidelines for others to implement the method themselves (Sect. 6 and Sect. 7).

2 Persona Use in Research and the Industry

Personas have been used in many research projects and lead to successful product developments. One of the goals of introducing the personas concept was to make designers focus design efforts on people who were not similar to themselves. Cooper [1] documented his idea of personas and how the products created via his technique have been used by many people.

Grudin and Pruitt documented three years of the use of personas inside Microsoft for a variety of projects [2]. Their colleagues and themselves had built on the personas process and asserted that personas helped engage team members, helped uncover design issues that other methods could not find, and could enhance the scenarios in a project by becoming the actors inside them. Earlier, Pruitt and Grudin [7] also argued that personas could be a powerful tool for participatory design, since creating personas required designers to engage with the people that would use the product and the work those people do. They warned, however, about reusing personas, since personas are created for a specific purpose with specific and situated choices, and reusing the personas may stretch them and blind designers to contradictory information about the new design situation. This has lead to textbooks that provide a detailed description of how to create and use personas [4, 8, 9].

Personas are increasingly used in the design of digital health services as well [10, 11]. Personas and scenarios are proposed as communication tools for multidisciplinary teams developing medical devices [12]. There is limited literature on co-creating personas with users. Donald et al. [13] had positive experiences of using personas in a consensus workshop with patients, and suggests using personas in patient-oriented research to explore their needs and preferences. Valaitis et al. [14] have involved patients and clinicians in persona-scenario workshops for a primary care intervention.

They conclude that this presents a promising alternative to active engagement of multiple stakeholders in the co-design of complex health interventions.

Although personas are normally used for product design and human-computer interaction (HCI), personas have found their way into fields like human-robot interaction (HRI). Specifically, personas have been created and formalized as models for the robot to know how to interact with a person [15].

Methods for creating personas have also been applied to create personas for people with disabilities. Some of the authors have documented a process used in several projects that created personas with different disabilities and different types of Assistive Technology [16].

The ÆGIS project (http://www.aegis-project.eu/) created a number of personas with different types of disabilities [17, 18]. These personas are available to others for inspiration to use in their projects. While some researchers do not recommend reusing personas, others may think that providing research-based personas to designers that do not have access to users with disabilities can be helpful. Others have created a set of personas that match a wide range of European Older Adults skills and disabilities based on demographic data [11, 19]. Gonzalez de Heredia et al. [11] propose quantitative measures to design personas for healthcare development and policy-making, based on several surveys of the aging population.

There have been some novel uses personas with disabilities. One project has used personas with disabilities as a guide for creating accessible content in Massively Open Online Courses (MOOCs) [20]. Participants would receive a persona description and attempt to create content that would be accessible to the persona's disabilities. This work was then checked by a peer who had access to the same persona. The HRI persona model has expanded to use a method for creating personas with disabilities [16] to create models of personas with dementia and paralysis [21]. Let us examine that method.

3   Previous Method for Creating Personas with Disabilities

Schulz and Fuglerud have presented their method for co-creating personas with disabilities [16]. This process consists of gathering information from people with disabilities, looking at the assistive technology (AT) that is used by people with disabilities, running a persona workshop with stakeholders, creating a persona skeleton based on the results from the workshop, and finally writing up the actual personas.

To gather information, Schulz and Fuglerud recommend combining standard user-centered design methods like observation, focus groups, interviews, and surveys. They note that when organizing for interview or focus group, it is important to carefully pick well-known locations that are easy to reach for people with disabilities. Similarly, an online survey tool needs to be universally designed so that it works with the AT people use to answer the questions. Knowledge about AT adds important insights, and Schulz and Fuglerud stressed the value of someone in the design team had actual experience working with people with disabilities, for example by learning to use an AT or by participating in user tests involving people using AT. If the team did not have a person with such knowledge, one could invite such a person as part of a persona workshop.

The persona workshop gathered stakeholders to help generate the beginning of the personas. The method described by Schulz and Fuglerud builds personas based on assumptions and factoids and is based on work from Adlin and Pruitt [4]. Assumptions are quotes, opinions, or goals that could come from a potential persona. These assumptions are usually based on the knowledge or experience of the stakeholder. Factoids are small facts or news articles that come from background research and material that is available at the workshop. Participants begin by looking through and rereading the background material, writing down factoids on items that are easy to rearrange (for example, writing one factoid on a post-it note, or nodes in a mind-mapping software). When the rate of extracting factoids slows enough, participants then begin writing assumptions. For each assumption, participants also add a possible persona name who may have this assumption.

Fig. 1. Examples of placing assumptions and initial clustering (left); these assumptions are later grouped with factoids into groups and themes are identified for persona skeletons (right).

When all the participants have finished with the factoids and the assumptions, the participants begin to build groups of similar assumptions (Fig. 1, left). Once all the assumptions have been put into groups, these groups are used as the starting point for grouping factoids. This usually results in another regrouping.

When this regrouping is finished, the groups are identified as themes (Fig. 1, right) and are used as a starting point for *persona skeletons*. Persona skeletons begin as an outline that contain the themes and keywords based on the assumptions and factoids from the different groups. This makes it easier to communicate between stakeholders to understand what the personas are going to look like and suggest changes. Once the basic skeletons are decided, they are filled out with more information. For example, a story may be developed for a persona to flesh out why that persona has a particular assumption with factoids providing a basis for the story. During this process, the personas presentation begins to take shape, and the persona's AT must also be selected and described, including the persona's expertise in using the AT.

Although Schulz and Fuglerud recommend co-creating personas with stakeholders, they do not explicitly include people with disabilities in that stakeholder group.

4 Persona Critiques

One frequent critique of personas is how they are used in the design effort. Cooper originally claimed that some designers would take a personas side and argue that a persona would never perform a particular action [9]. Bødker and her colleagues, however, found that personas didn't necessarily result in designers (or anyone) taking the persona's side, and that they may draw attention away from real participation of actual users [22]. Others have found that even projects that do not create personas end up with some designers creating an ersatz persona in their heads, with limited relevance for the users they sought to support [23]. One study found that practitioners used personas almost exclusively for communication, and not for design [24].

Some authors claim that personas with a personality reduces the need for human participants during design [25]. Others argue that personas cannot completely replace immersion in actual user data [24]. Using personas with some disabilities can even give the project group a false sense of understanding users, whereas, in reality, it creates an extra layer of interpretation between users and developers and thus can create a greater distance [26].

Another critique of personas is how they are created. Even though there are articles and textbooks on the subject [4], designers create personas in different ways [23]. Cooper himself laments that the one chapter he wrote to introduce the persona technique [9] was incomplete [1]. Given the different methods of persona creation, this raises the question of how representative and reliable persona is? That is, how much of a persona is real versus imaginary?

One way of ensuring representative personas is to base them on empirical and statistical data [7]. A statistically valid common behavior may stand stronger than an isolated account with unknown occurrence frequency [22]. Data-driven persona creation carries a risk that the researchers only look for data that confirms their assumptions. This results in the design of an ideal persona rather than a realistic one [27]. The data may also be contradictory, and some have found it difficult to remain true to a creation methodology when encountering contradictory evidence [28].

There is another reason to be cautious of only using quantitative data when creating a persona with disabilities: people with disabilities are rarely part of a statistical average, instead they are typically statistical outliers. Treviranus [29] has argued that creating personas based only on statistics and background research will not teach a designer enough about the individual struggle of a person with disabilities. An important concern in inclusive design is therefore to involve marginalized users in the design process [30]. Thus, from an inclusive and universal design perspective two main issues are how to generate data from users, and whether users themselves participate in their creation. Having users participate helps combat selection bias and imposing assumed traits, experiences and challenges over involving users directly.

The method described by Schulz and Fuglerud [16] set out to create personas with disabilities. However, it also can lead to processes where people with disabilities do not actively participate in the creation process. For example, feedback from people with disabilities might be restricted to before the persona workshop begins, rather than people with disabilities actually being part of the workshop. The people with disabilities feedback could be along as research material for the factoids, but the people themselves may be absent. Similarly, the AT expert can join the workshop, but this expert may only know how the AT works and not have to live with the AT as a way of interacting with the world. In addition, the most common method of creating assumptions and factoids (i.e., writing them on post-it notes and grouping them) may exclude people with reading, writing or mobility disabilities (e.g. people who are blind or have limited hand-function). It is not impossible to overcome these obstacles, but it requires planning and organization. Thus, we wanted to investigate whether involving users in the personas creation process could help counter some of the identified challenges, while retaining the main strengths of personas.

5   Involving Users with Disabilities in Creating Personas

In this section, we present our experiences with including users in the persona scenario creation process as part of the ongoing CAPABLE project [31]. The aim of the CAPABLE project is to create a digital tool that enable citizens to actively use their clinical and personal health information. The demonstration of the tool concentrates on three areas; medication, nutrition, and coordination of health service information.

An important goal for the CAPABLE solution is that it shall follow the principles of universal design, meaning that it shall be accessible and usable to as wide a range of people as possible, including people with disabilities. Therefore, the development of the CAPABLE tool is based on an inclusive user-centered design approach [30], emphasizing user involvement throughout the development cycle.

In the CAPABLE project, we follow a qualitative and interpretive research approach using different user-centered methods. In addition to five personas workshops, described in more detail below, we have run several other activities: (1) two focus groups, one with seven participants from an elderly council, and one with six participants from a disability council; (2) a design workshop with twenty-four young people, divided into five groups; (3) a pluralistic usability walkthrough of a low-fidelity prototype with four seniors from another senior council; and (4) a paper prototype user testing with a senior citizen. The participants represent citizens: (a) from adolescence to elderly, (b) with and without disabilities, (c) with varying degrees of health problems, (d) digital health literacy, and (e) in different stages of life: pupils, workers, next of kin and retirees. The participants were recruited through three municipalities that are partners in the project. The municipality recruited participants from their existing municipality councils (elderly, disability, youth).

For the persona workshops (Fig. 2), users were recruited from three non-governmental disability and health advocacy organizations (NGOs), which are also partners in the project. The plan was to develop six persona scenarios through two workshops in each NGO. We wanted the personas to be diverse in terms of sex, age, type of health challenge, disability and demonstration area (medication, nutrition and coordination of health service information). These parameters were therefore distributed across six very rough persona skeletons.

We ended up with five persona scenario workshops with different user groups recruited from the three NGO's: people with rheumatism, people with Chronic obstructive pulmonary disease (COPD), people with cardiovascular diseases (CVD), people with low vision, and people who are blind. There were three users in each workshop, fifteen in total. The workshop lasted around 2–3 h, including a break with some food, and the participants got a gift card as a compensation for their contribution.

Fig. 2. Co-creating persona scenario with users

The workshops were divided into two parts. In Part One, the persona concept was presented to the users. Their task was to create a fictional person that could be their peer, with realistic characteristics and challenges. They were introduced to the rough persona skeleton as a starting point, and were encouraged to discuss and create a mental picture of their persona, including the physical appearance, social environment, education, work, personality, interests, values, and information about health challenges and disability.

In Part Two, the persona were extended further with a focus on their health history, with details about medication, coordination, and food information needs. We explicitly asked the participants to think of concrete episodes and stories that could highlight challenges with health information management in the three demonstration areas for CAPABLE. While we wanted the persona description to be realistic, we would allow for the persona to have experienced somewhat more challenging situations than the participants considered usual for one single person. The aim of this was to encourage the participants to think of and discuss various situations that could be of relevance. Finally they were challenged to create scenarios for how they envisage that the CAPABLE tool could help the persona with some of the identified challenges.

The discussions were audiotaped and detailed notes and audio transcripts were used as a support for writing up the personas. For simplicity, we refer to the resulting persona descriptions including their health history and potential future CAPABLE usage scenarios as the *persona scenario*. These persona scenarios were distributed to the participants for comments and corrections. For documentation of user needs and to inform the design, we conducted a thematic analysis based on detailed field notes from all the activities, including the persona workshops. This is included in the basis material for the development of requirements for the CAPABLE tool.

We found that the discussions in the persona workshops provided detailed insight into the needs of the persona, and also of other persons with a similar disability or condition. Because the participants had experience from participating in peer-support and advocacy work through the NGOs, they could draw upon their insight into experiences and challenges among people with similar disabilities and conditions as themselves.

The discussions about the persona health history and various information needs and challenges were particularly detailed and provided useful insights and information for the project, and a different type of information than the information from the focus groups or usability walkthrough. There were quite some overlap between the themes emerging from the personas workshops and from the other methods. While the discussion in the focus groups often were quite high level, the usability walkthrough and design workshop gave concrete and detailed feedback to our PowerPoint prototype. The persona workshops on the other hand, gave detailed insight into concrete challenges during the life of the personas. The collected data represented a more coherent narrative, which showed challenges in dealing with health information over time and from the perspective of a person with a particular type of disability or health condition. This conversation was particularly different between focus groups and personas workshops.

The users' immediate feedback on the method was that it was fun and engaging. In the personas workshops, participants could talk about challenging experiences without disclosing one's or others' personal information. This made it easier to discuss potentially difficult and vulnerable issues. After all, the other participants could not know whether it was the participant's story or someone else's that they knew. In the focus groups, participants hesitated considerably to disclose their experiences. In both settings, the participants knew each other from before. Beyond the method, the number of participants present was the main aspect differing the two. This is another factor that could help explain the difference in the type of information that were discussed.

6 Discussion

As many have pointed out, there are inherent conflicts and tensions when trying to condense rich qualitative and quantitative data along many different axes into one or a few personas. Several authors have discussed the difficulty of creating a representative, coherent and believable personas based on such material, risking to create what Bødker describes as a kind of Frankenstein persona [22], or a persona that nobody is able to relate to. The idea of creating one or a few average personas to represent a large segment, will in a way break with the original idea of personas, namely that it is better to really understand and design for one person than to try to design for a general user. When reducing such materials into a few personas we are likely to lose important insights about people who are statistical outliers, such as people with disabilities, or people with special health conditions, and about time and context aspects that are important to understand their lived experience.

Some may dismiss having users participate in persona scenario creation as difficult or confusing for the users, or that it may be difficult to organize. Users in our workshops, however, quickly grasped the idea of personas scenario. Users seemed to enjoy themselves, participating actively in the workshop. One participant commented that she were reluctant in retelling her personal health history in a group, because it could be too personal and meant reliving traumatic events around her condition. She found it much easier and helpful for the co-design workshop to talk about such events in a fictive third person perspective, and create a persona scenario based on different stories she knows.

We experienced that co-creating personas scenarios, including a health history and future tool usage scenarios, provided a type of information that we could not derive from focus groups or usability walkthrough of the prototype. The co-created persona scenarios provided a narrative and insight into the lived experience of people with particular disabilities and health conditions, in a context and over time. This is in line with [14] who conducted similar types of persona-scenario workshops with patients and clinicians for a primary care intervention. They also found that this method provided rich descriptions and argue that the quality and quantity of ideas that were identified were significant and illustrate the added value and strength of this method.

This ties back to and answers to the critique from Treviranus [29] that personas created from background data lack the lived experience of the individual. Since the users co-create the personas with the experts, the participants' lived experiences are major components of the persona scenarios that we created. We found that creating persona scenarios with users gave high realism, and users were eager and willing to share information that would have been difficult to talk about in a more personal way. Co-creating personas with users with relevant, rich experience and/or functional declines can therefore be one of several methods to gather deep insights into the lived experience of potential users of the tool. This should provide the designers and developers with a better understanding of issues an individual with disabilities lives with every day.

As previously pointed out (Sect. 4) people with disabilities lie outside what is considered the average or typical user. We contend that there is no meaningful way to create an average person with disabilities. In inclusive and universal design, it is important to take into account diverse users with diverse needs and to make the design work for as broad a population as possible. A strategy to do this is to involve so-called "edge-users", "outliers" or "extraordinary users" in design activities [32]. These people can easily identify pain points in the current situation. The idea is that creating a solution to satisfy the universal design needs of such a persona will likely satisfy the needs of less demanding users as well. Treviranus [29] notes that the best people to have at the design table are people that have difficulty with a current solution. They are not invested in keeping the current solution, and they will help stretch or expand your design further. Co-creation with these people has the potential to spur new and innovative solutions [29, 32]. Therefore we asked the users in our persona scenario workshops to envision a persona that had been "a little unlucky", with perhaps multiple disabilities or challenges.

7 Conclusion

We have discussed the issue of collecting and representing the needs of marginalized user groups to support universal and inclusive design, and challenges related to gaining deep insight into their lived experience. A main critique of the persona method is the rather challenging task of condensing quantitative information into a few personas, and that this process can create increased distance to users rather than increased understanding.

We found that co-creating persona scenarios with users provided a type of information that we could not derive from focus groups, usability walkthrough of prototype or design workshop. The co-creation of persona scenarios gave us deeper insight into the lived experience of people with particular disabilities and health conditions, in a context and over time. While co-creating with users may increase the realism of the persona scenarios, it comes at the cost of statistical representativity. However, striving for this type of representativity may lead to personas that are not coherent and believable, and thus lose some of its potentially strongest properties, such as its ability to create deeper understanding, empathy and focus.

We suggest letting go of the idea that personas should reflect a quantitative segment, and rather use co-creation of persona scenario with users as a meaningful way to bring forth and discuss relevant and potentially sensitive information needs with users. We conclude that inclusive and participatory persona scenario creation can be a feasible and effective method to supplement other qualitative and quantitative methods to uncover user needs for universal and inclusive design purposes.

Acknowledgement. The work with this paper has supported by the Research Council of Norway through the CAPABLE project. We are grateful to the CAPABLE consortium, the municipalities and non-governmental organizations, which helped with recruiting participants to our workshops, and last but not least to the workshop participants for their valuable contributions.

References

1. The Origin of Personas. https://www.cooper.com/journal/2008/05/the_origin_of_personas/. Accessed 25 Jan 2020
2. Pruitt, J., Grudin, J.: Personas: practice and theory (2003). http://dx.doi.org/10.1145/997078. 997089
3. Miaskiewicz, T., Kozar, K.A.: Personas and user-centered design: how can personas benefit product design processes? Des. Stud. **32**, 417–430 (2011)
4. Adlin, T., Pruitt, J.: The Essential Persona Lifecycle: Your Guide to Building and Using Personas. Elsevier Inc., Amsterdam (2010)

5. Grudin, J.: Why Personas Work: The Psychological Evidence. The Persona Lifecycle. Morgan Kaufmann/Elsevier, Amsterdam (2006)
6. Bjerknes, G., Bratteteig, T.: User participation and democracy. A discussion of Scandinavian research on system development. Scand. J. Inf. Syst. **7**, 73–98 (1995)
7. Grudin, J., Pruitt, J.: Personas, participatory design and product development: an infrastructure for engagement. In: Proceedings of Participation and Design Conference (PDC 2002), Sweden, pp. 144–161 (2002)
8. Pruitt, J., Adlin, T.: The Persona Lifecycle: Keeping People in Mind Throughout Product Design (Interactive Technologies). Morgan Kaufmann, Burlington (2006)
9. Cooper, A.: The Inmates are Running the Asylum: Why High Tech Products Drive us Crazy and How to Restore the Sanity. Macmillan Publishing Co., Inc., Indianapolis (1999)
10. LeRouge, C., Ma, J., Sneha, S., Tolle, K.: User profiles and personas in the design and development of consumer health technologies. Int. J. Med. Inform. (2011). https://doi.org/10.1016/j.ijmedinf.2011.03.006
11. Gonzalez de Heredia, A., et al.: Personas for policy-making and healthcare design. In: Proceedings of the DESIGN 2018 15th International Design Conference, pp. 2645–2656. Faculty of Mechanical Engineering and Naval Architecture. University of Zagreb, Croatia, The Design Society, Glasgow, UK (2018)
12. Vincent, C.J., Li, Y., Blandford, A.: Integration of human factors and ergonomics during medical device design and development: it's all about communication. Appl. Ergon. **45**, 413–419 (2014)
13. Donald, M., et al.: Preferences for a self-management e-health tool for patients with chronic kidney disease: results of a patient-oriented consensus workshop. CMAJ Open **7**, E713–E720 (2019)
14. Valaitis, R., et al.: Health TAPESTRY: co-designing interprofessional primary care programs for older adults using the persona-scenario method. BMC Fam. Pract. **20**, 122 (2019)
15. Duque, I., Dautenhahn, K., Koay, K.L., Willcock, L., Christianson, B.: A different approach of using personas in human-robot interaction: integrating personas as computational models to modify robot companions' behaviour. In: 2013 IEEE RO-MAN, pp. 424–429 (2013)
16. Schulz, T., Skeide Fuglerud, K.: Creating personas with disabilities. In: Miesenberger, K., Karshmer, A., Penaz, P., Zagler, W. (eds.) ICCHP 2012. LNCS, vol. 7383, pp. 145–152. Springer, Heidelberg (2012). https://doi.org/10.1007/978-3-642-31534-3_22
17. Sulmon, N., Slegers, K., Van Isacker, K., Gemou, M., Bekiaris, E.: Using personas to capture assistive technology needs of people with disabilities. In: Persons with Disabilities Conference (CSUN), 22–27 January, 2010, San Diego (2010)
18. AEGIS - Open Accessibility Everywhere – Personas. http://www.aegis-project.eu/index.php?option=com_content&view=article&id=63&Itemid=53. Accessed 25 Jan 2020
19. Wöckl, B., Yildizoglu, U., Buber, I., Aparicio Diaz, B., Kruijff, E., Tscheligi, M.: Basic senior personas: a representative design tool covering the spectrum of European older adults. Presented at the Proceedings of the 14th International ACM SIGACCESS Conference on Computers and Accessibility, Boulder, Colorado, USA (2012)
20. Kelle, S., Henka, A., Zimmermann, G.: A persona-based extension for massive open online courses in accessible design. Procedia Manuf. **3**, 3663–3668 (2015)
21. Andriella, A., Torras, C., Alenyà, G.: Learning robot policies using a high-level abstraction persona-behaviour simulator. In: 2019 28th IEEE International Conference on Robot and Human Interactive Communication (RO-MAN), pp. 1–8 (2019)
22. Bødker, S., Christiansen, E., Nyvang, T., Zander, P.-O.: Personas, people and participation: challenges from the trenches of local government. Presented at the (2012)

23. Chang, Y.-N., Lim, Y.-K., Stolterman, E.: Personas: from theory to practices. In: Proceedings of the 5th Nordic Conference on Human-Computer Interaction Building Bridges - NordiCHI 2008, p. 439. ACM Press, New York (2008)

24. Matthews, T., Judge, T., Whittaker, S.: How do designers and user experience professionals actually perceive and use personas? In: Proceedings of the SIGCHI Conference on Human Factors in Computing Systems, pp. 1219–1228 (2012)

25. Anvari, F., Richards, D., Hitchens, M., Babar, M.A., Tran, H.M.T., Busch, P.: An empirical investigation of the influence of persona with personality traits on conceptual design. J. Syst. Softw. **134**, 324–339 (2017)

26. Bennett, C.L., Rosner, D.K.: The promise of empathy: design, disability, and knowing the "other." In: CHI 2019. https://doi.org/10.1145/3290605.3300528

27. Stickdorn, M., Hormess, M., Lawrence, A., Schneider, J.: This is Service Design Methods: A Companion to this is Service Design Doing. O'Reilly Media Incorporated, Newton (2018)

28. Vincent, C.J., Blandford, A.: The challenges of delivering validated personas for medical equipment design. Appl. Ergon. **45**, 1097–1105 (2014)

29. Treviranus, J.: The Three Dimensions of Inclusive Design, Part Two**. https://medium.com/@jutta.trevira/the-three-dimensions-of-inclusive-design-part-two-7cacd12b79f1. Accessed 31 Jan 2019

30. Fuglerud, K.S.: Inclusive design of ICT: the challenge of diversity. University of Oslo (2014). https://doi.org/10.13140/2.1.4471.5844

31. Janson, A.L., Moen, A., Fuglerud, K.S.: Design of the CAPABLE prototype: preliminary results of citizen expectations. In: Granja, C., Solvoll, T. (eds.) Proceedings of the 17th Scandinavian Conference on Health Informatics, p. 181. Linköping Electronic Conference Proceedings (2019)

32. Fuglerud, K.S., Sloan, D.: The link between inclusive design and innovation: some key elements. In: Kurosu, M. (ed.) HCI 2013. LNCS, vol. 8004, pp. 41–50. Springer, Heidelberg (2013). https://doi.org/10.1007/978-3-642-39232-0_5

Construction of an Inexpensive Eye Tracker for Social Inclusion and Education

Otthar A. N. Krohn[1], Vako Varankian[1], Pedro G. Lind[1], and Gustavo B. Moreno e Mello[2(✉)]

[1] Department of Computer Science, OsloMet Oslo Metropolitan University, Oslo, Norway
[2] Department of Mechanical, Electronic and Chemical Engineering, OsloMet Oslo Metropolitan University, P.O. Box 4, St. Olavs Plass, 0130 Oslo, Norway
gustavom@oslomet.no

Abstract. In this paper we described how to build an inexpensive eye-tracker and to apply it to social inclusion and educational activities in schools. The building of the device includes both the construction of the eye-tracking headset as well as the implementation of the code for translating eye trajectories into output data which can afterwards be analyzed and modeled. The procedure is cheap and can be easily implemented in high-schools and first-years undergraduate courses, to teach specific matters in computer sciences, physical sciences and mathematics. Moreover, we also discuss up to which extension such a cheap device can substitute commercial solutions for promoting social inclusion, particularly to develop empathy in communities by showing the difficulties behind eye-movement languages used by non-verbal paralyzed individuals.

Keywords: Eye tracker · Augmented communication · Accessibility · Social inclusion · Education

1 Introduction

Presently, eye-trackers are produced by different companies with particular purposes in the context of social equality. In particular, some commercial solutions allow paralyzed people, who are unable to use their hands, to use their eyes to control a computer through specialized human-computer interfaces (HCI). This kind of HCI maps eye-tracking records, as illustrated in Fig. 1, into computer commands according to an established eye-movement-based code. These eye-triggered commands can be used by non-verbal individuals with associated paralysis to control specialized software that enables them to type texts and convert it to speech. Thus, eye-tracking not only enables accessibility, but also augmented communication (AC) technologies, which might be the only possible mean of communication for some.

© Springer Nature Switzerland AG 2020
M. Antona and C. Stephanidis (Eds.): HCII 2020, LNCS 12188, pp. 60–78, 2020.
https://doi.org/10.1007/978-3-030-49282-3_5

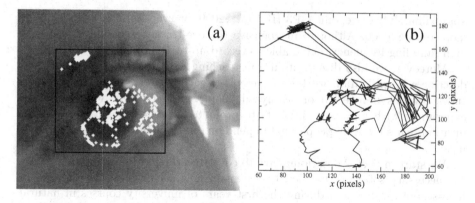

Fig. 1. (a) Illustration of one frame of eye-motion video (photo) superposed with the full set of locations of the pupil center during the same video recording, determined with our software. The region in the square is zoomed in (b) showing the only the full eye trajectory. A full description of the construction of such an eye-tracker as well as the algorithm for locating and keeping track of the pupil are presented in Sect. 2.

There are however two main drawbacks in AC application. First, although the technology enables communication and improvements have been done [1], it is yet far from supporting a comfortable and easy conversation [2–4]. The word selection process tends to be slow and prone to frequent mistakes. The speech synthesizer voice is often robotic and lacks emotional context, which makes substantial part of verbal communication. Finally, learning how to communicate through such a HCI is a challenging endeavour to the user, usually requiring special assistance and supervised training. These factors tend to decrease the chance for integration of non-verbal AC technology users, since the speaking community is typically not aware of the difficulties inherent in these limitations of the technology.

Second, the commercial eye trackers are typically expensive. While they can be used for many purposes, they are not affordable in several important situations, namely in high-school classes. Professors or teachers may want to use eye-trackers in their lectures as a mean to promote the engagement of the students. Nonetheless, they are dissuaded by the cost because, usually, the education budget cannot cover such investments in equipment. By providing a cheaper eye-tracker, one is able to open a new panoply of different tools and pedagogical approaches for teaching specific subject matters.

In this paper, we describe in detail how to build such an eye-tracker and explain how it can be used in classes of different participants, namely computer sciences, physics, mathematics. The total cost is approximately 100 NOK, i.e. 10 Euros, which corresponds to ~0.1% of the average price of a commercial device nowadays. As it will become clear, the eye-tracker here presented is easy and cheap to build. For comparison, one should be aware of some of the most typical commercial solutions namely PCEye Plus which costs $1700 approximately[1], Gazepoint GP3 HD[2] for \$2000, or even Tobii Pro X3-120[3] for more than \$16000. Although inexpensive the eye-tracker we build operates at high sampling frequency, being able to record up to 180 frames per second.

Moreover, we also discuss its use in teaching activities at high-schools and describe a possible framework for developing social awareness and positive attitudes towards non-verbal or paralyzed people. In particular, we propose an experiment with university students to promote awareness about the communication issues faced by people that depend on eye-tracking solutions to communicate.

We start in Sect. 2 describing how to construct the hardware and implement the necessary software. In Sect. 3 we explain how such device can be used in high-school lectures and during the first years of university courses in natural sciences, information technologies and engineering. In Sect. 4 the applicability of such cheap solution is discussed beyond the scope of the education sector, aiming at substituting commercial solutions for communication purposes, establishing an experimental design for promoting social empathy in a community of students. Section 5 concludes the paper.

2   How to Build A Cheap Head-Mounted Eye-Tracker?

In this section we describe how to build the hardware, how to implement the software, and describe its graphical user interface (GUI). We also communicate how the solution at hand is tested and validated, comparing its recorded eye trajectories with those obtained with a standard software, namely *EyeRecToo* [5]. Figure 2 shows the eye-tracker mounted on a subject at OsloMet.

2.1   Hardware

The hardware of the head-mounted eye-tracker is illustrated in Fig. 3(a) and includes:

- One <u>camera</u> (Fig. 3(a1)) such as PlayStation 3-eye, which can film in up to a resolution of 640×480 pixels with a sampling frequency of 60 Hz, up to a resolution of 320×240 pixels with 120 Hz.
- Accessory material for the <u>headset</u>:
  - <u>Frames</u> (Fig. 3(a2)) which form the skeleton of the headset.
  - A <u>supporting arm</u> (Fig. 3(a3)) for connecting the camera to the frames. This arm is composed by three parts, namely a camera holder, an L-shape arm and an adjuster.

---

[1] According to https://www.tobiidynavox.com/en-us/devices/eye-gaze-devices/pceye-plus-access-windows-control/.

[2] According to https://www.gazept.com/product/gp3hd/.

[3] Recently purchased by Faculty of Technology, Arts and Design of the Oslo Metropolitan University. Informations available at https://www.tobiipro.com/product-listing/tobii-pro-x3-120/.

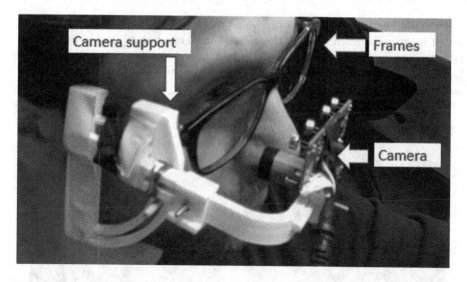

Fig. 2. Photo of the eye-tracker built at the AI Lab (OsloMet, Norway), showing its three main components, namely frames, a supporting arm and a camera. The cost of the camera is of the order of $10 and the cost of the other two components is negligible.

- One <u>PC station</u>, with standard specifications such as Acer Aspire V3-572G-50K9 15.6" 2015, Processor i5-5200U 2.2 GHz, Memory/RAM 8 GB 1600 MHz, a storage capacity of 1 TB or similar and a graphics card NVIDIA GT840M. We also install the PS3 eye drivers for *Windows*.

There are three important remarks regarding the choice or the printing of the components of the supporting arm. First, due to reasons that will become clear in the subsection about the software, it is important to avoid parts with dark coloring. Black frames and black components for the supporting arm interfere with the image, making it difficult to perfectly focus on the eye. Second, the focus length of the PlayStation 3 eye camera is exceptionally wide and do not provide good focus at short distance. This implicates that at the focus distance, the image capture areas of the face surrounding the eyes, which are irrelevant for eye-tracking purposes. To overcome this limitation we replaced the lens and used a custom 3D printed lens holder. This enabled to correct the focal length and the field of view, thus sharpening the image and maximizing area in the image occupied by the eye.

Third, we keep the number of different parts of the supporting arm to a minimum to simplify its assembly and minimize its cost. Apart the PC, commonly available in schools and institutions in general, the total cost of the camera is around $10 and the cost of the different parts of the supporting arm is negligible. The camera is mounted on the frame of normal glasses. One can recycle the frame of old glasses or shades, being enough to remove the lenses. Alternatively, cheap plastic frames can be found in any toy store or extracted from old glasses. As for the different parts of the supporting arm, they should be printed in a 3D

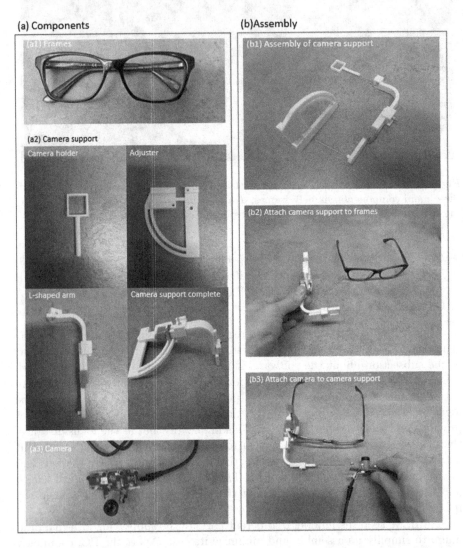

printer, but the supporting arm can be replaced by a 5 mm flexible copper wire, which is strong enough to hold the camera in place, but malleable to position adjustments. In fact, it is possible to even reduce the three components to the L-shaped arm solely, which is the fundamental component connecting camera and frames.

Fig. 3. (a) Illustration of the three components of the eye-tracker: (a1) frames, (a2) the supporting arm, including camera holder, adjuster and an L-shaped arm, and (a3) the camera. (b) Main steps for mounting the eye-tracker: (b1) assembly the supporting arm, (b2) attach the arm to the frames, and (b3) attach the camera to the arm.

The full mounting procedure is sketched in Fig. 3(b). One first assembles the three parts of the supporting arm, (Fig. 3(b1)). Next, one assembles the supporting arm to the frames (Fig. 3(b2)). Both these assemblies can be done using simple glue tape. The mounting is then finished by assembling the camera to the camera holder (Fig. 3(b3)).

Notice that, it is necessary to strip the camera from its unnecessary plastic to make it lighter, and only then attach it to the arm. In addition to reducing the weight of the camera, stripping away the plastic shell exposes a flat side that can be used to attach the headgear.

2.2   Back-End Software for the Segmentation Procedure

The full software is an open source code in Python (version 3.7.3) available at

https://github.com/OttharKrohn/Eye-tracking

which uses some of its standard packages and libraries from Anaconda distribution, including the usual libraries for this kind of software, namely *NumPy* (version 1.16.4) for scientific calculus, *CSV* for reading and writing csv-files, and *OS* and *Shutil* for handling files and folders. For the translation of sequences of images into eye trajectories we use the Python library *Open-CV 4.1.0*. This package is necessary for the fundamental parts of the algorithm, frame capturing, reading, writing and processing as well as performing these operations on videos. Additionally, several of its functions are used in the segmentation algorithm (see below).

The software applies an image-region segmentation procedure [6–8] to a set of frames composing the video of the motion of the eye. To better understand the segmentation procedure, it may be helpful to look at each frame of the video as a graph, or a matrix, instead of a picture. In our case the resolution of the pictures is 320×240 pixels, so they are two-dimensional data matrices with 320 columns (x-axis) and 240 rows (y-axis). The entries of this matrix are values, quantifying the color of the corresponding pixel. We use the RGB color-value system.

The segmentation procedure is illustrated in Fig. 4 and is divided into the following stages:

(a) The recording stage, when the set of frames are collected as set of matrices of color values (Fig. 4(a)). Using the RGB color-value system, each entry of a matrix is composed by a 3-tuple, $C = (R, G, B)$, given the values associated to each color of the RGB system, respectively red (R), green (G) and blue (B).

(b) The grayscale stage, when the algorithm converts the original color scale into a grayscale (Fig. 4(b)). Here one uses the function *grayscale* in *open-CV*, which stores only the intensity of light in each pixel, removing possible disturbing colors. More specifically, it converts the 3-tuple C value into a scalar, so-called the linear luminosity, Y_ℓ, which is given by a linear combination of the three values, R, G and B, and then redefines a new color-value of the pixel as the gray color $C_{new} = (Y_\ell, Y_\ell, Y_\ell)$.

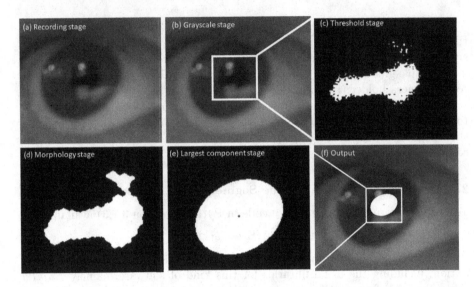

Fig. 4. The segmentation procedure: (**a**) In the first picture, you can see an image, a frame from a video of eye motion. (**b**) The first step is to convert the picture to gray scale, to make it easier to process. (**c**) The darkest parts of the picture is turned white, the rest is black. (**d**) Next, some smoothening is done with morphological transformations. (**e**) The largest connected component is selected and fitted to an ellipse. Center is marked with a red point. (**f**) The result is the superposition of the frame and the ellipse flagging the eye pupil. (Color figure online)

(c) The <u>threshold stage</u>, when the algorithm maps the gray image into a black-white set of pixels (Fig. 4(c)). The white pixels indicate the region where the pupil most likely is located. To that end the algorithm uses the light-intensity of the pixels and imposes a threshold $Y_\ell^{(th)}$, to color each pixel either black, $C = (0, 0, 0)$, if $Y_\ell < Y_\ell^{(th)}$ or white, $C = (255, 255, 255)$, if otherwise.

According to our empirical tests, the threshold should be chosen in the range between black and the dark gray around $C = (50, 50, 50)$. This range corresponds to the typically observed light-luminosity of the pupil. We fixed the threshold as $Y_\ell^{(th)} = 20$, which showed to be a reasonable trade-off between accuracy in localizing the pupil region in each frame and avoiding spurious regions with similar light luminosity. This stage is executed using the function *inRange* in *open-CV*. The threshold should be adjusted in each segmentation procedure, since different videos have different levels of light and shadow.

(d) The <u>morphology stage</u> starts with the set of black and white pixels and determines more accurately the region in the image where the pupil is located, coloring it in white (Fig. 4(d)). In the previous step one typically observes white points in the area covering the pupil, but without forming a connected region. To derive a connected region of white pixels, one uses morphological transformations, which evaluates if each pixel keeps its color or changes to the other one, depending on the surrounding pixels and according to a prescribed criterion. The criterion is implemented by defining a kernel, in our case a circle of pixels, and then the picture is scanned with this kernel. When the anchor point of the kernel (center of the circle) is white, the remaining points in the kernel are also white. This procedure is called dilation, since it leads to the increase of the number of white pixels. A complementary procedure leading to the decrease of white pixels, is erosion, which consists in coloring black all pixels inside the kernels whose center is black. Here, we choose the composition of one dilation with one erosion, both with a circle kernel with a radius of 7 pixels. In this stage, one uses the function *close* in *open-CV* and retrieves a connected white component to the next step.

(e) The largest component stage, when the connected white component is fitted to a "pupil-shaped" curve, namely an ellipse (Fig. 4(e)). This stage is important, since some frames or videos may have shadows or other dark areas, such as eyelids, yielding several connected components disconnected from each other. If the previous stages were properly implemented, the largest connected component should be the one with the highest probability of covering the region where the pupil is located. Moreover, the image of the pupil will often show some reflection, which induces a spurious variation in the luminosity resulting in a "deformed" image of the pupil. Therefore, the fitting of the ellipse is helpful, since it enables a more accurate representation of the pupil. The different connected components in one image can be determined using function *connectedComponentsWithStats* function in *open-CV*, which then selects the one with the largest number of pixels.

The fit of the largest component to an ellipse is done in two steps. In step one, using function *contours* in *open-CV*, one derives the set of points defining the boarder of the largest connected component. In step two, using the function *fitEllipse*, one derives the ellipse that best matches that boarder.

(f) The output of the segmentation procedure yields the superposition of the ellipse matching the pupil of the eye and the original image (Fig. 4(f)).

The center of the pupil is assumed to be given by the center of the ellipse, colored in red in Fig. 4(e) and 4(f). It is this pixel which is tracked in time, and the series of its coordinates define the so-called eye trajectory, as illustrated in Fig. 1. The segmentation procedure is repeated for every frame composing the video of eye-motion, writing out the coordinates for the pupil center in each frame, identified with the corresponding original image. By default, the code generates an output CVS-file with three columns: the frame number is stored in the first column, the x-coordinate of the center of the pupil is stored in the second column, and the y-coordinate in the third.

To summarize, the back-end part of our software segments a video of eye-motion, providing for each frame an estimate of the location of the pupil center, which is recorded as an output file. The software has a simple graphical user interface, which is described in the next section.

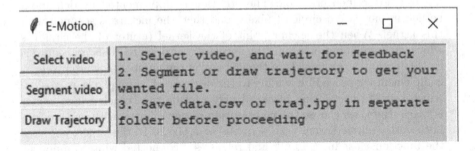

Fig. 5. Illustration of the Graphical User Interface as the front-end part of our software. The main functionalities are described in Sect. 2.3.

2.3 Front-End Software: The Graphical User Interface

At the front-end, the software opens a GUI window, shown in Fig. 5. The GUI window is made using Python's *Tkinter* (version 8.6), which uses an item-hierarchy to make the desired GUI. The interface shows a text box describing the main steps for performing the segmentation of a video, and three functionalities on the left:

– "Select video": This functionality allows one to select a video for segmentation, which is then read and stored as frames in a dedicated folder. Figure 4(a) shows a typical example of the frame of a video stored with this functionality. We also use the *Tkinter* functions to open a pop-up window which allows one to click and select the video. The video is then split up into frames by the *videoreader* class and the frames are saved as jpeg-files, in a dedicated folder, called *frames* by default.

Notice that, the program deletes and creates a new folder every time it reads a video, so as to avoid processing frames from two separate videos at the same time. The *videoreader* function also provides feedback if an error occurs, or when the storage of the video frames is finished.

– "Segment video": This functionality starts the segmentation of the chosen video, as described in Sect. 2.2 and retrieves the output CSV-file with the eye trajectory.

– "Draw trajectory": This functionality enables the possibility of drawing the eye trajectory, as the one shown in Fig. 4. For the user choosing this functionality a video of the trajectory is also shown. By default, points are drawn on the coordinates of the position of the center of the pupil (Fig. 1(a)) and lines are drawn between the points to illustrate the trajectory of the center of the pupil (Fig. 1(a)). Here, the algorithm reads the picture of the frame using function *imread* in *open-CV* and simultaneously reads the black slate generated during the segmentation procedure, indicating the area covering the pupil in white. It also reads the trajectory picture and shows the superposition using the *NumPy* "stitching function" called *horizontal stack* and also the function *imshow*.

By default, the black-white slate is defined with size of 320 × 240 pixels. This size should be adjusted depending on the resolution of the input video.

2.4 Testing the Cheap Eye-Tracker

For analyzing the accuracy of the eye-trajectories derived with our software, we compare it with the ones generated with the open-source software *EyeRecToo* [5]. This software is also designed for head-mounted eye-tracking devices.

The comparative analysis is done for examples of eye-motion videos recorded at 60 Hz and with frames of 320 × 240 pixels, as follows. For each specific eye-motion video, we extract the eye trajectory $r_{new}(n) = (x_{new}(n), y_{new}(n))$ with our software and another eye trajectory $r_{std}(n) = (x_{std}(n), y_{std}(n))$ with software *EyeRecToo* (ER2). Here n labels the frames composing the video.

Then, assuming trajectory $r_{std}(n)$ to be the "correct one", we measure the cumulative deviations of $r_{new}(n)$ from it during a time-span covering T frames. The left plots of Figs. 6(a) and 6(b) show two illustrative examples, signaling $r_{std}(n)$ and $r_{new}(n)$ with different colors.

The cumulative deviations between $r_{std}(n)$ and $r_{new}(n)$ are accounted by a quantity D, which we define as

$$D^2(T) = \sum_{n=1}^{T} |r_{new}(n) - r_{std}(n)|^2, \tag{1}$$

with $|\cdot|$ representing the vector norm. A perfect matching between both trajectories occurs when $D = 0$. Since all terms in the sum in Eq. (1) are positive, D is an increasing monotonic function of T. This monotonic behavior results from the increasing length of the eye-trajectory itself, since the total length L of a T-steps trajectory is given by

$$L(T) = \sum_{n=1}^{T} |\Delta r_{new}(n)| = \sum_{n=1}^{T} |r_{new}(n) - r_{new}(n-1)|, \tag{2}$$

and also increases monotonically with T. In Eq. 2, one uses the initial condition $r_{new}(0) = 0$. The middle panels of Figs. 6(a) and 6(b) illustrate the monotonic behavior of both quantities, D and L.

To properly account for a *relative* deviations, we consider a normalized quantity, which converges towards a constant (typical) value, for a large number T of frames. This normalized quantity is defined as

$$I(T) = \frac{D(T)}{L(T)}. \tag{3}$$

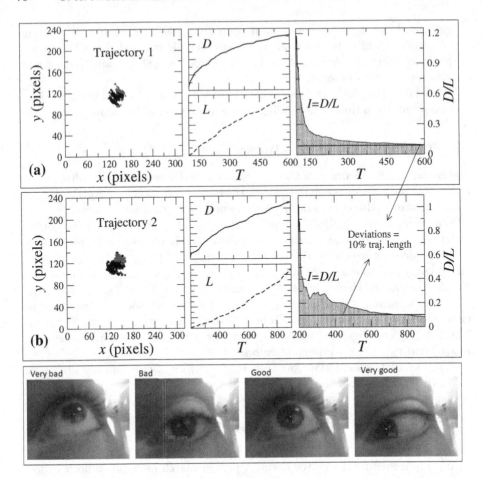

Fig. 6. Two illustrative examples, **(a)** and **(b)**, of eye-trajectories. **(Left)** The two-dimensional trajectories, colored in different colors, in the entire region of 320×240 pixels, to show the qualitative similarities. **(Middle)** The corresponding deviations, D, and total length, L, of the trajectories, as defined in Eqs. (1) and (2) respectively. **(Right)** The index which measures the relative deviations between both trajectories, as defined in Eq. (3), indicating the level of 10% deviation between the trajectory measured with our software and the one extracted with *EyeRecToo*. In **(c)** four examples of pupil's location illustrate the limitations of both ER2 and our algorithm.

The right panels in Fig. 6 show this converge, and typically we find deviations below 10%, which shows a reasonable accuracy of our software.

Neither our algorithm nor the ER2 software are exempt from errors and misdetections. As shown in Fig. 6(c), while for most of the frames in the movie sequences (around 70−90%) show a good or very good match between the center of the pupil and the pixel selected by ER2 or our algorithm, there are a few cases where either one or the other detection procedure fails an accurate detection. These few cases were filtered out in the trajectories shown in Fig. 6(a) and Fig. 6(b).

3   The Eye-Tracker as a Tool for Teaching

A cheap eye-tracker as the one described in previous sections is within reach of almost any consumer, in particular school communities that can use it for educational purposes. In this section we suggest some of the possible situations in high-schools and at the universities where such a device can be of use. The single input needed if the dataset of eye-positions $r(t)$ as a function of time t. While such dataset could be generated synthetically in any computer, the previous data collection through the usage of the eye-tracker promotes student engagement and motivation in the introduction of the topics afterwards. Furthermore, it also enables to bridge between scientific computing approaches for lectures in physics and mathematics and programming software in computer sciences.

A lecture on computer programming, such as Python or R, is becoming more and more ubiquitous at high-schools since the last years. Such a lecture could also profit from an eye-track device in two different ways.

First, at the programming level, the manipulation of the open-source code we provide in Github (see Sect. 2.2) could be used for basics of Python programming, namely working with variables and data types, reading and writing I/O data, introducing lists and data matrices, learning if-statements and while-loops, and defining and plotting functions.

Second, at the scientific computing level, the contents described in the scope of physics and mathematics could be imported also for the programming course. The specific matters that can be taught in a class of mathematics and physics are described next separately.

3.1   Physics

Since eye trajectories are typically trajectories in space, they can be used as real examples of trajectories from the physical world, where fundamental concepts in physics can be tested. Starting from the concept of trajectory itself, typically represented as a vector $r(t)$ whose coordinates are functions of time and correspond to the measurements collected by the eye-tracker itself, all basics of kinematics can follow:

- The computation of the velocity vector, which can easily be approximated as

$$v(t) = \frac{r(t) - r(t - \Delta t)}{\Delta t}. \tag{4}$$

Such approximation is acceptable for sufficiently small Δt. The camera was used with a sampling frequency of 60 Hz which implies $\Delta t \sim 17$ ms. A better approximation would be the implicit scheme

$$v(t) = \frac{r(t + \Delta t) - r(t - \Delta t)}{2\Delta t}. \tag{5}$$

Notice that while such a numerical scheme is implicit, it is easily to be computed from the set of values defining the recorded trajectory. Only the first and last trajectory position have no velocity defined.

- The computation of the acceleration vector, which could be done using a similar equation to Eq. (5), also known as Verlet scheme, which yields an acceleration approximated as

$$a(t) = \frac{r(t + \Delta t) + r(t - \Delta t) - 2r(t)}{(\Delta t)^2}. \tag{6}$$

- The computation of the curvature κ at each point of the trajectory, which can be parameterized by time, yielding

$$\kappa = \frac{\left|\frac{d^2 y}{dx^2}\right|}{\left(1 + \left(\frac{dy}{dx}\right)^2\right)^{3/2}}, \tag{7}$$

where x and y are the two coordinates of the eye position $r(t) = (x(t), y(t))$. As explained below, both the first and second derivatives of coordinate y with respect to the coordinate x can be computed directly from finite differences of the time derivatives of x and y.

- The computation of the trajectory's center of mass r_{CM}, which also follows from direct inspection of the dataset, namely

$$r_{CM}(T) = \frac{1}{T} \sum_{t=1}^{T} r(t). \tag{8}$$

Notice that since the eye trajectories are typically not closed, its center of mass is not static and has its own dynamics.

3.2   Mathematics

In a mathematics lecture, most of the basics in numerical analysis and statistics could also be approached with the output data from experiments with eye-trackers.

In numerical analysis, after introducing the basics of numerical differential calculus, with the discrete version of first and second derivatives with respect to an independent variable, such as time (see Eqs. (5) and (6)), more complicated derivatives can be introduced. For instance, with the motivation of computing the curvature along an eye trajectory one needs to compute numerically the derivative of one coordinate with respect to the other (see Eq. (7)). This is a different kind of derivative since we want to derive one dependent variable, y, with respect to *another* dependent variable, x.

However we can express $\frac{dy}{dx}$ and $\frac{d^2 y}{dx^2}$ in Eq. (7) as expressions with the first and second *time* derivatives of x and y. For the first derivate one has

$$\frac{dy}{dx} = \frac{dy}{dt} \frac{1}{\frac{dx}{dt}}, \tag{9}$$

and after substituting the discretization of the time derivatives, which are similar to Eq. (5), yields

$$\frac{dy}{dx} \simeq \frac{y(t + \Delta t) - y(t - \Delta t)}{x(t + \Delta t) - x(t - \Delta t)}. \tag{10}$$

Notice that Eq. (10) has singularities only for $x(t + \Delta t) = x(t)$, i.e. when eye pupils are exactly static which in practice never occurs.

For the second derivate one applies the chain rule twice, yielding

$$\frac{d^2 y}{dx^2} = \frac{dt}{dx} \frac{d}{dt} \left(\frac{dy}{dt} \frac{1}{\frac{dx}{dt}} \right)$$

$$= \frac{1}{\left(\frac{dx}{dt} \right)^2} \left(\frac{d^2 y}{dt^2} - \frac{dy}{dt} \frac{\frac{d^2 x}{dt^2}}{\frac{dx}{dt}} \right), \tag{11}$$

and substituting first and second time derivatives (see Eqs. (5) and (6)) for x and y yields

$$\frac{d^2 y}{dx^2} \simeq 4 \frac{y(t + \Delta t) + y(t - \Delta t) - 2y(t)}{(x(t + \Delta t) - x(t - \Delta t))^2}$$
$$- 4 \frac{(y(t + \Delta t) - y(t - \Delta t)) (x(t + \Delta t) + x(t - \Delta t) - 2x(t))}{(x(t + \Delta t) - x(t - \Delta t))^3}. \tag{12}$$

The choice of Δt in all calculations above has a lower bound given by the inverse of the sampling frequency of the sequence of the camera. However no upper boundary exists. Using different time increments, Δt, $2\Delta t$, $3\Delta t$, etc, the precision of the numerical calculus can be investigated and demonstrated how the global precision decreases with increasing time increment.

Finally, since the eye trajectory is typically a stochastic trajectory, it is characterized by specific *statistical* features. Consequently, basic statistical tools, such as the (two-dimensional) histogram of the most visited locations in space can be assessed.

4 Using Eye-Tracker for Promoting Social Inclusion

For severely physically disabled non-speaking people, eye tracking technologies in conjunction with letter boards [9] offer the possibility for communication. This augmented mean of augmented communication (AC) has yet many drawbacks that have not been surpassed by engineering. For instance, the slow rate of communication, the energy expenditure and the cognitive load during the transmission of messages using AC systems impacts the quality of the interactions between augmented communicators and others [10,11]. It has been observed that this issue can be mitigated by increasing the familiarity and ability of verbal speakers to communicate with a particular augmentative communication user [12,13]. Although a similar facilitation-by-familiarity also happens between

Fig. 7. E-Tran letter board interface in Norwegian: each color identifies a direction towards which the eye should move. The first move selects a group of characters and the second move selects a character within the group. (Color figure online)

two verbal speakers, part of the facilitation in the communication with the user of augmentative communication might be enabled by the understanding of the constraints imposed by the technology.

Here we propose that an eye-tracker can also be employed in educational activities to promote social inclusion of physically impaired and/or non-verbal people. By showing how the AC technology works, and how AC users communicate, we might increase the familiarization of students in a classroom regarding the communications issues. We can further allow verbal students to use the technology themselves in games, as if they had the impairment themselves, hence introducing the opportunity to empathize with AC users in a ludic and positive way. And we finally can follow up the motivation and awareness provided by the technology and the games to introduce information regarding the different health conditions that might lead to the need of AC technologies. These activities done in a class of students that is about to receive an AC user as a colleague, might severely diminish the alienation and the difficulties that AC users experience. What follows is a description of the interface, and the intervention protocols.

4.1   The Interfaces

We propose a digital version of E-TRAN lettering board [14] as AC interface, as sketched Fig. 7. E-tran boards are divided in nine segments, one central, con-

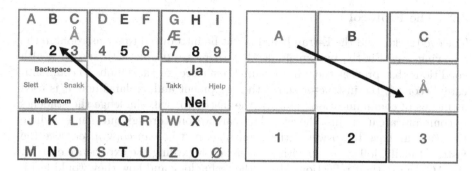

Fig. 8. Two-movements character selection process using an E-Tran letter board: once the group of characters is selected, the board changes replacing the groups by the characters of the group in their respective positions for selection. (**Left**) 1st eye movement: group of characters selection. (**Right**) 2nd eye movement: character selection.

sidered neutral, and eight peripheral sections. Each of these eight peripheral sections can be identified by direction or color (e.g., top-left: blue, top-center: white, top-right: yellow, middle-right: red, etc.). Within each one of these colored sections, groups of 6 to 8 characters are arranged by the same position and color rule of the eight initial sections of board. The user can communicate through two sequential eye-movements to key directions. First, the user moves the eyes towards the direction of the group of letters, and then to the direction that corresponds to the elected character.

Relative to other more sophisticated interfaces such as MinSpeak [9], the E-Tran interface has several advantages: it is relatively easy to learn, demands little effort because any letter can be chosen with two movements, and because only the direction of the eye is relevant for choice, it works well with eye-trackers with poor precision and accuracy. Additionally, because it does not require precise mapping of the eye-movement to the position on the screen, E-tran boards can be presented using any digital display. Thus, increasing its applicability into the educational setting. Figure 8 sketches the two-movements character selection.

Special functions, sentences and characters were introduced into the interface to account for the Norwegian language and to enable text editing capabilities (e.g., backspace, restart, space, etc.). Once the sentence is written, the user selects the speak command and the interface displays the entire sentence. Also, the interface speaks the typed sentence out loud using an open-source text-to-speech library, such as gTTS (Google Text-to-Speech) [15].

Additionally, other more limited interface can be implemented to explore the conditions of those with multiple limitations like associated blindness. In this second interface, there is no board. Letters are spoken to the user through a voice synthesizer. The user can chose the letter by looking down, go back the previous letter by looking left, start over by looking up, and say the message by looking right. The proprioceptive feedback from the eyes is enough for the user to know where they are looking to.

4.2   The Protocol

The eye-tracker and the E-tran board might be introduced to a classroom in the following way. Firstly, by explaining that there are people with special health conditions that prevent them from using their voices or their limbs to communicate. Secondly, the instructor shows the equipment and explains how it is used as means of communication. Thirdly, the instructor will challenge the students to communicate using just the eyes. This can be done through quiz games, where the students have to answer without mistake, or who can copy a sentence the fastest. Finally, following up with a discussion regarding the experience of using the AC device, their reflections about the technology and how they would feel if they needed to use AC technologies to communicate.

The instructor must pay special attention to insights regarding failures of the equipment and limitations of the interface. These points are important because they create awareness about the difficulties of the user and the need to assist them when the equipment is failing. Additionally, the instructor might ask what the students would change in the interface, or what other people should do to help someone that is using AC systems. In this way, the students are employing creative thinking towards an inclusive mindset, that might help in future difficult situations. This dynamic can take place few days before the introduction of a class member that needs to use AC devices.

5   Discussions and Conclusions

In this paper we describe how to build an eye-tracker using low-cost material solely, and provide the necessary software for localizing the eye-pupil in a series of frames composing a video. While we chose a head-mounted eye-tracker, there are other possible alternatives. The most common among them is the table-top mounted tracker, like the commercially available Tobii eye-tracker. Unlike the table-top mounted eye-tracker, the head-mount allows for freedom of movement and it is also more portable. Thus, we have made a design choice to develop around head-mounted setup because it offers more flexibility of use in the educational setting. A trade off between camera resolution/speed and its price and weight is an important factor. While there are cameras that are much lighter, faster and produce images with much higher resolution, these cameras are also very expensive. In our case, we re-purposed an old camera used for video-game applications. Because it is out-dated, it is exceptionally affordable, and it might be that the same strategy can be used in the future for cameras that are currently very expensive. This means that quality of image may increase using the same strategy without increasing the cost substantially. The integration of lighter and more capable cameras might support further developments, such as integrate it into virtual reality masks. This would now only allow to control the lighting around the eye, which may drastically improve accuracy and precision, but also integrate with all sorts of digital interfaces.

As important applications of the inexpensive eye-tracker, we described in some detail how it can be used for addressing specific contents at high-school classes or starting semesters of university studies in natural science. In particular, in physics the eye-tracker can be useful for teaching general kinematics and in mathematics it may increment engagement from the students when addressing basics in numerical analysis and statistics. In addition, the open-source code provided as the auxiliary software to process the eye-tracking recorded by the camera, can be manipulated by the students to implement additional functions discussed during the lecture.

Finally, we also proposed how such an eye-tracker can be adapted for performing specific experiments within universities. These experiments enable any student to access AC tools and in that way develop compassionate attitude towards AC users. The value of this approach in promoting empathy is yet to be assessed. But if it is proven valid, it will establish the eye-tracker as an important teaching tool for social inclusion.

References

1. Caligari, M., Godi, M., Guglielmetti, S., Franchignoni, F., Nardone, A.: Eye tracking communication devices in amyotrophic lateral sclerosis: impact on disability and quality of life. Amyotroph. Later. Scler. Frontotemporal Degener. **14**, 546–552 (2013)
2. Middendorp, J.J., Watkins, F., Park, C., Landymore, H.: Eye-tracking computer systems for inpatients with tetraplegia: findings from a feasibility study. Spinal Cord **53**, 221–225 (2015)
3. Caltenco, H.A., Breidegard, B., Jönsson, B., Struijk, L.N.S.A.: Understanding computer users with tetraplegia: survey of assistive technology users. Int. J. Hum.-Comput. Interact. **28**, 258–268 (2012)
4. Trojano, L., Moretta, P., Estraneo, A.: Communicating using the eyes without remembering it: cognitive rehabilitation in a severely brain-injured patient with amnesia, tetraplegia and anarthria. J. Rehabil. Med. **41**, 393–396 (2009)
5. Santini, T., Fuhl, W., Geisler, D., Kasneci, E.: EyeRecToo: open-source software for real-time pervasive head-mounted eye tracking. In: VISIGRAPP (6: VISAPP) 2017, pp. 96–101 (2017)
6. Garbin, S.J., et al.: Openeds: open eye dataset. arXiv preprint arXiv:1905.03702, 30 April 2019
7. Tonsen, M., Zhang, X., Sugano, Y., Bulling, A.: Labelled pupils in the wild: a dataset for studying pupil detection in unconstrained environments. In: Ninth Biennial ACM Symposium on Eye Tracking Research & Applications, 14 March 2016, pp. 139–142 (2016)
8. Luo, B., Shen, J., Wang, Y., Pantic, M.: The iBUG eye segmentation dataset. In: Imperial College Computing Student Workshop 2018, Imperial College Computing Student Workshop (ICCSW 2018), Schloss Dagstuhl-Leibniz-Zentrum fuer Informatik, Dagstuhl, Germany, pp. 7:1–7:9 (2019)
9. Trefler, E., Crislip, D.: No aid, an etran, a minspeak: a comparison of efficiency and effectiveness during structured use. Augment. Altern. Commun. **1**, 151–155 (1985)
10. Harris, D.: Communicative interaction processes involving nonvocal physically handicapped children. Topics Lang. Disord. **2**(2), 21–37 (1982). https://doi.org/10.1097/00011363-198203000-00005

11. Vanderheiden, G.C.: Non-conversational communication technology needs of individuals with handicaps. Rehabil. World **7**(2), 8–12 (1983)
12. Beukelman, D., Yorkston, K.: Non-vocal communication-performance evaluation. Arch. Phys. Med. Rehabil. **61**, 272–275 (1980)
13. Kraat, A.: Communication interaction between aided and natural speakers: a state of the art report. Canadian Rehabilitation Council for the Disabled, Toronto (1985)
14. Lloyd, L., Fuller, D.R., Arvidson, H.H. (eds.): Augmentative and Alternative Communication: A Handbook of Principles and Practices. Allyn & Bacon, Boston (1997)
15. gTTS - Google Text-to-Speech Python wrapper. https://pypi.org/project/gTTS/. Accessed 20 Jan 2020

Understanding Organizations Through Systems Oriented Design: Mapping Critical Intervention Points for Universal Design

Karina Ludwig[1], Miriam E. N. Begnum[1,2(✉)], and Linda Blaasvær[1]

[1] Department of Design, NAV Norwegian Labour and Welfare Administration,
Sannergt. 2, 0557 Oslo, Norway
`miriam@begnum.no`
[2] Department of Design, NTNU, Teknologiveien 22, 2815 Gjøvik, Norway
`https://www.nav.no`

Abstract. This paper discusses how organisations pro-actively can ensure compliance with disciplinary best practice and regulations on Universal Design (UD) of ICT. We apply system-oriented design to analyse and engineer organisational compliance. The focus is on how best practice – disclosed in theory on how to design for UD, as well as coming regulatory updates – relate to current practices and systems theory on where in a system to intervene in order to change systems most effectively. The aim is a blueprint for a compliant, stable and improved organizational system. The case for the study is the Norwegian Labour and Welfare Administration (NAV). The work presented is part of ongoing strategic work on UD for NAV. Two contributions are made; 1) a discussion on the success of the utilized approach to inform strategic work on intervention points, and 2) recommended system mechanisms for NAV and similar organizations in order to meet the intention of the UD legislation and current quality benchmarks.

Keywords: Universal Design · System thinking · Systems Oriented Design · GIGA mapping · Leverage points · Critical Success Criteria · Strategic design

1 Introduction

Universal Design (UD) is a dimension in the design of products, services, environments and solutions, so that these are usable for as many people as possible, regardless of the capabilities of users and their context of use [1]. This includes technical accessibility. In Norway, a basic level of UD has been a legal requirement for new websites and self-service machines since July 2014 [2]. These regulations are being updated and extended, and additional demands will come into force from 2021. As the legislation changes, organisations must continuously work to ensure UD of ICT in daily work and strategically meet new demands. One such organisation is the Norwegian Labour and Welfare Administration (NAV), whose increasing amount of web-based services are covered by the UD regulations.

There is no unified approach to analyse organisations in order to create internal systems that ensure a desired outcome. However, Systems Oriented Design (SOD) in

M. Antona and C. Stephanidis (Eds.): HCII 2020, LNCS 12188, pp. 79–97, 2020.
https://doi.org/10.1007/978-3-030-49282-3_6

the field of systemic design, offers a guide for businesses and organisations to create holistic understandings of their system mechanisms, rules and structures [3, 4]. Further, system thinking theory on leverage points shows us which mechanisms, rules and structures offer the strongest organisational impacts – and how they work together to create system stability over time [5, 6]. Such insights provide an opportunity to make informed decisions on any necessary changes, understanding the effects of interventions on system mechanisms, and deliver concrete plans for strategic alignment.

Research shows compliance to regulations is not sufficient to ensure usability for all, as these focus on technical accessibility. A distinction between technical and usable accessibility is recommended [7–12]. According to Fuglerud and Sloan [13] there is a heavy focus on adhering to the regulations and standards set forth by the legislations, and a lack of emphasis on the development process. Disciplinary best practice has thus been identified to complement regulations and bridge gaps between the legislative intent of UD and real-life results. A recently defined set of such guidelines are the Critical Success Criteria (CSC) for achieving universal design of IT-solutions [14, 15]. To inform strategic work on UD in NAV, we consider adherence to both disciplinary best practice and routines to ensure compliance with regulations. We ask: *How can NAV as an organizational system be improved and stabilized to reach its aims on delivering digital solutions to all inhabitants and comply with legal demands? In extension, what is needed to comply in time, and what is needed to comply over time?*

2 Background

NAV administers a third of the Norwegian national budget and a large proportion of social security schemes in Norway, such as unemployment benefits, work assessment allowances, assistive technologies, sickness benefits, disability and retirement pensions, child benefits and a range of other services related to life events. NAV provides services targeting diverse user groups, and has worked steadily to launch digitalized services to its users over the last decade [16–18].

The service digitalization has affected the internal organization of NAV. During the time-period 2013–2018, the NAV IT department has transformed. Development is shifting from being plan-based and outsourced, to agile in-house cross-disciplinary teams. In the era of big, waterfall IT projects, UD and accessibility were set as requirement to consultants delivering a service. NAV specified these requirements and tested for accessibility – combining accessibility inspections and user testing. These tests were mostly carried out by the UD team at NAV, consisting of 4–5 people. Considering the small size of the team, this meant only a small number of services could be tested thoroughly at once.

Since the transformation of NAV IT, this approach is no longer sustainable. Currently there are more than 40 agile teams in NAV. More autonomic, cross-functional teams are continuously formed. Instead of publishing large-scale IT solutions up to four times a year, new services can be published several times a day. The change rate is increased. As a consequence, the UD team changed their approach, concentrating on how to scale UD efforts and empower agile teams to build inclusive solutions. The agile development teams themselves are responsible for UD requirements, just as they are responsible for aspects such as security and privacy. The UD team focuses on educating NAV teams on the importance of UD and its relevance for the users, as well as how to assure UD. As of late, this has been developed into a service called "UD coaching"; teaching methods and tools and giving practical advice. The UD coaching stresses the importance of including users with special needs and those using assistive technologies, and arrange user testing with such edge-case users.

The UD team further helps assure the quality of the components in NAV's Design System and promotes its use. As accessibility is also an important part of the procurement requirements, and the UD team assists with educating the procurement staff and evaluating the accessibility of software that is considered. The UD team also contributes to building a new solution for forms used for applications for benefits, which at the time mostly consists of non-accessible PDFs.

Additionally, the NAV UD team explores future methods and tools, such as the possibilities of automated testing and artificial intelligence in UD testing. They work together with other state agencies to allow for reuse of measures and tools that have proven to be useful. Finally, they provide input to management on strategic plans. Current strategic work on UD of IT in NAV span two dimensions; 1) ensuring compliance to the coming **regulations**, and 2) promoting and incentivizing **best practice** for UD of IT in the agile development settings.

Related to regulations, NAV has announced compliancy since the introduction of 2013 regulations on UD of ICT [19]. NAV stipulate WCAG 2.0 AA-level compliance (with a few criteria exceptions) for web-based solutions [20]. From 2021, legacy systems will be covered by these regulations – not just new developments. This includes legacy documents, as documents as part of a web-based service are defined as web-content.

Concurrently, the Norwegian legislation on UD of ICT is updated in accordance with the European Web Accessibility Directive (WAD) [21]. This will introduce the following additional extensions on existing Norwegian legislation: a) new requirements from WCAG 2.1, b) provision and regularly update of an accessibility statement per webservice/mobile application, c) a user feedback feature on unsatisfactory accessibility, and d) UD requirements related to intranet and extranet.

Related to the second point on best practice, previous research articulated 15 Critical Success Criteria (CSC) for universal design (UD) in ICT-projects [14, 15]. These were identified through an interview study investigating the practices of IT-projects that had produced solutions of "high UD quality". The inclusion criteria were based on industry awards and assessment ratings, resulting in a sample 34 interviews across 23 IT-projects. A thematic content analysis pointed to a best practice for ensuring UD quality, both on a procedural level and related to organizational, personal and societal characteristics. The 15 most frequently mentioned characteristics were labeled CSC.

The assumption that these 15 CSC (see Table 1) represent success conditions was tested through a design-based research approach [22]. A tool predicting success based on CSC compliance was collaboratively developed through iterative expert analysis, user testing, focus group and phone interviews [23]. Though not perfect, the tool indicates likely successes and failure based on compliance. This strengthened our belief that CSC are indeed success conditions for IT projects and can be viewed as facilitating legal compliance (prior to 2021) and current "high quality" UD benchmarks.

Table 1. Summary of the 15 Critical Success Criteria (CSC)

CSC	Type	Category
1. Legislation	Societal	N/A
2. Awareness	Organizational	UD anchoring
3. Priority		UD strategy
4. Competence building		
5. Requirements specification	Procedural	Early & clear focus (on UD)
6. Needs integration		UD/UX integration
7. Continuous focus		Process qualities
8. Team collaboration		Quality control
9. User Testing		(Lack of) resources
10. Internal (evaluation)		
11. Time & budget		
12. Equipment & human resources		
13. Design for All (DfA) mindset	Personal	(Lack of) competence
14. Interested		Personal qualities
15. Enthusiastic		

3   Research Approach

The research approach outlined in this paper is viewed as a case study – an in-depth and contextual investigations of NAV. The work is qualitative and adhere to interpretive epistemology; focusing not on an objective and constant truth, but on reflexive analysis on shared perspectives. In other words, one tries to carefully interpret.

Hanington and Martin [24] present methods of design, and categorize their contributions as either exploring, evaluating or generating. Exploratory research approaches are typically used to investigate little-understood phenomena [25]. In contrast, generative research denotes the phase between exploratory and evaluating research where one generates concepts or early prototypes [24]. Generative research can be participatory, e.g. through workshops, which is descriptive for our research process [24]. In this paper we apply theory in the analysis of an empirical case, to create abstract insights and create strategizing concrete plans for change. We are thus both exploratory and generative. In terms of case study classification, we do a single case study, which is mainly an explaining case study (focusing on modeling and making visible), with traits from exploratory (focusing on novel insights) case studies [26].

The difference between a case study and other qualitative studies is the investigation is "bounded"; you can express (theoretically) a finite set of cases – e.g. number of people to be interviewed or observed [27]. In this case, we define the case and system of "NAV", more specifically NAV IT, as the internal organizational structures. A system is a set of interrelated elements organized to serve any particular function or goal (see Fig. 1). The system function or goal is sometimes not at all what the system or people in it would say it is, but rather the result that is clearly being produced by that system. Note, however, that this "system goal" may not always be in line with the goals of the people *in* the system, or the actors in the systems *environment*. Nonetheless, a system is scaffolded to support this overall "system goal". The system is organized towards it and is always trying to produce outcomes which are in line with it.

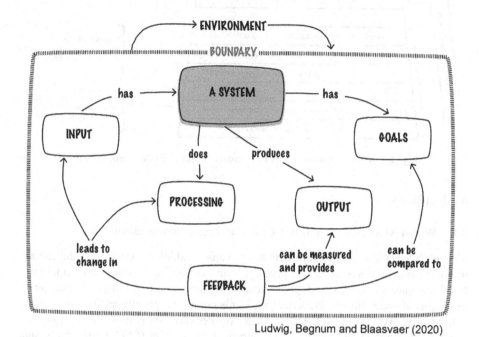

Ludwig, Begnum and Blaasvaer (2020)

Fig. 1. A concept model of a system

In order to analyse whether NAV has system mechanism in place facilitating legal compliance and success conditions for UD of ICT, we apply methods from SOD. Parts of the analysis was done by GIGA-mapping, a method that involves the visualization of exceedingly complex and rich data followed by the disclosure of patterns, couplings, functioning systems, nodes, flow, and so forth; in this paper referred to as "system mechanisms" [28, 30]. To answer our research questions, we investigated the following for the NAV system: A) Which mechanisms does the organization have to support CSC and legal requirements? B) Is there is a need to add, change, or remove mechanisms in order to comply? and C) Looking at the resulting system as a whole: Is there is a need to add, change, or remove mechanisms in order to stabilize the system? Extending the GIGA mapping of system mechanisms is a theoretical analysis of CSC in light of Meadow's 12 leverage points (see Fig. 2) [5, 6]. Leverage points are mechanisms in which small shifts can produce big changes on complex systems [6]. This enables prioritizing interventions according to their effectiveness as leverage points for systems change.

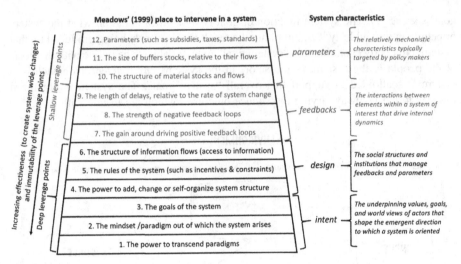

Fig. 2. System leverage points (in increasing order of effectiveness) [29]

4 Findings

4.1 Which Mechanisms Support CSC and Legal Requirements?

Meadow's top 3 leverage points are related to values and intent, which form the culture of an organization: system goals, paradigms and the ability to transcend paradigms. NAV emphasizes values and goals related to among other things user-centered development and inclusion. Nevertheless, UD is not a clear priority and requirement in high-level plans or strategies. UD mindsets on Personal (individuals) and Organizational levels (culture and management) appear partly present (CSC 2 Awareness and CSC 13 UD mindset). Critical design competencies from the Design Department seem underutilized in strategic value-based work. There are no clear aims for UD in the national political strategy on digitalization either [18], which would have trickled down into NAV's internal plans and goals.

The next 3 leverage points cover the social structures and institutions: the power of self-organization, system rules and information flows. In the current NAV structure, we identify few formalized requirements and rules to ensure legislative compliance (CSC 1 Legislation), or to ensure a desired level of UD focus, priority, and quality. The system seems to depend on informal mechanisms in this regard: The development teams are responsible for WCAG-compliance, but NAV lacks clear top-down requirements and consequences if solutions are not compliant. Most teams reflect too little on the UD quality of the service they build (CSC 10 Internal evaluation), even though many of them do user testing (CSC 9 User testing). Competence-building on UD is mostly ad-hoc, driven by personal enthusiasm (CSC 15 Enthusiasm), apart from information during onboarding. The UD-team offers coaching, but teams (mostly) have to put in requests for that. On procedural level, however, NAV has high-quality settings with self-organizing development teams, which checks some of the CSC best practice: agile and user-focused with cross-disciplinary collaboration (CSC 8 Team collaboration).

Leverage points 7 to 9 regard feedback, that is to say the interactions between elements within a system that drive internal dynamics: driving loops, balancing loops (relative to the impacts they are trying to correct) and length of delays (relative to the rate of system change). Here, we find leverage points operate with ad-hoc mechanisms. The system currently lacks mechanisms for meeting (balancing) any triggered (driving) demands on UD. For example, there is no way for the UD team to know when requests for support will come, or a set time for answering such team requests – this relies on the availability at the time. Increasing demand for UD support, for example as a result of possible mandatory reporting on UD status (CSC 1 Legislation and partly CSC 15 Enthusiasm), would trigger more constraints on the time available for the UD team, which thus had less opportunity to invest time into measures that could prevent UD errors and to educate development teams. This again would increase the demand for support from the UD team and so forth. Without any balancing loops, this driving loop would soon crash the capacity of the UD team, leading to a collapse of this part of the system. It could partly be balanced through people skilled in UD outside the UD team (CSC 14 Interest and CSC 15 Enthusiasm). Therefore, teams (especially team leaders) need to prioritize UD: Team members must be given time to build their UD competence and team leaders must encourage and demand UD efforts to build better solutions. Even if this could lead to slight delays in the publication of a service.

The final 3 leverage points are linear parameters, including the structure of material stocks and flows, and buffers. The Web Content Accessibility Guidelines can be seen as a parameter that enable teams to see if their solution is in accordance with the law (CSC 1 Legislation). We find NAV does not have an abundance of resources, nor any clear buffers, to rescue the system when unbalanced. Indeed, the limit on human and time resources is a constant challenge to ensure UD even under the present semi-structured system. This relates to CSC 11 Time and Budget, CSC 12 Equipment and human resources. How can one find the resources to meet new demands, and new goals?

Table 2. Mapping leverage points and Critical Success Criteria (CSC) for UD in NAV

Leverage point	Present mechanism supporting CSC/requirements	Challenge
1. Transcendence	*No CSC or legal requirements related to this*	
2. Paradigm – system mindset	CSC 2: organizational awareness – partly anchored CSC 13: personal UD mindsets – partly present	Negative UD mindsets & views also present
3. Goals of the system	*No CSC or legal requirements related to this*	Lacking formalized UD goals
4. Self-organization power	CSC 8: team collaboration – high procedural quality	Unknown UD focus
5. Rules of the system	CSC 1: legislation	Lacking UD-quality standards & competence assurance
6. Information flows	Procedural QA through CSC 9: user testing & 10: internal (expert) evaluation. Competence building through CSC 15: personal enthusiasm & UD coaching	Ad-hoc
7. Driving loops	CSC 1: legislation & CSC15: personal enthusiasm	Ad-hoc
8. Balancing loops	UD coaching & CSC 14: personal interest. CSC 3: Priority	Ad-hoc
9. Delays relative to changes	Too long – thus reducing UD quality	Overlong
10. Stock-and-flow Structure	CSC 12: equipment (test labs, licenses, platforms etc.)	Some strain
11. Buffers	Very few; mostly on CSC 12: human resources	Severe strain
12. Numbers	CSC 1: legislation, CSC 11: time & budget, and CSC 12: human resources are present, but not adequate	Insufficient

4.2 Is There a Need to Add, Remove or Change System Mechanisms?

A Strategy for UD, Anchored in High-Level Organizational Strategies. We conclude that NAV stresses, among other things, inclusion and user-centered development. But the existing goals and ambitions are vague, need to be interpreted and are too unspecific regarding UD. A strategy addressing the goals and paradigms in the system, focusing on diversity perspectives and societal responsibility to design for all of NAV's users should have a profound effect on the organization [6]. Cynically looking at compliance to the regulation on UD of ICT, the minimum necessitated change is to add organizational awareness on the legal demands. We propose establishing a strategy which expresses the desired UD aims for NAV, regardless of the scope of these aims. We also recommend more critical design thinking, needs analysis and service design in strategic phases (prior to solution procurement or development in order to reduce the risk of failed investments) given that these consider UD.

We believe a strategy for UD would fulfill CSC 2 (Awareness) on anchoring UD as part of organizational values and CSC 3 (Priority) on emphasize UD priority. Next, there is a need for mechanisms that ensure the desired UD aims and priority levels are being implemented.

Specify a UD Standard. The UD strategy could be translated to a UD quality standard for NAV, along with consequences or incentives for compliance. Specifically, NAV lacks system mechanisms to implement any CSC 5: requirements for UD. Today, there are no consequences if not complying to the legislation. This relates to the rules of the system: How absolute are requirements? What happens if teams de-prioritize UD? Who is responsible for ensuring legal compliance? Here, we recommend rules related to the end-result, but not rules related to a specific method or process for the teams. This would protect the agency of the teams, while promoting UD and ensuring compliance. The UD standard could also be part of or influence voluntary standards for several competence groups in NAV, such as Design standards or standards for Code Quality. However, we do recommend a structured and specified information flow and creating scalable best practice examples in the stock-and-flow structures (including the accessibility declaration).

Strategic Competence Building. NAV does not have a strategy for UD competence building, which is CSC 4. The relevant staff and departments must be made aware of the new UD strategy and aims, and the new rules of the system. Further, awareness on UD values and design for all mindsets are beneficiary. The relevant individuals must be offered UD training in order to be able to implement the strategy as desired. NAV wants teams to have true agency, and this is in fact itself a quality indicator for UD [15]. In addition, there are several procedural CSC, for example 8: Cross-disciplinary collaboration, 6: Viewing UD as part of user needs and UX, and 7: integrating UD/UX focus in work processes. This would support both information flow and self-organizing power.

4.3 Is There a Need to Add, Remove or Change System Mechanisms to Stabilize?

Today, the lack of priority given to UD creates ad-hoc driving loops for competence building and quality control, which is met by ad-hoc training and solutions. According to our analysis, UD fixes seem to be postponed mostly due to time constraints, lacking human resources within teams and lack of knowledge on how to find and fix errors. UD testing and error fixing in itself can lead to delays in publishing new parts or features of a service. If a development team experiences time constraints and is unsure how to test for and fix UD errors, there is an increased risk that the team only tests very little or skips the testing altogether.

However, if rules are introduced to ensure legal compliance and disciplinary best-practice, one must also ensure that there are buffers, balancing loops and delay mechanisms in place that can stabilize the system – so as to not break down but be sustainable over time.

Let us first look at the driving versus balancing feedback loops on UD in NAV. We find there are no clear system rules providing guidance on the degree to which teams need to do CSC 10: internal evaluations (expert inspections) of the UD quality of code, designs or service journeys, or CSC 9: testing with users. Procedures for checking compliance with regulations are not demanded. UD training is not required. **Key driving feedback loops for UD are as such not systematized.**

With the proposed changes outlined in Sect. 5.2, the system will look very different. Now, we will have a minimum of driving UD feedback loops, relative to the organizational goals (the standard) and rules (quality assurance). What is likely to happen when the teams start following these? First, teams need to find the time to educate themselves on UD. We foresee there will be an immediate need for CSC 11: Time. Teams are often hard pressured on the time at hand to increase their UD competence. Second, teams are pressured on the time to do QA work – user testing, for example, takes time to plan, conduct and evaluate. Third, the UD expert team is not able to buffer the time constraint the teams are under. Delays will continue and grow under the suggested change unless resources are increased. In our analysis, **time is completely lacking as a buffer in our system**.

The alternatives are finding more people with the necessary competence to get more done in the same amount of time. We now seem to have two choices; either pull resources from the organization or buy external competence. Let us then look at CSC 12: Equipment and human resources.

Internal UD Resources. There is a strain on human resources related to UD: NAV has a handful of UD experts who offer UD coaching (training) on demand to NAV's 40+ teams, in addition to strategic work, research, legal consultation, public sector collaboration and communication work. Though team support is prioritized by these experts, strategic work to reach legal compliance (such as piloting an accessibility statement and a feedback feature) and scalable efforts (such as supporting the Design System team) are expedited over timely response to single teams. Unfortunately, internal structures make it difficult for the UD team to get access to other resources like developers skilled in UD, which would be very beneficial for building and strengthening measures that prevent UD errors. Today, the UD expert team in NAV is not able to provide the necessary support in time to NAV IT teams, which hinders UD quality and competence building. The UD team could either restrict the number of agile teams receiving support, or the amount of support given to each agile team. As such, the **organization does not have that many internal UD resources to pull**.

External UD Resources. The second alternative then, is buying external competence. We do not have first-hand knowledge of NAV team budgets. Still, we believe there are as tight budgets for NAV as for public sector in general. We do not believe NAV has the budget to hire external experts to aid them on UD compliance in time.

Strategic Competence Building. There is, however a third option. By building UD competence in NAV IT over time, the delay in UD support – though continued – will be less critical. After all, a delay in a feedback process is only critical relative to what the feedback loop is trying to control. The necessary stabilizing mechanism is thus increasing the competence to independently secure UD in agile teams – thus over time diminishing the importance of the UD team.

In addition to the general strategic competence building for all of NAV IT, we find that NAV needs to utilize employees with interest in UD more. We suggest building a network of interested individuals, "**UD ambassadors**", that can discuss UD challenges and come up with improvements. This would support the leverage point of self-organization and could speed up innovation. We assume that this also would strengthen the will and ability of individuals to take responsibility for UD in their team.

Further, NAV could strengthen additional support mechanisms to support agile teams on UD, thereby adding more balancing mechanisms to the likely increased requests for the UD teams expert competence. NAV's **Design system** – including the frontend framework – provides a sound foundation for preventing common UD errors. A simple analysis of UD errors in older projects indicate that up to 70% of UD errors would not have occurred if the projects had used a Design system with "built-in UD". To comply with the coming legal requirements, the Design System needs to be updated. We recommend its broader use in NAV. Another way to support teams would be to **improve automatization of UD testing**. At the time of writing few UD criteria can be tested using automated tools; mostly technical WCAG criteria. If a higher percentage of UD errors can be detected using automated tools, this would reduce the stress on the development teams and the UD expert team. We recommend strengthened efforts to research and increase the coverage of automated testing.

5 Discussion

Looking at the time at hand, we have about 1 year left. Plainly put; strategic competence building is urgent for NAV to reach compliance in time! Since legal deadlines are finite, NAV will have **to apply for a (time-limited) exemption** from the requirements. To be granted an exemption, authorities demand NAV submits a **realistic plan on when and how to comply to the law**.

5.1 Towards a UD Strategy for NAV

Based on the possible leverage points, which measures will likely have the most profound positive effects on NAV's UD work? Let us look at intervention points both in the light of Meadow's [6] leverage points (LP) and the Critical Success Criteria (CSC) identified by Begnum [14].

Triggering Change. Meadows states that the higher-level the leverage point, the higher the intervention effect. Looking the relationship between leverage points and critical success criteria, a CSC may correspond to several LPs – and a LP may include several success criteria. As such, the relationship is a bit messy. Nevertheless, as shown in Table 2, most LPs and CSCs match very well, even regarding their priority. We find NAV is currently lacking system rules for ensuring legal compliance and that interventions to correct this corresponds to high-level leverage points; 2, 3 and 5. Meadows [6] and Begnum [14] are in alignment that a strategy and clear goals on an organizational level will likely trigger major changes in the organization fairly quickly.

Even so, it may be that these measures cannot lead to the necessary change in time, NAV may still have to apply for a time-limited exemption from at least some of the legal requirements.

Grassroot vs. top-down approach: According to Begnum [14] boosting CSC 13-14-15: UD mindset, UD interest and enthusiasm can create grassroot movements. Unfortunately, given the time left before the new regulations go into force, we do not believe a grassroot level movement would have the necessary effect *in time*. That being said, building competence is viewed as a bottom-up way to create the mindset and culture needed for organizational change, and therefore encouraged as part of the UD strategy in NAV. In addition, it would also be a way for NAV IT to protect the agency of their teams, an aspect that is threatened by a top-down approach to building system rules. A standard that works as a set of best practices to be educated on, instead of a rigid set of to-dos, could support the teams in prioritizing and conducting their own UD work as they see fit.

Sustaining Change. Meadows [6] warns of ensuring system stability. Similarly, Begnum finds that in order for triggers to succeed, there must also be sufficient possibilities (abilitating factors) in place in the organization [30]. Based on Fogg's Behavior Model for Persuasive Design, she hypothesizes this is A) related to enough time, money, equipment and human resources, and B) related to the cultural values of both the individual, the team and the organization. For a trigger to succeed, the abilitators are needed. We hypothesize that the identified strain on abilitating factors in NAV, has been hindering a grassroot movement. Our analysis shows resource factors are under strain in NAV. Any strategy must as such consider how these can be better aligned with the stated goals and rules. As such, the outlined top-down "strategy & rules approach" in NAV should consider resources and other system mechanisms as balancing factors (or abilitators) to be sustainable over time. Building up buffers in UD competence (by strategic competence building and an ambassador network) and measures that prevent UD errors to begin with (as the Design system and frontend framework) is thus considered critical for sustainability over time, even though they are on a lower level in Meadows´ hierarchy of leverage points.

In Conclusion, NAV Will Have to Work on Both Short-Time and Stabilizing Measures. The analysis highlights how adding *UD strategy, goals and rules* are the most powerful points to intervene in the NAV system to ensure expedient legal compliance to UD regulations. This is the argument focused on compliance **in** time. Further, in order for the outlined top-down "strategy & rules approach" to be sustainable, the strategy must trigger additional change in the system – such as the constants, flows, loops and buffers necessitated to follow and measure the rules. These are the foundation for all change to be sustainable over time. In particular, NAV has to focus on scaling UD in a way that teams can ensure UD quality of their solutions on their own, without extensive help of an expert team on a day-to-day basis. To ensure best practice and compliance **over** time, the analysis indicate that the most important thing NAV can do is boost abilitators. If not, Begnum and Meadows point to the same end – using terms such as "trigger failure" and "system collapse". Key interventions to answer the research questions *How can NAV as an organizational system be improved and stabilized to reach its aims on delivering digital solutions to all inhabitants and* comply with legal demands? and *In extension, what is needed to comply in time, and what is needed to comply over time?* is summarized in Table 3. Further, Fig. 3 provides an overview our empirical case. One expert team of 4–5 members serves NAV's 40+ agile teams.

Towards a sustainble system for complying with legal UD demands on digital solutions in NAV. Current, transistional and future state of UD expert team supporting agile teams.

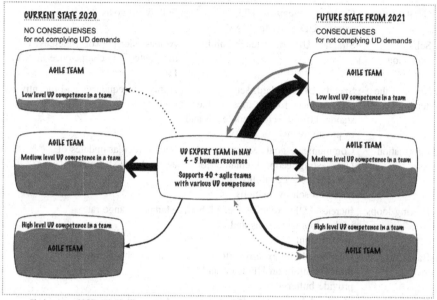

Black arrows 2020

Describes the pull on UD expertice in the current state of the system. The scenarios decribes teams with different levels of UD competence within the team from Low to High. There is little demand from teams with low competence as there are no consequences for not complying with legal UD demands.

LEGEND

Minimum demand for UD expertice · · · · · · · · ·
Some demand for UD expertice ———
High demand for UD expertice ▬▬▬
High and continouse demand for UD expertice ▬▬▬

Black arrows 2021

Describes an expected increase in pull on UD expertice as there will be consequences for not complying with legal UD demands from 2021.
Black arrows in the future state describes a transition phase that is not sustainable as there are litte or no feedback in the system.
The UD competence in agile teams appears to still be below medium, as the teams demand a lot of assistance from the UD expert team in order to build digital solutions that comply with UD regulations. These driving feedback loops operate within a system that has not built in time or other resources as buffers for the expert team to serve all agile teams in a time-ly manner. As such, the system is currently not sustainable.

Green arrows 2021

Describes a future state that includes feedback, testing, regular compe-tence building and providing practical advice. In this sceanrio time is built in as buffer for the UD expertise to handle requests from teams on how to comply with legal UD demands.

Ludwig, Begnum and Blaasvaer (2020)

Fig. 3. A graph derived from the rich data GIGA mapping process. The big black arrow indicates an exceedingly pull on UD expertise when all digital solutions need to comply with legal demands on UD in 2021.

Table 3. Summary of needed changes to NAV

Leverage point	To ensure legal compliance, we need:	To ensure system stability, we need:
1. Transcendence		Use critical design in strategic work
2. Paradigm – system mindset	Create a strategy for UD	Strengthen UD- and integration-related paradigms; include NAV's societal responsibilities into its strategies
3. Goals of the system	Create a strategy for UD; express UD goals for NAV	Follow up goals
4. Self-organization power	Strategic UD competence building	Ambassador network, increased distributed UD competence in NAV IT
5. Rules of the system	Specify UD standard, set consequences for not meeting the standard (for development teams and in procurement)	Apply consequences and incentives
6. Information flows	Communicate goals & system rules User testing/feedback channel for UD. Create accessibility statements based on self-evaluations.	Secure regular updates of accessibility statements
7. Driving loops	Increased UD expertise needed, both in development teams and procurement	Manage change rate
8. Balancing loops	Distributed UD expertise (to decrease strain on UD team and provide buffers)	Manage change rate
9. Delays relative to changes	Shorter delays in how long it takes to assist team that need UD support	Manage change rate
10. Stock-and-flow structure	Update the design system to be compliant with WCAG 2.1. Improved automatization of UD testing	Assure technical frameworks used in NAV support accessibility
11. Buffers	Access to internal resources skilled at UD that can support the UD team, both developers, designers and others Budget for needed software and for hiring external competence Apply for (time-limited) exemption from legal requirements	Time! Ambassador network
12. Numbers	Apt UD measurements	*Measure UD goals/rules*

5.2   Towards a UD Strategy for NAV

Without a shared organization-wide framework, it we see it will be difficult to set and follow up priorities in NAV. Therefore, UD needs a clear and stated mandate, just as privacy and security. NAV needs a framework that defines and ensures at least a minimum of quality in the solutions built. To achieve this, NAV has to stop viewing UD as technical requirements (the legally required minimum of technical accessibility), and start defining UD as a part of product and service development. This coincides with CSC regarding best praxis. Historically speaking, NAV has had a tendency to build big and inflexible frameworks to compensate for areas where NAV itself lacked expertise, in order to prevent errors. These static frameworks were supervised by strong control mechanisms and a project model which let little room for flexibility or autonomy. This led to a very low change, while opening for more thorough testing and quality assurance (of very few solutions), since things did not change as fast.

We do not see this as a fitting solution for UD work in NAV. Instead, UD has to be integrated into a system that can scale in a fast product development process. A scaffold which acts as a strong support mechanism for development teams is a critical factor to succeeding with competence building within several areas of competence. To succeed, the teams need help to see what they are not able to see for themselves – both in form of support structures (such as a template for an accessibility statement, the Design system and automated testing) and in form of strategic competence building (including possible help by the UD expert team). This should also be a scaffold that can be built down when the competence level within the teams is high enough, a bit like removing support wheels when one has learned to ride the bicycle. With this in mind, we suggest the following priorities: **(1) A UD strategy**, as part of an overall strategy at NAV, including a clear mandate for UD and the UD team, as well as consequences and incentives for meeting UD requirements. Both Meadows and Begnum indicate that a strategy will have severe effects on the UD work in NAV. We assume that it also will be critical for prioritizing UD in NAV and to build in time as a buffer, meaning that teams prioritize to use time both for UD testing and building UD competence. It should also include how to include internal resources using assistive technology better in the development process. (2) A plan for strategic competence building (based on today's UD coaching), which also should include the startup of an ambassador network. This has to be an ongoing process which will overlap with other measures. As argued above, this will be needed to achieve compliance over time and an essential measure to prevent a system collapse regarding strain on the UD expert team. (3) A UD standard, which outlines required outcomes and a recommended best praxis. (4) A template for an accessibility statement A UD quality assessment of all of NAV's services to achieve a more realistic picture of the status quo and to more easily be able to predict which teams will need how much and what kind of support. (5) An UD quality assessment of all of NAV's digital services, at least of all services that target end users (those are the services hat have to be compliant from 2021). This QA should use the accessibility statement template, and statements from different solutions should be able to generate statistic data that informs the UD team and NAV's leadership on the status quo. This data will be important to develop a realistic plan for UD fixes and be needed to **apply for a time-limited exemption** from the requirements. **(6) Updating the Design system**

and frontend framework. This will enable development teams to prevent UD errors and to improve the design quality of their solution with relatively little effort. **(7) Strengthen the efforts on automated UD testing**. This is also a measure to reduce the time and effort teams need to comply with UD requirements.

5.3   Reflections on Our Research Approach

In the previous section, we answered our research questions; This section represents a discussion on the success of the utilized approach to inform strategic work on intervention points. We also discuss whether we believe the recommended system mechanisms for NAV can be extended to similar organizations in order to meet the intention of the UD legislation and current quality benchmarks

Leverage Points and Critical Success Criteria as Indicators of Intervention Points. Both Meadows and Begnum point to similar areas that should be prioritized to leverage UD quality in an organisation. This indicates high-level LPs and CSCs are good starting points to guide strategic work on how to initiate change in the system. In order to balance the system, we identify additional interventions that are hypothesized to have a large effect on stabilizing the system. As NAV aims to create a strategy that both reaches timely compliance and is sustainable, bot the identified high leverage points and the insights into balancing factors inform the future strategy work on UD in NAV.

Value for Other Organizations. In-depth case based qualitative insights cannot scientifically be generalized to other cases. This article is not considering the external validity of our data. In this case-study we have utilized our knowledge of NAV as an organization and of its UD efforts to search for leverage points that could guide our future efforts to secure UD quality. It is likely that similar leverage points exist in similar organizations. However, we assume the greatest value for other organizations is the in showing how to apply systemic thinking to both consider effective measures to improve UD in their systems, and consider mechanisms to balance their systems. We theorize that if time is not an issue, the balancing mechanisms could be prioritized over high-level interventions, as they would work as abilitators to enable trigger success in a more sustainable environment. This approach could better facilitate grassroot movements.

GIGA Mapping. GIGA mapping visualizations made it possible for us see the holistic picture of the problematiques and utilized for further reflecting together, see interrelated functions, and to discuss content from which new questions emerged. Hence, GIGA mapping served as a medium for a reflective practice. GIGA mapping is applied in the Design Section and IT department at NAV. In addition, the method can be applied to other similar problematiques in other similar organizations. Accordingly, in addition to contribute to design research methodology within the area of UD, the reflections concerning our use of GIGA-mapping contributes to the design research within systemic design.

6   Conclusion

All over Europe, regulations on UD of IT is being updated and extended. These changes will come into force in Norway in 2021. The Norwegian Labour and Welfare Administration (NAV) is responsible for major social security schemes in Norway. NAV IT has been transformed to support the rapid speed of service digitalization. In this paper we have analyzed the emerged organizational system in NAV, and the degree to which current structures 1) facilitate best practice and 2) ensure legal compliance.

We find that NAV is lacking sufficient system mechanisms for ensuring legal compliance in the current system. Based on the findings, we discuss the prioritized places to intervene in the system to change this. We conclude that strategic plans that clearly express UD values and outline goals, clarify requirements and outlines system rules is needed to assure timely compliance. Based on theory this is considered the most important intervention, and the only strategy to achieve UD compliance in a short window of time. However, we do not only want to facilitate compliance with best practice and regulations *in time*, we also want to identify mechanisms necessary to stabilize the system *over time*. To do so, we advise NAV to prioritize balancing and abilitating factors. In particular, we would advise NAV to focus on strategic compretence building, to empower teams and make it possible to scale UD work to the desired speed of digitalization. We also recommend the support of measures that prevent UD errors or reduce time and effort needed for UD testing, such as NAV's Design system and automatization of UD testing where possible.

We believe the methodological approach applied in this paper showcases how theoretical and empirical knowledge can be merged using system thinking, in order to aid organisations in their strategic work to build up systems that are sustainable over time.

References

1. UN: Convention on the Rights of Persons with Disabilities (CRPD) (2006). https://www.un. org/disabilities/documents/convention/convoptprot-e.pdf
2. KMD: FOR-2017-09-13-1417, Forskrift om endring i forskrift om universell utforming av informasjons- og kommunikasjonsteknologiske (IKT)-løsninger, K.-o. moderniseringsde-partementet, Editor. Lovdata (2017). https://lovdata.no/dokument/LTI/forskrift/2017-09-13-1417
3. AHO and Halogen: Practicing Systems Oriented Design: A Guide for Businesses and Organisations that Want to Make Real Changes. Printhouse AS, Oslo (2014)
4. Blaasvær, L., Sevaldsson, B.: Educational planning for systems oriented design: applying systemic relationships to meta-mapping of GIGA maps. In: 21st International Conference on Engineering and Product Design Education (E&PDE 2019). E&PDE, Glasgow (2019)
5. Meadows, D.H.: Thinking in Systems: A Primer. Earthscan, UK (2009)
6. Meadows, D.: Leverage points: places to intervene in a system, Hartland (1999)
7. Røssvoll, T.H., Fuglerud, K.S.: Best practice for efficient development of inclusive ICT. In: Stephanidis, C., Antona, M. (eds.) UAHCI 2013. LNCS, vol. 8009, pp. 97–106. Springer, Heidelberg (2013). https://doi.org/10.1007/978-3-642-39188-0_11

8. Garrido, A., Rossi, G., Medina, N.M., Grigera, J., Firmenich, S.: Improving accessibility of web interfaces: refactoring to the rescue. Univers. Access Inf. Soc. **13**(4), 387–399 (2013)

9. Schulz, T., Fuglerud, K.S., Arfwedson, H., Busch, M.: A case study for universal design in the Internet of Things. In: Universal Design 2014: Three Days of Creativity and Diversity. IOS Press, Lund (2014)

10. Abascal, J., et al.: Rethinking universal accessibility: a broader approach considering the digital gap. Univers. Access Inf. Soc. **15**(2), 179–182 (2015)

11. Aizpurua, A., Arrue, M., Vigo, M.: Prejudices, memories, expectations and confidence influence experienced accessibility on the Web. Comput. Hum. Behav. **51**(1), 152–160 (2015)

12. Jung, B.K., Son, C.Y., Park, S.W., Kim, J.Y., Kang, B.G.: Analysis of ICT accessibility policy and implementation in South Korea. In: Information and Communication Technology Convergence (ICTC), Jeju, South Korea (2015)

13. Fuglerud, K.S., Sloan, D.: The link between inclusive design and innovation: some key elements. In: Kurosu, M. (ed.) HCI 2013. LNCS, vol. 8004, pp. 41–50. Springer, Heidelberg (2013). https://doi.org/10.1007/978-3-642-39232-0_5

14. Begnum, M.E.N.: Ensuring universal design of ICT: triggering the triggers!. In: UDHEIT - Universal Design and Higher Education in Transformation Congress. Awaiting Publication, Dublin (2018)

15. Harder, S.K., Begnum, M.E.N.: Promoting and obstructing factors for successful universal design. In: Norsk konferanse for organisasjoners bruk av IT (NOKOBIT). Open Journal Systems, Bergen, Norway (2016)

16. Thorgersen, A.: Digitale tjenester og brukerens tillit til NAV. In: Arbeid og velferd, nav.no. (2017)

17. KMD: St.meld. nr.27 (2015–2016) Digital agenda for Norge—IKT for en enklere hverdag og økt produktivitet, N.M.o.L.G.a.M.K.-o. moderniseringsdepartementet), Editor, Regjeringen. no (2015). https://www.regjeringen.no/contentassets/fe3e34b866034b82b9c623c5cec 39823/no/pdfs/stm201520160027000dddpdfs.pdf

18. KMD: Én digital offentlig sektor – Digitaliseringsstrategi for offentlig sektor 2019–2025, N. M.o.L.G.a.M.K.-o. moderniseringsdepartementet), Editor, Regjeringen.no (2019). https:// www.regjeringen.no/contentassets/db9bf2bf10594ab88a470db40da0d10f/no/pdfs/digitaliser ingsstrategi_for_offentlig_sektor.pdf

19. NAV. *Tilgjengelighet og universell utforming*. 2013 04.12.2019 [cited 2019 13.01]; Available from: https://www.nav.no/no/nav-og-samfunn/kontakt-nav/teknisk-brukerstotte/ nyttig-a-vite/tilgjengelighet-og-universell-utforming

20. W3C: Web Content Accessibility Guidelines (WCAG) 2.0. W3C (World Web Web Consortium) (2008). https://www.w3.org/TR/WCAG20/

21. EU: Directive (EU) 2016/2102 of the European Parliament and of the Council of 26 October 2016 on the accessibility of the websites and mobile applications of public sector bodies, EUR-Lex (2016). http://eur-lex.europa.eu/legal-content/EN/TXT/HTML/?uri=CELEX:3201 6L2102&from=EN

22. Leedy, P.D., Ormrod, J.E.: Practical Research Planning and Design, 10th edn. Pearson Education Limited, Essex (2014)

23. Begnum, M.E.N., Harder, S.K., Hjartnes, Ø.N.: Ensuring universal design of ICT: predicting the likelihood of universal design through measuring ICT-projects critical criteria compliance. Manuscripts submitted to Interacting with Computers

24. Hanington, B., Martin, B.: Universal Methods of Design: 100 Ways to Research Complex Problems, Develop Innovative Ideas, and Design Effective Solutions. Rockport, Beverly (2012)

25. Marshall, C., Rossman, G.B.: Designing Qualitative Research, 5th edn, p. 321. Sage, Los Angeles (2011)
26. Lazar, J., Feng, J.H., Hochheiser, H.: Research Methods in Human-Computer Interaction. John Wiley, West Sussex (2010)
27. Merriam, S.B.: Qualitative Research, a Guide to Design and Implementation, 2nd edn. Wiley, San Francisco (2009). Jossey-Bass, CA
28. Schön, D.A.: The Reflective Practitioner: How Professionals Think in Action. Arena, Aldershot (1995)
29. Abson, D.J., et al.: Leverage points for sustainability transformation. J. Hum. Environ. **46**(1), 30–39 (2016)
30. Sevaldson, B.: GIGA-mapping: visualisation for complexity and systems thinking in design. In: NORDES 2011. Nordic Design Research, Helsinki (2011)

Process Modelling (BPM) in Healthcare – Breast Cancer Screening

Inês Terras Marques[1]([⊠]), Carolina Santos[2], and Vítor Santos[1]

[1] Nova Information Management School, NOVA University of Lisbon,
Campus de Campolide, 1070-312 Lisbon, Portugal
{m20170211,vsantos}@novaims.unl.pt
[2] National School of Public Health, Public Health Research Centre, NOVA
University of Lisbon, Avenida Padre Cruz, 1600-560 Lisbon, Portugal
c.santos@ensp.unl.pt

Abstract. Breast cancer is a malignant epithelial neoplasm and it is a public health problem that has high incidence and mortality in women. Focusing the clinical performance on processes is proving to be the way to improve morbidity and mortality statistics. Business process management (BPM) is a management field that improves and analyzes business processes according to organizations' strategies. The early diagnosis of breast cancer is of great importance since it will enable more conservative treatments and a longer disease-free survival. Organized oncology screening programs, with all elements properly prepared, revealed to be more efficient than the opportunistic screenings. BPM usage will enable optimize and manage all processes from the screening until the diagnosis and treatment. The aim of this study is identification and modelling of BPM processes for the healthcare sector, namely, for Portuguese organized breast cancer screening. To achieve this goal, it was required the identification of the main processes by an interview to the employees and the development of "As-Is" diagrams. Some of the problems in a macroscopic way were detected and improvement suggestions were made.

Keywords: Business process management · Oncology · Frameworks

1 Introduction

Breast cancer is a public health problem since it's the most frequent cancer among women and one of the principal causes of cancer related death in women worldwide [1–3]. According to the International Agency for Research on Cancer (IARC), 2016, "before age of 75 years, 1 in 22 women will be diagnosed with breast cancer and 1 in 73 women will die from breast cancer, worldwide". In Portugal, in 2012, more than 6000 new cases appear and around 1600 women, per year, died with this disease [4].

Breast cancer is a malignant epithelial neoplasm, characterized by an uncontrolled growth of the abnormal breast cells with metastasis capacity [5]. The early diagnosis of breast cancer is of great importance since the detection of small tumors or tumors in evolutionary phase non-invasive, will enable treatments less mutilating, with more conservative surgeries and a longer disease-free survival [5]. Oncology screenings

M. Antona and C. Stephanidis (Eds.): HCII 2020, LNCS 12188, pp. 98–109, 2020.
https://doi.org/10.1007/978-3-030-49282-3_7

allow earlier diagnosis of the disease and aims the reduction of cancers' mortality [6]. Any screening program is dependent of a sequence of interventions, beginning in the identification of the target population until the post treatment [6].

Business process management (BPM) is a management field characterized for being a well-designed, implemented, executed, integrated, monitored and controlled approach, that improves and analyses business processes according to organizations' strategies [7, 8]. A business process is composed by structured and interconnected activities, which produce a service or product focused in the client's needs [8].

Targeting optimal patient outcomes is the aim of health service delivery. However, focusing the clinical performance on processes is proving to be the way to improve morbidity and mortality statistics [7].

Although the application of BPM techniques has been increasing in the healthcare sector, there are still some failures due to improper adoption of BPM and because of content and structural issues present in the health care sector [7]. BPM principles may be applied in hospitals, in primary care and public health [7].

With the current widespread of technology and its importance in several different areas, its usage in the diagnosis and treatment of oncology diseases can be an important feature to improve the quality and the implementation of preventive and screening actions. Organized screening programs, with all elements properly prepared, revealed to be more efficient than the opportunistic screenings (non-organized and unmonitored) [6]. It's here that BPM gets its importance since with this technique it will be possible to optimize and manage all processes from the screening until the diagnosis and treatment.

The goal of this paper is the identification and modelling of BPM processes for the healthcare sector, more precisely, processes for the breast cancer screening, by:

- Identification of the AS-IS model for the processes of the screening of breast cancer, according to the Portuguese League Against Cancer (LPCC);
- Description of each activity present in the process and the role of each stakeholder;
- Identification of bottlenecks and problems;
- Proposal of process improvements considering the available information and AS-IS model analysis.

The structure of the paper is as follows: Literature Review, Methodology, Critical analysis, Conclusion and Future Work.

2 Literature Review

2.1 Breast Cancer

The human body is composed of several millions of cells which coordinate between themselves to constitute tissues and organs [9]. Normal cells grow and divide for a period of time and then stop growing and dividing until its needed again to replace defective or dying cells [9, 10]. When this cell' reproduction become out of control and the cells lose their ability to stop dividing and spreading, a mass called tumor is formed and the cancer appears [9–11]. The tumor can be classified as benign or malign according to its features [9–11]. Breast cancer is a malignant cell growth in the breast tissue which has the capacity to spread to other areas of the body when left untreated [9, 10]. It is classified according to stages which describe the size of the tumor and if it has spread to lymph nodes or metastasized to distant organs. The risk of a woman develops breast cancer increase with the age, the majority of the cases appear in women older than 50 years, and the way to reduce its mortality is with an early detection and effective treatment [3, 10]. Breast cancer is one of the most treatable types of cancer when early detected [2].

2.2 Screening

Prevention of cancer can be reached through primary prevention, intended to prevent the occurrence of cancer, or through secondary prevention, which has the purpose of an earlier diagnosis of the cancer in order to reduce related mortality and distress [3]. The principal elements of secondary prevention are screening and early clinical diagnosis and they are essential components of any cancer control program [3].

Screening programs can enable the detection of cancer in earlier stages which allow the usage of suitable treatment [3]. The implementation of these programs has as expected outcome the decrease of mortality rates [12].

There are two types of screening programs, being classified as organized, also called population-based, or opportunistic screening programs. Organized screening programs are at national or reginal level, have a team responsible for health care and organization, a structure for quality assurance and an explicit policy while the opportunistic screenings result from a recommendation from a routine medical consultation, for an unrelated problem, based on a possibly increased risk of developing breast cancer (due to family history or other risk factors) [3]. Population-based screenings reach women who haven't participated in opportunistic screening and are the programs that enable more equity in access, guaranteeing that all women including those from lower socioeconomic groups obtain adequate diagnosis and treatment [3, 13]. However, it doesn't completely eliminate social inequalities access [3, 12].

Breast Cancer Organized Screening. Since the late 1980s, with the results of the effectiveness of the trials on breast cancer screening becoming available, that its programs have been in place in Europe [12]. The council recommendation of December 2nd, 2003, at European Union level, established a list of requirements to implement an organized, population-based breast cancer screening program [12].

Currently, the breast cancer screening with mammography alone is the population-based method used in the majority of the European countries for the early detection of this cancer [1]. Screening asymptomatic women includes the execution of mammography screening, at specified intervals, and referring those women with positive results for additional diagnostic investigations and possibly treatment [3]. A decrease on the breast cancer mortality in women aged 50 to 74 years has been shown [1].

The screening programs are offered to normal-risk women beginning with ages comprised between 40 to 50 years old and ending with ages between 69 to 74 years old and usually in intervals of two years [3]. Mammography can be used to check for breast cancer in women without signs or symptoms of the disease and is characterized for being an imaging modality specifically for breast tissue, which uses low energy X-ray

[11]. From all the breast cancers detected by mammography screening, less than one third would also be detectable by clinical examination [3]. Normally, in the screening programs, the mammography involves two views (X-ray images) of each breast and double reading [11]. With this technique it is possible the early detection of malignant tumours before the tumour spreads [11].

However, mammography screening has also some limitations and undesirable effects associated. As for example, it is not effective in detecting lesions in women with radiologically dense breasts, the radiation exposure and the false-negative or false-positive mammography results [1, 11, 14]. The reported rate of false-negative results in mammography is of at least 10% and false-positive results can lead to anxiety and psychological distress [11].

Challenges for Breast Cancer Organized Screening. Although mammography continues to be the gold standard of the screening methods [14], it has some limitations. Nowadays, research and discussions moved on to the use of digital breast tomosynthesis as routine for screening programs but until now no screening program has changed to routinely use it [3]. Digital breast tomosynthesis produces quasi three-dimensional images, reducing the effect of tissue superimposition, which allows better visualization and localization of potential lesions, improving mammography interpretation [3]. It improves the rate of cancer detection and reduce the proportion of patients' recall for additional imaging studies [15]. Although the radiation dose of digital mammography with tomosynthesis is around twice of the dose of mammography alone, it is considerably reduced by reconstruction of two-dimensional images from the three-dimensional images [3].

Another studies have shown that breast ultrasonography and breast Magnetic Resonance Imaging (MRI) are the best alternatives for mammography and may improve the breast cancer prognosis [16]. Breast ultrasonography screening have frequently focused on populations with mammographic density since dense breast tissue is a risk factor for breast cancer and reduces the sensitivity of mammography. Ultrasonography-only detected cancers were usually early-stage cancers, comparable or even in earlier stages than cancers detected through mammography [3]. Breast MRI have been proving to be a good alternative to mammography since it doesn't involve radiation exposure however, its specificity is too low and the interpretation is complex and not standardized, being recommended only for screening of high-risk women [16].

Molecular diagnostics are revolutionizing human oncology in order to enable early detection, target therapies or monitoring treatment [17]. Liquid biopsies, through the identification of genetic signatures associated with cancers, allow the detection of tumours in preclinical stages [17, 18].

In order to early and accurately identify the breast cancer it's important and needed the extraction of information from previous diagnosis data [9, 10]. Since machine learning techniques enable computers to learn from past data and patterns its usage in medical diagnosis is gradually increasing [10]. Computer-aided diagnosis systems are being proposed since it helps reducing the number of unnecessary breast biopsies [11]. As concluded by Mušić et Gabeljić [11], the use of neural network to classify mammographic tumors is beneficial and should be used by physicians to improve quality, accuracy and potentially the speed of digital mammography.

2.3   Portuguese League Against Cancer

The Portuguese league Against Cancer (LPCC) is a national entity of reference in the support for oncology patients and their family, in promoting health, in cancer prevention and in promoting research and training in oncology. It is composed by 5 regional nuclei: Azores, Centre, Madeira, North and South [19].

The LPCC is known as a reference organization in breast population-based screening program. LPCC screening activities are implemented in all geographic regions, excluding Algarve [20]. Their action is supported in protocols with Governmental Regional Health Administrations (North, Center, Lisbon and Tagus Valley, Alentejo) under the Ministry of Health.

In this paper the breast cancer screening process provided by the LPCC nuclei of the south will be used as a case study.

2.4   Business Process Management

Business Process Management (BPM) has gain power and interest to organizations due to its capacity to help achieve operational excellence, increase productivity and save costs [21].

When starting a BPM initiative, the first question that needs to be clarified should be: "Which business processes do we aim to improve?" [22]. Before applying BPM, the team needs to have an idea of what business processes may be causing the problems [22]. Considering this, it's important to start the BPM practices by describing the processes of the organization, building "AS-IS" models, and analysing them according to the organization's data and the knowledge of its employees [23]. A critical step in BPM is understand the value delivered by a process, by measuring it with process performance measures. There are four fundamental measurements [22, 24]:

- Time – Associated with process duration.
- Cost – Value associated with a process, which is typically a monetary value;
- Capacity – Amount or volume of a realistic output related to a process;
- Quality – Normally expressed as a percentage of actual to optimal.

With the previous analysis, an understanding of the issues in the process and the potential solutions can help prepare an improved process model, the "TO-BE" model [22, 23].

3   Methodology

3.1   Identification of Processes

The existing processes for Breast Cancer Organized Screening performed by LPCC were studied. In order to completely understand the processes an interview was done to the employees (Table 1).

Table 1. Identified processes of the Breast Cancer Organized Screening

Number	Name	Type
1	Patients' invitation	Process
2	Screening	Process
3	Reading of the exam	Process
3.1	Sending results	Sub-process
3.2	Check-up consultation	Sub-process
4	Sending results	Process
5	Check-up consultation	Process

3.2   Recognition of Entities

Within a business process, there are several organizational entities that can interact with each other. To analyse and transform a process, it's necessary to completely understand what are the entities present and their relationship.

The entities can be:

- Actors - people that perform the activities in the process;
- Systems - software used by the actors to perform their functions and to communicate with various stakeholders;
- Documents - methods used by the actors to share information that can be digital or non-digital documents (Tables 2, 3 and 4).

Table 2. Identified actors of the Breast Cancer Organized Screening

Actor	Description
Administrative technician	Person who gives administrative support for all the process
Radiologist technician	Person who is responsible for the screening exam
Radiologist	Person who is responsible for reading the exam and classify it
Family doctor	Person who will receive the letter with the screening result to deliver to the patient
Patient	Person submitted to the screening process

Table 3. Identified systems of the Breast Cancer Organized Screening

System	Description
SIRCM	Informatic system that monitors every activity in the screening program
Post mail	System used to send the invitation letters
Telephone	System used to re-invite eligible women for screening
Microsoft excel	Database of patients' information

Table 4. Identified documents of the Breast Cancer Organized Screening

Document	Description
Invitation letter	It is a printed letter sent to the women eligible for screening to invite her for the next screening in her residence area (15 days before screening)
Exam	It is a digital document with the exam
Letter with the result	Letter sent to family doctor with the screening result
Anamnesis	Printed form filled by the patient with personal information and relevant questions for the screening

3.3   Design of Diagrams

Modelling processes helps understand the process and share this understanding with the people involved in it while identifying and preventing issues. In this work, Bizagi will be used as software to develop the diagrams.

Macroprocess. The macroprocess is presented in Fig. 1 where several sub-processes can be seen. Each one of these sub-processes will be presented in the following chapters. In order to understand this macroprocess it's important to know what are the meaning of the exam's classifications: R1 - no abnormalities, R2 - benign findings, R3 - equivocal findings, R4 - suspected cancer and R5 - strongly suspected cancer.

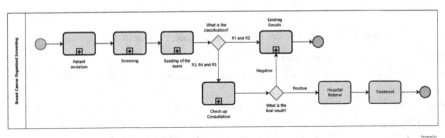

Fig. 1. Macroprocess for the Breast Cancer Organized Screening

Process "Patients' Invitation". The process "Patients' invitation" is performed by the administrative support unit which uses data provided by the ACES. The patients' database is sent as a Microsoft excel sheet and all that information is imported to the server SIRCM (Fig. 2).

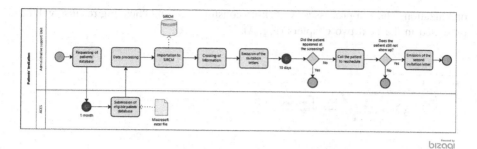

Fig. 2. Process "Patients' invitation"

Process "Screening". The process "Screening" is performed by an administrative technician and two radiologist technicians to an eligible woman which is called as patient. In this process there is one important document, the anamnesis that must be filled out by the patient every time she is screened (Fig. 3).

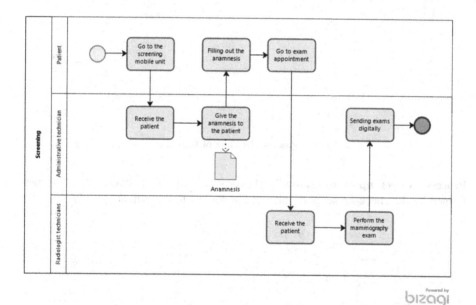

Fig. 3. Process "Screening"

Process "Reading of the Exam". The process "Reading of the exam" is performed by the radiologists but relies on the help of the reading, administrative and check-up support units. The consensus conference is done by the five radiologists of the organization. The sub-processes "Check-up consultation" and "Sending results" will be presented in the next two chapters (Fig. 4).

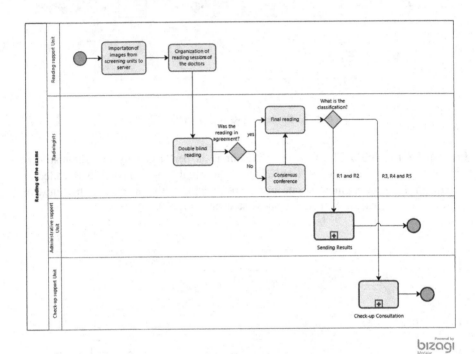

Fig. 4. Process "Reading of the exam"

Process "Check-up Consultation". The process "Check-up consultation" is performed by the check-up support unit and the doctors to the patient (Fig. 5).

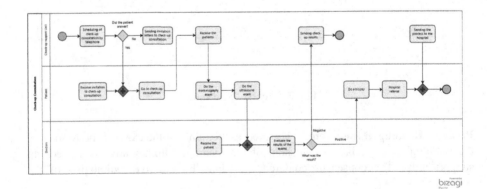

Fig. 5. Process "Check-up consultation"

Process "Sending Results". In the process "Sending Results" the radiologists, the administrative support unit and the family doctor will be involved in delivering the result to the patient. The results are delivered by the family doctor due to privacy issues (Fig. 6).

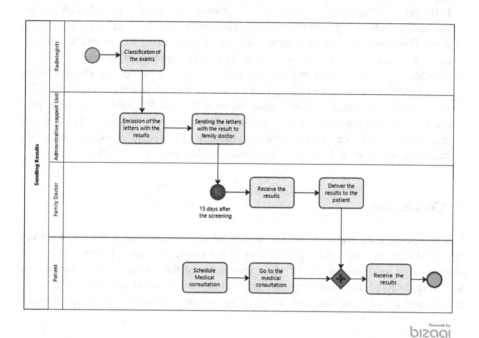

Fig. 6. Process "Sending Results"

4   Critical Analysis

Before updating a process is required a shared understanding of the current state of the process and if it's in agreement with the stated organization's objectives or not. This is achieved by process analysis [24].

The Breast Cancer Organized Screening under study follows the recommendation for the European countries, being well stablished the processes involved. However, breast cancer mortality rates can still be decreased, being an opportunity field to improve.

In the mainly important processes identified some critical analysis and improvements can be done as for example:

• In the process "Patients' invitation" an invitation letter is sent 15 days earlier to the patient but no telephone contact is done before the screening. The patient is only contacted by telephone if she didn't appear in the day of the screening. An improvement could be sending a message in the day before the screening, remembering the appointment, avoiding forgetfulness absences.

- In the process "Screening" the anamnesis is a printed form but it will be required in the process "Reading of the exams" where the radiologist will combine it with the mammography exams and previous information. The form could be changed into a digital format improving the file organization and crossing of information.
- In the process "Reading of the exam" it is necessary to combine the schedules of the five radiologists to organize the consensus conference what can delay the answering time. This time could be decreased using machine learning techniques to complement the evaluations in case of disagreement in the reading of the exam.
- Another aspect that could improve the time that all the process of Breast Cancer Organized Screening takes is the process that follows a classification higher than R3 in the exams. Currently classifications between R3 and R5 follows the same procedure however, knowing that R5 corresponds to a strong suspicious of cancer and that breast cancers can evolve quickly probably this type of classification should have priority or should do a biopsy already in the check-up consultation.

5 Conclusion

This is a positioning paper, where the mainly processes involved in the breast cancer organized screening with the appropriate entities (actors, systems and documents) were identified and modelled as "As-Is" diagrams. Some of the problems in a macroscopic way were detected and improvement suggestions were made in order to optimize the process and achieve the main objective of the process, the early detection of breast cancer.

6 Future Work

In future work a more detailed analysis will be performed in order to completely understand underlying issues and to allow the construction of high relevant "To-Be" models that could bring more efficiency to the screening processes.

References

1. Mathioudakis, A.G., et al.: Systematic review on women's values and preferences concerning breast cancer screening and diagnostic services. Psychooncology 28(5), 939–947 (2019)
2. Obaidullah, S.M., Ahmed, S., Gonçalves, T., Rato, L.: RMID: a novel and efficient image descriptor for mammogram mass classification. In: Kulczycki, P., Kacprzyk, J., Kóczy, L.T., Mesiar, R., Wisniewski, R. (eds.) ITSRCP 2018. AISC, vol. 945, pp. 229–240. Springer, Cham (2020). https://doi.org/10.1007/978-3-030-18058-4_18

3. IARC, H.W.: IARC HANDBOOKS Breast Cancer Screening. International Agency for Research on Cancer, 150 cours Albert Thomas, 69372 Lyon Cedex 08, France, vol. 15 (2016)
4. de Lacerda, G.F., et al.: Breast cancer in Portugal: temporal trends and age-specific incidence by geographic regions. Cancer Epidemiol. **54**, 12–18 (2019)
5. Cardoso, F.: 100 Perguntas chave no Cancro da mama, no. 2 (2017)
6. Miranda, N.: Relatório De Monitorização E Avaliação Dos Rastreios Oncológicos (2016)
7. Buttigieg, S., Dey, P.K., Gauci, D.: Business process management in health care: current challenges and future prospects. Innov. Entrep. Heal. **3**, 1 (2016)
8. Lopez-Sanchez, M., Campos, J., Musavi, A.: Approaches to hospital process management. Front. Artif. Intell. Appl. **202**(1), 409–418 (2009)
9. Devarriya, D., Gulati, C., Mansharamani, V., Sakalle, A., Bhardwaj, A.: Unbalanced breast cancer data classification using novel fitness functions in genetic programming. Expert Syst. Appl. **140**, 112866 (2019)
10. Bhardwaj, A., Tiwari, A.: Breast cancer diagnosis using genetically optimized neural network model. Expert Syst. Appl. **42**(10), 4611–4620 (2015)
11. Mušić, L., Gabeljić, N.: Predicting the severity of a mammographic tumor using an artificial neural network. In: Badnjevic, A., Škrbić, R., Gurbeta Pokvić, L. (eds.) CMBEBIH 2019. IP, vol. 73, pp. 775–778. Springer, Cham (2020). https://doi.org/10.1007/978-3-030-17971-7_115
12. Deandrea, S., et al.: Presence, characteristics and equity of access to breast cancer screening programmes in 27 European countries in 2010 and 2014. Results from an international survey. Prev. Med. (Baltim) **91**, 250–263 (2016)
13. WHO: WHO Position paper on mammography screening. Geneva WHO (2014)
14. Sadeghi, M., et al.: Feasibility test of dynamic cooling for detection of small tumors in IR thermographic breast imaging. Curr. Dir. Biomed. Eng. **5**(1), 397–399 (2019)
15. Ikejimba, L.C., et al.: A four-alternative forced choice (4AFC) methodology for evaluating microcalcification detection in clinical full-field digital mammography (FFDM) and digital breast tomosynthesis (DBT) systems using an inkjet-printed anthropomorphic phantom. Med. Phys. **46**, 3883–3892 (2019)
16. Jaglan, P., Dass, R., Duhan, M.: Breast cancer detection techniques: issues and challenges. J. Inst. Eng. Ser. B **100**(4), 379–386 (2019)
17. Wiley, C., Wise, C.F., Breen, M.: Novel noninvasive diagnostics. Vet. Clin. Small Anim. Pract. **49**, 781–791 (2019)
18. Gerratana, L., Davis, A.A., Shah, A.N., Lin, C., Corvaja, C., Cristofanilli, M.: Emerging role of genomics and cell-free DNA in breast cancer. Curr. Treat. Options Oncol. **20**(8), 68 (2019)
19. LPCC: Liga Portuguesa Contra o Cancro (2019). https://www.ligacontracancro.pt. Accessed 08 Nov 2019
20. Programa Nacional para as Doenças Oncológicas: Programa Nacional para as Doenças Oncológicas 2017 (2017)
21. Recker, J., Mendling, J.: The state of the art of business process management research as published in the BPM conference: recommendations for progressing the field. Bus. Inf. Syst. Eng. **58**(1), 55–72 (2016)
22. Dumas, M., La Rosa, M., Mendling, J., Reijers, H.A.: Fundamentals of Business Process Management. Springer, Cham (2018). https://doi.org/10.1007/978-3-642-33143-5
23. Szelągowski, M.: Evolution of the BPM lifecycle. In: Communication Papers of the Federated Conference on Computer Science and Information Systems, vol. 17, no. Ml, pp. 205–211 (2018)
24. ABPMP: BPM CBOK, 1st edn. (2013)

User Interfaces and Interaction Techniques for Universal Access

Brain-Computer Interfaces for Communication in Severe Acquired Brain Damage: Challenges and Strategies in Clinical Research and Development

Kirsten Brukamp[✉]

Protestant University of Applied Sciences,
Paulusweg 6, 71638 Ludwigsburg, Germany
k.brukamp@eh-ludwigsburg.de

Abstract. Brain-computer interfaces mediate interaction and communication via technology without relying on visible behavior. Thereby, they promise to benefit patients with neurological diseases that destroy motor functions. In particular, brain-computer interfaces may promote insight into mental states and cognitive functions in severe acquired brain damage, for example in disorders of consciousness (DOC), like the unresponsive wakefulness syndrome (UWS) and the minimally conscious state (MCS). The clinical research and development for brain-computer interfaces reveals multiple challenges, which are examined by methods of social science research. Strategies to cope with and to resolve obstacles are derived from contributions by caregivers, academic experts, and researchers. Challenges and strategies are identified and analyzed regarding the lack of validity in case of false results, the choice of communication topics, informed consent, well-being and avoidance of harm, transparency regarding restricted research resources, prevention of false hopes and beliefs, and data protection. Negative results concerning communication skills in the patient population with severe acquired brain damage are not valid for prognosis because of individual variants and the novel condition of the technology. Reasonable communication begins with exchanges about topics of everyday life and care. Informed consent, depending on legally authorized representatives, is legitimate in view of the potential benefit for the individual patient. Attention to the patients' levels of comfort during human-technology interaction fosters their quality of life. Regarding the research and development process, limited resources are to be made transparent, exaggerated expectations should be prevented, and data protection rules need to be followed.

Keywords: Human-technology interaction · Brain-Computer Interface (BCI) · Electroencephalography (EEG) · Severe acquired brain damage · Disorders of Consciousness (DOC) · Communication

M. Antona and C. Stephanidis (Eds.): HCII 2020, LNCS 12188, pp. 113–123, 2020.
https://doi.org/10.1007/978-3-030-49282-3_8

1 Introduction

The aim of this paper is to present empirical data on the challenges of clinical research situations in which brain-computer interfaces for communication are developed to benefit patients with severe neurological diseases. Thereby, the paper provides insights into strategies to translate basic research into practical innovations in the application area of neurotechnologies.

Research and development for brain-computer interfaces in health care are meant to support patients with diseases and disabilities. The clinical situations, in which these patients live and receive therapy, need to be taken into consideration in order to arrive at meaningful, effective, and responsible technologies. Consequently, the settings and contexts in health care facilities and nursing homes need to be examined. At the same time, the severely affected patients, who are the target group for communication by brain-computer interfaces, cannot normally voice their preferences and concerns reliably. Therefore, their wishes have to be deduced from multiple sources in order to provide them with adequate support by technologies.

The research and development project NeuroCommTrainer, which is an abbreviation for Training and Communication System for Nursing-Dependent Patients with Severe Brain Damage, is funded by the Federal Ministry for Education and Research in Germany from 2017 to 2020. The project part on implications regarding user experience and acceptance in NeuroCommTrainer is funded under grant no. 524-4013-16SV7791. The project aims at developing a brain-computer interface for communication and interaction with patients who suffer from severe acquired brain damage, including those ones with disorders of consciousness (DOC), such as the unresponsive wakefulness syndrome (UWS) and the minimally conscious state (MCS).

Severe acquired brain damage is a term that encompasses a wide variety of clinical manifestations as well as a range of causes. Typically, patients do not exhibit a stable state of consciousness, they do not reliably communicate in a meaningful manner, and they are nursing-dependent in their activities of daily living. Severe acquired brain damage results from diseases and conditions like stroke, traumatic brain injury, and hypoxic brain damage. The prognosis depends on the underlying disease process.

Disorders of consciousness (DOC) are extreme variants of severe acquired brain damage. In the unresponsive wakefulness syndrome (UWS), patients are awake, but they do not respond to attempts of verbal or non-verbal communication. In the minimally conscious state (MCS), patients can follow objects with their eyes, but they are unable to respond reliably as well. Humans with UWS and MCS are completely nursing-dependent. Whereas the term severe acquired brain damage is fairly broad, UWS and MCS are highly specific notions. Diagnosing these diseases requires specialized neurologists' expert knowledge. Nevertheless, behavioral characteristics occasionally fluctuate and thereby make a distinct diagnosis difficult [1].

The recovery is typically slow, requiring rehabilitation for many months after the insult (cf. [2]). Nevertheless, some patients have been reported to wake up from UWS years and decades after developing it. MCS carries a better prognosis than UWS, and traumatic causes are associated with better prognoses than non-traumatic ones in both UWS and MCS [3].

Previous studies demonstrated that some patients in UWS and MCS are capable of willfully modulating their brain activities [4]. In particular, one study examined 54 patients in Belgium and the United Kingdom with mental-imagery tasks by functional magnetic resonance imaging (fMRI) [5]. Of those, five patients could willfully modulate their brain activity, and one patient was capable to answer yes-or-no questions [5]. Therefore, the patients' brain activities could be utilized to elicit communication instead of non-existent verbal or non-verbal means.

The brain-computer interface in the project NeuroCommTrainer relies on electroencephalography (EEG), which renders it non-invasive, portable, and affordable, particularly in comparison to alternative technologies that measure brain signals, such as fMRI, which was employed in previous studies (cf. [5]). In the project, EEG data are related to the patients' mental states on a statistical level [6]. Long-term nursing home residents are firstly examined regarding their potential to benefit from a non-invasive brain-computer interface that is based on EEG. A select group secondly undergoes training, during which the patients' responses to auditory and haptic stimuli are measured.

NeuroCommTrainer is an interdisciplinary research and development project that involves partners from academia, health care and nursing, as well as small enterprises. Their educational training and their current professional activities are in areas as diverse as psychology, cognitive neuroscience, medicine, nursing, sociology, philosophy, computer science, and engineering.

The patients with severe acquired brain damage are not normally capable of expressing their wishes and desires. Therefore, methods of empirical social science research were utilized in the interaction with various target groups, including caregivers. The aim was to relate to user experiences, to gain an understanding of the patients' needs, to consider their interests, and to improve the complex research situation overall.

2 Methods

The project NeuroCommTrainer as a whole largely relies on quantitative methods in cognitive neuroscience, psychology, engineering, and computer science in order to analyze EEG data and to construct a brain-computer interface. For examining the social and psychological contexts of user experience, acceptance, and acceptability, the methods mainly stem from qualitative social science research. Methods included participant observations, project workshops, expert discourses, and interviews.

Participant observations took place in the nursing home during routine care, EEG measurements, and special events for residents. Observations were meant to enhance understanding of the research setting and to informally acquaint the researchers with the research setting in clinical care. Topics were deduced for the workshops, discourses, and interviews.

Workshops with structured and moderated discourses took place at the beginning and in the middle of the project. The first workshop helped to clarify aims in the project and sensitized for ethical, legal, and social implications (ELSI). The second workshop focussed on personas and research directions. In the first workshop [7], ten project researchers were introduced to the theoretical foundations of dimensions that are frequently applied to promote responsible research and innovation (RRI), namely beneficence, autonomy, safety and security, justice, privacy, participation, and self-image [8]. The structured and moderated discourse included presentations on these dimensions, as they were applied to the project, and a plenary discussion to place the dimensions in relation to each other [7]. For the second workshop, typical personas and research directions were derived from the intermittent project results. Twelve participants developed them further, based on the available results, e.g. from interview studies. For both workshops, participants' discussions and written comments were subsequently summarized and put into context with each other and the literature. In addition, an educational session on data protection took place for exchange among the project partners.

Contributions from three academic law experts were related to medical device law, data protection, and informed consent. The experts were chosen according to their legal specializations that complemented the interdisciplinary knowledge in the project team. Results from these discourses were subsequently put in context by relating them to the relevant literature.

Interviews were conducted with nurses, therapists, physicians, and relatives as well as with researchers in the project NeuroCommTrainer. An interview guide was developed based on previous project experiences, e.g. from participant observations. Interviews were recorded and documented in a written format by literal transcription. Qualitative content analysis (cf. [9]) was employed to identify topics and arguments, which were relevant for shaping and changing the processes in research and development for neurotechnologies. Here, anonymous results are presented from the interviews with seven researchers and six nurses because they are most aware of the research processes and the patients' clinical conditions, respectively [10]. Quotations given here are translated and paraphrased in order to improve understanding by presenting coherent sentences. The protocol for the interview studies received an affirmative voting from the responsible local research ethics committee.

The results summarized here constitute recurring themes from several sources in qualitative social science research. The topics stem from the application of the methods that are described above, and they are illustrated by appropriate quotations from the interview studies. Members of the institutional research group Health – Technology – Ethics contributed to team discussions about the results from workshops, discourses, and qualitative studies.

3   Results

Fundamental results regarding challenges in clinical research and development for brain-computer interfaces in severe acquired brain damage and strategies to overcome them concern the following realms, among others:

3.1   Lack of Validity for False Results

Challenge: Positive results, i.e. meaningful responses to stimuli and questions, may be interpreted as valid indicators of residual or improving cognitive abilities in patients. In contrast, negative outcomes cannot be interpreted as indicating an absence of cognitive capabilities. In some residents, the technological approach may not work for a number of reasons, e.g. general unsuitability of the technology, ignorance of sensitive wakeful phases, or the subjects' lack of ability to respond consistently.

Researchers are skeptical about both positive and negative findings: "Do answers imply conscious commitment? The system could deliver false-positive and false-negative results." (source: researcher) Negative results are particularly distressful: "What do we do with negative results? We could find nothing." (source: researcher) Even in cases where patients respond meaningfully, the extent of conclusions from their reactions remains in doubt: "Regarding legal and ethical questions, is the answer to a question about quality of life binding? What to do with it?" (source: researcher)

Strategy: No conclusions about the patients' mental states, or the lack thereof, can be deduced from negative results. A variety of reasons could hinder the human-technology interaction in this severely damaged and vulnerable patient population. Predictions concerning prognosis are not appropriate on the level of the individual subject. Positive responses need to be confirmed and interpreted carefully. While answers to simple questions may be reliable, far-reaching conclusions about complex issues like quality of life do not appear dependable, at least during the initial steps of communication training.

3.2   Choice of Communication Topics

Challenge: Challenges arise when deciding on the topics that patients should be presented with during the first attempts of establishing a yes-or-no answer paradigm. Literature in neuroscience provides only scarce and preliminary advice on this issue.

Strategy: Empirical data from this project suggest that relatives and health care personnel prefer concrete and practical questions regarding the circumstances of care, e.g. how to deliver nursing care and design the rooms. The nurses, who provide direct care to the patients and are in continuous contact with them, are interested in receiving a feedback on their daily work as well as the activities and interventions that they offer: "For example, the residents may say: I want it that way. What you are doing now, I do not want." (source: nurse) Therefore, simple questions about the patients' former lives and their current preferences seem most appropriate.

3.3   Informed Consent

Challenge: The patients cannot give their consent to participate in research studies. The subjective situations, in which the patients live, can hardly be understood by neurologically normal people. Communication is deeply disturbed, but is generally regarded as a value to promote autonomy, quality of life, and participation in society again. Conclusions from the workshops and several remarks from the interviews prove the positive attitude towards interaction: "I like it when communication helps to give people more autonomy." (source: nurse) "To improve quality of life, communication, life." (source: nurse)

Strategy: In theory, participating subjects could later give their own consent, should communication with them become possible again by human-technology interaction. For now, informed consent from legally authorized representatives is required, and it should take the patients' wishes into account. The predominant argument to gain consent consists of a promise to try bettering the situation by reestablishing communication to support autonomy, quality of life, and participation.

3.4   Well-Being and Avoidance of Harm

Challenge: The patients cannot willfully communicate when they are tired, uncomfortable, or in pain during participation in the EEG measurements. Dependable feedback in real time does not exist for the human-technology interaction during the early stages of the project. It is open to speculation what subjects perceive, as a researcher remarks: "Even something as common as a tactile stimulation, which can cause a vibration at the hand, may mean a disturbance or burden." (source: researcher) At the same time, EEG could help to identify responses that are otherwise not discernible: "There may be channels that still function, for hearing, feeling, tasting. We may be able to reach people and cause emotions. And we can measure those." (source: nurse)

Strategy: As a consequence, very limited non-verbal hints regarding the patients' conditions need to be considered in order to avoid unnecessary burdens. Researchers and nurses pay close attention to reactions during the measurements for research. They conclude the recordings in case the nursing home residents show signs of distress. Like a nurse recognizes, the research process requires "a high degree of attentiveness to do something good." (source: nurse)

3.5   Transparency Regarding Restricted Research Resources

Challenge: Relatives of nursing home residents are highly interested and frequently deeply involved in the current care. Almost all of them are very motivated to utilize novel technologies in order to promote positive changes for their loved ones. Nevertheless, the resources in research are limited. One brain-computer interface, which is built as part of the project, can only be offered to one resident at a time. In consequence, a few patients, who reveal promising results in the initial measurements, are chosen to continue testing. One researcher notes: "How to cope with the fact that there is choice involved? How to communicate that not everyone can have it?" (source: researcher)

Strategy: Relatives wish to be informed about all options that surface during research. Project partners in the nursing home have identified the need to address all concerns ahead of time. The scarce resources need to be explained to the relatives so that they do not expect too much. As a consequence, information sessions have been devised and held during which questions and concerns from relatives are addressed.

3.6 Prevention of False Hopes and Beliefs

Challenge: Personnel in the nursing home and the project find it important to prevent relatives from developing excessive hopes that brain-computer interfaces will heal the patients completely or better their situations significantly. At the same time, relatives need to understand that a lack of responses does not mean that clinical improvements are no longer possible. A researcher used an image to illustrate the relatives' hopes: "When all say farewell and leave, the baggage of expectations is left behind. It would be good to state early on what researchers can do and what they cannot do." (source: researcher)

Strategy: The nursing home personnel regard it as their responsibility to communicate both with the relatives and among themselves about the research setting: "It is part of our job to inform and accompany the relatives and to prepare the personnel." (source: nurse) Even after receiving formal consent from legally authorized representatives, the researchers maintain a stance of information and ask for persistent affirmation: "Conversations with relatives show that it is very important to continuously confirm that what we do is desired and that there is consent." (source: researcher) In consequence, educational sessions for legally authorized representatives and relatives are offered at the nursing home. Individual research results are documented in the patients' clinical files. Researchers are available to discuss questions, concerns, and preliminary outcomes, including negative ones.

3.7 Data Protection

Challenge: In this complex and multidisciplinary research and development project, diverse data are collected, analyzed, and generated at various sites with different methods. Clinical and EEG data are gathered from the patients with severe acquired brain damage, and interview data are collected from several target groups. EEG data need to be processed at several sites by different partners in order to contribute to the common goal of obtaining a brain-computer interface. Data stem both from the patients (e.g. clinical information, medical history, and current nursing care) and from the human-technology interaction (e.g. EEG measurements and recordings of activities).

Strategy: Data protection needed clarification in this project. The partners participated in an educational session on data protection by a recognized legal specialist for research settings. The pertinent law was reflected and applied to the project. A data protection statement was contrived and discussed with both the project partners and the nursing home, and it was finally approved there. One main result was the conclusion that a compromise was required between the subjects' right to privacy and some researchers' interests in collecting video recordings. The video recordings were restricted to a minimum extent, kept at one site only, transcribed to a written summary, and then deleted. In addition, data were transferred securely between the partner sites.

4 Discussion

In summary, the results reveal challenges in cognition-related research on an EEG-based, non-invasive brain-computer interface for patients with severe acquired brain damage. The themes presented repeatedly surfaced with several activities and methods of qualitative social science research during the course of the project. The interviewees partially identified hints at strategies to cope with the challenges, and the researchers in the project discussed the findings and devised clear-cut strategies to address the problems. Overall, the studies and activities demonstrate the importance of investigating the setting, into which a novel, meaningful technology is introduced, from the perspectives of various target groups in order to optimize human-technology interaction.

Concerning medical research with human beings, the Declaration of Helsinki [11], which contains widely recognized, but legally non-binding recommendations, states: "For a potential research subject who is incapable of giving informed consent, the physician must seek informed consent from the legally authorised representative. These individuals must not be included in a research study that has no likelihood of benefit for them unless it is intended to promote the health of the group represented by the potential subject, the research cannot instead be performed with persons capable of providing informed consent, and the research entails only minimal risk and minimal burden." ([11]: section 28) and "Research involving subjects who are physically or mentally incapable of giving consent, for example, unconscious patients, may be done only if the physical or mental condition that prevents giving informed consent is a necessary characteristic of the research group." ([11]: section 30).

Patients with severe acquired brain damage cannot typically give their consent for participation in research. Research with them is only performed in the project NeuroCommTrainer because their secluded condition is essential for the research and is meant to be altered significantly. These subjects are highly vulnerable because they cannot verbally express their wishes and concerns. Therefore, the informed consents from legally authorized representatives render the study legitimate. In the project NeuroCommTrainer, the personal benefit for each study participant is palpable. By entering the trial, every subject gets a chance to use the communication device, depending on the probability of a positive preliminary response.

Communication by brain-computer interfaces, which rely on brain activities in fMRI or EEG, is an example of motor-independent communication. This term implies that no movements take place, neither for verbal nor for non-verbal purposes. Quality criteria are the classic ones in psychological research, namely objectivity, reliability, and validity [12]. At present, the technology has not evolved to a state in which it allows stable long-term communication for patients with severe acquired brain damage. Therefore, no practical experiences are available from which meaningful recommendations can be drawn for facilitating, shaping, and interpreting communication. Nevertheless, the question how patients show competence to make their own decisions may be addressed prospectively and preliminarily on the theoretical level. Patients need to receive and understand information. Their comprehension is to be tested and confirmed. Moreover, the patients should experience consequences of their decisions. They need to receive confirmatory responses that their wishes are respected and followed.

Only then can they take questions about far-reaching decisions seriously and answer honestly rather than arbitrarily. Finally, the patients' preferences have to be seen in context with their whole situation as well as with the variety of treatment and communication options in order to benefit them most [12].

Relatives and nurses are frequently deeply involved in the care for patients with severe acquired brain damage. Their high degree of interest is discernible both in clinical contexts, like the nursing home in this project, and in the literature. Caregivers experience burdens regardless of the nursing setting, i.e., institutionalized versus care at home, with differential profiles of distress [13]. A study was conducted on narrative aspects in 29 articles that were published between 1990 and 2015 and dealt with the adaptation of caregivers in traumatic brain injury [14]. An evolution of four traditions in narration could be identified: burden/strain (1990–1999), appraisal/coping (2000–2005), quality of life (2006–2011), and resiliency (2012–2015) [14]. Social support, positive interpretations, and enjoyed activities could help caregivers in their situations [14]. A scoping review on family-oriented interventions after acquired brain injury identified more than 50 studies, which were heterogeneous and left a desire for a higher level of evidence [15]. Emotional support and education were named as core characteristics for family-oriented interventions [15]. The approach in this project is in line with these findings. Researchers and nursing home personnel focus on information, participation, and emotional support regarding the patients' relatives.

The requirements for data protection increased due to the advent of the General Data Protection Regulation (GDPR) in the European Union in 2016 [16]. In this project, the researchers developed the following recommendations: Data protection should be addressed early in the project. A dedicated educational session is highly informative, and a legal data protection specialist should provide the training. A written concept needs to be devised early in and revised during the project.

5 Conclusion

Brain-computer interfaces may mediate and improve interaction and communication for patients with severe acquired brain damage. Challenges for research and development as well as strategies to master them were identified in exchange with stakeholders, such as health care professionals, academic experts, and researchers. The results reveal the complex clinical situations in which the development of brain-computer interfaces for patients takes place. The outcomes lead to consequences and changes in the course of the patient- and user-oriented research. The experiences also prove informative regarding practical advice for comparable projects that work on novel neurotechnologies for clinical applications.

Human-technology interaction possesses the potential to benefit severely challenged patients with neurological diseases via brain-computer interfaces. When novel technologies are introduced into health care, the care settings need to be carefully examined in order to utilize technology meaningfully and successfully for the patients' welfare.

References

1. Giacino, J.T., Fins, J.J., Laureys, S., Schiff, N.D.: Disorders of consciousness after acquired brain injury: the state of the science. Nat. Rev. Neurol. **10**(2), 99–114 (2014). https://doi.org/10.1038/nrneurol.2013.279. Accessed 24 Feb 2020
2. Steppacher, I., Kaps, M., Kissler, J.: Against the odds: a case study of recovery from coma after devastating prognosis. Ann. Clin. Transl. Neurol. **3**(1): 61–65 (2015). https://doi.org/10.1002/acn3.269. Accessed 24 Feb 2020
3. Giacino, J.T., et al.: Comprehensive systematic review update summary: disorders of consciousness: report of the guideline development, dissemination, and implementation subcommittee of the American Academy of Neurology; the American Congress of Rehabilitation Medicine; and the National Institute on Disability, Independent Living, and Rehabilitation Research. Arch. Phys. Med. Rehabil. **99**(9), 1710–1719 (2018). https://doi.org/10.1016/j.apmr.2018.07.002. Accessed 24 Feb 2020
4. Chatelle, C., Chennu, S., Noirhomme, Q., Cruse, D., Owen, A.M., Laureys, S.: Brain-computer interfacing in disorders of consciousness. Brain Inj. **26**(12), 1510–1522 (2012). https://doi.org/10.3109/02699052.2012.698362. Accessed 24 Feb 2020
5. Monti, M.M., et al.: Willful modulation of brain activity in disorders of consciousness. N. Engl. J. Med. **362**, 579–589 (2010). https://doi.org/10.1056/nejmoa0905370. Accessed 24 Feb 2020
6. Finke, A., Steppacher, I., Kissler, J., Ritter, H.: Frequency band variations predict EEG single-trial classification performance in disorder of consciousness patients. In: Conference Proceedings – IEEE Engineering in Medicine and Biology Society 2018, pp. 1927–1930 (2018). https://doi.org/10.1109/embc.2018.8512719. Accessed 24 Feb 2020
7. Brukamp, K.: Responsible research and innovation for communication by brain-computer interfaces in severe brain damage. In: Boll, S., Hein, A., Heuten, W., Wolf-Ostermann, K. (eds.): Zukunft der Pflege – Innovative Technologien für die Praxis. Tagungsband der 1. Clusterkonferenz 2018, pp. 116–119. Future of Nursing – Innovative Technologies for Practice. Conference Proceedings of the First Joint Conference 2018, pp. 116–119. [German and English] Universität Oldenburg, Oldenburg (2018). https://www.pflegeinnovations zentrum.de/wp-content/uploads/2018/12/22.-Responsible-Research-und-Innovation-for-Communication-by-Brain-Computer-Interfaces-in-Severe-Brain-Damage.pdf. Accessed 24 Feb 2020
8. Manzeschke, A., Weber, K., Rother, E., Fangerau, H.: Ergebnisse der Studie „Ethische Fragen Im Bereich Altersgerechter Assistenzsysteme". Results of the study "ethical questions in the area age-appropriate assistive systems". [German] VDI/VDE Innovation + Technik Gmbh, Berlin (2013). https://www.technik-zum-menschen-bringen.de/dateien/service/broschuere-ethische-fragen-altersgerechte-assistenzsysteme.pdf/download. Accessed 24 Feb 2020
9. Mayring, P.: Qualitative content analysis: theoretical foundation, basic procedures and software solution. Klagenfurt, Austria (2014). nbn-resolving.de/urn:nbn:de:0168-ssoar-395173. Accessed 24 Feb 2020
10. Tirschmann, F., Brukamp, K.: Forschung an Neurotechnologien für erworbene Hirnschädigungen: Empirische Belege für die sozialen und ethischen Implikationen in der Pflegesituation. Research on neurotechnologies for acquired brain damage: empirical evidence for social and ethical implications in the nursing situation. [German] Pflege & Gesellschaft: Zeitschrift für Pflegewissenschaft Nurs. Soc. J. Nurs. Sci. [German] **24**(3), 218–236 (2019)

11. World Medical Association: WMA Declaration of Helsinki – Ethical Principles for Medical Research Involving Human Subjects. Fortaleza, Brazil (2013). https://www.wma.net/policies-post/wma-declaration-of-helsinki-ethical-principles-for-medical-research-involving-human-subjects. Accessed 24 Feb 2020

12. Brukamp, K.: Motorunabhängige Kommunikation durch körperlich hochgradig einges-chränkte Patienten. Neurowissenschaftliche Grundlagen und Patientenautonomie. Motor-independent communication by physically severely challenged patients: neuroscientific research results and patient autonomy. Der Nervenarzt Physician Neural Disord. [German] **84**(10), 1190–1195 (2013). https://doi.org/10.1007/s00115-013-3813-9. Accessed 24 Feb 2020

13. Steppacher, I., Kissler, J.: A problem shared is a problem halved? comparing burdens arising for family caregivers of patients with disorders of consciousness in institutionalized versus at home care. BMC Psychol. **6**(1), 58 (2018). https://doi.org/10.1186/s40359-018-0272-x. Accessed 24 Feb 2020

14. King, G., Nalder, E., Stacey, L., Hartman, L.R.: Investigating the adaptation of caregivers of people with traumatic brain injury: a journey told in evolving research traditions. Disabil. Rehabil. 2330–2367 (2020). https://doi.org/10.1080/09638288.2020.1725158. Accessed 24 Feb 2020

15. De Goumoëns, V., Rio, L.M., Jaques, C., Ramelet, A.S.: Family-oriented interventions for adults with acquired brain injury and their families: a scoping review. JBI Database System. Rev. Implement. Rep. **16**(12), 2330–2367 (2018). https://doi.org/10.11124/jbisrir-2017-003846. Accessed 24 Feb 2020

16. General Data Protection Regulation: Regulation (EU) 2016/679 of the European Parliament and of the Council of 27 April 2016 on the Protection of Natural Persons with Regard to the Processing of Personal Data and on the Free Movement of Such Data, and Repealing Directive 95/46/EC (General Data Protection Regulation) (2016). https://eur-lex.europa.eu/legal-content/EN/TXT/?uri=uriserv%3AOJ.L_.2016.119.01.0001.01.ENG&toc=OJ%3AL%3A2016%3A119%3ATOC. Accessed 24 Feb 2020

Evaluating Hands-On and Hands-Free Input Methods for a Simple Game

Mehedi Hassan[1(✉)], John Magee[2], and I. Scott MacKenzie[1]

[1] York University, Toronto, ON, Canada
mhassan@eecs.yorku.ca
[2] Clark University, Worcester, MA, USA

Abstract. We conducted an experiment to test user input via facial tracking in a simple computerized snake game. We compared two hands-on methods with a hands-free facial-tracking method to evaluate the potential of a hands-free point-select tool: *CameraMouse*. In addition to the experiment, we conducted a case study with a participant with mild cerebral palsy. For the experiment we observed mean game scores of 5.89, 3.34, and 1.94 for the keyboard, touchpad, and *CameraMouse* input methods, respectively. The mean game score using *CameraMouse* was 0.55 during the case study. We also generated trace files for the path of the snake and the cursor for the touchpad and *CameraMouse* pointing methods. In a qualitative assessment, all participants provided valuable feedback on their choice of input method and level of fatigue. Unsurprisingly, the keyboard was the most popular input method. However, positive comments were received for *CameraMouse*. Participants also referred to a few other simple games, such as *Temple Rush* and *Subway Surfer*, as potential candidates for interaction with the *CameraMouse*.

Keywords: Hands-free input · Face tracking · *CameraMouse* · Gaming

1 Introduction

The concept of human-computer interaction (HCI) is no longer confined to only physical interaction. While actions such as hovering the cursor of a mouse or touch-pad with our hands, clicking a button, typing, and playing games with our fingers are common forms of interaction, performing such tasks without physical touch is an intriguing idea. This is interesting both for non-disabled users and also for physically-challenged users.

We conducted an experiment with a simple yet well-known game: *Snake*. Since MIT student Steve Russel made the first interactive computer game, *Spacewar* in 1961 [7], computer games have evolved considerably. But, we did not conduct our experiment with a game that requires expensive graphics equipment or intense user interaction. For our study, the game was played with two hands-on methods and a hands-free method with facial tracking. We have re-created a version of

© Springer Nature Switzerland AG 2020
M. Antona and C. Stephanidis (Eds.): HCII 2020, LNCS 12188, pp. 124–142, 2020.
https://doi.org/10.1007/978-3-030-49282-3_9

Snake for this experiment. Our version is named *Snake: Hands-Free Edition*. This is a *Windows*-platform game. It can be played with three different input methods: keyboard, touchpad, and *CameraMouse*. The first two methods are hands-on and the third method is hands-free. By conducting this experiment, we explore the opportunities for accessible computing with hands-free input for gaming.

As part of our user study, we conducted a case study as well. The participant for this case study has mild cerebral palsy. Due to his physical condition, the case study was only conducted for the hands-free phase of our gaming experiment.

2 Related Work

Cuaresma and MacKenzie [3] compared two non-touch input methods for mobile gaming: tilt-input and facial tracking. They measured the performance of 12 users with a mobile game named *StarJelly*. This is an endless runner-style game. Players were tasked with avoiding obstacles and collecting stars in the game. A substantial difference was observed in the mean scores of the two input methods. Tilt-based input had a mean score of 665.8 and facial-tracking had a mean score of 95.1.

Roig-Maimó et al. [12] present *FaceMe*, a mobile head tracking interface for accessible computing. Participants were positioned in front of a propped-up *iPad Air*. Via the front-facing camera, a set of points in the region of the user's nose were tracked. The points were averaged, generating an overall head position which was mapped to a display coordinate. *FaceMe* is a picture-revealing puzzle game. A picture is covered with a set of tiles, hiding the picture. Tiles are turned over revealing the picture as the user moves her head and the tracked head position passes over tiles. Their user study included 12 able-bodied participants and four participants with multiple sclerosis. All able-bodied participants were able to fully reveal all pictures with all tile sizes. Two disabled participants had difficulty with the smallest tile size (44 pixels). *FaceMe* received a positive subjective rating overall, even on the issue of neck fatigue.

Roig-Maimó et al. [12] described a second user study using the same participants, interaction method, and device setup. Participants were asked to select icons on the *iPad Air*'s home screen. Icons of different sizes appeared in a grid pattern covering the screen. Selection involved dwelling on an icon for 1000 ms. All able-bodied participants were able to select all icons. One disabled participant had trouble selecting the smallest icons (44 pixels); another disabled participant felt tired and was not able to finish the test with the 44 pixel and 76 pixel icon sizes.

UA-Chess is a universally accessible version of the Chess game developed by Grammenos et al. [5]. The game has four input methods: mouse, hierarchical scanning, keyboard, and speech recognition. The hierarchical scanning method is designed for users with hand-motor disabilities. This scanning technique has a special "marker" that indicates input focus. A user can shift focus using "switches" (e.g., keyboard, special hardware, voice control). After focusing on an object another "switch" is used for selection. It currently supports visual and auditory output. A key innovative feature of this game is that it allows multi-player functionality.

Computer gaming inputs range from simple inputs to very intense interactions. For the hands-free interaction described herein, we focused not on the complexity or visual sophistication of the game, but rather on how participants would fare in a recreational environment with *CameraMouse*. Hence, we chose a simple game, *Snake*, similar to the simple games evaluated by Cuaresma and MacKenzie [3] and Grammenos et al. [5].

Our research on accessible computing was also aided by a literature review on "point-select tasks for accessible computing". Hassan et al. [6] compared four input methods using a 2D Fitts' law task in ISO 9241-9. The methods combined two pointing methods (touchpad, *CameraMouse*) with two selection methods (tap, dwell). Using *CameraMouse* with dwell-time selection is a hands-free input method and yielded a throughput of 0.65 bps. The other methods yielded throughputs of 0.85 bps (*CameraMouse* + tap), 1.10 bps (touchpad + dwell), and 2.30 bps (touchpad + tap).

MacKenzie [8] discusses evaluating eye tracking systems for computer input, noting that eye-tracking can emulate the functionality of a mouse. The evaluation followed ISO 9241-9, which lays out the requirements for non-keyboard input devices. Four selection methods were tested: dwell time, key selection, blink, and dwell-time selection. The throughput for dwell-time selection was 1.76 bits/s, which was 51% higher than the throughput for blink selection.

Gips et al. [4] developed *CameraMouse* which uses a camera to visually track any selected feature of the body such as the nose or tip of a finger. The tracked location controls a mouse pointer on the computer screen. These were early days in the development of *CameraMouse*. At this stage, the system did not have any tracking history. Cloud et al. [2] describe an experiment with *CameraMouse* with 11 participants, one with severe physical disabilities. Two application programs were used, *EaglePaint* and *SpeechStaggered*. *EaglePaint* is a simple painting application with the mouse pointer. *SpeechStaggered* is a program allowing the user to spell out words and phrases from five boxes that contain the entire English alphabet. A group of subjects wearing glasses showed better performance in terms of elapsed time than a group of subjects not wearing glasses.

Betke et al. [1] describe further advancements with *CameraMouse*. They examined tracking various body features for robustness and user convenience. Twenty participants without physical disabilities were tested along with 12 participants with physical disabilities. Participants were tested for performance of *CameraMouse* on two applications: *Aliens Game* which is an alien catching game requiring movement of the mouse pointer and *SpellingBoard*, a phrase typing application where typing was done by selecting characters with the mouse pointer. The non-disabled participants showed better performance with a normal mouse than with *CameraMouse*. Nine out of the 12 disabled participants showed eagerness in continuing to use the *CameraMouse* system.

Magee et al. [11] discussed a multi-camera based mouse-replacement system. They addressed the issue of an interface losing track of a user's facial feature due to occlusion or spastic movements. Their multi-camera recording system synchronized images from multiple cameras. For the user study, a three-camera version of the system was used. Fifteen participants were tested on a hands-free human-computer interaction experiment that included the work of Betke et al. [1] on *CameraMouse*. They tracked a user's head movement with three simultaneous video streams and software called *ClickTester*. They report that users put more effort into moving the mouse cursor with their head when the pointer was in the outer regions of the screen.

Magee et al. [10] did a user study with *CameraMouse* where dwell-time click generation was compared with *ClickerAID*, which detects a single intentional muscle contraction with an attached sensor. An evaluation tool called *FittsTask-Two*[1] [9, p. 291] was used for testing. Ten participants were tested and indicated a subjective preference for *ClickerAID* over dwell-time selection.

3 Software Systems

3.1 Camera Mouse

CameraMouse is a facial tracking application that emulates a physical mouse. Upon enabling *CameraMouse*, a point of the user's face is tracked. The preferable point of focus is usually the nose tip or the point between the eyebrows. If the user moves the tracked point of the face, the cursor moves on the screen accordingly. Figure 1 depicts how *CameraMouse* tracks a point on a user's face.

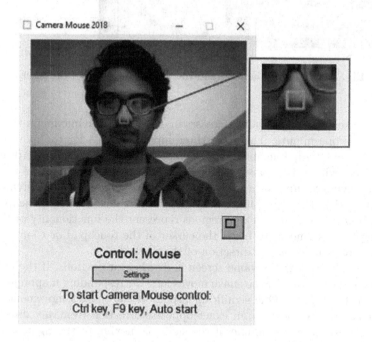

Fig. 1. Face-tracking by *CameraMouse*.

---

[1] https://www.yorku.ca/mack/HCIbook/.

3.2   Snake: Hands-Free Edition

We have remodeled the famous video game, *Snake*. We named our version of the game *Snake: Hands-Free Edition*. The idea remains the same as in the original game. In our version, a snake moves within the bounds of a surface. Two kinds of objects appear on this surface randomly. White objects are *fruits*, the black objects are *poisonous* objects (see Fig. 2). Colliding with a *fruit* will increase the snake's length and colliding with a *poisonous* object will kill the snake. The snake also dies if it collides with any wall or obstacle within the bounds of the surface.

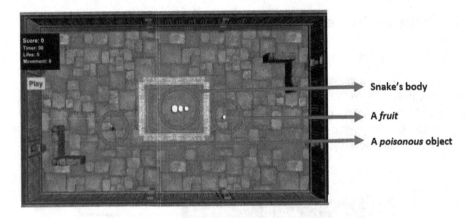

Fig. 2. The snake, the *fruit* and the *poisonous* object of the game.

The snake's speed gradually increases in each trial. The maximum time limit for a trial is one minute. There are three input methods for the movement of the snake: keyboard, touchpad, and *CameraMouse*. While altering directions of the snake with a keyboard, a user needs to press the four arrow keys of a standard keyboard: up, down, right, and left. The game window is divided into four regions (i.e., left, right, up, down) to aid movement with the touchpad and *CameraMouse* (see Fig. 3). These regions represent the functionality of the four arrow keys. A user needs to hover the cursor of the touchpad or *CameraMouse* over these regions to change direction of the Snake.

Figure 3 shows how the game screen is divided into regions. If the cursor is in the area marked as left, the snake moves left. Corresponding mappings occurs with the other regions. One significant aspect of the snake's movement is that it is not allowed to move to an exact opposite direction from any direction it is moving towards. For example, if the snake is moving to the right, it cannot directly move to the left by pressing the keyboard's left arrow key or by hovering the cursor on the area marked as left with the touchpad or *CameraMouse*. It would either have to go up or down first and then left to achieve movement to the left. This idea is consistent with how the original *Snake* game is played.

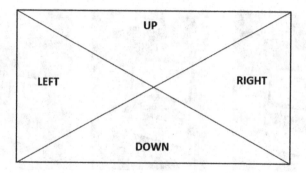

Fig. 3. Four screen regions for cursor control.

4   Methodology

4.1   Participants

We recruited 12 participants for the experiment. Eight were male and four were female. The participants were university students at undergraduate and graduate levels. They belonged to different geographic regions such as Bangladesh, Canada, India, and Pakistan.

4.2   Apparatus

For hardware, we used an *ASUS X541U* series laptop which has a built-in webcam. The experiment software was based on our *Snake Hands-free Edition* game, as described earlier (see Sect. 3.2). We used *CameraMouse* for facial tracking. Two software tools were used: *GoStats*[2] for statistical analyses, and the *Processing*[3] tool to generate trace files of the snake's movement and corresponding cursor movement for the touchpad and *CameraMouse*.

4.3   Procedure

The experimenter explained the steps of the experiment to each participant and demonstrated with a few practice trials. The counterbalancing group for each participant was chosen at random. Each participant was allowed some practice trials which were not part of the data analysis. Participants were tested over three sessions, one for each input method (see Fig. 4 parts a, b, and c). A maximum of two sessions was allowed within a day as long as there was a break of at least two hours between the sessions. Two consecutive sessions were not separated by more than two days. Each trial was one minute in duration.

---

[2] https://www.yorku.ca/mack/GoStats/.
[3] https://processing.org/.

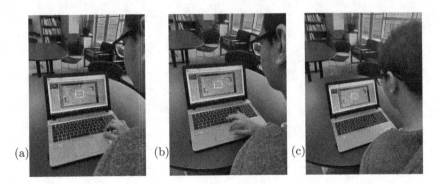

Fig. 4. A participant taking part in the Snake game with (a) keyboard, (b) touchpad, and (c) *CameraMouse*.

4.4 Design

The user study was a 3 × 8 within-subjects design. The independent variables and levels were as follows:

- Input method (keyboard, touchpad, *CameraMouse*)
- Block (1, 2, 3, 4, 5, 6, 7, 8)

There were three dependent variables: score, completion time (in seconds), and number of movements (count). The total number of trials was 1440 (3×8×5×12). The three input methods were counterbalanced with four participants in each group to offset learning effects.

5 Results and Discussions

5.1 Score

Whenever the snake eats a fruit, the score increases by one. The mean scores were 1.94 (*CameraMouse*), 5.89 (keyboard), and 3.34 (touchpad). See Fig. 5.

The effect of group on score was statistically significant ($F_{2,9} = 4.619$, $p < .05$), indicating an order effect despite counterbalancing. The effect of input method on score was statistically significant ($F_{2,18} = 83.569, p < .0001$). The effect of block on score was not statistically significant ($F_{7,63} = 1.225, p > .05$).

As seen in Fig. 5, the mean score is much higher for the keyboard compared with the touchpad and *CameraMouse* methods. The keyboard method is the closest simulation of the original snake game on Nokia mobile phones, where users had to press physical buttons to play the original game. This similarity likely played a part in the keyboard being the best among input methods in terms of score. The low score with *CameraMouse* is likely due to the newness of the method while playing such a game.

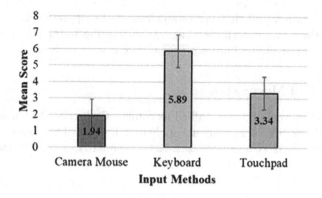

Fig. 5. Mean score by input methods. Error bars indicate ±1 *SE*.

5.2   Completion Time

Completion time signifies the time in seconds for which the snake was alive in each trial. In each trial, after 60 s, the snake would die automatically and the user would proceed to the next trial. The mean completion times were 35.38 s (*CameraMouse*), 40.79 (keyboard), and 39.32 (touchpad). See Fig. 6.

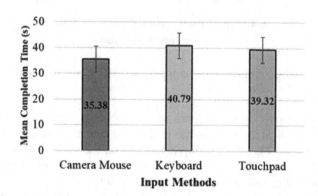

Fig. 6. Mean completion time (s) by input methods. Error bars indicate ±1 *SE*.

The effect of group on completion time was statistically significant ($F_{2,9} = 8.059, p < .01$), indicating again that counterbalancing did not adequately correct for order effects. However, the effect of input method on completion time was not statistically significant ($F_{2,18} = 2.185, p > .05$). The effect of block on completion time was also not statistically significant ($F_{7,63} = 0.865$, ns).

As stated earlier, the completion time for each trial signifies the in-game lifespan of the snake. The snake could die by hitting a poisonous object (black) or hitting a wall unless the allotted 60 s for a trial elapsed. The black objects appear on the game-screen randomly. Their appearance does not have any periodic or positional consistency and thus brings an element of surprise to the player. This is true for all three input methods; hence, as seen in Fig. 6, the mean completion times for each input method are not that different from each other.

5.3   Number of Movements

The number of movements were tallied as counts. Each time the snake changed direction, the number of movements increased by one. The mean number of movements was 21.57 (*CameraMouse*), 73.9 (keyboard), and 28.18 (touchpad). See Fig. 7.

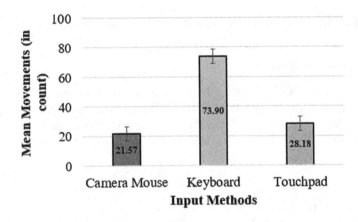

Fig. 7. Mean number of movements by input methods. Error bars indicate ±1 *SE*.

The effect of group on movements was not statistically significant ($F_{2,9} = 2.101, p > .05$), indicating that counterbalancing had the desired effect of off-setting order effects. The effect of input method on movements was statistically significant ($F_{2,18} = 65.157, p < .0001$). However, the effect of block on movements was not statistically significant ($F_{7,63} = 0.669$, ns).

The keyboard was the best performing input method for number of movements as well. The participants discovered that tapping diagonally positioned keys (i.e., left-up, up-right, left-down, down-right etc.) results in swift movement of the snake. They used this to move the snake faster in moving toward *fruits*. This resulted in a high number of movements with the keyboard. Participants struggled to bring this swift movement into control with the touchpad or *CameraMouse*, as covering the directional regions (see Fig. 3) was obviously not as easy as changing directions with the keyboard.

5.4 Learning

While analyzing learning over the eight blocks of testing, we found an improvement in some cases, but not all cases.

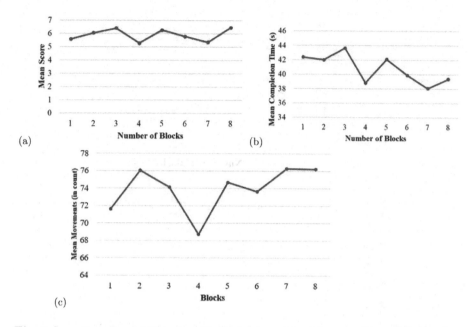

Fig. 8. Learning over eight blocks with the keyboard for (a) score, (b) completion time (s), and (c) movements (counts).

Beginning with the keyboard score (see Fig. 8a), there was very little learning effect for score during the first three blocks and the final two blocks. Otherwise, there were dips in the score. The reason behind this is a combination of familiarity with the game and fatigue coming into effect after four blocks. It is significant to note that many participants took a break of five minutes after the first four blocks of each session. Hence, when they restarted they did better. But, when fatigue increased, their performance took a dip again. Figure 8b shows that completion time gradually decreased across the eight blocks with the keyboard. The fatigue effect is evident here. It also signifies, looking back at Fig. 8a, that participants achieved a better score with less completion time during the final 2–3 blocks of the experiment while using the keyboard. For the number of movements with the keyboard, we see some learning taking place in Fig. 8c during the final 2–3 blocks but there is a large dip during the blocks in the middle of the experiment.

For score using the touchpad, the learning effects line was mostly flat. But very little learning was observed for completion time (see Fig. 9a) and number of movements (see Fig. 9b) while using the touchpad.

With *CameraMouse*, there was no significant improvement with practice for score. But completion time gradually decreased over the first few blocks and it fluctuated across the rest of the blocks (see Fig. 10a). Similar remarks can be made about movements while using the *CameraMouse* (see Fig. 10b).

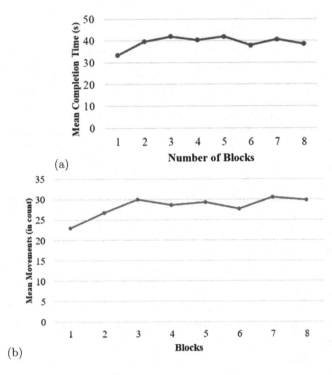

Fig. 9. Learning over eight blocks with touchpad for (a) completion time (s), and (b) movements (counts).

5.5   Traces of the Snake and Cursor

To further support our idea of dividing the game-screen into regions (see Fig. 3 for touchpad and *CameraMouse* control), we generated trace files. For the simplicity of presentation, we show some trace file examples in Fig. 11 and Fig. 12. These trace files were generated from relatively short trials from one of the *CameraMouse* sessions. The red and and blue dots in Fig. 11 and Fig. 12 decreased in size as time progressed along the trial. Note that the snake followed the cursor as the final point in the cursor's trace file was in the *UP* region and the final point of the snake's trace file shows that the snake was indeed going upwards. An overlapping trace file for both the cursor and the snake is depicted in Fig. 12. Similar images for longer lasting trials are shown in Fig. 13 and Fig. 14.

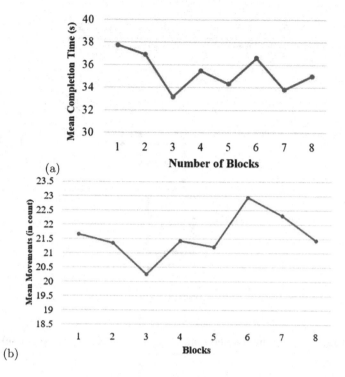

(a)

(b)

Fig. 10. Learning over eight blocks with *CameraMouse* for (a) completion time (s), and (b) movements (counts).

6   Participant Feedback

We collected participant feedback on a set of questions. Five of the 12 participants had no prior experience using *CameraMouse*. When asked about their preferred method of input, 11 of 12 participants chose the keyboard; only one participant chose the touchpad.

Participants also provided responses on two 5-point Likert scale questions. One question was on the participant's level of fatigue with *CameraMouse* (1 = *very low*, 5 = *very high*). The mean response was 2.67, closest to the *moderate fatigue* score. The second question was on the participant's rating of the hands-free phase of the experiment (1 = *very poor*, 5 = *very good*). The mean response was 3.25, just slightly above the *normal* score. Hence, it can be noted that the interaction with *CameraMouse* fared well.

We also asked the participants if they could name other games that they think can be played with the *CameraMouse*. Some interesting answers were given. Participants suggested games such as *Temple Rush*, *Subway Surfer*, and *Point Of View Driving* as possible candidates. However, 5 of the 12 participants thought *CameraMouse* could not be used in any other games. Participants were also asked about aspects of *CameraMouse* that they struggled with. The responses

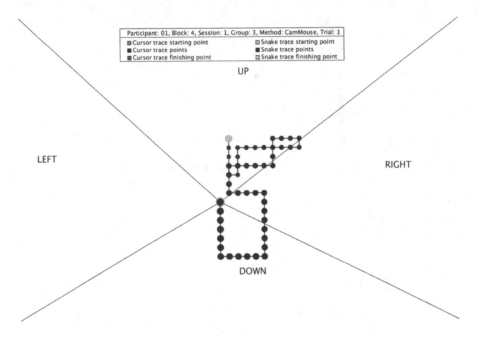

Fig. 11. Trace file for the snake's movement. (Color figure online)

were 'keeping track of the cursor', 'figuring out the required degree of head movement', 'horizontal movement', 'vertical movement', 'sensitivity of the cursor', etc. 'Keeping track of the cursor' and 'Figuring out the required degree of head movement' each received five responses. 'Sensitivity of the cursor' received nine responses.

7   Case Study

We conducted a case study along with our user study with a participant who has mild cerebral palsy. The participant is an undergraduate student. He is able to walk and has some use of his hands, but he does not have as much control in his hands as the 12 participants in the user study. Hence, he was only asked to do the hands-free session of the experiment (see Fig. 15). He took part in all eight blocks of the hands-free session. The hardware, software, and procedure were the same as in the user study.

7.1   Design

This was a 1 × 8 single-subject design. We had two factors for the case study. Their names and levels are:

- Input method (*CameraMouse*)

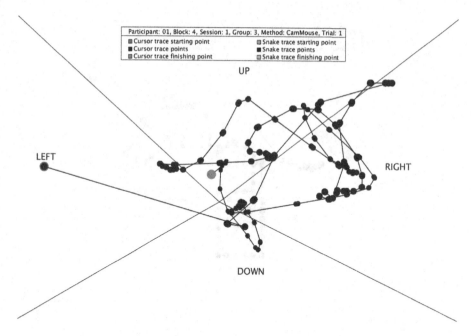

Fig. 12. Trace file for cursor movement. (Color figure online)

- Blocks (1, 2, 3, 4, 5, 6, 7, 8)

Of course, input method is not a factor, per se, since only one level was used. It is reported as such to be consistent with the earlier user study.

The performances measures were once again score, completion time (s), and number of movements (counts).

7.2   Results and Discussion

We compared the performance measures of the hands-free user study with the performance measures in the case study. As seen in Fig. 16a, the physically-challenged participant had a much lower mean score of 0.55 compared to the mean score for the hands-free session in the user study, which was 1.94. In terms of completion time, the case study had a mean completion time of 15.5 s whereas the user study's mean completion time for the hands free session was 21.57 s. See Fig. 16b. The case study had a mean number of movements of 21.08, but the user study had a mean number of movements at 35.38. See Fig. 16c. The physical condition of the participant of the case study obviously did not allow him to be as flexible as the non-disabled participants of the user study; thus, lower performance measures were observed during the case study.

The participant displayed very little learning in terms of completion time. See Fig. 17b. But, his performance fluctuated a lot in terms of score. See Fig. 17a. There was no significant learning effect observed for number of movements during the case study.

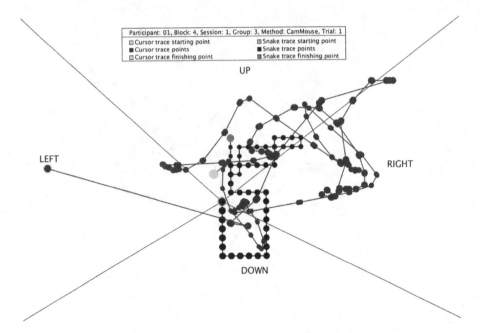

Fig. 13. Trace file for the snake's movement and cursor movement.

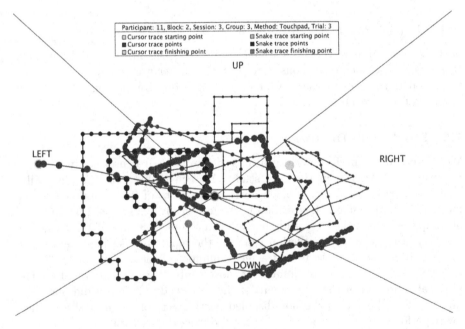

Fig. 14. Trace file for the snake's movement and cursor movement (longer lasting trial).

Fig. 15. Case study participant taking part in the experiment.

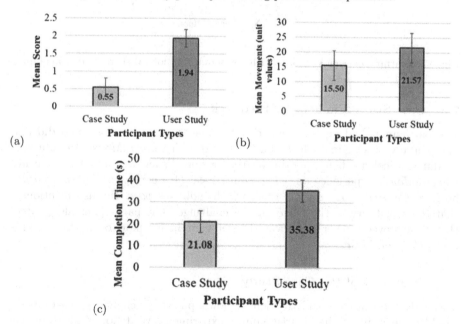

Fig. 16. Performance measure comparisons between the case study and the user study.

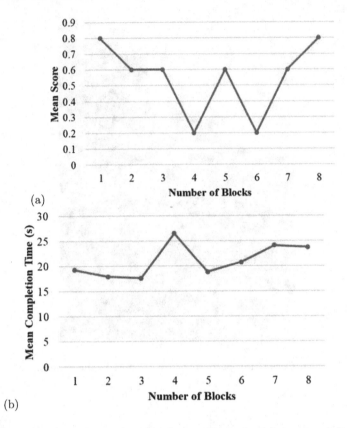

(a)

(b)

Fig. 17. Learning over eight blocks with *CameraMouse* for (a) score, and (b) completion time (s).

7.3 Case Study Participant Feedback

The participant had no prior experience using the *CameraMouse* and did not mention any other game which can be played with *CameraMouse*. He affirmed he did not feel much fatigue during the session. When was asked to rate his *CameraMouse* experience on a five-point scale: (1 = *very poor*, 5 = *very good*), he gave *CameraMouse* a score of 2, which indicates *poor*. He also mentioned that the sensitivity of the cursor was a challenge. The participant also stated that as he moved farther away from the web-cam, he felt more comfortable while using *CameraMouse*.

7.4 Summary of the Case-Study

We conducted this case study to identify how a physically-challenged participant would perform in our hands-free gaming experiment. We followed all standard experiment procedures for the case study and compared the performance measures in the case study with those in the user study. The performance measures in the case study were lower that those in the user-study, for all cases.

8 Conclusion

In this experiment, we compared *CameraMouse* with the touchpad and keyboard of a laptop computer to play a simple game: *Snake*. The keyboard was the best performing method among the three tested. The mean score for the keyboard was 5.89; the mean score for the touchpad was 3.34; and *CameraMouse* had the lowest mean score at 1.94. The mean completion time for the keyboard was 40.79 s; the mean completion time for the touchpad method was 39.32 s; and *CameraMouse* had a mean completion time of 35.38 s. The mean number of movements for the keyboard was 73.90; the mean number of movements for the touchpad method was 28.18; and *CameraMouse* had a mean number of movements of 21.57. We also conducted a case study with a physically challenged participant. The performance measures showed lower values in the case study compared to the results gathered in the hands-free session.

But considering participant feedback, opportunities were noted to try *CameraMouse* in other games, such as *Temple Run*, *Subway Surfers*, etc.

Voice command, gesture control, and brain-computer research are also significant forms of hands-free interaction. In the future, the door remains open to explore these forms of hands-free interactions against facial tracking methods. It is also worthwhile to mention that accessible computing does not necessarily mean that a user has to be completely apart physically from the machine. Hence, partially hands-free methods can also be valuable for user-interaction in the accessible computing domain.

References

1. Betke, M., Gips, J., Fleming, P.: The camera mouse: visual tracking of body features to provide computer access for people with severe disabilities. IEEE Trans. Neural Syst. Rehabil. Eng. **10**(1), 1–10 (2002)
2. Cloud, R., Betke, M., Gips, J.: Experiments with a camera-based human-computer interface system. In: Proceedings of the 7th ERCIM Workshop User Interfaces for All, UI4ALL, pp. 103–110. ERCIM (2002)
3. Cuaresma, J., MacKenzie, I.S.: A comparison between tilt-input and facial tracking as input methods for mobile games. In: 2014 IEEE Games Media Entertainment (GEM), pp. 1–7. IEEE, New York (2014)
4. Gips, J., Betke, M., Fleming, P.: The camera mouse: preliminary investigation of automated visual tracking for computer access. In: Proceedings Conference on Rehabilitation Engineering and Assistive Technology Society of North America, pp. 98–100. RESNA (2000)
5. Grammenos, D., Savidis, A., Stephanidis, C.: UA-Chess: a universally accessible board game. In: Universal Access in HCI: Exploring New Interaction Environments Proceedings 11th International Conference on Human-Computer Interaction (HCI International 2005), vol. 7 (2005)
6. Hassan, M., Magee, J., MacKenzie, I.S.: A Fitts' law evaluation of hands-free and hands-on input on a laptop computer. In: Antona, M., Stephanidis, C. (eds.) HCII 2019. LNCS, vol. 11573, pp. 234–249. Springer, Cham (2019). https://doi.org/10.1007/978-3-030-23563-5_20

7. Kent, S.L.: The Ultimate History of Video Games: From Pong to Pokemon and Beyond... The Story Behind the Craze That Touched Our Lives and Changed The World, vol. 2. Three Rivers Press, New York (2010)
8. MacKenzie, I.S.: Evaluating eye tracking systems for computer input. In: Majaranta, P., et al. (eds.) Gaze Interaction and Applications of Eye Tracking: Advances in Assistive Technologies, pp. 205–225. IGI Global, Hershey (2012)
9. MacKenzie, I.S.: Human-Computer Interaction: An Empirical Research Perspective. Morgan Kaufmann, Waltham (2012)
10. Magee, J., Felzer, T., MacKenzie, I.S.: Camera Mouse + ClickerAID: dwell vs. single-muscle click actuation in mouse-replacement interfaces. In: Antona, M., Stephanidis, C. (eds.) UAHCI 2015. LNCS, vol. 9175, pp. 74–84. Springer, Cham (2015). https://doi.org/10.1007/978-3-319-20678-3_8
11. Magee, J.J., Scott, M.R., Waber, B.N., Betke, M.: Eyekeys: a real-time vision interface based on gaze detection from a low-grade video camera. In: Conference on Computer Vision and Pattern Recognition Workshop, CVPRW 2004, p. 159. IEEE, New York (2004)
12. Roig-Maimó, M.F., Manresa-Yee, C., Varona, J., MacKenzie, I.S.: Evaluation of a mobile head-tracker interface for accessibility. In: Miesenberger, K., Bühler, C., Penaz, P. (eds.) ICCHP 2016. LNCS, vol. 9759, pp. 449–456. Springer, Cham (2016). https://doi.org/10.1007/978-3-319-41267-2_63

Affective Communication Enhancement System for Locked-In Syndrome Patients

Fanny Larradet$^{(\boxtimes)}$ 📵, Giacinto Barresi$^{(\boxtimes)}$ 📵, and Leonardo S. Mattos$^{(\boxtimes)}$ 📵

Istituto Italiano di Tecnologia, Genova, Italy
{fanny.larradet,giacinto.barresi,leonardo.mattos}@iit.it
https://www.iit.it/

Abstract. Patients with Locked-In Syndrome such as people with Amyotrophic Lateral Sclerosis (ALS) rely on technology for basic communication. However, available Augmentative and Alternative Communication (AAC) tools such as gaze-controlled keyboards have limited abilities. In particular, they do not allow for expression of emotions in addition to words. In this paper we propose a novel gaze-based speaking tool that enable locked-in syndrome patients to express emotions as well as sentences. It also features patient-controlled emotionally modulated speech synthesis. Additionally, an emotional 3D avatar can be controlled by the patient to represent emotional facial-expressions. The systems were tested with 36 people without disabilities separated into an affective group - full control of emotional voice, avatar facial expressions and laugh - and a control group - no emotional tools. The study proved the system's capacity to enhance communication for both the patient and the interlocutor. The emotions embedded in the synthesized voices were found recognizable at 80% on the first trial and 90% on the second trial. The conversation was perceived as more natural when using the affective tool. The subjects felt it was easier to express and identify emotions using this system. The emotional voice and the emotional avatar were found to help the conversation. This highlights the needs for more affective-driven communicative solutions for locked-in patients.

Keywords: Communication · Emotions · Gaze · Eye-tracking

1 Introduction

1.1 Motivations

Locked-In Syndrome (LIS) is a pathological condition where patients (for instance people in advanced stages of Amyotrophic Lateral Sclerosis - ALS) lost all capability to move any part of their body except the eyes [1]. When this last capability is lost, a state of Complete Locked-In (CLIS) is reached. LIS ad

This work was partially supported by Fondazione Roma as part of the project TEEP-SLA.

M. Antona and C. Stephanidis (Eds.): HCII 2020, LNCS 12188, pp. 143–156, 2020.
https://doi.org/10.1007/978-3-030-49282-3_10

CLIS patients' abilities are severely limited, including in terms of communication. Therefore, innovative communication systems for such patients are much needed to increase their communication capabilities and engagement with people around them. Considering this context, the main goal of this research is to build novel modalities of technologically mediated communication that are specifically designed to improve LIS patients' quality of life. In this paper we will focus on the skillset of LIS patients and exploit their ability to control their gaze as the input for computer-assisted communication systems [2]. Overall, the requirements for such solutions include the creation of novel user interfaces adapted to LIS patients capabilities to provide them with a more extensive, and complete communication system than the current state of the art. The solutions should improve their ability to express emotions as well as words.

1.2 State of the Art

The first communication systems for LIS patients consisted in codes using eye blinking to signify yes and no or more complex sentences using techniques such as Morse codes [3]. Other types of communication exist such as transparent letter board held by the interlocutor [3] (Fig. 1). In this case, the patient can indicate a letter by gazing at it. The interlocutor must then write down or remember the letters sequence to form words.

Fig. 1. E-TRAN letter board. (Image Courtesy of Low Tech Solutions)

The letter board is still widely used nowadays. Nonetheless, more advanced systems do exist. Notably, the ability of LIS patients to control their gaze was used to send commands to computer systems through eye-tracking cameras [2].

This technique enabled them to select letters on keyboards displayed on computer screens and to "read" the written sentence out loud using voice synthesis [2]. Such systems mostly focus on composing words letter by letter. However, when we communicate, we do not only use words but also a great range of additional non-verbal communications cues such as voice intonation, facial expression or body gesture [4]. Such additional input helps the interlocutor to properly understand the context of the message itself. A simple sentence such as "let's go now" can be read with excitement or anger and deliver a completely different message. This need for enriching words with emotional features has led to the creation of additional textual communication cues in Computer-Mediated Communication (CMC) such as emoticons [5]. These solutions are now widely used in text communications such as SMS or in social medias. For this reason, it is essential for LIS patients to also be able to communicate such affective state to their interlocutors in the most natural way possible. Focusing on the most common emotional cues in communication, voice and facial expression, we may find a great number of work in recreating such concept for CMC. For instance, emotional speech synthesis has been widely studied in the past [6–8]. Additionally, facial expression was often associated with avatars and 3D characters as a way to express emotions online [9–11]. The usage of those two technologies together were also studied in the past for CMC [12].

However, to our knowledge, those advances in technology related to emotion expression haven't been adapted for LIS patients yet. Augmentative and Alternative Communication (AAC) systems for persons with disabilities rarely provide tools for emotion expression [13]. Focusing on children with disabilities, [14] reviews the past studies on AAC and exposes the great need for emotional communication in such tools. Additionally, the effect of such affective capabilities on communication abilities for patients with LIS haven't been studied so far. To fill this gap in the literature we propose a novel open-source system controlled with eye gaze, including emotional voice synthesis and an emotional personalized avatar to enhance affective communication.

2 The Proposed Solution

In order to allow LIS patients to communicate their emotions in addition to words, we proposed a system including a gaze-based keyboard, an emotional voice synthesizer and a personalized emotional avatar. We focused on the 3 most common basic emotions: Happy, Sad and Angry. An additional option allowed the patients to generate a laughing sound. The laugh consists in a recorded sound and it is not created through the voice synthesizer. The system was created using the Unity3D platform[1], which is most notably know as a game development engine. However, this versatile platform is also very useful for the development of assistive user interfaces. (the work presented in this paper adopts the GUI developed through Unity3D for TEEP-SLA project[2].

---

[1] https://unity.com/ (Accessed Jan 14th 2020).
[2] https://teep-sla.eu/ (Accessed Jan 14th 2020).

a) AG display - Neutral

b) AG display - Happy

c) CG display

d) Dwell time settings menu

Fig. 2. General aspect of the keyboard display (AG: Affective Group; CG: Control Group).

2.1 Gaze-Based Keyboard

The general aspect of the keyboard can be found in Fig. 2. It uses a standard dwell time system for key selection [15]. A menu button enables the customization of this dwell time. Autocompletion words are proposed using the Lib-face library [16] and displayed in the center of the keyboard to reduce gaze-movements that have been proven to induce fatigue [17]. Additionally, according to preliminary data, the users would most likely see the proposed words positioned in this way rather than above all the keys as their gaze would often pass over the words.

2.2 Emotional Voice Synthesis

The open-source voice modulation platform Emofilt [8] was used to modulate the voice according to emotions. To tune the emotional voice, we took as an hypothesis that a great voice differentiation between emotions was primordial to insure the emotion recognition by the interlocutor in the long-term. The selected Emofilt settings for the happy (H), sad (S) and angry (A) voice can be found in Fig. 3.

		Angry	Sad	Happy
pitch	fORange	80		
	fOMean			230
	lastSylContour		30 - straight	
	variability			10
	firstWordLevel*			120
	lastWordLevel*	90		160
duration	durationUnstressedSyls	70	170	
	durationFocusStressedSyls	130	170	120
	durationWordstressedSyls		170	
	speechRate	110	90	110
	dur vowel		170	130
	durpause		200	
	lastSylDuration*		140	80
	durNasal			130
phonation	jitter	3		
	vocal effort	loud	soft	loud

Fig. 3. Emofilt settings.

The settings containing an asterisk are additions to the original system. The pitch were capped to a maximum and a minimum to avoid unnatural voices. The user are able to select the desired emotion using 3 emoticons buttons positioned above the keyboard (Fig. 2). If no emotion is selected the voice is considered as neutral.

2.3   Emotional Avatar

Because LIS patients are not able to communicate their emotion through facial expression, we decided to simulate this ability using a 3D avatar. To do so, the AvatarSDK Unity asset [18] was used. It allows to create a 3D avatar using a simple picture of the user or of someone else. 3D animations such as blinking and yawning are provided. We created additional 3D animations of the 3 previously cited emotions. An example of such avatar expressions can be found in Fig. 4. The avatar facial expressions are triggered using the same emoticons buttons used for the emotional voice. The selected facial expression is displayed until the emotion is disactivated by the user.

Original photo   Neutral   Happy   Sad   Angry

Fig. 4. Example of the emotional avatar generated from a picture.

3   Methodology

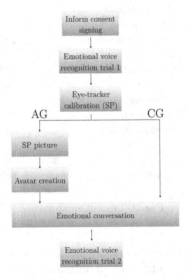

Fig. 5. Experimental flow (AG: Affective Group; CG: Control Group; SP: Subject Patient).

In order to test the capability of this system in enhancing patients' communicative abilities, we performed a between-subject study with 36 subjects (26 males, 10 females) separated into two gender-balanced group (5 females, 13 males, avg.

age 29 years): a control group (CG) and an affective group (AG). The experimental flow may be found in Fig. 5).

For the control group, unlike the affective group, the affective features (emoticon buttons, emotional voice, emotional avatar, laugh button) were hidden and therefore inaccessible. During each session, a subject was assigned to represent either "the patient" (SP) or "the healthy interlocutor" (SI). After signing the inform consent, we first tested the validity of the emotional voice. 5 sentences were randomly picked among 10 sentences (Table 1) and were each played in the 3 different emotions.

Table 1. Emotional sample sentences.

| He saw your father |
| We smelled your cake |
| She went this way |
| We came home early |
| You read the paper |
| You played the game |
| They made some food |
| She said my name |
| I know this person |
| I drove this car |

Therefore, in total, 15 sentences were played to the subjects in random order who had to decide if it was a Happy, Sad or Angry voice (Trial 1). Both SP and SI rated the emotional voices separately, in written form, without consulting each other. SP was then seated in front of a commercial eye-tracking monitor system (Tobii 4C [19]) and SI next to him. The eye-tracker was calibrated using the dedicated Tobii software. For the affective group, a picture of SP was taken using the camera from the computer. The 3D avatar was then built from this picture. A second screen displayed the emotional avatar positioned so that both subjects could see it. For both groups, the dwell time was originally fixed to 1 s but SP was able to adjust it at any time through the menu. They were then given a talk scenario designed to simulate an emotional conversation (Fig. 6).

The subjects were asked to have a conversation with each other. They were free to say whatever they desired while respecting the scenario. AG-SP was instructed to use the emotional buttons as much as possible. Once the conversation finished, both subjects were asked to answer a questionnaire on a 7-point Likert-type scale (Fig. 7). The first two questions were designed to compare the efficiency of the systems. The other questions were added to assess the user experience but will not be used to compare the systems. Such questions will be different between subjects and conditions to fit the context the subjects were experiencing. The first part of the study was then repeated with the remaining 5 sentences (Table 1) (Trial 2).

4   Results

4.1   Speech Synthesis Emotion Recognition

The control group (both interlocutors and patients) were able to recognize 81% of the emotions from the emotional voice synthesis in the first trial and 87% in the second trial. The affective group had a 80% recognition in the first trial and 92% in the second trial (Fig. 8).

SP	Your friend come to see you after not having seen you for a long time. This friend is in control of the company you spent your entire life building. You left him the control of the compagny when you started being sick because you trusted him. You are very happy to see him and express this joy to him. He will make a joke that makes you laugh. Then, he will tell you something that is very upsetting , you get angry at him. Finally after he explained the reason of his actions you forgive him but this situation made you very sad. You express this sadness to him
SI	You come to see an old time friend that has ALS. You tell him how happy you are to see him and start a casual conversation. You tell him a joke of how you fell in the parking lot on your way over. Later, you inform your friend that you have sold for money the company that he has built from his own hands. You defend yourself by explaining you sold the compagny because it was not bringing any money anymore and it was dommed. It was the only way to save it. You can't appologize enough.

Fig. 6. Conversation scenarios.

Subject "patient" (SP)		subject Interlocutor (SI)	
Control group	Affective group	Affective group	Control group
(Q1) The conversation was similar to a normal dialog (in terms of communication abilities, not in terms of scenario)			
(Q2-SP) I could express my emotions with the system		(Q2-SI) I could identify the emotions felt by my interlocuter	
(Q3-CG-SP) The ability to convey my emotions would have helped with the communication	(Q3-AG-SP) The ability to convey my emotions helped with the communication	(Q3-AG-SI) The ability to identify his/her emotions helped with the communication	(Q3-CG-SI) The ability to identify his/her emotions would have helped with the communication
-	(Q4-AG-SP) The emotions I tried to express were well represented by the emotional voice	(Q4 -AG-SI) I could identify the emotions felt by my interlocuter through the emotional voice	-
-	(Q5-AG-SP) The emotions I tried to express were well represented by the emotional avatar	(Q5-AG-SI) I could identify the emotions felt by my interlocuter through the emotional avatar	-
(Q6-CG-SP) A controlled animated 3D representation of myself virtually making facial expression would have helped with the communication	(Q6-AG) The emotional avatar helped with the communication.		(Q6-CG-SI) A controlled animated 3D representation of my interlocuter virtually making facial expression would have helped with the communication
(Q7-CG) An emotionaly modulated voice would have helped with the communication	(Q7-AG) The emotional voice helped with the communication		(Q7-CG) An emotionaly modulated voice would have helped with the communication

Fig. 7. Questionnaire.

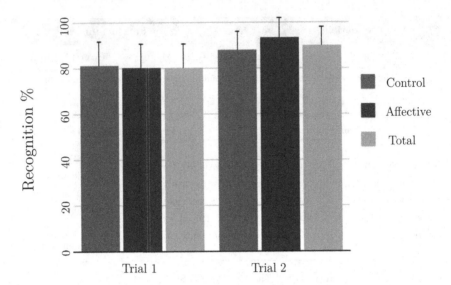

Fig. 8. Recognition rates of emotional sentences for each trial.

4.2 Questionnaire

In the questionnaire, only the first two questions aimed at comparing both systems and evaluating emotional communication efficiency. Results of these questions can be found in Fig. 9. The questionnaire results (ordinal scale measures, analyzed through Mann-Whitney U test) show the advantages of using the system proposed in this paper. The subjects considered the conversation significantly ($p < 0.05$) more similar to a normal dialog (in terms of communication abilities, not in terms of scenario) while they were using the expressive solution (Q1-AG-SP: 4.5 and Q1-AG-SI: 4.75 in average) compared to the control group (Q1-CG-SP: 3.375 and Q1-CG-SI: 3.25). This is true for both patient-like subjects ($U = 16$ with $p = 0.027$) and their interlocutors ($U = 12.5$ and $p = 0.012$).

The questionnaire data are analyzed through appropriate non-parametric tests because of the dependent variables are constituted by ordinal scale measures. The assumptions of the tests are checked.

The "patients" from the affective group found that they were more able to express their emotions (Q2-AG-SP: 5.875) compared to the control group (Q2-CG-SP: 3.25). A significant difference was found between the 2 conditions (AG and CG) (Mann-Whitney $U(16) = 1.5$ with $p < 0.001$).

The "healthy subjects" from the affective group found that they were more able to identify emotions from their interlocutors (Q2-AG-SI: 5.5) compared to the control group (Q2-CG-SI: 3.75). A significant difference was found between the 2 conditions (Mann-Whitney $U(16) = 10.5$ with $p = 0.008$).

Additional questions were asked aiming at collecting additional insights on both systems. The results can be found in Fig. 10.

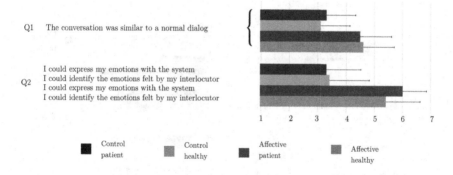

Fig. 9. Questionnaire results for significative systems comparison.

The "patients" in the affective condition found that the ability to convey their emotions helped with the communication (Q3-AG-SP: 5.875) and the ones from the control group thought that it would have helped (Q3-CG-SP: 5.2). The "healthy subjects" in that affective condition found that the ability to identify their interlocutor's emotion helped with the communication (Q3-AG-SI: 6.1) and the ones from the control group thought that it would have helped (Q3-CG-SI: 5.5).

5   Discussion

Firstly, we can see that the overall recognition of the emotional voice in the first task was sufficient for it to be used meaningfully in this experiment. Additionally, we can see that this recognition quickly increases with time since the recognition on task2 is much higher than the one on task1. This increase is higher for the affective group that had additional time to familiarize with the voice modulation during the scenario part of the experiment, reaching a score of 92%. This ability to successfully express emotion (Q4-AG-SP) and identify emotions (Q4-AG-SI) through the voice synthesizer were confirmed by the questionnaire. Furthermore, the affective group found this emotional voice helpful for the communication (Q7-AG) and the control group thought it would be a useful feature (Q7-CG). It confirms our hypothesis that strongly distinctive emotional voices are easily recognizable in the long term and improve communicative abilities.

The emotional avatar was found to successfully represent the desired emotion (Q5-AG-SP), to provide easily identifiable emotions (Q5-AG-SI) and to help with the communication in the affective group (Q6-AG). It is interesting to notice the affective group found the avatar to be more helpful for the communication than the voice (Q6-AG and Q7-AG).

Overall, the communication was found more natural to the affective group than to the control group (Q1). SP subjects found that they were more able to express their emotion (Q2-SP). It highlights the positive impacts of both the emotional avatar and the emotional voice on the communication which is

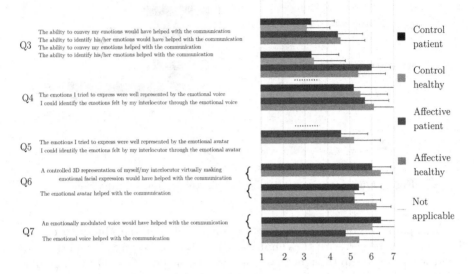

Fig. 10. Questionnaire results for additional insights.

confirmed by Q3-AG-SP and Q3-AG-SI. Concurrently, the control group that did not have access to any emotional tools, also found that the ability to express emotion (Q3-CG-SP) and to identify emotion (Q3-CG-SI) would have helped with the communication.

It is interesting to notice that in the affective group the "healthy" subject ranked higher how much the avatar and the voice helped (Q6-AG-SI and Q7-AG-SI) compared to the "patient" (Q6-AG-SP and Q7-AG-SP). This highlights the fact that this system is particularly useful for the interlocutor who is the one looking for cues about the emotion felt by the patient. The "patients" subjects often stated that they did not really pay real attention to the avatar as they were focused on writing on the keyboard.

6   Conclusions and Future Work

People in LIS have limited methods to communicate. In the past decades, technology has greatly improve their quality of life by providing a range of communication tools. However AAC are still constrained in communicating words and rarely include ways of expressing emotions. This work focused on studying the impact of expressing emotion on the communicative abilities of LIS patients. To do so we created a platform that allows the user to select an emotion between happy, angry and sad. A 3D avatar was then animated according to the selected emotion along-side with an emotionally modulated voice synthesis. This system was tested by 36 subjects who were successfully able to recognize the emotions from the voice modulation and the avatar. They found that the two emotional tools helped with the communication as they were more able to convey and identify emotions. This system is available in open-source [20] and also includes a gaze-based computer game [21] and a gaze-based web-browsing system [22]. While today the avatar is only expressing fixed emotions it shows the need for extending AAC tools to include more non-verbal communication cues. This system could in the future include additional animations such as lip synchronization, visual reaction to detected skin temperature (sweating, shivering), additional gesture (wink, hand gesture, raised eyes...), additional type of sounds ("waaaw", "uhm uhm", "oooh").

The avatar could therefore become an extensive communication tool as well as a quick visual aid for the interlocutor, family and caregiver to understand the internal state of the patient. Advanced avatar control could be used for instance to perform art [23].

While voice modulation and facial expression are the most common in non-verbal communication, other types of natural communication may be simulated such as physical contact. Indeed, systems such as heating wristbands placed on family and loved ones may be activated by the patient using gaze control to convey the idea of arm touching.

In the future, patients' emotions could be automatically detected for instance from physiological signals [24]. However, this should be investigated carefully as it would raise concerns regarding the patients' willingness to constantly display their emotion without a way to hide them from their interlocuter.

References

1. Smith, E., Delargy, M.: Locked-in syndrome. BMJ **330**(7488), 406–409 (2005)
2. Majaranta, P., Räihä, K.-J.: Twenty years of eye typing: systems and design issues. In: ETRA, vol. 2, pp. 15–22 (2002)
3. Laureys, S., et al.: The locked-in syndrome: what is it like to be conscious but paralyzed and voiceless? Prog. Brain Res. **150**, 495–611 (2005)
4. Mehrabian, A.: Nonverbal Communication. Routledge, New York (2017)
5. Lo, S.-K.: The nonverbal communication functions of emoticons in computer-mediated communication. CyberPsychol. Behav. **11**(5), 595–597 (2008)
6. Xue, Y., Hamada, Y., Akagi, M.: Emotional speech synthesis system based on a three-layered model using a dimensional approach. In: 2015 Asia-Pacific Signal and Information Processing Association Annual Summit and Conference (APSIPA), pp. 505–514. IEEE (2015)
7. Lee, Y., Rabiee, A., Lee, S.-Y.: Emotional end-to-end neural speech synthesizer. arXiv preprint arXiv:1711.05447 (2017)
8. Burkhardt, F.: Emofilt: the simulation of emotional speech by prosody-transformation. In: Ninth European Conference on Speech Communication and Technology (2005)
9. Neviarouskaya, A., Prendinger, H., Ishizuka, M.: Textual affect sensing for sociable and expressive online communication. In: Paiva, A.C.R., Prada, R., Picard, R.W. (eds.) ACII 2007. LNCS, vol. 4738, pp. 218–229. Springer, Heidelberg (2007). https://doi.org/10.1007/978-3-540-74889-2_20

10. Fabri, M., Moore, D.J., Hobbs, D.J.: The emotional avatar: non-verbal communication between inhabitants of collaborative virtual environments. In: Braffort, A., Gherbi, R., Gibet, S., Teil, D., Richardson, J. (eds.) GW 1999. LNCS (LNAI), vol. 1739, pp. 269–273. Springer, Heidelberg (1999). https://doi.org/10.1007/3-540-46616-9_24

11. Morishima, S.: Real-time talking head driven by voice and its application to communication and entertainment. In: AVSP 1998 International Conference on Auditory-Visual Speech Processing (1998)

12. Tang, H., Fu, Y., Tu, J., Huang, T.S., Hasegawa-Johnson, M.: EAVA: a 3D emotive audio-visual avatar. In: 2008 IEEE Workshop on Applications of Computer Vision, pp. 1–6. IEEE (2008)

13. Baldassarri, S., Rubio, J.M., Azpiroz, M.G., Cerezo, E.: Araboard: a multiplatform alternative and augmentative communication tool. Procedia Comput. Sci. **27**, 197–206 (2014)

14. Na, J.Y., Wilkinson, K., Karny, M., Blackstone, S., Stifter, C.: A synthesis of relevant literature on the development of emotional competence: implications for design of augmentative and alternative communication systems. Am. J. Speech-Lang. Pathol. **25**(3), 441–452 (2016)

15. Jacob, R.J.K.: Eye tracking in advanced interface design. In: Virtual Environments and Advanced Interface Design, pp. 258–288 (1995)

16. Matani, D.: An o (k log n) algorithm for prefix based ranked autocomplete. English, pp. 1–14 (2011)

17. Yuan, W., Semmlow, J.L.: The influence of repetitive eye movements on vergence performance. Vision. Res. **40**(22), 3089–3098 (2000)

18. ItSeez3D: Avatarsdk (2014). https://avatarsdk.com. Accessed 31 July 2019

19. Tobii Group: Tobii 4C (2001). http://www.tobii.com. Accessed 4 Mar 2019

20. Larradet, F.: Liscommunication (2019). https://gitlab.com/flarradet/liscommunication/. Accessed 27 Dec 2019

21. Larradet, F., Barresi, G., Mattos, L.S.: Effects of galvanic skin response feedback on user experience in gaze-controlled gaming: a pilot study. In: 2017 39th Annual International Conference of the IEEE Engineering in Medicine and Biology Society (EMBC), pp. 2458–2461. IEEE (2017)

22. Larradet, F., Barresi, G., Mattos, L.S.: Design and evaluation of an open-source gaze-controlled GUI for web-browsing. In: 11th Computer Science and Electronic Engineering (CEEC). IEEE (2018)

23. Aparicio, A.: Immobilis in mobili: performing arts, BCI, and locked-in syndrome. Brain-Comput. Interfaces **2**(2–3), 150–159 (2015)

24. Jerritta, S., Murugappan, M., Nagarajan, R., Wan, K.: Physiological signals based human emotion recognition: a review. In: 2011 IEEE 7th International Colloquium on Signal Processing and its Applications, pp. 410–415. IEEE (2011)

Perceived Midpoint of the Forearm

Ziyan Lu[1], Quan Liu[2], Roger Cholewiak[3], and Hong Z. Tan[1(✉)]

[1] Purdue University, West Lafayette, IN 47907, USA
{lu396,hongtan}@purdue.edu
[2] Rime Downhole Technologies, LLC, Benbrook, TX 76126, USA
quan.liu@rimetools.com
[3] Princeton University, Princeton, NJ 08544, USA
rcholewi@gmail.com

Abstract. The present study estimates the perceived midpoint of the forearm by asking participants to judge whether a touched point is closer to the wrist or the elbow. Our results show a perceived midpoint at 51.4% of the forearm length from the wrist, which is slightly shifted towards the elbow (by about 3 mm) from the geometric midpoint. This trend is consistent with some past studies that demonstrate mislocalization of tactors towards the more distal and mobile joints, but not consistent with others that show the opposite trend. For the design of an arm-worn tactor array where the tactor location is used to encode information, the shift in perceived midpoint is too small to warrant any adjustment in tactor spacing in order to ensure accurate tactor localization.

Keywords: Midpoint perception · Forearm midpoint · Haptic perception

1 Introduction

In our everyday life, localization of touches on the skin usually is important when a raindrop, insect, or a loved one comes close to us. In such cases, we are often relatively accurate in identifying "where" the contact happened. When homing in on, and swatting a mosquito away, the hand is usually large enough to make up for this "relative" error. However, the development of tactile communication systems that are intended to present language, location, or spatial orientation to augment or replace sensory input from the eyes, ears, or orienting systems, often require more precise localization of stimuli on the skin, in particular, the ability to locate the relative location of numerous sites through which information such as spatial orientation or speech might be presented (e.g., [1, 2]).

The accuracy of tactile localization and the influences of factors including body site, stimulus frequency, duration, force, and size of the contactor, have a long history of exploration in the psychological and physiological literature. Even the position of the body site in space relative to the body core can influence the perception of tactile stimuli (e.g., [3, 4]). One of Boring's histories of psychology [5] (p. 475) describes numerous early attempts to study many of these parameters and how they influence the

---

R. Cholewiak—Princeton University (Retired).

M. Antona and C. Stephanidis (Eds.): HCII 2020, LNCS 12188, pp. 157–167, 2020.
https://doi.org/10.1007/978-3-030-49282-3_11

accuracy of tactile localization, especially the detailed work of Weber [6]. From the literature on the physiology of the skin and psychophysical modeling, we also know that the underlying receptor populations at a particular location can affect tactile localization as well. More recent reviews (e.g., [7, 8]) underscore the facts that both stimulus parameters as well as intrinsic factors such as body/limb orientation or proximity to certain "anchor" points can affect judgments of location. For example, Cholewiak, Brill, and Schwab [9] showed that certain body landmarks (such as the midline of the abdomen or the spine) could serve as anchor points. In a more common test of tactile mislocalization, Cholewiak and Collins [10] demonstrated the influences of both the elbow and wrist joints on the localization of seven stimuli on the forearm and upper arm – the closer a stimulus was to the joint, the better the touched site was localized. They also were able to mimic this so-called "perceptual anchor" effect by introducing a change in the stimulus frequency at the more uncertain locations on the arm, in the middle of their linear array. Vignemont, Majid, Jola, and Haggard [11] explored our knowledge of our body parts and their segmentation with reference to body landmarks – specifically the arm vs the hand as divided by the wrist, an acknowledged anchor point. Judgments of apparent distance between caliper touches were greatest when presented spanning the wrist, but this effect only occurred tactually, not visually, and was reduced with hand-arm motion (which, they argue, unifies the surface into a single less-segmented functional unit). So they argue that tactual appreciation of the body surface is mediated by a representation of the body linked to the perception of the touch, while visual appreciation is direct and unmediated. Medina, Tame, and Longo [12] reported evidence of gaze-direction modulation of tactile localization bias where participants performed a tactile localization task on their left hand while looking at the reflection of their right hand in a mirror, a box through the mirror, and the right hand directly. Their results show that body surface representation is modulated by high-level representations of frame of reference and better somatosensory localization can be achieved when gaze is directed towards the body site being simulated.

There are some trends that have been noted in the pattern of mislocalizations across these stimulus dimensions. One of the more interesting ones is the likelihood that stimuli will be localized in a direction towards so-called "anchor points," like the wrist and elbow (e.g., [10]). Historically, anchor points have been related to the joints, that correspond to Vierordt's "law of mobility" [13] (cited by [5]). That is, stimuli are localized towards more "mobile" geometric structures. So, for example, a touch on the arm might be mislocalized closer to the shoulder or the elbow, predictable from its actual position on the arm. Lewy [14] and Parrish [15] have argued that the direction of mislocalizations tend to occur more in the distal direction on a limb (towards more mobile structures). Sadibolova, Tamè, Walsh, and Longo [16] demonstrated that localization errors or biases to paired touches on the back of the hand were large and occurred in the distal direction (towards the fingertips), in agreement with the historic notions. However, Hölzl, Stolle, and Kleinböhl [17] showed mislocalizations of all of their eight tactors on the forearm tended to occur in the proximal direction, and a post-publication analysis of the data from Cholewiak and Collins [10] also showed that mid-array stimulus errors on their forearm array of tactors also occurred more frequently towards sites near the elbow than towards the wrist. More recently, Wang et al. [18]

placed bands with two tactors touching the dorsal and the volar sides of the upper and lower left and right arms (a total of eight sites) and studied vibrotactile localization for each of these sites as well as combinations of them when presented simultaneously (similar to Geldard and Sherrick's [19] exploration of multiple presentations on the arms and legs). Tactors were located close to the elbow for the forearms, and close to the shoulder for the upper arms, and identification rates for the individual sites (only one stimulus presented) ranged from 87% to 100% with no clear pattern of variation over sites. More common errors occurred in mislocalizing stimuli on a single band – Was it the volar or the dorsal site on that particular band that was activated? This was also one of the more common types of errors reported by Fontana et al. [20] – confusion among "adjacent" stimulus sites across the forearm or upper arm, despite earlier data arguing better resolution for localization for these transverse sites on the limb rather than for those along the length of the arm [21]. So we apparently do not know "exactly" where we are touched.

Given this history, one might ask the question, do these data then argue that perceived nominal positions along the arm, such as the apparent midpoint, are somehow skewed away from the veridical geometric locations? This is the question that is asked in this project. Our finding is expected to inform the design of wearable haptic communication systems that use the location of tactors on the forearm to encode information.

2   Methods

2.1   Participants

Twelve participants (P1 to P12; 6 females; age 21.8 ± 1.4 years old) took part in the present study. All participants were right handed and have normal haptic perception by self-report. They gave informed consent using a form approved by the IRB at Purdue University. They were compensated for their time.

2.2   Apparatus

The experimental apparatus was a custom-built device with one horizontal stage that moved beneath and along the length of the participant's arm, and two synchronized vertical stages mounted on the moving horizontal stage (see Fig. 1). The horizontal stage (V-Slot® Mini V Linear Actuator from OpenBuilds Part Store) moved along the x-axis with a 0.091 mm accuracy. The vertical stages (two L12-R Micro Linear Servos by Actuonix with a 50 mm actuator stroke and 100:1 gear ratio at 6 V DC; see #2 in Fig. 1) were securely mounted on two bases (#1 in Fig. 1) attached to the horizontal stage and moved up-and-down along the z-axis with a repeatability of ±0.3 mm. The stimulus probe (#4 in Fig. 1) was a 175-mm long cylindrical hollow polycarbonate clear tubing with a tapered tip of 1.28 mm in diameter. The tube was filled with kitchen salt so as to weigh a total of 27 g. Two parallel aluminum rods (3.18 mm in diameter) went through the probe and rested on the two 3-D printed alignment forks (#3 in Fig. 1). An arm rest made from high-density polyethylene synthetic wood (26"L × 2.125"W × 0.875"H; #6 in Fig. 1) supported the participant's forearm and was clear from all moving parts.

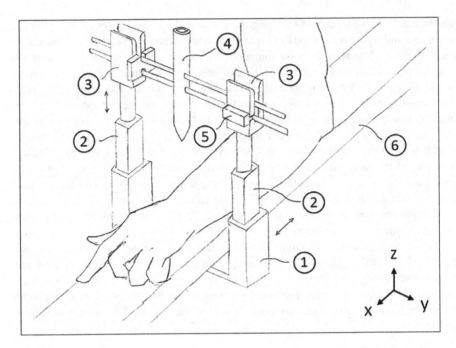

Fig. 1. Experimental apparatus: (1) vertical-stage base that is attached to the horizontal stage; (2) L12-R Micro Linear Servos; (3) alignment forks; (4) stimulus probe that is supported and kept vertical by the alignment forks; (5) infrared sensor; and (6) arm support. The V-Slot Mini V Linear Actuator for the horizontal stage is hidden by the arm support.

Past research has shown that force is the controlling factor in the perception of tactile intensity [22, 23], so our apparatus was designed to apply a consistent weight (27 g) to the skin. Since skin impedance differs over persons and locations, the resulting penetration depth varied, but was designed to be about 2 mm. LaMotte [24] used a 2-mm diameter probe that touched the finger pad for 900 ms to study magnitude estimation of skin indentation up to 1.6 mm. Our 2-mm indentation depth should therefore be clearly perceivable to all participants. To ensure sufficient contact time, the probe tip was allowed to press onto the skin for about 2 s [25, 26].

The horizontal stage served to position the stimulus probe on the desired skin location. The two vertical stages supported and lifted the probe off of the arm while the horizontal positioning stage moved. Once the probe reached its desired x position, the vertical stages lowered until the weight of the probe was fully supported by the skin on the arm. The vertical stage continued to move down for another 5 mm until the infra-red sensor (GP2Y0A41SK0F by Sharp; #5 in Fig. 1) no longer detected the bottom aluminum rod. At this point, the vertical stage was signaled to stop. The alignment forks supported the weight of the probe during the time it wasn't touching the skin. They also served to ensure that the probe remained vertical when the skin was supporting the probe's weight. At the end of the 2-s stimulus duration, the vertical stages lifted the probe off of the skin before the horizontal stage moved again. (Please see the supplemental video at https://youtu.be/RPhzymTr9jU that demonstrates the apparatus in action.)

The horizontal and vertical stages were controlled independently through an Arduino Uno R3 unit. A MATLAB program was developed to interface with the Arduino and to provide a GUI for the experiment.

2.3   Procedure

The participant sat next to a table and placed the non-dominant arm on the table, with either the dorsal or volar side facing up. We chose to test the non-dominant forearm because we envision most communication devices to be worn on the non-dominant forearm. The participant wore a noise-reduction earphone to block any possible auditory cues. An opaque screen blocked the participant's view of the forearm and the apparatus. Using a tape measure, the experimenter measured the length of the participant's forearm from the wrist (the crease at the volar base of the palm) to the elbow (the crease visible when the elbow is slightly bent), and the circumferences of the forearm at the elbow and the wrist. The experimenter then marked the wrist and elbow locations with ink. For bookkeeping, all positions were measured in mm from the wrist and then converted to percentage of total forearm length.

A one-interval forced-choice paradigm with a one-up one-down adaptive procedure was conducted. The thresholds obtained this way correspond to the 50 percentile point on the psychometric function (see [27], p. 470, left column, for a discussion of the pros and cons of the simple up-down procedure). Before each adaptive series, the probe touched the participant's wrist for 2 s, followed by a 2-s touch on the elbow, to ensure awareness of the exact positions of these two joints. On each trial, the stimulus probe contacted the skin at one point. The participant was asked to indicate whether the touched location felt closer to the "elbow" or the "wrist." If the participant responded "elbow" (or "wrist"), then the contact point was moved 10 mm away from the elbow (or wrist) on the next trial. After the first three reversals at the step size of 10 mm, the change in position was reduced to 5 mm. A reversal was defined as the contact location moving towards the elbow after having moved away from the elbow on the previous trial(s), or vice versa. The series ended after the participant had completed twelve (12) reversals at the smaller step size of 5 mm. If the participant's data did not converge by visual inspection of the stimulus vs. trial plot (e.g., see Fig. 2), the adaptive series was repeated. This happened to 4 participants (P3, P6, P9, P12).

Each participant completed four conditions: two starting positions (75% or 25% of the forearm length from the wrist) and two sides of the forearm (dorsal or volar). The order of the conditions was randomized over participants. The participant could take a break between the conditions. The entire experiment took two sessions, two conditions per session, for each participant and lasted a total of 1 to 2 h.

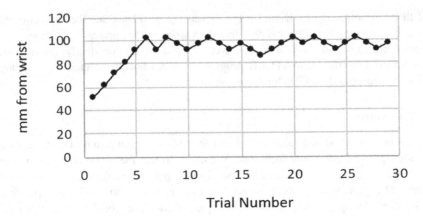

Fig. 2. One adaptive series for P10, with a starting point of 25% from the wrist, on the volar forearm. The measured forearm length is 210 mm. The estimated midpoint is 96.7 mm with a standard error of 0.3 mm, or 46.0% of forearm length from the wrist.

2.4   Data Analysis

The perceived midpoint on the forearm was estimated by averaging the peak and valley positions over the last 12 reversals. To determine the standard error of the perceived midpoint, six estimates were calculated from the six pairs of the peaks and valleys at the last 12 reversals. The average and standard error were then obtained from the six estimates (see [28] for a similar data processing method). Figure 2 shows a typical experimental series.

3   Results

The perceived midpoints in mm for each participant were first converted to percentage of forearm length for the participant. The measured forearm length varied from 180 to 225 mm for the twelve participants. Figure 3 is a scatter plot of perceived midpoints for all participants in percentage of forearm length from the wrist. For clarity, the data for the dorsal and volar sides of the forearm are slightly offset to the left and right, respectively, for each participant. It is evident that there are large differences in the data from the twelve participants. Three participants (P6, P7, P8) show a clear trend of having perceived midpoints at >50% over all conditions, which correspond to points closer to the elbow than to the wrist. Among the remaining participants, two (P1 and P12) exhibited different trends for dorsal (C1 and C2) vs. volar (C3 and C4) conditions. Yet others' data differed depending on the initial starting point at 75% from the wrist (C1 and C3) vs. 25% from the wrist (C2 and C4). These include P4, P5, P6, P7, P8, P10, and P11. Among the latter group whose data exhibited effect of starting point, some midpoint estimates hardly deviated from the starting points (e.g., C3 for P2, C2 for P11). Upon closer examination, the data that were most influenced by the starting position in these cases were from the randomly-selected first condition that the participants were tested on, reflecting a possible learning effect.

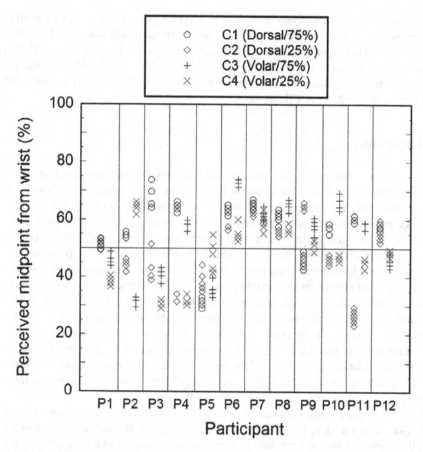

Fig. 3. Scatter plot of perceived midpoint estimates for each participant. The data for the dorsal side of the arm are slightly offset to the left of those for the volar side. There are six data points per condition, and some data points overlap.

The ranges of perceived midpoint were similar across the four experimental conditions, as shown in Table 1. The averages are above 50% for C1 and C3 (starting point at 75% from the wrist), and below 50% for C2 and C4 (starting point at 25% from the wrist). The standard errors are also similar across the four conditions. The average over all the participants and all the conditions shows a slight tendency (51.4%) toward the elbow.

Table 1. Perceived midpoint estimates for each experimental condition: Ranges, averages and standard errors over the twelve participants.

	Range	Ave ± std.err.
C1 (Dorsal, starting at 75% from wrist)	29.0–73.6%	56.4 ± 1.15%
C2 (Dorsal, starting at 25% from wrist)	23.1–65.8%	48.2 ± 1.38%
C3 (Volar, starting at 75% from wrist)	29.4–73.8%	53.2 ± 1.46%
C4 (Volar, starting at 25% from wrist)	29.2–66.1%	47.9 ± 1.20%

A repeated-measures analysis of variance (ANOVA) with the two factors starting point and side of forearm confirms significant inter-participant differences [F(11,273) = 16.77; p < .0001], a significant effect of starting point [F(1,273) = 43.34; p < .0001], but no significant effect of side of forearm [F(1,273) = 2.99; p = 0.0847]. A posthoc t-test comparing the perceived midpoints in percentage to 50% reveals a significant difference [t(287) = 2.07; p = 0.0390].

4 Discussions

The present study set out to ask the question of whether our perceived midpoint coincides with the geometric midpoint on the forearm. Past literature has shown tendency of mislocalization towards the more distal and mobile joint [5, 13–15]; in that a stimulated point at the geometric midpoint of the forearm is judged to be closer to the wrist. This suggests that in order for a point to be perceived as the midpoint, it needs to be located closer to the elbow, thereby suggesting a shift of perceived midpoint towards the proximal and less mobile joint (in our case the elbow). Other studies have shown the opposite trend [10] or no discernable pattern [18]. For example, a re-analysis of the localization errors for the mid-forearm tactor (#4) in the 7-tactor array from [10] showed that overall, there was a tendency for the tactile stimuli to be localized (incorrectly) in a direction closer to the elbow than to the wrist. That is, when Site 4 (at the physical midpoint of the arm) was stimulated, regardless of the magnitude of the error (1, 2, or 3 sites distant) it was more likely that the participant would respond that a site towards the elbow was stimulated than a site towards the wrist. This suggests a trend that the perceived midpoint was shifted towards the wrist.

While most past studies looked at tactor localization errors using one or more tactors placed on the skin, the present study directly asked the question of whether a touch that varied along the longitudinal direction (wrist to elbow) on the forearm felt closer to the wrist or the elbow. When the average was calculated over all the conditions and all the participants in the present study, we found a slight tendency for the perceived midpoint to be located in a direction towards the elbow; i.e., the average perceived midpoint was 51.4% of forearm length from the wrist. This finding was found to be significant in the post-hoc t-test analysis. Numerically, a 1.4% shift corresponded to a 3 mm displacement on the longest forearm (225 mm in length) among the participants tested. This slight shift of 3 mm is quite small, considering that most tactors have contact dimensions that are either similar to or larger than 3 mm. Therefore, for all practical purposes, we may conclude that the perceived midpoint and the geometric midpoint are quite close.

During the post-experiment debriefing, several participants commented that the tactile stimuli delivered by the weighted probe felt clearer on the volar side than on the dorsal side. This may be due to the slight differences in the detection thresholds at these two body sites. However our statistical analysis indicated that the side of forearm tested did not have a significant effect on the perceived midpoint estimates, presumably because the stimuli were well above thresholds on both sides of the forearm. Some participants were unsure about where the midpoint on the forearm was located. They pointed to a region rather than a point on the forearm as being in the "middle." Interestingly, when asked whether they could tell the location of a mosquito bite, more than half the participants (P1, P2, P3, P5, P6, P8, P12) said they couldn't.

5 Concluding Remarks

The results from the present study was useful to a tactile speech communication project where three locations on the forearm (near the wrist, middle of the forearm, and near the elbow) were used to encode phonemic information, in addition to other signal characteristics such as frequency and duration [29–31]. While it was clear that the tactors near the wrist and elbow could be easily localized, there was a question of whether the occasional mis-localization of the middle tactor could be attributed to a perceived midpoint that differed significantly from the geometric midpoint. Our finding is that the slight shift in perceived midpoint from the geometric midpoint (3 mm) is small compared to typical tactor sizes. Due to the variation among the participants and the different trends shown by individual participants (Fig. 3), it is conceivable that more data collected from additional participants may lead to a slightly different conclusion. However for the purpose of guiding the placement of tactors on an arm-worn array, there is sufficient evidence to determine that there is no need for adjusting the tactors placed in the middle of the forearm.

Acknowledgments.   This research was supported in part by Facebook, Inc. The authors thank Visheshta Malhotra for her assistance with literature search, Zhiyu Shao for his assistance with MATLAB coding, Juan Sebastian Martinez for his help with video editing, and Charlotte M. Reed for her helpful comments on an earlier draft of the paper.

References

1. Brill, J.C., Rupert, A.H., Lawson, B.D.: Error analysis for localizing egocentric multimodal cues in the presence of helicopter noise. Proc. Hum. Factors Ergon. Soc. Ann. Meet. **59**(1), 1297–1301 (2015)
2. Weisenberger, J.M., Broadstone, S.M., Kozma-Spytek, L.: Relative performance of single-channel and multichannel tactile aids for speech perception. J. Rehabil. Res. Dev. **28**(2), 45–56 (1991)
3. Rinker, M.A., Craig, J.C.: The effect of spatial orientation on the perception of moving tactile stimuli. Percept. Psychophys. **56**(3), 356–362 (1994)
4. Parsons, L.M., Shimojo, S.: Perceived spatial organization of cutaneous patterns on surfaces of the human body in various positions. J. Exp. Psychol. Hum. Percept. Perform. **13**(3), 488–504 (1987)
5. Boring, E.G.: Sensation and Perception in the History of Experimental Psychology. Appleton-Century, New York (1942)
6. Weber, E.H.: The Sense of Touch (De Tactu, HE Ross, Trans.; Der Tastsinn, DJ Murray, Trans.). Academic Press, New York (1826/1978)

7. Cholewiak, R.W., Collins, A.A.: Sensory and physiological bases of touch. In: Heller, M.A., Schiff, W. (eds.) The Psychology of Touch, pp. 23–60. Lawrence Erlbaum Associates, Hillsdale (1991)
8. Greenspan, J.D., Bolanowski, S.J.: The psychophysics of tactile perception and its peripheral physiological basis. In: Kruger, L. (ed.) Pain and Touch, pp. 25–104. Academic Press, San Diego (1996)
9. Cholewiak, R.W., Brill, J.C., Schwab, A.: Vibrotactile localization on the Abdomen: effects of place and space. Percept. Psychophys. 66(6), 970–987 (2004)
10. Cholewiak, R.W., Collins, A.A.: Vibrotactile localization on the arm: effects of place, space, and age. Percept. Psychophys. 65(7), 1058–1077 (2003)
11. Vignemont, F.D., Majid, A., Jola, C., Haggard, P.: Segmenting the body into parts: Evidence from biases in tactile perception. Quart. J. Exp. Psychol. 62(3), 500–512 (2009)
12. Medina, S., Tame, L., Longo, M.R.: Tactile localization biases are modulated by gaze direction. Exp. Brain Res. 236(1), 31–42 (2018)
13. Vierordt, K.: Die Abhängigkeit der Ausbildung des Raumsinnes der Haut von der Beweglichkeit der Körpertheile. Zeitschrift für Biologie 6, 53–72 (1870)
14. Lewy, W.: Experimentelle Untersuchungen über das Gedächtnis. Zeitschrift fur Psych. 8, 231–292 (1895)
15. Parrish, C.S.: Localization of cutaneous impressions by arm movement without pressure upon the skin. Am. J. Psychol. 8, 250–267 (1897)
16. Sadibolova, R., Tamè, L., Walsh, E., Longo, M.R.: Mind the gap: the effects of temporal and spatial separation in localization of dual touches on the hand. Front. Hum. Neurosci. 12(55) (2018). https://doi.org/10.3389/fnhum.2018.00055
17. Hölzl, R., Stolle, A., Kleinböhl, D.: From spatiotemporal tactile illusions to dynamic somatosensory maps. Program Abstracts/43. Kongress der Deutschen Gesellschaft für Psychologie, Lengerich [u.a.] (2002)
18. Wang, D., Peng, C., Afzal, N., Li, W., Wu, D., Zhang, Y.: Localization performance of multiple vibrotactile cues on both arms. IEEE Trans. Haptics 11(1), 97–106 (2018)
19. Geldard, F.A., Sherrick, C.E.: Multiple cutaneous stimulation: the discrimination of vibratory patterns. J. Acoust. Soc. Am. 37(5), 797–801 (1965)
20. Fontana, Juan M., O'Brien, R., Laciar, E., Maglione, L.S., Molisani, L.: Vibrotactile stimulation in the upper-arm for restoring individual finger sensations in hand prosthesis. J. Med. Biol. Eng. 38(5), 782–789 (2018). https://doi.org/10.1007/s40846-018-0374-1
21. Cody, F.W., Garside, R.A., Lloyd, D., Poliakoff, E.: Tactile spatial acuity varies with site and axis in the human upper limb. Neurosci. Lett. 433(2), 103–108 (2008)
22. Craig, J.C., Sherrick, C.E.: The role of skin coupling in the determination of vibrotactile spatial summation. Percept. Psychophys. 6, 97–101 (1969)
23. Poulos, D.A., et al.: The neural signal for the intensity of a tactile stimulus. J. Neurosci. 4(8), 2016–2024 (1984)
24. LaMotte, R.H.: Psychophysical and neurophysiological studies of tactile sensibility. In: Hollies, N.R., Goldman, R.F. (eds.) Clothing Comfort: Interaction of Thermal, Ventilation, Construction and Assessment Factors, pp. 83–105. Ann Arbor Science Publishers Inc., Ann Arbor (1977)
25. Hahn, J.F.: Tactile adaptation. In: Kenshalo, D.R., Thoma, C.C. (eds.) The Skin Senses—Proceedings of the First International Symposium on the Skin Senses, pp. 322–330 (1968)
26. Nafe, J.P., Wagoner, K.S.: The nature of pressure adaptation. J. Gen. Psychol. 25, 323–351 (1941)
27. Levitt, H.: Transformed up-down methods in psychoacoustics. J. Acoust. Soc. Am. 49(2), 467–477 (1971)

28. Brisben, A.J., Hsiao, S.S., Johnson, K.O.: Detection of vibration transmitted through an object grasped in the hand. J. Neurophysiol. **81**(4), 1548–1558 (1999)
29. Reed, C.M., et al.: A phonemic-based tactile display for speech communication. IEEE Trans. Haptics **12**(1), 2–17 (2019)
30. Jiao, Y., et al.: A comparative study of phoneme- and word-based learning of English words presented to the skin. Proc. EuroHaptics **2018**, 623–635 (2018)
31. Jung, J., et al.: Speech communication through the skin: design of learning protocols and initial findings. Proc. HCI Int. **2018**, 447–460 (2018)

Gen_braille: Development of a Braille Pattern Printing Method for Parametric 3D CAD Modeling

Kazunori Minatani[✉]

National Center for University Entrance Examinations,
Komaba 2-19-23, Meguro-ku, Tokyo 153-8501, Japan
minatani@rd.dnc.ac.jp

Abstract. The aim of this research is to establish a method that visually impaired people can use for shaping three-dimensional (3D) objects by themselves using programmable computer-aided design (CAD). In parametric CAD, variable definition and substitution are devised in a source code of the programmable CAD. If we prepare 3D data of assistive technologies (ATs) with the source code of the parametric CAD and also prepare an intuitive user interface for variable substitutions, we can realize a do-it-yourself AT useful for many visually impaired people. Thus, it is effective to place braille on the surface of a modeled object and use the 3D model as an AT for the visually impaired people.

In this research, a CAD module called gen_braille was created for the OpenJSCAD software. When an arbitrary braille character string is provided to this model, it outputs corresponding 3D dot patterns. The aim of this research is to realize a braille generation system that can be used for parametric CAD; therefore, a required area calculation function was implemented.

The author was able to produce an output of 32 square plates having sides of 2 cm each that displayed a single braille character. Debris, which could be misread, had adhered to 25 print results. The mean of the amount of the adhered debris was 1.08 (SD = 0.93). The debris could be removed with an ordinary post-printing process called manual removal. To prove that gen_braille could be used in parametric CAD, the tactile braille ruler creation system was made. By changing the value of the unit variable, it was possible to output a ruler with a freely chosen unit system (metric or inch).

Keywords: DIY assistive technology · Braille · Visually impaired people · Parametric CAD · Programmable CAD

1 Background

1.1 Effectiveness of Parametric CAD in Do-It-Yourself Assistive Technology for Visually Impaired People

In recent years, three-dimensional (3D) printing has attracted attention as a means for providing information to visually impaired people. In this study, the

© Springer Nature Switzerland AG 2020
M. Antona and C. Stephanidis (Eds.): HCII 2020, LNCS 12188, pp. 168–177, 2020.
https://doi.org/10.1007/978-3-030-49282-3_12

author has established a method that enables visually impaired people to shape 3D objects by themselves [1] by using computer-aided design (CAD)-type modeling. Specifically, in the CAD environment (where the input source code expresses the object called the programmable CAD), if the object shape is described without confirming the graphic output, CAD modeling can be performed even by visually impaired people. By using the proposed method, the do-it-yourself (DIY) assistive technology (AT) [2] method that has attracted a great deal of attention in recent years can also be applied to the field of vision impairment.

However, describing an object with programmable CAD requires a certain level of mastery and persistence. Therefore, it is important to refrain from directly expecting the use of programmable CAD in general for visually impaired people. The ability to use intuitive graphic CAD software that is commonly used among visually normal people is considered an important qualification for salary assessments at work. Taking this into account, we should not ignore the difficulty involved in using programmable CAD without checking the graphic output.

A method called parametric CAD is closely related to programmable CAD. Parametric CAD devises variable definitions and substitutions in the source-code descriptions of programmable CAD. Using this technique, the users can change the shape of the generated 3D object by using their ingenuity. For example, the technique corresponds to a source code that can output cases for arbitrary smartphones by assigning the height, width, and height values to the variables. If we prepare the 3D data of the welfare equipment and AT with the source code of the parametric CAD and also prepare an intuitive user interface for variable substitution, it would be possible to realize a DIY AT useful for many visually impaired people.

OpenJsCad [3] is a language processing system that can be a platform of DIY AT for the visually impaired. OpenJsCad is a software implemented by Javascript based on the language specifications of the programmable CAD environment OpenSCAD [4]. The CAD data are described according to the language specifications of the Javascript domain-specific language. The significant features of the OpenJsCad software are as follows:

- It can be executed on either the client side (on the web browser) or on the server side (using nodejs).
- The 3D objects can be stored in an array and given a shape.
- The functions included in the Javascript core language are available.

However, from the viewpoint of parametric CAD, the possibility of assigning a certain variable without changing the source code would be an important feature. In other words, when devising the description of the source code, certain values can be assigned to a variable by using the web form (when the variable is executed on the client-side web browser) and/or by using command-line parameter (when the variable is executed on the server side). Particularly, being able to specify the necessary input values to a web form on a web browser will be very promising for providing arbitrary object generation functions to users who are not proficient in CAD. A screenshot of the interactions of the OpenJsCad software with a web browser is shown in Fig. 1. Securing web accessibility for visually impaired people requires the use of advanced technology. Therefore, we can expect a user-friendly input environment for the CAD data that is highly simplified by using the web browser and the screen reader.

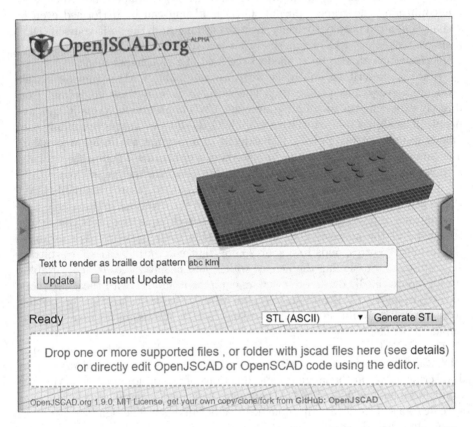

Fig. 1. Generating braille letters "abc" and "klm" using the gen_braille on OpenJS-CAD's web UI.

1.2   Displaying Braille on 3D Objects and Their Limitations in Parametric CAD Applications

To use the 3D model as AT for visually impaired people, it is effective to place braille on the surface of a modeled object.

Three studies and implementations based on these points of interest have already been conducted.

1. The author constructed a system that converted the data of the "embossed dot graphics" (drawn by arranging dots) into 3D data [5]. It was possible to output the braille characters as 3D objects. However, in this method, it was necessary to arrange the dots one by one, which makes it an inefficient

process because it was similar to writing a letter by arranging various lines (e.g., drawing a letter with SVG's path element). Also, the use of this method in the parametric CAD was not considered.

2. The 3D printed braille website provided by TouchSee [6] is a service that generates the braille 3D model as STL data on the web. It generates STL data by giving a character string from the web form. The service can provide output for 40 languages and braille notations. When a braille character string is automatically generated on a rectangular plate, its size is adjusted.

3. The 3D-braille software implementation [7] converts arbitrary English character strings to 3D braille data. The implementation generates STL data by giving an English character string as an argument from the command line. A braille character string is generated on a rectangular plate whose size is explicitly specified by the user. The character string that can be generated is limited to letters and numbers that are hard coded in the program.

The implementations 2 and 3 (stated above) were designed with a focus on the usability. In other words, a use case was assumed in which a user, who did not know braille, outputs a plate with braille, which could easily print 3D. The task could be performed by giving only a character string. The generated character string was integrated using the plate-like object as the foundation, and the generated data had the STL format. The possibility of the application of this string to parametric CAD was poor.

2 Development of Gen_braille

2.1 The Facility of the Gen_braille

In this research, the author created a CAD module called gen_braille for Open-JSCAD, which produced corresponding 3D dot patterns as the output when an arbitrary braille character string was provided. The module can comprehensively comply with languages and the braille notation supported by Its conversion utility Liblouis [8] and display screen reader BRLTTY [9].

A user of gen_braille can also specify braille by a method that directly specifies where he/she wants to place the dot. Using this feature, it is possible to output dot patterns that do not have any correspondence with the print letters. The method was implemented by using the OpenJsCad software; therefore, it can handle both the execution from web form and the execution from the command line. CAD data has the jscad format, which is the programmable CAD. By processing with OpenJsCad, it is possible to have an STL format output.

2.2 Additional Functions for Parametric CAD

The aim of this research is to realize a braille generation system that can be used for parametric CAD; therefore, we added a function for that in gen_braille. The size and shape of the object generated by the parametric CAD may be changed; therefore, the area where braille can be placed also may be changed.

To enable the braille system to include such changes, it is necessary to calculate the area that it requires. In some cases, the braille character string needs to be substituted according to the object. For this purpose, in addition to the braille output function, a required area calculation function is implemented. For the required area calculation function, two kinds of functions are provided: (i) a function to calculate the standard size of the braille cell as a required area and (ii) a function to calculate a minimum necessary area by considering a rectangular area where a dot exists.

3   Evaluation

3.1   Output Test

A character output test was performed. The author produced an output of square plates having sides of approximately 2 cm, which together displayed a symbol called the dot locator and a single character. The dot locator is a symbol in which all the six dots are embossed as criteria for checking the positions of the dots of the target braille characters. The author performed this test for 36 characters (i.e., the letters from A to Z and the digits from 0 to 9). The 3D printer used for this task was Ultimaker 3 [11]. The diameter of the extruder was 0.4 mm, and the molding material (filament) was polylactic acid (PLA) (Fig. 2).

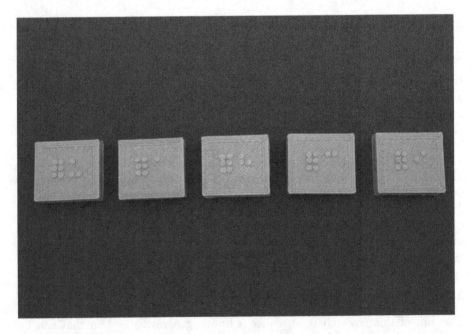

Fig. 2. Examples of the generated braille character blocks U, A, H, C, and I.

Figure 3 shows an enlarged photograph of the "o" character on a plate, which is suitable for observing the placement balance and dot dispersions as representations of the printing result.

Fig. 3. Enlarged photograph of the "o" character on a plate

Debris that adheres to the print results could be misread as braille dots. Debris had adhered to 25 print results. The mean of the amount of adhered debris was 1.08 (SD = 0.93). The debris could be removed using a common post-printing process described by the 3D printer's manufacturer.

The size of one braille character block was relatively small. It is desirable to print as many blocks of braille characters as possible at once. The size of a model that can be printed with a 3D printer was determined by the area and aspect ratio of the print bed of that printer (Fig. 4). To print as many blocks of braille characters as possible at once, it was necessary to arrange the optimal blocks according to each model of the 3D printer. This was automated by using parametric CAD. By providing the length and width of the print bed, we realized the script that optimally arranged the blocks for the 3D printer.

In addition, the same evaluation was performed using Original Prusa i3 MK3S [10] as a trial. The diameter of the extruder was 0.4 mm, and the molding material (filament) was PLA. The height of the printed braille dots was found to be lower than the height of the output obtained by using Ultimaker 3. However, the output could not be completed because of the lack of output materials. Therefore, the outputs of these two 3D printers could not be quantitatively compared.

3.2   Use in Parametric CAD

To prove that gen_braille can be used in parametric CAD, a tactile ruler script was made (see Listing 1.1) (Fig. 5).

Fig. 4. A consumer-grade 3D printer (Original Prusa i3 MK3S [10]) showing the names of the various parts

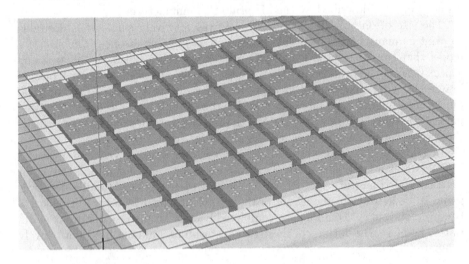

Fig. 5. Allocated braille blocks for printing with Ultimaker 3 [11]

Listing 1.1. An example of tactile ruler generator script with gen_braille

```
include("gen_braille.jscad");

function getParameterDefinitions () {
  return [
    { name: 'unit', initial: '10', type: 'digit', capti
      on: 'ruler unit length (mm)', size: 3 }
  ];
}

function main (param) {
    const unit=parseInt(param.unit);
    const len=160;
    const notchX=cellWidth*2+2;
    let ruler=[];
    ruler.push(cube({size: [notchX+10,len+3,3]}).transl
      ate([0,0,-3]));
    let uc=1;
    for (let i=unit; i < len ; i=i+unit) {
        ruler.push(cube({size: [10,1,1]}).translate([no
          tchX,i-0.5,0]));
        ruler.push(cube({size: [5,1,1]}).translate([not
          chX+5,i-(unit/2+0.5),0]));
        dp=getDotPatterns(parseInt(uc).toString());
        obj=getBrailleObj(dp);
        let [bw, bh]=getFootprint(parseInt(uc).toStrin
          g());
        x=cellWidth*2-bw;
        ruler.push(obj.translate([x,i-bh/2,0]));
        uc++;
    }
    return union(ruler);
}
```

The notches and the braille were aligned using a function that calculates the minimum required area. By changing the value of the unit variable, a ruler with a freely chosen unit system (metric or inch) could be output. The two rulers are shown in Fig. 6 as the printing results.

Some studies have evaluated DIY AT using parametric CAD for the visually impaired in more practical case studies [12]. The author has developed and evaluated a web-based system that can automatically generate STL data for the Banknote Identifier for Visually Impaired People application in any country.

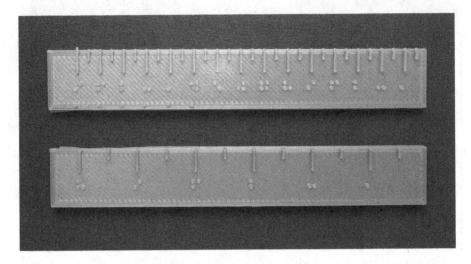

Fig. 6. Two rulers generated by the proposed OpenJSCAD parametric CAD system.

4   Conclusion and Future Research

The author developed a module that generated braille dot patterns for parametric CAD. The 3D printer output produced the expected dot patterns, and the debris could be removed by using a simple procedure. The module can be used with parametric CAD, which cannot be handled by the existing systems.

The output accuracy of the dot patterns corresponding to braille may depend on the 3D printer and the materials used. Therefore, it is important to grasp the characteristics of the facilities used for 3D printing.

Acknowledgments. This work was supported by KAKENHI (17H02005) and JST RISTEX Grant Number JPMJRX19I7, Japan.

References

1. Minatani, K.: Finding 3D CAD data production methods that work for people with visual impairments. In: Stephanidis, C. (ed.) HCI 2017. CCIS, vol. 713, pp. 548–554. Springer, Cham (2017). https://doi.org/10.1007/978-3-319-58750-9_76
2. Hurst, A., Tobias, J.: Empowering individuals with do-it-yourself assistive technology, In: Proceedings of The 13th International ACM SIGACCESS Conference on Computers and Accessibility, pp. 11–18 (2011)
3. OpenJSCAD.org. https://openjscad.org/. Accessed 27 Jan 2020
4. OpenSCAD - The programmers solid 3D CAD modeler. http://www.openscad.org/. Accessed 27 Jan 2020
5. Minatani, K.: A proposed method for producing embossed dots graphics with a 3D printer. In: Miesenberger, K., Kouroupetroglou, G. (eds.) ICCHP 2018. LNCS, vol. 10897, pp. 143–148. Springer, Cham (2018). https://doi.org/10.1007/978-3-319-94274-2_20

6. TouchSee - 3D printed braille. https://touchsee.me/. Accessed 26 Jan 2020
7. GitHub - OutsourcedGuru/3d-braille: a system for creating and exporting braille as a 3D-printable object. https://github.com/OutsourcedGuru/3d-braille/. Accessed 26 Jan 2020
8. Liblouis* - An open-source braille translator and back-translator. http://liblouis.org/. Accessed 26 Jan 2020
9. BRLTTY - Official Home. http://mielke.cc/brltty/. Accessed 26 Jan 2020
10. Original Prusa i3 MK3 kit. https://shop.prusa3d.com/en/3d-printers/180-original-prusa-i3-mk3-kit.html. Accessed 26 Jan 2020
11. Ultimaker 3. https://ultimaker.com/en/products/ultimaker-3. Accessed 26 Jan 2020
12. Minatani K.: Smart apps vs. renovated low-tech devices with DIY assistive technology: a case of a banknote identifier for visually impaired people. In: GoodTechs 2019: Proceedings of the 5th EAI International Conference on Smart Objects and Technologies for Social Good, pp. 96–101. (2019)

User Interfaces in Dark Mode During Daytime – Improved Productivity or Just Cool-Looking?

Lasse Apalnes Pedersen[1], Svavar Skuli Einarsson[1],
Fredrik Arne Rikheim[1], and Frode Eika Sandnes[1,2(✉)]

[1] Oslo Metropolitan University, 0130 Oslo, Norway
lasseap95@gmail.com, svavareinarsson@hotmail.com,
fredrik.rikheim@outlook.com, frodes@oslomet.no
[2] Kristiania University College, 0153 Oslo, Norway

Abstract. Applications are increasingly coming equipped with a so-called dark mode. Our observation is that many computer enthusiasts are under the impression that dark mode in a way is better than the traditional light mode. This study sets out to explore this belief by observing if dark mode indeed poses any improvements in terms of productivity and quantity of errors over light mode. A controlled experiment was designed involving a visually intensive text entry task using a virtual keyboard with an unfamiliar layout. The results indicate that there were no differences between dark mode and light mode in terms of productivity and quantity of errors.

Keywords: Dark mode · Dark UI · Dark theme · Productivity · Error rate · Text entry · Preference · Personalization · Color theme · High contrast mode

1 Introduction

According to Google Trends the term "Dark mode" emerged suddenly around the summer of 2018. During the last year or so there have been an increase in software applications and platforms that promote their dark mode configuration. For example, the widely used IOS and iPadOS platforms got a dark mode in their version 13 update.

In short, dark mode can be understood as an inverted text background-foreground configuration where the text in the foreground is bright and the background is dark, whereas light mode involves dark text in the foreground on a bright background.

One rationale for dark mode is that it is claimed to be better for the eyes when devices are used for prolonged periods under dim lighting conditions [1, 2]. For instance, children using their smartphones at night. Another rationale for using a dark mode is to save power [3]. Given display technologies where the background light of individual pixels can be turned off, such as with organic light emitting diodes (OLED) power can be saved if most of the pixels remain in an off-state, and hence black state [4].

Several development tools such as Eclipse also offer dark mode configurations, also called dark themes. Our impressionistic experiences are that computer science students often have opinions and preferences for or against dark mode. Some argue that dark

M. Antona and C. Stephanidis (Eds.): HCII 2020, LNCS 12188, pp. 178–187, 2020.
https://doi.org/10.1007/978-3-030-49282-3_13

mode is "better". The alleged benefits of dark mode in environments with low lighting does not necessarily apply to development tools when these are used during daytime in well-lit office spaces such as those found in workplaces, institutions, schools and universities. Also, the argument of power saving does not hold for mains-connected desktop computers.

There is not a shortage of opinions regarding dark mode and dark user interfaces although few opinions are based on empirical evidence documented in peer-reviewed sources. A blog post UX designers Niklos Phillips [5] identifies that dark mode is often used in interfaces related to film such as Apple TV and Netflix to achieve dramatic effect and as an convention often used in entertainment, as well as reasons of branding. Dark user interfaces are also commonly observed in gaming, probably for the similar reasons. Phillips argues that dark user interfaces work well for such entertainment contexts as content is often viewed at a distance in dimly lit rooms. He further argues that dark mode is not effective in text and data intensive applications and when there is a mix of different types of contents.

This study, therefore, was initiated to explore dark mode in the context of productivity under normal lighting conditions to determine whether dark mode during daytime leads to better productivity and fewer errors than the traditional light mode. Or, is dark mode just an esthetical gimmick that looks impressive?

The rest of this paper is organized as follows. The next section reviews related work, followed by a description of the experimental method, results and discussion. The conclusions section closes the paper.

2 Related Work

As revealed by Google Trends, «Dark mode» appears to be quite a recent term. At the time of writing, we were only able to identify two academic papers that mention dark mode explicitly in the title [6, 7]. Both studies addressed dark mode in terms of transparent heads up displays and transparent augmented reality displays. Although not mentioned explicitly, the notion that negative text polarity is better with technologies relying on beam splitting such as augmented reality, teleprompters, etc., is well known [8] as the dark background is not reflected by the beam splitter (half-mirror) while the bright text is reflected and overlaid with the background image.

Although the term dark mode appears recent, the idea of dark and light modes is far from new. The effects of positive and negative text polarity have been studied extensively, where positive text polarity is analogous to light mode and negative text polarity is analogous to dark mode. Interestingly, most of the literature on text polarity recommends positive text polarity over negative text polarity [9–11], that is, the studies recommend light mode for text reading tasks. Only in some cases, involving certain types of visual impairment, is negative text polarity found to improve readability [12] and some applications and operating systems have high contrast modes as well as some digital text magnifiers [13, p. 91]. For example, Microsoft Windows implements their high contrast mode using negative text polarity.

Note that these studies mostly focus on text in conjunction with extended reading tasks. Computer usage does indeed vary slightly as it involves also visual recognition tasks where user recognizes images and symbols besides reading text. Moreover, the readability studies are often based around the paper metaphor with either text in black ink on paper, or the background printed in black ink with the text as the paper-white background. In fact, modern display technologies are able to display millions of colors and hence a very large number of text-background combinations is possible. In one sense, the notion of dark mode must in such a context be understood as the brightness of the background being darker than the brightness of the foreground text. Usually, colors are adjusted according to three main parameters, namely their hue, brightness and saturation [14]. Although the brightness varies with the hue and various saturation settings, the main effect on brightness is via the brightness setting. Accessibility guidelines therefore focus on ensuring enough contrast between the background and the foreground [15–17] thereby resulting in various contrast tools [18–20]. There is comparatively little focus on negative versus positive text polarity.

Personalization is a much-studied topic [21, 22]. Personalization help accessing existing content on emerging platforms [23] and help individuals with reduced functioning to access content [24]. A study of smartphone personalization [25] revealed both gender differences in the way they are personalized and also that personalization has a positive effect on the perceived usability. Personalization has also been connected to adaptable systems [26].

3   Method

3.1   Experimental Design

A controlled 2 × 2 mixed experiment was designed with two independent variables and two dependent variables. The independent variables comprised the within-groups factor mode with the levels dark and light, and the between groups factor preference with the levels preference for dark mode and preference for light mode. Productivity in terms of words per minute (wpm) and error rates were measured as dependent variables.

3.2   Participants

A total of 16 participants was recruited for the experiment of which one was female. The participants were all computer science students at the authors' university, and they were all in their twenties. The narrow cohort of computer science students is particularly relevant for this experiment as we assumed that computer science students would be more familiar with the concept of dark mode compared to the general population. Participants were screened before the experiment in which they were asked about their preference for dark mode or light mode. This allowed us to recruit a balanced set comprising 8 participants with a preference for dark mode and 8 participants with a preference for light mode. The recruiting process revealed that there were slightly more people with a preference for light mode, yet it was relatively easy to recruit a completely balanced set of participants with both preferences.

Fig. 1. A screenshot of the virtual alphabetical keyboard in dark mode.

Fig. 2. A screenshot of the virtual alphabetical keyboard in light mode.

3.3 Task

In order to measure the difference with the use of dark versus light mode a visually intensive pointing task was set up involving text copying task using a virtual onboard keyboard. Text entry is a workload intensive task that most users understand which phenomena is studied extensively [27, 28]. To make it harder for the participants alphabetically ordered keyboards were used instead of a Qwerty keyboard as it was assumed that most users would be too familiar with the Qwerty layout [29, 30]. Studies have shown that users enter text significantly slower with alphabetical layouts [31, 32]. The lack of familiarity with the alphabetical keyboard was thus expected to induce a more intense visual search for the letters. MacKenzie and Soukoreff's commonly used list of 500 phases was used in the experiment [33].

3.4 Equipment

The experiment was conducted using a laptop computer and a mouse. The text was entered into OneNote using a virtual keyboard with an alphabetical layout. This keyboard could be configured to both light and dark mode, respectively. The customizable

Hot Virtual Keyboard was selected for the experiments (https://hot-virtual-keyboard.com/). The dark mode keyboard used is shown in Fig. 1 and light mode keyboard used is shown in Fig. 2. The text copying task was performed by controlling the pointer using a mouse. The text-copying task was timed using a stopwatch.

3.5 Procedure

Steps were taken to balance the experiment to avoid biases. The text phrases were divided into two sets. Half of the participants started in dark mode and finished in light mode, and vice versa. For each mode half the participants used the first set of text phrases and the other half the second set of text phrases. After the sessions the participants were briefly interviewed regarding their experiences during the session.

Participation was voluntary and anonymous. As the experiment was conducted in one session no identifying mechanisms had to be employed to link sessions. The General Data Protection Regulations (GDPR) therefore did not apply for this study.

3.6 Analysis

The results were analyzed using JASP version 0.10.0.0.

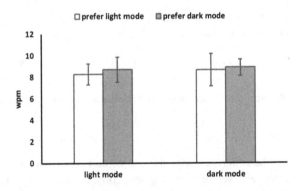

Fig. 3. Productivity in mean words per minute. Error bars show 95% confidence intervals.

4 Results

Figure 3 shows the results of the experiments in terms of productivity. Clearly, the mean words per minute for both groups under both conditions are quite similar and the 95% confidence intervals for all the point estimates overlaps. There is thus no evidence to support that there are any effects of either preference or mode of operation. A two-way mixed anova confirms the lack of significant effect both for mode of operation ($F(1, 14) = 0.680$, $p = .423$) and preference ($F(1, 14) = 0.189$, $p = .671$). The confidence intervals reveal that the participants who preferred dark mode exhibited a larger spread in the light mode condition, while similarly the participants who preferred light mode exhibited a larger spread in the dark mode.

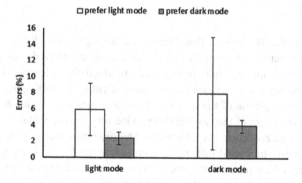

Fig. 4. Error rate in percent. Error bars show 95% confidence intervals.

Figure 4 shows the results of the error rate observations. Clearly, the error rates are similar for the light (left) and dark (right) modes. The mean point estimates for the participants who prefer light mode (white bars) is nearly twice as large as those of the participants who prefer dark mode (gray bars). However, the confidence intervals overlap, and one may therefore not conclude on any effective difference between the two groups. The participants who preferred light mode also exhibited a much larger spread than the participants who preferred dark mode. When comparing light mode with dark mode, there was a higher error rate with dark mode compared to the light mode for both groups. Again, the confidence intervals for the participants who preferred light mode overlaps too much for us to conclude that there are any significant differences. However, the confidence intervals for the participants who prefer dark mode overlap just slightly. A non-parametric Wilcoxon test confirms that there is no significant difference between light and dark mode for participants who preferred dark mode ($W = 10.5$, $p = .326$).

The following observations were made during the post session interviews of the participants. Nearly all the participants reported that they felt they improved using the alphabetical keyboard from the first to the second session, hence confirming a perceived learning effect. However, the experiment was balanced so this should have not affected the results. Participants' subjective opinions regarding the two keyboards varied. Most of the participants did not think that the mode affected their text entry speed nor error rate. However, they reported that one mode was more comfortable than the other. When asked about whether one mode made it easier to search and find the letters several participants responded positively, especially for the dark mode. But these were mostly participants who preferred dark mode in the first place. Our impressions from the interview is that users who prefer dark mode were more conscious about the aesthetical appearance and comfort rather than speed and errors.

5   Discussion

The results quite clearly confirm that there were no significant differences between productivity using dark mode or light mode. Our results therefore do not give support to the claim that dark mode results in improved productivity. Clearly, as revealed by the participant recruitment process users are quite divided in their opinions and preferences for the visual profile of the user interfaces as it was easy to locate participants with preferences for either of the two interfaces. One may thus speculate that the choice of dark mode is more an expression of a user's identity rather than a choice founded in ergonomic rationales. In shared office it is common to peek on colleagues' desktops, and dark mode may be a means for users to express their individuality or get the focus of attention. Some users may want their setup to be visually different and fancier than what is offered by the default configurations. Moreover, one may argue that people occasionally like variation and that a switch from light to dark mode can contribute to this perception of change.

However, some differences were observed. The fact that the participants exhibited a larger spread in the least preferred condition supports a speculation that participants exhibit more consistent results in their preferred mode. More consistent results under preferred conditions is a tendency one would expect.

Although not significantly different, the results for the participants with a preference for dark mode exhibited a higher performance in all conditions, that is practically higher text entry rates and lower error rates. Thus, one may speculate whether the preference for dark mode is a predictor of someone particularly computer savvy, or particularly enthusiastic about the use of computers. To be aware of dark mode someone is likely to actively follow recent technology trends and developments.

It is interesting to observe the (non-significant) practical difference in error rates between the two modes which indicates that there may be more errors associated with dark mode. However, the low number of participants may be one explanation for why we were unable to detect any significant differences. It may thus be worthwhile to explore this further in a follow up experiment with a larger number of participants. In fact, a higher ratio of errors in dark mode would be consistent with previous studies of how text polarity affects readability [9–11].

Clearly, as documented in the literature, there may be contexts where dark mode poses benefits over light mode, for instance, when a device is used in a room with little lighting at night over prolonged times [1, 2], when an economic power plan is needed with battery powered devices [3, 4] or when if a user has reduced vision [12]. However, issues related to lighting conditions, prolonged computer use, power consumption and disability is beyond the scope of this study.

5.1   Limitations

This study only included 16 participants, with only 8 participants in each group. This is a very small sample, and it is hard to even detect large significant differences with such few data points. Future work should therefore include more participants.

This study was also limited to a very narrow cohort expected to be more enthusiastic and aware of dark mode. The results therefore provide no foundations for how the results generalize to the general population of computer users. Further work should also include non-computer science users as dark mode is present in application targeted at the general population of computer users.

6 Conclusions

This study explored the effects of dark mode commonly found in modern user interfaces on productivity. A visually intensive pointing task involving text entry on a virtual keyboard in the two modes was conducted. The results indicate that there are no significant effects of dark mode on neither productivity nor errors. Although no observed effects on productivity, one should not underestimate users' perceived enjoyment and satisfaction with their personalized user interface configurations.

References

1. Mantiuk, R., Rempel, A. G., Heidrich, W.: Display considerations for night and low-illumination viewing. In: Proceedings of the 6th Symposium on Applied Perception in Graphics and Visualization, pp. 53–58. ACM (2009). https://doi.org/10.1145/1620993.1621005
2. Rempel, A.G., Mantiuk, R., Heidrich, W.: Display considerations for improved night vision performance. In: Color and Imaging Conference, vol. 2011, no. 1, pp. 191–194. Society for Imaging Science and Technology (2011)
3. Xu, J., Billah, S.M., Shilkrot, R., Balasubramanian, A.: DarkReader: bridging the gap between perception and reality of power consumption in smartphones for blind users. In: The 21st International ACM SIGACCESS Conference on Computers and Accessibility, pp. 96–104. ACM (2019). https://doi.org/10.1145/3308561.3353806
4. Dong, M., Choi, Y.S.K., Zhong, L.: Power-saving color transformation of mobile graphical user interfaces on OLED-based displays. In: Proceedings of the 2009 ACM/IEEE International Symposium on Low Power Electronics and Design, pp. 339–342. ACM (2009). https://doi.org/10.1145/1594233.1594317
5. Philips, M.: Dark UIs. The Good and the Bad. Dos and Don'ts. Downloaded, 7 January 2020. https://www.toptal.com/designers/ui/dark-ui
6. Riegler, A., Riener, A., Holzmann, C.: Adaptive dark mode: investigating text and transparency of windshield display content for automated driving. In: Mensch und Computer 2019-Workshopband (2019). https://doi.org/10.18420/muc2019-ws-612
7. Kim, K., Erickson, A., Lambert, A., Bruder, G., Welch, G.: Effects of dark mode on visual fatigue and acuity in optical see-through head-mounted displays. In: Symposium on Spatial User Interaction, pp. 1–9. (2019). https://doi.org/10.1145/3357251.3357584
8. Sandnes, F.E., Eika, E.: Head-mounted augmented reality displays on the cheap: a DIY approach to sketching and prototyping low-vision assistive technologies. In: Antona, M., Stephanidis, C. (eds.) UAHCI 2017, Part II. LNCS, vol. 10278, pp. 167–186. Springer, Cham (2017). https://doi.org/10.1007/978-3-319-58703-5_13
9. Buchner, A., Mayr, S., Brandt, M.: The advantage of positive text-background polarity is due to high display luminance. Ergonomics 52(7), 882–886 (2009). https://doi.org/10.1080/00140130802641635

10. Piepenbrock, C., Mayr, S., Mund, I., Buchner, A.: Positive display polarity is advantageous for both younger and older adults. Ergonomics **56**(7), 1116–1124 (2013). https://doi.org/10.1080/00140139.2013.790485

11. Tsang, S.N., Chan, A.H., Yu, R.F.: Effect of display polarity and luminance contrast on visual lobe shape characteristics. Ergonomics **55**(9), 1028–1042 (2012). https://doi.org/10.1080/00140139.2012.688876

12. Bangor, A.: Electronic text readability issues for the visually impaired. In: Proceedings of the Human Factors and Ergonomics Society Annual Meeting, vol. 43, no. 23, pp. 1372–1375. SAGE Publications, Los Angeles (1999). https://doi.org/10.1177/154193129904302323

13. Sandnes, F.E.: Universell utforming av IKT-systemer, 2nd edn. Universitetsforlaget, Oslo (2018)

14. Brathovde, K., Farner, M.B., Brun, F.K., Sandnes, F.E.: Effectiveness of color-picking interfaces among non-designers. In: Luo, Y. (ed.) CDVE 2019. LNCS, vol. 11792, pp. 181–189. Springer, Cham (2019). https://doi.org/10.1007/978-3-030-30949-7_21

15. Sandnes, F.E.: On-screen colour contrast for visually impaired readers: selecting and exploring the limits of WCAG2. 0 colours. In: Black, A., Lund, O., Walker, S. (eds.) Information Design: Research and Practice, pp. 405–416 (2016)

16. Sandnes, F.E.: Understanding WCAG2. 0 color contrast requirements through 3D color space visualization. Stud. Health Technol. Inform. **229**, 366–375 (2016). https://doi.org/10.3233/978-1-61499-684-2-366

17. Sandnes, F.E., Zhao, A.: An interactive color picker that ensures WCAG2. 0 compliant color contrast levels. Procedia Comput. Sci. **67**, 87–94 (2015). https://doi.org/10.1016/j.procs.2015.09.252

18. Sandnes, F.E., Zhao, A.: A contrast colour selection scheme for WCAG2. 0-compliant web designs based on HSV-half-planes. In: 2015 IEEE International Conference on Systems, Man, and Cybernetics, pp. 1233–1237. IEEE (2015). https://doi.org/10.1109/smc.2015.220

19. Sandnes, F.E.: An image-based visual strategy for working with color contrasts during design. In: Miesenberger, K., Kouroupetroglou, G. (eds.) ICCHP 2018, Part I. LNCS, vol. 10896, pp. 35–42. Springer, Cham (2018). https://doi.org/10.1007/978-3-319-94277-3_7

20. Hansen, F., Krivan, J.J., Sandnes, F.E.: Still not readable? An interactive tool for recommending color pairs with sufficient contrast based on existing visual designs. In: The 21st International ACM SIGACCESS Conference on Computers and Accessibility, pp. 636–638. ACM (2019). https://doi.org/10.1145/3308561.3354585

21. Bradley, K., Rafter, R., Smyth, B.: Case-based user profiling for content personalisation. In: Brusilovsky, P., Stock, O., Strapparava, C. (eds.) AH 2000. LNCS, vol. 1892, pp. 62–72. Springer, Heidelberg (2000). https://doi.org/10.1007/3-540-44595-1_7

22. Sunar, A.S., Abdullah, N.A., White, S., Davis, H.: Personalisation in MOOCs: a critical literature review. In: Zvacek, S., Restivo, M.T., Uhomoibhi, J., Helfert, M. (eds.) CSEDU 2015. CCIS, vol. 583, pp. 152–168. Springer, Cham (2016). https://doi.org/10.1007/978-3-319-29585-5_9

23. Hoh, S., Gillies, S., Gardner, M.R.: Device personalisation—where content meets device. BT Technol. J. **21**(1), 67–74 (2003). https://doi.org/10.1023/A:1022456327773

24. Cremers, A.H.M., Neerincx, M.A.: Personalisation meets accessibility: towards the design of individual user interfaces for all. In: Stary, C., Stephanidis, C. (eds.) UI4ALL 2004. LNCS, vol. 3196, pp. 119–124. Springer, Heidelberg (2004). https://doi.org/10.1007/978-3-540-30111-0_9

25. Tossell, C.C., Kortum, P., Shepard, C., Rahmati, A., Zhong, L.: An empirical analysis of smartphone personalisation: measurement and user variability. Behav. Inf. Technol. **31**(10), 995–1010 (2012). https://doi.org/10.1080/0144929X.2012.687773

26. García-Barrios, V.M., Mödritscher, F., Gütl, C.: Personalisation versus adaptation? A user-centred model approach and its application. In: Proceedings of the International Conference on Knowledge Management (I-KNOW), pp. 120–127 (2005)
27. Aschim, T.B., Gjerstad, J.L., Lien, L.V., Tahsin, R., Sandnes, F.E.: Are split tablet keyboards better? A study of soft keyboard layout and hand posture. In: Lamas, D., Loizides, F., Nacke, L., Petrie, H., Winckler, M., Zaphiris, P. (eds.) INTERACT 2019, Part III. LNCS, vol. 11748, pp. 647–655. Springer, Cham (2019). https://doi.org/10.1007/978-3-030-29387-1_37
28. Sandnes, F.E.: Evaluating mobile text entry strategies with finite state automata. In: Proceedings of the 7th International Conference on Human computer interaction with Mobile Devices & Services, pp. 115–121. ACM (2005). https://doi.org/10.1145/1085777.1085797
29. Sandnes, F.E., Aubert, A.: Bimanual text entry using game controllers: relying on users' spatial familiarity with QWERTY. Interact. Comput. 19(2), 140–150 (2006). https://doi.org/10.1016/j.intcom.2006.08.003
30. Ye, L., Sandnes, F.E, MacKenzie, I.S.: QB-Gest: qwerty bimanual gestural input for eyes-free smartphone text input, In: Antona, M., Stephanidis, C. (eds.) HCII 2020. LNCS, vol. 12188, pp. 223–242. Springer, Cham (2020). https://doi.org/10.1007/978-3-030-49282-3_16
31. Norman, D.A., Fisher, D.: Why alphabetic keyboards are not easy to use: keyboard layout doesn't much matter. Hum. Factors 24(5), 509–519 (1982). https://doi.org/10.1177/001872088202400502
32. Sandnes, F.E.: Effects of common keyboard layouts on physical effort: implications for kiosks and Internet banking. In: The Proceedings of Unitech2010: International Conference on Universal Technologies, pp. 91–100 (2010)
33. MacKenzie, I.S., Soukoreff, R.W.: Phrase sets for evaluating text entry techniques. In: CHI 2003 Extended Abstracts on Human Factors in Computing Systems, pp. 754–755. ACM (2003). https://doi.org/10.1145/765891.765971

Usability Evaluation of Short Dwell-Time Activated Eye Typing Techniques

Sayan Sarcar[✉]

University of Tsukuba, Tsukuba, Japan
mailtosayan@gmail.com

Abstract. Gaze-based interfaces introduce dwell time-based selection method to avoid the *Midas Touch* problem - it is a fixed amount of time the users must fixate their gaze upon an object before it is selected. In gaze-based text typing, spending such time on each character key composition effectively decreases the overall eye typing rate. Researchers proposed several interaction mechanisms to minimize or diminish the dwelling in the desktop environment, however, they lack in understanding the usability of such mechanisms for regular users, specifically in a constrained eye tracking setup. We conducted a within-subject usability evaluation of four such representative short dwell-time activated eye typing techniques. The results of the first-time usability study, longitudinal study and subjective evaluation conducted with 15 participants confirm the superiority of controlled eye movement-based advanced eye typing method (Adv-EyeK) compare to the other techniques.

Keywords: Gaze-based text entry · Short dwell-time · Usability

1 Introduction

In recent times, gaze-based interaction has evolved as an alternate user interaction modality. It has a significant impact in the field of text entry in the last few decades [14], due to its significant similarity and the only difference in the controlling organ, that is, eye instead of hand [11]. An advantage of the eye modality which may attract the developers is, with the same setup supporting able-bodied, we can develop systems for disabled users who are capable of visual interaction. Recently many applications were developed where controlling modality is eye gaze [13,16,32], even for mobile [5].

Unlike other input modalities, eye gaze supports few commands (as the eye is always moving and always activated, it is unnatural to hold the gaze for a long time, etc.) like eye movement, fixation, blinking and winking of an eye. In an eye-tracking setup, eyes are attached with the mouse pointer with the help of an eye-tracking device (i.e. camera) and gaze-tracking software. Eye gaze-based text composition can be performed in three ways namely a) direct gaze pointing or *Eye typing*, b) eye gesturing and c) continuous writing [2,11].

© Springer Nature Switzerland AG 2020
M. Antona and C. Stephanidis (Eds.): HCII 2020, LNCS 12188, pp. 188–210, 2020.
https://doi.org/10.1007/978-3-030-49282-3_14

1.1 Background

In *Eye typing* method, users require to perform text entry through an on-screen keyboard. There, selecting a key from the keyboard can be performed by placing eye pointer for a slightly prolonged duration, called as *dwell time* [11]. The other behavior used for selection is through *eye blink* performed on the desired key button. The second method, i.e. *Eye gesturing*, supports eye movements to draw a specific pattern (gesture) for selecting a character if that pattern matches. In *Continuous eye writing* method [2], commands are activated based on the natural movement of gaze (like positioning the gaze into an overlay button area selects a character, etc.). It is supporting the users' natural gaze movements as the eyes are always activated and roamed constantly [2]. Such continuous gaze behaviour (like continuous drawing with no lifting of a pen) can be chosen as a suitable platform to implement continuous tasks replaced by eye movement (e.g. using *Dasher* interface [34] for gaze-based text entry [31,35], where always it is needed to select the characters from the character stream). *Gaze-controlled continuous writing* method is different from *Eye typing* task as it does not require the eye pointer to be continuously active. In *Eye typing* method, rather after selecting a character, the eyes can stay which is not possible in other methods.

Minimizing speed-accuracy trade-off at different levels of cognitive complexity is one of the major concerns in dwell-based eye pointing [39]. Large dwell time prevents users from false selections most of the time, as well as brings tiredness in their eyes [15]. On the other hand, shorter dwell time increases the chance of *Midas Touch* problem (the classic eye tracking problem referring in our topic as wrong character selection from the keyboard through gaze pointing [7]). As a result, it is difficult to conclude that shorter dwell time always produces better text entry rate with accuracy. The fixed dwell time also sets the maximum typing speed limit as the user has to wait for the stipulated time on each character button before selecting it. Majaranta and Räihä [15] stated that most gaze typing evaluations were conducted with novices using a constant, fairly long dwell time (450–1000 ms). Wobbrock et al. [38] used a short dwell time (330 ms) and achieved fair text entry rate (7 wpm). Špakov and Miniotas [28], Majaranta and Räihä [15] and Panwar et al. [20] studied dynamic adjustment of dwell time. Although the typing result of those systems were better, they reported *delay* (participants committed that it was hard for them to change typing speed quickly as the system responded with a delay [29]) and *involuntary variation* (after selecting a key with less dwell time, users cannot move their eyes off the target. Thus, as the dwell time decreases, this adaptive adjustment becomes less convenient [29]) as critical problems. So, a trade-off still remains among dwell time, text entry rate and accuracy of the UI.

An effective way to increase the eye typing rate is to minimize dwell time. It has been observed by researchers that depending on the flexible cognitive complexity of users during the eye typing experiment, dwell time can be altered instead of fixing at a particular value [12]. Majaranta et al. [12] developed an interface which dynamically adjusts the dwell time. Their results revealed the effectiveness of the method in achieving faster eye typing rate. Further, researchers attempted to develop gaze-based interaction methods which can diminish dwelling task for selecting a character key. Effective execution of dwell-minimized methods can produce a moderate improvement of text typing rate. Urbina and Huckoff [32], Morimoto and Amir [17], Bee and Andrĕ [2], Kristensson and Vertanen [8], Sarcar et al. [24], Chakraborty et al. [3], Pedrosa et al. [21], Mott et al. [18], and Kurauchi et al. [9] proposed dwell-minimized eye typing mechanisms.

1.2   Usability Evaluation and the Current Work

According to Jacob Nielsen [19], *usability* is defined as a quality attribute that assesses how easy and learnable a user interface is. The word "usability" also points to methods for improving ease-of-use during the design process. Our motivation is to examine the effectiveness of existing character-level short dwell-time activated eye typing techniques, specifically to judge the usefulness over long-term use among regular computer users (with no experience in eye typing), through two usability studies (a *first-time usability study* followed by *longitudinal study*) for quantitative evaluation (i.e., eye typing rate and total error rate) and subjective measures. The *first-time usability study* is aimed to analyze the usability of representative eye typing methods/interfaces for short-time dwelling. On the other hand, the objective behind performing *longitudinal study* is to examine the combined effect of eye typing methods and on-screen keyboard layouts in accessing different eye typing interfaces of users over a long time. A subjective evaluation was performed using questionnaire responses collected during the experiment. From the results of usability between different dwell-minimized techniques examined in this comparative study, we find out the most effective technique which can further be used in developing efficient eye typing interfaces. It is to be noted that this work aims to understand the usability of four representative character-level eye typing techniques (nearly 'dwell-free') in a constrained hardware and software setup which (1) lacks accuracy compare to the professional eye trackers (e.g., Tobii, SMI) in terms of gesture recognition (e.g., swipe gesture), (2) focuses simply on the character-by-character text entry, not any other mechanism such as augmenting word prediction list or using 'swipe' gesture to compose words, and (3) lacks in recruiting expert user for controlled eye movement task (most of the participants exposed to the eye tracker for the first time). Thus, in this work, most recent eye typing mechanisms (such as [9,18,21]) are not considered for comparison.

The contribution of the paper is two-fold. First, it presents usability studies which were conducted first time with four eye typing techniques to analyze their efficacy in a constrained hardware and software setup. Further, this work shows a novel way to test short dwell-activation in different eye typing scenarios, such as 'in-the-wild', using the front camera of the smartphone or in a VR environment. Second, the studies shed light on the limitations in accessing such low-quality hardware and free software to control eye gestures precisely in the desktop environment.

2   Short Dwell-Time Activated Eye Typing Mechanisms

This section provides detailed methodology descriptions of dwell time diminishing mechanisms which are considered for the usability evaluation.

2.1   Iwrite

Iwrite [2,32] is a square-shaped interface for gaze-based text entry placing character buttons at the outer side and text area in the middle (Fig. 1(a)). The characters are selected by gazing toward the outer frame of the application. The text window is placed in the middle of the screen for comfortable and safe text review. The order of the characters, parallel to the display borders, reduces errors like the unintentional selection of items placed on the way to the screen button (e.g., [36]). The interface is very simple to use taking full advantage of the short saccade selection of character keys, leveraging continuous movement of eye gaze. The improved version of this interface - *pEYEWrite* which explores pie menus as keyboard [6] - is not considered for this study.

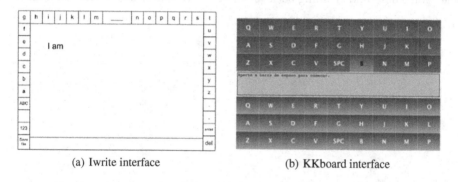

(a) Iwrite interface   (b) KKboard interface

Fig. 1. Different keyboard interfaces

2.2   KKBoard

Morimoto and Amir [17] proposed *Context Switch* (CS) concept to activate a key selection. The CS concept is based on *Key-focus* and *Key-selection* task-oriented eye movements. The *KKBoard* interface replicates same keyboard layout placed in two separate screen regions, called as contexts (see Fig. 1(b)) where the user needs to switch alternately for selecting a key. In the eye typing process, key-focus task, activated through short dwell time, is followed by key selection, which is made by switching contexts (a saccade to the other context). The key which is last in focus in the previous context is taken at the selection phase. Context switching task diminishes the effect of the *Midas Touch* problem. The CS-based text input replaces the traditional long dwell time with a short dwell followed by a context-switching saccade.

2.3   EyeK

Sarcar et al. [24] proposed the *EyeK* eye typing interface where they introduced
a dwell-minimized typing mechanism. According to the method, a key button
in the keyboard is selected automatically through specific interaction, which
activates while a user moves the eye pointer through the button areas in inside-
outside-inside fashion (see Fig. 2). As eye movement is faster than mouse or finger
movement, this interaction takes minimum effort and time, which is negligible
to the traditional dwell time. According to the example shown in Fig. 2, suppose
a user wants to select character 'C' While hovering on the character, key and
its overlay area are visible. The user starts moving the eye pointer within the
key area, goes to outside overlay area and again comes back inside to the key
area to complete the interaction phase (Fig. 2a, enlarged portion). After placing
the eye pointer inside the key area, character selection gets activated (Fig. 2b).
After selecting a character, visual feedback is given by changing its font color to
red, which remains up to next character selection. If users need to enter same
characters twice, they have to get out of the character initially and enter it
again in the similar manner. This proposed mechanism provides a facility that
the "going out" and "coming back" sides of a button may not be same and fixed.

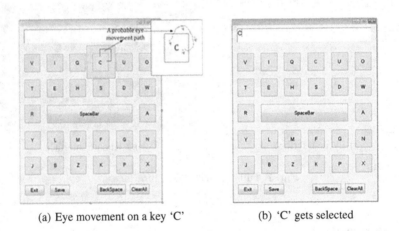

(a) Eye movement on a key 'C'   (b) 'C' gets selected

Fig. 2. Dwell-minimized eye typing in *EyeK* layout

2.4   An Effective Short Dwell-Time Activated Eye Typing Technique (*Adv-EyeK*)

A slight improvement over Sarcar et al.'s method [24] for dwell-minimized eye
typing was proposed by Chakraborty et al. [3] (throughout the article, we will call
it as *Adv-EyeK*, which is an advanced method of *EyeK*). The interaction pattern
for this advanced method is different from the previous method. It supports more
controlled eye movement for key selection (Fig. 3). In the overlay area which is
activated after hovering, a black point is placed at a fixed position (upper side

of the key, preferably at the center of the upper portion of the outer key area). After users hover on the intended key, they require to "go out" from the inner key, reach to that prominent point and after looking, "come back" inside the inner key area (preferably from same side) (Fig. 3a). A feedback system, same as the previous method, is applied to provide selection confirmation to the user (Fig. 3b). As an example, suppose, a user needs to select character 'C'. Then, on hovering 'C', the outer layer becomes visible and user "goes out" from the upper side, sees the point and "comes back" into the inner key from the same side. For the double selection of a single key, the same procedure used in the last method is followed.

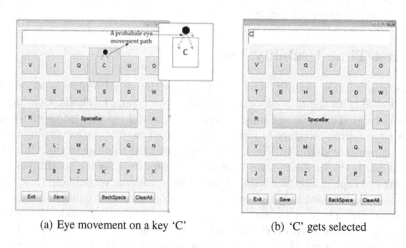

(a) Eye movement on a key 'C'   (b) 'C' gets selected

Fig. 3. Dwell-minimized eye typing in *Adv-EyeK* layout

Kriestensson and Vertanen [8] proposed a novel work in the related field, but they did not provide the working methodology of the system. So, we could not replicate the method. Bee and Andrě [2] mimicked the design methodology of *Quickwriting* text entry system for eye typing. We were unable to consider the system for our usability experiment also as it supports *Eye Writing* instead of *Eye typing* [2].

2.5 Low Cost Eye Tracking Solutions

Although the current study is not focused on developing low cost self-made eye tracking systems, however, here we mention a few ope-source gaze tracking programs which can further be used toward developing such systems. Agustin et al. [23] designed and evaluated a low-cost gaze tracking system based on a webcam mounted close to the user's eye. Schneider et al. [25] developed a portable low-cost head-mounted eye-tracking system based on extension of open-source ITU Gaze Tracker software with added functionality for calibration in space, scene recording, synchronization for eye and scene videos, and offline tracking. Providing a mobile device support, Tonsen et al. [30] developed a novel approach for mobile eye tracking leveraging millimetre-size RGB cameras which can be fully embedded into normal glasses frames.

We conducted two usability studies namely *first-time usability test* and *longitudinal user experiment* and analyzed the results. Our aim of conducting two experiments was to fulfill two objectives: a) to observe the efficacy of representative short dwell-time activated eye typing techniques with respect to user performance of eye typing task over a short time period and b) to also observe the user performance in a longitudinal study on combinations of three on-screen keyboards suitable for eye typing with these techniques. Detail descriptions of design, participants, apparatus, procedure, results, and discussions of both the usability studies are given below.

3   First-Time Usability Test

The purpose of this usability test was to study the speed, errors, and perception of usability in the first encounter with the eye typing methods. Conducting the short term study, we not only observed the initial reaction of users toward different eye typing interface but also judged the efficacy of the eye typing methods for immediate usability. We, in this study, wanted to observe the efficacy of different methods for short-term usability of users in different conditions (like accessing eye typing interface *without* and *with + without* verbal help (it is to be noted that we provided help through verbal instructions, not using hand gesture pointing on the screen or by any other means) etc.). The other side of conducting this short study with every user is to provide scope to get acquainted with different eye typing interfaces which would further help them while performing long-term studies.

3.1   Apparatus

Experiments were conducted in a low-cost eye-tracking setup using 2.2 GHz Intel Core2Duo processor with 15" screen LCD color monitor having 1440 × 900 resolution. Modified *Sony PlayStation Eye* webcam, original lens was replaced by Infrared (IR) filter lens (for gaze capturing), IR Lamp consists of a matrix of 10 IR LED, along with open source ITU GazeTracker software [1], developed by IT University of Copenhagen, were used for experiments. The keypress events and gaze positions were recorded automatically and stores into log files using separate event hooking programs. All experiments were performed in Windows 7 environment. Controlled light conditions and positioning of the setup were maintained.

Four applications were run during testing the efficacy of dwell-minimized typing methods namely *Iwrite* [32], *KKBoard* [17], *EyeK* [24] and *Adv-EyeK* method [3]. In each case, real-time eye movement was obtained with a tailored version of the application namely ITU GazeTracker. Apart from this, one C# application was run to display eye typing interfaces. Another application was used for presenting phrases during the typing session running. This program randomly presented a target phrase from a corpus of 500 to the user while simultaneously recording various text entry metrics for further analysis. Real-time (x, y) eye movements were converted to cursor coordinates by a C# program that simply masqueraded the gaze point as the mouse position to other Windows applications. The program was based on ITU Gaze tracker developed at IT University of Copenhagen [1].

Usability was measured by speed of text entry as words per minute (wpm) and total errors. In this study, we wanted to explore the effect of dwell-minimized eye typing methods on users' performance in short duration (in both without and with + without help situation). To judge user performance of traditional text entry systems, speed and accuracy are the basic and effective quantitative evaluation metrics. Thus, we collected user results on the basis of these two.

3.2 Participants

Eye typing experiments were performed by 15 participants (11 male, 4 female) recruited from the local university area. Participants ranged from 25 to 34 years (mean = 28.5). All were regular computer users, accessing on an average 4 h per day and did not have prior experience in composing text using eye typing techniques. All participants have normal or corrected-to-normal visual acuity. 14 participants were right-eye dominant and 1 was left-eye dominant, as determined from eye dominance test [4].

3.3 Keyboard Designs

Three representative keyboards namely, a) compact screen space-optimized full *Scrollable Keyboard* layout proposed by Špakov et al. [27] (Fig. 4a), b) Panwar et al.'s key size and space-optimized *EyeBoard* layout (Fig. 5) [20], incorporated in *EyeK* interface [24] and c) popular QWERTY layout (Fig. 4b) were considered for the evaluation. These keyboard layouts were chosen because of their design diversity in the gaze-supported keyboard domain. The size and space between key buttons were maintained same as specified in first two keyboards whereas for QWERTY, these were modified as 1.6 cm for both height and width and 0.6 cm for the distance between two keys, respectively [24]. During the first-time usability experiments, sentences to be typed were taken from MacKenzie and Soukoreff's phrase set [10]. The experiment was a within-subjects design. Participants were randomly assigned to keyboard and eye typing method.

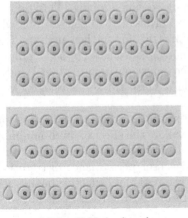

(a) Scrollable keyboard   (b) QWERTY keyboard

Fig. 4. Two keyboards used for *eye typing* experiments

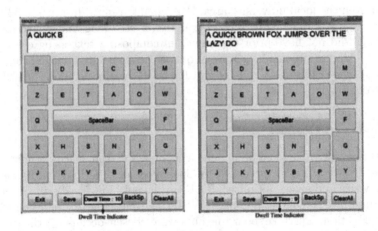

Fig. 5. EyeBoard keyboard design

3.4   Procedure

Every eye typing session was preceded by synchronization of the eye movement
with the gaze tracker through *Calibration*. During the typing session, users were
instructed to type as fast as possible allowing few errors and not to move their
eyes beyond the visibility range of the screen. To tackle this situation, users
wrote the to be typed phrase using pen and paper before the session began or
they listened to word-by-word from the instructor and composed them at runtime. Participants could only correct errors occurred due to wrong key selection
(no language level error considered) by erasing them using backspace and then
retyping them.

Participants spent the first few sessions before the experiment as training sessions where they were briefed about the nature of the experiment and then they completed a short demographic questionnaire. After that, they made themselves familiarized (with the initial help from the experimenter) with eye-tracking setup (fixing up the camera and Infrared lamp positions) and all eye typing methods applied on all keyboard interfaces by repeatedly accessing them. The total time for the interaction for each participant was about 20–25 min. Before typing, participants first practiced some phrases on pen and paper, taken from standard phrase set [10] (this phrase set contains 500 phrases, complete set is available in the web[1]) to memorize them and then composed these phrases for each of the three keyboards (to enhance the familiarity with keyboard-based eye typing and typing texts). We collected feedback from the participants after the training session. If after practice sessions, participants felt the strong attachment with the keyboards and eye typing methods, then we started the testing sessions.

In the testing phase of the first-time usability test, the initial speed of eye typing, errors, and perception of usability were studied. The first session of the initial usability test, on an average, took more than one hour, and data were not considered for analysis. Before starting of each session in short and long term test, users assured the instructors about their memorability of the practice setting. On average, each testing session took about 45 min. Among 12 texts selected in each experimental procedure for a user, 2 were taken from the in-domain Mackenzie and Soukreff's phrase set [10] and other 10 were taken from out-of-domain texts for judging the design efficacy.

This test was performed to prepare the participants for longitudinal eye typing tasks with on-screen keyboards following specific typing methods within the constrained hardware scenario. At starting, an initial assessment of eye typing familiarity of the users was done. For this, in any of the keyboards chosen randomly, users were required to search some character keys given by instructor through eye movement and then select by fixing their eyes on the key for some time. This task was termed as *first time test*. The eye typing experiment was planned such that participants were required to listen to the text and then typed it. Each user typed 20 words in a session (total 3 keyboards × 4 methods = 12 sessions). In this context, we divided the session into two subgroups where the order became random for each participant. One was to type 5 words, where we trained participants with single word typing after listening with no external help provided (*without help* phase). Here, key selections were performed through dwelling. When the task began, instructor uttered one word, and the user was expected to type it with his eye as fast as possible. Once finished, he gave the signal to the instructor for supplying the next word. If a word was typed correctly, the system played a "correct" sound. If the word was typed wrong on the first attempt, the system gave a "wrong" beep rang once, and instructor marked it wrong and asked them to type again. For the other method, known as *with + without help*, each user was given to type 3 phrase each containing 5 words. Here, the instructor read the phrases once, user listened to that and typed as

---

[1] http://www.yorku.ca/mack/PhraseSets.zip.

their own. Again, if users committed mistakes, instructors helped them to rectify those (this *with + without help mode* was allowed only for two attempts per word or phrase. If the user got the second attempt wrong as well, the current word was skipped and he had taken to the next word). The aforementioned eye typing methods were conducted at least two times each for a user and order of the keyboard selection was counterbalanced across participants. Although taken from the same corpus, the testing words or phrases were different from those chosen in the training session. We allowed a maximum of two days gap between two consecutive sessions of a user.

3.5 Dependent Measures

The dependent measures used in this experiment were words per minute (WPM) and the total error rate [26,37] which is an addition of corrected and uncorrected error rate.

3.6 Results

In the first-time usability test (15 participants × 20 words), total attempts can be categorized into a) successes without help, b) the proportion of successes without help, c) successes with and without help, and d) the proportion of successes with and without help for each keyboard. We averaged individual category results with respect to an user. Out of $300 \times 3 = 900$ attempts against each dwell-minimized method, *EyeK* and *Adv-EyeK* method proposed by Chakraborty et al. [3] earned best results in *success with + without help* as well as in *success without help* category. Using advanced *EyeK* method, users achieved 215 correct attempts (results ranging from 180 to 230, SD = 1.15) on an average which did not seek any help. The *EyeK* interface also performed better as it achieved on an average 205 attempts correct (range from 189 to 223, SD = 1.2) without seeking help out of 900 attempts. The results achieved in this category by *Iwrite* and *KKBoard* interface augmented dwell-time minimizing mechanisms were 189 attempts (range from 169 to 203, SD = 1.21) and 175 (range from 156 to 189, SD = 1.28), respectively. In *success with + without help* category also, users preferred controlled eye movement which was supported by *EyeK* augmented dwell-minimized method and advanced *EyeK* based efficient method. Users got on an average 290 correct attempts (results ranging from 285 to 294, SD = 1.08) and 296 (range from 187 to 205, SD = 1.05) toward entering text through these methods. In contrast, the other two methods i.e. *Iwrite* and *KKBoard* interface associated dwell-minimized methodologies achieved only 239 number of attempts (results ranging from 230 to 249, SD = 1.07) and 252 (values from 238 to 266, SD = 1.14) *with + without help* correct within 900 attempts. In this study, we observed no effect on different keyboard layouts while accessing dwell-minimized methodologies.

During the user performing a user study to empirically assess users' performance, we observed users' eye typing speed along with total error rate (combining corrected (number of backspaces pressed) and uncorrected (error remaining

Table 1. Average eye typing rates-first time usability study

Mode	Average eye typing rate (wpm)			
	Methods			
	Iwrite	KKBoard	EyeK	Adv-EyeK
Without help	3.58	4.14	4.9	5.6
With+without help	5.14	4.97	5.35	5.5

in the typed text) error rates) for all the methods. According to the scenario, all users typed in each keyboard augmented with every typing methodologies at least once. We gathered all user and keyboard-based results of eye typing rate and total error rate for a short dwell-time activated eye typing methods and averaged them. The average eye typing rate of users in the first-time study ranged from 3 to 6 wpm. For *without* as well as joint *with and without help* based interaction, controlled eye movement-based eye typing methods performed better.

In case of *without help*, *Iwrite* and *KKBoard* methods achieved average eye typing rate (see Table 1) as 3.58 (data varies from 3.2 to 3.9 wpm, SD = 1.09) and 4.14 (data varies from 3.76 to 4.36 wpm, SD = 1.19) wpm, respectively. The *EyeK* and *Adv-EyeK* achieved text entry rate as 4.9 (data varies from 4.2 to 5.4 wpm, SD = 1.09) and 5.6 (data varies from 5.2 to 6.0 wpm, SD = 1.08) wpm, respectively. The total error rate of the advanced method is 15.65% (value ranged from 14.74% to 16.25% SD = 2.08) which is lower than *EyeK* (20.81%) (value ranged from 18.74% to 22.53% SD = 3.12), *Iwrite* (28.16%) (value ranged from 26.78% to 31.36% SD = 4.12) and *KKBoard* (24.59%) (value ranged from 22.14% to 26.25% SD = 3.48).

Analyzing the user results for *with + without help* mode, we also found that the *Adv-EyeK* method performed better in terms of text entry rate and total error rate than other eye typing methods (see Table 1). It achieved text entry rate of 5.5 wpm (data varies from 4.8 to 6.8 wpm, SD = 1.15). The text entry rate of slightly different method associated with *EyeK* interface got a text entry rate result as 5.35 wpm (data varies from 5.2 to 5.6 wpm, SD = 1.06). The other two eye typing method associated with interface *Iwrite* and *KKBoard*, which are based on different principles than previous two, acquired text entry rate of 5.14 wpm (data varies from 4.8 to 5.4 wpm, SD = 1.09) and 4.97 wpm (data varies from 4.8 to 5.1 wpm, SD = 1.04), respectively. For the *with + without help* mode based user evaluation, the total error rate of the advanced method is 11.65% (value ranged from 10.37% to 13.43% SD = 3.0) which is less than *EyeK* (15.51%) (value ranged from 13.04% to 18.13% SD = 3.8), *Iwrite* (22.08%) (value ranged from 18.78% to 25.63% SD = 4.00) and *KKBoard* (22.17%) (value ranged from 20.05% to 24.29% SD = 3.00). Also, there lies no significant difference of total error rates between the methods ($F(3, 294) = 9.27$, n.s.).

3.7 Discussion

Results indicated that eye-typing with the *Adv-EyeK* interface was significantly faster and yielded less total error rate than three other eye typing methods - this concludes higher usability of the *Adv-EyeK* interface. The achieved high typing speed and low error rate can become more prominent with the number of sessions exercised by the users. Further, to explore the joint effect of eye typing method and augmented on-screen keyboard layouts, a longitudinal study was conducted.

4 Longitudinal Study

To analyze the effects on user performance on different dwell-minimized eye-typing schemes along with keyboards, we conducted a controlled experiment spanning 8 sessions attaching the methods with three different eye typing keyboards including QWERTY. Using these many sessions allowed us to assess the performance of the four methods over time, as we expected the learning rates of each method to be different. Individuals performed no more than 2 sessions per day. Maximum 48 h gap was kept between two consecutive sessions for a user. If two sessions were performed on the same day, at least two hours were kept between sessions.

4.1 Apparatus

The apparatus matches that of the first-time usability test.

4.2 Participants

All the participants participated in first-time usability tests were invited for the longitudinal test. We conducted the study one month after finishing the first-time usability study to make sure about less memorization of methods.

4.3 Designs

Same designs considered in the first-time test were used for this study. The study was a three-factor within-subjects design, with factors for Method (*Iwrite*, *KKBoard*, *EyeK* and *Adv-EyeK*), Keyboard (QWERTY, *Scrollable* and *Eye-Board*) and Session (1–8).

4.4 Procedure

In the longitudinal test, it was decided that evaluating the performance of the participants could be judged by typing the sufficient number of words through each of the three on-screen keyboards augmented with different eye typing methods because it was observed that a typical user would not put much effort in small trials to learn to type. We divided the task into 8 sessions for each user, each keyboard with each method. While most sessions ran on consecutive days, we ensured that 2 sessions could be completed for each user in a day. There could be a maximum gap of 2 days between any two sessions for a user. No training was provided before the task. Users were asked to input approximately 8 phrases (40 words) in a session as fast as possible. When the task began, the instructor spoke a phrase to the user which they listened and tried to type. No feedback, help or a second attempt was provided at the middle of typing a phrase. After completion of the phrase, participants pressed the "save" button, a sound was generated which alerted instructors for either declaring the session end or supplied the next phrases. Once the user had finished typing all the 8 phrases, it was shown how well he has done (what he was supposed to type, what he typed on the first attempt, what he typed on the second attempt if any, the errors if any, and the speed). Each session, on an average, lasted for 15–20 min a day. In this way, a participant who wanted to complete all the sessions, he required to type at least 3 keyboards × 4 methods × 8 sessions × 8 phrases in each session = 768 unique phrases taken from the standard phrase set. It was assured that instead of keyboard and method were selected randomly for a session, each user needed to type the same 768 phrases overall. During the study, keyboard and method presentation order were random and counterbalanced across participants. Each session lasted, on an average, approximately 45 to 60 min. A participant, who evaluated all keyboards with different typing methods, approximately took 2 to 4 months to finish (covering all the 8 sessions). It is also to be noted that a participant finished all 8 sessions in a particular method + keyboard combination before moving to the next one. Such a long duration is required to evaluate minimum 192 (2 trials × 3 keyboards × 4 methods × 8 sessions) trials per user. If the instructor, after a session, realized that user performance was not satisfactory (wasting more than 5 s to select a character key, for 3 consecutive times), he conducted the session again. After a session completion, the user was asked to rate the task on a scale of 1 to 5 for difficulty based on some demographic questionnaire. Then, the user was reminded to come for the next session before leaving.

4.5 Dependent Measure

Aligned with the pilot study, the dependent measures used in this experiment were words per minute, overhead time, total error rate (addition of corrected and uncorrected error rate) and subjective evaluation parameters like ease-of-use, distracting, fatigub.

4.6 Results

Within-subject experiments were performed with 3 keyboards each having 4 dwell-minimized methods measuring *eye typing rate*, *total error rate* and *overhead time* [8]. Data for each participant were averaged in each session to form a single measure per participant per session on a variety of metrics. Participants completed a total of 2 trials × 3 keyboards × 4 methods × 8 sessions = 192 trials. With 15 participants, the entire study comprised of 2880 trials. Also, for testing sessions, keyboard order was kept counterbalanced across participants. 3 sessions were performed per day by each participant. The whole study lasted for approximately 4 months. Each trial was made of 8 phrases taken randomly from new phrase set [33] (this phrase set, developed by Vertanen and Kristensson [33], contains a total of 2239 sentences and sentence fragments generally used in E-mails; it can be accessed online[2].)

Eye Typing Rate. The overall average eye typing rate achieved by participants with 4 methods applied on 3 different keyboards was ranged from 6 to 9 wpm (Fig. 6) (see Table 2). Using method applied in *Iwrite* [32], keyboards *Scrollable keyboard*, QWERTY and *EyeBoard* earned the eye typing rate ranging from 5.9 wpm to 7.1 wpm (mean = 6.6, SD = 1.05), 6.2 to 7.9 wpm (mean = 7.2, SD = 1.15) and 6.4 to 8.1 wpm (mean = 7.4, SD = 1.18), respectively (Table 2). Implementing *KKBoard* method, irrespective of users, 3 keyboards achieved 6.4 wpm to 7.9 wpm (mean = 7.1, SD = 1.02), 6.5 wpm to 8.2 (mean = 7.4, SD = 1.06) and 6.55 wpm to 7.8 wpm (mean = 7.1, SD = 1.17), respectively. In case of *EyeK* method, 3 keyboards achieved 6.8 wpm to 8.1 wpm (mean = 7.5, SD = 1.09), 6.7 wpm to 7.8 (mean = 7.3, SD = 1.06) and 7.1 wpm to 8.7 wpm (mean = 7.9, SD = 1.08), respectively. Finally, participants on an average achieved eye typing rate of 6.7 wpm to 7.8 wpm (mean = 7.3, SD = 1.07), 7.4 wpm to 8.3 (mean = 7.8, SD = 1.06) and 7.3 wpm to 8.9 wpm (mean = 8.1, SD = 1.08), respectively through 3 keyboards by using the *Adv-EyeK* method. For all the mechanisms, it was observed that participants' eye typing rates got improved in the first few sessions and then reached to saturation. The analysis of variance (ANOVA) on text entry speeds showed that there was no significant difference between the means of user's performance on different eye typing mechanisms ($F(3, 716) = 3.14$, n.s.).

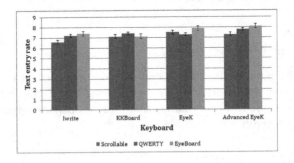

Fig. 6. Eye typing rate of different designs

---

[2] http://aactext.org/comm2/comm2.zip.

Overhead Time. Kristensson and Vertanen [8] stated the task completion time, apart from the dwelling, as overhead time. In our case, as key selection time for a large number of character entry took moderate time, key selection plus error correction time became overhead time. Throughout the sessions, we captured both key selection and error correction time and stored into a log file. The average overhead time for the 4 methods, irrespective of keyboard and participant were measured as 650 milliseconds (ms), 630 ms, 600 ms, and 530 ms, respectively.

Total Error Rate. Over the sessions, the total error rate, on an average over all the keyboards, became 26.29% in case of *Adv-EyeK* method and 33.15%, 33.18% and 30.73% for methods augmented with *Iwrite*, *KKBoard* and *EyeK* keyboard interfaces, respectively (Fig. 7). However, total error rates were dropped significantly over sessions ($F(7, 350) = 4.29$, $p < 0.05$). The results concluded the observation that using the *Adv-EyeK* method, users left fewer errors uncorrected in different keyboard designs, i.e., the number of corrected errors is more in case of associated interfaces. We also analyzed a number of errors left in the typed text for all the 4 methods applied on 3 keyboard designs. An analysis of variance revealed that there was no significant difference in total error rates between the keyboard designs ($F(2, 946) = 1.01$, n.s.)

Subjective Evaluation. We collected the subjective ratings from the participants with the *nonparametric Wilcoxon Matched Pairs Signed Ranks Test* [22] as Likert-scale data did not often conform to the assumptions required for ANOVA procedures. We talked with the participants before and after each session asking them about their eye strain and tiredness in a scale of 1 to 5. The level of tiredness was calculated by subtracting the first value from the later value. Analyzing the experimental results, we observed no significant difference between the average level of the tiredness, which was 0.52 in the first and 0.71 in the last session. We also calculated the text entry speed, ease of use, and general fatigue after each session using a questionnaire with a scale from 1 to 5. An increment of text entry rate of every user was observed (average from 3.1 to 4.3). By analyzing the participant preferences given in the Likert scale, *Adv-EyeK* method performed significantly better than other eye typing techniques in terms of easier to use

Table 2. Average eye typing rates

Methods	Average eye typing rate (wpm)		
	Keyboards		
	Scrollable	QWERTY	EyeBoard
Iwrite	6.6	7.2	7.4
KKBoard	7.1	7.4	7.8
EyeK	7.5	7.3	7.9
Adv-EyeK	7.3	7.8	8.1

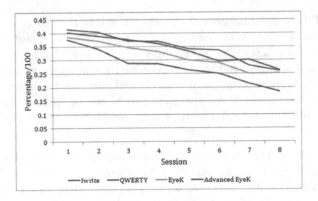

Fig. 7. Total error rate

Table 3. Average scores for survey responses in the range 1–5

Question	Iwrite	KKBoard	EyeK	Adv-EyeK
How easy did you find the eye typing interface? (5- much easier, 1- much harder)	3.31	3.14	4.08	4.21
How tiring did you find using the dwell-minimized eye typing method? (5- least tiring, 1- most tiring)	3.12	2.98	3.91	4.02
How faster did you compose the text? (5- very fast, 1- very slow)	3.22	3.17	4.07	4.29
How accurate was the composed text? (5- accurate, 1- inaccurate)	2.93	3.02	3.85	3.96
How useful was the dwell-minimized eye typing system? (5- very useful, 1- less useful)	3.32	3.38	4.14	4.32
How distracting did you find the eye typing? (5- very distracting, 1- less distracting)	2.55	2.46	2.13	2.08

($z = 42.00$, $p < .001$), faster ($z = 40.00$, $p < .01$), less distracting ($z = -47.00$, $p < .01$) and less fatiguing ($z = -55.00, p < .001$) (detail demographic questions and user feedbacks are shown in Table 3).

Finally, participants were again interviewed after completion of the series of sessions. Participants felt that the concept of key area increment and allowing user's eye to move through those areas in a pattern to select an object (here, key button in an on-screen keyboard) was much more intuitive than other methods. They also admitted that typing by gaze gesture was fairly easy and comfortable than their expectations and less boring than dwell-based eye typing methodologies, but the typing method is slower than using a conventional, hand-operated hardware/virtual keyboard.

Participants said that during the first few sessions, the *Adv-EyeK* and *EyeK* interfaces were felt to be more difficult for them in terms of selecting an intended key than other dwell-minimized eye typing methods. Soon, they started to control their eyes easily and after some time, usually took hold of the methods and gradually geared up the speed with them (as well as felt comfortable). Although the *Adv-EyeK* method was not known to participants previously, it can be pointed out as quickly learnable and perceived as easier to use than others. This might be for their simple going to a point and then coming back gesture of performing the selection task. Earlier, it might create a problem which soon got overcome.

Regarding *Iwrite* eye typing interface [32], participants expressed positive feedback about the simplicity and intuitiveness of it. But many of them said that they had difficulty to perform the interaction for selecting a key. The ambiguity between interaction and user's natural eye movement could hamper the eye typing process.

Participants, after performing eye typing task with *KKBoard* interface, admitted that in spite of the presence of popular QWERTY keyboard familiarity, the interface implemented two keyboard layouts which took double space than a normal keyboard size used in eye typing interface. Users suggested that the wastage of space should be minimized, but not that much where the keys become so small and inappropriate for use with eye trackers.

Learning Curve. To understand the learning of the selected dwell-minimized eye typing methods augmented with on-screen keyboards we performed a longitudinal study with those 4 methods augmenting QWERTY layout. Five new participants (who did not perform any of the previous experiments) having familiarity with QWERTY based text entry but unfamiliarity with eye-tracking methods performed the eye typing sessions with testing phrases selected from Vertanen's phrase set [33]. For each session, 5 phrases had been typed by each participant with each of the four methods. Each participant spent 60 more-or-less consecutive sessions. The average user result was depicted in Fig. 8. It indicates that the *Adv-EyeK* method needed more initial effort to learn compared to other methods. However, after 20 sessions, *Adv-EyeK* outperformed other methods. We derived standard regression models in the form of the power curve fitting as it followed the *Power law of learning*. The longitudinal study lasted for 60 sessions. The learning curve inevitably reflected the increasing efficiency of users after performing several sessions. The highest eye typing rate achieved through *Iwrite*, *KKBoard*, *EyeK* and *Advanced EeyK* methods were 6.55, 5.79, 7.31 and 8.01 wpm, respectively.

5   Discussion

Through user experiment, four dwell-minimized eye typing methods were compared in terms of performance measures and subjective usability criteria. The first time usability and longitudinal study results reflected that *Adv-EyeK* eye

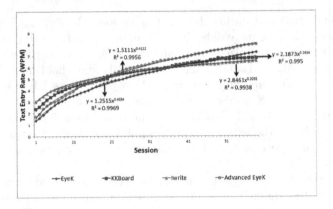

Fig. 8. Learning curve

typing mechanism performed better in eye typing rate, total error rate, and usability than other 3 methods. The interface with on-screen keyboard implementing the method was learned quickly because of a fixed pattern based selection for every key. The UI designers can leverage such eye gesturing behavior of users to select interface elements in very less time compared to mouse movement and selection task performance time.

Given users' subjective impressions, it is observed that they performed small eye pattern movement [3] well within a small region, after sufficient training. This scenario saves the screenspace offering an advantage over off-screen targets in limiting saccade distance to the dimensions of the attached keyboard's layout area. Further, subjective evaluations (feedback collected through 5-point Likert scale, see Table 3) confirm the superiority of *Adv-EyeK* design over others.

The main goal of this work is to empirically evaluate the usability of four gaze-based dwell-time minimized character-level text input techniques through the lens of text input rate, total error rate, and learnability. It is to be noted that the dwell-minimized eye typing technique proposed by Kristensson and Vertanen [8] and Kurauchi et al. [9] are focused on leveraging "continuous eye movement" phenomenon and they leverage a built-in word-level prediction method which predicts next characters and decodes the eye movement path (based on the proximity of the possible character keys) to the intended word sequences. In-spite achieving high text input speed, this technique requires an accurate 'swype' like movement of the eye and less occurrence of eye jitters, which our low-cost eye tracker can not handle effectively. In this work, we consider techniques which are based on quick eye fixation (not as long as dwell) on a particular character and no prediction involved in composing texts. We recently acquired a high-quality TOBII eye tracker thus plan to test the usability of such techniques in near future (Vertanen and Kristensson's work [8] and Mott et al.'s work [18] on shortening dwell time).

We did not find significant improvement in terms of both eye typing rate and total error rate over a few other short dwell-time activated eye typing mechanisms. The reason behind this is three-fold: (1) participant expertise: we recruited participants who are novice in performing character-level eye typing to observe their learning phase for four such mechanisms and (2) low-cost tracker: we used custom made low-cost eye tracking setup which posses less accuracy in tracing fixation and saccade position in real time; thus it is incomparable with the professional eye tackers (e.g., TOBII, SMI) as they offer little practice to users to get the eye movement and location information accurately, and (3) choosing eye typing method and text input enhancement technique: we chose such short dwell-based methods which can be easily implemented and evaluated in such setup and we ended up choosing four such methods; we did not implement word prediction as this could add more burden due to prolific attention switching between prediction list and text input area of the keyboard. Thus, it is the fact that such constraints did not provide us the maximum gain for the proposed Adv-EyeK method in terms of speed and accuracy in the current study.

One major problem in our longitudinal study is that while having a fully counterbalanced randomization of the independent variable combinations (3 keyboards, 4 techniques), we needed 12 participants or participants in the multiple of that number, however, we recruited 15 participants. Thus we repeated one ordering of the techniques for 3 participants. It is, however, to be noted that the performance results were not significantly different among most of the participants. We discarded three participants' data based on their average performance results, but it did not change the overall results significantly. So we kept the data as it is here, and learned that from the next time, we will be careful about the participant while recruiting them for such a longitudinal usability study.

6 Conclusion and Future Work

In this work, we present a usability study on four dwell-minimized eye typing mechanisms comparing them for eye typing rate, total error rate, ease-of-use, eye fatigue, etc. and collect results from short-term as well as longitudinal user experiments. The obtained user results reveal the suitability of *Adv-EyeK* eye typing method according to user's eye typing behavior. The learning rate and text entry rate of the *Adv-EyeK* method augmented with three on-screen keyboards are moderately higher than other eye typing techniques. This result undoubtedly supports the superiority of the method even while attached with any of the on-screen keyboards applied for eye typing. Also, due to the controlled nature, the underlying interaction can accurately be performed by users, once become familiarized.

In our study, we used our self-developed easy replicable low-cost eye-tracking set-up, as one of the initial objectives of this project was to develop low-cost eye typing task supporting hardware. Thus, we used low-cost apparatus and open-source software *ITU gaze-tracker*. However, the accuracy of the setup still is not up to the mark and thus, the validity of results confines within performing the experiments in controlled environments. To collect more accurate data from this low-cost setup, we introduced calibration before each session and also instructed participants not to see outside the screen area during the experiment. Irrespective of all these precautions, sometimes when we found that participants could not finish the experiment due to many errors committed, we had to conduct the same experiment again for each of them. Extending the current work, we can further improve the setup quality by many ways like fixing the infrared (IR) filters within visible range, placing the camera as close to the eye for more accurately detecting eye gaze during the calibration phase, etc.

References

1. Agustin, J.S., et al.: Evaluation of a low-cost open-source gaze tracker. In: Proceedings of ETRA, pp. 77–80. ACM, New York (2010)
2. Bee, N., André, E.: Writing with your eye: a dwell time free writing system adapted to the nature of human eye gaze. In: André, E., Dybkjær, L., Minker, W., Neumann, H., Pieraccini, R., Weber, M. (eds.) PIT 2008. LNCS (LNAI), vol. 5078, pp. 111–122. Springer, Heidelberg (2008). https://doi.org/10.1007/978-3-540-69369-7_13
3. Chakraborty, T., Sarcar, S., Samanta, D.: Design and evaluation of a dwell-free eye typing technique. In: CHI 2014 Extended Abstracts on Human Factors in Computing Systems, pp. 1573–1578. ACM (2014)
4. Collins, J.F., Blackwell, L.K.: Effects of eye dominance and retinal distance on binocular rivalry. Percept. Mot. Skills **39**, 747–754 (1974)
5. Drewes, H., Luca, A.D., Schmidt, A.: Eye-gaze interaction for mobile phones. In: Proceedings of the Mobility Conference, pp. 364–371. ACM (2007)
6. Huckauf, A., Urbina, M.: Gazing with pEYE: new concepts in eye typing. In: Proceedings of the 4th Symposium on Applied Perception in Graphics and Visualization, pp. 141–141. ACM (2007)
7. Jacob, R.J.K.: The use of eye movements in human-computer interaction techniques: what you look at is what you get. ACM Trans. Inf. Syst. **9**(2), 152–169 (1991)
8. Kristensson, P.O., Vertanen, K.: The potential of dwell-free eye-typing for fast assistive gaze communication. In: Proceedings of ETRA, pp. 241–244. ACM (2012)
9. Kurauchi, A., Feng, W., Joshi, A., Morimoto, C., Betke, M.: EyeSwipe: dwell-free text entry using gaze paths. In: Proceedings of the 2016 CHI Conference on Human Factors in Computing Systems, pp. 1952–1956. ACM (2016)
10. MacKenzie, I.S., Soukoreff, R.W.: Phrase sets for evaluating text entry techniques. In: Extended Abstracts on Human Factors in Computing Systems, pp. 754–755. ACM, Florida (2003)
11. Majaranta, P.: Text entry by eye gaze. Ph.D. thesis, Department of Computer Science (2009)
12. Majaranta, P., Ahola, U.K., Špakov, O.: Fast gaze typing with an adjustable dwell time. In: Proceedings of Conference on Human Factors in Computing Systems, pp. 357–360. ACM, Boston (2009)
13. Majaranta, P., Aula, A., Räihä, K.J.: Effects of feedback on eye typing with a short dwell time. In: Proceedings of ETRA, pp. 139–146. ACM (2004)
14. Majaranta, P., Räihä, K.J.: Twenty years of eye typing: systems and design issues. In: Proceedings of ETRA, pp. 15–22. ACM (2002)

15. Majaranta, P., Räihä, K.J.: Text entry by gaze: utilizing eye-tracking. In: Text Entry Systems: Mobility, Accessibility, Universality, pp. 175–187. Morgan Kaufmann, San Francisco (2007)
16. Miniotas, D., Spakov, O., Evreinov, G.: Symbol creator: an alternative eye-based text entry technique with low demand for screen space. In: Proceedings of INTER-ACT, pp. 137–143 (2003)
17. Morimoto, C.H., Amir, A.: Context switching for fast key selection in text entry applications. In: Proceedings of ETRA, ETRA 2010, pp. 271–274. ACM, New York (2010)
18. Mott, M.E., Williams, S., Wobbrock, J.O., Morris, M.R.: Improving dwell-based gaze typing with dynamic, cascading dwell times. In: Proceedings of the 2017 CHI Conference on Human Factors in Computing Systems, pp. 2558–2570. ACM (2017)
19. Nielsen, J.: Usability 101: introduction to usability (2010). www.nngroup.com/articles/usability-101-introduction-to-usability. Accessed Jan 2014
20. Panwar, P., Sarcar, S., Samanta, D.: EyeBoard: a fast and accurate eye gaze-based text entry system. In: Proceedings of IHCI, pp. 1–8. IEEE (2012)
21. Pedrosa, D., Pimentel, M.D.G., Wright, A., Truong, K.N.: Filteryedping: design challenges and user performance of dwell-free eye typing. ACM Trans. Accessible Comput. (TACCESS) 6(1), 3 (2015)
22. Phonetic Sciences IFA: The wilcoxon matched-pairs signed-ranks test (2014), available: http://www.fon.hum.uva.nl/Service/Statistics/Signed_Rank_Test.html. Accessed Jan 2014
23. San Agustin, J., et al.: Evaluation of a low-cost open-source gaze tracker. In: Proceedings of the 2010 Symposium on Eye-Tracking Research & Applications, pp. 77–80. ACM (2010)
24. Sarcar, S., Panwar, P., Chakraborty, T.: Eyek: an efficient dwell-free eye gaze-based text entry system. In: Proceedings of the 11th Asia Pacific Conference on Computer Human Interaction, pp. 215–220. ACM (2013)
25. Schneider, N., Bex, P., Barth, E., Dorr, M.: An open-source low-cost eye-tracking system for portable real-time and offline tracking. In: Proceedings of the 1st Conference on Novel Gaze-controlled Applications, p. 8. ACM (2011)
26. Soukoreff, R.W., MacKenzie, I.S.: Metrics for text entry research: an evaluation of MSD and KSPC, and a new unified error metric. In: Proceedings of the Conference on Human Factors in Computing Systems, pp. 113–120. ACM (2003)
27. Špakov, O., Majaranta, P.: Scrollable Keyboards for eye typing. In: Proceedings of COGAIN, Prague, Czech Republic, pp. 63–66 (2008)
28. Špakov, O., Miniotas, D.: On-line adjustment of dwell time for target selection by gaze. In: Proceedings of NordiCHI, pp. 203–206. ACM (2004)
29. Špakov, O., Miniotas, D.: On-line adjustment of dwell time for target selection by gaze. In: Proceedings of the third Nordic Conference on Human-computer Interaction, pp. 203–206. ACM (2004)
30. Tonsen, M., Steil, J., Sugano, Y., Bulling, A.: Invisibleeye: mobile eye tracking using multiple low-resolution cameras and learning-based gaze estimation. Proc. ACM Interact. Mobile Wearable Ubiquitous Technol. 1(3), 106 (2017)
31. Tuisku, O., Majaranta, P., Isokoski, P., Räihä, K.J.: Now dasher! dash away!: longitudinal study of fast text entry by eye gaze. In: Proceedings of the 2008 Symposium on Eye Tracking Research & Applications, pp. 19–26. ACM (2008)
32. Urbina, M.H., Huckauf, A.: Dwell time free eye typing approaches. In: Proceedings of COGAIN, pp. 3–4 (2007)

33. Vertanen, K., Kristensson, P.O.: A versatile dataset for text entry evaluations based on genuine mobile emails. In: Proceedings of the 13th International Conference on Human Computer Interaction with Mobile Devices and Services, pp. 295–298. ACM (2011)
34. Ward, D.J., Blackwell, A.F., MacKay, D.J.: Dasher-a data entry interface using continuous gestures and language models. In: UIST, pp. 129–137 (2000)
35. Ward, D.J., MacKay, D.J.: Artificial intelligence: fast hands-free writing by gaze direction. Nature **418**(6900), 838 (2002)
36. Ware, C., Mikaelian, H.T.: An evaluation of an eye tracker as a device for computer input. In: Proceedings of the CHI+GI, pp. 183–188. ACM (1987)
37. Wobbrock, J.O., Myers, B.A.: Analyzing the input stream for character-level errors in unconstrained text entry evaluations. ACM Trans. Comput.-Hum. Interact. (TOCHI) **13**(4), 458–489 (2006)
38. Wobbrock, J.O., Rubinstein, J., Sawyer, M.W., Duchowski, A.T.: Longitudinal evaluation of discrete consecutive gaze gestures for text entry. In: Proceedings of ETRA, pp. 11–18. ACM (2008)
39. Zhang, X., Ren, X., Zha, H.: Modeling dwell-based eye pointing target acquisition. In: Proceedings of the SIGCHI Conference on Human Factors in Computing Systems, pp. 2083–2092. ACM (2010)

A Comparative Study of Three Sudoku Input Methods for Touch Displays

Aslak Burheim Sommervold[1], Benjamin Nils Øvergaard[1],
Eskil Nysether[1], Mohamed Yusuf Nur[1],
and Frode Eika Sandnes[1,2(✉)] (iD)

[1] Oslo Metropolitan University, 0130 Oslo, Norway
aslak.sommervold@gmail.com, ben.overgaard@gmail.com,
{s330457,s333725,frodes}@oslomet.no
[2] Kristiania University College, Oslo, Norway

Abstract. Sudoku is a popular recreational game which is claimed to have positive health effects. It can be played using paper or electronically using computers. Only very few studies have explored Sudoku interaction methods. We therefore designed a controlled within-groups experiment involving $N = 18$ participants to empirically compare three Sudoku interaction methods implemented in a popular Sudoku smartphone app. Our results show that the participants entered digits faster when they selected the location first, followed by selecting the input digit, compared to selecting the digit first followed by selecting the cell location. Participants also preferred selecting cell first over selecting input digit first. No effects of error rates were found.

Keywords: Sudoku · Smartphone game design · Touch interaction · Cell first · Digit first · Game interaction · Preference

1 Introduction

Sudoku is a popular game that is believed to reduce cognitive aging and help train working memory [1]. It is a game of numbers that involves placing digits on a grid. The traditional Sudoku grid comprises 9×9 cells divided into nine squares of 3×3 cells. The game involves inserting digits from 1 to 9 such that all vertical rows and horizontal columns contain each of the 9 digits exactly once. At the same time the player must adhere to a set of digits already inserted into the board. The difficulty of the game is controlled by the way the fixed digits are inserted into the Sudoku grid. Sudoku can also be played using letters, words or symbols instead of digits.

Traditionally, Sudoku puzzles were printed in newspapers or in special Sudoku puzzle books. Several electronic computer-based Sudoku games have also been developed. To the best of our knowledge, there are only a handful of studies addressing the interaction aspects of Sudoku and little is therefore known about Sudoku game interactions. This study therefore set out collect empirical data about three interaction methods implemented in a popular Sudoku app.

We have coined the three input methods *digit first*, *cell first* and *popup*. The *digit first* input method involves first selecting the digit at the bottom of the screen organized

M. Antona and C. Stephanidis (Eds.): HCII 2020, LNCS 12188, pp. 211–222, 2020.
https://doi.org/10.1007/978-3-030-49282-3_15

in two rows (see Fig. 1 (a)) and then select the cell in which the digit is to be inserted. Once a digit is selected, this digit can be inserted in multiple cells without having to re-select the digit. Hence, the digit first method holds potential for reducing the users' workload. With the *cell first* method the user first selects the cell on the Sudoku board where the digit is to be placed, followed by selecting the input digit (see Fig. 1 (b). To insert another digit the cell-digit selection process needs to be repeated. *Popup* is similar to the *cell first* method in that the user first selects the cell where the digit is to be input. Next, a digit-selection popup is presented to the user (see Fig. 1 (c)) in the form of a numeric keypad. Again, the entire process is repeated to insert additional digits.

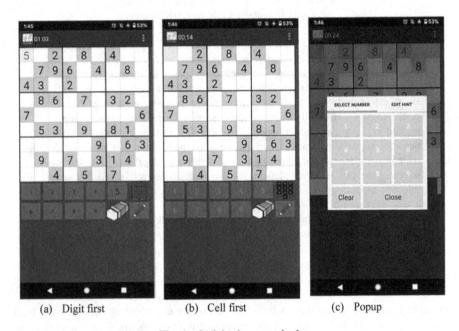

(a) Digit first   (b) Cell first   (c) Popup

Fig. 1. Sudoku input methods.

This study thus set out to explore if there are any differences in the mean time to use these input methods, the errors involved and users' preferences for the three methods. This paper is organized as follows. The next section reviews related work, followed by a description of the method used and the results obtained. Next, the results are discussed. The conclusions section closes the paper.

2   Related Work

Sudoku has received much attention in the research literature, see for instance [2–4]. Within computer science most of the attention has evolved around algorithms for the automatic solution of Sudoku puzzles [5–7], for example using metaheuristics [8].

A Sudoku inspired encoding has also been used for information hiding [9]. The potential of Sudoku as a pedagogical resource for learning computer science has also been discussed [10].

Comparatively, little has been written about Sudoku interaction. One exception is Norte and Lobo's [11] Sudoku game aimed at users with reduced motor function where the game is controlled via switches and scanning or via voice input. Sudoku has also been studied for visually impaired players [12], and very challenging problem as it is difficult to effectively communicate two-dimensional structures such as tables with non-visual means [13]. Echtler et al. [14] discussed a Sudoku interface for tabletop displays allowing users to move items around or access the game using a mobile device. Kondraju [15] proposed a possible extension of Sudoku into three dimensions. Bernsen and Dybkjær [16] addressed usability testing with Sudoku as a case. A doctoral dissertation [17] (written in Slovenian) was devoted to the implementation of an Android Sudoku app.

Traditional Sudoku uses digits and the interaction can in some ways be considered a specialized form of digit input. The problem of digit input has been studied extensively as it is a commonly performed task in many domains. Issues that have been studied includes speech-based digit input [18], written digit recognition [19] and keyboard layouts for digit input [20, 21]. It has been demonstrated that numeric keypads are more efficient than the number keys found on small laptop computers [21]. In Norway digit copying and input is heavily used when performing bank transactions, both for copying temporary passcodes [22] and long customer identification numbers [23]. The copying and input of numbers also appear in other domains such as prescription parameters in medical equipment [24–28].

One of the input methods studied herein includes popups. Popup messages versus in text messages have been measured systematically [29]. Specialized methods for setting quantities has also been studied such as setting the time [30] and color values [31, 32].

3 Method

3.1 Experimental Design

A controlled within-groups experiment was conducted with input method as an independent variable with three levels, namely *cell first*, *popup* and *digit first*. Previous experience playing Sudoku was also used as a secondary between-groups independent variable. Three dependent variables were measured, namely the time to input digits, error rate the participants' subjective input method preferences.

3.2 Participants

A total of 18 participants was recruited for the experiment. There nearly a balance of female and male participants (with slightly more males) and mostly in their twenties, and a few in their thirties. The participants were all computer science students at the authors' university. Of the participants, 13 had played Sudoku before, while 5 have never played Sudoku. Of the 13 participants who had played Sudoku 4 had also used the app before.

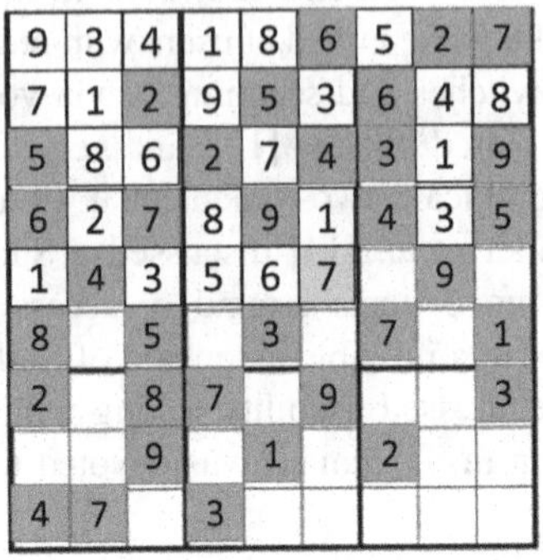

Fig. 2. The cell with its content highlighted in yellow as used in the Sudoku copying task. The empty cells on the board were traversed left-to-right, top-to-bottom.

3.3   Equipment

The Classic Sudoku Pro (No Ads) Android app was used for the experiments. The experiments were run on a Google pixel 2 smartphone. The numbers to be input were presented using a Microsoft PowerPoint presentation on a laptop computer placed on a desk in front of the participants. This PowerPoint presentation contained 146 pages shown in sequence. For each page the cell with the digit to be input was highlighted (see Fig. 2). Hence, the participants simply had to copy what was shown on the PowerPoint. The cells were filled in from left-to-right, top-to-bottom. Google forms was used to collect the users' preferences for the various input methods.

3.4   Procedure

Each participant was tested individually in a quiet room. They were seated in front of a laptop computer and was asked to hold the smartphone with the Sudoku app. The participants were asked to input 47 digits displayed in the PowerPoint presentation into the app. Hence, the participants did not have to solve the Sudoku puzzle, but rather focus on copying the digits into their respective positions. Each participant completed the Sudoku board with each of the three input methods. The order of the input methods was varied to minimize learning effects and biases. There are six possible combinations with the three input methods and the 18 participants were recruited so that each combination was executed by three participants. The task completion times for the entire Sudoku boards were measured using a stopwatch. This total board completion time was used to calculate the time per digit for each participant. Errors were observed manually and counted. After completing the session with the three interfaces the participants were asked to indicate their subjective preference for the three interfaces using a 5-point Likert scale using Google forms, i.e., how easy they found each interface to use, respectively. The questionnaire also asked if the participants had played Sudoku before, and if they had used this app or similar apps before.

Participation was voluntary and anonymous. As the experiment was conducted in one session no identifying mechanisms had to be employed. The General Data Protection Regulations (GDPR) therefore did not apply for this study.

3.5 Analysis

The results were analyzed using JASP version 0.10.0.0. The task completion times were analyzed using a repeated measures anova with Bonferonni post-hoc tests, while the error rates and preference data were analyzed using a Friedman test with Connovers post hoc testing since the error rates and Likert data did not satisfy the assumptions of the parametric testing procedures. The non-parametric Spearman correlations and Mann Whitney tests were also used for the same reasons.

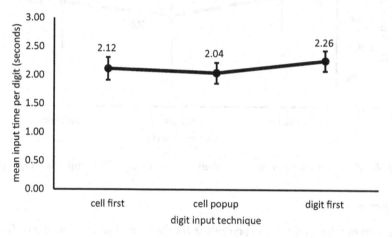

Fig. 3. Mean time to input a digit with the three interfaces. Error bars show 95% confidence intervals.

4   Results

4.1   Digit Input Time

Figure 3 shows the results of the digit input time measurements. A repeated measures anova shows that the digit input times with the three interfaces were significantly different ($F(1, 34) = 11.17, p < .001, \eta^2 = 0.397$). Bonferroni post-hoc tests reveal that the mean digit input time with the *digit first* interface ($M = 2.26$ s, 95% CI [2.08, 2.44]) was significantly different to both the *cell first* interface ($M = 2.12$ s, 95% CI [1.92, 2.32], $p = .027$, Cohen's $d = -0.694$) and the *popup* interface ($M = 2.04$ s, 95% CI [1.86, 2.23], $p = .002$, Cohen's $d = -0.961$), while the *cell first* and *popup* interface were not significantly different ($p = .188$). In other words, the *digit first* input method was the slowest, while the *popup* digit input method was the fastest, although not significantly faster than the *cell first* input method.

Pearson correlations showed that participants who were faster with one type of input method were also faster with the other input methods. That is, digit input time with *digit first* correlated strongly and positively with digit input using *cell first* ($r(18) = 0.876$, $p < .001$), *digit first* correlated strongly and positively with *popup* ($r(18) = 0.833$, $p < .001$) and *cell first* correlated strongly and positively with *popup* ($r(18) = 0.936$, $p < .001$).

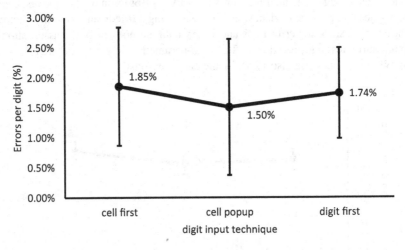

Fig. 4. Mean percentage of errors per digit. Error bars show 95% confidence intervals.

4.2 Errors

Figure 4 shows the error rates in percentage for the three digit input methods. Overall, the error rates with the digit input methods were below 2%. The *popup* interface appears to have been associated with the fewest mean number of errors, although this input method also had the largest spread. The confidence intervals for the three methods overlap greatly and a Friedman test confirms that there was no significant difference in error rate between the three digit input methods ($\chi^2(2) = 0.905$, $p = .636$).

There was also a significant positive medium to strong correlation between the digit input times and error rates for the three methods, namely *digit first* ($r(18) = 0.729$, $p < .001$), *cell first* ($r(18) = 0.645$, $p = .004$) and *popup* ($r(18) = 0.578$, $p = .010$). Clearly, participants who perform the task faster also makes more mistakes.

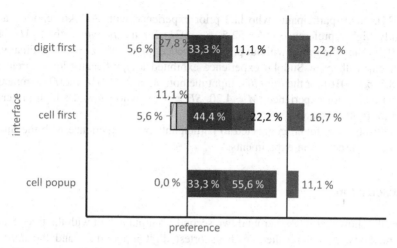

Fig. 5. Diverging stacked bar graph showing the distribution of preferences in percentages (left: negative, middle: positive and right: neutral).

4.3 Preferences

Figure 5 shows the participants' subjective preferences for the digit input methods. Clearly, the *popup* method was associated with the most positive responses as there were no negative responses and it exhibited the lowest quantity of neutral responses. *Popup* is followed by the *cell first* digit input method. *Digit first* was associated with the lowest preference with a balanced set of negative and positive responses as well as being the input method with the most neutral responses. A Friedman test reveals that there is a significant difference between the preferences for the three methods ($\chi^2(2) = 8.716$, $p = .013$, Kendall's $W = 0.137$). Connover's post hoc tests show that the low preference for *digit first* was significantly different to *popup* ($p = .007$) which was the most preferred. However, there were no significant differences between *popup* and *cell first* ($p = .124$) and *cell first* and *digit first* ($p = .186$).

Spearman correlations also revealed a significant positive medium correlation between digit input times using the digit first input method and preference for the digit first input method ($r_s(18) = 0.566$, $p = .014$).

4.4 Prior Sudoku Experience

Of the participants, 13 had played Sudoku before while 5 had never played the game. In terms of digit input time a mixed repeated measures anova did not reveal any between-group effects ($F(1, 16) = 1.437$, $p = .248$), however, an interaction between digit input times and past experience with Sudoku was found ($F(1, 32) = 8.601$, $p < .001$).

To explore other between-groups effect a series of non-parametric Mann Whitney tests were performed. Three significant differences were observed. First, the number of errors were significantly lower with the *popup* method for participants who had played Sudoku before compared to those who had not played the game before ($W = 12.00$,

$p = .024$). Next, participants who had prior experience with Sudoku reported a significantly higher preference ($W = 52.5$, $p = .031$) for the *popup* method ($M = 4.69$, $SD = 0.48$) than the group without prior experience ($M = 3.8$, $SD = 0.84$). Finally, the participants with prior Sudoku experience exhibited a significantly lower preference ($W = 8.5$, $p = .016$) for the *digit first* input method ($M = 2.77$, $SD = 1.09$) compared to those without prior experience ($M = 4.20$, $SD = 0.45$) who showed a high preference for the *digit first* method.

No effects were found connected to participants prior experience with the Sudoku app that was used in the experiments.

5   Discussion

The results show that it takes around two seconds to input a digit with the three Sudoku input methods. *Popup* resulted in the shortest digit input times and the *digit first* method resulted in the longest digit input times, although the difference between the *popup* and *cell first* methods was practical and not statistical. Moreover, the results showed that participants who are faster with one method is also faster with the other methods, suggesting that there was an underlying effect of individual skill.

The error rate results did not show any differences between the methods. We are therefore unable to claim any effect of input method on error. Instead, the results showed that participants who entered digits faster also made more mistakes. This observation is consistent with what one would expect.

The input time observations were consistent with the preference observations, namely that the *popup* method is the fastest, and also the most preferred, while the *digit first* method was the slowest and least preferred method. One may speculate that a faster interface is more likely to be preferred over a slower interface, although this may not always be true such as has been demonstrated in the text entry literature where time has demonstrated that faster optimized keyboard layouts cannot compete with the ubiquitous but slower Qwerty keyboard [20].

One explanation for why *digit first* yielded the slowest digit entry times and lowest preference scores is that a participant primarily focus on the Sudoku board and its location first and the digit to be inserted second. Therefore, asking a participant to first select the digit before selecting the location on the board may violate the mental models of users. Hence, the intended time saving made possible by inserting the same digit into multiple cells does not justify the added cognitive load of violating the cognitive model of the users.

Clearly, the *popup* method was only practically faster and more preferred than the *cell first* method and not significantly faster. A possible explanation for this small, but insignificant difference could be the following. First, the user may have been more familiar with the numeric popup dialog as it had the visual appearance of a traditional numeric keypad, while the two-row numeric layout used with the two other methods was not standardized and therefore not as recognizable. Another explanation may be that the popup immediately drew the users' attention towards the digit input step after selecting a cell. While with the *cell first* method the user must explicitly initiate a selection of a digit from the bottom of the screen.

It is indeed interesting that participants who performed worse with the *digit first* input method also preferred this input method. Perhaps one explanation is that for participants who were generally faster would prefer one of the other two input methods while the participants who were generally slower preferred the *digit first* method.

These observations are also consistent with the between-groups results, namely that the participants with prior experience with Sudoku exhibited a higher preference for the *popup* method compared to those that had not played Sudoku before, while those who had not played Sudoku before preferred the *digit first* method to a much higher degree than those who had Sudoku experience. A noticeable between groups effect was also observed for the *popup* method further confirming experienced participants' confidence with this method over the inexperienced participants. One reason for these differences could be that the participants with Sudoku experience approached the task in a Sudoku manner, although they were not asked to solve the Sudoku puzzles, while the participants without Sudoku experience approached the task as a simple digit entry task where digits displayed had to be mechanically placed on the board without placing any particular significance with regards to the board locations.

5.1 Limitations and Future Work

This experiment essentially comprised a digit copying task. The nature of the task may have affected the results as the performance of the participants may have been different if they were exposed to an actual game context rather than digit copying context.

The cohort was limited to relatively young computer science students. It is therefore unlikely that the results generalize as computer science students are likely to be more enthusiastic about using computers and more computer literate than a typical computer user. Future work should therefore also consider broader sampling.

It would also have been relevant to explore effects over time through a longitudinal study. One may expect that the practical differences between the popup numeric keypad and the two row digit layout in the cell first method would disappear with practice as users would learn to locate the desired digits with equal speed, while the mental mismatch of asking for the digit before the location may be less likely to disappear.

It would have been interesting to explore Sudoku game interaction using digit handwriting as it would be more directly related to the traditional paper-based Sudoku games. Touch displays also affords handwriting. With direct handwriting on a Sudoku board the selection of location and insertion of the digit would be done in one integrated step. Although more physical effort may be needed to articulate the digit gestures compared to the two display presses needed to select location and content, such digit gestures are an established part of most people's fundamental skill set utilizing their motor memory.

6 Conclusion

Sudoku game interaction was studied. Three input methods for placing digits on Sudoku boards were explored. The results show that user performed the task faster and also prefered to first select the location of the digits followed by selecting the digit. On the contrary, users without Sudoku experience preferred to enter the digits first and location second. Small non-significant, but practical differences were found in favor of numeric keypad popups over the two-line row of digits at the bottom of the screen. One possible implication of the results is that this type of games should be designed with the principle of going from broad/global to narrow/local, i.e., from location to content.

References

1. Grabbe, J.W.: Sudoku and working memory performance for older adults. Activit. Adaptat. Aging **35**(3), 241–254 (2011). https://doi.org/10.1080/01924788.2011.596748
2. Delahaye, J.P.: The science behind Sudoku. Sci. Am. **294**(6), 80–87 (2006)
3. Felgenhauer, B., Jarvis, F.: Mathematics of sudoku I. Math. Spectrum **39**(1), 15–22 (2006)
4. Herzberg, A.M., Murty, M.R.: Sudoku squares and chromatic polynomials. Notices AMS **54** (6), 708–717 (2007)
5. Geem, Z.W.: Harmony search algorithm for solving Sudoku. In: Apolloni, B., Howlett, R.J., Jain, L. (eds.) KES 2007. LNCS (LNAI), vol. 4692, pp. 371–378. Springer, Heidelberg (2007). https://doi.org/10.1007/978-3-540-74819-9_46
6. Simonis, H.: Sudoku as a constraint problem. In: CP Workshop on Modeling and Reformulating Constraint Satisfaction Problems, vol. 12, pp. 13–27 (2005)
7. Felgenhauer, B., Jarvis, F.: Enumerating possible Sudoku grids (2005). http://www.afjarvis. staff.Shef.ac.uk/sudoku/sudoku.pdf
8. Lewis, R.: Metaheuristics can solve sudoku puzzles. J. Heuristics **13**(4), 387–401 (2007). https://doi.org/10.1007/s10732-007-9012-8
9. Chang, C.C., Chou, Y.C., Kieu, T.D.: An information hiding scheme using Sudoku. In: 2008 3rd International Conference on Innovative Computing Information and Control, pp. 17–17. IEEE (2008). https://doi.org/10.1109/icicic.2008.149
10. Kurmas, Z., Dulimarta, H., Tao, Y.: Sudoku: nifty tools. J. Comput. Sci. Colleges **23**(1), 109–110 (2007)
11. Norte, S., Lobo, F.G.: Sudoku access: a sudoku game for people with motor disabilities. In: Proceedings of the 10th International ACM SIGACCESS Conference on Computers and Accessibility, pp. 161–168. ACM (2008). https://doi.org/10.1145/1414471.1414502
12. Libuša, A.: Sudoku for visually impaired, Doctoral dissertation, Masarykova univerzita, Fakulta informatiky (2008)
13. Sandnes, F.E.: Universell Utforming av IKT-Systemer, 2nd edn. Universitetsforlaget, Oslo (2018)
14. Echtler, F., Nestler, S., Dippon, A., Klinker, G.: Supporting casual interactions between board games on public tabletop displays and mobile devices. Pers. Ubiquit. Comput. **13**(8), 609–617 (2009). https://doi.org/10.1007/s00779-009-0246-3
15. Kondraju, V.K.M.K.: An exploration of HCI design features and usability techniques in gaming. IOSR J. Comput. Eng. **15**(3), 53–57 (2003)

16. Bernsen, N.O., Dybkjær, L.: Intermezzo 5: sudoku usability evaluation. In: Multimodal Usability, pp. 387–412. Springer, London (2010). https://doi.org/10.1007/978-1-84882-553-6_17

17. Bartol, M.: Aplikacija uganke Sudoku za Android, Doctoral dissertation, Univerza v Ljubljani (2012)

18. Ainsworth, W.A.: Optimization of string length for spoken digit input with error correction. Int. J. Man Mach. Stud. 28(6), 573–581 (1988). https://doi.org/10.1016/S0020-7373(88)80061-0

19. LeCun, Y., et al.: Handwritten digit recognition with a back-propagation network. In: Advances in Neural Information Processing Systems, pp. 396–404 (1990)

20. Sandnes, F.E.: Effects of common keyboard layouts on physical effort: implications for kiosks and Internet banking. In: The proceedings of Unitech2010: International Conference on Universal Technologies, pp. 91–100 (2010)

21. Tsang, S.N., Chan, A.H.S., Chen, K.: A study on touch screen numeric keypads: effects of key size and key layout. In: International MultiConference of Engineers and Computer Scientists, vol. 324 (2013)

22. Vinbæk, E.O., Pettersen, F.M.B., Carlsen, J.E., Fremstad, K., Edvinsen, N., Sandnes, F.E.: On online banking authentication for all: a comparison of BankID login efficiency using smartphones versus code generators. In: Antona, M., Stephanidis, C. (eds.) HCII 2019. LNCS, vol. 11572, pp. 365–374. Springer, Cham (2019). https://doi.org/10.1007/978-3-030-23560-4_27

23. Sandnes, F.E.: A memory aid for reduced cognitive load in manually entered online bank transactions. In: Norsk informatikkonferanse. Tapir Academic Pubhlishers (2012)

24. Sandnes, F.E.: An error tolerant memory aid for reduced cognitive load in number copying tasks. In: Stephanidis, C., Antona, M. (eds.) UAHCI 2013. LNCS, vol. 8010, pp. 614–623. Springer, Heidelberg (2013). https://doi.org/10.1007/978-3-642-39191-0_66

25. Oladimeji, P.: Towards safer number entry in interactive medical systems. In: Proceedings of the 4th ACM SIGCHI Symposium on Engineering Interactive Computing Systems, pp. 329–332. ACM (2012). https://doi.org/10.1145/2305484.2305543

26. Sandnes, F.E., Huang, Y.P.: A computer supported memory aid for copying prescription parameters into medical equipment based on linguistic phrases. In: 2013 IEEE International Conference on Systems, Man, and Cybernetics, pp. 3447–3451. IEEE (2013). https://doi.org/10.1109/smc.2013.588

27. Taxis, K., Barber, N.: Incidence and severity of intravenous drug errors in a German hospital. Eur. J. Clin. Pharmacol. 59(11), 815–817 (2004). https://doi.org/10.1007/s00228-003-0689-9

28. Wiseman, S., Cairns, P., Cox, A.: A taxonomy of number entry error. In: Proceedings of the 25th BCS Conference on Human-Computer Interaction, pp. 187–196. British Computer Society (2011)

29. Hofseth, K.Å., Haga, L.K., Sørlie, V., Sandnes, F.E.: Form feedback on the web: a comparison of popup alerts and in-form error messages. In: Chen, Y.-W., Zimmermann, A., Howlett, R.J., Jain, L.C. (eds.) Innovation in Medicine and Healthcare Systems, and Multimedia. SIST, vol. 145, pp. 369–379. Springer, Singapore (2019). https://doi.org/10.1007/978-981-13-8566-7_35

30. Skogstrøm, N.A.B., Igeltjørn, A., Knudsen, K.M., Diallo, A.D., Krivonos, D., Sandnes, F.E.: A comparison of two smartphone time-picking interfaces: convention versus efficiency. In: Proceedings of the 10th Nordic Conference on Human-Computer Interaction, pp. 874–879. ACM (2018). https://doi.org/10.1145/3240167.3240233

31. Brathovde, K., Farner, M.B., Brun, F.K., Sandnes, F.E.: Effectiveness of color-picking interfaces among non-designers. In: Luo, Y. (ed.) CDVE 2019. LNCS, vol. 11792, pp. 181–189. Springer, Cham (2019). https://doi.org/10.1007/978-3-030-30949-7_21
32. Hansen, F., Krivan, J.J., Sandnes, F.E.: Still not readable? an interactive tool for recommending color pairs with sufficient contrast based on existing visual designs. In: The 21st International ACM SIGACCESS Conference on Computers and Accessibility, pp. 636–638. ACM (2019). https://doi.org/10.1145/3308561.3354585

QB-Gest: Qwerty Bimanual Gestural Input for Eyes-Free Smartphone Text Input

Linghui Ye[1], Frode Eika Sandnes[1,2(✉)] ⓘ, and I. Scott MacKenzie[3]

[1] Department of Computer Science, Oslo Metropolitan University,
0130 Oslo, Norway
yelinghui1987@gmail.com, frodes@oslomet.no
[2] Institute of Technology, Kristiania University College, 0153 Oslo, Norway
[3] Department of Computer Science, York University, Toronto,
ON M3J 1P3, Canada
mack@cse.yorku.ca

Abstract. We developed QB-Gest, a bimanual text entry method based on simple gestures where users drag their thumbs in the direction of the desired letter while visualizing the Qwerty-layout. In an experiment with four sessions of testing, 20 users achieved text entry rates of 11.1 wpm eyes-free and 14.1 wpm eyes-on. An expert user achieved an eyes-free rate of 24.9 wpm after 10 rounds of entering the-quick-brown-fox phrase. The method holds potential for users with low vision and certain types of reduced motor function.

Keywords: Mobile text entry · Eyes free text · Gestures · Qwerty

1 Introduction

Smartphones have become an important tool in modern society by facilitating communication independent of time and place. Many smartphone tasks require text input, such as searching the web, sending emails, or messaging. Text input typically uses a default virtual keyboard. Yet, many users find it hard to use virtual smartphone keyboards compared to physical desktop keyboards [1], because input requires accurately hitting keys without tactile feedback. Virtual smartphone keys are smaller than physical desktop keys; so, input is both visually intensive and requires careful eye-motor coordination [2]. Techniques that require limited visual demand, such as touch typing, are desirable in many situations. Eyes-free operation is an absolute necessity for blind users [3, 4]. In addition to situational impairments, visual acuity and pointing accuracy reduce with age. Another goal is to free up the valuable display real estate occupied by soft keyboards for displaying other information.

Gestures have been proposed as a means of reducing visual demand in text entry tasks [5–7]. Instead of hitting keys at absolute positions, the user inputs simple gestures as relative finger movements. Such gestures, often resembling the graphical shape of letters, can be input eyes-free. Usually, gesture alphabets must be learned, and this requires the user to invest effort. In the proposed approach we instead rely on users' familiarity with the Qwerty layout, thus reducing the need to learn new gestures. Users

© Springer Nature Switzerland AG 2020
M. Antona and C. Stephanidis (Eds.): HCII 2020, LNCS 12188, pp. 223–242, 2020.
https://doi.org/10.1007/978-3-030-49282-3_16

visualize the Qwerty layout and move a thumb in the direction of the required character within either the left or right half of the layout (see Fig. 1).

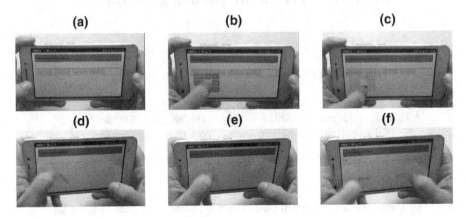

Fig. 1. Top: Input of *c* in eyes-on mode by (a) pressing left thumb, (b) displaying the left side of the Qwerty keyboard centered around the thumb, (c) dragging the thumb down towards *c* and releasing the thumb. Bottom: Inputting the word *we* in eyes-free mode by (d) the left thumb northwest for *w*, (e) left thumb north for *e*, (f) both thumbs outwards for *space*.

High text entry rates can be achieved when both hands are used collaboratively to input text. Expert smartphone users often input text with two thumbs [8]. However, it is difficult to input complex gesture shapes bimanually as users typically need their dominant hand for fine motor tasks. Since the proposed method only requires simple directional gestures it is envisaged that bimanual input is possible. An experiment was designed to determine if users who are familiar with Qwerty can visualize the layout and produce the corresponding directional gestures. These observations were contrasted against a group of users who used the technique with visual feedback.

In the next section we review work related to smartphone text entry. This is followed by a description of the proposed QB-Gest prototype. Then, we describe a user study to test the prototype followed by an analysis of the results.

2   Related Work

Qwerty is the most common layout on smartphones, although alternatives have been proposed [9]. Since users resist change [10, p. 187], research focuses on compromises that leverage users' familiarity and the reduced visual search afforded by both alphabetical [11] and Qwerty [12] layouts. Other work experimented with adding keys dynamically according to current input using a language model [13].

Virtual or soft keyboards on smartphones are small with limited space for each key. Key width is especially small when the device is in portrait mode. Clearly, to successfully hit small keys, visual cues are required for key locations. Ordinary smartphone virtual keyboards are a challenge for individuals with low vision and or reduced motor function [14]. As vision and motor control reduce with age, smartphone text entry is particularly challenging for older individuals [1].

Input on a virtual keyboard is a pointing task where users move a finger or stylus to hit a key. With physical keyboards, the fingers feel the keys before acting; with practice, ten-finger touch-typing is possible. However, virtual keyboards have no such tactile feedback: The first touch is recorded as a keypress. Input using virtual keyboards is therefore a visually intensive target acquisition task. Fitts' law predicts the relationship between the distance to the target, the width of the target, and the speed [15]; hence, the faster the pointing task is performed, the less likely is the user to hit the target. With smaller targets, accurate target acquisition requires slowing down. Hence, Fitts' law explains why smartphone text entry is slower than using ordinary physical keyboards.

Experiments on ten finger touch-typing on touch surfaces have used Markov-Bayesian models [16]. Although entry rates were high, at 45 wpm, achieving adequate accuracy was a challenge. Attempts have also been made to input text through eyes-free thumb input relying on motor memory [17]. Again, accuracy is a challenge.

The small size of smartphones means that ten finger touch typing is not possible. Instead, input uses a single index finger, two thumbs, or a single thumb. Azenkot and Zhai report that text entry rates reach approximately 50 wpm with two thumbs, 36 wpm with a single index finger, and 33 wpm with one thumb [8]. Two thumbs are faster as the keyboard area is divided in two and each thumb traverses shorter distances. Two thumb input is also associated a higher error rate (11%) compared to using a single index finger (8%) and or a single thumb (7%). The authors also found that the participants hit consistently below the targets, with larger horizontal offsets at the edges. This implies that participants tend to minimize the finger distance travelled. Approaches for supporting input on tiny virtual keyboards include zooming in using a callout where an enlarged version of the acquired key is displayed above the finger. Callouts may also include neighboring keys [2].

Zhu et al. [18] explored if users were able to enter text on a smartphone eyes-free using their memory of the Qwerty layout. Experiments with their Invisible Keyboard achieved 31.3 wpm during the first session and 37.9 wpm during the third session without visual feedback. An invisible smartphone keyboard relies on skill transfer from smartphone text entry. It is not likely that ordinary Qwerty typing skills will transfer to the smartphone form factor. Text entry methods such as Apple's VoiceOver or Android's TalkBack support blind or low-vision individuals. Users move their finger over the keyboard and receive speech feedback to explore the layout until the desired letter is spoken. One of the first accounts of this technique is found in the Slide Rule project [19]. Such exploratory strategies are slow with a study on blind users revealing a text entry rate of 2.1 wpm with VoiceOver using a Qwerty layout [4]. Proposed improvements include two-handed input with separate male and female voices for each hand [20] and using pseudo-force to separate exploration and taps, where the touch area of the fingertip is used as a measure of finger pressure [6]. An alternative to keyboard input is speech, with rates about $5\times$ faster than VoiceOver [3]. Moreover, speech input was preferred by blind users [3].

There are comparatively fewer studies addressing smartphone text entry for individuals with reduced motor function. Graphical approaches such as Dasher [21] are visually intensive. The literature on text entry with reduced motor function is dominated by keyboard scanning where virtual keyboards are automatically traversed in regular steps and once the desired key or key-group is highlighted a selection is made with a single key or switch [22]. Hence, the user only makes a time-dependent selection and there is no need to hit an absolute target. Clearly, scanning is slow compared to other techniques. Chording [23, 24] offers potentially high text entry rates and is suitable for certain types of reduced motor function, such as loss of a hand, and can also be performed eyes-free. Chording has been used for eyes-free numeric input on smartphones [5]. Unfortunately, learning the chords is required and chording is therefore not widely adopted despite effective mnemonic aids such as using the graphical shape of letter [24] and Braille codes [25].

Another avenue of text entry research is gestures [26, 27]. Gestures are simple dragging motions performed on the touch display. The motions are relative and do not require hitting specific targets. Thus, gesture input is applicable to users with low or no vision. Also, gestures can be employed by users with reduced motor function who are unable to accurately hit targets. Approaches such as Graffiti [26, 28] and EdgeWrite [27, 29] rely on gestures that resemble the shape of letters. It is easier to remember gestures that mimic symbols users already know. On the other hand, these gestures can resemble complex shapes with twists and turns. Simpler gestures such as UniStrokes are faster (15.8 wpm) than the more complex Graffiti gestures (11.4 wpm) as there is less distance for the fingers to travel [28].

Attempts exist to input text using single-stroke gestures, for example navigating menu hierarchies to retrieve a specific letter using multiple simple gestures [30, 31]. With Swipeboard [31] the user selects letters by navigating menus on very small touch displays using multiple swipe gestures. Absolute pointing tasks and gestures have also been combined, such as Swype, where the user drags the finger along the keys of a keyboard using a continuous stroke to produce a word shape. Bimanual mechanisms have been explored but are slower than the methods relying on one hand [32]. Lai et al. [33] investigated if simple gestures with audio feedback could be used for entering text eyes free on a smartphone using one hand. Their system, ThumbStroke, presented letters alphabetically in groups around a circle with the thumb dragged in the direction of the desired letter. After 20 sessions users reached 10.85 wpm eyes-free. Banovic et al. [34] combined absolute pointing with relative gestures for eyes-free text entry. With their Escape-Keyboard, the user first points at one of four regions on the display, then performs a simple gesture in one of eight directions. Input used one thumb. Users were given audio feedback and after six training sessions reached 7.5 wpm.

A study where a physical keyboard was compared to a virtual keyboard and gestures [35] found that the physical keyboard (48.6 wpm) was more than 2× faster than the virtual on-screen keyboard (21.0 wpm), which again was faster than using gestures (16.5 wpm). As found in performance measures with smartphones [8], the virtual keyboard and gestures were input with one hand, while the keyboard task was conducted bimanually. However, an 8-in. tablet was used instead of a smartphone.

The study reported herein allows text entry with simple gestures. It was inspired by a text entry method proposed for dual joystick game controllers [36], where the user visualizes the Qwerty keyboard. If the desired key is on the left side of the keyboard, the user uses the left hand and left joystick, and vice versa. In inputting a specific letter the user imagines that the left and the right joysticks are located between D-F and J-K, respectively. To retrieve a specific letter, the respective joystick is moved in the direction of the letter. Dictionaries resolve ambiguities as several of the directions are assigned multiple characters. Experiments with joysticks showed that with little practice participants reached 6.8 wpm [36]. The present study employed the same principle except using finger touch gestures. One benefit is that the gestures require less finger movement than traditional UniStroke-type gestures. Moreover, they are bimanual in nature. There is thus potential for high text-entry speeds. However, touch gestures are different from manipulating dual joysticks as used in the earlier study [36]. Joysticks provide tactile feedback since they move in the direction pushed, and stop once the maximum displacement is achieved, with the stick returning to the home position when released. Moreover, each joystick has a square guide allowing users to feel if they have found the diagonal corners. Thus, joysticks offer tactile feedback. Also, with joysticks the response appears on the display with the user mapping joystick motion with display feedback. With touch input, visual feedback can be provided near the finger, thus allowing for a close mapping between the physical movement and visual feedback. The benefit of building eyes-free text entry on the smartphone is the wide applicability and availability of this technology, where special-purpose input devices such as joysticks are impractical.

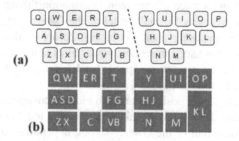

Fig. 2. Qwerty layouts showing (a) customary left-right division for two-handed touch typing and (b) *QB-Gest* letter positions for bimanual gestural input.

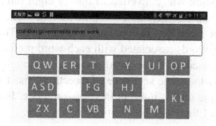

Fig. 3. QB-Gest with visual hints in the eyes-free mode.

3 QB-Gest System Description

QB-Gest was implemented in Java and tested on a Huawei C8817E smartphone with a 5-in. display running Android 4.4 KitKat. The UI included a text region and a gesture region, along with two entry modes: eyes-free and eyes-on. The text region contained fields for the presented and transcribed text, and a word region showing four suggested words. The word region was only implemented for the eyes-on mode.

The gesture region was located below the text region and was divided into a left and right side. The left side was for letters on the left side of the Qwerty layout and the right side was for letters on the right side of the Qwerty layout. Figure 2a shows the usual Qwerty left-right division of input for two-handed touch typing. Figure 2b shows the QB-Gest left-right positions for gestural input. Although practical, the assignment of letters to direction is not optimal from an information theoretic perspective. In particular, left-west is assigned three high-frequency letters, ASD, while left-south is assigned just the letter C. The rationale was to exploit users' familiarity with Qwerty. Consequently, the letter-to-direction assignments are limited. An alternative is to change the groups ASD:FG to AS:DFG, but then one would also need to change the right-side assignments from HJ:KL to HJK:L to maintain symmetry across the two hands. There is an obvious trade-off between information theoretic optimization and assignments that leverage users' mental model of the Qwerty keyboard [36].

For eyes-free input, the letter positions in Fig. 2b are hidden and do not appear during input. However, the user can request visual hints using a two-thumb swipe-up gesture. In this case, the letter positions appear for 1.5 s. Figure 3 shows the QB-Gest application in eyes-free mode with visual hints shown.

For eyes-on input, the letter positions are also hidden, but appear immediately when the user's thumb touches the display to make a gesture. On touch, the display shows the letters for the left or right half of the Qwerty layout, depending on the touch location. Each half shows eight boxes around the touch point. By dragging the thumb in one of the eight directions, the respective box of letters is selected once the finger is released. In the eyes-free mode, a short beep is heard each time a letter is entered.

The angle of the gesture was converted to one of eight directions by dividing the space into eight equal sectors centered on compass directions. A trie data structure [37] mapped the sequence of directions to words is a dictionary. The trie is a special tree data structure that stores words associated with each word prefix. In the eyes-on mode, words were suggested based on these word prefixes. Although there are ambiguities caused by words sharing the same sequence of directions, most sequences are unique. Figure 4 gives an example of text input in the eyes-on mode. In eyes-free mode, entry proceeds similarly except the letter positions do not appear.

3.1 KSPC Analysis

Since QB-Gest positions 26 letters on $2 \times 8 = 16$ keys, the entry of some words is ambiguous. However, the ambiguity is considerably less than that of a phone keypad where 26 letters are positioned on 8 keys.

Keystrokes per character (*KSPC*) is an established metric that captures the keystroke efficiency of a text entry method [38]. Of course, "keystrokes" is "gesture strokes" in the present context. For ambiguous keyboards, *KSPC* reflects the overhead in resolving the ambiguity when a key sequence corresponds to more than one word.

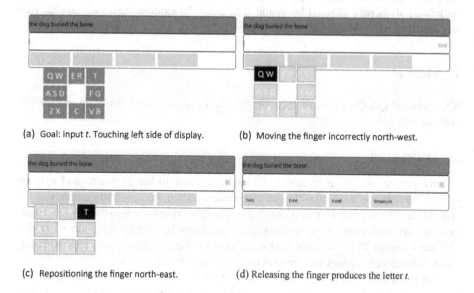

(a) Goal: input *t*. Touching left side of display.

(b) Moving the finger incorrectly north-west.

(c) Repositioning the finger north-east.

(d) Releasing the finger produces the letter *t*.

Fig. 4. QB-Gest example input in eyes-on mode.

As an example, for English text entry using a 10,000 word dictionary, a phone keypad has *KSPC* = 1.0072 [38]. In other words, the overhead, on average, is just 7.2 keystrokes per 1000 keystrokes. This is for T9-style input, where the user navigates an ordered list of words when ambiguities occur.

A similar calculation for QB-Gest yields *KSPC* = 1.0037, for an overhead of 3.7 keystrokes per 1000 keystrokes. So, ambiguous words, or "collisions", are rare. Examples for QB-Gest include {king, lung}, {edge, rage} and {rise, ride, rude}. See Fig. 2. Since collisions are rare, we have not implemented a disambiguation method for eyes-free input in our prototype. We expect a full implementation could use linguistic context to resolve the occasional collision that does occur.

3.2 Special Inputs

As well as the two-thumb gesture to request visual hints, we used special inputs for SPACE, BACKSPACE, and ENTER. Two-thumb gestures were chosen to reduce conflicts with letter input. Through some experimentation it was found that symmetric gestures worked better than non-symmetric gestures [39]. The two-thumb gestures are

SPACE	both thumbs moving outward to the sides
BACKSPACE	both thumbs moving inward
ENTER	both thumbs moving down
HINTS	both thumbs moving up

Our research questions are as follows: Can users leverage their knowledge of the Qwerty layout to perform bimanual gestural input on a smartphone? To what degree can users perform eyes-free text entry? Is the error rate affected by visual feedback? Are the gesture dynamics affected by visual feedback? To explore these, we conducted a user study, as now described.

4 Method

We evaluated QB-Gest in both the eyes-free and eyes-on entry modes over four sessions of text entry.

4.1 Participants

Twenty participants were recruited, 10 each assigned to the eyes-free and eyes-on groups. Participants were recruited among students from the university campus of the first author. There were 11 males and 9 females split equally (approximately) between the eyes-free and eyes-on groups. Ages ranged from 10 to 54 years with most participants between 25 to 34 years. The mean ages for the two groups was approximately equal. All the participants had normal or correct-to-normal vision.

The participants were screened for text input skill and Qwerty familiarity as this was a prerequisite for participating in the experiment. Responses were self-assessed on a six-point Likert scale, with higher scores for greater skill/familiarity. The responses are summarized thus:

Text input skill
    Eyes-on group ($M = 4.3$, $SD = 0.68$)
    Eyes-free group ($M = 4.6$, $SD = 0.52$)

Qwerty familiarity
    Eyes-on group ($M = 4.2$, $SD = 1.14$)
    Eyes-free group ($M = 5.2$, $SD = 0.79$)

Using a Mann Whitney U test, there was no significant difference between the responses of the two groups in terms of self-assessed text entry skill ($z' = -1.023$, $p = .306$). However, the slightly higher mean response for the eyes-free group on Qwerty familiarity was statistically significant ($z' = -2.053$, $p = .0401$). Although the two groups exhibit different Qwerty skills which may confound results, our main focus was to study eyes-free text entry with the eyes-on entry as a reference.

4.2 Task

The participants performed a text copy task using a standard 500-phrase set [40]. Phrase were selected at random and appeared in the presented text field. The user entered the phrase using QB-Gest in the assigned mode with the result appearing in the transcribed text field (see Figs. 3 and 4). At the end of a phrase, participants employed the ENTER gesture to move to the next phrase. The participants in the eyes-free group could use the HINTS gesture to receive a visual hint wherein the full Qwerty letter pattern was shown for 1.5 s.

4.3 Procedure

Testing was done in a quiet room. The first session included a briefing where participants signed a consent form and completed a questionnaire asking for demographic information and a text entry skill self-assessment. Next, participants practiced QB-Gest for 10 min to enter text using either the eyes-free or eyes-on entry mode, depending on the participant's group. After practicing, the measured text entry sessions began. Sessions were time-limited to 20 min with the measured text entry part of the session taking about 5 min. The number of phrases entered in a session varied from 6 in session 1 to 11 in session 4.

The four sessions for each participant were a few days apart in a concentrated time-period to avoid confounding effects. The entire experiment involved 80 sessions and ran over three months. The participants where asked about their opinions on QB-Gest using a 6-point Likert scale after the fourth session. No monetary reward was given.

4.4 Apparatus

The hardware and QB-Gest user interface described earlier were used in the experiment. The software logged all the interactions performed on the smartphone during the experiment, including the spatial and temporal details of the individual gestures as well as high-level statistics such as text entry speed (in words per minute), error rate (percent of incorrect letters) [41], and requests for hints.

To minimize word collisions (particularly for the eyes-free mode), QB-Gest was configured with a small dictionary that contained only the 1168 unique words in the phrase set. In this configuration, the T9-style $KSPC = 1.0023$.

4.5 Design

The experiment was a 2×4 mixed design with the following independent variables and levels:

Entry mode	Eyes-free, eyes-on
Session	1, 2, 3, 4

The assignments were between-subjects (entry mode) and within-subjects (session). Entry mode was assigned between-subjects to avoid interference between the two conditions.

The dependent variables were text entry speed in words per minute (wpm), error rate (%), hint requests (count per character), output/input gain resulting from using word suggestions (difference in number of output and input symbols over number of output symbols) and gesture length (cm). Error rate was measured using the minimum string distance metric, comparing the presented and transcribed text phrases.

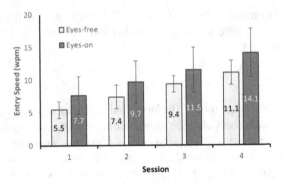

Fig. 5. Text entry speed (words per minute) by session and entry mode. Error bars show ±1 *SD*.

5   Result and Discussion

5.1   Performance

The grand mean for text entry speed was 9.55 wpm. By session, the means increased from 6.60 wpm (session 1) to 12.60 wpm (session 4). By entry mode, the means were 8.35 wpm (eyes-free) and 10.75 wpm (eyes-on). The results show a significant improvement in text entry performance with practice ($F(3, 54) = 106.5$, $p < .001$, $\eta^2 = .851$) and also a significant difference between entry modes ($F(1, 18) = 4.917$, $p = .040$, $\eta^2 = .215$). Text entry speed was about 29% higher for the eyes-on entry mode (see Fig. 5). Bonferroni post-hoc tests showed that all the sessions are significantly different from each other ($p < .001$).

Table 1. Eyes-free text mobile text entry results (*Results with a MacBook).

Mode	Hands	Entry Speed (wpm) by Session				
		1	2	3	4	> 5
Invisible Keyboard [18]	2	31.3	35.7	37.9		
Blindtype (PR) [17]	1	22.8				
Graffiti (delayed) [7]*	1	11.1				
Escape [34]	1	6.9	9.3	10.4	11.1	
QB-Gest	2	**5.5**	**7.4**	**9.4**	**11.1**	**24.9**
Thumb Stroke [33]	1	7.2				10.8
EdgeWrite [33]	1					7.8
Qwerty [4]	1	2.1				
NoLookNotes [46]	1	1.32				
VoiceOver [46]	1	0.66				

The improvement with practice appears close to linear. It is thus likely that further practice would yield further improvements. However, with prolonged training one would expect the improvement to be logarithmic, that is, with increased practice the improvement becomes smaller [10, p. 274]. A logarithmic regression model suggests that the mean entry speed may exceed 20 wpm after 18 sessions.

The performance in the eyes-free entry mode seems to match that of the preceding session for the eyes-on entry mode. Another interesting observation is that the spread for eyes-on is larger than the spread for eyes-free. One would expect the spread to be somewhat higher with higher mean values. Also, one could expect a higher spread for the eyes-free mode since the task is more difficult. We suspect that the difference in spread is a result of between-group sampling bias and not necessarily an effect. There was no Session × Entry Mode interaction effect on entry speed ($F(3, 54) = 0.63$, ns).

We compared our results to other studies of eyes-free mobile text entry. See Table 1. Clearly, the Invisible Keyboard yields text entry speeds much above the other methods as it directly leverages users' Qwerty skills. However, such high mobile text entry speeds are mostly found among expert users, typically young individuals. Older smartphone users typically yield lower performance [1]. The Invisible Keyboard is also the only other reported bimanual input method. Very fast rates were also obtained with an enhanced version of Graffiti. QB-Gest has a similar performance to the Escape-keyboard at the fourth session, while QB-Gest has more rapid improvement. QB-Gest performs marginally better than Thumb Stroke. All these recent methods yield higher performance than older methods such as EdgeWrite and VoiceOver. Comparison of error was not possible as the studies report different error metrics.

5.2 Errors

Error rate was calculated from the minimum-string distance between the presented and transcribed text phrases [41]. The grand mean for error rate was 10.8%. By session, the means decreased from 15.9% (session 1) to 6.90% (session 5). By entry mode, the means were 15.2% (eyes-free) and 6.3% (eyes-on). The errors rates by session and entry mode are shown in Fig. 6.

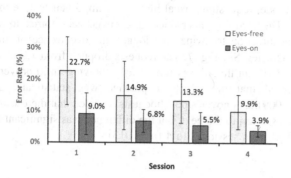

Fig. 6. Error rates (%) by session and entry mode. Error bars show ± 1 *SD*.

As seen, the error rates with eyes-free entry are nearly twice as high as with eyes-on entry. Higher error rates for eyes-free entry agree with other studies [4, 19].

Training also affects the error rate as there is a reduction from the first to last session for both eyes-free and eyes-on entry. A Levene's test showed that the data lacked equality of variances. The measurements were therefore transformed using the aligned rank transform (ART) [45]. Mauchly tests showed that the data aligned according to session did not satisfy the assumption of sphericity and a Greenhouse-Geisler correction was therefore applied. There was a significant effect on practice (session) for eyes-on entry ($F(2.156, 38.813) = 13.941$, $p < .001$, $\eta^2 = .426$). Bonferroni post-hoc tests show that the error reduction from the first to the second session is significant ($p = .013$) while not from session 2 to 3 and from session 3 to 4. The reduction in error is also significant from session 2 to 4. There is also a significant effect of mode ($F(1, 18) = 13.34$, $p = .002$, $\eta^2 = .426$) as well as a significant interaction between session and mode ($F(3, 54) = 3.874$, $p = .014$, $\eta^2 = .167$).

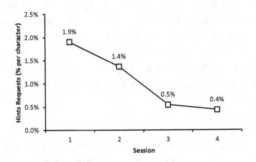

Fig. 7. Percentage visual hints requests by session (% per character).

5.3   Visual Hints

In the eyes-free mode, requesting visual hints is an important feature in learning QB-Gest (see Fig. 3). The need for hints reduces as users get accustomed to which thumb to use and in which direction to swipe. We logged the occurrence of hint requests by session and by character. See Fig. 7. The requests dropped from 1.9% per character in the 1st session to 0.4% in the 4th session, clearly showing an improvement. A Friedman test confirmed that the effect of practice was statistically significant (χ^2 (3) = 11.61, $p = .009$). Connover's post hoc tests revealed that there was no significant different from one session to the next, but the difference was significant from session 1 to 3 ($p = .007$) and from session 2 to 4 ($p = .013$).

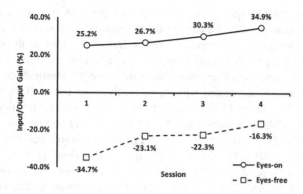

Fig. 8. Output/input gain resulting from word suggestions and BACKSPACE use.

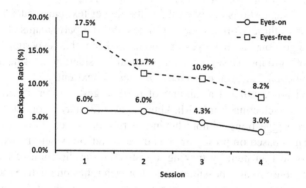

Fig. 9. Backspace ratio.

5.4 Word Suggestions

In the eyes-on mode participants could select words based on prefixes by directly pressing the displayed suggestion. To assess the effect of the suggestions, the input gain for both the eyes-on and eyes-free modes were calculated. We define input gain as the difference between the number of outputs (characters) and the number of inputs (gestures) over the total number of inputs (gestures). All the participants in the eyes-on experiment utilized word suggestions. As illustrated by Fig. 8, the suggestions resulted in a gain of 25.2% in the first session, increasing to a gain of 34.9% in the fourth session. The eyes-free mode yielded a negative gain of −34.7% during the first session that decreased to −16.3% during the fourth session. Clearly, practice had a significant effect on output/input gain ($F(3, 54) = 8.626$, $p < .001$, $\eta^2 = .309$). However, Bonferroni post-hoc testing revealed that only the first and last sessions were significantly different ($p < .001$). There was a significant difference between the output/input gains for the eyes-on mode vs. the eyes-free mode ($F(1, 18) = 151.1$, $p < .001$, $\eta^2 = .894$).

The negative output/input gains observed with the eyes-free mode can be partly explained by BACKSPACE use. If a user inputs a, followed by BACKSPACE and b, that's 3 gestures producing just 1 character. To explore BACKSPACE further, the ratio of BACKSPACE inputs to all inputs is plotted in Fig. 9. The observations did not show equivalence of variances and the observations were therefore transformed using ART [45]. The eyes-free mode is associated with significantly more use of BACKSPACE than the eyes-on mode ($F(1, 18) = 15.72$, $p < .001$, $\eta^2 = .466$). During the first session the eyes-free mode exhibited a mean rate of 17.5% BACKSPACE inputs, while the eyes-on mode only exhibited 6.0% BACKSPACE inputs. Practice had a significant effect on the use of BACKSPACE ($F(3, 54) = 13.196$, $p < .001$, $\eta^2 = .415$). Post-hoc tests show that the two first sessions were significantly different ($p = .041$) but not the other two consecutive sessions. Again, session two and four were significantly different ($p = .003$). During the fourth session the BACKSPACE ratio dropped to 8.2% in the eyes-free mode and 3.0% in the eyes-on mode. A significant interaction was also observed between practice and mode ($F(3, 54) = 4.718$, $p = .005$, $\eta^2 = .195$).

Having word suggestions partly explains the higher text entry rates in the eyes-on mode compared to the eyes-free mode. In hindsight, the participants should not have been given suggestions in the eyes-on mode to keep this experimental condition constant for both groups. However, as a practical consideration, using word suggestions is clearly beneficial, even expected, for eyes-on text entry.

The eyes-on mode utilized a mixture of relative gestures for character input and absolute targets for selecting words. Marking menus [42] may be one way of providing users with word suggestions without having to rely on direct pointing. The Marking menus approach is based on presenting menu items radially when the user touches the display. Users select an item by making a gesture in the direction of the menu item. Hierarchal selections are also possible. This approach relies on relative motions instead of absolute pointing. With practice, users select items without looking. To avoid confusing word selections with character input, a different region of the display could be allocated for these selections, for example the top middle of the display.

The incorporation of effective word suggestions in eyes-free mode is still an open problem. The user needs feedback on the word suggestions while entering text. Without visual feedback this information must be conveyed using other modalities. The most obvious modality is audio. Further research is needed to uncover how such audio feedback might interfere with the text entry task.

5.5   Gesture Dynamics

To compare the gesture dynamics of the eyes-on and eyes-free modes, detailed gesture information were extracted from the logs and aggregated into mean gesture lengths (cm) and mean gesture angles. See Figs. 10 and 11. There are several noticeable differences between the two modes. First, the gesture lengths in the eyes-on mode are shorter ($M = 1.0$, $SD = 0.2$) than the eyes-free gestures ($M = 1.2$, $SD = 0.2$), and the difference is significant ($F(1, 10) = 5.474$, $p = .041$, $\eta^2 = .354$). There is no significant difference in gesture length across the two hands for the eyes-on mode ($F(1, 3) = 4.889$, $p = .114$). A visual inspection of the eyes-on gestures in Fig. 10 shows that the four diagonal gestures are slightly longer than the four horizontal/vertical gestures.

The endpoints of the gestures appear to fall on the boundary of an approximate square for both hands. One explanation is that the visual feedback on the display guides the fingers toward the displayed targets and hence constrains finger movement.

Figure 11 shows that the gesture patterns in eyes-free mode are different from those in eyes-on mode. The two gestures along the adjacent diagonals are longest while the gestures along the perpendicular diagonals are shortest. This pattern mirrors across the hands, explained as follows. There are no visual guides in the eyes-free mode; the user therefore executes the gestures more freely in a comfortable manner. The left thumb has a higher dexterity along the northwest-southeast diagonal as it involves abductions and adductions, while moving the left thumb along the southwest-northeast direction is anatomically more difficult as it involves flexion and extensions. These southwest-northeast motions are thus smaller. The same holds for the right thumb although the patterns are mirrored vertically resulting in longer gestures along the southwest-northeast diagonal.

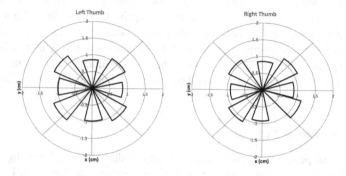

Fig. 10. Mean gesture lengths (cm) and angles in eyes-on mode.

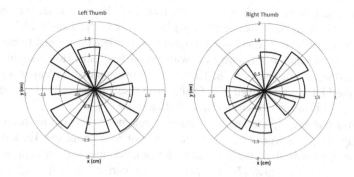

Fig. 11. Mean gesture lengths (cm) and angles in eyes-free mode.

The gesture angles were not noticeably different across the eyes-on and eyes-free modes. However, the plots reveal that the vertical up-down gestures tilted slightly left for the left thumb and slightly right for the right thumb with both modes (an offset of 3–9°). This is probably a result of the thumb origin being in the bottom left corner for the left hand resulting in arc-like shapes and vice versa for the right hand.

These results may help improve the accuracy of gesture recognition. In addition to using just the angle and a minimum distance to detect gestures, the length may help improve the discrimination of neighboring eyes-free gestures. The vertical detection angles should also be adjusted accordingly. Another possibility is to redesign the visual feedback in the eyes-on mode to better align with the hand ergonomics.

5.6   Subjective Assessment

After completing four sessions of testing, participants were asked several questions on their impressions of QB-Gest. Responses were on a 6-point Likert scale. Participants in each group were asked if they felt the entry method (eyes-free or eyes-on) was "easy to use". A Mann Whitney U test revealed no significant difference between the responses from the two groups ($z' = -1.336$, $p = .182$). They were also asked to self-assess their typing skill on the entry mode they were using. Again, there was no difference in the self-assessed performance between the two entry modes ($z' = -1.413$, $p = .158$). All the responses were in the upper part of the Likert scale from 3 to 6, indicating a good overall impression with QB-Gest. A positive but non-significant correlation was found between how easy the participants found the method to use and errors ($r_s(20) = .402$, $p = .079$).

5.7   Improvement with Practice

The longitudinal performance measurements suggest that prolonged training will yield further improvements as there was no sign of the flattening as typical in longitudinal studies. It is thus likely that the observed performance is not representative of what is practically possible. For reference, we also measured the peak performance of an expert QB-Gest user in the eyes-free mode (one of the authors) who managed to input the phrase "the quick brown fox jumps over the lazy dog" 10 times at an average rate of 24.9 wpm. The mean performance observed in the user study, namely 14.1 wpm with visual feedback wpm in session 4, is by no means exceptional compared to the 50 wpm obtained with two-thumb text entry [8] with visual feedback. However, in terms of eyes-free text input, our results are better than 2.1 wpm reported for VoiceOver [4] and similar to the 11.1 wpm obtained with Graffiti with visual feedback [28] and better than the 8.34 wpm obtained with Graffiti in eyes-free mode [7].

The error rate was high in the no-visual feedback mode. This means that a practical system employing this type of text-entry needs robust error correction. Error correction is commonly employed in the text-entry domain, for instance through word-level correction of gesture input [7], full-phrase error correction [43], and word-level chording errors [44].

Users who rely on eyes-free text entry are not likely to continuously monitor and detect mistakes in the inputted text and it is thus appropriate to employ error correction techniques where the entire phrase is checked and corrected instead of individual words [43] as this gives more robustness.

6   Conclusions

We presented QB-Guest – a method for inputting text on small smartphone displays using simple Qwerty bimanual gestures. The user visualizes the Qwerty keyboard and gestures with the left or the right thumb in the direction of the desired character from the gap between D-F and J-K keys as the left and right points of origin.

A user study demonstrated that text could be input both with visual feedback at a rate of 14.1 wpm and eyes-free at a rate of 11.1 wpm during the fourth session. An expert user entered text eyes-free at 24.9 wpm.

The error rate was 9.9% for the eyes-free mode and 3.9% for the eyes-on mode during the fourth session. Participants relied little on visual hints in the eyes-free mode as only 0.4% of the inputted characters required hints during the fourth session. The results are comparable to other results obtained with gestures, but the longitudinal data suggest that higher text entry rates are possible with additional training. All participants in the eyes-on mode relied on word suggestions and during the fourth session this led to an output/input gain of 34.9%. The results also indicate that the visual guides in the eyes-on mode constrained the physical movement of the thumbs.

Text entry on smartphone virtual keyboards is visually demanding as there are small targets and no tactile feedback. QB-Gest holds potential for rapid smartphone text entry with low visual attention, for example, in situations where users are multitasking and attention is limited. As QB-Gest can be used eyes-free, it holds potential for blind users. Although the participants herein were not visually impaired, their ability to enter text eyes-free is a convincing indicator; however, further user studies involving blind users are needed.

References

1. Smith, A.L., Chaparro, B.S.: Smartphone text input method performance, usability, and preference with younger and older adults. Hum. Factors **57**(6), 1015–1028 (2015)
2. Leiva, L.A., Sahami, A., Catala, A., Henze, N., Schmidt, A.: Text entry on tiny QWERTY soft keyboards. In: Proceedings of the 33rd Annual ACM Conference on Human Factors in Computing Systems (CHI 2015), pp. 669–678. ACM, New York (2015)
3. Azenkot, S., Lee, N.B.: Exploring the use of speech input by blind people on mobile devices. In: Proceedings of the 15th International ACM SIGACCESS Conference on Computers and Accessibility (ASSETS 2013), Article 11. ACM, New York (2013)
4. Oliveira, J., Guerreiro, T., Nicolau, H., Jorge, J., Gonçalves, D.: Blind people and mobile touch-based text-entry: acknowledging the need for different flavors. In: The proceedings of the 13th International ACM SIGACCESS Conference on Computers and Accessibility (ASSETS 2011), pp. 179–186. ACM, New York (2011)
5. Azenkot, S., Bennett, C.L., Ladner, R.E.: DigiTaps: eyes-free number entry on touchscreens with minimal audio feedback. In: Proceedings of the 26th Annual ACM Symposium on User Interface Software and Technology (UIST 2013), pp. 85–90. ACM, New York (2013)
6. Goh, T., Kim, S.W.: Eyes-free text entry interface based on contact area for people with visual impairment. In: Proceedings of the Adjunct Publication of the 27th Annual ACM Symposium on User Interface Software and Technology (UIST 2014 Adjunct), pp. 69–70. ACM, New York (2014)

7. Tinwala, H., MacKenzie, I.S.: Eyes-free text entry with error correction on touchscreen mobile devices. In: Proceedings of the 6th Nordic Conference on Human-Computer Interaction: Extending Boundaries (NordiCHI 2010), pp. 511–520. ACM, New York (2010)

8. Azenkot, S., Zhai, S.: Touch behavior with different postures on soft smartphone keyboards. In: Proceedings of the 14th International Conference on Human-Computer Interaction with Mobile Devices and Services (MobileHCI 2012), pp. 251–260. ACM, New York (2012)

9. MacKenzie, I.S., Zhang, S.X.: The design and evaluation of a high-performance soft keyboard. In: Proceedings of the SIGCHI Conference on Human Factors in Computing Systems (CHI 1999), pp. 25–31. ACM, New York (1999)

10. MacKenzie, I.S.: Human-Computer Interaction: An Empirical Research Perspective. Morgan Kaufmann, Waltham (2013)

11. Zhai, S., Smith, B.A.: Alphabetically biased virtual keyboards are easier to use: layout does matter. In: CHI 2001 Extended Abstracts on Human Factors in Computing Systems (CHI EA 2001), pp. 321–322. ACM, New York (2001)

12. Bi, X., Smith, B.A., Zhai, S.: Quasi-qwerty soft keyboard optimization. In: Proceedings of the SIGCHI Conference on Human Factors in Computing Systems (CHI 2010), pp. 283–286. ACM, New York (2010)

13. Raynal, M.: KeyGlasses: semi-transparent keys on soft keyboard. In: Proceedings of the 16th International ACM SIGACCESS Conference on Computers & Accessibility (ASSETS 2014), pp. 347–349. ACM, New York (2014)

14. Kane, S.K., Jayant, C., Wobbrock, J.O., Ladner, R.E.: Freedom to roam: a study of mobile device adoption and accessibility for people with visual and motor disabilities. In: Proceedings of the 11th International ACM SIGACCESS Conference on Computers and accessibility (Assets 2009), pp. 115–122. ACM, New York (2009)

15. MacKenzie, I.S., Buxton, W.: Extending Fitts' law to two-dimensional tasks. In: Proceedings of the SIGCHI Conference on Human Factors in Computing Systems (CHI 1992), pp. 219–226. ACM, New York (1992)

16. Shi, W., Yu, C., Yi, X., Li, Z., Shi. Y.: TOAST: ten-finger eyes-free typing on touchable surfaces. Proc. ACM Interact. Mob. Wearable Ubiquitous Technol. 2(1) (2018). Article 33

17. Lu, Y., Yu, C., Yi, X., Shi, Y., Zhao, S.: BlindType: eyes-free text entry on handheld touchpad by leveraging thumb's muscle memory. Proc. ACM Interact. Mob. Wearable Ubiquitous Technol. 1(2) (2017). Article 18

18. Zhu, S., Luo, T., Bi, X., Zhai, S.: Typing on an invisible keyboard. In: Proceedings of the 2018 CHI Conference on Human Factors in Computing Systems (CHI 2018), Paper 439. ACM, New York (2018)

19. Kane, S.K., Bigham, J.P., Wobbrock, J.O.: Slide rule: making mobile touch screens accessible to blind people using multi-touch interaction techniques. In: Proceedings of the 10th International ACM SIGACCESS Conference on Computers and Accessibility (Assets 2008), pp. 73–80. ACM, New York (2008)

20. Guerreiro, J., Rodrigues, A., Montague, K., Guerreiro, T., Nicolau, H., Gonçalves, D.: TabLETS get physical: non-visual text entry on tablet devices. In: Proceedings of the 33rd Annual ACM Conference on Human Factors in Computing Systems (CHI 2015), pp. 39–42. ACM, New York (2015)

21. Ward, D.J., Blackwell, A.F., MacKay, D.J.C.: Dasher—a data entry interface using continuous gestures and language models. In: Proceedings of the 13th Annual ACM Symposium on User Interface Software and Technology (UIST 2000), pp. 129–137. ACM, New York (2000)

22. Polacek, O., Sporka, A.J., Slavik, P.: Text input for motor-impaired people. Univ. Access Inf. Soc. 16(1), 51–72 (2017)

23. Lyons, K., et al.: Twiddler typing: one-handed chording text entry for mobile phones. In: Proceedings of the SIGCHI Conference on Human Factors in Computing Systems (CHI 2004), pp. 671–678. ACM, New York (2004)
24. Sandnes, F.E.: Can spatial mnemonics accelerate the learning of text input chords? In: Proceedings of the Working Conference on Advanced Visual Interfaces (AVI 2006), pp. 245–249. ACM, New York (2006)
25. Frey, B., Rosier, K., Southern, C., Romero, M.: From texting app to braille literacy. In: CHI 2012 Extended Abstracts on Human Factors in Computing Systems (CHI EA 2012), pp. 2495–2500. ACM, New York (2012)
26. Goldberg, D., Richardson, C.: Touch-typing with a stylus. In: Proceedings of the INTERACT 1993 and CHI 1993 Conference on Human Factors in Computing Systems (CHI 1993), pp. 80–87. ACM, New York (1993)
27. Wobbrock, J.O., Myers, B.A., Aung, H.H., LoPresti, E.F.: Text entry from power wheelchairs: edgewrite for joysticks and touchpads. In: Proceedings of the 6th International ACM SIGACCESS Conference on Computers and Accessibility (Assets 2004), pp. 110–117. ACM, New York (2003)
28. Castellucci, S.J., MacKenzie, I.S.:. Graffiti vs. unistrokes: an empirical comparison. In: Proceedings of the SIGCHI Conference on Human Factors in Computing Systems (CHI 2008), pp. 305–308. ACM, New York (2008)
29. Wobbrock, J.O., Myers, B.A., Kembel, J.A.: EdgeWrite: a stylus-based text entry method designed for high accuracy and stability of motion. In: Proceedings of the 16th Annual ACM Symposium on User Interface Software and Technology (UIST 2003), pp. 61–70. ACM, New York (2003)
30. Sandnes, F.E., Tan, T.B., Johansen, A., Sulic, E., Vesterhus, E., Iversen, E.R.: Making touch-based kiosks accessible to blind users through simple gestures. Univ. Access Inf. Soc. 11(4), 421–431 (2012)
31. Chen, X., Grossman, T., Fitzmaurice, G.: Swipeboard: a text entry technique for ultra-small interfaces that supports novice to expert transitions. In: Proceedings of the 27th Annual ACM Symposium on User Interface Software and Technology, pp. 615–620. ACM (2014)
32. Bi, X., Chelba, C., Ouyang, T., Partridge, K., Zhai, S.: Bimanual gesture keyboard. In: Proceedings of the 25th Annual ACM Symposium on User Interface Software and Technology (UIST 2012), pp. 137–146. ACM, New York (2012)
33. Lai, J., Zhang, D., Wang, S., Kilic, I.L., Zhou, L.: A thumb stroke-based virtual keyboard for sight-free text entry on touch-screen mobile phones. In: Hawaii International Conference on System Sciences (2018)
34. Banovic, N., Yatani, K., Truong, K.N.: Escape-keyboard: a sight-free one-handed text entry method for mobile touch-screen devices. Int. J. Mob. Hum. Comput. Interact. 5(3), 42–61 (2013)
35. Armstrong, P., Wilkinson. B.: Text entry of physical and virtual keyboards on tablets and the user perception. In: Proceedings of the 28th Australian Conference on Computer-Human Interaction (OzCHI 2016), pp. 401–405. ACM, New York (2016)
36. Sandnes, F.E., Aubert, A.: Bimanual text entry using game controllers: relying on users' spatial familiarity with QWERTY. Interact. Comput. 19(2), 140–150 (2007)
37. Fredkin, E.: Trie memory. Commun. ACM 3(9), 490–499 (1960)
38. MacKenzie, I.S.: KSPC (keystrokes per character) as a characteristic of text entry techniques. In: Paternò, F. (ed.) Mobile HCI 2002. LNCS, vol. 2411, pp. 195–210. Springer, Heidelberg (2002). https://doi.org/10.1007/3-540-45756-9_16

39. Matias, E., MacKenzie, I.S., Buxton, W.: Half-QWERTY: typing with one hand using your two-handed skills. In: Plaisant, C. (ed.) Conference Companion on Human Factors in Computing Systems (CHI 1994), pp. 51–52. ACM, New York (1994)
40. MacKenzie, I.S., Soukoreff, R.W.: Phrase sets for evaluating text entry techniques. In: CHI 2003 Extended Abstracts on Human Factors in Computing Systems (CHI EA 2003), pp. 754–755. ACM, New York (2003)
41. MacKenzie, I.S., Soukoreff. R.W.: A character-level error analysis technique for evaluating text entry methods. In: Proceedings of the Second Nordic Conference on Human-computer Interaction (NordiCHI 2002), pp. 243–246. ACM, New York (2002)
42. Kurtenbach, G., Buxton, W.: User learning and performance with marking menus. In: Proceedings of the SIGCHI Conference on Human Factors in Computing Systems (CHI 1994), pp. 258–264. ACM, New York (1994)
43. MacKenzie, I.S., Castellucci, S.: Reducing visual demand for gestural text input on touchscreen devices. In: CHI 2012 Extended Abstracts on Human Factors in Computing Systems (CHI EA 2012), pp. 2585–2590. ACM, New York (2012)
44. Sandnes, F.E., Huang, Y.-P.: Chording with spatial mnemonics: automatic error correction for eyes-free text entry. J. Inf. Sci. Eng. 22(5), 1015–1031 (2006)
45. Wobbrock, J.O., Findlater, L., Gergle, D., Higgins, J.J.: The aligned rank transform for nonparametric factorial analyses using only anova procedures. In: Proceedings of the SIGCHI Conference on Human Factors in Computing Systems (CHI 2011), pp. 143–146. ACM, New York (2011)
46. Bonner, M.N., Brudvik, J.T., Abowd, Gregory D., Edwards, W.K.: No-look notes: accessible eyes-free multi-touch text entry. In: Floréen, P., Krüger, A., Spasojevic, M. (eds.) Pervasive 2010. LNCS, vol. 6030, pp. 409–426. Springer, Heidelberg (2010). https://doi.org/10.1007/978-3-642-12654-3_24

Web Accessibility

Exploring WAI-Aria Techniques to Enhance Screen Reader Interaction: The Case of a Portal for Rating Accessibility of Cultural Heritage Sites

Marina Buzzi[1], Barbara Leporini[2(✉)], and Francesca Romano[2]

[1] IIT-CNR, via Moruzzi, 1, 56124 Pisa, Italy
marina.buzzi@iit.cnr.it
[2] ISTI-CNR, via Moruzzi, 1, 56124 Pisa, Italy
barbara.leporini@isti.cnr.it, fq.romano@gmail.com

Abstract. Cultural heritage sites (museums, archaeological parks, exhibition spaces, etc.) do not always guarantee accessibility to all users, regardless of their abilities. Often services are not really as usable and functional as expected. Currently there is no website offering accessibility information on heritage sites in a format accessible to all. People with disability or their caregivers are forced to spend considerable time and effort to obtain accessibility information, sometimes encountering difficulties. The Axem portal aims to fill this gap by offering information on the degree of accessibility of cultural sites (museums, archaeological parks, libraries, art galleries, places of worship, exhibition spaces, etc.). It has been designed as a facility for people with disabilities and in general for all individuals who have special needs and require specific services. In this paper the Axem web site is presented as a case study to (1) investigate the use of web techniques for enhancing screen reading interaction, and (2) propose a portal to collect information on accessible services supported by the cultural sites. Regarding web accessibility, the use of WAI ARIA, an accessible web design, is discussed in order to improve screen reading interaction. Accessibility functions and features as well as the ranking algorithm for easy search and the rating mechanism are presented. This work offers a further contribution to the web accessibility field, while proposing a portal which could be exploited by cultural heritage sites and promote their accessible services to people with disability.

Keywords: Accessibility · WAI-ARIA · Screen reader · Cultural heritage sites

1 Introduction

Accessibility is crucial for guaranteeing fair opportunities to all regardless of one's ability, at school, work and cultural and social life. About 15% of the world's population lives with some form of disability [1]. This data shows the urgent need to close the access gap worldwide.

In recent years, many researchers have focused on the accessibility of cultural heritage sites. Technology has recently greatly enhanced accessibility for people with

© Springer Nature Switzerland AG 2020
M. Antona and C. Stephanidis (Eds.): HCII 2020, LNCS 12188, pp. 245–260, 2020.
https://doi.org/10.1007/978-3-030-49282-3_17

disability. Digitization, 3D printing and sensors offer visitors an augmented environ-ment enhancing their perception with an audio-tactile experience [2]. In the last decade, information related to artifacts in museum collections has been increasingly made available to visitors using mobile guides or smartphones via wireless networks, exploiting RFID technology [3, 4], or beacons [5]. In addition, 3-D printing enables blind people as well as children, to explore artifact copies that can be touched and handled [6], offering a multisensory experience that enables learning by experience [7]. However, little attention has been devoted to personalizing user experience according to different user abilities when exploring digital resources [8], nor to making accessi-bility information of cultural sites truly accessible to people with disabilities.

Cultural heritage sites (museums, archaeological parks, libraries, art galleries, places of worship, exhibition spaces, etc.) do not always guarantee accessibility to all users, regardless of their abilities. Often services are not as usable and functional as expected. Currently no web website offers accessibility information on heritage sites in a format accessible to all. People with disability or their caregivers are forced to spend much time and effort to obtain accessibility information, sometimes encountering difficulties.

The Axem website aims to bridge this gap by offering information on the degree of accessibility of Italian cultural sites (museums, archaeological parks, libraries, art galleries, places of worship, exhibition spaces, etc.). It would be an accessible website that delivers information on accessible services of Italian cultural heritage sites.

This paper illustrates the design model driving the creation of the Axem website, its services, accessibility functions and features, the ranking algorithm for easy search and the rating mechanism. Both benefits and limitations will be discussed. Since benefits for people with disability are obvious in terms of saving time and increasing the enjoyment of a cultural site experience, and are factors that can help orient their visit, the limits merit a brief discussion. The major limit in the spread of the Axem website is persuading managers of cultural heritage sites to provide the metadata related to their accessibility services. Axem aims to offer an environment for promoting an interactive community on accessibility topics.

In this study, the Axem case study is exploited to investigate WAI-Aria techniques used to enhance screen reader interaction. In previous works, WAI-Aria attributes and roles have applied to enhancing screen reader interaction with Google Docs [9] and Wikipedia editing [10]. Herein, a further study is presented to explore other attributes in the web page design.

In short, this work offers a further contribution to the web accessibility field, while proposing a portal that could be used by cultural heritage sites to promote accessible services and functions to people with disability.

This paper is organized into six sections. Section 2 introduces the related work, and Sect. 3 describes the method driving this study. In Sect. 4 the Axem website is described highlighting new aspects introduced in its design concept, while in Sect. 5 its most relevant features are discussed in detail. Conclusions and future work end the paper.

2   Related Work

Information and Communication Technologies (ICTs) can greatly enhance the museum experience [11]. Technology can actually enhance user interaction and stimulate learning in the museum by eliciting emotions, inspiring people and provoking curiosity with the aim of promoting knowledge among users with different backgrounds, interests, and skills [12]. Due to people's diversity and preferences, it is important to deliver a personalized experience in order to increase the possibility of actively involving users [13]. However, the creation of accessible cultural experiences requires a systematic approach, and the possibility of offering equal access to cultural heritage for persons with disabilities is unfortunately still not mature [14].

Kabassi carried out an accurate literature review by analyzing the state of the art of museum websites. In fact, if not appropriately designed to guarantee access for all, technology may create obstacles and make interaction difficult, causing museums to lose visitors [15]. Considerable research focuses on how to create accessible and usable information for online museums and evaluation of museum websites. Website evaluation frameworks have been proposed by a number of researchers such as those who proposed 35 criteria for museum websites, grouped into six categories: Content, Presentation, Usability, Interactivity & Feedback, e-Services, and Technical, designed for driving experts in implementing inspection evaluation MuseumQual [16].

Museums usually provide visitors with brochures or audio guides. Visits to museums are sometimes boring since it is difficult for museum curators to catch the attention of all visitors and define in advance a tour for all, since interests vary from person to person according to age and interests [17]. Interactive and personalized museum tours can be developed by exploiting the Internet of Things (IoT). The system proposed by the authors can enhance the user experience by delivering not only artwork details such as title, artist, date, but also details of scenes in large paintings aimed at individual visitors or through multimedia walls in the room for a group. The user can store his/her spontaneous feelings and share this cultural experience on social networks. Such an augmented reality application can make the visitor experience more accessible to everyone. The user is equipped with a wearable device, which captures images, able to trigger location-aware services.

One most appealing technology exploited in museums is Virtual Reality (VR). "VR relies on technologies (such as computer science, 3D graphics, robotics, etc.) to create a digital environment in which users feel completely immersed, and with which they can interact" [18].

Besides web accessibility, an increasing number of museums are building accessible services for visitors. For instance, for the blind a number of solutions have been implemented in order to make collections accessible by combining tactile exploration, audio descriptions and mobile gestures [19]. However, one problem is the scalability of these solutions; for instance 3-D printing is still expensive depending on the materials selected and it is difficult to maintain high definition when reproducing large and complex artifacts (on a smaller scale).

Descriptions of items can be provided in Braille (although vocal description maybe more comfortable and rapid when moving around a museum), and AAC (Alternative and Augmentative Communication) is useful for describing artifacts in an accessible way for people with autism, while large readable fonts might facilitate reading not only for visitors with dyslexia, but also for old people and children.

Are all these services really accessible for anyone? Physical and technical barriers can negatively impact on visitors with special needs. People with disability need to look for information when visiting a cultural site, to enjoy their cultural experience. This is time-consuming and can be difficult for a person with an impairment. Autonomy is very important for anyone and crucial for people with disability who are dependent on help of caregivers.

Italy is very rich in cultural heritage sites, offering a vast number of public and private collections. Thus it is important to have a point where services are recorded and can be easily explored.

The Axem website would collect this information to benefit persons with disability and spread the culture of accessibility. In the following, features characterizing this website as well as innovative design items are described in detail.

3 Method

The website has been developed using WordPress, a very popular Content Management System. Accessibility was taken into account from the website's earliest design phases. First of all, the accessibility of the templates made available by WordPress were evaluated. Thus, some templates were first selected according to the layout typology preferred for the Axem website. Next, they were modified to obtain a more accessible and usable layout via screen reader. More specifically, to resolve some accessibility issues encountered while interacting via screen reader, several changes were needed.

Accessibility was taken into account when designing the website. Accessibility requirements by WCAG 2.1 [20] were applied. Despite meeting accessibility requirements, some interaction problems via the screen reader were still encountered. For this reason, some changes to the templates, as well as the WAI-ARIA technology [21] application were necessary to improve interpretation and navigation through screen readers.

More specifically, in WordPress only one standard template and three plugins were installed: Loco Translate[1] (translation editor, https://it.wordpress.org/plugins/loco-translate/), Ajax Search Lite[2] (is a responsive live search engine, which improves the user experience exploiting Ajax calls, https://it.wordpress.org/plugins/ajax-search-lite/) that replaces the default WordPress search engine; PODS[3] Plugin to create and manage personalized content (custom post types, custom taxonomies and advanced content types, https://it.wordpress.org/plugins/pods/). Then three taxonomies ("Places", "Services", "Categories") and two custom post types ("Cultural Places" and "Ratings") were created in the website.

The necessary changes were coded via PHP functions which had been integrated with those provided by the CMS (WordPress). Doing this, the types of posts (pages and articles) available in the CMS had been extended so as to have specific pages for the website (data forms and rating system). The result was to offer website features that can be interacted with by the end-user (e.g., the person editing the pages to insert cultural site data) via a graphical interface.

Web Content Accessibility Guidelines (WCAG) and WAI-ARIA (Web Accessibility Initiative - Accessible Rich Internet Applications) functions were applied to simplify the interaction of people using screen readers or having cognitive difficulties.

The intent was to experiment WAI-ARIA to improve the user interface experience, in order to make navigation via screen reader simpler and more effective while keeping the user interface pleasant and graphically appealing.

4   The Axem Website Prototype

The Axem website has been designed as a supporting tool for people with disabilities or temporary limitations, and in general for all individuals who have special needs and need specific services. It is intended to be an information point which connects users with disabilities to facilities, in order to improve the quality and the spread of information about accessible services related to cultural heritage sites. This should encourage cultural centers to become more accessible (through the incentive of an accessibility rate).

For each cultural site, AXEM website is therefore designed to collect information about the services offered for each specific disability. For instance, a museum offers braille labels for blind visitors, but does not have writings suitable for people who require communication via AAC (Augmentative and Alternative Communication). Also, another museum might offer video guides for hearing-impaired people but lacks an interactive audio guide for those with a vision impairment. In short, any site should include this type of information in their forms to add to the website. Thus, when retrieving the desired information the user can obtain the results according to the type of disability selected in the search form.

4.1   Novel Aspects

Axem is a centralized digital gateway for gathering data about the accessibility of cultural heritage sites. The new aspects considered when designing the AXEM website are related to (1) functionalities offered to the user when getting information, and (2) features to enhance the screen reader user interaction with the user interfaces (UIs). In designing the Axem pages, several techniques to improve screen reading interaction have been used and tested.

First, innovative functional aspects of the Axem website include:

- A search procedure based on filters for enabling search according to user preferences – for instance, the possibility of selecting and retrieving those cultural sites offering a specific accessible service, or located in a geographic area.
- A Review system combined with accessibility aspects.
- A combined algorithm for ranking score processing based on the level of accessibility.

Secondly, regarding screen reading interaction with the user interfaces, the new design aspects include:

- Visual flow differing from what is perceived via screen reader in order to get a more accessible and pleasant visual layout. This feature has been tested for the "about" page and the search results.
- Aural feedback to improve the user experience; this functionality has been applied to the success/failure for the search results as well as when selecting the review score.

5 AXEM Development

5.1 Search Interface

The main function of the Axem website is the search, and so this was designed with particular attention (developing a sophisticated algorithm). Figure 1 shows the Search page. The user can access the search by scrolling the home page or clicking the item "Search" on top menu.

The interface is simple and minimal in order to make interaction easy and efficient for all, including via screen reader and keyboard. It displays two buttons in order to offer two different search modalities:

(a) free "Search", i.e., a text box to edit the cultural heritage place for which accessibility services are desired;
(b) "Search with Filters", which is composed of a three-item drop-down menu (Category, Region, and City) and four checkboxes for selecting disability type (intellective, motor, hearing and visual disabilities) as shown in Fig. 2.

5.2 Accessibility Score

Each cultural heritage site has an accessibility score assigned by an algorithm designed to not penalize sites that for any reason have no accessibility services. The rating reflects the actual quality of the available services, since the evaluation is performed for each service and not globally, as shown below (Fig. 3 and Fig. 4).

The overall rating is the overall mean generated by the arithmetic mean of the scores associated with each service for a specific disability (from 0 to 4). Those scores are defined by the ratings proposed by the users.

The rating system accepts the score and comments related to a single disability per time. This feature differentiates the Axem website from those allowed by other rating systems: to improve accuracy, the scores are based on the user experience of each single service. There is no overall evaluation of the visit.

The review for a cultural site can also comprise more comments to evaluate more services of a disability area.

To this aim, the search form is composed of a title and a checkbox showing the available services by disability category. For any selected category, a score field and a text box are shown by the interface for inserting data.

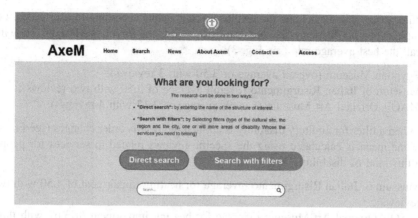

Fig. 1. The search page. Search by name (direct search) or search by filters

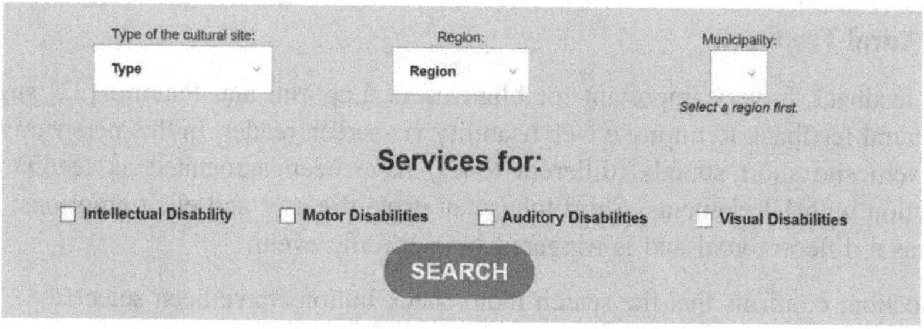

Fig. 2. The search page: search by filters

5.3 Results and Ranking

The "Direct Search" returns the accessibility data related to the target cultural site the user was looking for, while the search with filters produces multiple results, which are ordered with a conditional control on two parameters, arranged then in a decreasing order.

The algorithm acts in this way:

- if a generic search is performed (i.e., no one disability category is selected), results are ordered on the arithmetic mean (scores associated to all disability services offered by the structure);
- if one or more disabilities are selected, results are ordered based on the mean of the relative mean (i.e., the mean of the mean score associated to the selected disabilities).

In practice, this means that the results ranking adapts according to user needs. For example, when no filters are selected, the first result is the Egyptian Museum, showing overall the best average rate (see Fig. 3):

1. Egyptian Museum (overall average of 3.50 with 3 reviews);
2. Museum of Italian Risorgimento (overall average of 3.50 with two reviews);
3. MAO - Oriental Art Museum (overall average of 3.17 with 4 reviews).

When a filter for auditory disability is applied the results order changes (see Fig. 4) since the mean is calculated using the specific reviews related to services for people with this kind of disability:

1. Museum of Italian Risorgimento (average for hearing impairment of 4.50 with two reviews);
2. MAO - Oriental Art Museum (average for hearing impairment of 3.67 with three reviews);
3. Egyptian museum (average for hearing impairment of 2.50 with two reviews).

5.4   Aural Feedback

Aural feedback is very important for blind users. Leporini and Paternò [22] suggest using aural feedback to improve web usability via screen reader. In this perspective, in the Axem site short sounds (different tones) have been associated as feedback of interaction with UI elements. Short tones can drive the user and elicit emotions; each tone has a different goal and is triggered by a specific event:

- selection: confirms that the search radio/check buttons have been selected;
- search: confirms the search is started;
- rating: provides immediate feedback to the user (via an increasing and decreasing tone according to the level of score) while selecting the radio buttons related to the different scores and thus confirms review upload. Specifically, different tones for delivering the number of stars selected for the review: ascending tone for 5 stars, descending tone for 1 star, increasing incrementally adding stars.

5.5   Enhancing Reading Flow via Screen Reader

The most important target of Axem is accessibility. To make the site accessible via screen reader, html native features to provide basic semantic information and WAI-ARIA attributes have been exploited. Specifically, "aria-live", for live regions (areas that dynamically change client-side) and "aria-labelledby", to link objects to their labels assuring the correctness of the announced content have been used. We considered these features while designing the Axem pages. The "About Axem" page is an example (Fig. 5).

Active filters

No filters selected ..

37 results

1) Egyptian Museum

Location: Torino (Piedmont)

Type: Museum

Description:
The Egyptian Museum of Turin is the oldest museum in the world, entirely dedicated to the Nileticcivilization and is Considered, for the value and quantity of the exhibits, the most important in the world after the one in Cairo.

Motor Disabilities

Ramps

Auditory Disabilities

Language Descriptions of the signs

Visual Disabilities

Audio guides | Descriptions works or information materials in Braille | Embossed Guide

Go to the site

Accessibility
(3 reviews)

2) The National Museum of the Italian Risorgimento

Location: Torino (Piedmont)

Type: Museum

Description:
The National Museum of the Italian Risorgimento is the largest exhibition space of Italian national history,the oldest and most important museum dedicated to the Italian Risorgimento Because of the richness and representativeness of its collections and the only One That officially has the title of "national". Founded in 1878, it is located in Turin inside the historic Palazzo Carignano.

Intellectual Disability

Easy reading | Paths for People with Intellectual Disabilities

Auditory Disabilities

Language Descriptions of the signs | Opera written descriptions

Visual Disabilities

Audio guides | embossed Guide | Tactile paths

Go to the site

Accessibility
(2 reviews)

3) MAO - Museum of Oriental Art

Location: Torino (Piedmont)

Type: Museum

Description:
The MAO - Museum of Oriental Art is one of the most recent museums in Turin. Located right in the center, it is housed in the historic Palazzo Mazzonis and houses one of the most interesting Asian art collections in Italy.

Intellectual Disability

Paths for People with Intellectual Disabilities

Motor Disabilities

Elevators | Ramps | Services and tools suited to height

Auditory Disabilities

Interpreter LIS | Video with subtitles

Visual Disabilities

Descriptions works or information materials in Braille

Go to the site

Accessibility
(4 reviews)

Fig. 3. Search without filters

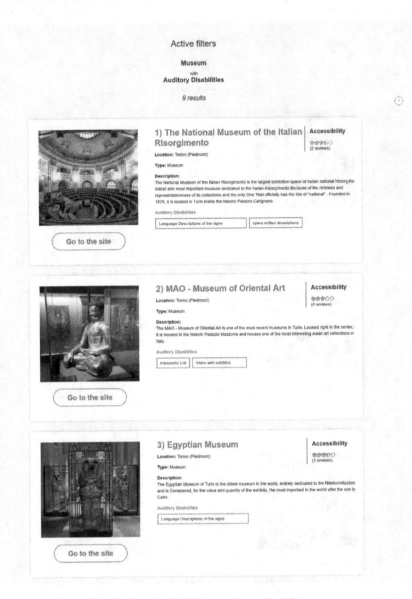

Fig. 4. Search with filters: auditory disability

Fig. 5. The 'About Axem' page

The "About Axem" page is structured with two containers: a list on the right side and a text area on the left showing dynamically the content associated to the link selected from the items in the right list. So, visually the current text is shown on the left, while the list of possible choices is on the right. When designing such a structure, the screen reader announces first the current content, and next the right list. In this way, a blind user reads the content beforehand and only afterward the list of all the possible choices to select.

This organization is very functional visually but was disorienting when reading the page via screen reader, which announces sequentially content by first detecting the text on the left and next the menu list on the right. In this way, the user is unable to perceive the appropriate content uploaded according to the user selection on the left. The right logical order to be perceived should be (1) the list of items, and (2) the main content uploaded according to the item selected from the list. To fix this problem the <div> elements have been inverted in the order to assure the correct sequence of the reading via screen reader, while the graphical appearance was arranged in the CSS using "float left" and "float right" attributes.

The text appears/disappears thanks to a Java Script function associated with the paragraph id that modifies the "display" element ("block" or "none" values) and links the focus() method to the document object related to the id of the associated text. With "focus" it's possible to move the cursor (focus) on a Web page element. The text section is a live region. In this way, the screen reader user is able to suitably perceive all the dynamically updated content, while the sighted one can see the same nice layout, as no change was made. The Fig. 6 shows a portion read by the screen reader in the correct order. The words in italics announced by the screen reader to provide information on the user interface. Also, to facilitate the movement via keyboard, an "accesskey" has been associated with the list. This attribute creates a shortcut for accessing the target item quickly (accesskey = "x" tabindex = "0").

Figure 7 shows portions of code of the axemscript.js and about.php files. Figure 8 reports a portion of the CSS file.

Main region
Questions and answers
Link What is AxeM?
Link How research works
Link Evaluation of the accessibility of a place of culture
Link How are contents updated?
Link The purpose of the project and expectations
Link Guidelines

Heading level 1 What is AxeM?
AxeM is a web portal that provides information on the level of accessibility of cultural sites such as state archives, libraries, ...
...
Main region end

Fig. 6. Portion read by the screen reader

```
file axemscript.js
...
function visualizza(id){
switch (id) {
  case 'testo_scomparsa1':
  document.getElementById('testo_scomparsa1').style.display = 'block';
  document.getElementById('testo_scomparsa2').style.display = 'none';
  document.getElementById('testo_scomparsa3').style.display = 'none';
  document.getElementById('testo_scomparsa4').style.display = 'none';
  document.getElementById('testo_scomparsa5').style.display = 'none';
  document.getElementById('testo_scomparsa6').style.display = 'none';
  document.getElementById('titolo1_content_about').focus();
break;
  case 'testo_scomparsa2': [...] // (repeat for each pop-up section)


file About.php
<main role="main" class="pagina-about pagina-faq">
<div style="width: 100%; height:200px; display: block; background:url('<?php
echo get_site_url(); ?>/wp-content/uploads/2019/03/Collage.jpg'); background-
repeat:no-repeat; background-size:cover; background-position: center;"></div>
 <div class="row content_single_luogo_cultura">
 <div class="col-md-12">
 <div class="row">
<!—column 2-->
 <div class="menu_about col-md-5 order-md-12" role="menu" accesskey="x"
tabindex="0" accesskey="q">
<?php echo '<h1 id="titolo_menu_faq" class="titoli_verdi">' ._(' Questions and
answers
', 'axem') . '</h1>'; ?>
<ul id="menu_about">
 <li aria-label="uno" role="menuitem"><a href="#titolo1_content_about"
onclick="visualizza('testo_scomparsa1');"> What AxeM?</a></li>
 <li aria-label="due" role="menuitem"><a href="#titolo2_content_about"
onclick="visualizza('testo_scomparsa2');"> How does the search</a></li>
 <li aria-label="tre" role="menuitem"><a href="#titolo3_content_about"
onclick="visualizza('testo_scomparsa3');"> Accessibility Evaluation of a place of
culture</a></li>
[...] // (repeat for each title)
 <li aria-label="sei" role="menuitem"><a href="#titolo6_content_about"
onclick="visualizza('testo_scomparsa6');"> Guidelines</a></li>
</ul>
</div>
<!—column 1 -->
 <div class="content_about_testo col-md-7 order-md-1">
 <div  aria-live="assertive"  id="testo_scomparsa1"  style="display: block;  text-
```

Fig. 7. Java Script and WAI-Aria code portions

```
align: justify;">
 <h1  tabindex="-1"  class="titolo_content_about"  id="titolo1_content_about"  >
What AxeM?</h1>
<p> [...] </p>
<div  aria-labelledby="titolo_menu_faq"><img  style="width:  5px;"  src ="<?php
echo get_site_url(); ?> /wp-content/uploads/2019/04/bianco.png "/>
</div>
</div>
...
```

Fig. 7. (*continued*)

```
#content_about {
    max-width: 1440px;
    margin: 0 auto;
    min-height: unset;
    padding: 60px 0;
}
.content_about_testo {
    float: left!important;
}
.menu_about {
    float: right!important;
}
...
```

Fig. 8. Portion of CSS file

6   Conclusions and Future Work

The Axem website has been designed as a supporting tool for people with disabilities or temporary limitations and in general for all individuals who have special needs and need specific services. It is intended to be an information point, which connects users with disabilities to facilities, in order to improve the quality and the spread of information about accessible services related to cultural heritage sites. This should encourage cultural places to become more accessible (through the incentive of an accessibility rate). In this context, users' reviews and ranking are a crucial functionality available in the Axem portal.

Currently, the Axem site structure is complete with its main components and functions. The portal is ready to be populated and tested by curators of places of culture and to be optimized, thanks to the users' feedback. Concerning the user interface, the WAI-Aria attributes used to enhance screen reader interaction resulted in a suitable solution to be considered when developing accessible web pages and layout. In particular, the two attributes "aria-live" and "aria-labelledby" combined with the property "float left" are useful to design a pleasant graphical interface, while maintaining a logical sequence in reading via assistive technology.

The model used to design the Axem site could also be applied to other domains, such as in the educational context, in which accessibility and usability principles can improve the user experience and make the learning process simpler for people with disability.

Future work will include the development of additional features to support the users in searching and obtaining details and information of the services offered by the cultural site, creating a link with other people in the community, designing public and private communication features, and so on. Furthermore, other WAI-Aria attributes will be explored to investigate additional accessibility features.

References

1. WHO 2019: World Health Organization. Report on disability. https://www.who.int/disabilities/world_report/2011/report/en/. Accessed 10 Oct 2019
2. D'Agnano, F., Balletti, C., Guerra, F., Vernier, P.: Tooteko: a case study of augmented reality for an accessible cultural heritage. Digitization, 3D printing and sensors for an audio-tactile experience. Int. Arch. Photogramm. Remote Sens. Spat. Inf. Sci. **40**(5), 207 (2015)
3. Karimi, R., Nanopoulos, A., Schmidt-Thieme, L.: RFID-enhanced museum for interactive experience. In: Grana, C., Cucchiara, R. (eds.) MM4CH 2011. CCIS, vol. 247, pp. 192–205. Springer, Heidelberg (2012). https://doi.org/10.1007/978-3-642-27978-2_17
4. Ghiani, G., Leporini, B., Paterno, F.: Supporting orientation for blind people using museum guides. In: CHI 2008 Extended Abstracts (2008)
5. Asakawa, S., et al.: An independent and interactive museum experience for blind people. In: Proceedings of the 16th Web For All 2019 Personalization-Personalizing the Web, p. 30. ACM (May 2019)
6. Rossetti, V., Furfari, F., Leporini, B., Pelagatti, S., Quarta, A.: Enabling Access to cultural heritage for the visually impaired: an interactive 3D model of a cultural site. Procedia Comput. Sci. **130**, 383–391 (2018)
7. Dindler, C., Iversen, O.S., Smith, R., Veerasawmy, R.: Participatory design at the museum: inquiring into children's everyday engagement in cultural heritage. In: Proceedings of the 22nd Conference of the Computer-Human Interaction Special Interest Group of Australia (OZCHI 2010), pp. 72–79. ACM, New York (2010)
8. Buzzi, M.C., Buzzi, M., Leporini, B., Marchesini, G.: Improving user experience in the museum. In: Proceedings of the IADIS—Interfaces and Human Computer Interaction, pp. 327–331 (2013)
9. Buzzi, M.C., Buzzi, M., Leporini, B., Mori, G., Penichet, V.M.R.: Accessing Google docs via screen reader. In: Miesenberger, K., Klaus, J., Zagler, W., Karshmer, A. (eds.) ICCHP 2010. LNCS, vol. 6179, pp. 92–99. Springer, Heidelberg (2010). https://doi.org/10.1007/978-3-642-14097-6_17

10. Buzzi, M., Leporini, B.: Editing Wikipedia content by screen reader: easier interaction with the Accessible Rich Internet Applications suite. Disabil. Rehabil.: Assist. Technol. **4**(4), 264–275 (2009)
11. Chiang, H.H., Tsaih, R.H., Han, T.S.: Measurement development of service quality for museum websites displaying artifacts. In: Managing Innovation and Cultural Management in the Digital Era, pp. 100–127. Routledge (2016)
12. Falk, J.H., Dierking, L.D.: Learning from Museums. Rowman & Littlefield, Lanham (2018)
13. Bohnert, F., Zukerman, I.: Non-intrusive personalisation of the museum experience. In: Houben, G.-J., McCalla, G., Pianesi, F., Zancanaro, M. (eds.) UMAP 2009. LNCS, vol. 5535, pp. 197–209. Springer, Heidelberg (2009). https://doi.org/10.1007/978-3-642-02247-0_20
14. Partarakis, N., Klironomos, I., Antona, M., Margetis, G., Grammenos, D., Stephanidis, C.: Accessibility of cultural heritage exhibits. In: Antona, M., Stephanidis, C. (eds.) UAHCI 2016. LNCS, vol. 9738, pp. 444–455. Springer, Cham (2016). https://doi.org/10.1007/978-3-319-40244-4_43
15. Kabassi, K.: Evaluating websites of museums: state of the art. J. Cult. Herit. **24**, 184–196 (2017)
16. Fotakis, T., Economides, A.A.: Art, science/technology and history museums on the web. Int. J. Digit. Cult. Electron. Tour. **1**(1), 37–63 (2008)
17. Alletto, S., et al.: An indoor location-aware system for an IoT-based smart museum. IEEE Internet Things J. **3**(2), 244–253 (2015)
18. Carrozzino, M., Bergamasco, M.: Beyond virtual museums: experiencing immersive virtual reality in real museums. J. Cult. Herit. **11**(4), 452–458 (2010)
19. Anagnostakis, G., et al.: Accessible museum collections for the visually impaired: combining tactile exploration, audio descriptions and mobile gestures. In: Proceedings of the 18th International Conference on Human-Computer Interaction with Mobile Devices and Services Adjunct, pp. 1021–1025. ACM (September 2016)
20. W3C: WCAG 2.1 1.1. https://www.w3.org/TR/WCAG21/
21. W3C: WAI-ARIA 1.1. https://www.w3.org/TR/graphics-aria-1.0/#bib-wai-aria-1.1
22. Leporini, B., Paternò, F.: Applying web usability criteria for vision-impaired users: does it really improve task performance? Int. J. Hum.-Comput. Interact. **24**(1), 17–47 (2008)

Impact of Sentence Length on the Readability of Web for Screen Reader Users

Bam Bahadur Kadayat and Evelyn Eika[(✉)]

Faculty of Technology, Art and Design, Oslo Metropolitan University,
Oslo, Norway
{S310223, evelyn.eika}@oslomet.no

Abstract. Readability of text is generally believed to be connected to sentence length. Most studies on readability are based on visual reading. Less is known about text readability for users relying on screen readers, such as users who are blind. This study therefore set out to investigate the effect of sentence length on the readability of web texts accessed using screen readers. A controlled within-subjects experiment was performed with twenty-one participants. Participants used a screen reader to read five texts with different sentence lengths. The participants' comprehension and perceived workload were measured. The findings reveal that there is a significant effect of sentence length and most participants exhibit the highest comprehension and lowest workload with sentences comprising 16–20 words. Implications of these results are that web content providers should strive for sentence length of 16–20 words to maximize readability.

Keywords: Readability · Workload · Sentence length · Screen reader · Blind · Accessibility · Universal design

1 Introduction

Readability is the measure of ease or difficulty with which the text can be read and understood by an intended reader who is reading for a specific purpose [1]. Readability is affected by several factors such as content, structure, readers' knowledge, vocabulary, layout, and design [2]. It can be challenging to read web content using screen reader software. Screen reader users also have difficulties re-tracking the reading content as software does not read it back. Users may not recall what they read, which leads to comprehension difficulties. This study investigates web readability for screen reader users, in particular, the factor of sentence length: its impact and its appropriate length.

2 Background

Most studies indicated that sentence length affects the readability where long sentences are harder to read than shorter sentences [3–5]. Shorter sentences, however, do not necessarily improve readability because of other factors such as vocabulary and

© Springer Nature Switzerland AG 2020
M. Antona and C. Stephanidis (Eds.): HCII 2020, LNCS 12188, pp. 261–271, 2020.
https://doi.org/10.1007/978-3-030-49282-3_18

coherence. Word difficulty is another factor that is commonly mentioned. A sentence with difficult words is harder to read compared to one without. The sentence and the word length are the two attributes that are used in readability measures [3] such as the Flesch-Kincaid reading ease index. This popular readability measure is designed to quantify how difficult it is to comprehend a reading passage. The score ranges between 0 and 100, where a high score indicates easy to read and low score hard to read [6]. However, such readability measures tend to be over simplistic and are mostly used for printed text [3]. Also, text on web is read differently compared to printed text [7].

2.1 Screen Reader Users and the Web

About 45 million blind people worldwide access websites using screen reader technology [8]. Text is a significant part of the web and reading through web applications is an especially challenging task for blind users. An accessible and readable web content thus allows blind users to access and understand its information. Also, web developers and designers were often unaware about the impact of non-visual web content for blind users hindering accessibility of Websites [8]. WCAG 2.0 offers a broad set of recommendations for making the web content accessible and readable [9].

2.2 Readability on the Web

Gottron and Martin [10] employed content extraction algorithms to determine the readability of web documents. They analyzed 1114 documents from five websites and compared quantitative readability measures along with their adjusted content filters (i.e., the adapted content code blurring and document slope curves algorithms). They showed that embedding adjusted content extractions for SMOG and Flesch Reading Ease indexes yielded more accurate readability estimates. The results support a solution where corpus statistics is employed on the web to achieve language-independent measures of readability.

de Heus and Hiemstra [11] used the Automated Readability Index (ARI) to determine the mean grade level needed to understand a website. They used MapReduce for real-time calculation of the readability of more than a billion webpages. The datasets called *Common Crawl* included 61 million domain-names, 92 million PDF documents, and seven million Word documents. About 60% of the information originated from commercial, organization, and network websites. The cumulative results showed that 12-year-olds, 23-year-olds, and 18-year-olds can comfortably comprehend 25%, 75%, and 50% of the content on web, respectively.

Chung, Min, Kim, and Park [12] investigated the readability of text-based web documents for deaf people. They proposed a newscasting display technique which converted difficult sentences into easy sentences and indicated the relationship with the help of visual illustration. They developed a system consisting of a graphical representation module and a structural simplification module to visualize the relationships between simple fragmented sentences. However, the system was found not easy to use for low literacy deaf people.

2.3   Readability for Blind Users

Guerreiro and Goncalves [13] investigated whether increasing speech rates affected content scanning with concurrent speech. They recruited 30 visually impaired participants and focused on relevance scanning from two-hundred Portuguese news with three main topics (sports; politics and economy; and television, celebrities, and arts). The results showed that concurrent speech (two and three-voices) of a speech rate slightly higher than the default rate greatly increased scanning speed for relevant information. Their findings suggest that two-voices with a rate 1.75 times the default-rate (ca. 278 words per minute) enables the appropriate scanning without loss in performance.

2.4   Optimal Sentence Length

Mikk [14] examined young adults' cognitive load involving sentence length. A total of 37 students (17–18 years old) participated in their study. A total of 30 texts were taken from scientific books. Cloze tests were carried out where the participants needed to fill in the blanks with deleted words. The results showed that 50–130 characters were appropriate for these students. The findings also demonstrated that the too short and too long sentences were not suitable for participants' memory workload.

Cutts [15] did not recommend an upper limit sentence length, even though sentence lengths exceeding 40 words discouraged readers. A better goal for an average sentence length is said to be 15–20 words. Cutts argued that the word length is an average and it is not necessary for all the sentences to be in this range. Other ranges are possible.

2.5   Impact of Sentence Length on Readability

Oelke, Spretke, Stoffel, and Keim [16] presented a tool named VisRa to assist authors to make their writing easier to read. This tool indicated complex paragraphs and sentences which were harder to comprehend. VisRa provided feedback for correcting a text. The feedback showed not only issues on sentences, but also it explained why sentences were hard to read. VisRa gives the following features: word length (the mean number of characters per word), vocabulary difficulties (the percentage of terms not listed in the common list), nominal forms (the noun ratio), and sentence length (the number of words in a sentence).

Sherman (as cited in DuBay [17]) compared older writers with modern writers and observed a trend where sentences have become shorter over time by statistically analyzing sentence lengths. His analyses showed that on average 50 words were used per sentence before the Elizabethan era, and it reduced to an average of 29 words per sentence during Victorian times and to 23 words during 1893 [17]. Currently, the average sentence length is 20 words per sentence.

In this study two questions were asked: Does sentence length affect the readability of web in terms of workload for screen reader users? What is the appropriate sentence length that makes web content readable and understandable for screen reader users? To answer the questions, two predictions were formed. First, there is a significant impact of sentence length on web readability for screen reader users. Second, a minimum of sentence length is most suitable for screen reader users to read and comprehend web content in terms of subjective workload. We therefore formulated the following two null-hypotheses:

1. H_0: There is no significant impact of sentence length on the readability of the web for screen reader users.
2. H_0: Minimum sentence length on the web will not be appropriate for screen reader users in terms of subjective workload.

3 Method

A controlled within-subject [21, 22] experiment was conducted to collect quantitative data. The data included (a) workload perceived by participants while reading each prototype and (b) comprehension test after reading each prototype. The word length was the independent variable with five levels: 10–15 words, 16–20 words, 21–25 words, 26–30 words, and 30 or more words. The two dependent variables included the comprehension score and NASA-TLX scores. A one-way repeated measures ANOVA was employed to verify whether sentence length has impact on the readability of the web for screen reader users. It was assessed based on the workload that participants experienced while reading the content of five prototypes through a screen reader technology.

3.1 Participants

Thirteen males and eight females participated in the study ($N = 21$) with a mean age of 28 years (13 from 26–30 years; 5 from 31–35 years; and 1 from 20–25, 36–40, and 41 and above, respectively). The participants were recruited from Oslo Metropolitan University. All participants were non-native speakers but read English fluently (1 at intermediate level and 20 at an advanced level). Most were from the Master program of Universal Design of Information and Communication Technology, and few were from other educational background. Twenty participants were master students, and one was a bachelor student. None was recognized as a blind participant.

3.2 Materials

Five webpages were chosen for each test prototype. Five comprehension tests were constructed for each reading task. The NVDA (non-visual desktop access) screen reader was used as assistive tool.

Figure 1 shows the five prototypes (webpages) of different sentence length that were created for the experiment (Prototype A, 10–15 words; Prototype B, 16–20 words; Prototype C, 21–25 words; Prototype D, 26–30 words; and Prototype E, 30 words or more). The contents of all the prototypes were taken from online news portals including BBC, Yahoo, Norway today, New York Times, and The Local. All the pages addressed different topics (e.g., technology, education, and entertainment) but they had similar layout. Each prototype consisted of two same-length sentences.

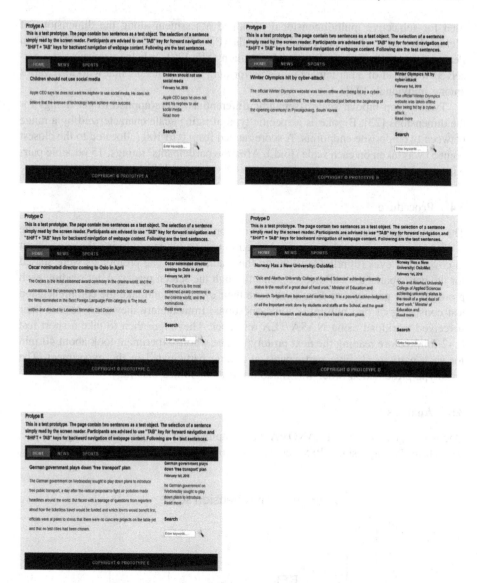

Fig. 1. The five prototype webpages with different sentence lengths: (a) 10–15 words, (b) 16-20 words, (c) 21–25 words, (d) 26–30 words, and (e) 30 words or more.

3.3   Observations

A Comprehension test was used to assess the participants' ability to read and understand the content of the prototypes. Each test consisted of two multiple-choice questions.

NASA-TLX was used to measure the perceived workload of the participants in the experiment process. It is a standardized tool used by many studies in Human Factors and Ergonomics [18]. It is shown to be highly reliable and valid [19]. Moreover, it is used for subjective multidimensional workload assessment along the dimensions of Mental Demands (Md), Physical Demands (PD), Temporal Demands (TD), Own Performance (OP), Effort (EF), and Frustration (FR) [20]. It helps determine the perceived workload of a participant while performing a task since mental workload varies among individuals [22].

Twenty step bipolar scales (semantic differentials) were applied to get ratings for the dimensions [23]. Bipolar is a specific type of rating scale characterized by a range between two opposite endpoints. A score ranged from 0 to 100 (allocated to the closest point 5) was taken on each scale (Ibid.). After the participants' ratings, 15 possible pairwise comparisons were conducted in terms of six scales [18].

3.4 Procedure

The participants were first given an information sheet and then familiarized with the NVDA screen reader tool. They were asked to use an eye-mask during the experiment to cover their eyes (blindfolded) during the reading task. The prototypes were started for the participants to read their contents through the screen reader. After reading each prototype, the participants were to remove their eye-mask and take the comprehension test consisting of two multiple-choice questions. Immediately they were to rate their perceived workload using NASA-TLX on paper. They were then to take a short rest (1–2 min) before reading the next prototype. The whole experiment took about 40 min for each participant. Five participants at a time participated in the experiment. The prototype presentation order was randomized to minimize bias [23].

3.5 Analysis

One-way repeated measures ANOVA were employed to verify sentence length impact on web readability using SPSS version 24.0 for Windows [27].

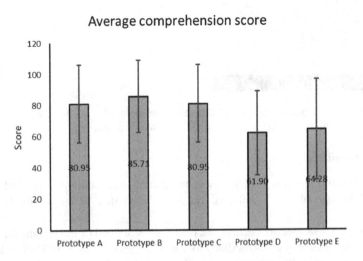

Fig. 2. Mean comprehension test score for the five prototypes. Error bars show standard deviation.

4   Results

4.1   Comprehension Scores

Figure 2 showed the average comprehension test score of each prototype. The total score was 100, and all participants scored above 50% in each test. There was a significant difference in comprehension score among prototypes B, D, and E but prototypes A and C had the same mean score. The results showed that prototype B had the highest mean score ($M = 85.7$, 16–20 words) whereas the prototype D had the lowest mean score ($M = 61.9$, 26–30 words). Based on comprehension scores, the results suggested that web contents with shorter sentences tended to be easier to comprehend than those with longer sentences.

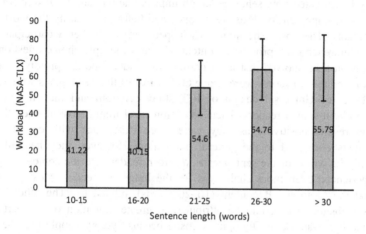

Fig. 3. NASA-TLX workload scores for the five prototypes. Error bars show standard deviation.

4.2   NASA-TLX Workload Scores

The NASA-TLX scores are shown in Fig. 3. Mauchly's test of sphericity revealed that the assumption of sphericity was violated ($\chi^2(9) = 28.17$, $p < .001$) for the TLX observations. A Greenhouse-Geisser correction was therefore applied [24, 25] since the epsilon was less than 0.75. The results showed that there was a significant effect of sentence length on average workload ($F(2.26, 45.27) = 19.77$, $p < .001$). Descriptive statistics for the five-level independent variables (prototypes A to E) showed that the participants used less workload on prototype B ($M = 40.15$, $SD = 18.45$) compared to other prototypes. Post-hoc tests revealed that prototype B was significantly different compared to the other prototypes ($p < .001$) apart from prototype A ($p = .67$). Prototype A ($M = 41.22$, $SD = 15.30$) had just a slightly higher workload than prototype B.

The highest workload was observed for prototype E ($M = 65.79$, $SD = 17.77$) which was significantly different to the other prototypes ($p < .001$) apart from prototype D ($p = .76$). Similarly, prototype C ($M = 54.60$, $SD = 14.79$) and prototype D

($M = 64.76$, $SD = 16.51$) exhibited a significantly mean difference of 10.14 ($p < .01$). Prototype B had the lowest workload mean among all the prototypes.

The results indicated statistically significant differences of mean workload across the five prototypes, except in between prototypes A and B (towards the shortest length), and between D and E (towards the longest length). The overall findings illustrated that the participants experienced significantly less workload with prototype B (second shortest) while reading sentences on web compared to prototypes A, C, D, and E. This evidence supports the hypothesis that sentence length significantly impacts readability of the web for screen reader users.

5 Discussion

This study investigated how sentence length impacts the readability of web for screen reader users. Comprehension tests were conducted before measuring the workload of the participants. The comprehension tests helped verify whether a participant could read and comprehend the prototype contents through multiple-choice questions. The comprehension tests showed that most participants understood the prototype contents as their comprehension scores were above 60%. Most of the participants were students in the Master of Universal design of ICT study program and they therefore had knowledge about screen readers. Their education level might have affected the comprehension results positively as they were more experience with comprehending complex texts compared to the general population. However, they had difficulties recalling all the words of the sentences as a screen reader read the content only once. They experienced even more challenges for the longer sentences. Most participants understood the prototype B content (16–20 words), related to "The official Winter Olympics website." This could be attributed to greater attention of the participants towards the cyber-attack of Olympics website because young people may be highly attracted to games and sports.

The ANOVA results indicate a significant impact of sentence length over five prototypes. There was a considerable mean difference across five prototypes in terms of subjective workload. The results based on the subjective workload mean that the first null hypothesis (H_0) can be rejected and instead the alternative hypothesis (H_1) can be accepted. It suggests that screen reader users' comprehension can be affected by sentence length. Thus, it is advisable that web content authors use appropriate sentence length to create web content to assist screen reader users. The post-hoc tests indicate that prototypes D and E had the smallest mean difference, followed by A and B (second smallest mean difference). The increasing mean difference across prototype A through prototypes B, C, D and E signifies an increasing degree of complexity in readability of the text.

Overall prototype B (with sentence length of 16–20 words) had the desired preferences for reading by the participants as all the participants exhibited the least physical demand workload. This might be because of less body movement required of the participants. The temporal demand was also the lowest with prototype B compared to other prototypes. Also, prototype B exhibited the overall lowest workload thereby featuring the maximum readability. However, the sentence length of prototype B was not the shortest among the prototypes. Hence, this result does not support the second hypothesis that the shortest sentence length will be most appropriate for the screen reader users on the readability of the web. Nevertheless, it is evident that the length of sentences on the web for the screen reader users has impact on readability. Concerning the appropriate sentence length, it also depends on the readers' language proficiency, reading skills, and memory workload.

One limitation of this study concerns recruiting fully blind participants, which is a challenging task. It was thus decided to recruit sighted participants which were blindfolding with an eye-mask. The findings may have been different if actual blind users were recruited as blind users depend mainly on their auditory and touch senses to substitute their lack of visual hints while interacting with the environment [26] and blind users are likely more experienced using screen readers. As also noted, some participants found it awkward to be blindfolded. Another factor that might have affected the results is the complexity of the measurement scales. As the NASA-TLX workload measurement scale relies on subjective perceptions of the participants, there might be individual differences in understanding and completing the measurement scales. As observed, some participants experienced difficulties using the NASA-TLX bipolar scales (20 steps) ratings from 0 to 100 scores. Immediately after the reading tests, the participants needed to circle the factor which affected the workload of the task. A skilled participant may find it easy to perform these tasks whereas others might find it challenging to perform the same task in the same situation. Some participants also found that the physical demand factor was not relevant because they did not perform any physical strenuous task during the experiment (except using the screen reader and manually filled in the forms).

6   Conclusion

This study examined the impact of sentence length on the readability of the web for screen reader users and explored suitable word lengths. The results indicate that there is a significant difference in the workload of the participants over five prototypes (websites) of varied sentence lengths. Regarding the appropriate length of sentences, it is not mandatory for sentence length to be as short as possible. Prototype B with sentence lengths of 16 to 20 words shows the lowest workload thereby exhibiting maximum readability. The result thus suggests that using sentences of 16-20 words may be appropriate for screen reader users when performing reading tasks on the web. Future work may address additional web content types with more varied word lengths and sentence lengths. Future studies might also address in-depth analysis of NASA-TLX.

References

1. Pikulski, J.J.: Readability. 10 January 2020
2. Owu-Ewie, C.: Readability of comprehension passages in Junior High School (JHS) English textbooks in Ghana. Ghana J. Linguist. 3(2), 35–68 (2014)

3. Eika, E., Sandnes, F.E.: Assessing the reading level of web texts for WCAG2.0 compliance —can it be done automatically? In: Di Bucchianico, G., Kercher, P. (eds.) Advances in Design for Inclusion, pp. 361–371. Springer, Cham (2016). https://doi.org/10.1007/978-3-319-41962-6_32

4. Eika, E., Sandnes, F.E.: Authoring WCAG2.0-compliant texts for the web through text readability visualization. In: Antona, M., Stephanidis, C. (eds.) UAHCI 2016. LNCS, vol. 9737, pp. 49–58. Springer, Cham (2016). https://doi.org/10.1007/978-3-319-40250-5_5

5. Eika, E.: Universally designed text on the web: towards readability criteria based on anti-patterns. Stud. Health Technol. Inform **229**, 461–470 (2016)

6. Kincaid, J.P., Fishburne, R.P., Rogers, R.L., Chissom, B.S.: Derivation of new readability formulas (automated readability index, fog count, and flesch reading ease formula) for Navy enlisted personnel. Research Branch report 8–75. Chief of Naval Technical Training: Naval Air Station Memphis (1975)

7. Gottron, T., Martin, L.: Readability and the web. Fut. Internet **4**(1), 238–252 (2012)

8. Babu, R., Singh, R., Ganesh, J.: Understanding blind users' Web accessibility and usability problems. AIS Trans. Hum.-Comput. Interact. **2**(3), 73–94 (2010)

9. World Wide Web Consortium: Web content accessibility guidelines (WCAG) 2.0 (2008)

10. Gottron, T., Martin, L.: Estimating web site readability using content extraction. In: Paper presented at the Proceedings of the 18th international conference on World wide web (2009)

11. de Heus, M., Hiemstra, D.: Readability of the web: a study on 1 billion web pages. In: Paper presented at the DIR (2013)

12. Chung, J.W., Min, H.J., Kim, J., Park, J. C.: Enhancing readability of web documents by text augmentation for deaf people. In: Paper presented at the proceedings of the 3rd international conference on web intelligence, mining and semantics profile data, vol. 24, no. 2, pp. 95–112 (2013)

13. Guerreiro, J., Gonçalves, D.: Faster text-to-speeches: enhancing blind people's information scanning with faster concurrent speech. In: Paper presented at the proceedings of the 17th international ACM SIGACCESS conference on computers & accessibility (2015)

14. Mikk, J.: Sentence length for revealing the cognitive load reversal effect in text comprehension. Educ. Stud. **34**(2), 119–127 (2008)

15. Cutts, M.: Oxford guide to plain English. OUP, Oxford (2013)

16. Oelke, D., Spretke, D., Stoffel, A., Keim, D.A.: Visual readability analysis: how to make your writings easier to read. IEEE Trans. Visual Comput. Graph. **18**(5), 662–674 (2012)

17. DuBay, W.H.: The Principles of Readability. Online Submission (2004)

18. Hart, S.G.: NASA-task load index (NASA-TLX); 20 years later. In: Proceedings of the Human Factors and Ergonomics Society Annual Meeting, vol. 50, no. 9, pp. 904–908. Sage Publications, Los Angeles (2006)

19. Longo, L.: On the reliability, validity and sensitivity of three mental workload assessment techniques for the evaluation of instructional designs: a case study in a third-level course (2018)

20. Hart, S.G., Staveland, L.E.: Development of NASA-TLX (Task Load Index): results of empirical and theoretical research. In: Advances in Psychology, vol. 52, pp. 139–183. Elsevier (1988)

21. MacKenzie, I.S.: Within-subjects vs. between-subjects designs: which to use? Hum.-Comput. Interact. Empir. Res. Perspect. **7**, 2005 (2002)

22. Raluca, B.: Between-subjects vs. within-subjects study design (2018). https://www.nngroup.com/articles/between-within-subjects/

23. Suresh, K.: An overview of randomization techniques: an unbiased assessment of outcome in clinical research. J. Hum. Reprod. Sci. **4**(1), 8 (2011)

24. Greenhouse, S., Geisser, W.: On methods in the analysis of profile data. Psychometrika **24** (2), 95–112 (1959)
25. Huynh, H., Feldt, L.S.: Estimation of the Box correction for degrees of freedom from sample data in randomized block and split-plot designs. J. Educ. Stat. **1**(1), 69–82 (1976)
26. Nielsen, J.: Cloze test for reading comprehension (2011). https://www.nngroup.com/articles/cloze-test-reading-comprehension/
27. Green, S.B., Salkind, N.J.: Using SPSS for Windows and Macintosh. Books a la Carte. Pearson, Upper Saddle River (2016)

Towards Universal Accessibility on the Web: Do Grammar Checking Tools Improve Text Readability?

Hitesh Mohan Kaushik[1], Evelyn Eika[1],
and Frode Eika Sandnes[1,2(✉)] (iD)

[1] Oslo Metropolitan University, 0130 Oslo, Norway
hmkaushik@yahoo.com, {evelyn.eika, frodes}@oslomet.no
[2] Kristiania University College, 0153 Oslo, Norway

Abstract. Readable text is a key ingredient in a universally accessible web. WCAG2.1 recommends that text should be readable by someone with basic schooling, a criterion that is hard to quantify and implement. Writers rely on qualitative clear-language recommendations, their own experience, and tools. This study set out to investigate if one class of such tools, automatic grammar checkers, has a measurable effect on the readability of text. A controlled experiment was conducted employing 15 participants who brought a piece of their own writing to the experiment tasked with improving the text using a grammar checker. Changes in readability of the text before and after applying the grammar tool were measured. Results show that there were significant reductions in error rates by applying the grammar tool, while there were no significant effects on readability. The results suggest that other automatic tools beside grammar checkers are needed to improve readability. These results have implications for web content providers.

Keywords: Universal accessibility · Readability · Web texts · Grammar checkers · Clear language · Writing assessment

1 Introduction

With increased access to digital devices, information is more available than ever, governments have been pushing towards digital societies. While it is the fastest medium to share information on the internet, it should also be of concern to make that information accessible to everyone [45]. Acknowledging this, US government in 1998 announced a plan for implementing a system of plain language for the writing of government regulations. The objective of plain language is to make regulations clearer and easier for the average person to understand [37]. According to WCAG2.1 guideline 3.1, content providers should "make text content readable and understandable" [52]. Guideline 3.1.5 addresses the reading level and implies that the limit is centered around "lower secondary education level". When a text requires the reader to have an education level beyond this, content providers are recommended to offer an alternative simplified version of the texts. This is challenging [15–166] as it is both difficult to quantify and also language dependent. WCAG2.1 also addresses unusual words (3.1.3) and abbreviations (3.1.4).

According to Statistics Norway 2019, about 34.1% of the Norwegian population above 16 years of age had higher education. In the United States 32.2% of all adults of age 18 and above had higher education as per 2018. As per 2011 census, only 6.7% of the population in India attained higher education. In order to prevent information discrimination in society, it is important that the information is accessible and succinct. Additionally, governments and organizations such as hospitals and businesses are also providing online services. Meade and Smith [38] described the importance of readable and understandable texts in healthcare. Text provides vital information, including advice on how to prevent unhealthy habits and actively participate in diagnosis processes. Health-care summaries that are difficult to read prevent patients from becoming active and responsible partners that make informed conscious decisions.

Quality writing is a challenging task, be it for academics or professionals, for business or private communications [13]. Graduates often lack necessary writing skills for business across disciplines including public relations, journalism, and communication [25]. Ideally, a good quality text is comprehensible, readable, and communicative. Words on paper help establish a bond between sender and receiver, and this bond breaks if the writer attempts to persuade a reader with poorly structured sentences that fail to forge trust and create coherence [25]. It is essential to address the different factors that improve text quality and readability. These include vocabulary, sentence structure, subject verb agreement, use of correct tense, content, and other grammar conventions. Improved writing skills help the writer to express the ideas more clearly and accurately. Writing is intended for sharing information; it might be in the form of a personalized letter, examination paper, published news, or a research article. It is the responsibility of an author to ensure that the text is legible and easily understood by the target group, such as a newspaper article which has the general public as an audience. This large audience includes readers with different backgrounds, education, literacy levels, disabilities, and people with English as a foreign language.

Although the notion of readability is relatively easy to comprehend as "easy to read", what exactly constitutes a readable text in practice is less obvious. Klare [32] defines readability as the level of difficulty of written text. Various factors affect text readability such as vocabulary, sentence length, semantics, readers' area of interest [24], education level and experience. Usage of widely known words and shorter sentences help make texts easier to read and understand [34]. Readability refers to how much sense the words and sentences make to readers, how clear the vocabulary and grammar are [7]. Readable texts benefit not only persons with limited education but also readers with learning disorders, cognitive disabilities, dyslexia, and ADHD [3, 4, 22]. Highly readable and concise texts are also beneficial for visually impaired readers who rely on screen reading technologies as it provides these users with a more rapid access to the texts [31].

A grammar checker is a type of writing aid. Web content providers may deploy such tools to improve content readability. Word-processors such as Microsoft Word come equipped with simple integrated spelling and grammar checkers. There are also third party specialized commercial grammar checkers such as Grammarly and Ginger. Open source tools such as Language Pack provided the Open Office family of word-processors. The rationale for this study was to investigate if such tools have a measurable effect on the actual readability of texts. One of the widely used tools, Grammarly Premium claims to offer over 400 types of checks. It checks grammatical errors, provides vocabulary enhancement suggestions, detects plagiarism, and provides citation suggestions [19]. Moreover, Grammarly claims to provide writer support for improving the readability of the text by reducing sentence length and employing simple and exact words in all contexts [19]. Other products include GingerSoftware and WhiteSmoke, with similar claims of helping writers write better English. Based on this we formulated the following research questions:

1. Do grammar tools help improve readability?
2. Do writers' self-assessed writing abilities correspond with their actual writing abilities?
3. Do grammar tools help writers learn about writing?

2 Related Work

2.1 Readability Formulas

Dale [111] discussed three aspects affecting readability, namely typography, readers' interest, and writing style. Typography refers to the choice of font, text size, text color, background color, spacing, line length, and line spacing. Typography is concerned with both the legibility of the text and its aesthetics. Legibility and readability concern the speed at which users can read the printed matter. Color contrast has been an important issue for readable texts on the web [6, 23, 42, 46–50]. Interest regards what grabs the readers' attention. Gilliland [18] inferred that readability when studied as interest leads to the analysis of subject matter and themes preferred by specific groups of readers. The style of writing concerns what types of vocabulary, sentence structure, and other expressional elements best suit the abilities of readers.

In order to determine difficulty level, three widely cited readability formulas were developed: the Flesch–Kincaid readability tests, the Dale-Chall readability formula, and the Gunning FOG Index. Flesch [17] introduced the two-part readability formula. The first part, the reading ease formula, uses only two variables, the number of syllables and the number of sentences for each 100-word sample. It predicts reading ease on a scale from 1 to 100, with 30 being very difficult and 70 being easy. The second part of Flesch's formula predicts human interest by counting the number of personal words (e.g., pronouns and names) and personal remarks (e.g., quotes, exclamations, and incomplete sentences). Dale-Chall formula was designed to correct certain shortcomings in the Flesch Reading Ease formula. It uses a sentence-length variable plus a percentage of hard words not found on the Dale-Chall list of 3,000 easy words, of which 80% are known to fourth-graders. The Gunning FOG Index [21] uses two variables: average sentence length and the number of words with more than two syllables per 100 words. Mc Laughlin [36] deduced that readability could be expressed as a relationship between two variables which are measures of the difficulty experienced by people reading a given text and a measure of the linguistic characteristics of that text. They proposed the SMOG readability formula which was derived using regression analysis. SMOG was intended to eliminate the problem in existing formulas where one long word or sentence affects the readability of an easier text more than it will of a harder text.

To study the independent impact of different text attributes on readability, Pitler and Nenkova [43] identified six factors affecting readability: word length and sentence length, vocabulary, syntactic features, lexical coherence, entity coherence, and discourse relations. Of these, vocabulary and discourse relations had the strongest impact, followed by the average number of verb phrases and text length. The authors claimed that using word length and sentence length were less effective than the other features, while using a combination of all features produces the best results.

2.2 Readability Beyond Formulas

Traditional readability formulas are regarded too simplistic and possibly do more harm than good as they do not consider other factors such as vocabulary, grammar, and background knowledge [1, 51]. Wright [54] pointed out that readability formulas do not consider key factors such as document type, layout, acronyms, and abbreviations. Further, some longer words (e.g., *understanding*) are given low readability scores with the formulae but are easy to read, while short but less frequent words (e.g., *grasp*) are given a higher readability score but may be harder to read. In addition, proper nouns such as people's and place's names should not count negatively towards readability. A standard test of readability measure is how well its prediction matches with readers' actual comprehension using existing texts [2].

2.3 Readability on the Web

Jatowt and Tanaka [29] compared readability of three websites, namely Wikipedia, simple Wikipedia, and Britannica. They used both syntactical (Flesch Reading Ease) and familiarity-based approaches (New Dale-Chall formula) to determine the readability index. They found that the average word and sentence lengths were much higher on Wikipedia texts compared to those of simple Wikipedia. Britannica was also easier to read compared to Wikipedia. The study suggested that Wikipedia's emphasis on accuracy and coverage may have reduced readability compared to the other resources.

To study the impact of typographic features on readability, Yu and Miller [55] introduced a Firefox Extension named Froggy. The extension removed distractions from the web pages in the form of advertisements and transformed the text into a more readable format. The participants were positive towards the Jenga format, and they considered it easier to read and understand compared to the standard format. There was also a slight improvement in comprehension without affecting reading speed.

Chung et al. [10] focused on simplifying the text on news websites for improved readability for deaf people. They developed an online news display system simplifying syntactic structures and providing graphical representations. The system simplified complex sentences by identifying embedded clauses, and relocating them for simpler structure, and then visually presenting the relationships among clauses. The evaluation showed that tested sentences were mostly correctly restored. More than half of the erroneous sentences were false relocations of adverbial clauses. The participants responded positively concerning system adequacy.

2.4 Evaluating Writing

Writing assessment can be implemented based on holistic or analytic scales. The holistic evaluation involves reading to gain an overall impression of a writer's skill [9]; in contrast, the analytic scoring involves an itemized analysis to help identify weaknesses in a student's writing [33]. In holistic scoring, the rater makes an overall judgment concerning the quality of performance. In analytic scoring, the rater assigns a score to each of the dimensions being assessed [30]. These evaluations are often conducted using scoring rubrics to help analyze writing in a reliable and consistent manner [39]. A well-established scoring scheme for writing assessment included five categories: content, organization, vocabulary, language use, and mechanics [26]. Weigle [53] described this as one of the best known and most widely used analytic scales in ESL.

2.5 Grammar Checkers and Efficacy

Schraudner [40] examined the role of automated correction tools as a teacher's assistant to supplement efficient learning for English language learners. The participants were asked to weekly read a portion of a book and electronically respond with an explanation of the content. The results showed that commonly occurring errors were related to punctuation, conjunctions, and pronouns. Grammarly's category for sentence structure found direct translation errors. Sentence structure was created as object-subject-verb or subject-object-verb. The tools were deemed useful for the students' learning and planning; in particular, word choice, word frequency, and spelling were easy to monitor and target, except handling irregular past tense verbs. The tools helped improve learners' lexical abilities and the use of punctuations and prepositions.

Dale [12] conducted a comparative study of ten proofreading systems including Grammarly, Ginger, ProWritingAid, ClearEdits, Editor, Correct English, GrammarBase, GrammarCheck.net, SpellCheckPlus, and Style Writer 4. The study observed that the performance of these programs was unsatisfactory. Grammarly and Ginger performed better than the others.

Cavaleri and Dianati [8] surveyed the students' perceptions of Grammarly use in writing assignments. Students had mostly positive feedback with a few exceptions. The survey indicated long-term benefits as explanations and hints were helpful in understanding grammar rules. Some responded that they would only use Grammarly for proofreading. The grammar mistakes detected appeared to be minor and could have been resolved if they had read them carefully themselves. Some Grammarly recommendations were deemed incorrect or unclear.

Oneill and Russell [41] explored the role of feedback on grammar for those using Grammarly. The results were compared for those who received automatic advice from Grammarly and those who manually received advice from the advisors. The students who received non-Grammarly advice were satisfied, but the students with Grammarly advice were strongly satisfied. Students' experience was largely positive regarding the use of Grammarly; they claim it improved their confidence. The major concern was the accuracy of the feedback. They also identified issues with passive voice, complex sentences, and vocabulary choices. Some students were not satisfied with the performance of Grammarly and even preferred feedback from MS Word over Grammarly.

Students' prior knowledge of the English language also had effect on their responses. Students with a low IELTS score were highly satisfied with Grammarly. Students with the lowest scores who studied English at the university were most critical of Grammarly.

3 Method

3.1 Experimental Design

A controlled experiment was configured with a pre-test/post-test design. Automatic grammar tool was the independent within-groups variable with two levels, namely without tool and with tool. The dependent variables included ratio of errors per word, Grammarly readability score, Gunning Fog Index, SMOG readability score, and raters' language scores.

3.2 Participants

Fifteen participants were recruited; six were female and nine were male. All were students at Oslo Metropolitan University, randomly selected from graduate programs where English was the language of tuition. Most participants were in the 27 to 34 age range, with the youngest being 21 and the oldest close to 50. The participants had minimum qualification of English proficiency with experience in academic writing. Participants either had at least a TOEFL score of 90 or had been studying English for more than 13 years. None of the participants reported having any reading disabilities such as dyslexia.

Eleven participants reported having English as their second language (L2), three participants reporting having English as their third language (L3), while one participant reported using English as the fourth language (L4). Nine participants heard about readability, while six participants were unfamiliar with this term. Moreover, ten participants had heard about grammar checking tools such as Grammarly, while five reported that they had not heard about such tools.

3.3 Equipment

A Thinkpad laptop computer with screen size of 13 in. and touchpad was used for the experiments with Microsoft Word word-processor and a full version of Grammarly installed. An initial test revealed that there were minimal functional differences between Grammarly and Ginger, and Grammarly was chosen as it appears to have a larger market share. Grammarly also has its own built-in readability metric. The screen activity was recorded using ShareX video recording software.

3.4 Task

The participants were asked to bring a recently written text document on a USB stick. This text was to be academic coursework as part of their studies. These texts were used as a pre-experiment sample. Participants' own writing was chosen to make the experiment more engaging and help motivate the participants as they had a chance to improve their own writing.

The grammar-checking task involved editing their own text using the feedback from the grammar tool. The grammar tool would suggest simple grammar corrections and other changes such as restructuring sentences to improve clarity. Participants had the option of accepting suggestions, reject suggestions, or edit the text based on the feedback.

3.5   Procedure

Potential participants were contacted personally and briefed about the purpose and tasks for this project. A suitable time to perform experiment was agreed upon, which allowed potential participants extra time to decide about their participation.

The participants conducted the tasks individually at the university campus in a meeting room, which reduced the influences of external noise and ensured constant conditions for each participant. This setup was controlled in a natural environment since all the participants were students at the university. Participants were given a copy of consent form explaining the purpose of the study. Consent was given orally. The experiment was completed in a single session for each participant. Each session started with a questionnaire to gather information about the participant's understanding of readability and their self-assessment of proficiency in written English (How much help is needed with vocabulary, grammar, sentence formation, punctuations, content, writing style, and voice). It also included questions about common writing issues and any prior experiences with grammar checker software.

Next, the text sample was loaded, and the participant was asked to run Grammarly on the text sample they had brought to the session. The participants were asked to use the feedback and improve the text as per their understanding. Participants were encouraged to work independently, but on-spot guidance was provided. The computer screen was recorded without audio enabled to facilitate in-depth analyses of the users' interaction with the grammar tool.

After completing the grammar-check, the participants were asked to answer a post-test questionnaire about their overall experience and their opinions about the problems identified and corrections suggested by the software.

Participation was voluntary and anonymous. The participants' identities were not recorded and the meta-information in the participants text documents were deleted. Therefore, no personal identifying information was stored, and the General Data Protection Regulations (GDPR) did not apply.

3.6   Observations

The number of errors in the documents was reported by Grammarly and verified by a review of the screen recordings. The ratio of errors per word per writing was computed by taking the number of errors reported divided by the number of words in the text. This allowed the error scores to be compared across writings with varying lengths. The Gunning FOG Index was calculated using an online tool (http://gunning-fog-index.com/fog.cgi) and the Grammarly readability scores were provided directly by the software tools. The SMOG scores were computed using online readability checker tool (https://readabilityformulas.com/).

The texts were also manually assessed based on a scoring rubric of five criteria. A scoring rubric guides assessors what features to scrutinize as they read; these descriptors are useful because they give evaluators a sense of what aspects of a student's writing should be critiqued [30, 33]. Style, vocabulary, grammar, mechanics, and clarity are the criteria identified for evaluation. These categories are tweaked version of scoring rubric from [26], which is widely used in its original or adapted form [5, 11, 27, 33, 35, 44]. This study excludes the content criterion and uses analytic scoring as content evaluation involves testing subject-specific knowledge, which is not affected by grammar checker tools.

3.7 Analysis

The observations were analyzed using the statistical analysis software JASP version 0.11.0.0 [28].

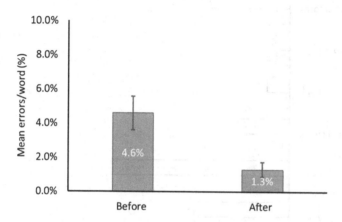

Fig. 1. The mean number of errors before and after applying the grammar checker. Error bars show 95% confidence intervals.

4 Results

Shapiro Wilks tests revealed that the Grammarly readability scores ($W = 0.433, p < .001$) and Gunning FOG scores ($W = 0.769, p = .002$) were not normally distributed, while the ratio of errors per word and SMOG measurements did not deviate from the normal distribution. The pre-check and post-check scores for Grammarly readability and Gunning FOG were therefore analyzed using non-parametric procedures, while the errors per word and SMOG measurements were analyzed using paired t-tests.

A paired t-test test revealed that grammar checking had a significant effect on the percentage of errors per word ($t(14) = 6.437$, $p < .001$, Cohen's $d = 1.662$), as there were nearly three times the percentage of errors per word (see Fig. 1) in the pre-checked texts ($M = 4.6$, $SD = 1.8$) compared to the post-checked texts ($M = 1.3$, $SD = 0.8$). In terms of percentage, the results show that the participants followed about one third of the advice provided by the grammar tool ($M = 31.8$, $SD = 18.3$) but rejected the remaining advice. It is also worth noting that the rate of error per word prior to grammar checking correlated strongly with language levels (L2, L3, and L4) of the participants (r (15) = .656, $p = .008$), confirming that less experienced learners made more mistakes than more experienced learners.

No significant effect of the grammar checker could be observed for the Grammarly readability score ($W = 15.0$, $p = .93$); the scores before checking ($M = 38.7$, $SD = 10.7$) were marginally larger than the scores after checking ($M = 37.2$, $SD = 12.4$). Similarly, no significant effect of the grammar checker could be observed on the Gunning FOG index ($W = 39$, $p = 1.0$); the scores before checking ($M = 15.157$, $SD = 2.319$) were nearly the same as the scores after checking ($M = 15.153$, $SD = 2.33$).

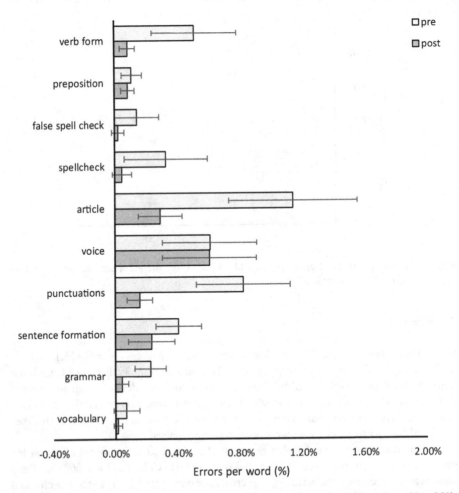

Fig. 2. Distribution of mean errors types before and after grammar check. Error bars show 95% confidence intervals.

There was also no significant effect of the grammar tool on the SMOG measures (t (14) = 1.317, p = .209) as the mean pre-check score (M = 11.693, SD = 1.65) was nearly identical to the mean post-check score (M = 11.633, SD = 1.616). The SMOG score did not correlate with the participants' self-reported English writing skills; however, the SMOG readability scores correlated positively (r(15) = .524, p = .045) with the participants' language level (L2, L3, or L4).

Figure 2 shows the distribution of error types before and after applying the grammar tool. As can be seen, verb form, article, and punctuations are error categories that were effectively eliminated by the grammar tool. Voice, preposition, and vocabulary were associated with only minimal improvements. Figure 2 also shows that the spread in ratio of errors was generally smaller for the texts after the grammar check.

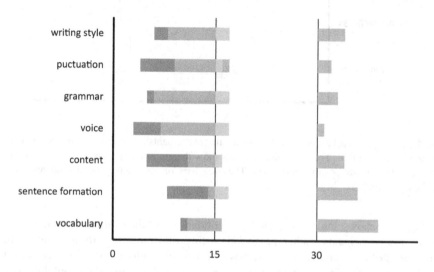

Fig. 3. Diverging stacked bar chart showing participants' self-reported writing abilities. The Grey-blue left bars show the number of negative responses and the blue right bars show positive responses. The grey bars on the right show neutral responses. (Color figure online)

Figure 3 shows the participants' self-reported English writing abilities. Overall, all the responses strongly leaned towards the negative side with the fewest positive ratings of participants' own abilities in terms of content. The largest number of negative responses was associated with voice, while vocabulary was associated with the fewest negative responses. Clearly, voice was the feature of writing with the fewest neutral responses while vocabulary was associated with the largest number of neutral responses.

We also correlated the participants' self-reported writing abilities with the objective readability metrics. The only significant positive correlation was observed between writing style and the Grammarly readability score (r_s(15) = .553, p = .033) and a significant negative correlation between writing style and the Gunning FOG scores (r (15) = −.514, p = .05). Participants' self-reporting writing style correlated positively with the error rate after grammar checking (r_s(15) = .556, p = .031).

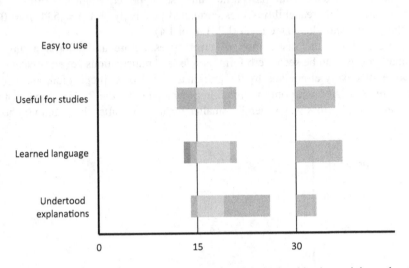

Fig. 4. Diverging stacked bar chart showing the participants' subjective opinions about the grammar-checking tool. The Grey-blue left bars show the number of negative responses and the blue right bars show positive responses. The grey bars on the right show neutral responses. (Color figure online)

Figure 4 shows the participants' perceptions about the grammar-checking tool. Unlike the participants' rather pessimistic rating of their own writing abilities, the perceptions of the grammar tool were positive with all results strongly leaning towards positive responses. None of the participants reported that they found the tool difficult to use, and only one participant reported that they did not understand the explanations given by the tool. Although also tending towards positive responses, the two questions related to learning (i.e., if the tool would be useful for their studies and if they learned language using the tool) were associated with mostly neutral responses.

Correlation analyses show that the participants' responses to the question about whether the grammar tool helped the text correlated positively with the percentage of advice followed (r_s(15) = .533, p = .041). The error rate before correlated negatively with the participants' perception of how helpful the tool was for improving text (r_s(15) = −.688, p = .005). The error rate before also correlated negatively with the participants' perception of how relevant the advice provided by the tool was (r_s(15) = −.560, p = .030).

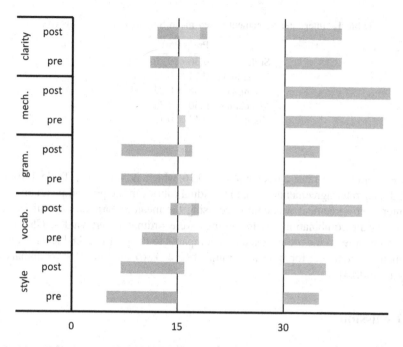

Fig. 5. Diverging stacked bar graph showing the median scores based on the three raters for the five-item scoring rubric (style, vocabulary, grammar, mechanics, and clarity). The Grey-blue left bars show the number of negative responses and the blue right bars show positive responses. The grey bars on the right show neutral responses. (Color figure online)

Figure 5 shows the median ratings of the texts based on the three raters. The median ratings of the three raters for each text were used in the analysis as it was a more robust measure than the mean. Analyses show that there was only a significant improvement effect of the grammar checker in terms of vocabulary and language ($W = 0.0$, $p = .018$) which started with a lower mean score ($M = 2.867$, $SD = .743$) and it ended with a higher score ($M = 3.2$, $SD = .676$) after the grammar checking. The diverging stacked bar graph in Fig. 4 shows that most of the scores on the negative side of the scale became neutral. A visible improvement can also be spotted for clarity and style, although these improvements are not statistically significant. Moreover, Fig. 4 shows that there were very little change in terms of mechanics and grammar. In fact, the post-grammar check scores for mechanics were slightly lower than the pre-check scores.

The median ratings of the texts before checking were correlated with the participants' self-assessed writing abilities. Style was found to correlate negatively with sentence formation ($r_s(15) = -.543$, $p = .036$) and positively with voice ($r_s(15) = -.557$, $p = .031$), and clarity was correlated negatively with sentence formation ($r_s(15) = -.686$, $p = .005$). There were no significant correlations between the automatic readability indices (FOG, SMOG, and Grammary readability score) and the manual ratings of the texts.

Table 1. Inter-rater agreement based mean Spearman correlations (ρ).

	Pre	Post
Style	0.36	0.20
Vocabulary	0.14	0.12
Grammar	0.36	0.22
Mechanics	0.30	−0.33
Clarity	0.14	0.12

The overall inter-rater agreement was 0.16 which is very low. Table 1 lists the detailed inter-rater agreements for the individual rubrics in the pre and post conditions. The inter-rater agreement was computed using the mean Spearman correlations of all three rater-pair combinations as the ratings were ordinal Likert values. Clearly, the raters agree more on the pre-checked text compared to the post-checked texts. Next, the agreements were higher for style and grammar ($\rho = 0.36$) and lower for vocabulary and clarity ($\rho = 0.14$).

5   Discussion

The significant effect of a grammar checker on the reduction of errors is as one would expect, as the purpose of a grammar checker is to identify and help correct errors. Similarly, the positive effect of the grammar tool on the writers' vocabulary improvement is as expected and as also reflected in the raters' assessment since the grammar tool suggests alternative words and phrases. Readability, or the lack of readability, on the other hand is not an error; the results clearly show that there is no significant effect of the grammar tool in terms of readability. One could argue that errors and readability represent two perpendicular dimensions: It is possible to envisage a grammatically correct and error free text that is very hard to read, and a text that is very easy to read but with many trivial grammar and spelling mistakes. In other words, our results do not give support to the claims made by the tool developers that the tool helps improve readability.

It is interesting to observe that most of the participants had a negative perception of their own writing abilities, while they had an overall positive perception of the grammar tool. It would be interesting to also contrast the results with a cohort of native English speakers. Perhaps we would observe the opposite pattern, namely a positive perception of their own writing ability and a negative perception of the tools. Put differently, those who are aware of their shortcomings may be more perceptible to assistance compared to those who may not have such shortcomings and hence will not find the tools valuable.

The danger of this positive perception of the grammar tool is that they may give a false sense of security for learners of English, especially because of the advertising claim that the tools help improve readability. Users may perceive that the texts are improved as many changes are suggested and feedback is provided. However, the elimination of grammar errors should not be mistaken for readability enhancement.

The fact that the percentage of advice followed was far from 100% suggests that participants do not blindly follow the advice provided by the tool. They make individual assessments of the suggestions and reject some proposals. This is an encouraging result. The positive connection between the perceived helpfulness of the tool to improve the text and the percentage of advice followed shows that participants who followed more advice were also more satisfied with the tool. Most of the participants gave positive feedback about the tool, while one of them was highly critical and did not find it effective. Six of the participants raised the issue of false-positives and said they were overwhelmed with the amount of errors reported. Three participants also noted that the tool lacks technical vocabulary.

It is not clear as to why the number of errors before the grammar check correlates negatively with the participants' perception of the helpfulness of the tool and the relevance of the advice. This result seems to suggest that participants who made fewer errors initially had a more positive perception of the tool than participants who made many mistakes initially.

Clearly, grammar tools did not help with improving readability. It seems that content providers still need to rely on language expertise and manual editorial review work on their content in order to ensure universally accessible text with high level of readability.

It is also interesting to observe that the SMOG scores correlated with the participants' reported language level (L2, L3, L4) while both FOG and Grammarly scores correlated with the participants' self-reported writing style. It would be worthwhile to explore this in more detail, but it may be advisable to base any speculation on a larger sample of participants.

6 Limitations

This study was conducted with a relatively small sample of participants. The observations of the dependent variables did not adhere to a normal distribution. It could be that a larger sample would yield normally distributed observations. If so, parametric testing procedures could be applied. Although the cohort is narrow in the sense that it only included students, the cohort was still quite wide in that it included both undergraduate and postgraduate students from a range of disciplines. Our goal was to narrow the cohort to a single class, but not enough participants volunteered to participate.

Another potential limitation lies in the texts provided by the participants. These were on a diverse set of topics and contexts. Although this was a necessary practical adaptation, it would have been beneficial if these texts were on the same topics and contexts.

The inter-rater agreement appears to be low, suggesting that the devised manual rating procedures need to be further refined. One problem may have been that some of the rubrics overlapped and no instructions were given on what the various levels of the scales meant, leaving the scoring up to personal interpretation. Moreover, the different cultural and academic backgrounds of the raters could have been an influencing factor on the inter-rater agreement. Also, as the manual ratings did not correlate with the automatic readability measures, less emphasis has been placed on the manual rating results. Finally, this study was based on English, while the WCAG readability requirement is language neutral. Hence, it may differ concerning how to approach readability in various languages.

7 Conclusions

This paper investigated the effects of the grammar checking tool on the readability of texts. As expected, the results reveal that the grammar tool has a positive effect on reducing the ratio of errors. However, no significant effect on readability is detected. Our results therefore do not agree with the claims that these tools help readability. It is recommended that web content providers do not rely on grammar checking tools to ensure readability. Content providers are advised to consult manual editorial work involving language competences in order to contribute towards universal accessibility of web contents.

References

1. Bailin, A., Grafstein, A.: Grammar and readability. In: Readability: Text and Context, pp. 65–96. Springer, London (2016). https://doi.org/10.1057/9781137388773_3
2. Benjamin, R.G.: Reconstructing readability: recent developments and recommendations in the analysis of text difficulty. Educ. Psychol. Rev. **24**, 63–88 (2012)
3. Berget, G., Sandnes, F. E.: Searching databases without query-building aids: implications for dyslexic users. Inf. Res. **20**(4) (2015). http://www.informationr.net/ir/
4. Berget, G., Mulvey, F., Sandnes, F.E.: Is visual content in textual search interfaces beneficial to dyslexic users? Int. J. Hum Comput Stud. **92**, 17–29 (2016)
5. Boye, A.: Teaching, Learning, & Professional Development Center. https://www.depts.ttu.edu/tlpdc/Resources/Teaching_resources/TLPDC_teaching_resources/StudentWriting.php (2017)
6. Brathovde, K., Farner, M.B., Brun, F.K., Sandnes, F.E.: Effectiveness of color-picking interfaces among non-designers. In: Luo, Y. (ed.) CDVE 2019. LNCS, vol. 11792, pp. 181–189. Springer, Cham (2019). https://doi.org/10.1007/978-3-030-30949-7_21
7. Brinck, T., Gergle, D., Wood, S.D.: Writing for the web. In: Usability for the Web: Designing Web Sites that Work, pp. 244–301. Morgan Kaufmann, San Francisco (2003)
8. Cavaleri, M.R., Dianati, S.: You want me to check your grammar again? The usefulness of an online grammar checker as perceived by students. J. Acad. Lang. Learn. **10**, A223–A236 (2016)
9. Charney, D.: The validity of using holistic scoring to evaluate writing: a critical overview. Res. Teach. Engl. **18**, 65–81 (1984)
10. Chung, J.-W., Min, H.-J., Kim, J., Park, J.C.: Enhancing readability of web documents by text augmentation for deaf people. In: Proceedings of the 3rd International Conference on Web Intelligence, Mining and Semantics, pp. Article 30. Association for Computing Machinery, Madrid, Spain (2013). https://doi.org/10.1145/2479787.2479808
11. Dale, E., Chall, J.: The concept of readability. Elementary Engl. **26**(1), 19–26 (1949)
12. Dale, R.: Checking in on grammar checking. Nat. Lang. Eng. **22**, 491–495 (2016)
13. Dubay, W.: The Principles of Readability. CA 92627949, 631-3309 (2004)

14. Eika, E., Sandnes, F.E.: Assessing the reading level of web texts for WCAG2.0 compliance —can it be done automatically? In: Di Bucchianico, G., Kercher, P. (eds.) Advances in Design for Inclusion, pp. 361–371. Springer, Cham (2016). https://doi.org/10.1007/978-3-319-41962-6_32

15. Eika, E., Sandnes, F.E.: Authoring WCAG2. 0-compliant texts for the web through text readability visualization. In: International Conference on Universal Access in Human-Computer Interaction, pp. 49–58. Springer, Cham (2016)

16. Eika, E.: Universally designed text on the web: towards readability criteria based on anti-patterns. Stud. Health Technol. Inform 229, 461–470 (2016)

17. Flesch, R.: A new readability yardstick. J. Appl. Psychol. 32(3), 221–233 (1948)

18. Gilliland, J.: The concept of readability. Reading 2, 24–29 (1968). https://doi.org/10.1111/j.1467-9345.1968.tb00749.x

19. Grammarly: Write your best with Grammarly (n.d.). https://www.grammarly.com/

20. Gray, W.S., Leary, B.E.: What Makes a Book Readable?. University Chicago Press, Oxford (1935)

21. Gunning, R.: The Technique of Clear Writing. McGraw-Hill, New York (1971)

22. Habib, L., et al.: Dyslexic students in higher education and virtual learning environments: an exploratory study. J. Comput. Assist. Learn. 28(6), 574–584 (2012)

23. Hansen, F., Krivan, J.J., Sandnes, F.E.: Still not readable? an interactive tool for recommending color pairs with sufficient contrast based on existing visual designs. In: The 21st International ACM SIGACCESS Conference on Computers and Accessibility, pp. 636–638. ACM (2019). https://doi.org/10.1145/3308561.3354585

24. Hargis, G.: Readability and computer documentation. ACM J. Comput. Document. 24, 122–131 (2000)

25. Hines, R., Basso, J.: Do communication students have the "Write Stuff"?: practitioners evaluate writing skills of entry-level workers. J. Promot. Manag. 14, 293–307 (2008). https://doi.org/10.1080/10496490802625817

26. Jacobs, H., Zinkgraf, S., Wormuth, D., Hearfiel, V., Hughey, J.: Testing ESL Composition: A Practical Approach. Newbury House Publishers, Inc., Rowley, Massachusetts (1981)

27. Janssen, G., Meier, V., Trace, J.: Building a better rubric: Mixed methods rubric revision. Assess. Writ. 26 (2015). https://doi.org/10.1016/j.asw.2015.07.002

28. JASP Team: JASP (Version 0.11.1) [Computer software] (2019)

29. Jatowt, A., Tanaka, K.: Is Wikipedia too difficult? comparative analysis of readability of Wikipedia, simple Wikipedia and Britannica. In: Proceedings of the 21st ACM International Conference on Information and Knowledge Management, pp. 2607–2610. Association for Computing Machinery, Maui (2012). https://doi.org/10.1145/2396761.2398703

30. Jönsson, A., Svingby, G.: The use of scoring rubrics: reliability, validity and educational consequences. Educ. Res. Rev. 2, 130–144 (2007). https://doi.org/10.1016/j.edurev.2007.05.002

31. Kadayat, B.B., Eika, E.: Impact of sentence length on the readability of web for screen reader users. In: International Conference on Universal Access in Human-Computer Inter-action. Springer, Cham (2020). LNCS 12188

32. Klare, G.: The measurement of readability: useful information for communicators. ACM J. Comput. Doc. 24, 107–121 (2000). https://doi.org/10.1145/344599.344630

33. Klimova, B.: Evaluating writing in English as a second language. Procedia Soc. Behav. Sci. 28, 390–394 (2011). https://doi.org/10.1016/j.sbspro.2011.11.074

34. Lidwell, W., Holden, K., Butler, J.: Universal principles of design, revised and updated: 125 ways to enhance usability, influence perception, increase appeal, make better design decisions, and teach through design. Rockport Pub 198 (2010)

35. Mahon, R.: A grading system for composition papers. Clear. House **69**, 280–282 (1996). https://doi.org/10.1080/00098655.1996.10114317
36. Mc Laughlin, G.H.: SMOG grading-a new readability formula. J. Read. **12**, 639–646 (1969)
37. McKinley, V.: Keeping it simple: making regulations write in plan language. Regulation **21**, 30 (1998)
38. Meade, C., Smith, C.: Readability formulas: cautions and criteria. Patient Educ. Couns. **17**, 153–158 (1991). https://doi.org/10.1016/0738-3991(91)90017-Y
39. Moskal, B., Leydens, J.: Scoring rubric development: validity and reliability. Pract. Assess. Res. Eval. **7** (2000). https://doi.org/10.7275/q7rm-gg74
40. Schraudner, M.: The online teacher's assistant: using automated correction programs to supplement learning and lesson planning. CELE J. **22**, 128–140 (2014)
41. ONeill, R., Russell, A.: Stop! grammar time: university students' perceptions of the automated feedback program Grammarly. Australasian J. Educ. Technol. **35**, 42–56 (2019). https://doi.org/10.14742/ajet.3795
42. Pedersen, L. A., Einarsson, S. S., Rikheim, F. A., Sandnes, F. E.: User interfaces in dark mode during daytime – improved productivity or just cool-looking? In: Antona, M., Stephanidis, C. (eds.) HCII 2020, LNCS, vol. 12188, pp. 178–187. Springer, Cham (2020)
43. Pitler, E., Nenkova, A.: Revisiting readability: a unified framework for predicting text quality. In: Proceedings of the Conference on Empirical Methods in Natural Language Processing, pp. 186–195. Association for Computational Linguistics, Honolulu, Hawaii (2008)
44. Rakedzon, T.: To make a long story short: a rubric for assessing graduate students' academic and popular science writing skills. Assess. Writ. **32** (2017). https://doi.org/10.1016/j.asw.2016.12.004
45. Sandnes, F.E.: Universell utforming av IKT-systemer, 2nd edn. Universitetsforlaget, Oslo (2018)
46. Sandnes, F.E.: On-screen colour contrast for visually impaired readers: selecting and exploring the limits of WCAG2.0 colours. In: Black, A., Lund, O., Walker, S. (eds.) Information Design: Research and Practice, pp. 405–416 (2016)
47. Sandnes, F. E.: Understanding WCAG2. 0 color contrast requirements through 3D color space visualization. Stud. Health Technol. Inform. **229**, 366–375 (2016). https://doi.org/10.3233/978-1-61499-684-2-366
48. Sandnes, F. E., Zhao, A.: An interactive color picker that ensures WCAG2.0 compliant color contrast levels. Procedia Comput. Sci. **67**, 87–94 (2015). https://doi.org/10.1016/j.procs.2015.09.252
49. Sandnes, F.E., Zhao, A.: A contrast colour selection scheme for WCAG2. 0-compliant web designs based on HSV-half-planes. In: 2015 IEEE International Conference on Systems, Man, and Cybernetics, pp. 1233–1237. IEEE (2015). https://doi.org/10.1109/smc.2015.220
50. Sandnes, F.E.: An image-based visual strategy for working with color contrasts during design. In: Miesenberger, K., Kouroupetroglou, G. (eds.) ICCHP 2018. LNCS, vol. 10896, pp. 35–42. Springer, Cham (2018). https://doi.org/10.1007/978-3-319-94277-3_7
51. Schriver, K.A.: Readability formulas in the new millennium: what's the use? ACM J. Comput. Doc. **24**, 138–140 (2000)
52. W3C: Web Content Accessibility Guidelines (WCAG) 2.1, 5 June 2018. https://www.w3.org/TR/WCAG21/
53. Weigle, S.C.: Assessing Writing. Cambridge University Press, Cambridge (2002)
54. Wright, N.: Free eBook: StyleWriter's New BOG INDEX Readability Formula: Readability Software. http://www.stylewriter-usa.com/bog-index-readability-formula.php
55. Yu, C.-H., Miller, R.C.: Enhancing web page readability for non-native readers. In: Proceedings of the SIGCHI Conference on Human Factors in Computing Systems, pp. 2523–2532. Association for Computing Machinery, Atlanta, Georgia, USA (2010). https://doi.org/10.1145/1753326.1753709

Investigating the Effect of Adding Visual Content to Textual Search Interfaces on Accessibility of Dyslexic Users

Mona Muftah and Ahamed Altaboli[✉]

Industrial and Manufacturing Systems Engineering Department,
University of Benghazi, Benghazi, Libya
ahmed.altaboli@uob.edu.ly

Abstract. The problem of the study is to investigate whether adding visual content such as icons to textual search user interfaces improves performance for dyslexic users. Eight dyslexics and eight non-dyslexics (controls) Benghazi-school students, of ages twelve to seventeen years, completed sixteen search tasks in four conditions: word, icon, word/icon, and icon/word in a list layout. Results showed that both dyslexics and non-dyslexics generally benefited from using icons in the interface. Particularly, for both groups, significantly shorter search times were recorded in the icon and the word/icon conditions than the word condition. There were no significant differences in search times between the word/icon and the icon/word conditions. Also, both groups preferred the two mixed icon-word conditions over the word or the icon conditions. These results suggest that accessible search interfaces should use icons and words (text) rather than only words; this should satisfy users' performance and preference for both dyslexics and non-dyslexics.

Keywords: Dyslexia · Accessibility · Search user interfaces

1 Introduction

Dyslexia is a specific learning disability that not related to intelligence. (Ramachandran 2002). It is characterized by difficulties of reading and poor spelling abilities. The typical cause of these difficulties is the deficit in the phonological component of language that is usually irrelative to other cognitive abilities and the provision of effective classroom education (International Dyslexia Association 2014).

1.1 Web Accessibility and Dyslexic Users

Nowadays, web access is important in education, work and everyday life. Therefore it is necessary to ensure and improve access to web for all members of the society (Takagi and Asakawa 2015). Web accessibility means that websites should be designed so that people with disabilities can perceive, understand, navigate, and interact with the Web (Iriarte et al. 2016).

M. Antona and C. Stephanidis (Eds.): HCII 2020, LNCS 12188, pp. 289–299, 2020.
https://doi.org/10.1007/978-3-030-49282-3_20

People with dyslexia can face problems in interacting with web pages that have heavy textual content and poorly built navigation structures. Various navigation aids have been used by web sites in order to facilitate the navigation process, however; it is still unclear whether these aids are useful for dyslexic users (Al-Wabil et al. 2007).

Although it is estimated that up to 7.7% of special-needs school-aged children in Benghazi are diagnosed with dyslexia (Department of Education and Inclusion of Special-Needs in Benghazi, personal communication 2018), to the best of the authors' knowledge, there have been no significant academic research projects involving those children and aiming at investigating and studying how to facilitate dyslexic users' access to the web. Such research projects should include investigating how websites designs could be improved and become more accessible for dyslexic users. This, in turn, would require determining what types of websites design and navigation aids could be considered useful for dyslexic users.

This study claims to be one contribution in this regard. The aim of this study is to investigate the possibility of improving web accessibility for dyslexic users by adding visual content such as icon to the user interface. The concentration was on textual search interfaces; with the objective of investigating whether adding icons to lists of textual search results would improve dyslexic users' performance.

2 Literature Review

The reviewed previous work concerned with improving web accessibility for dyslexic users can be divided into three categories; design of interface tools to aid dyslexic users, studies aiming at developing and improving accessibility recommendations and guidelines, and studies evaluating specific interface features using user testing.

2.1 Design of Interface Tools to Aid Dyslexic Users

Santana et al. (2013) designed a tool bar called Firefixia to support people with dyslexia. The Firefixia contains no text. All the features in the toolbar are offered via image buttons, it allows users to define preferred attributes involving: font size, font type, text alignment, space between lines, space between characters, background color, text color, link color, visited link color, line width, border of block elements, and eliminate italics. Opinions of participants regarding the Firefixa were not bad, but there is still a need to confirm the success of the Firefixa tool bar by conduct qualitative and quantitative studies on large number of dyslexic users.

Avelar et al. (2015) has developed a web help dyslexia tool bar to help people with dyslexia adapt web content to make it easier to read. The tool included features to change font size, font type, remove text decoration such as italics, bold and under-lining, changing foreground and background colors, change paragraph spacing, length and alignment, highlighting text, fading text to focus on specific parts and searching for synonyms for words. The evaluations showed that the features were very useful.

2.2 Studies Aiming at Developing and Improving Accessibility Recommendations and Guidelines

Rello and Baeza-Yates (2015) presented a set of recommendations to make text on a screen readable for dyslexic people. These recommendations were based on the results of an eye tracking study involving testing the effect of eight text presentation parameters on objective readability and subjective preferences for people with and without dyslexia. Study conclusions indicated that larger font sizes significantly improve readability, especially for people with dyslexia (ranging from 18 to 24 points for Arial font type). Conclusions also showed that larger character spacing significantly improves readability for people with and without dyslexia.

Venturini and Gena (2017) made experiments to improve the level of web accessibility for dyslexic users. They set guidelines that in their opinion should be added to current criteria in order to improve the level of web accessibility for dyslexic users. These guidelines are adding complete, exhaustive, and intuitive glossaries; increasing the minimum font and line spacing size; decreasing the number of characters for each text column; giving precise guidelines for designing a clear layout, i.e. how to separate page sections (color, border), and fix the maximum number of columns that must be implemented.

Benmarrakchi et al. (2017) set guidelines for accessibility of digital Arabic content for students with specific learning disabilities. One guideline refers to offer the possibility for dyslexic readers to adjust the electronical text size and the font types so as to create texts that are easy to read.

2.3 Studies Evaluating Specific Interface Features Using User Testing

Zikl et al. (2015) compared reading speed and efficiency using two different fonts (the standard writing fonts and open dyslexic font). They found that the use of the font Open Dyslectic, which was designed specifically for pupils with dyslexia did not lead to any marked improvement of reading speed or error rates in comparison with the commonly used font.

Berget et al. (2016) investigated whether the visual content in search user interfaces enhances performance among dyslexics, they test performance of participants (dyslexic and non-dyslexic) in four conditions: icons only in a grid layout, words only in a grid layout, and both icons and words in a grid layout and icons and words in a list layout. They concluded that presenting icons and words in a list layout will benefit both dyslexics and non-dyslexic users in terms of search performance over any kind of grid - like format.

3 Method

3.1 Objective and Hypotheses

Berget et al. (2016) that was mentioned in previous studies (in Sect. 2.3) investigated whether the inclusion of visual content in textual search user interfaces enhances performance among dyslexics. They tested performance of participant (dyslexics and non-dyslexics) in four condition (a) icons only in a grid layout, (b) words only in a grid layout, and both icons and words in dual-modality displays in (c) a grid and in (d) list layout. They found that presenting icons and words in a list layout will benefit both dyslexic and non-dyslexic users, but they did not investigate the effect of switching the locations of word and icon (displaying icon first instead of words in the list layout).

This study continued the work of Berget et al. (2016); the objectives included confirming findings of Berget et al. (2016) and investigating the effect of switching the locations of words and icons.

The work in this current study included testing performance. Task search times and number of errors were used as measures of performance of participants in four conditions: words only, icons only, both words and icons in two arrangements (words/icons) and (icons/words). Each was presented in a list layout as part of a search user interface. The purpose of the last two conditions is to investigate whether displaying the icons first than the words (icons/words) will give better performance for dyslexic users (without reducing performance of non-dyslexic users) than displaying the words first than the icons (words/icons). Participants included both dyslexic users and non-dyslexic users (as controls). An experiment was designed to test the following hypotheses:-

- H_1: Dyslexics locate targets more efficiently and effectively in search tasks displayed by mixed words and icons (in both conditions) than in search tasks with only words or icons.
- H_2: Dyslexics locate targets more efficiently and effectively in search tasks displayed by (icons/words) than in search tasks with (words/icons).
- H_3: Non-dyslexics locate targets more efficiently and effectively in search tasks displayed by mixed words and icons (in both conditions) than in search tasks with only words or icons.
- H_4: Non-dyslexics locate targets more efficiently and effectively in search tasks displayed by (words/icons) than in search tasks with (icons/words).
- H_5: Dyslexics prefer search interfaces containing mixed words and icons (in both conditions) over interfaces containing only words or icons.

3.2 Participants

Sixteen students (eight with dyslexia and eight non-dyslexic who are a control group) of basic (preparatory) education and middle (secondary) education schools in Benghazi participated in the experiment. Students with dyslexia were recruited through the Department of Education and Integration of Special Needs in Benghazi. The control group was matched as much as possible with the dyslexic group according to age, gender, and school grade.

Half the participants in each group were females. The range of age of the participants was twelve to seventeen years with an average of 14 years and a standard deviation of 1.69 years in the control group and an average of 14.25 years and a standard deviation of 1.58 years in the dyslexic group.

3.3 Design of Experiment and Procedure

According to the experimental conditions, four test screens with different visual content: word, icon, word/icon, and icon/word (for simplicity, the singular form will be used to name the conditions) were designed using Cascading Style Sheets (CSS) language. Each screen represents a list of Seventeen items. Arial font (24 point size) was used, distance between words and icons was 1.5 cm, and the visual angle was 0.43° for each icon (see Fig. 1). Since Arabic language is the native language of all participants the test screens were design with a right to left direction.

The experiment was done in a normal office (during school hours) with the participant sitting in front of a desk at a viewing distance of 65 cm in front of a laptop with 15.6 in. screen size and 768 × 1366 resolution. Google Chrome was used as an Internet browser in offline mode.

Pilot experiments were conducted first to verify and adjust the experimental setup and procedure. In the main experiment, a set of search tasks was developed and each participant completed twenty tasks in the four conditions (word, icon, word/icon, and icon/word) presented in a list layout. Instructions were provided verbally for each participant and the experiment began with one training search trial with four search tasks (one in each of the four conditions), followed by four search trials; each consisting of four search tasks (one for each condition). Participants were instructed to use "pg up" and "pg dn" buttons to scroll up and down to ensure that all use the same method of scrolling. A screen recorder was used to record the test screen while participants perform tasks.

The sequence of the search trials and tasks was arranged using a Latin-Squares-Crossover Design. This design ensured that each participant tested all the targets in all the test screens. One target was presented in each task and doesn't appear again as a distracter in the next tasks after being used as target in the previous tasks.

A structured interview was conducted with each participant after finishing the search tasks to collect the demographic information and to obtain participants' opinions regarding the four types of test screens.

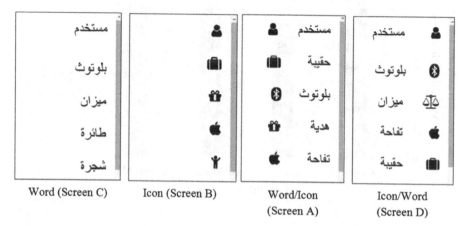

| Word (Screen C) | Icon (Screen B) | Word/Icon (Screen A) | Icon/Word (Screen D) |

Fig. 1. The four types of test screens (according to the four experimental conditions).

4 Results

4.1 Results of the Experiment

Search times of the four tasks in each condition for each participant were calculated by analyzing the recorded videos. Search time of each task was calculated from the time the screen appeared on the display in front of the participant until the time the participant placed the mouse pointer on the target.

All participants identified targets correctly in all search tasks in all screens (conditions) and there were no errors.

Between Groups Analysis
Figure 2 shows mean search times for the dyslexic and control groups. In all conditions, dyslexics mean search times are longer than mean search times of the control group.

The t-test was performed to compare mean search times between controls and dyslexics. Results of t-tests (shown in Table 1), indicated that dyslexic group took significantly longer times than control group to find search target in all conditions.

Within Group Analysis
Paired t-test was performed to compare mean search times between each two conditions within each of the two groups. Result of within groups paired t-tests for both control group and dyslexic group are shown in Table 2. Results of the tests indicated that the control group was significantly slower in the word condition compared with all the other conditions. While dyslexics were significantly slower in the word condition compared with the icon and the word/icon conditions and they were significantly faster in the icon condition than the icon/word condition.

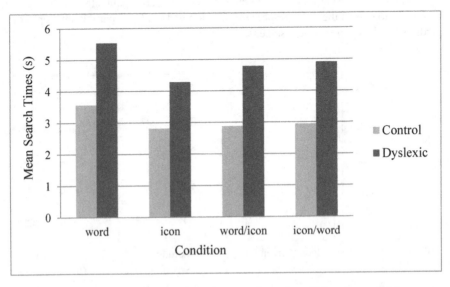

Fig. 2. Mean search times for both groups in each condition (in seconds).

Table 1. Results of t-test between mean search times (in seconds) of the two groups.

Condition	Control group		Dyslexic group		t-test		
	Mean	Standard deviation	Mean	Standard deviation	Degrees of freedom	t	p-value
Word	3.56	0.49	5.53	1.03	14	−4.87	<0.01
Icon	2.81	0.32	4.28	0.85	14	−4.57	<0.01
Word/icon	2.87	0.35	4.78	0.90	14	−5.57	<0.01
Icon/word	2.94	0.37	4.90	0.85	14	−5.97	<0.01

Table 2. Results of within-group paired t-test.

Conditions Pair	Control group			Dyslexic group		
	Degrees of freedom	t	p-value	Degrees of freedom	t	p-value
Word – icon	7	4.79	0.002	7	3.03	0.019
Word – word/icon	7	4.66	0.002	7	2.51	0.04
Word – icon/word	7	3.99	0.005	7	2.34	0.052
Icon – word/icon	7	−0.80	0.45	7	−1.97	0.09
Icon – icon/word	7	−1.32	0.23	7	−3.12	0.017
Word/icon – icon/word	7	−0.42	0.68	7	−0.62	0.55
Word – icon	7	4.79	0.002	7	3.03	0.019

4.2 Results and Analysis of the Interview Responses

All participants expressed their satisfaction with the design in general, size of words and icons was appropriate in their opinion and they said that they didn't have any difficulty in identifying the words and icons.

Table 3 and Fig. 3 show numbers and percentages of participants, in the two groups, according to their preferred type of test screen (condition). It is clear that most participants in the two groups preferred the two mixed icon-word conditions; with the largest percentage preferring the icon/word condition.

Table 3. Numbers and percentages of participants according to their preferred type of test screen (condition).

Type of test screen (condition)	Control group		Dyslexic group	
	Number	Percentage (%)	Number	Percentage (%)
Word	0	0	1	12.5
Icon	1	12.5	0	0
Word/icon	3	37.5	2	25
Icon/word	4	50	5	62.5

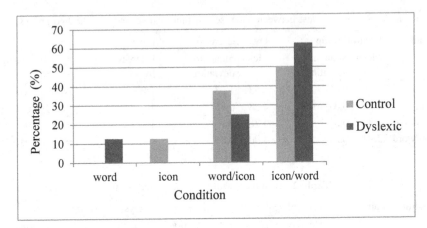

Fig. 3. Percentages of participants according to their preferred type of test screen (condition).

4.3 Results of Study Hypotheses

- **H_1:** This hypothesis assumes that dyslexics locate targets more efficiently and effectively in search tasks displayed by mixed words and icons (in both conditions) than in search tasks with only words or icons. Results of the experiment partially support this hypothesis in the word condition and contradict it in the icon condition. Results of the experiment showed that dyslexics located targets faster in the two mixed conditions than the word condition; however, this was only statistically significant in the word/icon condition. Results also showed that they located targets faster in the icon condition than the two mixed conditions, with statistical significance found with the icon/word condition.

- **H_2:** This hypothesis assumes that dyslexics locate targets more efficiently and effectively in search tasks displayed by (icons/words) than in search tasks with (words/icons).

  Results of the experiment indicate that there was no significant difference in search times between the icon/word and the word/icon conditions, although larger percentage of dyslexics preferred the icon/word condition.

  This finding contradicts with this hypothesis and indicates that there is no effect of switching the locations of words and icons.

- **H_3:** This hypothesis assumes that non-dyslexics locate targets more efficiently and effectively in search tasks displayed by mixed words and icons (in both conditions) than in search tasks with only words or icons. Results support this hypothesis in the word condition, but not in the icon condition.

  The results showed that non-dyslexic located the targets significantly faster in the two mixed conditions (word/icon and icon/word) than in the word condition. Also, they located targets in the icon condition faster than the two mixed conditions (word/icon and icon/word); although there were no statistically significant differences.

- H_4: This hypothesis assumes that non-dyslexics locate targets more efficiently and effectively in search tasks displayed by (words/icons) than search with (icons/words).
  Results showed that non-dyslexic located targets faster in the word/icon condition than the icon/word condition; however, since this difference was not statistically significant the hypothesis could not be confirmed.
- H_5: This hypothesis assumes that dyslexics prefer search interfaces containing mixed words and icons (in both conditions) over interfaces containing only words or icons. Results confirmed this hypothesis.

4.4 Discussion

Dyslexics located targets significantly faster in search tasks displayed by icons only compare with the word and the icon/word conditions and non-dyslexics (control) were fastest in the icon condition in comparison with the word condition; this indicates that it is simpler to locate targets in the icon condition.

The results showed that non-dyslexics located targets significantly faster than dyslexics in all conditions. Also, for both dyslexics and non-dyslexics, significant differences were found in search times between the word and the icon conditions. This is different from the findings of Berget et al. (2016), who found that no significant difference in search times between dyslexic and control in the icon condition, also found no significant difference in search times between the word and the icon conditions for dyslexics; the reasons behind this might be due to the differences in culture/language, age of the participants or that the conditions of the performance test of this study are different than conditions of the performance test of Berget et al. (2016).

There were no errors in locating targets in all conditions for both groups. This means that all screens were clear and size and type of font were suitable. This result supports recommendations of Rello and Baeza-Yates (2015) on use of Arial font with 24 point size.

The largest percentage of participants preferred the two mixed icon-word conditions; because, according to their opinion, they were more arranged.

Although, for the dyslexics, no significant differences were found between mean search times of the word/icon and the icon/word conditions; percentage of dyslexics that preferred the icon/word condition was larger than who preferred the word/icon condition.

5   Conclusions

This study examined the effect of adding visual content to textual search user interfaces on performance of dyslexic and non-dyslexic users. Performance was tested in four conditions (word, icon, word/icon, icon/word) presented in a list layout. Also, the effect of switching the locations of words and icons was investigated.

Results of the study indicated that, in general, adding visual content to textual search interfaces produced better performance. Specifically, better performance (for both dyslexics and non-dyslexics) was obtained when icons (representing the visual content) were used in the interface compared to using only words (text) in the interface.

Switching the locations of words and icons had no effect on performance; i.e. the same level of performance was obtained whether words were placed before icons or icons were placed before words. However, both non-dyslexics and dyslexics performed better in the word/icon interface than the word interface. The non-dyslexics, also, performed better in the icon/word interface than the word interface, while the dyslexics performed better in the icon interface than the icon/word interface.

Also, results of the study revealed that both dyslexics and non-dyslexics preferred interfaces containing both text and visual elements (mixed words-icons) over interfaces containing only text (words) or only visual elements (icons). Moreover, from the two mixed word-icon interfaces, they chose the icon/word as the most preferred one.

Based on these findings, this study recommends that developers and designers should use both icons and words in search interfaces targeting dyslexics instead of using only words. This should make the search interface more accessible for dyslexics and also improves performance of non-dyslexics.

6   Recommendations for Future Work

One limitation of this study is that it was difficult to reach larger numbers of dyslexic students. In future works, solutions to this difficulty should be sought and larger numbers of participants with wider range of age should be reached. This should help confirm results of the current study. It is also recommended that real-case search interfaces should be used.

It is also recommended that in future work, an eye tracker device should be used It would aid in measuring eye positions and movements during tasks search. This should help further in analyzing and understanding the results; including measurement of the mental load of the participants during performance of the experiments.

Another issue that could be investigated in future work is the effect of the distance between word and icon (in the mixed word-icon interface) on performance.

References

Ramachandran, V.S.: Encyclopedia of the Human Brain. Academic Press, San Diego (2002)

International Dyslexia Association. https://dyslexiaida.org/ida-dyslexia-handbook/. Accessed 18 Jan 2020

Takagi, H., Asakawa, C.: New challenges in web accessibility. Univ. Access Inf. Soc. 16(1), 1–2 (2015)

Iriarte, E.G., McConkey, R., Gilligan, R.: Disability and Human Rights: Global Perspectives. Palgrave Macmillan, London (2016)

Al-Wabil, A., Zaphiris, P., Wilson, S.: Web navigation for individuals with dyslexia: an exploratory study. In: Stephanidis, C. (ed.) UAHCI 2007. LNCS, vol. 4554, pp. 593–602. Springer, Heidelberg (2007). https://doi.org/10.1007/978-3-540-73279-2_66

Santana, V.F.D., Oliveira, R.D., Almeida, L.D., Ito, M.: Firefixia: An accessibility web browser customization toolbar for people with dyslexia. In: 10th International Cross-Disciplinary Conference on Web Accessibility. Association for Computing Machinery, Rio de Janeiro, Brazil (2013)

Avelar, L.O.D., Rezende, G.C., Freire, A.P.: WebHelpDyslexia: a browser extension to adapt web content for people with dyslexia. Procedia Comput. Sci. **67**, 150–159 (2015)

Rello, L., Baeza-Yates, R.: How to present more readable text for people with dyslexia. Univ. Access Inf. Soc. **16**(1), 29–49 (2015)

Venturini, G., Gena, C.: Testing web-based solutions for improving reading tasks in students with dyslexia. In: 12th Biannual Conference on Italian SIGCHI Chapter. Association for Computing Machinery, Cagliari (2017)

Benmarrakchi, F., Kafi, J.E., Elhore, A.: Communication technology for users with specific learning disabilities. Procedia Comput. Sci. **110**, 258–265 (2017)

Zikl, P., et al.: The possibilities of ICT use for compensation of difficulties with reading in pupils with dyslexia. Procedia – Soc. Behav. Sci. **176**, 915–922 (2015)

Berget, G., Mulvey, F., Sandnes, F.E.: Is visual content in textual search interfaces beneficial to dyslexic users? Int. J. Hum.-Comput. Stud. **92–93**, 17–29 (2016)

A Comparative Study of Accessibility and Usability of Norwegian University Websites for Screen Reader Users Based on User Experience and Automated Assessment

Prabin Parajuli and Evelyn Eika[✉]

Faculty of Technology, Art and Design, Oslo Metropolitan University,
Oslo, Norway
prabin.b9@gmail.com, evelyn.eika@oslomet.no

Abstract. Websites are essential for learners' access to information. However, due to the lack of accessibility and usability of websites, students with disabilities who solely rely on screen readers face challenges accessing webpage contents. This study explores accessibility and usability issues frequently encountered by screen reader students while interacting with Norwegian university webpages. An evaluation using automated tools showed that none of the university websites met the minimum WCAG 2.1 guidelines. Sixteen visually impaired participants were recruited and assigned five usability tasks on four different university websites. The results show that participants encountered usability and accessibility issues on all four websites. Recommendations for increased accessibility are proposed based on the findings.

Keywords: Web accessibility · Web usability · WCAG 2.1 · Universal design · University websites · Screen reader · Blind · Visually impaired

1 Introduction

The web is an essential part of the current day education system as it aids students to access information, offering the flexibility in times and locations for learning and personal growth [1]. Easily accessible and useable higher educational websites are essential because they assist a wide range of students with diverse abilities to use and access these websites. University websites facilitate teaching, learning, and communication [2]. Despite this, a digital divide exists in context of accessing information on webpages because many educational websites are not accessible and usable to all students, particularly to the blind users who rely on assistive technologies to navigate websites [1]. Early work uncovered basic usability problems with learning management systems (LMS) [3]. This study investigates the accessibility level of Norwegian university websites and addresses accessibility and usability issues that screen reader users commonly face.

M. Antona and C. Stephanidis (Eds.): HCII 2020, LNCS 12188, pp. 300–310, 2020.
https://doi.org/10.1007/978-3-030-49282-3_21

Universal design concept emerged from North Carolina State University in 1997, and the expert group of advocates developed its seven well-known principles. They coined universal design as "the design of products and environments to be usable by all people, to the greatest extent possible, without the need for adaptation or specialized design". More refined definition of universal design focusing on all people has also been proposed. According to Steinfeld and Maisel [4], universal design is defined as a process which authorizes a wide range of people by enhancing individuals' potential, health, and involvement in various social sectors.

Web accessibility refers to websites and tools to which people with disabilities are able to use [5]. People with disabilities are able to get all information and use all the functionality available to users without disabilities, such as links, buttons, and form controls [1]. Web accessibility empowers individuals with disabilities or special needs to operate the web contents, making web accessibility a fundamental matter in web design [6]. W3C [7] elaborates on the accessibility requirements for people with disabilities as follows: (a) Websites should work well with assistive technologies such as screen reader tools, screen magnifiers, and voice recognition tools for the text input; and (b) General usability principles should be included. One factor for successful delivery of web accessibility is developers' awareness of the aspects involved [8]. The level of web accessibility is often low in many websites although various tools have been developed to help increase accessibility [9].

The term *usability* refers to the extent to which a product or system can be used by particular users with a specified objective in a particular situation with effectiveness, efficiency, and satisfaction [10]. Usability is also defined as the state of ease of use [11]. A product in a given context is considered usable if a person is satisfied using it. When a person purchases products, he/she expects them to function well and be easy to use in order to meet his/her needs [12]. Nielsen [13] defined usability using five key components: *Learnability*–How easy is it for users to accomplish tasks the first time they encounter the design? *Efficiency*–Once users have learned the design, how quickly can they perform tasks? *Memorability*–When users return to the design after a period of not using it, how easily can they reestablish proficiency? *Errors*–How many errors do users make, how severe are those errors, and how easily can they recover from the errors? *Satisfaction*–How pleasant is it to use the design?

Web accessibility means people with disabilities can perceive, understand, navigate, and interact with the websites' tools and features without barriers [14]. Inclusive web design gives people with disabilities equitable access to the functionality of the web as those without disabilities. Web usability concerns users' experience when they browse a website in terms of ease of use. According to Kamal, Alsmadi, Wahsheh, and Al-Kabi [6], web accessibility and web usability share common concerns, but they are not identical.

This study investigated the accessibility level of Norwegian university websites using two automated tools against Web Content Accessibility Guidelines (WCAG) 2.1. The study also addresses common accessibility and usability issues screen reader users encounter. The following research questions are asked: (1) To what level of compliance do the Nordic university websites meet the criteria for successful inclusive web design following WCAG 2.1 guidelines using automated tools? (2) What are common accessibility barriers screen reader users face when interacting with the different

Norwegian university webpages based on user experience and automated tools? (3) Are there assessment discrepancies between the two automated tools employed?

2 Related Work

There is a vast body of work on accessibility on the web. Some studies have addressed the assistive technology in use such as screen readers [15]. This study is concerned with the content. Kurt [16, 17] evaluated the accessibility of ten university websites over an interval of 5 years based on two automated tools, namely AChecker and Sortsite. In the first study [16], none of the assessed websites met the minimum success criteria. The follow-up study [17] showed that the same websites had not improved much over the 5-year period, and there was even a marginal decrease in accessibility.

Larzar, Allen, Kleinman, and Malarkey [18] investigated challenges faced by 100 screen reader users by collecting time diary data. The researchers identified five causes of user frustration when interacting with the website using screen reader software: (a) design of the page resulting in confusing screen reader response, (b) incompatibility of screen reader software with the internet browsers, (c) poorly designed unlabeled forms, (d) missing alternative text for images, and (e) inaccessible PDF-files and screen reader crashes. The results also showed that it took on average of 30.4% longer to use the websites due to frustrations.

Thompson, Burgstahler, and Moore [19] evaluated the homepages of 127 higher education websites over a 5-year period with experts' manual accessibility checks. They found significant accessibility improvement. However, most issues involved keyboard navigation which the researchers assumed to be caused by emerging new dynamic web contents.

Kesswani and Kumar [20] and Masood Rana, Fakrudeen, and Rana [21] noted that many educational institutes did not conform to recommended accessibility standards. The comparative analysis of top university websites of different countries showed that most schools met less than half of the accessibility recommendations.

Ismail and Kuppusamy [22] evaluated web accessibility of 302 Indian universities using three automatic tools (WAVE, AChecker, and Webpage Analyzer). Common errors were uncovered based on WCAG 2.0 conformance level guidelines. The results showed that none of the university websites tested met the WCAG 2.0 accessibility criteria. Design recommendations for accessibility were then proposed as follows: (a) Text alternatives for all non-text web content should be provided; (b) Headers need to be included for each page, including sections and tables; (c) Color contrast and other keyboard functionalities need to be supported; (d) Well-structured forms with interactive features should be considered; (e) Adjustment control of color contrast should be included and clearly visible in webpages; and (f) Media players should allow users to have full control to resize and reposition media in videos/audios.

Harper and DeWaters [23] evaluated accessibility of 12 university homepages in the United States by using the Watchfire Bobby automated tool according to the WCAG 1.0 guidelines. The results showed that only one university met all the accessibility criteria against WCAG 1.0 three priority levels A, AA, and AAA. Only

50% of the websites met priority 1 and priority 2 criteria; 33% of the websites met priority 1 conformance.

Menzi-Çetin, Alemdağ, Tüzün, and Yıldız [24] conducted a usability evaluation of a university website with six screen reader users employing interviews, usability tasks, and satisfaction questionnaires. The results showed that the most challenging task was finding the final exam dates on the university calendar, and the most time-consuming task was locating the course schedule on the webpage. The participants complained regarding missing search form on each page and suggested that a text version for all pages and proper link-list be provided.

Lazar, Olalere, and Wentz [25] evaluated the accessibility and usability of online job portal sites across eight states in USA. Sixteen participants applied for at least two jobs using automated tools. The results showed that most usability issues were the same for visually impaired users and people without disabilities. Also, user testing was fruitful when the participants performed the tasks including navigation between the various webpages and when they thought out loud during testing. The study deemed that most online accessibility and usability issues are easy to locate and can be fixed with little effort by web designers.

Another avenue of research relates to text readability [26–28] which in principle is covered by WCAG. However, it is hard to assess text readability in a practical and consistent manner.

3   Method

3.1   Participants

Ten partially blind and four fully blind participated in the study ($N = 16$) with a mean age of 19.5 years. Fifteen of the participants were from Nepal and one was from Oslo Metropolitan University. All the participants had at least a bachelor's degree and were proficient English readers. All participants used their own personal computer for the user testing. Nine participants used the NVDA screen reader tools and seven used the JAWS screen reader.

3.2   Material

Four internationally recognized Norwegian university websites were chosen for this research: University of Stavanger (UiS, https://www.uis.no/), University of Tromso (UiT, https://en.uit.no/), University of South-Eastern Norway (USN, https://www.usn. no/), and University of Adger (UiA, https://www.uia.no/).

The above-listed websites were chosen arbitrarily. We evaluated the homepages, contact pages, and about pages using two automated tools. The homepages were evaluated first because it is the portal through which the users access the websites. If the home page is inaccessible, disabled user may find it challenging to access the remaining part of the website [29]. Only 1-level pages were evaluated. As noted, the homepage alone does not represent the accessibility and usability of the entire website, but the homepage and level-1 represent the site [30].

3.3 Equipment

Two automated tools WAVE (Web Accessibility Evaluation Tool) [31] and Total Validator [32] were used to evaluate the accessibility of the university webpages. Automated tools are essential for checking the minimal accessibility level of the website; however, relying only on automated tests may not be sufficient as automated tools cannot thoroughly check accessibility issues of the webpages [17, 33]. Total Validator is a free software for web accessibility testing. It checks if the website uses valid HTML and CSS with no broken links and complies with WCAG 2.1 [34]. Similarly, WAVE is a free web accessibility evaluation tool which presents a visual description of accessibility issues [34]. Both tools test webpages against the latest WCAG 2.1 guidelines, support direct URL submissions, and generate detailed WCAG 2.1 conformance level reports (A, AA, and AAA).

3.4 Measurements

Web accessibility metrics indicate the accessibility level of websites [35]. WAVE and Total Validator were used to evaluate the different webpages of university websites against WCAG 2.1. The guidelines are categorized into four principles: perceivable, operable, understandable, and robust. These are subdivided into 13 guidelines. Among those guidelines, we selected the checklists for screen reader users. In this study, only conformance Level AA of the webpage is tested. According to the guidelines' documentation [36], Level AAA conformance is not a must as a general policy for the whole website as it is not practicable to meet the whole Level AAA Success Criteria for some content. We thus chose Level AA conformance because it fulfills both Level A and Level AA conformance of the webpages.

The System Usability Scale (SUS) is a 5-Likert scale consisting of 10 questions; it provides the overall view of subjective assessments of usability of system [37]. SUS score indicates usability interpretation regarding effectiveness, efficiency, and satisfaction [38].

A web accessibility questionnaire was devised. The questionnaire was inspired by structural issues given [40] and included the following checks: (a) page title; (b) image text alternatives; (c) heading, contrast ratio, and text sizing; (d) keyboard access and visual focus, forms, labels, and errors; and (e) moving, flashing, or blinking content, multimedia alternatives, and basic structure checks.

3.5 Procedure

Both face-to-face and remote sessions were conducted. The four university webpages were first evaluated using two automated tools. The most reoccurring results of each webpage from automated tools were then extracted. The participants were given five sets of tasks for each university. Then they were provided with the SUS questionnaire to measure the usability of each website. Further, they were provided with accessibility questionnaires and open-ended questions to assess the accessibility of the website. The face-to-face session lasted approximately 1.5 h. Remote sessions lasted longer (Fig. 1).

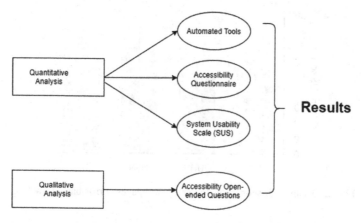

Fig. 1. Experimental procedure overview.

4 Results

4.1 Automated Accessibility Testing

Table 1 shows the results obtained with WAVE and Total Validator tools on the four university websites. The number of errors reported by Total Validator ($M = 46.75$, $SD = 24.65$) was higher than that of WAVE ($M = 36.5$, $SD = 23.35$). In contrast, the number of warnings reported by WAVE ($M = 50.5$, $SD = 33.13$) was higher than those reported by Total Validator ($M = 45.75$, $SD = 28.91$). Total Validator reported that the number of errors was relatively more severe than the warnings generated, which need to be minimized to achieve successful accessibility.

Table 1. Mean and standard deviation of automated tools report

Automated tools	WAVE			Total validator	
	Errors	Alerts	Contrast	Errors	Warnings
Mean	36.5	50.5	21.5	46.75	45.75
Standard Deviation	23.35	33.13	22.12	24.65	28.91

4.2 Perceived Usability

Figure 2 shows the perceived usability results of the four university websites based on the participants' responses to the SUS questionnaire. Following the usability interpretation [41], the usability score showed that only University of Adger (UiA) website was acceptable ($M = 69.53$, $SD = 7.14$). The other three university websites (UiS, UiT, and USN) fell below the average of usability scale (i.e., $M = 68$). Only USN came close to the average usability scale ($M = 67.81$, $SD = 10.95$), and UiS ($M = 54.37$, $SD = 10.7$) and UiT ($M = 51.25$, $SD = 8.36$) were much below average.

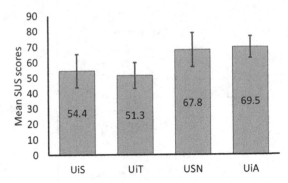

Fig. 2. Mean SUS scores for university webpages. Error bars show SD.

4.3 Interviews

After the online survey, the participants were asked open-ended questions on commonly occurring issues they encountered on the university websites. The results can be summarized as follows: Frist, the video played automatically and the pages did not have the option to pause the video. Next, some instances of duplicate page titles were observed. As a result, the users who relied on screen reader tools had difficulty distinguishing the pages. Instances of unstructured linked lists and headings were also reported. The users thus had to scan the entire page with the screen reader to find the desired content. Further, the screen reader read the webpage with a Norwegian accent. Some of the breadcrumbs were poorly designed which again confused the screen readers. There were also browser compatibility issues with the screen readers. Some participants had to switch to other browsers to complete some tasks when they could not accomplish them in one browser. Finally, the search form within the website did not provide relevant results. Instead, when searching using the widely available google search engine, they were able to accomplish the pertinent contents.

After participants completed the online accessibility questionnaire, they were asked two open-ended questions related to accessibility issues. The accessibility problems encountered included poor heading structures, poor link list structures, ambiguous links, screen reader incompatibility in the browser itself, and inaccessible keyboard navigation.

5 Discussion

This study aimed to uncover common accessibility and usability issues screen reader users experience when interacting with the contents provided by typical Norwegian university webpages. The results employing the two automated tools indicate that all four universities had accessibility level A checkpoint issues of 1.1.1 (non-text content). This checkpoint has been found to be the most commonly violated issue in other university websites [16, 17, 41–43]. This accessibility problem is frustrating for people with disabilities, especially screen reader users; therefore, fixing this issue would enable users to more effectively perceive the web content.

Level A checkpoint 1.3.1 (info and relationships) and level AA 3.3.2 (labels or instructions) were outlined as distinct issues, as also found in other educational institute websites [22, 41–43]. These issues should also be entailed to increase accessibility for users relying on screen reader tools. Note that USN and UiT had slightly different ratings compared to the other two universities: the UiT homepage had a 3.3.1 issue (instead of 3.3.2) reported by both tools and its contact page had no 3.3.2 issue according to WAVE. USN's homepage and contact page had no 3.3.2 issue according to WAVE, while both pages had such issues according to Total Validator. Additionally, there appears to be a trend where more level AA 1.4.3 (contrast) issues were detected by WAVE while more 1.4.4 (resize text) issues were detected by Total Validator.

Further, level A checkpoint 2.4.4 (link purpose) was violated by all four university websites. Entailing this checkpoint would ensure that all the links have a meaningful purpose and the potential users can understand the context of the links. This checkpoint issue has also been identified in other websites [22, 40, 41]. Also, 2.4.6 (headings and labels) was the only level AA checkpoint issue detected on all selected websites by WAVE only, except USN's contact page which was instead detected by Total Validator. This issue has also been a major issue in other university websites [41–43].

The participants responded that navigation was the most reoccurring issue they experienced when accessing the Norwegian university websites with screen readers. This issue acknowledges earlier research [18] which confirms that navigation is one of the most frustrating challenges screen reader users face when accessing the web. Previous studies [45–47] also point out that the navigation issue should be considered in educational websites.

In addition, the participants experienced that the screen reader tool read all the links and headings when browsing the webpages, which was annoying. Previous studies [18, 24, 48] also report that the users get frustrated when the pages are read out every time the webpage is loaded. Inclusion of a *skip* link within a webpage is recommended [18] such that screen reader users can bypass unwanted links.

Another common usability issue is incompatibility of screen reader software with the internet browsers. A few students were observed switching between browsers to complete the task. This reveals a violation of one of the usability principles, i.e., *learnability*, coined by [13], as also addressed in other studies [18, 24].

During the testing, it was observed that most participants visited external search engines to locate the desired information which they could not find using the internal search engine of the website. Most were able to accomplish the tasks via the search engines. Menzi-Çetin and colleagues [24] detected similar usability barriers.

The automated tools revealed that none of the university websites investigated met the minimum WCAG accessibility guidelines. The tools reported inconsistent accessibility issues and warnings. This finding is in agreement with that of Molinero and Frederick [44] who used three automated tools to evaluate 50 websites with different results. They warn that simply relying on one automated tool is risky since different tools seem to provide different accessibility results.

In this study we recruited only fully blind and partially blind participants. Other participant groups who may also rely on screen reader tools (e.g., motor impaired and users with cognitive disorders) were not included. Most of the tests were performed remotely. A remote study can be error prone and it is difficult to observe all the issues and sessions during the tasks [49]. Further, all four tested websites are dynamic; their contents are frequently updated daily. The results could differ when evaluations are performed over time. Moreover, the evaluation was performed only on three webpages of each university website. Including more evaluation tools and manual evaluations may also help reaffirm the findings. Further analysis of the open-ended questions may also help clarify related issues.

6 Conclusion

Our experiment suggests that the accessibility level of higher educational websites at the time of the study was inadequate. It was observed that none of the evaluated sites met the minimum WCAG 2.1 guidelines. Additionally, entirely relying on automated tools is probably not the optimal practice for uncovering website accessibility issues. This study reveals that the most common usability issues universities need to consider are clear labelling of page titles, ease of keyboard access on navigation, presenting the breadcrumb easy to locate, and proper interface and results of search form design. Also, universities should focus on accessibility aspects including organizing the heading and link structures, proper labelling of headings and links, and keyboard navigation. It is advisable that the screen reader developers design the software compatible with most browsers. Future work includes assessing larger samples and conducting face-to-face interviews to gather more complete impressions. Also, manual evaluations may help in-depth analyses of accessibility issues. Future studies may address individuals with different disabilities who also rely on screen reader tools to access web information, with different assistive tools and evaluation tools.

References

1. Kuakiatwong, S., Whittier, D.: Evaluating web accessibility and usability for totally blind users at Thailand Cyber University. ProQuest Dissertations Publishing (2011)
2. Carmel, T., Alan, B.: The school website: facilitating communication engagement and learning. Br. J. Edu. Technol. 47(2), 421–436 (2016)
3. Sandnes, F., Jian, H., Hagen, S., Talberg, O.: Student evaluation of the learning management system fronter from an HCI perspective. In: International Conference on Engineering Education–ICEE (2007)
4. Steinfeld, E., Maisel, J.D.: Universal Design: Creating Inclusive Environments. Wiley, Hoboken (2012)
5. W3C: Introduction to Web Accessibility (2019). https://www.w3.org/WAI/fundamentals/accessibility-intro/. Accessed 22 Apr 2019
6. Kamal, I.W., Alsmadi, I.M., Wahsheh, H.A., Al-Kabi, M.N.: Evaluating web accessibility metrics for Jordanian Universities. Int. J. Adv. Comput. Sci. Appl. 7(7), 113–122 (2016)
7. W3C: Accessibility, Usability, and Inclusion: Related Aspects of a Web for All (2016). https://www.w3.org/WAI/intro/usable. Accessed May 2018
8. Sierkowski, B.: Achieving web accessibility. In: Proceedings of the 30th Annual ACM SIGUCCS Conference on User Services, pp. 288–291. ACM (2002)

9. Lazar, J., Dudley-Sponaugle, A., Greenidge, K.-D.: Improving web accessibility: a study of webmaster perceptions. Comput. Hum. Behav. **20**(2), 269–288 (2004)
10. ISO.: Ergonomics of human-system interaction - Part 11: Usability: Definitions and concepts (ISO 9241–11:2018) (2018)
11. Martyn, C., Chetz, C., Anne, J.: Embedding accessibility and usability: considerations for e-learning research and development projects. Res. Learn. Technol. **15**(3), 231–245 (2007)
12. Sunil, B., Ravi, B., Edna, W.: Mapping product usability. Int. J. Oper. Prod. Manag. **22**(10), 1071–1089 (2002)
13. Nielsen, J.: Usability 101: Introduction to Usability. CRC Press, Boca Raton (2003)
14. W3C: Accessibility, Usability, and Inclusion (2016). https://www.w3.org/WAI/fundamentals/accessibility-usability-inclusion/. Accessed 15 May 2019
15. Kadayat, B.B., Eika, E.: Impact of sentence length on the readability of web for screen reader users. In: Antona, M., Stephanidis, C. (eds.) HCII 2020, LNCS, vol. 12188, pp. 261–271. Springer, Cham (2020)
16. Kurt, S.: Accessibility of Turkish university Web sites. Univ. Access Inf. Soc. **16**(2), 505–515 (2017)
17. Kurt, S.: The accessibility of university web sites: the case of Turkish universities. Univ. Access Inf. Soc. **10**(1), 101–110 (2011)
18. Lazar, J., Allen, A., Kleinman, J., Malarkey, C.: What frustrates screen reader users on the web: a study of 100 blind users. Int. J. Hum. Comput. Interact. **22**(3), 247–269 (2007)
19. Thompson, T., Burgstahler, S., Moore, E.J.: Web accessibility: a longitudinal study of college and university home pages in the northwestern United States. Disabil. Rehabil. Assist. Technol. **5**(2), 108–114 (2010)
20. Kesswani, N., Kumar, S.: Accessibility analysis of websites of educational institutions. Perspect. Sci. **8**, 210–212 (2016)
21. Masood Rana, M., Fakrudeen, M., Rana, U.: Evaluating web accessibility of university web sites in the Kingdom of Saudi Arabia. Int. J. Technol. Knowl. Soc. **7**(3), 15 (2011)
22. Ismail, A., Kuppusamy, K.: Accessibility of Indian universities' homepages: an exploratory study. J. King Saud Univ. Comput. Inf. Sci. **30**(2), 268–278 (2018)
23. Harper, K.A., DeWaters, J.: A quest for website accessibility in higher education institutions. Internet Higher Educ. **11**(3–4), 160–164 (2008)
24. Menzi-Cetin, N., Alemdağ, E., Tüzün, H., Yıldız, M.: Evaluation of a university website's usability for visually impaired students. Univ. Access Inf. Soc. **16**(1), 151–160 (2017)
25. Lazar, J., Olalere, A., Wentz, B.: Investigating the accessibility and usability of job application web sites for blind users. J. Usabil. Stud. **7**(2), 68–87 (2012)
26. Eika, E., Sandnes, F.E.: Assessing the reading level of web texts for WCAG2.0 compliance —can it be done automatically? In: Di Bucchianico, G., Kercher, P. (eds.) Advances in Design for Inclusion, pp. 361–371. Springer, Cham (2016). https://doi.org/10.1007/978-3-319-41962-6_32
27. Eika, E., Sandnes, F.E.: Authoring WCAG2.0-compliant texts for the web through text readability visualization. In: Antona, M., Stephanidis, C. (eds.) UAHCI 2016. LNCS, vol. 9737, pp. 49–58. Springer, Cham (2016). https://doi.org/10.1007/978-3-319-40250-5_5
28. Eika, E.: Universally designed text on the web: towards readability criteria based on anti-patterns. Stud. Health Technol. Inform **229**, 461–470 (2016)
29. Lazar, J., Greenidge, K.-D.: One year older, but not necessarily wiser: an evaluation of homepage accessibility problems over time. Univ. Access Inf. Soc. **4**(4), 285–291 (2006)
30. Hackett, S., Parmanto, B.: Homepage not enough when evaluating web site accessibility. Internet Res. **19**(1), 78–87 (2009)
31. WebAIM.: WAVE Web Accessibility Tool (2019). https://wave.webaim.org/. Accessed 05 Apr 2019

32. Total Validator: Total Validator (2019). https://www.totalvalidator.com/. Accessed 08 Apr 2019
33. Vigo, M., Brown, J., Conway, V.: Benchmarking web accessibility evaluation tools: measuring the harm of sole reliance on automated tests. In: Proceedings of the 10th International Cross-Disciplinary Conference on Web Accessibility. ACM (2013)
34. W3C: Web Accessibility Evaluation Tool Lists (2006). https://www.w3.org/WAI/ER/tools/. Accessed 05 Apr 2019
35. W3C: Research Report on Web Accessibility Metrics (2012). https://www.w3.org/TR/accessibility-metrics-report/. Accessed 11 Apr 2019
36. W3C: Understanding Conformance|Understanding WCAG 2.0. https://www.w3.org/WAI/WCAG21/Understanding/conformance. Accessed 12 Apr 2019
37. Brooke, J.: SUS-a quick and dirty usability scale. Usabil. Eval. Ind. **189**(194), 4–7 (1996)
38. UIUX Trend: Measuring and Interpreting System Usability Scale (SUS) (2017). https://uiuxtrend.com/measuring-system-usability-scale-sus/. Accessed 7 Apr 2019
39. Sauro, J.: Measuring usability with the system usability scale (SUS) (2011). https://measuringu.com/sus/. Accessed 22 Nov 2018
40. W3C: Easy Checks - A First Review of Web Accessibility (2017). https://www.w3.org/WAI/test-evaluate/preliminary/. Accessed 24 Apr 2019
41. Ismailova, R., Inal, Y.: Accessibility evaluation of top university websites: a comparative study of Kyrgyzstan, Azerbaijan, Kazakhstan and Turkey. Univ. Access Inf. Soc. **17**(2), 437–445 (2018)
42. Verkijika, S.F., De Wet, L.: Accessibility of South African university websites. Univ. Access Inf. Soc. **19**(1), 201–210 (2018). https://doi.org/10.1007/s10209-018-0632-6
43. Alahmadi, T., Drew, S.: Accessibility evaluation of top-ranking university websites in world, Oceania, and Arab categories for home, admission, and course description webpages. J. Open Flex. Dist. Learn. **21**(1), 7–24 (2017)
44. Molinero, A.M., Frederick, G.K.: Reliability in automated evaluation tools for web accessibility standards compliance. Issues Inf. Syst. **7**(2), 218–222 (2006)
45. Hasan, L.: Evaluating the usability of educational websites based on students' preferences of design characteristics. Int. Arab J. e-Technol. **3**(3), 179–193 (2014)
46. Zhang, P., Dran, G.V., Blake, P., Pipithsuksunt, V.: A comparison of the most important website features in different domains: an empirical study of user perceptions. In: AMCIS 2000 Proceedings (2000)
47. Pearson, J.M., Pearson, A., Green, D.: Determining the importance of key criteria in web usability. Manag. Res. News **30**(11), 816–828 (2007)
48. Tanyeri, U., Tüfekçi, A.: Bir yükseköğretim uzaktan eğitim programının görme engellilerin kullanımı açısından değerlendirilmesi: GÜUEP örneği. Antalya, Turkey (2010)
49. Jard, C., Jéron, T., Tanguy, L., Viho, C.: Remote testing can be as powerful as local testing. In: Wu, J., Chanson, S.T., Gao, Q. (eds.) Formal Methods for Protocol Engineering and Distributed Systems. IAICT, vol. 28, pp. 25–40. Springer, Boston (1999). https://doi.org/10.1007/978-0-387-35578-8_2

Usability of User-Centric Mobile Application Design from Visually Impaired People's Perspective

Hammad Hassan Qureshi[✉] and Doris Hooi-Ten Wong

Razak Faculty of Technology and Informatics, Universiti Teknologi Malaysia,
54100 Kuala Lumpur, Malaysia
h.qureshi-1979@graduate.utm.my, doriswong@utm.my

Abstract. All over the world smartphone-based mobile applications
increasing rapidly. In the context of this rapid growth, these mobile applications are progressively important in daily life to look for using social
media, searching for medical information, applying for new opportunities,
online shopping, and becoming well informed with their surroundings. In
order to strengthen the interaction, accessibility, and usability for Visually Impaired People (VIP), the assistive mobile phone applications are
materializing this trend. The Visually Impaired People (VIP) are encouraged to act many functions with the help of these mobile applications.
According to the World Health Organization (WHO) estimated in the
year 2018 that worldwide there are approximately 1.3 billion people have
affected by near and distance vision impairment. The quality of their life
has suffered from visual impairments. Sometimes they have problems in
their ability to work and establish in their personal relationships. Due
to visual impairment, there are about 48% of people completely or moderately cut off from the people and things around them. These Visually
Impaired People (VIP) are taking an interest in the use of mobile applications. The mobile applications that are available nowadays, they are
totally inaccessible for VIP. The usability in these mobile applications is
limited and these applications do not follow the accessibility guidelines
of mobile. There is a serious need for a user-centric design of mobile
applications that creates easiness for Visually Impaired People (VIP)
to access mobile applications. The objective of this study is to describe
the user-centric mobile application design with the involvement of VIP.
There are two parts to this experiment. In the first part, VIP used the
original mobile applications which are available on their mobile phones.
After finishing and during the user interaction with original mobile phone
applications, user feedback, observation, interview answers, and design
recommendations were obtained. In the result of observation and interview in the first part, there are a lot of usability and accessibility problems during using mobile applications. In the second part, according to
the results of the first part and with the involvement of VIP developed a
user-centric design of a mobile application. The usability and time consumed on each task of this new design model were tested again by VIP.
Results show that the performance of VIP improved with the use of a

© Springer Nature Switzerland AG 2020
M. Antona and C. Stephanidis (Eds.): HCII 2020, LNCS 12188, pp. 311–322, 2020.
https://doi.org/10.1007/978-3-030-49282-3_22

user-centric design model of mobile applications. System Usability Scale shows that the usability of VIP is increased with the use of a user-centric design of mobile applications. Finally, this paper focused attention on establishing equal opportunities, that the user-centric mobile application design should be implemented. In the future, this user-centric design of a mobile applications will be used to develop improved mobile applications for VIP. It would be also needed for mobile application developers to follow the user-centric design to develop new mobile applications for VIP.

Keywords: Visually Impaired People · Human-Computer Interaction · Mobile applications · Usability · Accessibility · Visual impairment

1 Introduction

There are many kinds of research available on the design of mobile applications from many years, design guidelines are still producing difficulties and challenges for VIP. A VIP use these mobile applications to fulfill their needs with some help. Designing mobile applications for VIP involves specific challenges that are different from the designer of a mobile application. These challenges are expectations, experience, needs, and environment in which VIP use mobile applications. Mobile applications should be planned to developed according to the needs and continuous collaborations with VIP. The development of mobile applications is growing faster and its use becomes more widely due to its independence, in order to access the information and new technologies for visually impaired people(VIP). For VIP there are many organizations and individuals have tried to develop the mobile application accessibility instructions. The latest report by the World Health Organization [1] on dated 18 Oct 2018, there were about 1.3 billion people have lived with some visual impairment. This is a large portion of the total population but this portion remains cut off from new mobile development and research design technology. There is proof that VIP [2,3] faced many problems while using mobile applications. There were many types of research that have explored the wishes and requirements of VIP with respect to the requirements of mobile phone applications. In this exploration, they found the multi-functional abilities that are not available in old mobile phone applications. From practical research especially on the accessibility of mobile phone user interface design guidelines for VIP, there is no extensive contract. For VIP, global designing access should be allowed in mobile application designing. The people's quality of life has changed due to the appearance of mobile applications. The people can enjoy social network services, online shopping, mobile group chats, and email reading like services through these mobile applications. However, the visual interface is very prominent in all these mobile applications, therefore VIP has difficulties to access these mobile applications.

According to a survey on the accessibility of information systems [4], there is a need for extraordinary enhancement in the accessibility of mobile applications for VIP. In order to make progress the usability and accessibility problems in mobile applications, the usability guidelines provide by mobile phone companies like Google, Apple, and Samsung. There is deep darkness on the availability of these guidelines with respect to developers and designers due to that they are not aware of these rules and regulations. There are no international guidelines and standards for accessibility of a mobile application for VIP, such as Web Content Accessibility Guidelines(WCAG)[5]. The work done in the past for VIP is mainly focus on the graphical interfaces of mobile applications, and there are no implemented features in mobile applications for VIP. This study evaluates the accessibility and consequence of mobile applications on VIP and comparison the use of mobile applications by them. The main goal of this study explores the difficulties faced by VIP during the use of the mobile application in which the usability of different mobile applications from VIP's perspective was evaluated.

The remaining part of this paper is organized as follows. Section 2 describes the background and literature review. Section 3 describes the methodology of the experiment. VIP's interaction with original mobile applicatios in Sect. 4. Designing a new prototype of mobile application in Sect. 5.The Results and Discussion are described in Sect. 6. The conclusion and feature direction are described in Sect. 7.

2   Background and Literature Review

VIP are faced with difficulties in order to obtain their specific results while using mobile applications. They take a longer time to complete their tasks, performance to complete a task is also slow [10]. The PACMAD (People At the Centre of Mobile Application Development) is proposed by Harrison et al. [7] in which they described that mobile environments do not follow the usability standards. They also insist that effectiveness, efficiency, and satisfaction should be included to measure the usability of mobile applications. There was a vast investigation upon the mobile application design domain for VIP by researchers. In order to improve accessibility and interaction between touch-screen based smartphones and VIP, an investigation analyzed by Chiti et al [6] in 2012. An idea of a low vision mobile application portal was proposed for the development method by Sanchez et al [8]. VIP can gain access with the help of the developer's designed API to a, particularly designed mobile application accessibility feature. In modern software design, many kinds of research have communicated the major feature of mobile application development with user-centered design principles [11,12]. In order to provide self-reliance, privacy, and real-world metaphor research presented the guidelines that can be used to evolve accessible mobile devices for VIP [9]. However, in the real process of developing these guidelines are very common. Kane et al. [10] in an account for better use of touchscreen-based gestures manage a study in which they compared that how sighted people and VIP use the touch screen gestures. They proposed the design guidelines for accessible touch screen mobile applications that are mainly focused on gestures such as flick, multitouch, symbol, and shapes. Accessibility guidelines and standards of mobile applications promote and develop by an organization Web Accessibility Initiative (WAI) associated with World Wide Web Consortium (W3C). Mobile Web Accessibility Guideline (MWAG) 2.0 is proposed by WAI. There are four criteria of mobile environment guidelines depends on Mobile Web Accessibility Guideline (MWAG) 2.0 like operable, understandable, namely perceivable, and robust [5]. However, these guidelines are not particularly for mobile applications but somehow these guidelines are used for sorting out the accessibility problems in mobile webpages. iOS is provided a gesture-based screen reader is called VoiceOver [13]. VIP is able to navigate and type text input with the help of VoiceOver. VIP can adjust the focus of an object by moving the cursor position up, down, right, and left. The focuses object's description and name listen by the VoiceOver. When a user touches the character on a keyboard for input, VoiceOver pronounces that characters. In iOS VoiceOver handles both third-party integrated applications and built-in applications. Online mobile applications have pointed out that VIP uses those mobile applications to removing the disruptions of social life. The accessibility of Facebook on different mobile interfaces is evaluated by Wentz et al [14] with the help of 15 VIP. They suggested the desktop version of Facebook less accessible than a mobile interface. The uses of VizWiz mobile application is also evaluated by VIP, they classify the asked questions and used these questions as a Q&A platform for VIP.

3   Methodology

There are two phases in the experimentation. The first phase consists of, the participants were asked to use the original mobile applications as it is. At the end of user interaction with original mobile applications, user feedback, design recommendations, and user suggestions were obtained. In the next phase according to the user's response and feedback, a new prototype of a mobile application is designed. That newly designed mobile application prototype is again evaluated by the VIP.

3.1   Participants

In this study, the target people were visually impaired and have been evaluated the usability of different mobile applications from VIP's perspective. The VIP took part in the study with their own will. A pre-experiment interview has been taken from the participants to evaluate their level of knowledge with mobile applications. This interview helped to point out which participant can communicate and handle the mobile applications easily. On the basis of the interview, thirty-three participants were excluded out of 143. Thirteen participants found totally blind and severely visually impaired. Ten participants were facing difficulties when they interact with a touch screen mobile interface, they could not control the touch screen mobile keyboard. Six participants have no experience with the use of touch screen mobile phone applications. Finally, four participants have been refused due to their age was not between 18 and 45 years.

3.2 Materials

All participants used touch-screen mobile phones (Android) with the same android version 7.1. Audio and video demonstration of each task is given before a task is started. The study was organized in a lab. Five mobile applications used in this experiment. It was informed to all participants that if they want to quit at any stage of the experiment, or they feel that any task is more than their expectations or competency and they want to withdraw from that task then participants should quit with informed to their mentor.

1. Settings of any pre-installed application.
2. Chrome (Mobile web browser, pre-installed application).
3. Whatsapp (Messenger) used for mobile communication application.
4. Daraz (Online Shopping Portal, people use this portal for shopping).
5. Facebook (Social Network Service) .

In order to better understanding the feelings particulars in this study, observed participant behavior patterns and interviewed the participants after the use of each mobile application. The participants were asked to perform each task listed below. The result of observation recorded the time consumed to complete each task and a number of successfully completed tasks. When participants declared to finish tasks then the recording is also stopped.

3.3 Tasks

Table 1. Tasks with assinged applications.

Task	Application	Description
Task 1	The setting of mobile application	Task 1 is consisted of setting an existing mobile application, in which all the participants perform the Bluetooth and Wi-Fi switch On or Off
Task 2	Chrome Browser	Task 2 is related to a mobile web browser Chrome, in which participants searching the first picture of the computer
Task 3	Whatsapp Messenger	Task 3 is related to mobile messenger, in which all participants sending and receiving the voice message to each other
Task 4	Daraz Shopping Portal	Task 4 is related to an online shopping portal, in which participants perform the process of purchase a mobile phone
Task 5	Facebook	Task 5 is related to a social network service (Facebook), in which each participant update his current status and place a comment on it

4   VIP's Interaction with Original Mobile Applications

All participants perform the tasks on original mobile applications. The activities performed by VIP were observed closely by a mentor. In order to make sure that VIP performed the assigned tasks by themselves and the smooth operations, the mentor was responsible for it. In order to get the reviews from VIP, post-experiment interviews were organized at the end of completing tasks. It is observed that the VIP has faced difficulties in order to perform tasks. The average time spent on an individual task by VIP and task completed by VIP is shown in Table 1.

4.1   Usability Problems in Performing the Tasks

According to the interview that was conducted after the experiment, it is concluded that VIP had the following difficulties in performing tasks on mobile applications.

4.1.1   Typing Issue

In typing 67 VIP had difficulties in typing due to layout of keypad is very concentrated. Seven VIP who said that they have well familiar with mobile keypad, they had a ten-second delay in typing also. 35 VIP had difficulty in to see the output of what they were typed.

4.1.2   Vocal Problem

In interview 48 VIP recommended that voice instructions must be included in different languages while the manufacturing of mobile applications. The usage of mobile applications is more comfortable with voice instructions for VIP.

4.1.3   Need for Assistance

There are almost 34 VIP appeal and highlighted this issue that there is a person who should collaborate them in completing their tasks.

4.1.4   Difficulties in Operation

There were 20 VIP people cannot found the Bluetooth and WiFi buttons for operating. In mobile messenger, around 34 could not found the send text image due to it has no label on that button. In order to perform the online shopping 83 VIP could not select the mobile phone for purchasing. 35 VIP could not start the voice control to place their instructions.

4.1.5   Complex Structures of Mobile Applications

There were 46 VIP people had problems on how to update their status on Facebook. 52 VIP had a problem to place a comment on their friend's status. 36 VIP had difficulty in finding a specific friend from a list, in order to send a voice message. The bigger font size was suggested by many 25 VIP and 31 VIP had a problem in reading the text. The usability problems found in existing mobile applications by VIP, shown in Fig. 1.

USABILITY PROBLEM IN MOBILE APPLICATION

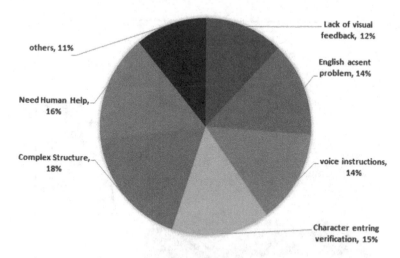

Fig. 1. Overall percentage of Usability Problems highlighted by VIP.

4.2   Design Recommendations

From the VIP's feedback, the following design guidelines were collected to improve the usability of the mobile application.

1. The place of home and power button should be fixed.
2. There are proper spaces between buttons and edges of buttons are clear.
3. The popup/voice message of error notification should be proper.
4. The cursor should be blink at the entry area.
5. The entered character's name must be heard.
6. When VIP touched an item its name should be heard.
7. Sound feedback can easily turn off if it is no more required.

5   Designing a New Prototype of Mobile Application

The response from VIP, about the use of the original mobile application, is a reason to design a new prototype of the mobile application. A new prototype of a mobile application was designed for the help of VIP. In the very first interaction of VIP with a new prototype of mobile application, the operating instructions will be clearly provided to operate the mobile application. A newly designed prototype was tested on Samsung A50, Huawei P10 Lite, and OPPO. This prototype will be used to enhance the usability of mobile applications for VIP, due to designing this prototype will increase the accessibility of mobile applications. Following requirements references of VIP were considered in designing the new android prototype. The adopted process in a newly designed prototype is sum up in Fig. 2.

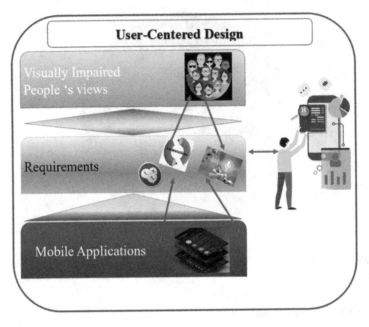

Fig. 2. User-Centered Design approach for newly designed mobile application prototype.

In the implementation of basic functionalities, a virtual keypad was taken more attention. The basic functions like add contacts, place a call, write and read messages are done with the help of a virtual keypad. In the virtual keypad, it was decided that there is a fixed number of keys and in order to utilize a mobile screen the size of keys was maximized instead of using a standard layout. In the result of VIP's feedback, it is decided that there is a fixed place of a keypad on a mobile screen. This solution was very much impressive and fast to use. A more comprehensive analysis was compulsory in order to make voice feedback effective for VIP. In order to perform scrolling in the contact list, VIP received a very quick voice response in moving from one button to another button. It was decided to maintain the gap between two adjacent buttons. When VIP used the soft keyboard there are interesting results were obtained that VIP have difficulties in selecting the appropriate key after locating the key. In order to overcome this situation, many VIP used voice commands but this is not fruitful. The usage of vibrotactile feedback was used to overcome this problem. When VIP performed Task2 and Task5 they have difficulties after selecting a text box when they entered characters in it. There is no confirmation message that their entering character wrote into the text box or not. In order to overcome this problem in a new prototype, VIP listens to the pronunciation of those characters which are entered into the textbox.

5.1 Evaluation of New Mobile Prototype

The mobile application prototype was evaluated on the task time consumed to complete a task, performance with System Usability Scale (SUS) rating. Brooke in 1996 described that SUS is a global assessment for the usability of a system because it is a reliable and low-cost usability scale [15]. In order to create ease for usability professionals, SUS is a highly flexible and powerful tool. According to Miller and Kortum in 2008 SUS has been used for a wide range of user evaluations like mobile applications, web pages, and web applications [16]. In order to provide authentic results according to the sample size, SUS is the simplest questionnaire [17]. There are 10 questions with five response options on the Likert scale, it is chosen for this study because it has simple in structure. In a newly developed prototype, it was observed that how many time VIP take help from our team. In the results section, the comprehensive facts and figures are shown.

6 Results and Discussion

The results have shown in Table 2 are related to the original mobile applications that were installed on their mobile phones. In Task 1 104 VIP successfully completed in 45 s and 10% help was needed by VIP from our team. In Task 1 VIP had a problem to locate the position of WIFI icon. In Task 2 78 VIP have completed the task successfully and 25% help was needed by VIP from our team. In Task 2 VIP taken 678 s due to they have faced problems in finding the web browser and inserting the text in a search bar. Some VIP had used the voiceover but due to its linear nature, they also had to wait to perform their task. In Task 3 88 VIP have completed their task successfully and 17% help was needed by VIP from our team. In Task 3 VIP taken 543 s to complete the task due to they do not find both buttons like the contact list and send items buttons. In Task 4 only 2 VIP completed the task and 63% help is needed by VIP from our team. In Task 4 unlimited time was taken by VIP due to the complex structure of a web page and VIP had difficulties to select their specific item. In Task 5 46 VIP completed their task successfully and 31% help was needed by VIP from our team. In Task 5 VIP taken 894 s to complete their task due to they have problems in finding the comments of their fellow and also had a problem in confirmation of the comment which they entered in the text field.

The results have shown in Fig. 3 is a comparison of how much time was consumed by VIP to complete their tasks both on original and newly developed mobile prototype. In Task1 VIP consumed four minutes on an original mobile

Table 2. Time spend, number of task completion and help needed.

Task	Task Completion (Min)	Total Number of VIP Complete the Task (N=110)	Percentage of help needed during Task
Task 1 (WIFI Setting)	4	104	10%
Task 2 (Chrome Browser)	9	78	25%
Task 3 (Whatsapp Messenger)	11	88	17%
Task 4 (Daraz Shopping Portal)	24	2	63%
Task 5 (Facebook)	10	46	31%

application and two minutes on a newly developed prototype. In Task2 VIP consumed nine minutes on an original mobile application and six minutes on a newly developed prototype. In Task3 VIP consumed 11 min on an original mobile application and eight minutes on a newly developed prototype. In Task4 VIP consumed 24 min on an original mobile application and 12 min on a newly developed prototype. In Task5 VIP consumed 10 min on an original mobile application and six minutes on a newly developed prototype.

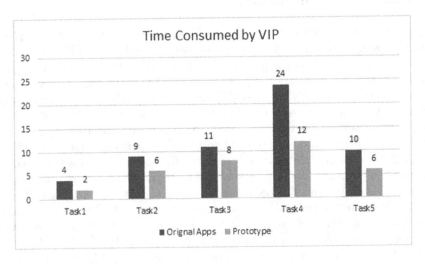

Fig. 3. Time Consumed by VIP to Complete the Tasks.

The results have shown in Fig. 4 are a usability percentage of tasks that are taken from the SUS questionnaire. After completing all tasks SUS questionnaire was filled in order to collect the feedback of VIP regarding usability. The usability of Task1 on an original mobile application is 63% and 93% on a newly developed prototype. The usability of Task2 on an original mobile application is 53% and

73% on a newly developed prototype. The usability of Task3 on an original mobile application is 62% and 79% on a newly developed prototype. The usability of Task4 on an original mobile application is 30% and 54% on a newly developed prototype. The usability of Task4 on an original mobile application is 46% and 87% on a newly developed prototype.

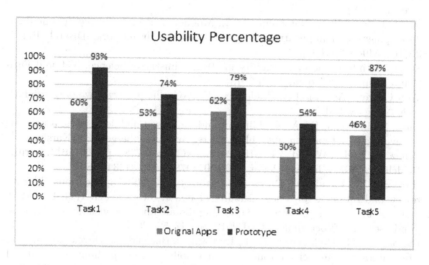

Fig. 4. usability percentage to Complete the Tasks.

7   Conclusion

The usability of user-centric mobile application design with respect to visually impaired people, the main goal of this study is to provide easy access to mobile applications for VIP. This study was conducted into two phases. In the first phase, VIP use the original mobile applications from their smartphones. In this phase, VIP has faced many difficulties in using the mobile application. VIP described their experiences for a better understanding of post-experiment interviews. It was observed that VIP had difficulties in accessibility features of mobile application design, particularly when they used the virtual keyboard for typing. In the second phase, a new prototype of a mobile application was designed according to the suggestion of VIP with the help of two expert mobile application developers. This mobile application prototype again used by VIP and it was observed that there is much improvement in the usability of the newly developed mobile application prototype. In conclusion, it believed that the contribution of this study lies in producing a new effective design of mobile applications. These designs of mobile applications are referred to mobile application designers and developers, in order to develop more usable and accessible mobile applications for VIP. In order to improve the recent situation of mobile applications for VIP, there is a serious need for making international standards with the involvement of VIP.

References

1. World Health Organization (WHO), Visual Impairment and Blindness Fact Sheet (2089). http://www.who.int/mediacentre/factsheets/fs282/en
2. McGookin, D., Brewster, S., Jiang, W.: Investigating Touchscreen Accessibility for People with Visual Impairments. Paper presented at the NordiCHI 2008 Lund, Sweden (2008)
3. Smith-Jackson, T.L., Nussbaum, M.A., Mooney, A.: Accessible cell phone design: development and application of a needs analysis framework. Disabil. Rehabil. **25**(10), 549–560 (2003)
4. Survey on information accessibility in 2012, Ministry of Science, ICT and Future Planning in South Korea, April 2013
5. Web Content Accessibility Guidelines (WCAG). http://www.w3.org/standards/techs/wcag#w3call
6. Chiti, S., Leporini, B.: Accessibility of android-based mobile devices: a prototype to investigate interaction with blind users. In: Miesenberger, K., Karshmer, A., Penaz, P., Zagler, W. (eds.) ICCHP 2012. LNCS, vol. 7383, pp. 607–614. Springer, Heidelberg (2012). https://doi.org/10.1007/978-3-642-31534-3_89
7. Harrison, R., Flood, D., Duce, D.: Usability of mobile applications: literature review and rationale for a new usability model. J. Interact. Sci. **1**(1), 1–16 (2013)
8. Sanchez, J., de Togores, J.S.R.: Designing mobile apps for visually impaired and blind users. In: Proceedings ACHI 2012, pp. 47–52 (2012)
9. Piccolo, L.S.G., De Menezes, E.M., De Campos Buccolo, B.: Developing an accessible interaction model for touch screen mobile devices: preliminary results. In: Proceedings IHC&CLIHC 2011, Brazilian Computer Society, pp. 222–226 (2011)
10. Kane, S.K., Wobrock, J.O., Ladner, R.E.: Usable gestures for blind people: understanding preference and performance. In: Proceedings CHI 2011, pp. 413–422. ACM Press (2011)
11. Krajnc, E., Feiner, J., Schmidt, S.: User centered interaction design for mobile applications focused on visually impaired and blind people. In: Leitner, G., Hitz, M., Holzinger, A. (eds.) USAB 2010. LNCS, vol. 6389, pp. 195–202. Springer, Heidelberg (2010). https://doi.org/10.1007/978-3-642-16607-5_12
12. Liimatainen, J., Häkkinen, M., Nousiainen, T., Kankaanranta, M., Neittaanmäki, P.: A mobile application concept to encourage independent mobility for blind and visually impaired students. In: Miesenberger, K., Karshmer, A., Penaz, P., Zagler, W. (eds.) ICCHP 2012. LNCS, vol. 7383, pp. 552–559. Springer, Heidelberg (2012). https://doi.org/10.1007/978-3-642-31534-3_81
13. Apple - Accessibility (VoiceOver for iOS). https://www.apple.com/accessibility/ios/voiceover
14. Wentz, B., Lazar, J.: Are separate interfaces inherently unequal?: an evaluation with blind users of the usability of two interfaces for a social networking platform. Paper presented at the Proceedings of the 2011 iConference (2011)
15. Brooke, J.: SUS-A quick and dirty usability scale. Usability Evaluation in Industry, pp. 189–194 (1996)
16. Bangor, A., Kortum, P.T., Miller, J.T.: An empirical evaluation of the system usability scale. Int. J. Hum. Comput. Interact. **24**, 574–594 (2008)
17. Tullis, T.S., Stetson, J.N.: A comparison of questionnaires for assessing website usability. In: Usability Professional Association Conference, pp. 1–12 (2004)

Virtual and Augmented Reality for Universal Access

Large Scale Augmented Reality for Collaborative Environments

Arnis Cirulis[✉]

Faculty of Engineering, Vidzeme University of Applied Sciences,
Valmiera, Latvia
arnis.cirulis@va.lv

Abstract. The purpose of this paper was to test UWB (ultra wide-band) tracking technology in augmented reality mode to achieve an environment where more than two users can interact with virtual content (3D models, intelligent avatars) in large rooms or open-air environments. The study showed that there is much potential for this technology despite precision not being very high. Position measurements and participant experience confirmed that these visualization and tracking technologies can be successfully used in Smart City infrastructures, collaborative training environments and other use cases.

Keywords: Augmented reality · Position tracking · Multi-user environment · Collaboration · Smart Cities

1 Introduction

Whether in cities or rural areas, there are no processes and activities that cannot be monitored, controlled or automated by the use of Internet of Things (IoT). By monitoring air pollution, it is possible to control carbon dioxide emissions of factories, pollution emitted by cars and toxic gases generated in farms. To detect potential fire hazards, combustion gasses and preventive fire conditions can be monitored to define alert zones. By monitoring vibrations and the state of materials in buildings, bridges and cultural heritage sites, structural conditions can be estimated. Driving and walking routes can be optimized by predicting traffic congestion using vehicle and pedestrian flow monitoring. Smart parking allows using parking space more effectively. Smart roads can display warning messages and provide diversions based on climate conditions and unexpected events like accidents or traffic jams. For waste management it is possible to determine rubbish levels in containers to optimize trash collection routes. Water quality and water suitability in rivers and the sea can be analysed for fauna and potability. Detection of liquid outside tanks and pressure variations along pipes. Smart lightning provides street light operation based on necessity. Real time sound monitoring in high activity areas. These are just a few examples [1] which we do not even notice in everyday life.

In the whole context of IoT technologies, when life is assigned to the world of physical things, it is important to provide a natural interface between humans and IoT elements through the use of visualization technologies. In communication where people, things, processes and data are involved, feedback is crucial. The lower the

M. Antona and C. Stephanidis (Eds.): HCII 2020, LNCS 12188, pp. 325–335, 2020.
https://doi.org/10.1007/978-3-030-49282-3_23

communication barrier between human and IoT elements, the more precise and correct the decisions that will be made [2]. Wide uses of smart phones and mobile applications foster guidelines for development of Smart City IoT applications. IoT technologies enable better Smart City applications, but the heterogeneity and dynamic nature of Smart City devices and infrastructure, as well as their large-scale deployment, make building Smart City applications difficult [3]. In future Smart Cities, technologies will need to be applied in a distributed manner, covering each other in response to users' real-time demands, in order to provide low-latency and high-performance computing for services. These activities will facilitate the residents' quality of life and improve the efficiency of services to meet their needs [4]. One of the main technological actors within the Smart City is the Internet of Things (IoT) paradigm, which proposes including physical objects as a new actor of the Internet, connecting them with people, information systems, and among themselves, so still the focus is on the interactions between people and simple objects [5]. For visualization and onsite interaction potential augmented reality could be used, but still lot of challenges arise if these technologies are used outdoors in city-wide distances, not only using smartphones, but AR HMDs as well, like *MagicLeap*, *Hololens 2* or *Nreal*, to visualize augmented information in the correct position, so that an observer still could move and do things naturally.

Around sixteen categories of sensors are used to provide Smart Cities' and smarter world's applications, where 3% are position and proximity sensors and 9% are acceleration and tilt sensors [6]. Present position sensors are not precise enough to provide projection of 3D models in correct positions, but the inside-out-tracking AR devices are not suitable for large distances. In this paper ultra wide band tracking technology is analysed and tested as a potential IoT sensor for position tracking of participants and elements in AR environment of Smart City. Cities are dynamic environments, which means that the surroundings are ever changing and technology should handle these changes in real time. These changes involve movement of people and transport, changes in weather and lighting conditions, which are difficult to filter or ignore. That is why a sensor-based solution is more appropriate than computer vision technologies in this case. A free room concept for entertainment in virtual reality ensures larger distances using optical tracking technologies, but this solution is not suitable for outdoor use and costs increase rapidly as the area grows. Instead, UWB anchors and sensors can be used outdoors in various weather conditions.

2   Methods to Clarify Potential Requirements for Collaborative Environments and Engagement of Participants

More topical in modern interactive environments is the potential of interaction among several participants in the same environment. Most current augmented reality environments provide individual user experiences but for real-life use cases collaboration is very important, whether this environment provides safety training on construction sites or decision making for city infrastructure, teamwork functionality should also be provided in augmented reality. It means that the position of multiple participants should be tracked fast and accurately, and virtual content should be multiplied and synchronized to involved augmented reality devices.

In recent years, high precision has been achieved in UWB tracking, meaning that this technology could be suitable not only for sports tracking and for logistics, but also for multiple-user collaborative VR/AR environments. Ultra-wideband uses short-range radio communication. Compared to Bluetooth Low Energy and Wi-Fi, position determination is not based on measuring signal strength (Receive Signal Strength Indicator, RSSI), but on a runtime method Time of Flight (ToF) or time-difference-of-arrival (TDoA). It measures the time light propagates between an object and several anchors. At least three receivers are required for the exact localization of an object using trilateration. A direct line of sight between the receiver and transmitter is required [7]. UWB utilizes a train of impulses rather than a modulated sine wave to transmit information. This unique characteristic makes it perfect for precise ranging applications. Since the pulse occupies such a wide frequency band (3–7 GHz according IEEE 802.15.4a standard), its rising edge is very steep and this allows the receiver to very accurately measure the arrival time of the signal. The pulses themselves are very narrow, typically no more than two nanoseconds [8]. UWB positioning systems offer 5–30 cm accuracy both indoors and outdoors and enable to get both 2D and 3D data [9]. Companies like Sewio, Eliko, Insoft, Decawave offer setups for implementing UWB wireless real-time locating systems.

A real test bed was set up in the Virtual reality technologies laboratory at Vidzeme University of Applied Sciences. Test bed floor size is 6 × 10 m equipped with four ultra wide band (UWB) anchors. With additional anchors the area can be expanded to cover much larger distances of over 100 m (see Fig. 1). The placement of anchors depends on area conditions. If it is a playground or construction area with direct line of sight, less anchors are needed, if it is a floor with offices or a warehouse with shelves, more anchors with various placement options are required.

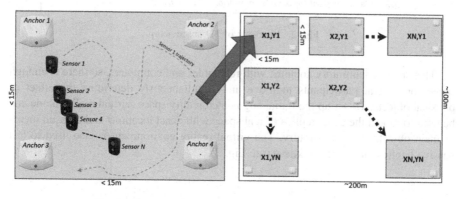

Fig. 1. Real-time location system (UWB) testbed setup.

The current AR UWB test bed allows testing the operation of advanced augmented reality scenarios (see Fig. 2) with two or more participants wearing Magic Leap or MS Hololens AR head mounted displays (HMD). An UWB sensor that is attached to the headset tracks participant position. As this is an augmented reality mode, the room can be equipped with furniture and different types of natural objects and at the same time be populated with virtual objects and avatars in form of 3D models. By placing a physical UWB sensor at any position in the room, the associated 3D model is moved to a new position. Predefined static objects can be placed before running merged worlds.

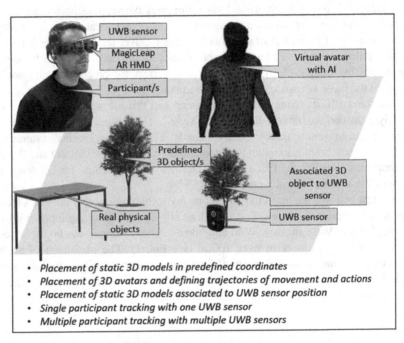

- Placement of static 3D models in predefined coordinates
- Placement of 3D avatars and defining trajectories of movement and actions
- Placement of static 3D models associated to UWB sensor position
- Single participant tracking with one UWB sensor
- Multiple participant tracking with multiple UWB sensors

Fig. 2. Elements of 3D space setup.

This specific laboratory contains with real tables and computers, so there is enough space for several participants to move and simultaneously determine the effect of physical objects. To set up the initial augmented reality space, virtual reality mode can be used to model the exact replica of real space with exact locations and measurements of main objects in the laboratory. The virtual reality environment is also used to test passive haptics and cyber sickness (see Fig. 3).

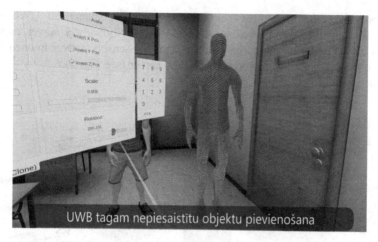

Fig. 3. Object and sensor management in virtual reality mode.

Runtime object management functionality is provided in AR mode. It is possible to replace present 3D models with other models from a database. Newly added models can be adjusted by changing their location, rotation and scale (see Fig. 4). New static models that are not associated with any UWB sensors can be placed in the scene.

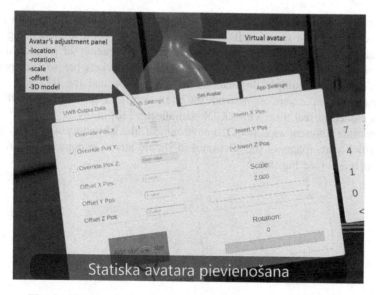

Fig. 4. Object and sensor management in augmented reality mode.

To provide collaboration between two or more participants, all UWB sensor position data should be delivered to all AR HMDs. Normally a server calculates positions of UWB sensors based on blink information sensors deliver to anchors and anchors to the real-time locating system (RTLS) server (see Fig. 5).

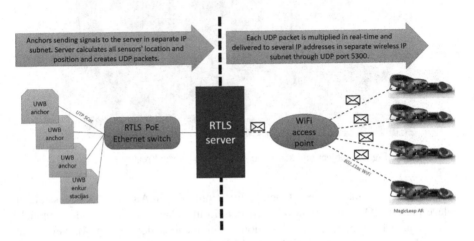

Fig. 5. Position data packet cloning to multiple AR headsets.

The calculated position of each sensor is encompassed in a JSON data packet, which is delivered to a specified IP address via the UDP protocol. Depending on the configuration the of the UWB system and server, the frequency of position data per second can vary starting from 10 position JSON data packets per second, per each sensor. To achieve multiple destinations all AR HMDs and the RTLS server are connected to the same wireless network (802.11n or 802.11 ac) and each UDP JSON packet is cloned in real time with a UDP samplicator [10] utility.

To measure different aspects of the environment, the laboratory was marked at 20 points, which participants of the environment should attend in consecutive order and pointed direction (see Fig. 6).

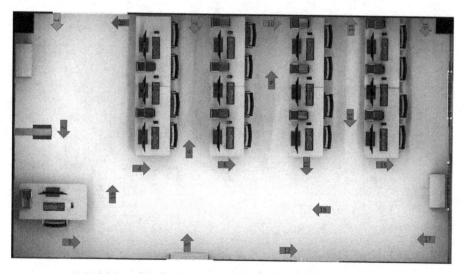

Fig. 6. Marked positions for precision and experience testing.

To analyse the tracking precision, position data was extracted from the JSON data stream, filtering only "*pressed*" events, which means each user triggered his/her position by pressing a button on the UWB sensor when reaching the exact position. A UWB sensor was attached to the right side of a *MagicLeap* headset. All data streams can be used to analyse user trajectories in depth.

3   Results of UWB Tracking Technology in the AR Environment

The group participating in the experiment was comprised of 26 people (female-10, male-16). All participants were between the ages 18 and 25. All participants were secondary school or university students, who are mostly familiar with technology and also have some experience and knowledge about virtual and augmented reality technologies. Completing the task took 4 to 6 min. The process was monitored from the server to make sure that all positions are activated only once without double "*pressed*" events. All 26 trajectories for 20 spots are depicted in Fig. 7. Position standard deviation varies from 0,10 m to 0,19 m. Higher data scattering can be observed in corners or closer to walls where spot marks were placed almost under the UWB anchor.

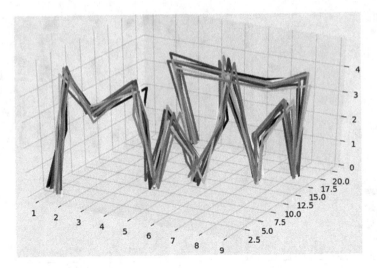

Fig. 7. 3D representation of all marked 20 locations for 26 participants.

The second experiment involved qualitative evaluation of user experience issues. Participants were divided into groups of two, where each one was wearing a *MagicLeap* headset connected to the same WiFi network. The experiment did not include very strict instructions or sequence. It was more about gaining experience in a safe way. The scenario included two static 3D models, two 3D models associated with UWB sensors and one walking avatar. Before the experience the user received basic instructions and a list of tasks they should try. Main tasks included walking around and observing physical and virtual objects, using UI to select different 3D models for the sensors, using UI to adjust virtual object position, use a controller to change object position, taking a UWB sensor and placing it in different positions, watching other participant's activity and talking with them, observing virtual object movement together with UWB sensor and avatar movement on a predefined trajectory, walking around virtual objects. The experiment took approximately 10 min for each group.

A survey included six questions based on object control and movement, navigation, UI and communication (see Fig. 8) and possible answers included the following: strongly agree, agree, not sure, disagree and strongly disagree. As depicted in Fig. 8, the amount of "disagree" or "strongly disagree" is low for all answers. However, participants were not highly satisfied with use of UI, and in some positions object movement was not smooth enough.

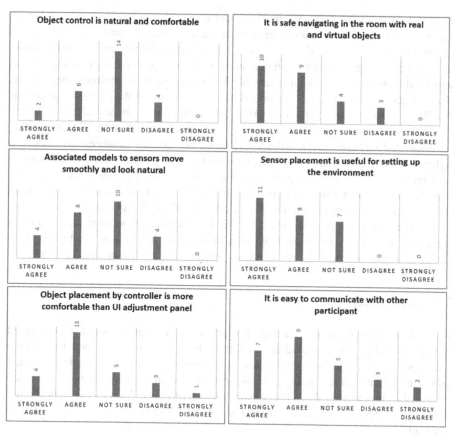

Fig. 8. Participant feedback about multiuser AR environment.

4   Discussion of UWB Tracking Suitability for Large-Scale AR Solutions

The purpose of these experiments was to understand whether UWB position tracking could be used for augmented reality scenarios, which take place in large rooms or outdoor environments with two or more participants. After the development of the first prototype for the Meta2 headset and then for *MagicLeap* it was clear that there is potential. Depending on UWB RTLS system configuration, manufacturers expressed the tracking precision around 30 cm [8], sport tracking companies [11] in some configurations have achieved 5 cm precision. When preparing experiment testbeds, the goal was not to achieve the highest precision but to understand whether there is a noticeable influence on the augmented environment from a participant's point of view. As the systems server applies the *Kalman* filter for position calculation, it also makes noticeable improvements for 3D model visualization, as it would be without the *Kalman* filter. For virtual object positioning stability is more important than precision and based on experiment data offsets of up to 20 cm or in some cases even up to 30 cm do not make a crucial difference in 3D model depiction and interaction, so a participant's experience in such a multiuser environment is natural. Next it is important to understand the limitations of what kind of interaction scenarios can be carried out in such an environment. Besides determination of X, Y position data, it is possible to acquire altitude values, but with noticeably less precision, so in environments without plain surfaces correct object depiction will not work. Rotation data is also available as the UWB sensor's casing contains a 9 axis IMU (Inertial Measurement Unit) [8], which is useful to determine view direction and virtual object orientation for 3D models that are associated with specific UWB sensors based on their ID numbers. To achieve a higher level of interaction it is not enough to know the position and orientation of a participant's head. Other body parts should also be tracked. For now, optical tracking technologies can deal with it. In the case of AR UWB headset controllers are a good option for hand gesture recognition with the headsets' depth cameras.

For future research an outdoor testbed will be setup to analyse more than two users interacting in larger area with more dynamic movements. In addition, a full networking service is in development to provide virtual object synchronization among users.

5   Conclusions

Technologies used for sports tracking or logistics can be adapted for use in augmented and virtual reality modes providing much more use cases in various industries. Large scale tracking and VR/AR visualization technologies are important for future Smart Cities and collaborative training environments. Research approbation will be carried out in collaboration with AR/VR companies like *Overly* and *Exonicus* to implement a solution for open-air museum, construction site and decision training for first aid in battlefields.

Acknowledgements. This work is post doctorate research project funded by ERAF, project number: 1.1.1.2/VIAA/1/16/105. Project name: Dynamic 3D visualization of the Internet of Things (IoT) elements in outdoor augmented reality (AR) modes. Research activities take place at the Faculty of Engineering at Vidzeme University of Applied Sciences, and specifically, in the virtual reality technologies laboratory. The project relates to Latvia's Smart Specialization Strategy (RIS3). Specifically, the project aims to contribute to the number 4 priority and number 5 specialization "Modern Information and Communication Technologies".

References

1. Libelium Comunicaciones Distribuidas, Libelium Smart World infographics. http://www.libelium.com/resources/top_50_iot_sensor_applications_ranking/#show_infographic
2. Cirulis, A.: Ultra wideband tracking potential for augmented reality environments. In: De Paolis, L.T., Bourdot, P. (eds.) AVR 2019. LNCS, vol. 11614, pp. 126–136. Springer, Cham (2019). https://doi.org/10.1007/978-3-030-25999-0_11
3. Giang Nam, K., et al.: On building smart city IoT applications: a coordination-based perspective. In: Proceedings of the 2nd International Workshop on Smart, pp. 1–6 (2016)

4. Naranjo, P.G.V., et al.: FOCAN: a Fog-supported smart city network architecture for management of applications in the Internet of Everything environments. J. Parallel Distrib. Comput. **132**, 274–283 (2019)
5. Rashid, Z., et al.: Using Augmented Reality and Internet of Things to improve accessibility of people with motor disabilities in the context of Smart Cities. Future Gener. Comput. Syst. **76**, 248–261 (2017)
6. Liu, X., et al.: Overview of spintronic sensors with Internet of Things for smart living. IEEE Trans. Magn. **55**(11), 1–22 (2019)
7. Reitmayr, G., Drummond, T.: Going out: robust model-based tracking for out-door augmented reality. In: Proceedings of the 5th IEEE and ACM International Symposium on Mixed and Augmented Reality. IEEE Computer Society (2006)
8. UWB Technology: Sewio Networks, s.r.o. (2018). https://www.sewio.net/uwb-technology/
9. Ultra Wideband Positioning: Eliko Tehnoloogia - Sensing The Future (2018). https://www. eliko.ee/services/ultra-wideband-positioning/
10. Leinen, S.: Samplicator. https://github.com/sleinen/samplicator/commits?author=sleinen
11. Eschosports. http://www.echosports.eu/#how-it-works

Walking Support for Visually Impaired Using AR/MR and Virtual Braille Block

Katsuya Hommaru[✉] and Jiro Tanaka

Graduate School of IPS, Waseda University, Kitakyushu, Japan
hommarukatsuya@fuji.waseda.jp, jiro@aoni.waseda.jp

Abstract. In recent years, the number of visually impaired people has been increasing, and supporting the movement of visually impaired people will be indispensable for the future society. At present, for visually impaired people, a general-purpose walking support is a combination of a braille block and a white cane; however, it is not enough. In this research, we provide a system that expands the above combination by utilizing the technologies of a see-through head-mounted display (HMD) and Augmented Reality/Mixed Reality (AR/MR). Specifically, utilizing the features of AR/MR, a virtual 3D object is projected as a braille block (virtual braille block) on the walking surface of visually impaired people via an HMD. Subsequently, when the white cane waved by visually impaired people and the virtual braille block intersect (collision), the guidance of forwarding, left, right, and turn is returned as feedback by voice and vibration. By realizing these, the goal is to provide a system that enables visually impaired people to move freely in the walking space.

Keywords: Augmented Reality · Mixed Reality · Visual impairments · Blind navigation · Accessibility

1 Introduction

Various measures have been taken for a long time to assist the mobility of visually impaired people. However, in recent years, it has become a social problem. For instance, traffic accidents while walking and fall accidents at the platform of train stations occur one after another. Many of the causes are misrecognition of braille blocks, difficulty walking due to obstacles, and misjudgments due to changes in the surrounding environment. To solve the problem, it is required to install braille blocks on the sidewalk and install platform doors at the station; however, it takes time and cost to develop the infrastructure.

Therefore, this research focuses on improving the mobility of visually impaired people without maintaining infrastructure and provide a walking support system for visually impaired people using AR (Augmented Reality)/MR (Mixed Reality).

M. Antona and C. Stephanidis (Eds.): HCII 2020, LNCS 12188, pp. 336–354, 2020.
https://doi.org/10.1007/978-3-030-49282-3_24

2 Goal and Approach

2.1 Background

According to official statistics from the World Health Organization (WHO) in 2013, there are about 285 million visually impaired people in the world, of which about 14% are blind, and 86% are of low vision [1, 2]. In addition, WHO's latest announcement (August 2019) shows that the total number has increased significantly to about 2.2 billion [3]. The reason is that not only congenital, but also acquired disorders, are increasing.

Based on these backgrounds, research using ICT has been accelerated in recent years, such as research aimed at improving navigation accuracy for visually impaired people [4, 5], and research on avoiding collision with visually impaired people based on walking prediction [6].

2.2 Research Goal

In this research, we focus on the combination of a white cane and a braille block, which is a general-purpose walking support for visually impaired people [7, 8]. For example, in Japan, walking of visually impaired people is required by the Road Traffic law, with the assistance of a guide dog or the walking with a white cane [9].

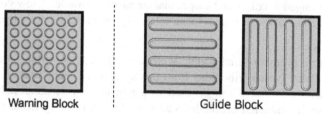

Warning Block   **Guide Block**

A dotted block indicates that there is a brunch point or an obstacle,
and a linear block indicates that the direction of the protrusion is the path.

Fig. 1. Two types of braille blocks

Braille blocks (see Fig. 1) were invented in Japan in 1965, and are used by visually impaired people to walk on the road in front of them while waving a white cane. At present, it is a highly versatile system that is installed not only in Japan but also in over 100 countries around the world. However, there are the following restrictions and problems [10–12]:

- Space and environment are limited, depending on the installation cost.
- Due to design priorities, colors that are difficult to see for low vision people may have to be used.
- Warning block and guide block placement rules are not uniform.

To solve these problems, this research extends a general-purpose walking support using braille block and white canes using a see-through head-mounted display (HMD) and AR/MR technologies. Specifically, utilizing the features of AR/MR, a virtual 3D object is projected as a braille block (virtual braille block) on the walking surface of visually impaired people via an HMD. Subsequently, when the white cane waved by visually impaired people and the virtual braille block intersect (collision), the guidance of forwarding, left, right, and turn is returned as feedback by voice and vibration. By realizing these, the goal is to provide a system that enables visually impaired people to move freely in the walking space [13].

2.3   Assumed Users of This System

Users of this system are assumed to be visually impaired people, with mainly low vision [14]. The reason for it is that about 90% of visually impaired people will obtain low vision in the future, and there will be cases where they can recognize the virtual object projected on the HMD.

2.4   Novelty

In this system, the advantages of wearing HMD and walking support for visually impaired people by virtual braille blocks utilizing AR/MR technology are as follows:

- Braille blocks can be placed independently of space and environment.
- It can be changed to colors and shapes that are easily viewable by low vision people.
- Comprehension of proper placement rules, complementation of physical braille blocks.

Furthermore, even for blind people who cannot recognize virtual braille blocks, receiving feedback (voice, vibration) from this system will help walking assistance. Another advantage is that it can be used as a tool to provide comfortable walking spaces for visually impaired people by road managers and facility managers.

For these reasons, it can be said that this research, which wears HMD and supports walking for visually impaired people using AR/MR technology, has certain novelty and usefulness.

3   Related Work

3.1   Collision Avoidance Support System Based on Collision Prediction

Many kinds of research of walking support for visually impaired people assume their own use, such as guiding a walking route, detecting obstacles, and avoiding collisions —however, Kayukawa et al. [6] take an approach to inform other pedestrians that visually impaired people are walking and to encourage the pedestrians to avoid the collisions.

This research, which focuses on collisions with pedestrians, provides visually impaired people with a suitcase that includes image recognition and depth information acquisition functions. By tracking the position and movement of pedestrians facing each other, warning sounds are generated in various patterns according to the distance. It is beneficial for notifying a pedestrian who is touching a smartphone while walking or a group talking while walking that visually impaired people are walking. In our system, we refer to the distance to pedestrians (obstacles) and warning patterns.

3.2   Stair Walking Support System Using AR

Focusing on the difficulty of walking on stairs for visually impaired people (low vision), Yuhang Zhao et al. [15] have proposed stair walking support using two different AR platforms. One is a projection-based AR using a small projector, and the other is a smart-glass-based AR.

In projection-based AR, light using five animation patterns is projected at the edge of the steps of the stairs to alert visually impaired people. In smart-glass-based AR, the direction of the stairs and the number of stairs are notified to visually impaired people, and the stairs are classified into seven stages, centered on the top, middle, and bottom, and each is color-coded.

A comparison of the two shows that projection-based AR can move up and down at fast walking speeds. However, walking with a projector in hand is not easy, and AR using smart glasses is realistic. Although this system is limited to stairs, AR-based alerts using animation and the method of segmenting and visualizing colors in each experiment are effective.

4   System Design

This system provides the following two devices to visually impaired people with a white cane to assist in moving freely in the walking space.

- Microsoft HoloLens
- Smartphone

Microsoft HoloLens [16] is a see-through HMD that provides AR/MR technology. It projects virtual braille blocks dynamically generated as 3D objects onto real space, and use it as a device for notifying voice and beep sound source feedback. The smartphone is used as a device to alert the user during walking by blinking the screen and vibrating. The reason for choosing a smartphone is that the number of visually impaired people who use mobile phones or smartphones daily is increasing, and it is a device that they always carry with them [17, 18]. The functions and procedures for implementing this system are as follows.

4.1   Determination of Walkable Area

For visually impaired people to move freely in the walking space, it is necessary to determine whether the surrounding space is a walking area. In this system, obstacles (walls) and floors in space are identified as the first process to determine the walkable area.

Fig. 2. Field of view immediately after application launch

Figure 2 shows the real space in the field of view immediately after launching the application via Microsoft HoloLens. Then, using the combination of the depth sensor installed in Microsoft HoloLens and the Spatial Mapping/Understanding library of the Mixed Reality Toolkit (MRTK) [19], feature points of the surrounding space shape are extracted and accumulated. Figure 3 shows meshes based on the accrued feature points in the space.

Fig. 3. Mesh generated from feature points of the surrounding space shape

Subsequently, to improve the processing speed and reduce memory consumption, unnecessary mesh vertices are thinned out. Finally, the remaining mesh space is classified into walls and floors by flat surface processing. Figure 4 shows the state where this processing is added to Fig. 3, where the wall surface is drawn in red, and the floor surface is drawn in blue. The blue floor surface is the walkable area defined in this section. In this system, the environment data of the surrounding space is updated in real-time by repeating these processes once every three seconds.

Fig. 4. Walkable Area: walls and floors classified by flat surface processing (Color figure online)

4.2   Obstacle Detection

In addition to the walkable area, safe walking for visually impaired people requires detection of obstacles that obstruct the walking of the visually impaired. In this system, we define walls and physical objects as obstacles.

Wall as an Obstacle. For the recognition of the wall, the Raycasting function of Unity [20] is used to determine the collision (Physics.Raycast) between the wall object generated by flat surface processing and the gaze of visually impaired people. The gaze vector originating from the camera coordinates (Camera.main.transform.position) of Microsoft HoloLens always follows the movement of the HMD and measures the positions and distances of all the walls in the field of view. If there is a wall in forwarding direction and the distance to a wall is within 10 m, the wall is defined as an obstacle.

Figure 5 shows a state in which the gaze point shown in (1) collides with the front wall (red). In this case, the distance from the wall is about 3.3 m, as shown in the log (2), the wall is regarded as an obstacle, and the virtual warning braille block and the direction guide braille block are placed on the floor.

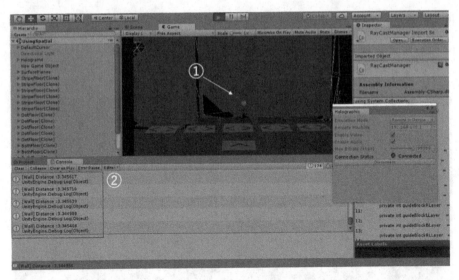

Fig. 5. Walkable area: walls and floors classified by flat surface processing (Color figure online)

Physical Objects as Obstacles. For recognizing physical objects in the field of view, we use the Azure Custom Vision Service – Object Detection [21], which is provided as a cloud service by Microsoft. Azure Custom Vision Service reads an image into a learning model of a physical target object. It determines whether the physical target object exists in the image by comparing the feature values.

This system uses the video camera function of Microsoft HoloLens to post the view image of visually impaired people captured every three seconds via the WebAPI to the created learning model. When the result is recognized as an obstacle, the object is notified by voice (see Fig. 5). Visually impaired people need sufficient time to avoid obstacles. Therefore, in this system, the condition threshold is set when there is a physical object within 5 m from the current position.

4.3   Virtual Braille Block

This system uses AR/MR technology to extend a braille block (see Fig. 1) and project it on a floor in real space as a virtual 3D object braille block (virtual braille block). In the walkable area, virtual forward guide braille blocks indicating the moving direction are projected. When walking is obstructed by obstacles, virtual warning braille blocks and direction guide braille blocks are projected. In this system, a virtual braille block is projected at 60 FPS to follow the gaze of visually impaired people.

Generating of Virtual Forward Guide Braille Blocks. Figure 6 shows that the gaze of visually impaired people collides with a floor object existing in the walkable area. Calculate the distance from the collision point (a) to the vertical point (b) from the HMD, and the angle of the HMD following the head movement. Then, virtual forward guide braille blocks are dynamically generated continuously on the floor between the points (a) and (b) in the direction of the gaze.

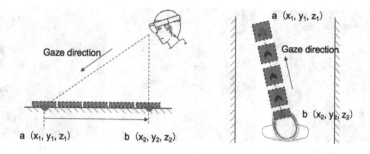

Fig. 6. Generating of virtual forward guide braille blocks

Generating of Virtual Warning and Direction Guide Braille Blocks. As shown in Fig. 7, the blocks that guide direction change of visually impaired people are a combination of virtual warning braille blocks (red) and direction guidance braille blocks (arrow).

These combinations consist of four patterns. If there is an obstacle such as a wall in the front and right-hand direction (1), the block displays direction change to the left. Similarly, if there is an obstacle such as a wall in the front and left-hand direction (2), the block displays direction change to the right.

On the other hand, if there is an obstacle such as a wall in the front but no obstacle in both sides (3), the block displays direction change to left and right both. If there is an obstacle such as a wall in the front and both sides (4), the block displays turn as a terminal.

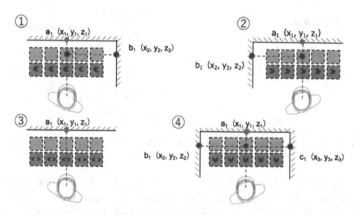

Fig. 7. Generating of virtual warning and direction guide braille blocks (Color figure online)

4.4   Change Color of Virtual Braille Block

Whether the braille block is easy to see or hard to see varies depending on the degree of color vision impairment and low vision. Utilizing the features of the system using AR/MR, this system can change the color of the virtual braille block, as shown in Fig. 8. This function is reflected by voice commands via Keyword Recognizer/Voice Recognizer.

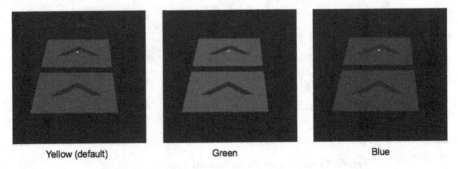

Yellow (default)   Green   Blue

Fig. 8. Change color of virtual braille block by voice command

4.5 Intersection (Collision) Judgment of White Cane and Virtual Braille Block

This system focuses on visually impaired people walking while waving a white cane to rub the road in front. In this section, we use AR/MR to judge the intersection (collision) between the generated and placed virtual braille block, and the white cane waved by visually impaired people. In this system, the movement of the white cane is not detected by the system. Apply the feature that the tip of the white stick is on the extension of the hand of visually impaired people.

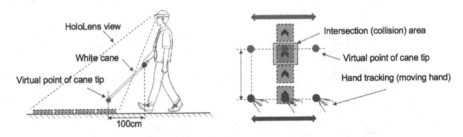

Fig. 9. Intersection (collision) judgment of white cane and virtual braille block

Assuming that the distance from the hand to the tip of the white cane is about 100 cm, the tip is the virtual point of the white cane. Subsequently, the horizontal movement of the hand holding the white cane is tracked. The virtual point at the tip of the white cane follows the movement of the hand, making it possible to determine the intersection (collision) with the virtual braille block (see Fig. 9).

To determine the intersection (collision), use Unity's Physics.Raycast from the virtual point at the tip of the white cane to the floor surface direction.

4.6   Feedback to Visually Impaired People

If the intersection (collision) between the white cane and the virtual braille block is determined, Microsoft HoloLens play the voice and beep sound and also notify feedback to the smartphone.

Voice and Beep Feedback via Microsoft HoloLens. If the intersection (collision) between the white cane and the virtual braille block is determined, the voice and beep sound feedback are sent to visually impaired people via Microsoft HoloLens according to the conditions in Fig. 7. Figure 10 shows the voice and beep sound patterns generated by this system.

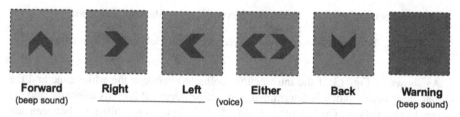

| **Forward** | **Right** | **Left** | **Either** | **Back** | **Warning** |
| (beep sound) | | | (voice) | | (beep sound) |

Fig. 10. Voice and beep sound patterns

Forward guidance and warning play two beeps. To notify right, left, either, and turn, use Microsoft HoloLens' Text-to-Speech API to play four types of voice guidance (Right/Left/Either/Turn).

Feedback to Smartphone. Similarly, if the intersection (collision) between the white cane and the virtual braille block is determined, the blinking screen and the feedback by vibration are notified to visually impaired people via a smartphone (see Fig. 11).

Fig. 11. Feedback to smartphone

This system uses WebSocket as a method of communication from Microsoft Hololens to a smartphone. As shown in Fig. 12, WebSocket Server is built on the cloud, and two-way communication is realized by connecting the Android application and Microsoft Hololens application to WebSocket Server.

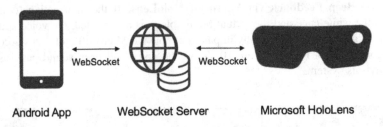

Fig. 12. Two-way communication between Microsoft Hololens and smartphone.

As shown in Fig. 13, if the intersection (collision) between the white cane and the virtual guide braille block is determined, a vibration occurs at 200 ms intervals, and the screen blinks yellow. On the other hand, if the intersection (collision) between the white cane and the virtual warning braille block is determined, a vibration occurs at 1,000 ms intervals, and the screen blinks red.

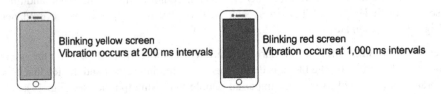

Fig. 13. Vibration and blinking screen (Color figure online)

The purpose of this blinking screen is not to notify the visually impaired, but to make the pedestrian aware that visually impaired people are walking around during walking at night.

4.7 Structure of Multi-thread Processing

In this section, we explain the timing of the above spatial recognition, generation of virtual braille blocks, obstacle detection, and hand tracking.

Figure 14 shows the multi-thread processing structure in this system. The gaze tracking starts immediately after the application and performs at 60 FPS (real-time) as the main thread. After that, a thread that performs spatial recognition (flat surface processing), obstacle detection, and hand tracking starts. Spatial recognition and obstacle detection are repeated once every 3 s, and hand tracking performs at 60 FPS (real-time) as with gaze tracking.

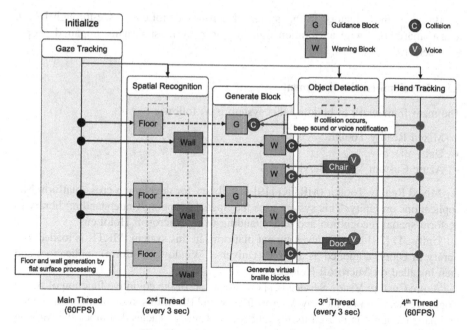

Fig. 14. Vibration and blinking screen

If the collision between the floor object generated by flat surface processing and the gaze of the visually impaired people is determined (Floor), the virtual direction guidance braille block is generated each time (G). If the collision between the wall object and the gaze of the visually impaired people is determined (Wall), the virtual warning braille block is generated each time (W). Similarly, if the physical object is detected by obstacle detection (Chair/Door), the virtual warning braille block is generated, and the obstacle is notified by voice (V).

On the other hand, hand tracking tracks the movement of the hand, waving the white cane. If the movement intersects (collides) with the virtual braille block (C), feedback to the voice, beep sound, and smartphone occur.

5   Hardware

The functions required for the device to be worn for this research are as follows:

- Sensor for extracting feature points in space
- Camera capture function for image recognition
- HMD capable of generating and projecting 3D objects
- Hand tracking
- Play audio/sound and Vibration function

Based on these factors, in this system, Microsoft HoloLens, a see-through HMD, and a smartphone with a vibration function worn by most visually impaired people were selected as devices.

5.1 Development Environment

The main framework in building this system is as follows:

- Mixed Reality Toolkit
- Unity 3D
- Azure Custom Vision Service

Mixed Reality Toolkit (MRTK) [19] is a library for developing cross-platform MR applications on Unity. This system uses the Spatial Mapping/Understanding library to perform spatial recognition and understanding using Microsoft HoloLens.

Unity 3D [20] is a 3D development platform. In this system, MRTK is loaded as a library in Unity, compiled as a UWP (Universal Windows Platform) application, and then installed on Microsoft HoloLens.

Azure Custom Vision Service [21] can use a part of the cognitive function of Azure Cognitive Service provided by Microsoft as WebAPI. In this system, object detection by image recognition is used in this function to detect obstacles that block the walking of visually impaired people.

5.2 Judgment of Walkable Area and Obstacle Detection

Judgment of Floor. To determine the floor surface as a walkable area, it is necessary to use the normal vector of the mesh plane generated based on the feature points of the surrounding space shape. This system refers to HoloToolkit.Unity.SpatialMapping. SurfacePlane class provided by MRTK. Whether the normal vector of the mesh plane is closer to the horizontal or vertical is determined by the direction of the normal and the threshold. When it is vertical and upward, it is determined to be the floor.

Wall Detection. To detect a wall, use the Raycasting function of Unity to determine the collision (Physics.Raycast) between the wall object generated by flat surface processing and the gaze of visually impaired people. Judge whether the gaze and the wall object collide within a distance of 10 m or less. If it is determined that a collision has occurred, it is regarded as an obstacle.

Obstacle Detection with Azure Custom Vision Service. Azure Custom Vision Service creates a learning model of a physical target object in advance. It determines whether the physical target object exists in a newly given image for the model. Figure 14 shows the result of the Azure Custom Vision Service determining the chair as a physical target object.

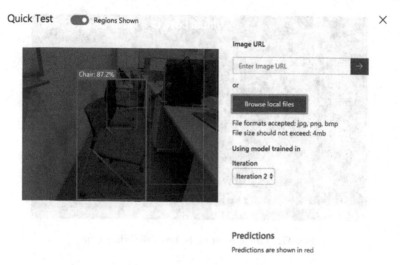

Fig. 15. Image recognition using Azure Custom Vision Service

After the image is determined, the identified object is surrounded by a red frame, and the accuracy is displayed. In this example, the chair in the center of the image has the highest accuracy (87.2%). In this system, obstacles that appear in the field of view once every three seconds are determined via WebAPI.

5.3 Generation and Placement of Virtual Braille Block

In this system, three types of virtual braille block models are created in advance as 3D objects and registered as Unity resources (see Fig. 15).

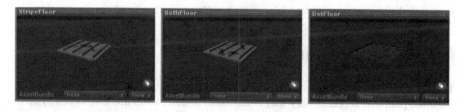

Fig. 16. Three types of virtual braille block models

These are called out from resources according to the conditions and are dynamically placed on the floor.

5.4 Intersection (Collision) Judgment of White Cane and Virtual Braille Block

In this system, the spherical 3D object in Fig. 16 is defined as a virtual point at the tip of the white cane of visually impaired people (Fig. 17).

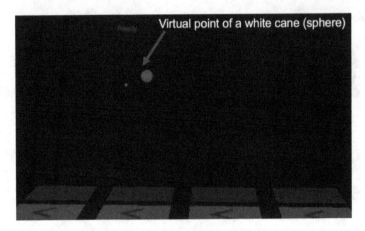

Fig. 17. Virtual point at the tip of the white cane

This sphere follows the horizontal hand movement while keeping a certain distance in the Z-axis direction (forward direction) from the hand of the visually impaired people who wave the white cane (see Fig. 9). Ray is cast vertical (Camera.main.-transform.up*-1) to the floor from the virtual point (x, y, z) at the tip of the white cane, and it is considered as an intersection (collision) if it collides with the virtual braille block layer.

5.5 Change the Color of Virtual Guided Braille Block by Voice Command

In this system, there is a function to change the color of the virtual guide braille block mainly for people with low vision. This function uses voice commands. It is because it is assumed visually impaired people operate without closing hand.

6 Preliminary Evaluation

This chapter introduces interviews with the viewpoint and convenience of visually impaired people and preliminary user evaluations to design and implement this system.

6.1 Interviews

We interviewed the Kobe Eye-light Association [22], a non-profit organization specializing in low vision and visual impairment support, for the problem of walking with white canes.

About Walking with White Canes. The white cane consists of three parts: a grip, a shaft, and a tip. There are about 150 types depending on the shape, weight, and length. For this reason, visually impaired people select those that are easy to use individually while receiving appropriate walking instructions. In our sense, it appears to be waving a white cane, but it is an action of rubbing or exploring the road. In addition to judging obstacles ahead, it also judges whether the road surface is asphalt or cobblestone.

About Walking with Guide Dog. Trained guide dogs are excellent, but they are expensive and can depend on their daily relationship with their owners, and only 1,000 are utilized in Japan. Therefore, it is not a realistic.

About Braille Blocks. We reconfirmed that the braille block is the most effective guide for visually impaired people with a white cane, but there is a problem with the number of braille blocks needed. Also, we found that a pedestrian crossing where braille blocks could not be installed was a problem. As a countermeasure for pedestrian crossings, a road crossing zone (escort zone) [23] for guiding the visually impaired has been introduced. Currently, the number of installations is small, and a new solution is required.

About Color Information. We reconfirmed that the color appearance differs depending on the visually impaired (low vision). We also found that the relationship between contrast, inversion, and the complementary color was important among colors.

About Mobile Phones. We reconfirmed that 90% of visually impaired people have a mobile phone and can be operated with voice guidance. However, visually impaired people often put their smartphones in their bags or pockets while walking to concentrate their consciousness on checking the road surface conditions. In this system, the vibration of a smartphone is used as a feedback notice. Still, we received advice that only auxiliary information (voice) that does not hinder concentration should be used.

About the Effectiveness of this System. We interviewed Kazunari Mori, the director of this association, who is a gait trainer and provides guidance in gait training, about his impressions of using this system. He said there was a problem with the response of hand tracking due to the limited viewing angle of HoloLens. However, he said that it would be practical and useful if the device could be miniaturized, expressed contrast, and adapted to the escort zone.

6.2 Preliminary Evaluation Participants

We invited eight participants (two women and six men) in their 20s and 50s to evaluate the usability and efficiency of the system. Participants did not include visually impaired people. However, it is crucial to simulate visual impairment [24]; therefore, in this preliminary experiment, participants temporarily removed the correction with eyeglasses and contact lenses and wore glasses for experiencing visual impairment.

6.3 Task and Questionnaire

All participants received a brief introduction to the system and instructions for operating Microsoft HoloLens. After the participants got used to the device, they walked using the system in the corridor and conducted a questionnaire after the experiment.

The questionnaire had the following five questions, which were evaluated by grading from 1 to 5 (1 = very negative, 5 = very positive).

1. Do you think this system is easy to use?
2. Do you feel that the virtual braille blocks complement the walking space where there is no braille block?
3. Do you think this system is attractive?
4. Do you think it is effective for walking assistance for visually impaired people?
5. Do you want to introduce this system to your acquaintances?

6.4   Result

Table 1. Questionnaire.

	P1	P2	P3	P4	P5	P6	P7	P8	Avg
Q1	4	4	4	5	3	4	4	4	4
Q2	4	4	4	4	4	5	5	5	4.38
Q3	5	4	4	4	5	5	5	5	4.63
Q4	4	3	4	4	4	5	4	5	4.13
Q5	4	5	4	4	5	5	5	5	4.63

Question 1 is about the usability of this system. The average score of 4 shows that the system is easy to use. However, concerning hand tracking, two participants pointed out that it takes time to get used to operating Microsoft HoloLens. Question 2 is about whether the virtual braille block can be a complement for the walking space where there is no braille block. The average score of 4.38 shows that this system can substitute braille blocks. Participants replied that they are particularly effective in unknown lands and environments. Questions 3, 4, and 5 are about the usefulness of this system. The average score of Q3 was 4.63, Q4 was 4.13, and Q5 was 4.63, which shows that this system is attractive and useful as a means to support walking support for visually impaired people (see Table 1).

Based on the results of these preliminary evaluation experiments, questionnaires, and interviews, this research aimed at realizing walking support for the visually impaired using AR/MR, despite a pseudo-visual impairment situation, received a certain high evaluation. In addition, it was shown that the system has utility and potential as a system to substitute braille blocks.

7   Conclusion and Future Work

In this research, we first focused on the fact that the combination of a braille block and a white cane is a general-purpose walking support for the visually impaired. Next, we showed that the walking space where there is no braille block could be complemented using AR/MR technology. In the implementation, the walkable area was determined by spatial recognition and obstacle detection. Based on the results, virtual guide braille blocks and warning braille blocks placed on the floor, and the system notified feedback of the intersection (collision) between them and the white cane by voice and vibration.

At present, the limitations and rules regarding the installation of braille blocks are a social problem. Based on the results of interviews and preliminary evaluations, this research, a walking aid using AR/MR and virtual braille blocks, can be a novelty and useful alternative to braille blocks.

We will apply the image recognition used in obstacle detection to the determination of road surface conditions in the future, and the color change of the virtual braille block is improved to a system that considers the relation of contrast, inversion, and the complementary color. In addition, by utilizing the features of this system, we will also consider a method to supplement the escort zone space that has not been installed, aiming to realize safer and more accurate guidance for visually impaired people.

Acknowledgments. The authors deeply thank IPLAB members, Kazunari Mori, Ken Fujioka, Shohei Fujii, and Nayon Cho, for their valuable advice and cooperation.

. References

1. World Health Organization: Universal eye health: a global action plan 2014–2019 (2013)
2. Bourne, R.R.A., Flaxman, S.R., Braithwaite, T., et al.: Magnitude, temporal trends and projections of the global prevalence of blindness and distance and near vision impairment a systematic review and meta-analysis. Lancet Glob. Health **5**, e888–e897 (2017)
3. World Health Organization: Blindness and vision impairment. https://www.who.int/en/news-room/fact-sheets/detail/blindness-and-visual-impairment. Accessed 9 Jan 2020
4. Bai, J., Liu, D., Su, G., et al.: A cloud and vision-based navigation system used for blind people. In: Proceedings of the International Conference on Artificial Intelligence, Automation and Control Technologies, Wuhan, China, 7–9 April 2017, pp. 1–6 (2017)
5. Guerreiro, J., Ahmetovic, D., Sato, D., et al.: Airport accessibility and navigation assistance for people with visual impairments. In: Proceedings of the 2019 CHI Conference on Human Factors in Computing Systems, Glasgow, Scotland, UK, 4–9 May 2019, Paper No. 16 (2019)
6. Kayukawa, S., Higuchi, K., Guerreiro, J., et al.: BBeep: a sonic collision avoidance system for blind travellers and nearby pedestrians. In: Proceedings of the 2019 CHI Conference on Human Factors in Computing Systems, Glasgow, Scotland, UK, 4–9 May 2019, Paper No. 52 (2019)
7. Japan Federation of the Blind: About Braille Block. http://nichimou.org/impaired-vision/barrier-free/induction-block/. (published in Japanese). Accessed 9 Jan 2020
8. Traffic Safety Research Center: What is a Braille Block? http://www.tsrc.or.jp/. (published in Japanese). Accessed 9 Jan 2020
9. Ministry of Internal Affairs and Communications: The Road Traffic Law in Japan. https://elaws.e-gov.go.jp/search/elawsSearch/elaws_search/lsg0500/detail?lawId=335AC0000000105. (published in Japanese). Accessed 9 Jan 2020
10. Tokuda, K., Mizuno, T.: Braille Blocks - From Japan for Visually Impaired People to Safely Walk the World. Fukumura Shuppan Inc. (2011). (published in Japanese)
11. Mizuno, T., Tokuda, K., Nishidate, A., et al.: Installation errors and corrections in tactile ground surface indicators in Europe, America, Oceania and Asia. IATSS Res. **32**(2), 68–80 (2008)

12. The Asahi Shimbun Company: Developed easy-to-read Braille Blocks, 17 Colors. https://www.asahi.com/articles/ASKDQ4JF5KDQULBJ00W.html. (published in Japanese). Accessed 9 Jan 2020
13. Hommaru, K., Tanaka, J.: Walking support for visually impaired using virtual braille block. In: Forum on Information Technology 2019, J-020, Fascicle3, pp. 277–278 (2019)
14. Colenbrander, A.: Visual standards aspects and ranges of vision loss with emphasis on population surveys. In: International Council of Ophthalmology at the 29th International Congress of Ophthalmology, Sydney, Australia, April 2002 (2002)
15. Zhao, Y., Kupferstein, Y., et al.: Designing AR visualizations to facilitate stair navigation for people with low vision. In: UIST 2019, New Orleans, LA, USA, pp. 387–402 (2019)
16. HoloLens | Documentation. https://docs.microsoft.com/ja-jp/hololens/. Accessed Jan 9 2020
17. Watanabe, T., Yamaguchi, T., et al.: Survey of mobile phone usage by blind people 2017. The Telecommunications Advancement Foundation Research Report No. 29 (2014). (published in Japanese)
18. Watanabe, T., Kaga, H., et al.: Survey on smartphone and tablet usage by blind people 2017. IEICE technical report, WIT2017-42, vol. 117, no. 251, pp. 69–74, October 2017. (published in Japanese)
19. Getting Started with MRTK | Mixed Reality Toolkit Documentation. https://microsoft.github.io/MixedRealityToolkit-Unity/Documentation/GettingStartedWithTheMRTK.html. Accessed Jan 9 2020
20. Unity | Documentation. https://docs.unity3d.com/Manual/index.html. Accessed Jan 9 2020
21. Microsoft Azure | Custom Vision. https://docs.microsoft.com/ja-jp/azure/cognitive-services/custom-vision-service/. Accessed Jan 9 2020
22. Kobe Eyelight Association. https://eyelight.eek.jp/. Accessed Jan 9 2020
23. Okayama Prefectural University: Secret of Road Crossing Zone (Escort Zone) for Visually Impaired Guidance. http://tans.fhw.oka-pu.ac.jp/topics/topic002.htm. (published in Japanese). Accessed 9 Jan 2020
24. Sandnes, F.E., Eika, E.: Head-mounted augmented reality displays on the cheap: a DIY approach to sketching and prototyping low-vision assistive technologies. In: Antona, M., Stephanidis, C. (eds.) UAHCI 2017. LNCS, vol. 10278, pp. 167–186. Springer, Cham (2017). https://doi.org/10.1007/978-3-319-58703-5_13

Effect of Background Element Difference on Regional Cerebral Blood Flow While Viewing Stereoscopic Video Clips

Fumiya Kinoshita[1(✉)], Honoka Okuno[1], Hideaki Touyama[1],
Masumi Takada[2], Masaru Miyao[3], and Hiroki Takada[4]

[1] Toyama Prefectural University, 5180 Kurokawa, Imizu,
Toyama 939-0398, Japan
f.kinoshita@pu-toyama.ac.jp
[2] Yokkaichi Nursing and Medical Care University, 1200 Kayoucho, Yokkaichi,
Mie 512-8045, Japan
[3] Nagoya Industrial Science Research Institute, 2-10-19 Sakae, Naka,
Nagoya 460-0008, Japan
[4] University of Fukui, 3-9-1 Bunkyo, Fukui 910-8507, Japan

Abstract. Stereoscopic video clips cause discomfort, such as headache, vomiting, and eye fatigue, based on their image elements and viewing conditions. The symptoms are termed as 3D motion sickness, and the mechanism of their occurrence is not elucidated to date. To watch stereoscopic video clips safely, it is essential to verify the effects of stereoscopic video clips on the body. In the study, we created two types of stereoscopic video clips with different background elements to verify the research hypothesis that information from the peripheral visual field significantly affects 3D motion sickness. Additionally, the regional cerebral blood flow while viewing stereoscopic video clips was measured via functional near-infrared spectroscopy (fNIRS). Thus, it was confirmed that the difference in the background element in the peripheral visual field when viewing stereoscopic video clips affected the regional cerebral blood flow from the occipital lobe to the prefrontal cortex. This suggests that visual information on depth perception by the dorsal visual pathway can be overloaded while viewing stereoscopic video clips with background elements.

Keywords: Stereoscopic video clips · 3D motion sickness · Regional cerebral blood flow · Peripheral visual field · Dorsal visual pathway · functional Near-Infrared Spectroscopy (fNIRS)

1 Introduction

Recently, there were significant improvements in the display technology of stereoscopic images, and it is used in various fields such as movies, televisions, and games. The concept of binocular stereovision was proposed by the British physicist Charles Wheatstone in 1832 and spans a history exceeding 150 years [1]. Until the first half of the 20th century, stereoscopic vision implied almost stereoscopic display technology. However, terms such as "augmented reality" and "artificial reality" also recently

© Springer Nature Switzerland AG 2020
M. Antona and C. Stephanidis (Eds.): HCII 2020, LNCS 12188, pp. 355–365, 2020.
https://doi.org/10.1007/978-3-030-49282-3_25

appeared as stereoscopic display technologies [2]. The application of stereoscopic display technology is active in a wide range of fields such as medical care, education, and amusement.

Several studies examine the method of presenting stereoscopic video clips. However, binocular stereo that expresses a stereoscopic effect by presenting two images that mainly differ by the parallax of both eyes is generally used. With respect to the content using stereo-scopic images, the movie "Avatar" was released in 2009 and became a record hit. In 2010, the world's first full high-definition 3D TV was launched and indicated signs of the trend of stereoscopic images. However, 3D television was not adopted. There are various reasons for this including safety concerns. Stereoscopic video clips cause discomfort, such as headache, vomiting, and eye fatigue, based on their image elements and viewing conditions [3, 4] .The symptoms are termed as 3D motion sickness. In 2008, the 3D Consortium publicly published "3DC Safety Guidelines for Dissemination of Human-friendly 3D" [5]. Revised versions of the safety guidelines were published in December 2009 and April 2010. However, only a few theories are described as causes of 3D motion sickness, and a significant improvement was not achieved [6, 7]. To safely view stereoscopic video clips, it is essential to verify the effects of stereoscopic video clips on the body.

Conventionally, 3D motion sickness is considered to occur while viewing stereoscopic video clips, and this is considered as the reason for the mismatch between the crystalline lens adjustment function and convergence movement. In normal natural vision, accommodation reflex and vergence reflex are simultaneously performed due to near vision reaction. Conversely, in the explanation based on the vergence-accommodation conflict theory, the crystalline lens adjustment function while viewing stereoscopic video clips is fixed to the screen on which the video clips is presented, and convergence is fixed to the protruding virtual object. Thus, it is considered that visual fatigue occurs because the difference in appearance from natural vision continues while viewing stereoscopic video clips. The hypothesis of the vergence-accommodation conflict theory is traditionally described as a cause of visual fatigue when viewing stereoscopic images and is described in many documents such as safety guidelines [5]. Conversely, in 2013, Shiomi et al. established a simultaneous measurement method of crystalline lens accommodation and convergence movement while viewing video clips and compared them with real objects, 2D video clips, and 3D video clips [8]. Thus, the results confirmed that the crystalline lens adjustment during stereoscopic viewing in young individuals was linked to the pop-out and retraction of the virtual object in a manner similar to the natural vision state. Hence, it was confirmed that the discrepancy is absent between crystalline lens accommodation and vergence movement [9].

Currently, explanation via sensory conflict theory is commonly considered as the mechanism of 3D motion sickness [10, 11]. This is because spatial orientation becomes unstable when the combination of information input from the visual system, vestibular system, and somatosensory system does not match the combination of sensory system information as established by previous experience. Thus, this leads to symptoms such as headache or vomiting. As a recent trend in the VR field, efforts focus on perceiving the theory of sensory conflict theory as the root cause of 3D sickness and modifying information input to sensory organs to avoid sensory inconsistency. For example, studies investigate the control of discomfort symptoms by applying a weak current to the head (vestibular system) by using vestibular electrical stimulation (Galvanic Vestibular Stimulation; GVS) to impart a feeling of inclination or movement to the user and on using a large simulator to add a feeling of inclination by actually rotating the user based on the visual information [12, 13]. However, although the aforementioned approaches are effective in increasing the immersion and presence of the user, they are not effective solutions for 3D motion sickness.

Previous studies reported that information from peripheral vision can affect 3D motion sickness [14]. A previous study performed a comparison between viewing stereoscopic video clips using peripheral vision and viewing stereoscopic video clips using pursuit vision. Thus, the scores related to video sickness and center of pressure of body sway as per the subjective questionnaire significantly increased while viewing stereoscopic video clips using peripheral vision. This suggested a relationship between 3D motion sickness and background elements of peripheral vision. Specifically, among the visual pathways in the cerebral cortex, the dorsal visual pathway is known to be involved in the perception of depth [15]. Hence, it is possible to evaluate the effect of stereoscopic video clips on peripheral vision function by measuring the local cerebral blood flow in the dorsal visual tract. In the study, to verify the research hypothesis that information from the peripheral visual field significantly affects 3D motion sickness, we created two types of stereoscopic video clips with different background elements. The regional cerebral blood flow while viewing stereoscopic video clips was measured by functional near-infrared spectroscopy (fNIRS).

2   Experimental Method

2.1   Subjects and Materials

The subjects included 14 healthy young men and women (21.0 $\pm$ 1.8 years old). The experiment was described to all subjects and written informed consent was obtained in advance.

The measurement equipment used corresponded to LABNIRS (Shimadzu Corporation, Kyoto). The NIRS probes are arranged as shown in Fig. 1. Time series data of oxy-Hb and deoxy-Hb as measured by LABNIRS were recorded with a time resolution corresponding to 55 Hz.

The stereoscopic video clips used in the experiment corresponded to Sky Crystal fabricated by Olympus Memory Works Corp. The Sky Crystal induces crystalline lens accommodation via presenting a sphere with a smooth movement between distal and proximal. In the experiment, a comparison was performed between stereoscopic video clips, namely one in which the background element was removed from Sky Crystal (video clips without background) and the other in which the background element moved periodically (video clips with background) (Fig. 2). The video clips were presented using a 3D display 55UF8500 (LG Electronics) installed at a distance corresponding to 2.1 m from the subject, and the display method corresponding to a circular polarization method using 3D glasses (Fig. 3).

The experiment was performed in a sitting position, and the three conditions including closing the eyes (state-I), watching the sphere with tracking (state-II), and watching the sphere with peripheral vision (state-III) were continuously performed for 70 s each (total 210 s). The protocol was used as 1 trial and a total of 5 trials were successively performed (Fig. 4). Given the effect of the order, the experiment order of the video clips with background and the video clips without background was randomized for each subject.

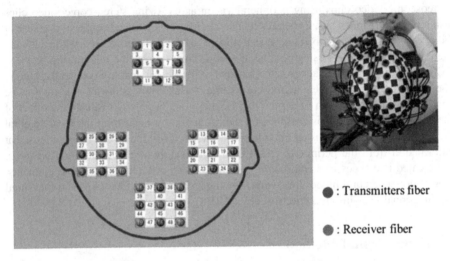

● : Transmitters fiber

● : Receiver fiber

Fig. 1. Probe arrangement of LABNIRS

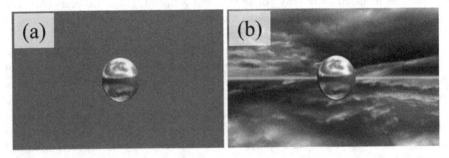

Fig. 2. Experimental video clips (a) Video clips without background, (b) Video clips with background

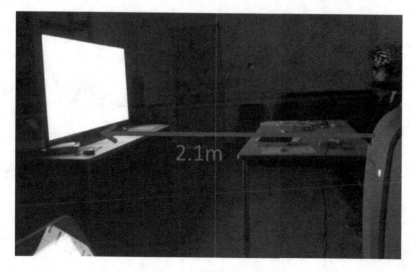

Fig. 3. Visual distance is set as 2.1 m.

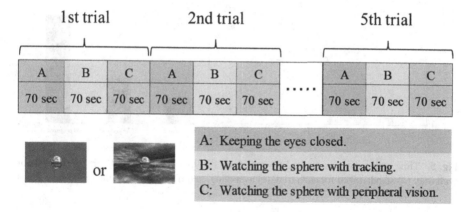

Fig. 4. Experimental protocol

2.2 Analytical Indices

In the experiment, time-series data of oxy-Hb and deoxy-Hb were recorded with a time resolution of 55 Hz using LABNIRS. The obtained time-series data of oxy-Hb (Fig. 5a) and deoxy-Hb of all 48 channels were subjected to noise removal via a 0.15 Hz low-pass filter (Fig. 5b). Subsequently, time series data of oxy-Hb and deoxy-Hb for a total of 5 trials were divided for each trial (Fig. 5c). Each divided time series was standardized (mean ± standard deviation, 0 ± 1) for each trial (Fig. 5d), and averaging was performed between the trials (Fig. 5e). In the study, the integrated value of the time series after the averaging process was calculated for each state, and the value was used as the representative value.

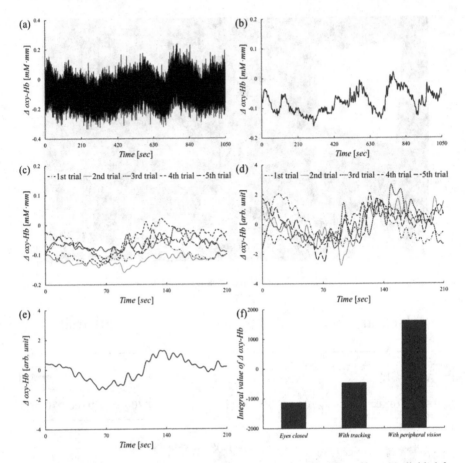

Fig. 5. Time series analysis method (a) raw data, (b) 0.15 Hz low-pass filter, (c) divided for each trial, (d) standardized for each trial, (e) averaging, and (f) integrated value of the time series

3   Results

With respect to the oxy-Hb and the deoxy-Hb time series after the averaging process, the integrated values of the time series were calculated for each state. Comparisons were performed using Wilcoxon signed rank-sum test for the video clips with background and video clips without background. The significance level in the study was set to 0.05.

Figure 6 shows channels in which values significantly fluctuated from State-I to State-II at the oxy-Hb. In the prefrontal cortex, the value significantly decreased in ch3 and ch5 when the video clips were viewed without a background, and the value significantly decreased in ch3, ch4, ch5, and ch8 when the video clips were viewed with a background ($p < 0.05$). In the right and left temporal lobes, the value significantly increased in ch25 when the video clips were viewed without a background, and it significantly decreased in ch23, and ch36 when the video clips were viewed with a background (p < 0.05). In the occipital lobe, the value significantly increased in ch41 when the video clips were viewed without a background, and it significantly increased in ch38, ch39, ch40, ch41, and ch43 when the video clips were viewed with a background (p < 0.05).

Subsequently, Fig. 7 shows channels in which values significantly fluctuated from State-I to State-II at the deoxy-Hb. In the prefrontal cortex, the value significantly increased in ch1, ch2, and ch7 when the video clips were viewed without a background while the value significantly increased in ch1, and ch12 when the video clips were viewed with a background (p < 0.05). In the right and left temporal lobes, the value significantly decreased in ch13, ch14, ch15, ch16, ch18, ch19, ch20, ch21, ch23, ch25, ch26, ch28, ch29, ch30, ch31, ch33, and ch34 when the video clips were viewed without a background, and it significantly decreased in ch13, ch14, ch16, ch18, ch19, ch20, ch28, ch29, ch30, ch31, ch34, and ch36 when the video clips were viewed with a background (p < 0.05). In the occipital lobe, the value significantly increased in ch47 when the video clips were viewed without a background (p < 0.05) although there were no channels wherein the value significantly fluctuated when the video clips were viewed with a background.

Figure 8 shows channels in which values significantly fluctuated from State-II to State-III at the oxy-Hb. In the prefrontal cortex, the value significantly increased in ch3, ch4, ch5, ch6, ch7, ch10, and ch12 when viewing the video clips without background (p < 0.05) although there were no channels wherein the value significantly fluctuated when the video clips were viewed with a background. In the right and left temporal lobes, the values significantly increased at ch22, ch23, ch24, ch27, ch30, ch32, ch33, and ch35 when the video clips were viewed without a background, although there were no channels wherein the value significantly fluctuated when the video clips were viewed with a background. In the occipital lobe, the values significantly increased at ch38, ch40, ch42, ch43, ch45, and ch48 when the video clips were viewed without a background (p < 0.05), although there were no channels wherein the value significantly fluctuated when the video clips were viewed with a background.

Subsequently, Fig. 9 shows channels in which values significantly fluctuated from State-II to State-III at the deoxy-Hb. In the prefrontal cortex, the value significantly decreased in ch9, ch11, and ch12 when viewing the video clips without background, and it significantly decreased in ch9 when the video clips were viewed with a background (p < 0.05). In the right and left temporal lobes, the values significantly decreased at ch14, ch17, ch24, ch27, and ch35 when the video clips were viewed without a background, and it significantly decreased in ch14, and ch27 when the video clips were viewed with a background (p < 0.05). In the occipital lobe, the values significantly increased at ch40, ch41, ch42, ch43, ch44, ch45, and ch46 when viewing the video clips without a background, and it significantly increased in ch39, ch41, ch43, ch44, and ch45 when the video clips were viewed with a background (p < 0.05).

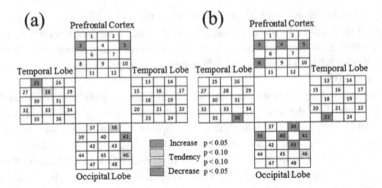

Fig. 6. Channels in which the value significantly fluctuated from State-I to State-II in oxy-Hb. (a) without background and (b) with background

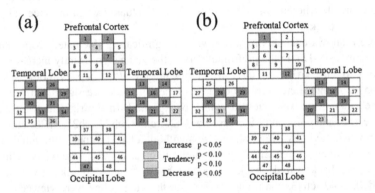

Fig. 7. Channels in which the value significantly fluctuated from State-I to State-II in deoxy-Hb. (a) without background and (b) with background

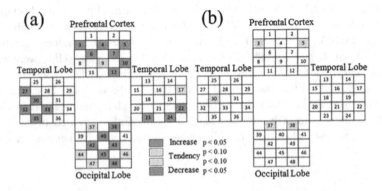

Fig. 8. Channels in which the value significantly fluctuated from State-II to State-III in oxy-Hb. (a) without background and (b) with background

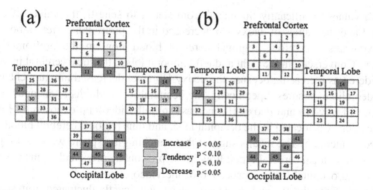

Fig. 9. Channels in which the value significantly fluctuated from State-II to State-III in deoxy-Hb. (a) without background, (b) with background

4 Discussion

Stereoscopic video clips cause discomforts, such as headache, vomiting, and eye fatigue, based on their image elements and viewing conditions. The symptoms are termed as 3D motion sickness, and the mechanism of their occurrence is not elucidated to date. In order to safely view stereoscopic video clips, a study verifying the effects of stereoscopic video clips on the body is essential. Currently, a common explanation involves sensory conflict theory as the mechanism of 3D motion sickness. In a recent trend in the VR field, efforts focus on perceiving the theory of sensory conflict as the root cause of 3D sickness and modifying information input to sensory organs to avoid sensory inconsistency. However, although the aforementioned approaches are effective in increasing the immersion and user presence, they do not correspond to effective solutions for 3D motion sickness.

Previous studies reported that information from peripheral vision can affect 3D motion sickness. A previous study compared viewing stereoscopic video clips using peripheral vision and viewing stereoscopic video clips using pursuit vision. Thus, the scores related to video sickness and center of pressure of body sway as per a subjective questionnaire significantly increased while viewing stereoscopic video clips using peripheral vision. This suggests a relationship between 3D motion sickness and background elements of peripheral vision. Specifically, among visual pathways in the cerebral cortex, the dorsal visual pathway is known as involved in the perception of depth. Hence, it is possible to evaluate the effect of stereoscopic video clips on peripheral vision function via measuring the local cerebral blood flow in the dorsal visual tract. In the study, to verify the research hypothesis that information from the peripheral visual field significantly affects 3D motion sickness, we created two types of stereoscopic video clips with different background elements. Additionally, the regional cerebral blood flow while viewing stereoscopic video clips was measured via fNIRS.

Based on the blood oxygenation level-dependent (BOLD) effect, changes in oxygen metabolism at the site of nerve activity increase oxyhemoglobin when nerve activity starts and subsequently decrease hemoglobin [16]. With respect to the channels in which values significantly fluctuated from state-I to state-II, the values of oxy-Hb increased and the values of deoxy-Hb decreased in the prefrontal cortex in both video clips exposures. Therefore, regional cerebral blood flow in the prefrontal cortex decreases. Conversely, in the right and left temporal lobes, the local cerebral blood flow is considered as increasing because the deoxy-Hb level decreased in many channels in both video clip exposures. Specifically, the occipital lobe exhibits a tendency wherein the values of oxy-Hb and deoxy-Hb increase in both video clip exposures. However, the visual cortex is located in the occipital lobe, and thus regional cerebral blood flow is observed to increase. The results suggest that watching the sphere with tracking leads to a decrease in local cerebral blood flow in the prefrontal cortex and an increase in the temporal and occipital lobes irrespective of the video exposure.

With respect to the channels in which values significantly fluctuated from state-II to state-III, the values of oxy-Hb increase and the values of deoxy-Hb decrease when exposed to video clips without background, and a consistent trend is absent when exposed to video clips with background. In the right and left temporal lobes, the value of oxy-Hb increases and the value of deoxy-Hb decreases when exposed to video clips without background, and a consistent tendency is not observed when exposed to video clips with a background. In the occipital lobe, oxy-Hb and deoxy-Hb increase in both video clip exposures. The results suggest that while watching the sphere with peripheral vision, local cerebral blood flow increases in the prefrontal cortex and temporal and occipital lobes when compared with watching the sphere with tracking when exposed to video clips without background. Conversely, a consistent tendency is absent with the exception of the increase in the occipital lobe when exposed to video clips with background.

In the study, we created two types of stereoscopic video clips with different background elements to verify the research hypothesis that information from the peripheral visual field significantly affects 3D motion sickness. Additionally, the regional cerebral blood flow while viewing stereoscopic video clips was measured via fNIRS. Thus, it was confirmed that the difference in the background element in the peripheral visual field when viewing stereoscopic video clips affects the regional cerebral blood flow from the occipital lobe to the prefrontal cortex. This suggests that visual information on depth perception via the dorsal visual pathway can be overloaded while viewing stereoscopic video clips with background elements.

Acknowledgements. This work was supported by JSPS KAKENHI Grant Number 19K20620.

References

1. Oguchi, T., Tanishima, M., Haibara, M.: 3D seiki -Kyoi rittai eiga no 100nen to eizo shin seiki-, Borndigital (2012)
2. Tamura, H., Ohta, Y.: Mixed reality. J. Inst. Image Inform. TV. Eng. **52**(3), 266–272 (1997)
3. International Standard Organization: IWA3: 2005 image safety-reducing determinism in a time series. Phys. Rev. Lett. **70**, 530–582 (1993)
4. Lambooij, M., Jsselsteijn, W., Fortuin, M., Heynderickx, I.: Visual discomfort and visual fatigue of stereoscopic displays: a review. J. Imaging Sci. Technol. **53**(3), 1–14 (2009)

5. D Consortium: 3DC Safety Guidelines for Popularization of Human-friendly 3D (2008)
6. Yano, S., Emoto, M., Mitsuhashi, T.: Two factors in visual fatigue caused from stereoscopic image. J. Inst. Image Inform. TV. Eng. **57**(9), 1187–1193 (2003)
7. Yano, S., Ide, S., Hal, T.: A study of visual comfort and visual fatigue at the point of accommodation response in viewing stereoscopic image. J. Inst. Image Inform. TV. Eng. **55** (5), 711–717 (2001)
8. Shiomi, T., et al.: Simultaneous measurement of lens accommodation and convergence in natural and articial 3D vision. J. Soc. Inform. Display **21**(3), 120–128 (2013)
9. Miyao, M.: Lens accommodation while viewing 3D video clips. In: Takada, H., Miyao, M., Fateh, S. (eds.) Stereopsis and Hygiene. CTEHPM, pp. 13–24. Springer, Singapore (2019). https://doi.org/10.1007/978-981-13-1601-2_2
10. Reason, J.T., Brand, J.J.: Motion Sickness. Academic Press, London (1975)
11. Takeda, N.: Motion sickness and vomiting reflex. Practica oto-rhino-laryngologica, Supplement **41**, 197–207 (1991)
12. Nakayama, Y., Aoyama, K., Kitao, T., Maeda, T., Ando, H.: How to use multi-pole galvanic vestibular stimulation for virtual reality application. In: Proceedings of the VRIC, Laval, France (2018)
13. Nakagawa, C., Ohsuga, M., Takebe, T.: Basic study on autonomic responses of 'Sickness' induced by visual and motion stimuli: using four projected screens and a 6-DOF motion base. Trans. Virtual Reality Soc. Jpn. **6**(1), 27–35 (2001)
14. Takada, M., Tateyama, K., Kinoshita, F., Takada, H.: Evaluation of cerebral blood flow while viewing 3D video clips. In: Antona, M., Stephanidis, C. (eds.) UAHCI 2017. LNCS, vol. 10279, pp. 492–503. Springer, Cham (2017). https://doi.org/10.1007/978-3-319-58700-4_40
15. Kato, T., Kamei, A., Takashima, S., Ozaki, T.: Human visual cortical function during photic stimulation monitoring by means of near-infrared spectroscopy. J. Cereb. Blood Flow Metab. **13**, 516–520 (1993)
16. Zardecki, A.: Multiple scattering corrections to the beer-lambert law. In: Proceedings of the SPIE, 103–110 (1983)

Dementia: I Am Physically Fading. Can Virtual Reality Help? Physical Training for People with Dementia in Confined Mental Health Units

Maria Matsangidou[1(✉)] [iD], Eirini Schiza[1] [iD], Marios Hadjiaros[1] [iD], Kleanthis C. Neokleous[1] [iD], Marios Avraamides[1] [iD], Ersi Papayianni[2] [iD], Fotos Frangoudes[1] [iD], and Constantinos S. Pattichis[1] [iD]

[1] Research Centre on Interactive Media, Smart Systems and Emerging Technologies (RISE), Nicosia, Cyprus
m.matsangidou@rise.org.cy
[2] Archangelos Michael Elderly People Nursing Home/Rehabilitation Centre for Patients with Alzheimer (AMEN), Nicosia, Cyprus

Abstract. In recent years, there has been growing interest in designing non-pharmacological interventions to improve the quality of life for People with Dementia (PwD) who face motor impairments. This paper investigates the feasibility of using Virtual Reality (VR) technologies for the rehabilitation of 20 patients with moderate to severe dementia residing in a confined psychiatric hospital and discusses the impact of this interactions on motor training. To accomplish this, we present three interrelated studies that refer to: (1) System requirement analysis carried out through a workshop with experts in dementia care; (2) System interaction method assessment by testing two different types of interaction in Virtual Reality, to identify the most suitable for People with Dementia; and (3) A pilot study with patients performing three upper limb physiotherapy tasks in Virtual Reality. The issues encountered during the design, testing and execution of the experimental tasks are discussed and a set of guidelines and recommendations for the future deployment of VR in healthcare services is provided.

Keywords: Virtual Reality · Dementia · Long-term care

1 Introduction

Dementia is an umbrella term that includes a set of symptoms linked to disorders of the brain that progress over time and refers primarily to impairments of cognitive and motor functions [38]. A 2017 report suggested that 50 million people live with dementia worldwide [45] and this number is expected to rise to 132 million within the following thirty years [45]. This growth has made imperative the need for hospitalization and support of people with moderate to severe dementia with cognitive and motor function impairments. Even though hospitalization is necessary in some cases for

© The Author(s) 2020
M. Antona and C. Stephanidis (Eds.): HCII 2020, LNCS 12188, pp. 366–382, 2020.
https://doi.org/10.1007/978-3-030-49282-3_26

People with Dementia (PwD), it is associated with negative effects on cognition and negative impact on the physical state of the person [1, 11, 19, 31, 50]. Therefore, hospitalization presents challenges that need to be addressed.

Exercise and physical activity in general have been associated with several benefits in mental and physical health for PwD. Many studies highlight that PwD who exercise on a regular basis have improved motor functions, including stronger upper and lower body muscle strength and better walking balance compared to those who do not engage in any type of physical activity [35, 39]. In addition, many studies report a negative relationship between cognitive decline and exercise, suggesting that cognitive decline could be delayed through systematic physical activity [22, 34, 35]. Thus, regular physical activity can improve functionalities related to the brain, preventing the further development of neurological conditions and cognitive decline [23].

Even though the benefits of physical activity and exercise are well documented, research also demonstrates that people living with dementia may experience several difficulties in taking up or continuing physical training. Indeed, barriers may arise from mental and physical impairments that limit or prevent patient engagement in exercise. In particular, as the disease progresses, PwD encounter difficulties with orientation, which can affect their understanding of the exercise task [40]. Attention, memory and language processing difficulties also interfere with their understanding. Therefore, it is especially challenging for a person with dementia to comprehend the exercise instructions given by the physician during the physical activity [48]. Another impediment related to dementia symptoms, is the increase of apathy, loss of motivation and interest in the self [5, 7, 20, 30] which contributes to patient reluctance to engage in any form of physical activity. As a result, most of the PwD find physical training to be boring and tedious [32, 42].

Interventions that aim to enhance the quality of life for people living with dementia can become difficult to achieve in more rigid settings including hospitals, where environmental and procedural restrictions are implemented depending on the risk that individuals may pose. As a result, further research is needed to develop novel interventions that can support and enhance care within confined environments. With this study, we aim to explore the use of Virtual Reality (VR) as a novel intervention to improve physical activity and therefore enhance the quality of life for patients with moderate to severe dementia who reside in a psychiatric hospital.

1.1 Related Work

Several studies that investigated the use of technology for physical training have shown promising results. One study [14] showed that the memory of PwD can be improved by playing a bowling game on Nintendo Wii on a regular basis. Another study [46] revealed that cognitive levels were improved by performing upper and lower limbs exergaming tasks, such as catching virtual coins or playing drums in front of a screen using customized controllers. Finally, improvements in cognition, gait and balance in PwD were also reported by a study which used the Wii Fit to compare virtual to normal walking tasks. This improvement was attributed to the high levels of presence experienced by PwD and was associated with exposure to the Virtual Environment [15]. It follows from these studies that VR can be an effective tool in improving the quality of life for PwD.

VR as a technology has been also used to improve physical training in healthy adults and athletes with promising results [27–29]. In general, most of the research related to VR and dementia focuses on the enhancement of specific skills which tend to decline within the course of the condition. Such skills include cognition [4, 6, 22, 23, 34], memory [33], spatial navigation [8, 49], executive functions, such as planning activities [25] and attention enhancement [10, 24].

Within the context of Human-Computer Interaction (HCI), research mostly focuses on the specific needs of PwD interacting with technology. Past studies have examined the important elements that a virtual environment should incorporate in terms of design and development in both semi-immersive and fully-immersive modalities. An overall conclusion from past studies is that special focus should be placed on creating personalized experiences that take into account the preferences and skill level of each individual user [12, 13, 18, 43].

Our objective here is to discuss the applicability of VR for the physical training of people with moderate to severe dementia and to communicate our experiences in designing such a system. We present a set of guidelines, based on the issues encountered during the design, testing and execution of the experimental tasks, to enable the future development of VR applications for PwD in healthcare environments. To accomplish this, we present three interrelated studies that refer to: (1) System requirement analysis carried out through a workshop with experts in dementia care; (2) System interaction method assessment by testing two different types of interaction in VR, to identify the most suitable for PwD; and (3) A pilot study with patients performing three upper limb physiotherapy tasks in VR. To conclude, this paper presented an examination of issues encountered during the design, testing and execution of a VR system for physical training for people with moderate to severe dementia.

2 Apparatus

An Oculus Rift CV1 VR[1] head-mounted-display (HMD) was used to display the physical training tasks while interactions were effected using two Oculus Touch Controllers. Differences in Range of Motion (ROM) capabilities were measured with a goniometer (see Study 3, Materials) to avoid any frustration and enable PwD to successfully perform the exercise task based on the range of motion they were able to perform.

The VR experience was delivered using the Unity3D[2] game engine and the 3D models were created in Maya[3]. The experience was also streamed to a laptop screen, mirroring the user's real-time virtual interactions. This allowed the clinical staff and the researchers to observe silently the procedure.

---

[1] https://www.oculus.com/rift/.

[2] https://unity.com/.

[3] https://www.autodesk.com/products/maya/.

3 Study 1. System Requirements Analysis

3.1 Study Design and Procedure

First, we conducted a thorough systematic literature review to inform the design of the VR application for a range of patients with neurodegenerative diseases, including those with dementia [41]. Then, a workshop was conducted to discuss potential VR environments and to identify the most suitable types of VR content with respect to the needs of people with moderate to severe dementia, informed by the knowledge gained from the systematic review.

3.2 Materials

Notes were taken by an HCI researcher during the workshop discussions. The aim of these observations was to identify potential VR environments and activities according to the needs of PwD.

3.3 Participants

Thirty-nine medical and paramedical personnel including clinical psychotherapists (n = 3), physiotherapists (n = 4), occupational (n = 2), speech (n = 2) and music/arts (n = 4) therapists, social workers (n = 1), gymnasts (n = 1) and caregivers (n = 22) attended the workshop.

3.4 Findings and Discussion

Study 1 included a 30-min consultative workshop to brainstorm about the suitable type of VR content for PwD. During the workshop, an HCI researcher provided an introduction of the potential uses of VR technology including information about what types of virtual environments were reported by previous literature as suitable for use with dementia patients. Environments included a cathedral, a forest, a beach, and a countryside [31, 50]. Then, all attendees rated the virtual environments independently (possible range between 0–2, where 0 = not suitable, 1 = neutral, and 2 = suitable). The highest-rated virtual environment was the forest. Therefore, it was agreed to use a forest as the backdrop to this study. A snapshot of the selected virtual environment is shown in Fig. 1.

Then, the HCI researcher observed the regular physical training of five different PwD. After the training, four physiotherapists, two occupational therapists and a gymnast agreed on three essential tasks that a VR training session should include. The selected exercises were:

1. Overhead arm-stretching: Climbing up a vertical rope with 40 knots/targets. Each target represents each overhead arm-stretching move (Fig. 1A).
2. Overhead arm-raising: Climbing up a wall with 40 blocks/targets (Fig. 1B).
3. Seated cable row: Pulling a horizontal rope with 40 knots/targets towards their side (Fig. 1C).

Fig. 1. The three exercises performed during the training session.

All training activities involved upper body movements which can be performed actively from a seated position and are similar to the regular training routine. Seated position exercise training is mostly preferred in hospitalization training to avoid the risk of falling.

4 Study 2. System Interaction Method Assessment

4.1 Study Design and Procedure

The aim of this study was to assess the usability of different interaction methods in VR by PwD. Participants were asked to perform a boxing exercise via two conditions: (a) Touch Condition: Participants held a controller and touched a virtual ball by extending their hands, and (b) Touch and Grab Condition: Once participants touched the ball, as in the Touch Condition, they had to grab it using the grip button of the controller. Visual feedback was provided for each successful attempt by changing the colour of the ball from red to green (Fig. 2).

The study used a within-subject design and the order in which the two conditions were performed was counterbalanced to equate potential carry-over effects. The experiment lasted about 20 min. The findings prescribed the design factors for Study 3.

4.2 Materials

Accuracy and latency data from task execution were logged automatically by the computer. Additional data – independence, SQE and VAS – were collected by an HCI researcher located in the room where the VR physical training session took place. The metrics collected in each session were the following:

1. **Task Performance.** Assessed the ability to perform the boxing exercise correctly for 20 repetitions within a two-minute timeframe.
2. **Task Independence.** Evaluated by taking into account the number of times assistance was provided by the physiotherapist to the patient to perform the boxing exercise. More assistance yielded a lower score on this measure.
3. **Time.** Time was measured in seconds, from the first time that participants successfully performed the exercise until they completed it.
4. **The Single Ease Question (SEQ) [44].** SEQ assessed the level of difficulty for each interaction on a 7-point Likert scale (1 = very difficult and 7 = very easy).
5. **Visual Analog Scale (VAS) [6].** VAS was used as a psychometric response scale of depicted emoji to measure emotions (0 = happy and 5 = sad). The scale was used

to allow patients to express their emotions towards each method of interaction. We asked patients to point to the specific emoji which matched their emotional state before and after each task execution.

4.3 Participants

Ten people with moderate to severe dementia (Male = 5; Female = 5), with ages between 75 to 85 years (M = 78.90, SD = 3.81), participated in this study. Their average number of years of living with dementia was 3.4 years (SD = 2.01) and ranged between 1–8 years. The mean Global Deterioration Scale rating (GDS; [36]) was 4.80 (SD = .92) "moderate to severe dementia" (range = 3–6: "mild to moderately severe"). Primary diagnoses included dementia in Alzheimer's disease (n = 10) and secondary diagnoses included depressive episodes (n = 3), clinical anxiety (n = 3), and paranoid schizophrenia (n = 1). No participant had any prior experience using VR.

4.4 Findings and Discussion

Task Performance, Independence and Simplicity. Only seven dementia patients were happy to use the VR system. The remaining reported experiencing claustrophobia (see Sect. 6) and did not complete the study.

An independent sample t-test revealed that patients scored significantly higher when performing the boxing exercise in the touch condition (M = .91, SD = .15) than in the touch and grab (M = .34, SD = .34); t (12) = 4.04, p = .002. In addition, an independent sample t-test revealed that PwD were depending more on the physiotherapist assistance in order to perform the exercise task correctly during the touch and grab condition than during the touch condition (M = 13.86, SD = 6.36) than during the touch and grab conditions (M = 1.86, SD = 2.91); t (12) = −4.54, p = .001. Finally, a significant difference was found in the scores of difficulty PwD encountered during the touch (M = 6.29, SD = 1.25) and the touch and grab (M = 2.57, SD = 2.44) conditions; t (12) = 3.58, p = .004.

Fig. 2. Study 2 setting with a virtual ball turning green with each successful interaction (Color figure online)

The results suggest that PwD were able to complete the exercise tasks successfully, and with less assistance from the physiotherapist when simple interactions were assigned to the VR system. Our study validates the recommendation made by a previous study that suggested avoiding the use of buttons as control input when an interaction is required by people with mild dementia [13]. We also encourage researchers and developers to deliver simple interactions, avoiding the use of buttons as a control input.

In addition, we observed that, during the touch and grab condition, five out of seven PwD accidentally pressed the trigger button instead of the grip. Therefore, when buttons are considered necessary for the design, we propose to use the "trigger button" which is positioned to the front of the oculus controller instead of the "grip button" which is positioned to the side. We believe that patients naturally positioned their fingers to the front side of the controller because of the reduced finger mobility that is common with old age.

Learnability and Emotional Affect. Task performance can also be assessed based on the time the PwD took to perform each task. Results showed that the time needed for the first completion in the touch condition (M = 2 s) was significantly lower than the touch and grab condition (M = 55 s); t (12) = −2.80, p = .016. Overall, most of the PwD were able to perform the task for the first time within 10 s of the experimental session in the touch condition, compared to about a minute for the touch and grab condition. Similarly, the analysis of the total time needed to complete the tasks revealed a significant difference between the touch condition (M = 38 s) and the touch and grab condition (M = 102 s); t (12) = −4.49, p = .001.

The response time affected, either positively or negatively, the intensity of the task performance. Therefore, and based on our findings, we suggest that it's best to avoid complicated interactions with the use of buttons. To the best of our knowledge, this is the first study which examines the response time of the people with moderate to severe dementia for a given exercise task. Simple interactions where natural movements are used were found to provoke much more positive emotions to the PwD. This statement was validated by a 2 × 2 within-subjects ANOVA which compared the effect of the method of interaction on the patients' emotions (VAS) at a pre- and post-exposure level. The results revealed a significant main effect of the method of interaction [F(1, 12) = 7.67, p = .017] with the touch condition evaluated as more enjoyable (M = 0.86, SD = 1.06) than the touch and grab (M = 3.28, SD = 2.06).

Based on the above results, we conclude that linking the buttons with the control input of the device is not a suitable solution for people with moderate to severe dementia. Therefore, we developed the VR system of Study 3 in accordance with these findings.

5   Study 3. A Pilot Study with Patients Confined at a Psychiatric Hospital Performing Physical Training in Virtual Reality

5.1   Study Design and Procedure

Patients were invited to use the VR system along with their own physiotherapist in a familiar room of the hospital. Their psychologist was also present to reduce the risk of behavioural disturbance and anxiety.

The experimental procedure followed six steps: First, patients were screened for inclusion. Then, a researcher observed each patient in care for 15 min prior to the session and recorded the person's mood. PwD who were judged to be in a relatively good mood proceeded to a VR familiarization session. This was done to ensure that patients were able to use VR without any side effects (e.g., nausea).

Once the familiarization session was completed, patients took part in the VR physical training session (Overhead arm-stretching, Overhead arm-raising and Seated cable row as described in Sect. 3.4) (Fig. 3). During the session, quantitative data about task performance, reaction time, and independence of the patient were collected. Once the intervention was completed, patients returned to care where a familiar caregiver observed them for 15 min to record their mood. The maximum duration of the physical training session was set to 20 min to reduce the risk of adverse effects. Overall, each session lasted approximately 30 min.

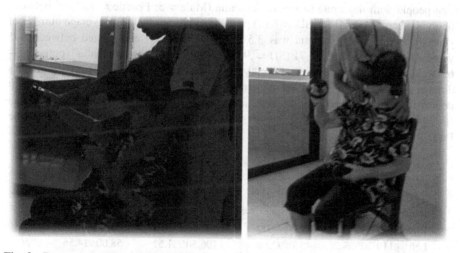

Fig. 3. Dementia patients performing an overhead arm stretching exercise. Left: the physiotherapist assists the patient. Right: the patient performs the task on her own.

5.2   Materials

1. **Goniometer.** A goniometer was used by the physiotherapist to assess ROM for each task. Each exercise task was personalized based on the pre-set ROM of each patient to ensure that training was carried out with the appropriate ROM and difficulty.
2. **Task Performance.** Measured by the number of times each task was performed correctly out of 40 repetitions.
3. **Task Independence.** As in Study 2, it was computed based on the number of times assistance was offered by the physiotherapist to the patient to perform the boxing exercise. ore assistance yielded a lower score on this measure.
4. **Time.** The time was measured in seconds and included: (1) the time participants needed to perform the exercise correctly for the first time (first repetition), (2) the overall time participants spent on each exercise, and (3) on the full VR session.
5. **The Single Ease Question (SEQ).** SEQ assessed the system usability (1 = very difficult and 7 = very easy).
6. **Visual Analog Scale (VAS).** VAS assessed the participants' emotional state. The scale was administered before and after each session.
7. **Observation Notes.** Detailed observation notes were taken by an HCI researcher to classify the patient's interactions and behavioural responses to the VR experience.

5.3   Participants

Ten people with moderate to severe dementia (Male = 5; Female = 5), aged between 65 to 90 years (M = 80.10, SD = 7.11) participated in Study 3. The average number of years of living with dementia was 3.5 years (SD = 1.35) and ranged between 1–5 years. The GDS mean was 4.71 (SD = .95) "moderate to severe dementia" (range = 3–6: "mild to moderately severe"). Primary diagnoses included: dementia in Alzheimer's disease (n = 6) and unspecified dementia (n = 4). Secondary diagnoses included: depressive episodes (n = 4); clinical anxiety (n = 4) and paranoid schizophrenia (n = 1). Table 1 presents descriptive statistics about the goniometer data of the PwD ROM.

Table 1. Goniometer data (means and standard deviations).

Hand	Flexion (M/SD)	Extension (M/SD)	Abduction (M/SD)	Adduction (M/SD)
Right	114.20°/45.98	47.00°/4.00	102.50°/34.80	60.80°/15.30
Left	119.20°/38.26	45.70°/2.80	106.50°/31.51	58.00°/14.56

5.4   Findings and Discussion

Task Performance, Independence and Simplicity. The overall mean success of patients in performing the overhead arm stretching exercise was .74 (SD = .22), for the seated cable row exercise .78, (SD = .21) and for the overhead arm raise exercise .84 (SD = .25). The high rates of VR task performance demonstrate the ability of people with moderate to severe dementia to use VR technology for their daily exercises.

In addition, and similarly to the usual care, assistance was requested in order to perform the tasks accurately. In particular, patients were in need of assistance approximately 14 times out of 40 during the overhead arm stretching exercise (M = 13.71, SD = 13.09), 12 times during the seated cable row exercise (M = 11.57, SD = 13.41) and 11 times during the overhead arm raise exercise (M = 11.00, SD = 15.69). However, it should be noted that even though assistance was required in order to perform the exercise tasks correctly, participants, in general, reported low difficulty in carrying out the exercises (M = 5.00, SD = 1.63).

These results suggest that VR can enhance and support the PwD physical training when assistance is provided by the physiotherapist. Coupled with the findings of Study 2, these results suggest that less complicated tasks can reduce the need for assistance and lead to improved levels of independence by the patients.

Learnability and Emotional Affect. A paired sample t-test revealed a significant difference in the scores of the emotional state of PwD in pre- (M = 1.46, SD = .55) and post- (M = .76, SD = .29) VR exercising exposures, suggesting that VR exercise can significantly improve patient emotional states; t (6) = 3.26, p = .017. Previous research suggested that approximately half of the long-term hospitalized PwD are diagnosed with depression, which contributes negatively to the progression of the disease [20]. In the past, clinical research has shown that VR has been used successfully to enhance the treatment of mental health disorders such as depression, anxiety, and phobias [21, 26]. Here, we found that VR can have a positive effect on PwD. We consider this finding to be of vast importance since research has shown that depression leads to increased apathy and loss of motivation in dementia patients, which impacts negatively the engagement to physical activity [20, 30]. If VR can reduce the negative emotional responses in dementia, this could have a positive effect on the deceleration of the disease.

We also measured the time participants needed to successfully complete each exercise task for the first time. This was done to validate the simplicity of the requested task and to assess the understanding of task instructions. Descriptives statistics are presented in Table 2.

Table 2. Measured time means in seconds of the three exercise tasks by PwD.

Time (s)	Overhead arm stretching (M/SD)	Overhead arm raises (M/SD)	Seated cable row (M/SD)
First repetition	19.63/17.24	13.26/07.20	11.96/08.21
Overall	74.92/30.82	82.41/34.69	54.70/22.87

6 Implications and Recommendations Based on Content Analysis

A qualitative content analysis of the observational data was also conducted to discuss in depth the problems faced during the design, testing and execution of the experimental tasks and present recommendations for future deployment in healthcare services. Observed experiences regarding the more optimum design of the experimental setup were elaborated with quotes from our observational notes. The data were anonymized, and participants referred to as [PwD Number and Physiotherapist/Psychologist Number]. For example, a quote by the first patient and his/her physiotherapist is presented as: [Patient 1, Physiotherapist X].

Accept that VR is not for every PwD. In contrast to other kinds of digital technologies, such as flat-screen interfaces, tablets and mobile devices, fully-immersive VR systems envelop the users view completely. Because of the material factors of the system, three out of ten PwD, all women with a mean age of 78.2 (SD = 3.78), refused to put on the HMD. These three patients reported suffering from severe clinical anxiety.

> *"Please, please my dear remove this thing from my head, it makes me feel like I cannot breathe, I cannot breathe..."*
> [Patient 4, Physiotherapist 2].
> *"No, no, no, no, no... Take this off of me, you are going to blind me!"*
> [Patient 5, Physiotherapist 1].
> *"Where are you? Why did you leave me here alone?". [The physiotherapist softly responded] "I am right here!" [The PwD puts her arms into the air and tried to grab the physiotherapist, she looked around and once she failed to find the physiotherapist, she took off the VR system and threw it away from her intensely].*
> [Patient 9, Physiotherapist 3].

This is not the first time such responses were observed in PwD. Previous research on VR and patients with mild dementia reported that handheld systems (i.e., being able to hold the HMD with their hands) were preferred [18] since the system can link to a sense of claustrophobia [43]. However, and based on the nature of our study, such a solution was not an option, since patients had to perform upper body exercise tasks. We believe that building an exoskeleton to hold the VR display might increase participants tolerance and acceptance towards the device. It could also reduce the incidence of catastrophic behaviour, which yields a risk for the patient, the staff and the system.

Give Constant Feedback. As dementia progresses, cognitive functions such as attention, memory and language comprehension, decline and interfere with the understanding of the exercise tasks [40, 48]. Therefore, to overcome such barriers, feedback for the upcoming movement should be provided to the PwD as a reminder. Our VR system used arrows to provide visual feedback for each target and to remind participants of their next move. We found that the visual feedback was confusing for one patient who often reached to grab the arrows instead of the targets. We observed that verbal instructions which were given by the physiotherapist to the PwD during the VR session, helped patients' attention to the exercise task and improved performance.

> *[The patient tried to grab the arrow pointing to the target, a couple of times. The physiotherapist then grabbed the PwD hand and placed it on the target. The physiotherapist instructed the patient:]* "This, grab this…", *[PwD giggles and respond]* "Ohh my hand!" *[She remained silent for a while observing the virtual hand which closed once it grabbed on the target. The physiotherapist response again:]* "Yeah, that is your hand. Grab another target with your other hand" *[The PwD remained silent and the physiotherapist instructed he again:]* "Show me your other hand!" *[The patient with dementia raised her other hand to the air. The physiotherapist said:]* "Good, good grab the target now" *[The PwD grabbed the target, and the physiotherapist reacted happily:]* "Bravo! Grab the other target and climb up, climb up the rope!". *[The PwD raised her hands alternately and started climbing. She managed to perform the task correctly for a couple of times and then stopped. The physiotherapist intervened again:]* "Bravo! Bravo!" *[The PwD continued to do the exercise until she reached the top].*
> [Patient 3, Physiotherapist 4].

These observations demonstrated that the verbal reward, via positive words such as "Bravo and Good", might increase the PwD's motivation to continue performing the given task. Previous research suggests that positive emotions activate brain areas related to reward, playing a critical role in motivation [2]. It is also documented that pleasant activities and rewards can relieve stress and improve motivation [47]. We, therefore, suggest incorporating in VR design, expressions that will present some form of motivation and approval for PwD.

Boost the Visual Targets. Comparing the findings across Studies 2 and 3 we conclude that it is better to present the virtual targets as big shapes, with sharp colours and within the front field of view of PwD. Targets should also be stable as this is shown to improve performance. With respect to the observational data, during the seated cable row exercise, one patient grabbed the virtual rope and pulled it downward. The physiotherapist had to bring the patient back to the correct seated position to prevent hitting the ground.

> *Physiotherapist:* "[Name of PwD] let's get back to your chair. I want you to stay on your chair". *PwD:* "But I want to grab the rope…". "Here is the rope. Let's do the exercise together" *[The physiotherapist held the PwD hands and together they performed a few exercises moves].* *Physiotherapist:* "Bravo! Continue on your own. Bravo!".
> [Patient 6, Physiotherapist 1].

In addition, it was observed that at some point during the exercise, all the patients tended to get confused and repeated the same steps for a couple of times. Patients repeatedly moved first in one direction and then in the opposite direction, instead of moving forward. In these cases, the physiotherapist assisted the patient. Based on this observation, we recommend avoiding the use of moving targets. We developed the VR system to simulate real-world interactions, and follow real-world physics rules. However, we suggest simplifying some interactions to avoid confusing PwD.

> *[PwD is moving frontward and backwards, this happened a couple of times]. Physiotherapist: "Where do you need to go?", PwD: "Up". Physiotherapist: "So what do you need to grab to climb up? [PwD thinks but doesn't respond, physiotherapist intervenes again] Grab the next target. Up! Up!" [PwD followed the physiotherapist instructions and continued correctly the exercise].*
> [Patient 4, Physiotherapist 2].

Include Content of Natural Environments. Another impediment related to dementia symptoms are the experience of depressive episodes, the increased apathy and loss of motivation, along with the negative attitudes towards the engagement in physical activity [20, 30]. Therefore, to create an engaging and fun VR physical training we used a natural environment which was found to motivate PwD [16] while offering a pleasant experience with positive psychological effects, such as decreased tension, anger, and depression [3, 9, 17]. Our patients were found to enjoy the natural environment view.

> *"Olalla! Look at the trees and the birds and the sky... Olalla! the sky... look at the sky, so blue, and the air..." Researcher intervene: "Do you feel the air?". PwD: "Oh, yes, it's a nice breeze! Olalla, there are so many, so many, so many things in here!".*
> [Patient 1, HCI Researcher].

Content of the Process of Reminiscence. It was also observed that VR was able to trigger old memories for PwD. This is not the only study to suggest that VR is able to evoke positive memories on topics of family, geographical origins and travels [37]. In the past, research suggested that the recreation of experiences via VR could be very beneficial for PwD [18]. Therefore, we suggest that the design community aims to deliver personalised VR environments that might trigger memories of past experiences.

> *"I am in Disneyland again! I am close to the ice-mountains!" Researcher intervene: "Have you been at Disneyland?" [PwD giggles and nods her head:] "Long time ago when my children were still young!"*
> [Patient 7, HCI Researcher].

Offer a Smooth Transition to Reality. It is well documented by the literature that after VR exposure, PwD might experience a sense of disorientation [4, 43]. Once the VR HMD was removed from their head, our patients exhibited some disorientation.

> PwD: "ooo, where are the... the... the..." researcher intervene: "The trees?"
> PwD: "Yes, where are they?" researcher: "Did you liked them?" PwD: "Yea! Oh,
> here they are!" [PwD pointed to a tree out of the window]. Researcher: "Are these
> the trees you saw?" [the PwD didn't respond and the researcher repeated: "[Name
> of PwD], is this the tree you saw?" PwD: "No". Researcher: "Do you want to put the
> system back on to see the trees?". PwD: "Yes!" [He laughs].
> [Patient 3, HCI Researcher].

We acknowledge the importance of smoothly transitioning PwD back to the physical space. Since this incident of disorientation happened at the very first patient's exposure we then asked the physiotherapist and/or psychotherapist to inform the PwD when the experiment was over, and then to remove the HMD. No visual cues were presented to the PwD during the time the staff was informing them of the end of the session. We found that providing verbal prompts before removing the VR HMD improves the patient's transition to the physical space. Having PwD for a couple of seconds without any visual cues might also improve smooth transition. We recommend for future VR development to incorporate features that will explain to the PwD that the experience is over. For example, a blue screen with a congratulatory message might appear. A soft voice might enhance this by informing participants that the experiment is over.

7 Conclusion

This paper presented an examination of issues encountered during the design, testing and execution of a VR system for physical training for people with moderate to severe dementia. The system was deployed into a confined mental health unit and thus the paper presents recommendations for designing VR systems for healthcare services. An iterative participatory design process was followed with input from health experts coming from diverse fields and from 20 people with moderate to severe dementia. Two methods of interaction and three different types of exercise were designed and tested in VR. Our analysis revealed the potential of VR physical training for PwD and presented a set of guidelines and recommendations for the future deployment in healthcare services: 1) continuous feedback should be provided to the PwD in order to perform the task correctly and without much supervision and assistance from the clinical staff; 2) visual targets should be stable, visible, and within the frontal field of view of the PwD so that the patients could interact easier and appropriately with the system; 3) personalised virtual environments relevant to the PwD's interests and past memories improve the patient's immersion and engagement, and 4) transitioning smoothly the PwD back to reality is of vast importance to reduce the risk of distress and disorientation.

The current study contributes to the emerging body of research in the use of VR technology with people with moderate to severe dementia. We trust that this paper lays the foundations for the future deployment of VR to enhance physical training for PwD in confined psychiatric hospitals.

Acknowledgements. We thank the "Archangelos Michael" Dementia and Alzheimer psychiatric hospital for providing the support to conduct this research. Special thanks to the hospital staff Kouyoumdjian Maria, Nicolaou Christiana and Xynari Katerina, for their dedication to the study. We also thank all PwD who participated in the study and their families. This project has received funding from the European Union's Horizon 2020 Research and Innovation Programme under Grant Agreement No 739578 and the Government of the Republic of Cyprus through the Directorate-General for European Programmes, Coordination and Development.

References

1. ACEMA (Aged Care Evaluation and Management Advisors): Examination of length of stay for older persons in the acute and sub-acute sector. Report for the AHMAC Working Group on the Care of Older Australians. Department of Health, Canberra (2003)
2. Berridge, K.C.: Pleasures of the brain. Brain Cogn. **52**(1), 106–128 (2003)
3. Calogiuri, G., Chroni, S.: The impact of the natural environment on the promotion of active living: an integrative systematic review. BMC Public Health **14**(1), 873–900 (2014)
4. Cherniack, E.P.: Not just fun and games: applications of virtual reality in the identification and rehabilitation of cognitive disorders of the elderly. Disabil. Rehabil.: Assist. Technol. **6**(4), 283–289 (2011)
5. Clarke, D.E., et al.: Apathy in dementia: clinical and sociodemographic correlates. J. Neuropsychiatr. Clin. Neurosci. **20**(3), 337–347 (2008)
6. Crichton, N.: Visual analogue scale (VAS). J. Clin. Nurs. **10**(5), 697–706 (2001)
7. Crombie, I.K.: Why older people do not participate in leisure time physical activity: a survey of activity levels, beliefs and deterrents. Age Ageing **33**(3), 287–292 (2004)
8. Cushman, L.A., Stein, K., Duffy, C.J.: Detecting navigational deficits in cognitive aging and Alzheimer disease using virtual reality. Neurology **71**(12), 888–895 (2008)
9. Bowler, D.E., Buyung-Ali, L., Knight, T.M., Pullin, A.S.: Urban greening to cool towns and cities: a systematic review of the empirical evidence. Landsc. Urban plan. **97**(3), 147–155 (2010)
10. Doniger, G.M., et al.: Virtual reality-based cognitive-motor training for middle-aged adults at high Alzheimer's disease risk: a randomized controlled trial. Alzheimer's Dement.: Transl. Res. Clin. Interv. **4**, 118–129 (2018)
11. Ehlenbach, W.J., et al.: Association between acute care and critical illness hospitalization and cognitive function in older adults. JAMA **303**(8), 763–770 (2010)
12. Eisapour, M., Cao, S., Domenicucci, L., Boger, J.: Virtual reality exergames for people living with dementia based on exercise therapy best practices. In: Proceedings of the Human Factors and Ergonomics Society Annual Meeting, vol. 62, no. 1, pp. 528–532 (2018)
13. Eisapour, M., Cao, S., Domenicucci, L., Boger, J.: Participatory design of a virtual reality exercise for people with mild cognitive impairment. In: Extended Abstracts of the 2018 CHI Conference on Human Factors in Computing Systems, CS15, pp. 1–9. ACM (2018)
14. Fenney, A., Lee, T.D.: Exploring spared capacity in persons with dementia: what WiiTM can learn. Act. Adapt. Aging **34**(4), 303–313 (2010)
15. Flynn, D., Van Schaik, P., Blackman, T., Femcott, C., Hobbs, B., Calderon, C.: Developing a virtual reality-based methodology for people with dementia: a feasibility study. Cyberpsychol. Behav.: Impact Internet Multimed. Virtual Real. Behav. Soc. **6**(6), 591–611 (2003)
16. Gladwell, V.F., Brown, D.K., Wood, C., Sandercock, G.R., Barton, J.L.: The great outdoors: how a green exercise environment can benefit all. Extrem. Physiol. Med. **2**(1), 3–10 (2013)
17. Hitron, T., et al.: Does participating in physical activity in outdoor natural environments have a greater effect on physical and mental wellbeing than physical activity indoors? A systematic review. Environ. Sci. Technol. **45**(5), 1761–1772 (2018)
18. Hodge, J., Montague, K., Hastings, S., Morrissey, K.: Exploring the design of tailored virtual reality experiences for people with dementia. In: Proceedings of the 2018 CHI Conference on Human Factors in Computing Systems, pp. 514–526 (2019)

19. King, B., Jones, C., Brand, C.: Relationship between dementia and length of stay of general medical patients admitted to acute care. Australas. J. Ageing **25**(1), 20–23 (2006)
20. Kitching, D.: Depression in dementia. Aust. Prescr. **38**, 209–211 (2015)
21. Lindner, P., et al.: Creating state of the art, next-generation Virtual Reality exposure therapies for anxiety disorders using consumer hardware platforms: design considerations and future directions. Cogn. Behav. Ther. **46**(5), 404–420 (2017)
22. Littbrand, H., Stenvall, M., Rosendahl, E.: Applicability and effects of physical exercise on physical and cognitive functions and activities of daily living among people with dementia: a systematic review. Am. J. Phys. Med. Rehabil. **90**(6), 495–518 (2011)
23. Loprinzi, P.D., Herod, S.M., Cardinal, B.J., Noakes, T.D.: Physical activity and the brain: a review of this dynamic, bi-directional relationship. Brain Res. **1539**(20), 95–104 (2013)
24. Manera, V., et al.: A feasibility study with image-based rendered virtual reality in patients with mild cognitive impairment and dementia. PLoS ONE **11**(3), e0151487 (2016)
25. Manera, V., et al.: Kitchen and cooking, a serious game for mild cognitive impairment and Alzheimer's disease: a pilot study. Front. Aging Neurosci. **7**(24), 1–10 (2015)
26. Maples-Keller, J.L., Bunnell, B.E., Kim, S.J., Rothbaum, B.O.: The use of virtual reality technology in the treatment of anxiety and other psychiatric disorders. Harv. Rev. Psychiatr. **25**(3), 103–113 (2017)
27. Matsangidou, M., Ang, C.S., Sakel, M.: Clinical utility of virtual reality in pain management: a comprehensive research review. Br. J. Neurosci. Nurs. **13**(3), 133–143 (2017)
28. Matsangidou, M., Ang, C.S., Mauger, A.R., Intarasirisawat, J., Otkhmezuri, B., Avraamides, M.N.: Is your virtual self as sensational as your real? Virtual Reality: the effect of body consciousness on the experience of exercise sensations. Psychol. Sport Exerc. **41**, 218–224 (2019)
29. Matsangidou, M., Ang, C.S., Mauger, Alexis R., Otkhmezuri, B., Tabbaa, L.: How real is unreal? In: Bernhaupt, R., Dalvi, G., Joshi, A., Balkrishan, D.K., O'Neill, J., Winckler, M. (eds.) INTERACT 2017. LNCS, vol. 10516, pp. 273–288. Springer, Cham (2017). https://doi.org/10.1007/978-3-319-68059-0_18
30. Muliyala, K.P., Varghese, M.: The complex relationship between depression & dementia. Ann. Indian Acad. Neurol. **13**(6), 69–73 (2010)
31. Nichol, B., Lonergan, J., Mould, M.: The use of hospitals by older people: a casemix analysis. Occasional Papers, New Seriesno, vol. 11. Commonwealth Department of Health and Aged Care, Canberra (2000)
32. Nyman, S.R.: Psychosocial issues in engaging older people with physical activity interventions for the prevention of falls. Can. J. Aging/La Rev. canadienne du vieillissement **30**(1), 45–55 (2011)
33. Optale, G., et al.: Controlling memory impairment in elderly adults using virtual reality memory training: a randomized controlled pilot study. Neurorehabil. Neural Repair **24**(4), 348–357 (2010)
34. Pitkälä, K.H., et al.: Effects of the Finnish Alzheimer disease exercise trial (FINALEX): a randomized controlled trial. JAMA Intern. Med. **173**(10), 894–901 (2013)
35. Potter, R., Ellard, D., Rees, K., Thorogood, M.: A systematic review of the effects of physical activity on physical functioning, quality of life and depression in older people with dementia. Int. J. Geriatr. Psychiatry **26**(10), 1000–1011 (2011)
36. Reisberg, B., Ferris, S.H., de Leon, M.J., Crook, T.: The global deterioration scale for assessment of primary degenerative dementia. Am. J. Psychiatr. **139**(9), 1136–1139 (1982)
37. Rose, V., Stewart, I., Jenkins, K.G., Tabbaa, L., Ang, C.S., Matsangidou, M.: Bringing the outside in: the feasibility of virtual reality with people with dementia in an inpatient psychiatric care setting. Dementia (2019). https://doi.org/10.1177/1471301219868036

38. Rose, V., Stewart, I., Jenkins, K., Ang, C.S., Matsangidou, M.: A Scoping review exploring the feasibility of Virtual Reality technology use with individuals living with dementia. In: ICAT-EGVE 2018 - International Conference on Artificial Reality and Telexistence and Eurographics Symposium on Virtual Environments (2018)

39. Santana-Sosa, E., Barriopedro, M.I., López-Mojares, L.M., Pérez, M., Lucia, A.: Exercise training is beneficial for Alzheimer's patients. Int. J. Sports Med. **29**(10), 845–850 (2008)

40. Savva, G.M., Zaccai, J., Matthews, F.E., Davidson, J.E., McKeith, I., Brayne, C.: Prevalence, correlates and course of behavioural and psychological symptoms of dementia in the population. Br. J. Psychiatr. **194**(3), 212–219 (2009)

41. Schiza, E., Matsangidou, M., Neokleous, K., Pattichis, C.S.: Virtual Reality applications for neurological disease: a review. Front. Robot. AI **6**(100), 1–14 (2019)

42. Suttanon, P., Hill, K.D., Said, C.M., Byrne, K.N., Dodd, K.J.: Factors influencing commencement and adherence to a home-based balance exercise program for reducing risk of falls: perceptions of people with Alzheimer's disease and their caregivers. Int. Psychogeriatr. **24**(7), 1172–1182 (2012)

43. Tabbaa, L., et al.: Bring the outside in: providing accessible experiences through VR for people with dementia in locked psychiatric hospitals. In: Proceedings of the 2019 CHI Conference on Human Factors in Computing Systems, pp. 1–15 (2019)

44. Tedesco, D., Tullis, T.: A comparison of methods for eliciting post-task subjective ratings in usability testing. Usability Professionals Association (UPA), pp. 1–9 (2006)

45. World Health Organization. Dementia: Fact Sheet No. 362 (2017). WHO. http://www.who.int/mediacentre/factsheets/fs362/en/. Accessed 2 Sep 2019

46. Yamaguchi, H., Maki, Y., Takahashi, K.: Rehabilitation for dementia using enjoyable video-sports games. Int. Psychogeriatr. **23**(4), 674–676 (2011)

47. Yamaguchi, H., Maki, Y., Yamagami, T.: Overview of non-pharmacological intervention for dementia and principles of brain-activating rehabilitation. Psychogeriatrics **10**(4), 206–213 (2010)

48. Yu, F., Kolanowski, A.: Facilitating aerobic exercise training in older adults with Alzheimer's disease. Geriatr. Nurs. **30**(4), 250–259 (2009)

49. Zakzanis, K.K., Quintin, G., Graham, S.J., Mraz, R.: Age and dementia related differences in spatial navigation within an immersive virtual environment. Med. Sci. Monit. **15**(4), 140–150 (2009)

50. Zekry, D., et al.: Does dementia predict adverse hospitalization outcomes? A prospective study in aged inpatients. Int. J. Geriatr. Psychiatr.: J. Psychiatr. Late Life Allied Sci. **24**(3), 283–291 (2009)

A Virtual Rehabilitation System for Occupational Therapy with Hand Motion Capture and Force Feedback

Implementation with Vibration Motor

Kouki Nagamune[(✉)] and Shinto Nakamura

University of Fukui, Fukui 9108507, Japan
nagamune@u-fukui.ac.jp

Abstract. We have reported the development of virtual rehabilitation system using motion capture and vibration motor. The rehabilitation occupational therapy in our study is moving the box. Subjects recognize as a grasping motion by bending their finger near the box. At that time, in the grasping operation, feedback control was performed such that feelings of touching the virtual box is given to the subjects with the activation of the vibration motor.

The purpose of this research is to add force feedback to virtual rehabilitation system for increasing reality. In the experiment, measurements were performed by three healthy adult men, and the effect of the presence or absence of force feedback on the results was confirmed.

Keywords: Virtual rehabilitation system · Hand motion · Virtual reality

1 Background

1.1 Rehabilitation for Stroke

There are more than 1.17 million patients with cerebrovascular disease in Japan, and many people need rehabilitation. However, hospital rehabilitation due to cerebrovascular disorder has a limited number of days, and home rehabilitation and its evaluation are required [1]. However, the test for evaluating upper limb function requires special equipment, and it is expensive and cannot be easily performed. Therefore, we created and evaluated the Box and Block test (BBT), one of the upper limb function evaluation tests, in a virtual environment. Virtual rehabilitation has few restrictions on the location of equipment, and it is easy to change the level of rehabilitation by human. In this study, normal BBT only evaluates the number of time blocks tested. The evaluation focused on the hand trajectory in BBT.

1.2 Occupational Therapy

BBT is one of the occupational therapies. Occupational therapy is useful for treatment of patient with dementia which is derived from some diseases such as Parkinson's disease [2]. In occupational therapy, an examiner (occupational therapist) assigns a

M. Antona and C. Stephanidis (Eds.): HCII 2020, LNCS 12188, pp. 383–392, 2020.
https://doi.org/10.1007/978-3-030-49282-3_27

motion task based on standard procedure to a patient. The motion task aims to recover the motor function of the patient. Usually, the motion task requires that the examiner should explain the motion task and measure the operational time to finish the motion task. If this operation can be realized with a computer instead of the examiner, it can support to decrease the daily work of the occupational therapist. We already proposed a new virtual therapy with force feedback [3]. The difference between conventional and proposed occupational therapy is shown in Fig. 1.

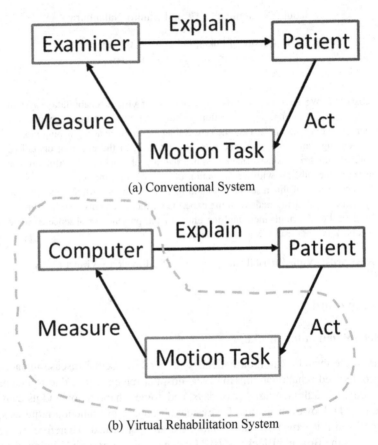

(a) Conventional System

(b) Virtual Rehabilitation System

Fig. 1. Virtual rehabilitation system for occupational therapy

2   Methods

The basic concept of the proposed system [3] is shown in Fig. 2. In the general virtual reality, a subject acts to object. Then the change as the result is projected through visual sense. In this case, it is difficult to recognize the relationship between the body and objects where the a part of body is placed in front of the objects along visual line.

Obstacles often exist in the field of view. To overcome this problem, the proposed system provides additionally force feedback to the fingers of the subject.

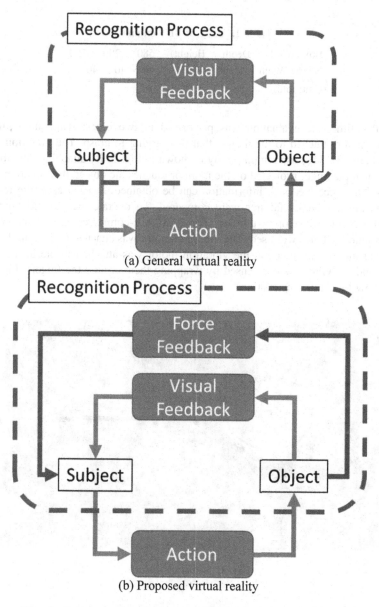

(a) General virtual reality

(b) Proposed virtual reality

Fig. 2. Basic concepts of (a) general and (b) proposed virtual reality

In this study, we repeated the operation of grasping an object on a monitor and moving it to a predetermined position using a Leap Motion controller (Leap motion)

and the development platform Unity 2019.3.0a4 (Unity Technologies). For the shape, we referred to Box & Block Test [4], a simple upper limb function method. Table 1 shows the scales created on Unity.

Table 1. Scale of BBT on unity

Box (Width × Depth × Height)	580 × 290 × 190
Block (Width × Depth × Height)	40 × 40 × 40

(Unit: mm)

At that time, the evaluation was performed in two cases: with and without a vibration motor attached to the fingers that were trying to grasp. The vibration motor (Tokyo Parts, FM34F) used in this study is shown in Fig. 3. By attaching the vibration motor, when the finger projected on the monitor touches the object, the vibration motor vibrates. The force feedback information can be obtained. In each case, the required time and the number of failures were compared. To operate the vibration motor, a KKHMF UNO R3 development board (Apple Trees E-commerce co., LT) compatible with Arduino UNO R3 was used. The vibration motor was attached to the thumb, index finger and middle finger. First, the vibration motor was attached to the inside of the Velcro, and the vibration was sensed by wrapping them around the fingers. Figures 4 and 5 show the actual installation.

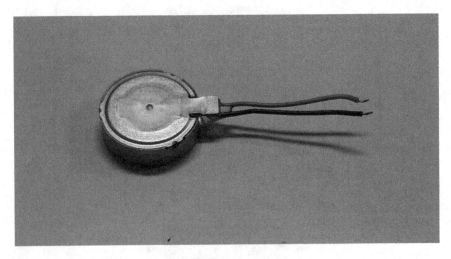

Fig. 3. Vibration motor.

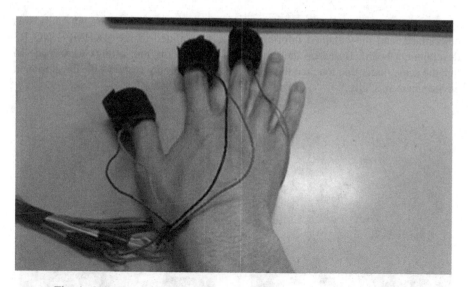

Fig. 4. Vibration motors are attached to the fingers by using Velcro straps.

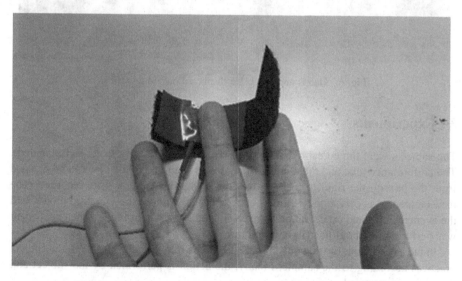

Fig. 5. A vibration motor is placed on the nail side of the finger.

Judging which finger touched the block displayed on the monitor via Unity was determined, and the obtained information was transmitted to the KKHMF UNO R3 development board. Based on the transmitted information, the settings were made so that the same finger that touched the monitor vibrated. Figure 6 shows the development environment in Unity.

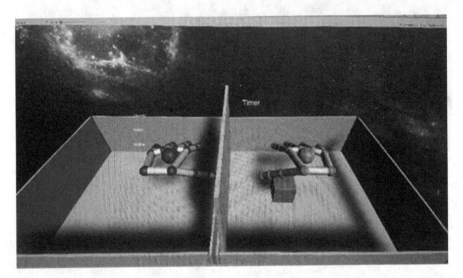

Fig. 6. Hands and block are displayed on virtual space.

3   Experiments

The subjects were three healthy subjects (male, (21.6 ± 0.5) years old, right-handed). The performance time and the number of failures when moving the block to be grasped from the box on the right to the left over the wall from the box were recorded. The measurement was performed 10 times each with and without the vibration motor, and the average and standard deviation were calculated as shown in Fig. 7. The experiment was performed without the vibration motor.

In the experiment, the demonstration is first shown to the subjects. Next, the subject practices according to the sample. Finally, the action is performed by the subject and the action is recorded.

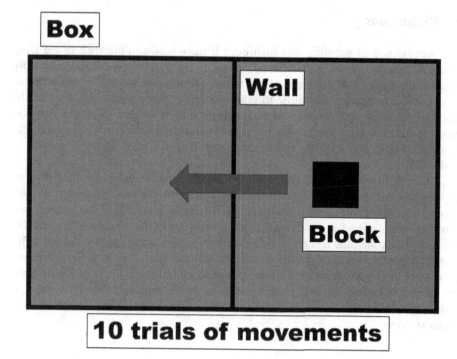

Fig. 7. Experiment outline

4 Results

Table 2 shows the results of the experiment. There was no significant difference in the measurement time between the case with and without the vibration motor. However, the number of missed grasping attempts was greater when the vibration motor was not installed. The standard deviation was about 1 s when no vibration motor was installed.

Table 2. Results of the performance.

		Performance time (s)	Number of failures
Subject 1	With vibration	3.3 ± 0.9	9
	Without vibration	3.5 ± 0.4	2
Subject 2	With vibration	5.1 ± 0.9	1
	Without vibration	4.0 ± 1.1	2
Subject 3	With vibration	7.1 ± 4.4	10
	Without vibration	6.5 ± 2.5	2

5 Discussions

The success rate of grasping was high even if there was no difference in the measurement time by attaching the vibration motor to the three fingers. This is probably because the finger was touched and the finger was not touched before grasping the object, and a correction was made to grasp the object more firmly. Referring to the standard deviation, the variation in measurement time is smaller when the vibration motor is attached, and it can be seen from the obtained information that it is intended to be used reliably. This suggests that behavior with feedback plays an important role in daily life.

Figure 8 shows the configuration of performance time. Performance time consists of cognitive time, judgment time, and reaction time. In our past reports [5], it took about 1 s from cognitive time to reaction time. Therefore, about 1 s of this performance time can be considered as the time related to recognition of the position of the box. On the other hand, the time related to the recognition of the contact of box did not differ greatly depending on the presence or absence of force feedback. In the experiments, two out of three persons showed shorter performance time with force feedback. Also, the number of failures showed a very small value in the remaining one. From these, it can be considered that force feedback works very effectively for the virtual rehabilitation system.

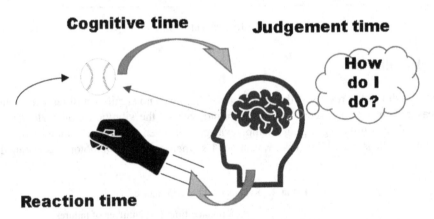

Fig. 8. Configuration of performance time.

In this experiment, force feedback gave a constant vibration regardless of whether the contact was strong or weak. On the other hand, in the real world, a strong grasping produces a large reaction, while a weak grasping produces a small reaction. To achieve the same situation, the same effect can be expected by giving a strong vibration when holding strongly and giving a small vibration when holding weakly as shown in Fig. 9.

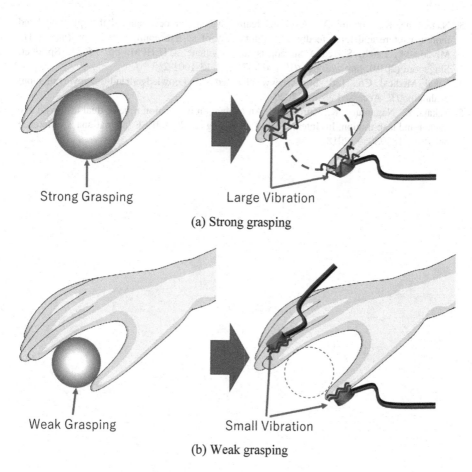

(a) Strong grasping

(b) Weak grasping

Fig. 9. Concept of vibration intensity

6   Conclusion

In this study, we explained the concept of virtual rehabilitation system including force feedback. Force feedback was realized using a vibration motor. In the experiment, it was applied to three subjects and the results were recorded. As a result, it was shown that force feedback is effective for virtual rehabilitation system. The future task is to adjust the strength of force feedback according to the contact situation.

References

1. Japan preventive association of life-style related disease. http://www.seikatsusyukanbyo.com/guide/cerebral-infarction.php. Accessed 23 Feb 2020
2. Ingrid, H.W.M., et al.: Efficacy of occupational therapy for patients with Parkinson's disease: a randomised controlled trial. Lancet Neurol. **13**(6), 557–566 (2014)

3. Nagamune, K., Uozumi, Y.: A virtual reality system for occupational therapy with hand motion capture and force feedback: a pilot study of system configuration. In: Takada, H., Miyao, M., Fateh, S. (eds.) Stereopsis and Hygiene. CTEHPM, pp. 25–31. Springer, Singapore (2019). https://doi.org/10.1007/978-981-13-1601-2_3
4. Sakai Medical Co., Ltd. https://www.sakaimed.co.jp/knowledge/hand-therapy/evaluation/evaluation03/. Accessed 23 Feb 2020
5. Takata, K., Nagamune, K., Kuroda, R.: An evaluation of reaction time of dual task with eye tracker and leap motion. In: International Proceedings of 2018 IEEE International Conference on SMC, 18398059 (2018)

iVision: An Assistive System for the Blind Based on Augmented Reality and Machine Learning

Jinyang Shen, Zhanxun Dong[⊠], Difu Qin, Jingyu Lin,
and Yahong Li

School of Design, Shanghai Jiao Tong University, Shanghai 201101, China
dongzx@sjtu.edu.cn

Abstract. In this paper, an assistive system iVision for the blind is proposed, which can solve one of the main problems faced by the visually impaired. We use augmented reality technology to create a three-dimensional model of the surrounding space and machine learning model to find the object of interest in the image taken by the camera. Then we combine these data to get the actual spatial location of the objects. This location information can be used by visually impaired people to search for objects of interest and avoid dangerous obstacle. The system uses speech and audio to feedback the spatial location to the user. Voice user interfaces (VUIs) is designed for iVision which allow the user to interact with a system through voice or speech commands. We verified the usability of the proposed system in evaluation experiments and noted its innovations and limitations.

Keywords: Assistive device · Visually impaired · Augmented reality · Machine learning

1 Introduction

According to the latest estimates by the World Health Organization, there are currently 285 million visually impaired people, 39 million of whom are blind. The number of blind and visually impaired people increases rapidly as the global population and the number of elderly people increases. Global number of blind people likely to increase to 115 million by 2050.

It is well known that impaired vision means difficult interpersonal communication and limited mobility. Visually impaired people will encounter various difficulties in their daily activities, such as object location, navigation and obstacle avoidance [1]. Questionnaire have shown that the current assistive equipment for visually impaired people is difficult to satisfy the need: navigating in unknown environments, locating objects or obstacles, and identifying similar objects [2].

Developing tools to assist blind people can greatly improve their quality of life. Positioning and navigation systems for visually impaired users have been extensively studied. Several techniques have been proposed for blind navigation system. Researchers

M. Antona and C. Stephanidis (Eds.): HCII 2020, LNCS 12188, pp. 393–403, 2020.
https://doi.org/10.1007/978-3-030-49282-3_28

use GPS [3], depth sensing and sonification [4], RFID tag [5, 6] and other technologies to get the direction and location of the object of interest and planning routes.

The prevalence of smartphones featuring various kinds of sensors and the improvements in the computation capabilities of those devices makes it possible to deploy new computer technologies such as computer vision, mobile phone-based augmented reality and deep learning models on mobile phones. For example, Google Lens [7] can analyze the camera screen, identify the characteristics of objects and search for users to understand the surrounding world, such as identifying animals and plants, translating text, scanning QR codes and barcodes.

In this paper, we propose and design a blind assistant system iVision based on augmented reality and machine learning models with mobile phones as the system operation platform (Can also run on Android smartphones).

We use AR framework to create and track a correspondence between the real-world space the user inhabits and machine learning model to find the object of interest in the camera screen. Combine these data to get the actual spatial location of the objects. This location information can be used by blind people to search for objects of interest and avoid dangerous objects. The system feedbacks the angle and distance information of the object relative to the mobile phone to the user through voice over a text-to-speech engine. Full voice user interfaces (VUIs) is designed for iVision which allow the user to interact with a system through voice or speech commands.

2   Related Work

As mentioned earlier, obstacle avoidance, object location and navigation are the main difficulties and core needs of visually impaired people. Guide dogs and guide sticks can only be used to find obstacles in front, and it is difficult to obtain more information. From early research, Electronic Travel Aids (ETA) and Electronic Orientation Aids (EOA) as the main type of assistive equipment for the visually impaired have been classified in three classes: obstacle detectors or clear-path indicators, environmental sensors and navigation systems [8, 9], which try to solve the problem of the blind. As far as the site is concerned, these devices and systems can be divided into two categories: outdoor and indoor systems.

One type of blind assistance system is based on RFID. The system proposed by Sakmongkon Chumkamon et al. [5] embeds RFID tags in the sidewalk. An RFID reader with antenna is integrated into the blind stick to read RFID tags. The navigation server receives the information on the tags of the current position and the destination position and then uses the shortest path algorithm to obtain the shortest path. The RFID information grid designed by S. Willis and S. Helal [6] does not rely on a remote database and can convey precise locations and detailed attributes about the surrounding area.

Computer vision is also often discussed. Boris Schauerte et al. [10] combine color- and SIFT-based object detection to find specific objects. VizWiz::LocateIt [10] uses Speeded Up Robust Features (SURF) for object recognition. When a blind person takes a picture and seeks assistance to find a specific object, the image with the user's request will be transferred to Amazon's Mechanical Turk. The remote worker will get the outline of the object and then estimate the position of the object automatedly in the environment to guide the user to interact with it.

Many methods rely on GPS, and it is easy to understand that this method can only be applied to outdoor systems. "map-in-the-hat" [3] is a wearable computer with augmented realities in an outdoor environment (WCAROE) to Support Terrestrial Navigation. It uses GPS to know the current location, which greatly improves the ability to draw current location information on a map. National University of Singapore's research team uses the Google Maps API in navigation systems for the visually impaired. The API can generate web-based maps and provide visualization capabilities. This project converts the navigation information generated by the Google Maps API into blind navigation information.

In addition, some projects use other techniques and methods. S. Ram and J. Sharf [11] use pyroelectric and ultrasonic sensors to distinguish between biological obstacles (human) and non-biological obstacles (non-human) in the path. This can eliminate the trouble of the walking stick from reaching the pedestrian.

A major limitation of these systems discussed so far is that they are dependent on original and dedicated hardware devices, and even require hardware sensors to be set up in the environment in advance. Although some studies advocate the use of wearable computing devices such as smartphones for sensing and computing, they still cannot be completely separated from additional hardware. This limitation makes these systems more expensive and difficult to deploy in the real lives of visually impaired people.

3   Design of iVision

3.1   System Overview

Here we present our work on iVision, a prototype system based on augmented reality and machine learning to help blind people locate any recognizable items in their environments.

iVision hardware has one and only one iPhone. iVision's prototype is developed on iOS platform. Because the software uses Vision, Core ML, ARKit, etc. framework, which make prototyping easier. iVision needs to run on an iOS device with A9 processor or better configuration, including iPhone 6 s and above, iPad 2017 and above and all iPad Pro. In fact, all the functions of iVision can be ported to Android devices. But you need to rewrite the code using Vuforia, ARCore and other augmented reality frameworks that support the Android platform.

We used an iPhone 7 with iOS 13 to run iVision. The 12-megapixel camera includes optical image stabilization on iPhone 7, and a $f/1.8$ aperture and 6-element lens can capture clear photos and videos. iPhone 7 uses the Apple A10 Fusion 64-bit system-on-chip. In addition, sensors in mobile phones, including gyroscopes, compasses, and accelerometers, calculate and determine the location of the device.

Considering that the environment for the visually impaired people to use the device is complicated, iVision software can perform offline operations without relying on external resources such as the network.

iVision's software includes real-time object detection and hit-testing in augmented reality, and a voice interaction process designed for the scenario of blind person seeking. Figure 1 shows iVision's software framework working on iOS.

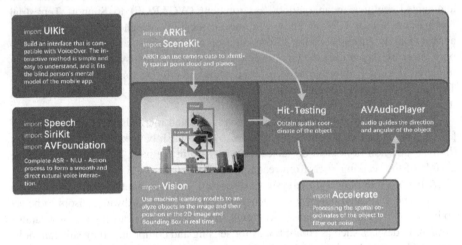

Fig. 1. Block diagram of system framework

At the same time, based on the use habits of visually impaired users and the functions of iVision prototype, we have constructed a set of voice user interfaces to guide users to complete tasks.

3.2   Object Detection

Object detection is a computer technology related to computer vision and image processing. It is used to detect instances of specific classes of semantic objects (such as people, buildings, or cars) in images and videos. In simple terms, it automatically finds specific objects from videos and images. At present, the main research directions of object detection include face detection and pedestrian detection, which can be used in areas such as video surveillance and home intelligence.

Object recognition can solve the problem that visually impaired people cannot see the objects in the surrounding environment and can also find some potential dangers (such as sharp tools, high-temperature flames, and other dangerous items). It would be very convenient to implement object recognition on our hardware basis.

When users use this application, they should scan the surrounding environment by holding the iPhone, so a challenge that needs to be solved is that we need to run a real-time target detection instance on the iPhone. That is, we need to respond to the images captured by the camera in real-time There must not be too much delay, otherwise it will greatly affect its availability and reliability.

The object detection method we use is called You only look once (YOLO). YOLO is a real-time object detection, which is extremely fast and accurate [12]. On a Pascal Titan X, YoloV3 processes images at 30 FPS. And it has a mAP of 57.9% on COCO test-dev. With YoloV3, you can get the detected object name, bounding box, confidence and the time it takes. This model can be accurately identified many commonly used items such as cups, mice, and bananas. In iVision, we set it to identify 20 common items in life such as TV monitor, chair, potted plant, cup, banana, apple, book, bag, mouse, keyboard, laptop, orange, bed, mobile phone. because these items are also often needed to locate the visually impaired.

In our development tests, we found that on iPhone 7, YoloV3 can maintain a recognition speed of 10 frames per second. Although this speed will slow down as the program runs for a long time, the phone will overheat and reduce the frequency, but it will still meet the requirements for the visually impaired.

As mentioned above, firstly, we use the Vision framework and the Core ML framework provided by iOS to capture real-time images from the camera, and the YoloV3 deep learning model is used to obtain the name of a specific object, the position and size of the bounding box in the two-dimensional image. After filtering the results with lower confidence, you can get the picture as shown left picture in Fig. 2.

3.3 Cloud Point and Hit-Testing in AR

For users with visual impairments to know where they are looking for or the danger is, object detection is not enough. We need to come up with a way to find the spatial location of this item. In essence, the job is to label the objects in the three surrounding spaces. In the part of object detection, we have completed the task of identifying the objects in the camera screen (the surrounding environment). What needs to be done now is to project the semantic information of the items in the two-dimensional image into the three-dimensional space.

In the past few decades, AR has become a hot topic. Technology giants such as Microsoft, Facebook, Google, and Apple are all laying out Augmented Reality (AR) technology, which may be one of the next new technologies that disrupt human life. AR is a 3D technology that can combine the physical world and digital world in real-time. AR can be defined as a system that fulfills three basic features: the combination of real and virtual worlds, real-time interaction, and accurate 3D registration of virtual and real objects [13]. The most common AR is image-based augmented reality, which requires identification marks or specific objects (such as plane or wall) to display digital information, which coincides with our appeal. But specific objects without marks are more complex and changeable.

On smartphones, the currently available AR SDKs are ARCore from Google, ARKit from Apple, and Vuforia from PTC (Before ARKit became popular, Vuforia was the most popular AR SDK for developers). These frameworks, without exception, build point clouds of the surrounding environment. They can detect the characteristic points of visual difference in the captured camera image, which are selected from the points in the image that have large differences in light, dark, color, and grayscale. Over time, a 3D model of the user's surroundings can be established to achieve the purpose of environmental understanding. This 3D model is composed of many feature points, which is the feature point cloud.

ARKit provides hit testing method, which means that a 2D point in the image coordinates can refer to any point along a 3D line that starts at the device camera and extends in a direction determined by the device orientation and camera projection. Hit testing is often used to implement click and drag operations between users and virtual models in AR.

Therefore, combining point cloud and hit testing, we use the ARKit augmented reality framework to find feature point cloud in space. Then use the data of the bounding box returned by YoloV3 for hit-testing to find real-world surfaces corresponding to a point in the camera image. The two-dimensional coordinates in the screen can be converted to points in three-dimensional space by the hit-testing methods. When the number of recognition points is enough, the real spatial position of the object is finally obtained.

Although this application does not bring fascinating visual effects on headsets or other wearable devices like augmented reality applications in the strict sense, we still believe that this does not depart from the definition of the emerging field of augmented reality. In fact, the capabilities of the augmented reality framework are used here as a technical means to build iVision.

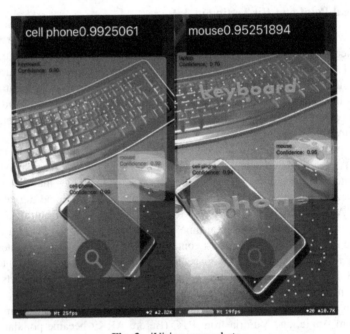

Fig. 2. iVision screenshots

The right picture in Fig. 2. iVision Screenshots shows the process by which the iVision app recognizes the mouse, keyboard, smartphone and marks its spatial location. And as the camera screen changes and the point cloud information becomes complete, the location of the item's anchor point will become more accurate.

3.4   Voice User Interface

Combined with the point cloud generation and hit testing methods provided by the augmented reality framework, and the specific object bounding box information in the two-dimensional image obtained by the machine learning model, we have obtained the coordinate information of the object. Obviously, this is not enough. Next, we need to consider how to make the visually impaired users understand this location information and guide them to the target location or away from the dangerous location.

The spatial position of the anchor point relative to the mobile phone position can be represented by distance and angle, and visual information need to be translated into audio information. When the target is identified, iVision will broadcast the distance and angle of the object through the TTS engine, such as "Apple is 2 m to the left of your front" and "Cup is 0.2 m to the front of you".

At the same time, iVision starts to play rhythmic beeping sounds. As the user (mobile phone) approaches the target, iVision calculates the distance to the target in real-time and changes the frequency of beep. The closer the distance, the faster beep's frequency. Figure 3 shows that the frequency of the beeping sound suddenly becomes 5 Hz at 0.3 m, indicating that the distance between the user and the item is very close. In this way, the user can perceive the distance to the target through hearing, and finally, find the object through the beeping audio.

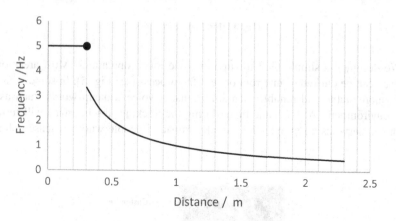

Fig. 3. The relationship between frequency and distance

Because blind people use touch screens with low efficiency and can't use traditional UI as smoothly as a sighted person, the system uses voice interfaces to build interactive processes. Figure 4 is the interactive process of iVision prototype.

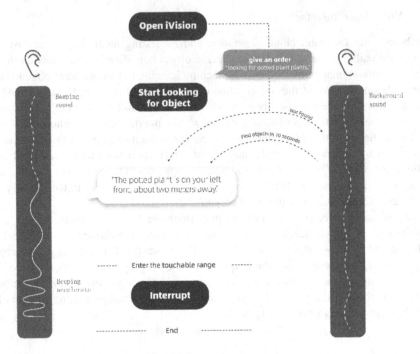

Fig. 4. Interactive process

We designed a simple GUI to support some touch operations. Most areas on the interface can be clicked to interrupt or start the process (see Fig. 5). In some scenarios, this is more stable and reliable than simply using voice wakeup words, such as in a noisy environment. At the same time, during the tracking, the interface will turn red, which can serve as a reminder for visually impaired people who can sense color and light.

Fig. 5. GUI of iVision

The speech-based interface combines real-time object detection model and augmented reality, into an interactive speech-based positioning and navigation device.

4   Evaluation

Fig. 6. Find randomly placed objects

The evaluation experiments for iVision prototype were performed by three blind people and three sighted people in the indoor space.

Firstly, they learned how the iVision App interacts and how to use it. They were asked to use the iVision App to complete the task of finding a specific object in an indoor space.

The table is about 3 m long, 2 m wide and 1.2 m high. It is placed 2 m away from the starting point. Various objects were randomly placed on the table. Participants were told that there was a flowerpot on the table, and they needed to touch it as fast as possible. To avoid some of the photosensitivity of the visually impaired participants from interfering with the experiment, everyone needs to cover their eyes with an eye mask (see Fig. 6).

The grouping of experiments is as follows:

1. The blind use iVision to find flowerpots
2. Sighted people with use iVision to find flowerpots
3. In addition, blind people need to perform a controlled experiment without using the iVision App.

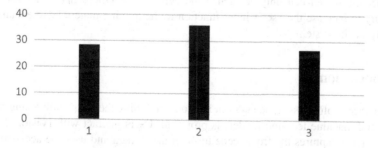

Fig. 7. Time needed to complete the task

The experimental results are shown in Fig. 7. Three groups of participants successfully completed their respective tasks.

When using the iVision App, blind people perform better than sighted people who have blindfolded eyes. Using iVision (the second group) takes slightly longer than finding a flower pot without using any equipment (the third group), mainly because users need time to interact with iVision. It is worth noting that the search process of the third group seems more chaotic and untargeted.

Participants said that using iVision can quickly understand the location of surrounding objects, increasing the sense of security and understanding of the surrounding space. This experiment shows that the availability of the system is sufficient for the device to be used in the real life of the blind.

5   Discussion

The novelty of the research lies in two aspects.

Firstly, the mobile phone has advantages such as low cost, universal type, powerful function, wide application range compared with the previous blind object positioning and navigation method and device. In this paper, we use the iPhone as the operating platform, but the framework of iVision can also be ported to the Android platform, which can lower the threshold for use. At the same time, this platform has strong expandability. Under this framework, application scenarios including the use of specific scenarios such as differentiation of similar items, shopping, and blind spot positioning can be implemented.

Secondly, an interactive app is designed and prototyped in this paper. which received positive feedback through user testing.

There are still several shortcomings in this research and some parts worthy of further study. Although the system can obtain the spatial position of the actual object, it is not intuitive and easy to understand the way to guide the blind user. Later studies can consider more interactive ways of somatosensory instead of visual guidance for sighted people.

At the same time, the point cloud data of other objects recognized by AR is not fully utilized to help the blind find the best route. The narrow viewing angle of the camera reduces the efficiency of recognition and becomes a limitation of the use scene.

In this paper, we use the trained model to identify the object, ignore the difference between the individual living environment, and cannot identify some special items. For example, the model can only recognize the cup of a specific shape. Therefore, it is necessary to increase the user's input function to the training material and enhance the usability of the system.

6   Conclusion

In this paper, a blind assistance system iVision combining the latest mobile augmented reality and machine learning models is proposed. Users interact with iVision through voice. iVision captures the front scene through the camera and uses the accelerometer to obtain the three-dimensional point cloud. At the same time, it uses the deep learning framework to obtain the coordinates of the objects of interest in the picture. Combine the two data to know the spatial position of the object, and finally use audio to feedback the position of the object to the visually impaired user.

Preliminary experiments of the prototype show that iVision can play an effective role for blind people in situations such as avoiding dangers and finding lost objects in strange environments.

Acknowledgement. Supported by Zhejiang Provincial Key Laboratory of Integration of Healthy Smart Kitchen System (Grant No: 2017F02).

References

1. Elbes, M., Al-Fuqaha, A.: Design of a social collaboration and precise localization services for the blind and visually impaired. Procedia Comput. Sci. **21**, 282–291 (2013)
2. Dramas, F., et al.: Designing an assistive device for the blind based on object localization and augmented auditory reality. In: Proceedings of the 10th International ACM SIGACCESS Conference on Computers and Accessibility, Halifax, Nova Scotia, pp. 263–264. Association for Computing Machinery, Canada (2008)
3. Thomas, B., et al.: A wearable computer system with augmented reality to support terrestrial navigation. In: Digest of Papers. Second International Symposium on Wearable Computers (Cat. no. 98EX215). IEEE (1998)
4. Brock, M., Kristensson, P.O.: Supporting blind navigation using depth sensing and sonification. In: Proceedings of the 2013 ACM Conference on Pervasive and Ubiquitous Computing Adjunct Publication. ACM (2013)
5. Chumkamon, S., Tuvaphanthaphiphat, P., Keeratiwintakorn, P., Blind, A.: Navigation system using RFID for indoor environments. In: 2008 5th International Conference on Electrical Engineering/Electronics, Computer, Telecommunications and Information Technology (2008)
6. Willis, S., Helal, S.: RFID information grid for blind navigation and wayfinding. In: Ninth IEEE International Symposium on Wearable Computers (ISWC 2005) (2005)
7. Google: Google Lens. https://lens.google.com/
8. Dunai, L., et al.: Real-time assistance prototype—a new navigation aid for blind people. In: IECON 2010-36th Annual Conference on IEEE Industrial Electronics Society. IEEE (2010)
9. Ran, L., Helal, S., Moore, S.: Drishti: an integrated indoor/outdoor blind navigation system and service. In: 2004 Proceedings of the Second IEEE Annual Conference on Pervasive Computing and Communications (2004)
10. Bigham, J.P., et al.: VizWiz::LocateIt - enabling blind people to locate objects in their environment. In: 2010 IEEE Computer Society Conference on Computer Vision and Pattern Recognition - Workshops (2010)
11. Ram, S., Sharf, J.: The people sensor: a mobility aid for the visually impaired. In: Digest of Papers. Second International Symposium on Wearable Computers (Cat. No. 98EX215) (1998)
12. Redmon, J., Farhadi, A.: Yolov3: an incremental improvement. arXiv preprint arXiv:1804.02767 (2018)
13. Azuma, R.T.: A survey of augmented reality. Presence: Teleoperators Virtual Environ. **6**(4), 355–385 (1997)

Relationship Between Eye Movements and Individual Differences in Motion Sickness Susceptibility While Viewing Stereoscopic Movies Under Controlled Consciousness

Akihiro Sugiura[1(✉)], Kunihiko Tanaka[1], and Hiroki Takada[2]

[1] Department of Radiological Technology, Gifu University of Medical Science, Seki, Japan
asugiura@u-gifu-ms.ac.jp
[2] Graduate School of Engineering, University of Fukui, Fukui, Japan

Abstract. In our previous study, we found it is possible to affect subjective feelings of visually induced motion sickness (VIMS) by controlling visually evoked postural responses (VEPRs) by changing conditions of consciousness of body sway. Thus, in this study, we verified the relationship between eye movements, body sway, and the susceptibility to motion sickness. Controlling consciousness of body sway while participants viewed stereoscopic movies revealed the involvement of three related theories for VIMS or motion sickness: sensory conflict theory, postural instability theory, and eye movement theory. Participants filled in a motion sickness susceptibility questionnaire short form (MSSQ-short). Thereafter, in the demonstration experiment, participants watched a three-dimensional movie consisting of several colored balls that moved sinusoidally at 0.25 Hz in the horizontal direction for 3 min after pre-instruction. Pre-instructions included "uncontrolled consciousness", "keep a static, upright posture", and "sway body in the same/opposite direction". This study recorded both body sway and electrooculography (EOG) data. Recorded EOG data were converted to eye movement velocity. The main result showed that susceptible participants exhibited a decreased frequency of optokinetic nystagmus (OKN) under conditions prone to the occurrence of OKN from correlated analysis for eye movements. Hence, we concluded that sensory conflict induced by decreases in the frequency of OKN is the primary cause of VIMS as OKN has a role in postural maintenance. This is a different hypothesis than the traditional eye movement theory.

Keywords: Sensory conflict theory · Postural instability theory · Eye movement theory · Body sway · Optokinetic nystagmus (OKN) · Visually Induced Motion Sickness (VIMS) · Consciousness

1 Introduction

Human beings can enjoy virtual experiences that produce feelings of presence, defined as a "sense of being there" [1]. However, there has been an increase in the presentation of symptoms similar to motion sickness (nausea, burping, sweating, and so on), often

© Springer Nature Switzerland AG 2020
M. Antona and C. Stephanidis (Eds.): HCII 2020, LNCS 12188, pp. 404–416, 2020.
https://doi.org/10.1007/978-3-030-49282-3_29

referred to as visually induced motion sickness (VIMS) or cyber-sickness [2, 3], which are experienced by users during or after virtual activities. Stanney reported that 88% of virtual environment participants developed VIMS when viewing virtual reality movies for over an hour [4]. Thus, in their current state, some people find virtual experiences meant for amusement to be stressors.

The genesis of VIMS and the reasons for the onset of its complex symptoms are not sufficiently understood. However, there are three major hypotheses for VIMS and motion sickness: sensory conflict theory, postural instability theory, and eye movement theory. The sensory conflict theory, which was first proposed by Irwan [5], suggests that the unpleasant symptoms are caused by the presence of conflicts among the afferent inputs of sensory modalities. VIMS is evoked when the information relayed by the visual system is contradictory to information from the other senses. The unpleasant symptoms caused by conflict between a sense of equilibrium or somatosensation and other senses while riding some kind of vehicle is called motion sickness. In addition, Reason et al. pointed out that this mechanism involved current sensory conflict situation as well as the gaps between current and past similar experiences (perception) [6]. Currently, the sensory conflict theory is estimated to be the main explanation for the genesis of VIMS.

Postural instability theory, first proposed by Riccio and Stoffregen [7], indicates that postural instability attributes to VIMS and motion sickness. They hypothesized that motion sickness occurred when an individual was unable to maintain control of their posture for a sustained period of time. They limited postural instability theory to predicting conditions that will induce motion sickness and did not attempt to explain why those conditions produced particular symptoms. Stoffregen et al. pointed out that body sway before motion sickness and VIMS symptoms in itself become a cause for VIMS and motion sickness [8]. Riccio et al. reported a positive correlation between the degree of postural instability and that of motion sickness [7].

Eye movement theory, which was first proposed by Ebenholtz et al. [9], indicates that reflective eye movements, such as optokinetic nystagmus (OKN) attributes to VIMS and motion sickness. They indicated that OKN evoked by moving visual patterns stimulated the vagus nerve. The excess neural activity prompts the unpleasant symptoms. Hence, OKN is not simply related to but rather a cause of VIMS and motion sickness. Hu et al. reported varying the amount of OKN in their participants following different velocities of an optokinetic drum. Their results showed increased motion sickness severity when the drum rotated with a faster velocity [10]. Furthermore, Flanagan et al. and Webb et al. respectively reported that suppressing the OKN by visual fixation point reduces VIMS [11, 12].

We are currently investigating ways to control VIMS. Our previous study found it was possible to affect subjective feelings of VIMS by controlling visually evoked postural responses (VEPRs) by changing conditions of consciousness of body sway [13]. Many related studies on the mechanisms underlying the appearance of VIMS have had inconsistent conclusions. The above three theories are not necessarily exhaustive, and elements of each theory may be true in certain situations. Thus, in this study, we verified the relationship between eye movements, body sway, and suscep- tibility and history of motion sickness. We controlled consciousness of body sway while participants viewed stereoscopic movies in order to reveal the involvement of each theory in this condition. This work is an extension of our work originally pre- sented in HCI International 2019 for analytical approaches [14].

2 Material and Method

2.1 Participants

Eleven participants (3 males and 8 females; 21–27-years-old) who did not have vision or equilibrium problems participated in this study. The study was approved by the Research Ethics Committee at the Gifu University of Medical Science. Oral and written consent was obtained from the participants after the purpose and significance of the study and the nature and risk of the measurements were explained. In addition, the study was conducted in accordance with the 1964 Declaration of Helsinki and its later amendments or comparable ethical standards.

2.2 Visual Stimulation

Figure 1 is a screenshot of the movie, used for visual stimulation in this study. The visual stimulation was delivered via a movie created using the 3ds Max 2017 computer graphics software (Autodesk, San Rafael, CA, USA). The movie consisted of several colored balls placed at random positions in 3-dimentional computer graphics space. We produced the horizontal sinusoidal round-trip movement of the balls at 0.25 Hz in the movie by moving camera-simulated ocular globes (the balls themselves did not move). The amplitude of the sinusoidal motion was set to 200 according to the software setting.

The experimental setup is shown in Fig. 2. We performed the experiments in a controlled environment (illuminance: under 10 lx) in order to limit the variations to visual input. The movie was displayed on an LCD monitor that was positioned (42LW5700, LG, Seoul, Korea) 50 cm in front of the participant. The displayed movie size was 93.30 cm × 52.62 cm with a resolution of 1,920 × 1,080 pixels. The participants watched the experimental three-dimensional (3D) movies with their peripheral vision.

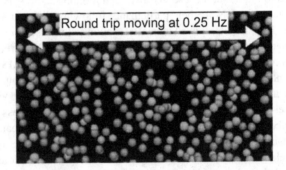

Fig. 1. Screenshot of the movie used in this study. A large number of balls were located at random positions. The balls moved sinusoidally round-trip at 0.25 Hz in a horizontal direction in the videos.

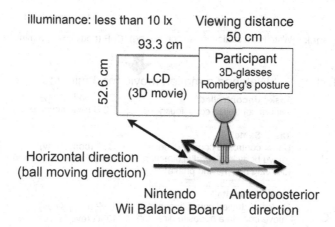

illuminance: less than 10 lx   Viewing distance
50 cm

93.3 cm

52.6 cm

LCD
(3D movie)

Participant
3D-glasses
Romberg's posture

Horizontal direction
(ball moving direction)

Nintendo
Wii Balance Board

Anteroposterior
direction

Fig. 2. Diagram of the experimental setup. The movie was displayed on an LCD monitor 50 cm in front of the participant. The participants watched the experimental 3D movies using 3D glasses. In order to measure the position of the center of pressure (CoP), participants were asked to stand on a Wii Balance Board with Romberg's posture.

2.3   Procedure and Design

Before experimental study, participants filled in a motion sickness susceptibility questionnaire short form (MSSQ-short) produced by Golding [15]. Specifically, participants rate the frequency of previous episodes during travel (never traveled, never felt sick, sometimes felt sick, frequency felt sick, always felt sick) with respect to various transport types (e.g., riding in a car, on a merry-go-round, on a boat). Participants fill in the short form twice, once for the memory of occurrences during their childhood (prior to the age of 12) and once for the past decade of adult life. In this study, the total MSSQ-Short score (childhood score + adult life score) was calculated for each participant as an index for their susceptibility to motion sickness.

The study procedures are shown in Fig. 3. The participants stood on the Wii Balance Board with Romberg's posture and watched a static (nonmoving) movie for three minutes as the Pre-task in order to check participant's equilibrium function. The experimental task was divided into four tasks (A, B, C, and D) following different pre-instructions about body motion. For Task A ("Uncontrolled"), participants watched the motion movie for 3 min with uncontrolled consciousness. For Task B ("Same"), participants watched the movie for 3 min after pre-instruction to sway their body in a direction parallel to the ball's movement while maintaining Romberg's posture. For Task C ("Opposite"), participants watched the movie for 3 min based on the pre-instruction to sway their body in a direction opposite to the ball's movement while maintaining Romberg's posture. For Task D ("Controlled Static"), participants watched the movie for 3 min based on the pre-instruction to maintain a static, upright pose while maintaining Romberg's posture. Participants performed the four tasks (Task A to D) in a random sequence to avoid order effects. Intervals between tasks was set at more than 5 min.

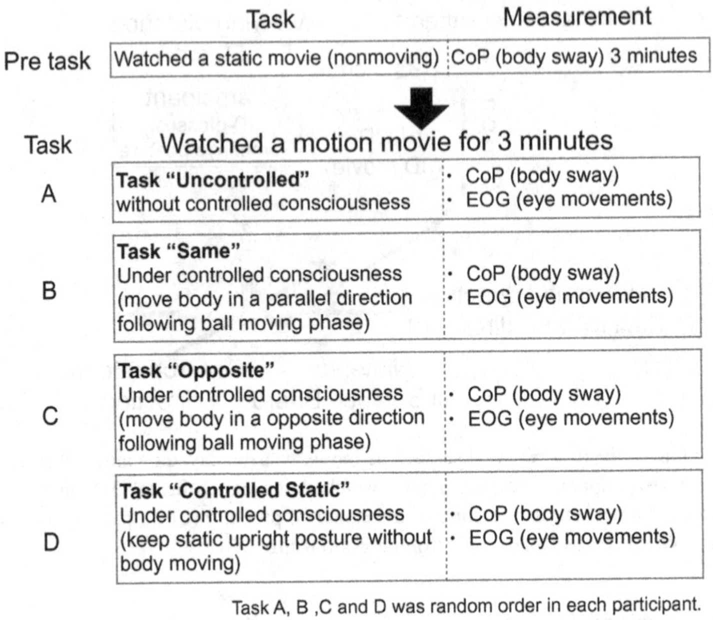

	Task	Measurement
Pre task	Watched a static movie (nonmoving)	CoP (body sway) 3 minutes

⬇

Task	Watched a motion movie for 3 minutes	
A	**Task "Uncontrolled"** without controlled consciousness	• CoP (body sway) • EOG (eye movements)
B	**Task "Same"** Under controlled consciousness (move body in a parallel direction following ball moving phase)	• CoP (body sway) • EOG (eye movements)
C	**Task "Opposite"** Under controlled consciousness (move body in a opposite direction following ball moving phase)	• CoP (body sway) • EOG (eye movements)
D	**Task "Controlled Static"** Under controlled consciousness (keep static upright posture without body moving)	• CoP (body sway) • EOG (eye movements)

Task A, B ,C and D was random order in each participant.

Fig. 3. Study protocol and measurements.

2.4 Measurement and Analysis

This study recorded both the center of pressure (CoP), as body sway, and electrooculography (EOG), as eye movements. The CoP was continuously measured by the Wii Balance Board for each Task. The CoP measurements were recorded at 20 Hz, which is the basic setting for sampling in clinical gravimetric tests. The continuous CoP data were separated by intervals of 1 min of viewing time to analyze each time segment. CoP data were analyzed for instability of postural maintenance. The total locus lengths in the horizontal direction were calculated as indexes of postural instability. Changes in the total locus length were induced by visual stimulation from the movie or each pre-instruction. Statistical tests were performed using ORIGIN Pro 8.5 software (OriginLab, Corporation, Northampton, MA, USA) with the two-way repeated measures ANOVA and post-hoc comparisons to confirm differences among each task and time segment.

EOG measures the electric potential changes caused by eye movements [16]. The EOG requires multiple electrodes to be attached to facial muscles. We only measured conjunctive horizontal eye movements in this study because the motion components in the movie were only in the horizontal direction. Thus, electrodes were attached on the outer corners of both eyes and in the middle of the eyebrows. Changes in the electric potential were recorded at 200 Hz using LabChart 7.3.7 software (ADInstruments, Dunedin, Otago, New Zealand) after the biological signal was amplified and software-filtered with a hum-filter at 60 Hz with EBA-100 (Unique Medical Co., Ltd., Tokyo, Tokyo, Japan).

A flow diagram for measurement and processing procedures are shown in Fig. 4 and Fig. 5. Eye movements are generally evaluated by eye movement velocity because differences in eye velocity reflect differences in neural activity. Measured electric potential data must be converted to eye velocity to determine changes in eye movements. Thus, this study performed four steps for the conversion: (1) Participants looked 30° to the right and to the left with each repetition to accrue data, which was then converted to electric potential to degree of visual line. (2) Measured electric potential data was converted degree of visual line following pre-measurements. (3) A low-pass filter (LPF) at 50 Hz was applied to the data to reduce high-frequency noise. Then, in order to obtain eye velocity data, the data that were filtered with LPF were differentially processed using five measured points in a 0.025 s window. The continuous eye velocity data were separated by 1 min-intervals of viewing time to analyze each time segment. For analysis of eye movements, the processed eye velocity data were roughly divided into 2 components: low velocity component induced by smooth pursuit eye movement (SPM), and high velocity component induced by OKN. Differences in the task expectedly appeared as differences in configuration of the histogram constructed by the eye velocity components because of changes in its. Hence, the individual's interquartile range, represented by the width of histogram, was adopted as an index of the eye movements, shown in Fig. 5.

To research the relationship between eye movements, body sway and susceptibility of motion sickness, Pearson's product-moment correlation coefficient was calculated from the interquartile range (the index of eye movement) or the total locus length (index of body sway) for each MSSQ-short total score respectively using ORIGIN Pro 8.5.

1. Pre-measurement for data conversion

Watched right 30-degree to left 30-degree with each repetition to match measured voltage value and degree of visual line.

2. Calculation for eye movement velocity

Convert measured EOG data (voltage data) to degree of visual line following result of No. 1.

Utilize low-pass filter at 50 Hz to reduce high-frequency noise components.

Differentiate with 0.025 second time window (5 measured points)

Fig. 4. Method for data conversion from EOG to eye velocity data.

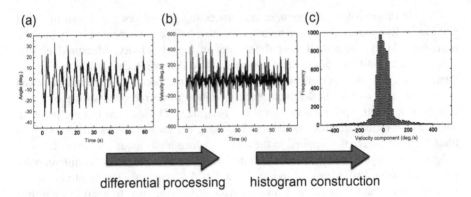

differential processing   histogram construction

Fig. 5. Example of data processing. (a) time-series of visual angle, (b) time-series of eye velocity, and (c) histogram for eye movement velocity.

3   Results

3.1   Body Sway

Figure 6 shows a summary of changes in the locus length in the horizontal direction in different tasks based on the pre-instruction. The results of both the Same and the Opposite tasks showed significantly long locus length in the horizontal direction, compared to the Uncontrolled consciousness and the Controlled static tasks ($P < 0.01$). By contrast, significant changes in postural instability were not found among the groups with increases in recording time.

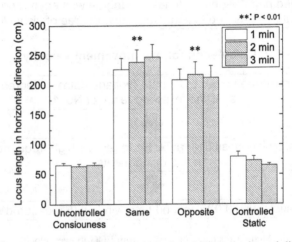

Fig. 6. Summary of changes in the locus length in the horizontal direction.

3.2   EOG

Figure 7 summarizes the results of the interquartile ranges (eye movement velocity) during different tasks. The interquartile range increased in the following order: the Same task < the Controlled Static task = the Uncontrolled task < the Opposite task. The results of the Opposite task showed a significantly longer interquartile range compared to the others (P < 0.01). The Uncontrolled task and the Opposite task tended to increase the interquartile range according to the recording time. However, these changes in the interquartile range were not statistically significant.

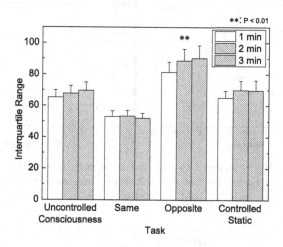

Fig. 7. Summary of the interquartile range results from the different tasks.

3.3   Correlation Analysis

The average and standard deviation of the total MSSQ short score were 18.6 and 11.7, respectively. Figure 8 shows typical results in a 3 min-duration of the correlation analysis between the locus length (index of the postural instability) and MSSQ-Short score. Additional characters in Fig. 8 represent different tasks: (a) represents the Uncontrolled task, (b) represents the Same task, (c) represents the Opposite task, and (d) represents the Controlled static task. The result in the Uncontrolled task indicated the highest positive correlation (r = 0.52), without statistical significance, of all tasks. However, the other tasks showed decorrelation (r ≈ 0).

As with Fig. 8, the typical results between the interquartile range and MSSQ-short score are shown in Fig. 9. Unlike the correlation analysis between the locus length and MSSQ-Short, all tasks indicated negative correlations. Especially, both the Uncontrolled task, the Opposite task and the Controlled static task represented statically negative correlations (P < 0.05). Results in the Opposite task had the strongest relationship (r = −0.74, P < 0.01).

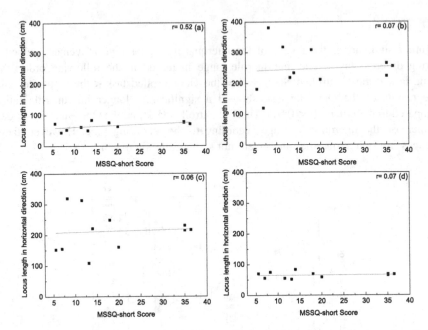

Fig. 8. Typical results (3 min-duration) of the correlation analysis between the locus length and MSSQ-Short. (a) to (d) represent different tasks: (a) is the Uncontrolled task, (b) is the Same task, (c) is the Opposite task, and (d) is the Controlled static task.

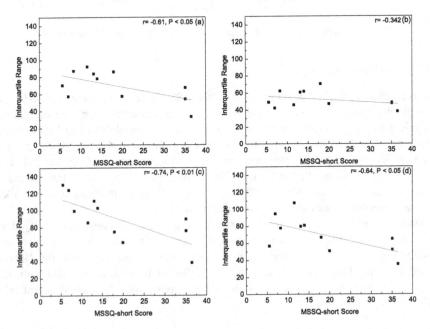

Fig. 9. Typical results (3 min-duration) of the correlation analysis between the interquartile range and MSSQ-Short. Additional characters are the same as in Fig. 8.

Table 1 shows the overall results of the correlation coefficient between the locus length and MSSQ-Short score. The correlation coefficients in the case of the Uncontrolled task were relatively high regardless of viewing time duration. A significant correlative relationship was not found in all cases. In addition, changes in the correlation coefficients were not also found following increases in recorded time.

Table 2 shows the correlation coefficients between the eye movement velocity index (interquartile range) and MSSQ-Short score. All correlation coefficients were negative values, and except for the Same task, some durations of each task showed significant correlations. The highest correlation coefficient was found in the Opposite task in the 3-min duration.

Table 1. List of correlation coefficients between body sway index and MSSQ-Short score.

Duration	Task A Uncontrolled	Task B Same	Task C Opposite	Task D Controlled static
1 min	0.354	0.145	0.282	0.062
2 min	0.518	0.139	0.148	0.042
3 min	0.515	0.223	0.150	-0.036

Table 2. List of correlation coefficients between eye movement velocity index and MSSQ-Short score.

Duration	Task A Uncontrolled	Task B Same	Task C Opposite	Task D Controlled static
1 min	−0.629	−0.380	−0.487	−0.507
2 min	−0.676*	−0.287	−0.657*	−0.547
3 min	−0.615*	−0.342	−0.739**	−0.644*

**: $P < 0.01$, *: $P < 0.05$

4 Discussion

This section deals with interpretation of the results in this study based on each theory. Table 3 shows the relationship between the experimental task and each theory for VIMS and motion sickness. Order numbers in the Table 3 indicate mean susceptibility to motion sickness in order from 1 to 4 (strong to weak), following each theory.

For the sensory conflict theory, our supposition of the order of sensory conflict was the following: the Opposite task > the Controlled static task > the Uncontrolled consciousness > the Same task. Both the Opposite task and the Controlled static task induced promotion of conflict between vision and equilibrium sense because these tasks caused participants to suppress the role of VEPRs. On the other hand, the Uncontrolled task and the Same task lead participants to normal and promoted VEPRs. Our previous study suggested that VEPRs are just a conflict correction response from our experimental verification [17]. We assumed that controlling VEPRs was effective method to control VIMS. Hence, those doing the Opposite task were the most likely to acquire VIMS, and doing the Controlled static task was second easiest way to get VIMS.

For the postural instability theory, the order of postural instability measured from results in this study were the following: the Opposite task = the Same task > the Uncontrolled task = the Controlled static task (Fig. 7). The reason was that the influence of the pre-instructions appeared to be much stronger than that of the vision information. Body movements attributed with pre-instructions in the Same and Opposite task consisted mainly of volitional movements, different from body motion in the Uncontrolled task. Body sway in the Controlled static task was the most stable of all tasks. The postural instability theory states that one of the causes of motion sickness is low-frequency external motion stimulus, such as ship shaking [18]. As for VIMS, visually low-frequency motion stimulus leads to VIMS, as the case of motion sickness [19]. In general, body sway was supposed to be an effective index for detecting VIMS [20, 21]. This body sway is basically involuntary movements induced by vision information. By contrast, as previously described, periodic motion observed in the Same task and Opposite task was autokinesis following the characteristics each pre-instruction. Significantly positive or negative correlations between the degree of motion sickness susceptibility and postural instability definitely were not found, regardless of the kind of experimental task (Fig. 8 and Table 1). However, this issue should also be carefully considered because it might be out of the application range of the postural instability theory.

For the eye movement theory, the order of the amount of eye movement (interquartile range of the velocity histogram) considered from results in this study was following: the Opposite task > the Uncontrolled task = the Controlled static task > the Same task. This order followed the frequency of OKN because OKN is a reflex fast motion, compared to SPM. A previous study demonstrated that an increase in the frequency of OKN (also expressed as slow-phase velocity of OKN) accedes to an increase in velocity of vision stimulus [22, 23]. In this study, relative velocity (between body motion velocity and movie motion velocity) changed only due to the kind of pre-instruction, because the same experimental movie was used in each task. As some previous studies demonstrate, the frequency of VIMS increase with increases of OKN, a major reason for VIMS based on eye movement theory [10, 22]. OKN is one of the functions of postural maintenance because OKN prevents retinal image blurring. In correlated analyses for eye movements, under conditions prone to occurrences of OKN, susceptible subjects indicated decreased tendency of the frequency of OKN, compared to insusceptible subjects, shown through significantly negative correlations. Hence, we suggest sensory conflict induced by a decrease in the frequency of OKN is the main cause of VIMS. This is a different hypothesis than the traditional eye movement theory.

Table 3. Relationship between experimental task and theory for VIMS and motion sickness.

Task	Related theory		
	Sensory conflict	Postural instability	Eye movement
Uncontrolled consciousness	3	2	2
Same	4	1	3
Opposite	1	1	1
Controlled static	2	2	2

5 Conclusion

In this study, we verified the relationship between eye movements, body sway, and the susceptibility of motion sickness. Controlling consciousness of body sway while participants viewed stereoscopic movies also revealed the involvement of each theory. The following conclusions can be drawn:

Susceptible subjects indicated decreased tendencies of OKN frequency under conditions prone to OKN occurrence, as compared to insusceptible subjects. This study offers a new perspective to the traditional eye movement theory in that the findings suggest the possibility that sensory conflict induced by decrease in the frequency of OKN is the main cause of VIMS.

Acknowledgments. This work was supported by a JSPS KAKENHI Grant-in-Aid for Scientific Research (C) (18K11971 and 17K00715).

References

1. Bowman, D.A., McMahan, R.P.: Virtual reality: how much immersion is enough? Computer (Long. Beach. Calif) **40**, 36–43 (2007). https://doi.org/10.1109/mc.2007.257
2. Kennedy, R.C.S., Drexler, J., Kennedy, R.C.S.: Research in visually induced motion sickness. Appl. Ergon. **41**, 494–503 (2010). https://doi.org/10.1016/j.apergo.2009.11.006
3. Stanney, K.M., Kennedy, R.S., Drexler, J.M., Harm, D.L.: Motion sickness and proprioceptive aftereffects following virtual environment exposure. Appl. Ergon. **30**, 27–38 (1999). https://doi.org/10.1016/S0003-6870(98)00039-8
4. Stanney, K.M., Kingdon, K.S., Kennedy, R.S.: Dropouts and aftereffects: examining general accessibility to virtual environment technology. Proc. Hum. Factors Ergon. Soc. Annu. Meet. **46**, 2114–2118 (2002). https://doi.org/10.1177/154193120204602603
5. Irwin, J.A.: The pathology of sea-sickness. Lancet **118**, 907–909 (1881). https://doi.org/10.1016/S0140-6736(02)38129-7
6. Reason, J.T.: Motion sickness adaptation: a neural mismatch model. J. R. Soc. Med. **71**, 819–829 (1978). https://doi.org/10.1177/014107687807101109
7. Riccio, G.E., Stoffregen, T.A.: An ecological theory of motion sickness and postural instability. Ecol. Psychol. **3**, 195–240 (1991). https://doi.org/10.1207/s15326969eco0303_2
8. Stoffregen, T.A., Faugloire, E., Yoshida, K., Flanagan, M.B., Merhi, O.: Motion sickness and postural sway in console video games. Hum. Factors. **50**, 322–331 (2008). https://doi.org/10.1518/001872008x250755
9. Ebenholtz, S.M., Cohen, M.M., Linder, B.J.: The possible role of nystagmus in motion sickness: a hypothesis. Aviat. Space Environ. Med. **65**, 1032–1035 (1994)
10. Hu, S., Stern, R.M., Vasey, M.W., Koch, K.L.: Motion sickness and gastric myoelectric activity as a function of speed of rotation of a circular vection drum. Aviat. Space Environ. Med. **60**, 411–414 (1989)
11. Flanagan, M.B., May, J.G., Dobie, T.G.: Optokinetic nystagmus, vection, and motion sickness. Aviat. Space Environ. Med. **73**, 1067–1073 (2002)
12. Webb, N.A., Griffin, M.J.: Optokinetic stimuli: motion sickness, visual acuity, and eye movements. Aviat. Space Environ. Med. **73**, 351–358 (2002)

13. Sugiura, A., Tanaka, K., Ohta, K., Kitamura, K., Morisaki, S., Takada, H.: Effect of controlled consciousness on sense of presence and visually induced motion sickness while viewing stereoscopic movies. In: Antona, M., Stephanidis, C. (eds.) UAHCI 2018. LNCS, vol. 10908, pp. 122–131. Springer, Cham (2018). https://doi.org/10.1007/978-3-319-92052-8_10

14. Sugiura, A., Tanaka, K., Takada, H.: Changes in eye movements and body sway while viewing stereoscopic movies under controlled consciousness. In: Antona, M., Stephanidis, C. (eds.) HCII 2019. LNCS, vol. 11572, pp. 657–668. Springer, Cham (2019). https://doi.org/10.1007/978-3-030-23560-4_48

15. Golding, J.F.: Predicting individual differences in motion sickness susceptibility by questionnaire. Pers. Individ. Dif. **41**, 237–248 (2006). https://doi.org/10.1016/j.paid.2006.01.012

16. Hale, K.S., Stanney, K.M.: Handbook of Virtual Environments. CRC Press, Boca Raton (2014). https://doi.org/10.1201/b17360

17. Sugiura, A., Tanaka, K., Wakatabe, S., Matsumoto, C., Miyao, M.: Temporal analysis of body sway during reciprocator motion movie viewing. Nihon Eiseigaku Zasshi. **71**, 19–29 (2016). https://doi.org/10.1265/jjh.71.19

18. Golding, J.F., Mueller, A.G., Gresty, M.A.: A motion sickness maximum around the 0.2 Hz frequency range of horizontal translational oscillation. Aviat. Space. Environ. Med. **72**, 188–192 (2001)

19. Diels, C., Howarth, P.A.: Frequency characteristics of visually induced motion sickness. Hum. Factors. **55**, 595–604 (2013). https://doi.org/10.1177/0018720812469046

20. Stoffregen, T.A., Smart, L.J.: Postural instability precedes motion sickness. Brain Res. Bull. **47**, 437–448 (1998). https://doi.org/10.1016/S0361-9230(98)00102-6

21. Takada, H., Miyao, M.: Visual fatigue and motion sickness induced by 3D video clip. Forma. **27**, S67–S76 (2012)

22. Ji, J.T.T.T., So, R.H.Y.Y., Cheung, R.T.F.F.: Isolating the effects of vection and optokinetic nystagmus on optokinetic rotation-induced motion sickness. Hum. Factors **51**, 739–751 (2009). https://doi.org/10.1177/0018720809349708

23. Nooij, S.A.E., Pretto, P., Oberfeld, D., Hecht, H., Bülthoff, H.H.: Vection is the main contributor to motion sickness induced by visual yaw rotation: implications for conflict and eye movement theories. PLoS ONE **12**, e0175305 (2017). https://doi.org/10.1371/journal.pone.0175305

HoloPrognosis - An AR-Based Serious Exercise Game for Early Stage Parkinson's Disease Patients

Marios Thomos[1], Vasileios Charisis[1(✉)], Stelios Hadjidimitriou[1],
Dimitrios Iakovakis[1], Sevasti Bostantzopoulou[2],
and Leontios Hadjileontiadis[1,3]

[1] Department of Electrical and Computer Engineering,
Aristotle University of Thessaloniki, Thessaloniki, Greece
mthomos@outlook.com, vcharisis@ee.auth.gr,
stellios22@gmail.com, dimiiakol2@gmail.com
[2] Third Neurological Clinic, G. Papanikolaou Hospital, Thessaloniki, Greece
bostkamb@otenet.gr
[3] Department of Electrical and Computer Engineering,
Khalifa University of Science and Technology, Abu Dhabi, UAE
leontios.hadjileontiadis@ku.ac.ae

Abstract. Augmented Reality (AR) is a novel technology that experiences rapid bloom in the last years. By using an AR electronic device, we can blend the real world with a virtual one in real time. Gamification in healthcare interventions helps patients adopt a healthier lifestyle in various aspects of their lives. In this direction, there is ample space for exploration in the field of alternative treatments for diseases like Parkinson's disease (PD). Among the various game categories targeting PD patients' rehabilitation, exergames, that focus on the main exercises employed in the interventions phase of early-stage PD patients, gain great popularity. The reason is that physical activity is a key concept for delaying motor and functional loss of early-stage PD patients.

In this context, this work presents HoloPrognosis, an AR-based serious exercise game targeting the mitigation of upper limbs motor impairment of early-stage PD patients. More specifically, the game motivates the patients to reach large amplitude movements progressively while tracking their performance and collecting data related to hand movement for further analysis. Unlike other similar efforts, AR offers the advantages of augmented engagement and user experience, real first-person experience and authentic human body controls.

Keywords: Parkinson's disease · Serious game · Augmented Reality

1 Introduction

1.1 Serious Games

Serious or applied games (SGs) are primarily designed to serve a serious purpose rather than to entertain users. The designation "serious" is added to indicate that the player can 1) familiarize herself/himself with an unused process or object, 2) develop new

© Springer Nature Switzerland AG 2020
M. Antona and C. Stephanidis (Eds.): HCII 2020, LNCS 12188, pp. 417–430, 2020.
https://doi.org/10.1007/978-3-030-49282-3_30

mental or physical skills and 3) exercise utilizing a scientific methodology to mitigate the negative impact of a disease.

Serious games are used in areas such as defense, politics, marketing or healthcare and they have successfully replaced written instruction manuals and audiovisual guidance, because in SGs, players are active mentally or physically, unlike other conventional methods, where they are passive.

HoloPrognosis can be considered as a SG since it has been designed at its core with a serious goal in mind, exercise of the upper limbs of PD patients.

1.2   Augmented Reality

Augmented Reality (AR) technology provides a real-time view of the natural environment whose elements have been augmented with additional artificial ones, generated by an electronic device. These elements can be images or sounds and can have either static or dynamic behavior. In other words, their state can be altered according to the changes in the physical/real environment as well as the user's interactions, either kinetic or phonetic, with them. AR serves two main purposes: 1) to create a virtual graphical interface which can provide to the user additional real-time information for her/his environment and 2) to create an augmented environment based on the physical one.

Towards this direction, inside the augmented user space, as mentioned above, there are artificial elements with which the user can interact via voice, body movements, eyes or using an input device, such as a keyboard. According to Azuma and Ronald T. in their 1997 research on AR technology [1], a device that can be used for this purpose should have the following capabilities: 1) combine the virtual world with the real world, 2) provide real time interactions and 3) register the generated virtual world in the real world in all 3 spatial dimensions.

AR is usually used to guide users in complex actions as well as to ease learning of new skills. There is intense research to develop AR solutions for various sectors such as education, medicine, advertising, and military exercise simulation and it has been already applied in various complex procedures that are performed daily.

Currently, AR wearable devices have holographic technology lenses for displaying virtual elements. Through the lenses, the user can see the augmented environment. Such a device is the Microsoft HoloLens which has been used in this work.

1.3   The i-Prognosis Paradigm

Parkinson's disease (PD), one of the commonest neurodegenerative diseases, is a chronic and progressive disease that often begins with mild symptoms that advance gradually over time. Symptoms can be so subtle in the early stages that they go unnoticed, as there are no PD-related biomarkers and findings on routine magnetic resonance imaging and computed tomography scans are unremarkable, leaving the disease undiagnosed for years. In the same context, early diagnosis of PD can lead to early interventions that may delay the progress of PD symptoms and levodopa treatment.

Motivated by the latter, i-PROGNOSIS project has a dual objective: i) design and develop early and unobtrusive Parkinson's disease detection tests based on the interaction of users with their everyday technological devices, ii) design and develop interventions to help PD patients sustain their quality of life over the course of the disease [2].

The i-PROGNOSIS interventions include, among others, a personalized game suite (PGS). PGS consists of games based on the existing physical training methodology for PD patients. That is, the i-Prognosis games can be reasonably considered SGs, since they have been built to serve a "serious" purpose with an entraining way.

1.4 Existing Interactive Practice Methods for Parkinson's Disease

Currently, the implementation of interactive training techniques in PD interventions is at its dawn and a lot of research efforts focus on designing new PD interventions based on well-established methodologies used in other sectors of healthcare.

A noteworthy technique is the interactive metronome (IM) [3], an evidence-based assessment and training tool that measures & improves neurotiming for cognitive, communicative, sensory & motor performance. As the individual activates a trigger in time with a steady auditory beat, IM technology provides real-time auditory and visual feedback for millisecond timing. Knowing whether she/he is hitting before, after, or exactly in sync with the beat to the millisecond allows the individual to make immediate, online corrections to improve timing & rhythm over the course of training. Existing IM training programs are designed with A-B-A [4] principles to ascertain to any signs of improvement to patient's condition after training.

Exergaming [5] is another intriguing game genre which relies on advanced software and hardware to track body movement or reaction. This genre has been credited with upending the stereotype of gaming as a sedentary activity, and promoting an active lifestyle. Exergames usage in PD interventions play a beneficial role in improving quality of life and everyday functional activities [5].

1.5 Proposed Application

This paper presents a novel AR based serious training game namely HoloPrognosis, targeting early-stage PD patients having a training routine to sustain upper limbs motor operation [6, 7]. HoloPrognosis collects user data during the game to track hand usage and interactions. The data can be stored externally for future analysis purposes. HoloPrognosis is designed on the innovative principles of the i-PROGNOSIS project for developing interventions while evolving the original idea [8] further with the utilization of robust hardware and AR technology to offer higher user engagement with authentic human body controls [9].

2 Scenario/Architecture of HoloPrognosis Serious Game

2.1 Game Scenario

During this serious training game, user's goal is to pick apples from a tree and carry them towards a circular target following a specific procedure. The game is divided into rounds depending on the number of apples. At each round, a specific apple must be moved with a specific hand. Both hand and apple are selected by the application as described below and the user is informed about their selection at the beginning of every round.

Initially the apple tree is being rendered in the space. It has dynamic size and number of apples depending on the size of scanned area. Initially, oral information is provided to the user about the target hand (that should be used to manipulate the apple) and, at the same time, the target apple gets a highlighted outline in order to stand out from the rest apples on the tree. The user moves closer to the tree in order to pick the target apple. Upon success, the user lowers her/his hand until it forms a 90° angle with the body. Then, the user executes a 90° body turn towards the circular target. The user remains still for 3 s and then she/he is being informed by voice to release the apple.

The above description defines a single round of the game. A new round is executed as long as there are available target apples on the tree. The set of target apples consists of those that are located on the tree at a height that is the same or higher than the height defined by the vertically stretched hand(s) of the user. The latter is recorded during calibration step (see Sect. 2.2, "Calibration Process"). In case the user plays the game with both hands, two different sets of target apples are defined, one for each hand, based on the height of each vertically stretched hand.

The game is terminated when there are not any available apples on the tree or upon user selection via the dedicated menu. Game stats are presented to the user, including successful and failed movements. At the same time, hand movement data are being stored to the internal storage of the device for later use.

2.2 Introductory Stages

Spatial Mapping Phase. After application startup, user enters the spatial mapping phase. As previously referred, AR can blend the virtual and physical world to a new augmented one and in this stage, she/he is instructed to move around so the HoloLens can scan the space. For user's ease, the mapped area is being overlaid by a graphical mesh so the she/he can perceive how well an area has been scanned or she/he can identify the unmapped area. When the space requirements have been covered, user is notified to terminate this process. Again, for user's ease, the process can only be terminated manually by the user so extra space can be mapped or already scanned area can be remapped better.

Main Menu and Game Start. After the termination of spatial mapping, the main menu appears. From the menu, the game can be started, the application options can be accessed the language can be toggled between Greek and English. When user selects to start the game, she/he is being asked about the hands she/he want to use during training. Finally, she/he is being asked about using demo mode before training.

Demo Mode. During demo mode, user is instructed how to execute the hand gestures needed for the training or how to pick an apple. To accelerate her/his familiarization with gestures, she/he can infinitely attempt to pick and move a demo apple. Additionally, the demo includes a toggle for appearing a circular target like the one being used during the actual game. The demo mode can only be terminated by the user through a menu.

Calibration Process. Before game starts, it is necessary to obtain data to observe any progress after the execution of the game. This data entails the length of the horizontally stretched hand and the height of the upwards vertically stretched hand.

Initially the user is instructed by voice to stretch her/his hand horizontally forming a 90° angle with her/his body and remain still for 3 s. Then she/he is instructed to raise the hand as high as possible, when the maximum height is achieved, she/he opens the palm to finalize the calibration. This process is executed for each hand separately. After the successful calibration, the game starts.

2.3   User Interaction

In AR, user can interact with the virtual objects using hands, voice or gaze. In the context of HoloPrognosis, the user uses gaze focus and hand gestures in order to navigate through menus and handle the apples during gameplay.

With gaze focus, device can identify in real time which object user is looking at and make necessary changes according to the defined usage scenario. For example, during game, the device can acknowledge, based on gaze focus, which apple the user is looking at and enable its movement. For user's ease, a circular cursor is being used so the user can perceive the area or object the device assumes she/he is looking at. This assumption is correct, only if she/he always looks only through HoloLens lenses.

The hand gestures provide a more natural approach to the user to interact with the virtual elements. For the implementation of the hand gestures two main factors have been considered: 1) they must be easy to executed by PD patients and 2) HoloLens can detect them almost instantaneously, providing a pleasant overall user experience.

The first user gesture is for hand detection and real time position tracking. The user places her/his hand in front of the device, the hand pointer must be stretched vertically upwards, the thumb must be free to the outside of the hand and the other fingers must be closed. When the hand is successfully detected, HoloLens is placing a holographic cube at the center of the palm so the she/he can acknowledge the position of the palm in the AR space.

The second gesture is about handling the apple. The user should previously execute the hand detection gesture, to interact with an apple. He can pick it by closing her/his palm, when the hand holographic cube is touching the apple or is close enough to it. For user's ease, when user's intention to pick an apple is detected, hand holographic cube and apple highlight have the same color and it varies according to the distance between them. If the hand is moving closer to the apple, color becomes more greenish otherwise it becomes more magentish. User can successfully pick the apple when this color is fully green and as long as the palm is closed, the user can move the apple, the same way as she/he does in the real world. She/he just opens his palm to release it.

Moreover, a selection gesture called Air Tap has been implemented for the menu navigation. It emulates the same behavior like the left click of the mouse input device for a computer, a familiar and fundamental action for almost every user.

2.4   UI

The user interface (UI) of the application was designed to be simple and clearly visible to a PD patient. All menus appear at the same position, preferably on the wall for consistency. Specifically, every menu follows a button – option scheme, where a button corresponds to an option. The buttons are large, filled with a solid color and accompanied with a white text. This option can be a functionality or a navigation toggle. Visual elements like images are being used only during demo mode because they can provide information to the user more pleasantly.

The main menu is showed to the user as showcased in Fig. 1, after application startup. Using it, the user can start the game, access the application options and toggle application language between Greek and English.

Selecting the Options button, she/he enters to options menu as portrayed in Fig. 2. There, she/he can enable/disable the voice instructions during game and enable/disable the use of the HoloLens clicker, an input device which in HoloPrognosis can be used for instructive purposes.

After selecting green start button from the main menu, pre-game menu appears as pictured in Fig. 3 and through it, user can set the hand(s) for training and progress to the game.

Before game, user is being asked about entering or skipping the demo mode through a new menu as shown in Fig. 4. Of course, she/he can return to the main menu with the corresponding button.

During demo mode (Fig. 5), a corresponding menu appears containing buttons for terminating demo mode, toggling the circular target status and returning to the menu. Additionally, instruction pictures are included, providing hints for hand gestures.

During training, a small menu as pictured in Fig. 6 appears and contains only one button for game termination.

In Fig. 7, the results menu appears after the game finalization, where user can see game stats and can return to the main menu.

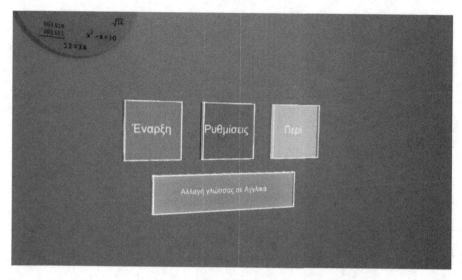

Fig. 1. The main menu. The green button corresponds to the game start (Έναρξη), the blue one (Ρυθμίσεις) opens the options menu and the yellow one is an about section placeholder (Περί). Using the big grey button, application language can be toggled between English and Greek (Αλλαγή γλώσσας σε αγγλικά). (Colour figure online)

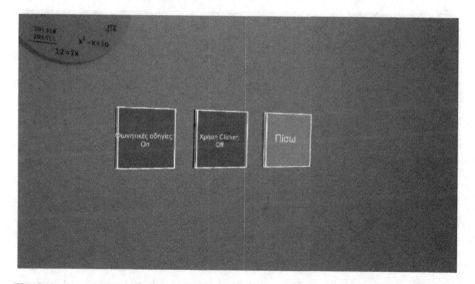

Fig. 2. In the options menu, the left blue button (Φωνητικές οδηγίες: On) controls audio instructions playback and the right blue button (Χρήση Clicker: Off) corresponds to HoloLens clicker usage. Using the red button, user returns to the main menu. (Colour figure online)

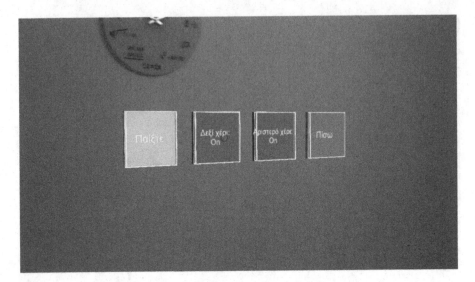

Fig. 3. In the pre-game menu, the green button (Παίξτε) corresponds to game start, using the two blue buttons, right and/or left hand(s) can be selected for the game accordingly. (Δεξί χέρι: On, Αριστερό χέρι: On). Also, using the red button (Πίσω), main menu appears. (Colour figure online)

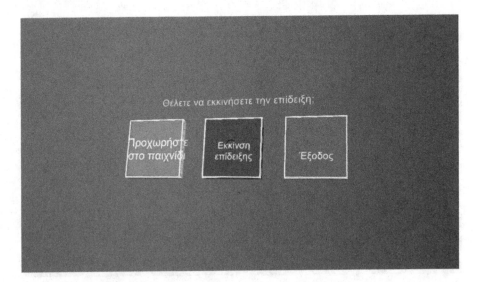

Fig. 4. The demo asking menu. The green button (Προχωρήστε στο παιχνίδι) skips demo mode and initiate calibration process, the blue one (Εκκίνηση επίδειξης) start the demo mode and the red one (Έξοδος) corresponds to the return to main menu. (Colour figure online)

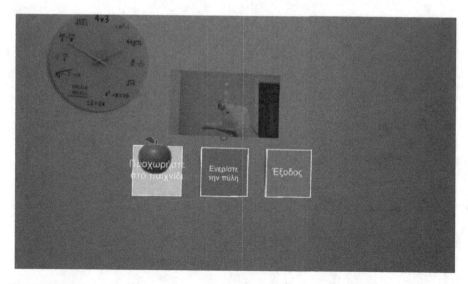

Fig. 5. The demo menu contains a green button (Προχωρήστε στο παιχνίδι) for game initialization, a blue button (Ενερ/στε την πύλη) for toggling circular target status and a red button (Εξοδος) for demo termination and return to main menu. Furthermore, pictures hinting hand gestures are being shown above the buttons. (Colour figure online)

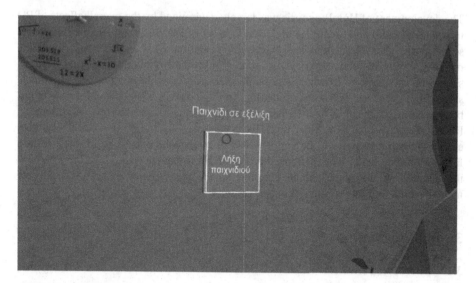

Fig. 6. The only button of the game menu (Λήξη παιχνιδιού), terminates the game prematurely. (Colour figure online)

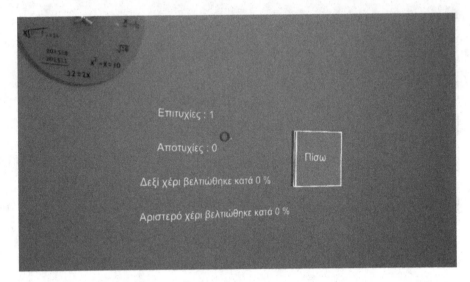

Fig. 7. The results menu contains text fields presenting game stats along with a red button (Πίσω) for returning to the main menu. (Colour figure online)

2.5   Constraints Originating from Parkinson's Disease

The development of HoloPrognosis was largely determined by the overall effects of PD in patient's health and quality of life. That is, a set of PD constraints defined the game scenario, the user interactions and their implementation. First and foremost, since the majority of PD patients experience tremor, rigidity and bradykinesia, hand gestures should be as simple to execute as possible. Secondly, a large number of PD patients suffer from decreased color discrimination. In this context, a specific color palette has been used in HoloPrognosis interface elements, as cursors and buttons. Additionally, PD patients, especially the elder ones, have decreased mental ability. So, it was necessary the game scenario to be simple, easy to understand and to be inspired from a familiar or even better an experienced procedure from patient's life. Last but not least, the duration of the game should be short so the patients not to get physically or mentally tired and to avoid any kind of discomfort.

3   Implementation

3.1   Microsoft HoloLens

The Microsoft HoloLens (Fig. 8) is a head-mounted device providing mixed reality capabilities. It contains a pair of semi-transparent lenses for the projection of virtual objects and a camera array for spatial mapping and hand tracking. Speakers for audio playback, internet connection capability and a specialized processing unit for processing the data obtained from the device sensors and cameras are also being included.

HoloLens software provides application programming interfaces (APIs) for access to camera buffers and to the integrated software for spatial mapping and hand tracking.

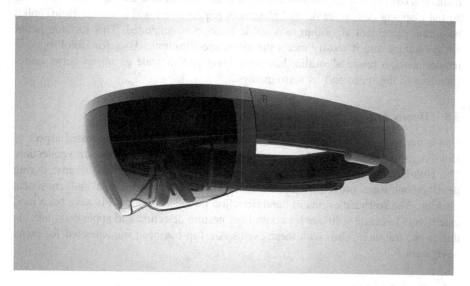

Fig. 8. Microsoft HoloLens

3.2 Unity and HoloToolkit

Unity, a 3D/2D industry leading game engine, supports natively Microsoft HoloLens and its APIs. It provides a simple interface and workflow for rendering, placing and manipulating graphical objects in the physical space obtained by the spatial mapping. Generally, Unity is being preferred for non-graphics-oriented research projects because of its already feature-rich implemented functionality like object collision and lighting. Along with Unity, HoloToolkit has been used which is a set of Unity packages, containing scripts using HoloLens APIs.

3.3 Spatial Mapping

Spatial mapping is about transferring the physical space to the virtual – computer based one. Using data from the camera array and HoloLens APIs, continuous fixed time scans can be conducted to map new area or remap the scanned one more accurately. The outcome of spatial mapping can be used to identify room parts like a wall or furniture which can be used for holograms placement. Furthermore, with spatial mapping, the physical dimensions of a scanned area can be stored and used for placement purposes.

3.4 Holograms Placement

Holograms placement is crucial for an AR application because its effective implementation can provide an intuitive and natural user experience. Taking advantage of the
spatial mapping data to set desired placement requirements and using the HoloToolkit
hologram placement algorithm, a possible location is generated. This location is not
always unique and it mostly meets the given specifications. Also, for HoloPrognosis
requirements, a resize algorithm has been developed to scale an object better corresponding to the space and its surroundings.

3.5 Hands Tracking and Gestures Recognition

Hands tracking can be considered as the most significant and complicated aspect of
HoloPrognosis, both from a user experience standpoint as well as about data collection.
The HoloLens integrated hand detection mechanisms were preferred because during
development were proved to be the most viable solution for fast and consistent
tracking. The software events of hand detection provided by the APIs have been used
extensively to create software for controlling gesture detection and apple manipulation
during the training. Also, with these events Air Tap has been implemented for menu
navigation.

3.6 Gaze Tracking

It is extremely important to be known where the user is starring at, so the candidate
objects for interaction should be prepared for use. HoloLens does not provide eye
tracking, but using its APIs, the user's straight look can be obtained if it is assumed that
the holographic screen is being viewed fully by the user. If she/he wishes to focus on an
object outside the field of the lenses view, head or body movement is necessary. The
consequences of this lack will be mentioned below along with other hardware
limitations.

3.7 Limitations of Software and Hardware

Microsoft HoloLens, a development platform for AR applications using experimental
hardware and software, affected significantly the development approach. Firstly, device
size and weight make HoloLens uncomfortable for long-minute use, limiting the
training duration. The viewing range of the semi-transparent lenses is small, limiting
the number of objects that user can see fully. Perforce, during training user must avoid
to look more than one objects. Furthermore, because of limited resources, the only
viable solutions for spatial mapping and hands tracking are the integrated HoloLens
mechanisms because only these can take advantage of the specialized hardware for
accelerating these operations. Last but not least, lack of eye tracking, requires from the
user to look always straight through the transparent lenses so the device can
acknowledge to which direction she/she/he is looking at.

4 Conclusion

This work presents an approach of a novel interactive game-like training and it is expected to assist PD patients trying to maintain their kinetic abilities. Also, this work may form the basis for future research since the application can collect hand movement data for further analysis about observing the patient's condition or events that the patient has not yet realized and to predict future possible changes about his state.

The first version of HoloPrognosis has been demonstrated to the Thessaloniki General Hospital "G. Genimatas – Agios Dimitrios" and the Agrinio General Hospital. More specifically, 10 PD patients have been volunteered to use the demo mode and play the training game under doctor surveillance after first having received an introduction to the game and instruction for using the device properly. Afterwards, they completed a System Usability Scale (SUS) questionnaire [10] in order to provide feedback. The SUS has been adopted HoloPrognosis needs and two more questions were appended. The analysis of the SUS results denoted rather satisfactory user acceptance (3.8/5) and engagement (4.3/5), mandatory usage of instruction during training (5/5), extremely slow adaptation process (1.2/5) and certain presence of another person to give guidance until her/his familiarization with the application (4.3/5).

Additional observations have been made while the PD patients were being watched during training. PD patients had encountered problems to perceive correctly the distance between their hand and the focused holographic apple, therefore, they failed to grab the apple. Furthermore, all patients complained for comfort and viewing issues, which are related to the specific AR device used.

5 Future Work

Future improvements could be made to provide a more pleasant experience to the PD and to advance the training game. The use of a more advanced device and a more mature development platform could solve a variety of issues encountered during application development. For example, the next generation HoloLens which is significantly lighter, provides wider viewing range and more advanced finger tracking, can be used to implement a more immersive and intuitive scenario for the user. It goes without saying that improvements could be made to the instructions given to the user, to enrich the environment with additional artificial elements. Furthermore, more training games can be implemented focus on PD movements effects or mental retardation.

Acknowledgements. This project has received funding from the European Union's Horizon 2020 research and innovation programme under grant agreement No 690494.

References

1. Azuma, R.T.: A survey of augmented reality. Presence Teleoper. Virt. Environ. **6**(4), 355–385 (1997)
2. Dias, S.B., et al.: Personalized game suite: a unified platform to sustain and improve the quality of life of parkinson's disease patients. In: SAN2016 Meeting (2016). https://doi.org/10.3389/conf.fnhum.2016.220.00023
3. Kim, A., Lee, H.-S., Song, C.-S.: Effects of interactive metronome training on postural stability and upper extremity function in Parkinson's disease: a case study. J. Phys. Ther. Sci. **29**(1), 168–171 (2017)
4. A-B-A Design (ABA). https://www.appliedbehavioranalysisprograms.com/faq/what-is-the-a-b-a-design-in-applied-behavior-analysis
5. Dias, S.B., et al.: Serious games as a means for holistically supporting Parkinson's Disease patients: the i-PROGNOSIS personalized game suite framework. In: 2017 9th International Conference on Virtual Worlds and Games for Serious Applications (VS-Games), pp. 237–244. IEEE (2017)
6. Riley, D., Lang, A.E., Blair, R.D., Birnbaum, A., Reid, B.: Frozen shoulder and other shoulder disturbances in Parkinson's disease. J. Neurol. Neurosurg. Psychiatry **52**(1), 63–66 (1989)
7. Rigidity (Stiffness). https://www.parkinson.org/Understanding-Parkinsons/Symptoms/Movement-Symptoms/Rigidity-Stiffness
8. Keus, S., et al. European physiotherapy guideline for Parkinson's disease. The Netherlands: KNGF/ParkinsonNet (2014)
9. Alamri, A., Cha, J., El Saddik, A.: AR-REHAB: an augmented reality framework for poststroke-patient rehabilitation. IEEE Trans. Instrum. Meas. **59**(10), 2554–2563 (2010)
10. System Usability Scale (SUS). https://www.usability.gov/how-to-and-tools/methods/system-usability-scale.html

A Feasibility Study on the Application of Virtual Reality Technology for the Rehabilitation of Upper Limbs After Stroke

Le Wang[1,2], Jean-Lon Chen[3], Alice M. Wong[2,3(✉)], and Kevin C. Tseng[2,4(✉)]

[1] Department of Design, National Taiwan Normal University, Taipei, Taiwan
[2] Product Design and Development Laboratory, Taoyuan, Taiwan
ktseng@pddlab.org
[3] Department of Physical Medicine and Rehabilitation, Chang Gung Memorial Hospital, Taoyuan, Taiwan
walice@cgmh.org.tw
[4] Department of Industrial Design, National Taipei University of Technology, Taipei, Taiwan

Abstract. The purpose of this study was to explore the clinical feasibility of virtual reality (VR) for the rehabilitation of upper limbs of stroke. In this study, it was found and suggested that future research should focus on the content design and application of VR rehabilitation games. While using VR to increase the interestingness of rehabilitation, one can also integrate VR and other technologies to achieve complementary benefits. In addition, in terms of the design of VR rehabilitation games, it was suggested that VR rehabilitation game researchers investigate the needs of the target users and design VR games that meet the needs of the target users in future work. Finally, this study demonstrates the clinical feasibility of applying VR technology for the rehabilitation of upper limbs after stroke, as well as highlights the aspects that still need to be addressed by researchers. These aspects are important targets of designing a VR system suitable for stroke upper limb rehabilitation.

Keywords: Stroke rehabilitation · Virtual reality (VR) · Games

1 Background

According to the World Health Organization, 15 million people worldwide suffer a stroke each year. Studies have shown that 86% of stroke patients will suffer from upper limb dysfunction after the onset of the disease [1] and that 30% [2] to 66% [3, 4] still suffer from upper limb dysfunction 6 months after the onset of the disease. Upper limb dysfunction can seriously affect a patient's motor function and daily life. Therefore, upper limb rehabilitation is particularly important.

Rehabilitation therapy is characterized by high intensity, repeatability, functionality and task specificity [5, 6]. Traditional rehabilitation methods not only lack interestingness but also fail to give patients successful feedback and experience [7]. Previous

© Springer Nature Switzerland AG 2020
M. Antona and C. Stephanidis (Eds.): HCII 2020, LNCS 12188, pp. 431–441, 2020.
https://doi.org/10.1007/978-3-030-49282-3_31

research studies have shown that the participation and enthusiasm of stroke patients are key factors affecting the rehabilitation outcome, and there is a significant positive correlation between patients' active continuous participation and the rehabilitation effect [8]. Therefore, it is of great significance to identify an active and effective rehabilitative method for improving the upper limb function of stroke patients. Researchers have proposed the application of VR technology for the rehabilitation of upper limbs after stroke as one such method [9–11].

VR is a computer simulation technology that can create virtual worlds and experiences within them, and it has three basic aspects: immersion, interaction and imagination [12]. Users interact with the virtual environment created by computers in a variety of ways to create an immersive feeling [13, 14]. With the application of VR technology, patients can transmit their actions to the computer through input devices (such as data gloves, motion capture devices, and computer mice) and receive sensory feedback, such as visual, auditory or touch feedback, from the output device [6]. Furthermore, the visual and proprioceptive feedback received by the users can also encourage target behaviours of the users, maintain their motivation and enthusiasm, and help them achieve a happy, successful emotional experience, thereby encouraging them to practice continuously until they learn the behaviours. VR provides technical support for three key elements of rehabilitation: repetition, performance feedback and motivation maintenance. This training method not only considerably reduces the amount of human and material resources needed for training but also increases the interestingness of the treatment to stimulate the enthusiasm of the patients, transform passive treatment into active treatment, and improve treatment efficiency [15].

Although increasingly more research studies on VR applications in rehabilitation have been conducted in recent years, most studies have focused on the effect of rehabilitation after stroke, and there are few studies on how to design VR systems for upper limb rehabilitation. Thus, the aim of this study was to review and analyse the existing literature to explore the clinical feasibility of VR applications in stroke upper limb rehabilitation and determine which VR systems are suitable for the rehabilitation of upper limbs after stroke.

2   Clinical Applications of VR Rehabilitation Technology

The effect of VR on the rehabilitation of upper limbs in stroke has been confirmed by many clinical studies. Saposnik et al. believe that the combination of VR and video games is a novel and potentially useful technology that can be combined with traditional rehabilitation treatments to improve the function of upper limbs after stroke [11]. Because this kind of training is more interesting, patients show stronger rehabilitation motivation in the VR environment than in the traditional rehabilitation environment [16]. In addition, Laver et al. conducted a systematic evaluation of the clinical trials of VR application in stroke rehabilitation in recent years, and the results showed that there was a trend suggesting that higher dose (more than 15 h of total intervention) was preferable as were customised virtual reality programs [17]. Hatem also demonstrated through a systematic literature review that the combination of VR with other rehabilitation therapies is superior to rehabilitation therapy alone [18].

The Application of VR Combined with Other New Technologies. The combination with other new technologies has yielded complementary effects, indicating the range of potential applications is large. The three main combinations involving VR are as follows:

- *Combination of VR and rehabilitation robot technology.* At present, rehabilitation robot technology has been widely used in the field of clinical rehabilitation. In these systems, mechanical feedback, visual feedback and tactile feedback devices are mostly used as input and output devices so that patients can carry out rehabilitation training assisted by rehabilitation robots in a virtual environment [19]. The assistance of the machine makes it possible for patients with severe motor dysfunction to participate in rehabilitation training; in addition, it can also correct poor postures and movements of patients and improve the rehabilitation effect [20].
- *Combination of VR and telerehabilitation technology.* VR telerehabilitation systems can facilitate convenient and economical exchanges of information and rehabilitation training platforms for patients and rehabilitation therapists. Patients can use VR equipment to participate in rehabilitation training in a virtual environment, as required. For rehabilitation therapists, after they receive the relevant parameters and videos the of patients' movements, they can select and tailor the rehabilitation training mode according to patients' individual conditions. Therefore, the combination of VR technology and telerehabilitation technology is helpful to solve the problem that scientific rehabilitation training cannot be carried out because of the geographical remoteness and limited rehabilitation conditions [21, 22].
- *Combination of VR and brain-computer interface technology (BCI).* The BCI technology can be used to detect the electroencephalogram (EEG) signals generated by the brain when planning volitional movements, identify the signals corresponding to patients' movement intentions by extracting and classifying the signal features, and convert these signals into control commands to control external devices, thereby assisting patients in generating the corresponding actions [23]. The brain signals generated by the patients during motion planning is processed and realized through the VR system. The combination of these two techniques can help patients with minimal residual motor function complete rehabilitation and promote the remodelling of neural function.

VR can provide patients with more active, colourful and inspiring situational feedback. Therefore, VR and other rehabilitation technologies can be combined to enhance the efficacy of this rehabilitation technology.

In addition, VR technology may be used to develop a relatively objective evaluation standard for efficacy. There are more than 40 evaluation methods for the rehabilitation of upper limbs after stroke, and the most commonly used methods include the Fugl-Meyer (FMA), Wolf Motor Function Test (WMFT), and EQ-5D [24]. However, these scales all depend on the subjective evaluation of rehabilitation physicians, so it is difficult to evaluate the curative effect of the treatment comprehensively and objectively. In contrast, the parameters collected by VR equipment are relatively objective. In the future, the parameters collected during of exercise can be calculated as evaluation indexes of the rehabilitation effect.

3   Feasibility Analysis of the Application of VR in the Rehabilitation of Upper Limbs After Stroke

When VR is used in the rehabilitation of upper limbs after stroke, appropriate hardware and software devices should be selected so that the patients can interact with the system.

3.1   Hardware Selection

Hardware devices, including display devices and input devices, are tools used by the user to interact with the virtual environment (software) and are means of communication between the user and virtual reality system.

Display Device. High immersion is a feature of VR. At present, VR display devices can be categorized as either immersive or non-immersive devices. The immersive devices completely isolate the user's vision from reality. What the user sees is a computer-generated virtual environment with a wide field of vision, which makes the user feel as if he or she is in a brand-new environment. Non-immersive devices display the virtual environment on a computer or TV screen [10]. There are different opinions on the immersive and non-immersive devices. Some studies have pointed out that there are three problems in using immersive devices [25]: (1) high requirements for 3D images in virtual environments increase the difficulty and cost of system development; (2) a certain amount of space on the ground may be required for training; and (3) VR technology can cause slight adverse reactions, such as transient dizziness. However, other studies tend to use immersive devices because compared with non-immersive devices, immersive devices are more attractive to patients and more beneficial to patient recovery.

With the rapid development of 3D imaging technology, VR software development is not difficult. In terms of the hardware, those of immersive VR devices need to be upgraded frequently, and immersive portable devices have become the mainstream VR devices. Therefore, if portable immersive devices are used for rehabilitation, they will not take up additional space. Dizziness can be resolved by avoiding jitter in the virtual screen and limiting the use time. All the problems existing in the application of immersive devices in the rehabilitation of upper limbs of stroke that are mentioned above can be solved. Therefore, immersive devices are a better choice.

Input Device. The VR system interface is a tool for users to interact with the virtual environment and a communication channel between users and virtual reality. It is related to the gameplay of games. Low usability of a VR system interface design will affect the consistency of operation. Currently, VR devices that are on the market have different input methods due to the different brands and different system designs used. For example, the interaction mode of Google Cardboard is gaze and click; HTC Vive uses two six-degree of freedom controllers; Oculus uses the Xbox One controller but will eventually use the 6DOXF dual controller. All of these systems enable users to use a more advanced immersive interaction mode. In addition, there are other types of input devices, such as hand tracking devices.

As shown in Table 1, when VR technology is applied to stroke rehabilitation, its common input devices include computer mice [26], motion capture devices [10], data gloves [27], and rehabilitation robots [28]. When a mouse is used as the input device, the hand is fixed due to the posture needed to hold the mouse, which is not conducive to the rehabilitation of the patient, and the applications are relatively limited. Motion capture devices are suitable for rehabilitation with a large range of motion, as data on finger movements and other fine movements cannot be monitored. The positions of hand tracking devices can be flexibly adjusted according to the needs of the user, and they have better flexibility and portability in tracking the movements during rehabilitation. When VR is combined with a rehabilitation machine, the data collected by the rehabilitation machine is more accurate. For example, it can measure joint mobility, the average joint movement speeds, and other kinematic parameters during specific training tasks (motion accuracy, motion trajectory smoothness, motion trajectory length, movement coordination, etc.), making it easier for people to monitor the rehabilitation effect.

3.2 Software Design

The interaction logic of different software is very different. The type of VR software selected determines the interaction mode between the patients and VR rehabilitation system.

VG or VE. There are two main types of VR that have been applied in the field of stroke upper limb rehabilitation. One is a virtual reality game (VG), in which there are settings for barriers, difficulty, rewards and leaderboards. The other is a simple virtual reality environment (VE), in which people and objects operated by the users simply interact with the objects in the virtual environment. As we mentioned earlier, patients' own motivation plays an important role in determining the outcome of treatment [8], so it is necessary to compare the two types of applications and determine which one is more likely to motivate patients for rehabilitation.

According to the flow theory proposed by Hungarian psychologist Csikszentmihalyi [29], when a person is completely immersed in an activity, he or she will ignore the existence of other things. This state is called flow in which there is great joy, and people are often willing to pay a great price to experience this state. When people are fully engaged in an activity and are filtering out all irrelevant perceptions, we say that they enter a state of immersion. And, it is in this state that they are at their happiest moment. VE presents tasks in a repetitive manner, which makes it difficult for patients to stay interested in prolonged exercise. Compared with VE, VG is more interactive and interesting. In the process of completing the game level, patients constantly challenge themselves, improve their skills and immerse themselves in the game.

When experiencing VG, stroke patients have visual feedback information, including scores, feedback on user actions (whether they are correct or not), tips on how activities should be carried out and incentives, as well as feedback sounds such as key triggers and alarms, which are designed to attract users' attention and encourage

Table 1. Input device in upper limb rehabilitation

Input device	Application	Research
Mouse		Cho et al., 2013
Motion capture instrument		Trombetta et al., 2017
Data gloves		Harley et al., 2011
Rehabilitation machine		Shi et al., 2018

them to complete tasks easily. The game has difficulty level or barrier settings, which can arouse the patient's internal drive for excellence and enhance the patient's motivation to complete rehabilitation.

VG Design for Rehabilitation. The only criterion used to judge whether a game is good or not is whether the players like the game. In game design, the enjoyment of players is the most important issue [30]. Based on Cziksentmilalyi's flow theory, Sweetser proposed the game flow model, which contains eight core elements [30]:

- *Focus.* The game should require concentration, and players should be able to focus on the game.
- *Challenge.* The game should be sufficiently challenging and meet the player's skill level.
- *Player skills.* The game must support the development and mastery of the player's skills.
- *Control.* Players should have a sense of control over their actions in the game.
- *Clear goals.* The game should provide clear goals for players at the appropriate time.
- *Feedback.* Players must receive the appropriate feedback at the appropriate time.
- *Immersion.* Players should experience in-depth and relaxed efforts in the game.
- *Social interaction.* The game should support and create opportunities for social interaction.

This model is universal for game design, but designing games for rehabilitation patients has its particularity; that is, the design of rehabilitation games should not only satisfy the users' needs for playing games but also achieve the goal of rehabilitation.

Although there is no uniform standard for the design of stroke rehabilitation games, it can be concluded from the relevant research that the following attributes are desirable in stroke rehabilitation games:

- *Direct game cues.* Although games have immediate and continuous feedback, the majority of stroke users are elderly people, and it is difficult for them to understand indirect action cues [9]. For example, it is difficult for them to understand how to perform vertical motions (raising and lowering arms) to control the motion of a game character in a horizontal position. Therefore, the cues in the game should be intuitive to most stroke rehabilitation patients.
- *Difficulty settings for rehabilitation.* The difficulty of the game should be set according to the rehabilitation course of the target stroke patient. Some researchers think that the difficulty of the game should be determined by the rehabilitation physician, and the difficulty of the game should be set according to a set of basic difficulty values provided by the rehabilitation doctor [9]. However, after communicating with rehabilitation doctors, we learned that they do not know all the rehabilitation methods, many of which are summarized by long-term medical practice. Therefore, when a game is used in rehabilitation, if the combination of the rehabilitation method and game is not familiar to the rehabilitation doctor, many tests need to be performed to set the difficulty level and duration according to the rehabilitation doctor's advice.
- *Fun but low-intensity games.* Through more than 300,000 questionnaires, QuanticFoundry Company found that the main motivation of players over the age of 36 is fantasy and completion and that completion is the most stable game motivation, which does not weaken with age and is ranked as one of the top three motivations for both male and female players. Research has pointed out that older video game players prefer simple games, and games designed for elderly people should also take into account their decreased sensitivity and longer response time (e.g., using large font, allowing delayed response) [31].

All of these are useful for VR rehabilitation game design. In addition, Steam Store is considered the database of the game world, and player evaluation is the best screening procedure. Although the VGs on Steam are not designed for stroke patients, the VG reviews can help us understand the problems of VG. There are many VR games on Steam that receive many poor reviews. By analysing a large number of player reviews on Steam, we determined that the problems are related to the following three aspects:

- *VR technology, such as picture quality and action control.* The immersive experience of VR games is based on the advancement of science and technology. There are some problems in the technology used in games that received poor reviews. In addition to dizziness, delay and other problems mentioned above, the problems also include rough pictures, the system freezing and loopholes. An unreasonable motion control designs are another major problem of VG. If the game control design is unreasonable, players will often collide with objects in the game or even walk through objects directly. Some specific situations can cause discomfort for the users, such as being in high or narrow spaces.
- *Specific designs, such as plot and level designs.* Regarding VR systems, the game concept and design itself are the core aspects of the game, and they are what lead the players to have fun. Some games with overstep stories, boring repetitive operations and poor designs commonly receive poor comments from Steam players.
- *Cooperation between the VR hardware and game operation.* The operations of some games are not coordinated with the configuration of VR hardware devices, leading to players' difficulty in operation.

Therefore, in the design of stroke upper limb rehabilitation games, attention should be paid to avoiding the above problems.

Besides, stroke patients have support needs for immersive training, because a large portion of them are elderly and they are not familiar with modern new technologies. The training program should account for the patients' education level, life and working experience of the elderly. Thus, they could be provided with suitable learning support need and, therefore, are more likely to obtain amusement by choosing different immersion programs from the VR game.

4   Conclusions

In conclusion, the application of VR in the field of stroke rehabilitation can make the long-term rehabilitation process interesting rather than boring and can stimulate the enthusiasm of patients to improve the efficiency of treatment. Therefore, in-depth discussions on the content designs and applications of VR rehabilitation games and methods of increasing the interestingness of rehabilitation may be important directions of future research. In addition, the VR and other technologies can also be integrated to achieve complementary benefits. For example, one can try to combine VR with rehabilitation robot and brain computer interface technologies. There are still many unresolved issues to be studied and discussed regarding the integration n of VR with other technologies.

Furthermore, regarding VG design, no studies on the needs of stroke patients as a user group have been conducted. This study can only summarize the characteristics of VR and existing problems in the context of rehabilitation of upper limbs after stroke. Therefore, it is suggested that in the future, researchers who develop VR rehabilitation games investigate the needs of target users, such as the preferred game types, screen styles, and game music. After the user needs are determined, the background, scenes, elements, tasks, levels, rules, and interface for the game and the user control method can be designed according to the user's specific needs and the gameplay enjoyment model. Therefore, it is expected that a VG design that meets the needs of the target users can be designed.

In this feasibility study, the findings showed the clinical feasibility of the application of VR for upper limb rehabilitation after stroke, as well as the existing problems that need to be solved. These problems are important targets of designing a VR system suitable for stroke upper limb rehabilitation.

Acknowledgments. The author(s) disclosed receipt of the following financial support for the research, authorship, and/or publication of this article: This work was supported in part by the Ministry of Science and Technology of Taiwan, ROC under Contracts MOST 108-2410-H-027-024-MY3, MOST 106-2628-H-003-009-MY3 and MOST 108-2622-8-003-001-TM1, by the Chang Gung Medical Foundation (grant nos. CMRPD3E0373, CMRPG5E0083, CMRPD2F0211, CMRPG5F0142, CMRPG5F0143, and CMRPD2F0212 CMRPD2F0213). The funders had no role in the study design, data collection and analysis, decision to publish, or preparation of the manuscript.

References

1. Nichols-Larsen, D.S., et al.: Factors influencing stroke survivors' quality of life during subacute recovery. Stroke **36**(7), 1480–1484 (2005). https://doi.org/10.1161/01.STR.0000170706.13595.4f
2. Heller, A., et al.: Arm function after stroke: measurement and recovery over the first three months. J. Neurol. Neurosurg. Psychiatry **50**(6), 714–719 (1987). https://doi.org/10.1136/jnnp.50.6.714
3. Wade, D.T., et al.: The hemiplegic arm after stroke: measurement and recovery. J. Neurol. Neurosurg. Psychiatry **46**(6), 521–524 (1983). https://doi.org/10.1136/jnnp.46.6.521
4. Sunderland, A., et al.: Arm function after stroke. An evaluation of grip strength as a measure of recovery and a prognostic indicator. J. Neurol. Neurosurg. Psychiatry **52**(11), 1267–1272 (1989). https://doi.org/10.1136/jnnp.52.11.1267
5. Maclean, N.: A critical review of the concept of patient motivation in the literature on physical rehabilitation. Soc. Sci. **12** (2000)
6. Langhorne, P., et al.: Motor recovery after stroke: a systematic review. Lancet Neurol. **8**(8), 741–754 (2009). https://doi.org/10.1016/S1474-4422(09)70150-4
7. Hesse, S., et al.: Robot-assisted arm trainer for the passive and active practice of bilateral forearm and wrist movements in hemiparetic subjects. Arch. Phys. Med. Rehabil. **84**(6), 915–920 (2003). https://doi.org/10.1016/S0003-9993(02)04954-7
8. Rose, F.D., Attree, E.A., Johnson, D.A.: Virtual reality: an assistive technology in neurological rehabilitation. Curr. Opin. Neurol. **9**(6), 461–467 (1996)

9. Lohse, K., et al.: Video games and rehabilitation: using design principles to enhance engagement in physical therapy. J. Neurol. Phys. Therapy 37(4), 166–175 (2013). https://doi.org/10.1097/NPT.0000000000000017

10. Trombetta, M., et al.: Motion Rehab AVE 3D: a VR-based exergame for post-stroke rehabilitation. Comput. Methods Programs Biomed. 151, 15–20 (2017). https://doi.org/10.1016/j.cmpb.2017.08.008

11. Saposnik, G., Levin, M.: Virtual reality in stroke rehabilitation. Stroke 42(5), 1380–1386 (2011)

12. Burdea, G.C., Coiffet, P.: Virtual Reality Technology, 2nd edn. Wiley, New York (2003)

13. Shirzad, N., Van der Loos, H.F.M.: Error amplification to promote motor learning and motivation in therapy robotics. In: 2012 Annual International Conference of the IEEE Engineering in Medicine and Biology Society, San Diego, CA, pp. 3907–3910. IEEE (2012). https://doi.org/10.1109/EMBC.2012.6346821

14. Burke, J.W., et al.: Optimising engagement for stroke rehabilitation using serious games. Vis. Comput. 25(12), 1085–1099 (2009). https://doi.org/10.1007/s00371-009-0387-4

15. Mirelman, A., et al.: Effects of training with a robot-virtual reality system compared with a robot alone on the gait of individuals after stroke. Stroke 40(1), 169–174 (2009). https://doi.org/10.1161/STROKEAHA.108.516328

16. Jang, S.H., et al.: Cortical reorganization and associated functional motor recovery after virtual reality in patients with chronic stroke: an experimenter-blind preliminary study. Arch. Phys. Med. Rehabil. 86(11), 2218–2223 (2005). https://doi.org/10.1016/j.apmr.2005.04.015

17. Laver, K.E., et al.: Virtual reality for stroke rehabilitation. Cochrane Database Syst. Rev. (2017). https://doi.org/10.1002/14651858.CD008349.pub4

18. Hatem, S.M., et al.: Rehabilitation of motor function after stroke: a multiple systematic review focused on techniques to stimulate upper extremity recovery. Front. Hum. Neurosci. 10, 442 (2016)

19. Jiang, T.T., et al.: Analysis of virtual environment haptic robotic systems for a rehabilitation of post-stroke patients. In: 2017 IEEE International Conference on Industrial Technology (ICIT), Toronto, ON, pp. 738–742. IEEE (2017). https://doi.org/10.1109/ICIT.2017.7915451

20. Díaz, I., et al.: Lower-limb robotic rehabilitation: literature review and challenges. J. Robot. 2011, 1–11 (2011). https://doi.org/10.1155/2011/759764

21. Krpič, A., et al.: Telerehabilitation: remote multimedia-supported assistance and mobile monitoring of balance training outcomes can facilitate the clinical staff's effort. Int. J. Rehabil. Res. 36(2), 162–171 (2013). https://doi.org/10.1097/MRR.0b013e32835dd63b

22. Kairy, D., et al.: Maximizing post-stroke upper limb rehabilitation using a novel telerehabilitation interactive virtual reality system in the patient's home: study protocol of a randomized clinical trial. Contemp. Clin. Trials 47, 49–53 (2016). https://doi.org/10.1016/j.cct.2015.12.006

23. Shih, J.J., et al.: Brain-computer interfaces in medicine. Mayo Clin. Proc. 87(3), 268–279 (2012). https://doi.org/10.1016/j.mayocp.2011.12.008

24. Veras, M., et al.: Scoping review of outcome measures used in telerehabilitation and virtual reality for post-stroke rehabilitation. J. Telemed. Telecare 23(6), 567–587 (2016). https://doi.org/10.1177/1357633x16656235

25. Li, B.J., Li, F.: Application progress of virtual reality rehabilitation technology in upper limb dysfunction after stroke. Chin. J. Contemp. Neurol. Neurosurg. 17, 245–248 (2017)

26. Cho, S., et al.: Development of virtual reality proprioceptive rehabilitation system for stroke patients. Comput. Methods Programs Biomed. 113(1), 258–265 (2014). https://doi.org/10.1016/j.cmpb.2013.09.006

27. Harley, L., Robertson, S., Gandy, M., Harbert, S., Britton, D.: The design of an interactive stroke rehabilitation gaming system. In: Jacko, J.A. (ed.) HCI 2011. LNCS, vol. 6764, pp. 167–173. Springer, Heidelberg (2011). https://doi.org/10.1007/978-3-642-21619-0_22
28. Shi, P., et al.: A virtual reality training system based on upper limb exoskeleton rehabilitation robot. In: i-CREATe 2018: Proceedings of the 12th International Convention on Rehabilitation Engineering and Assistive Technology, pp. 138–141 (2018)
29. Cziksentmihalyi, M.: Flow – The Psychology of Optimal Experience (1990)
30. Sweetser, P., Wyeth, P.: GameFlow: a model for evaluating player enjoyment in games. Comput. Entertain. 3(3) (2005). https://doi.org/10.1145/1077246.1077253
31. Flores, E., et al.: Improving patient motivation in game development for motor deficit rehabilitation. In: Proceedings of the 2008 International Conference in Advances on Computer Entertainment Technology - ACE 2008, Yokohama, Japan, p. 381. ACM Press (2008). https://doi.org/10.1145/1501750.1501839

Robots in Universal Access

Usable and Accessible Robot Programming System for People Who Are Visually Impaired

Juliana Damasio Oliveira[1]($\boxtimes$), Márcia de Borba Campos[2],
and Vanessa Stangherlin Machado Paixão-Cortes[1]

[1] Pontifical Catholic University of Rio Grande do Sul (PUCRS),
School of Technology, Porto Alegre, Brazil
{juliana.damasio,vanessa.stangherlin}@acad.pucrs.br
[2] Inedi College – CESUCA, Cachoeirinha, Brazil
marciabcampos@hotmail.com

Abstract. In the 1960s, Papert introduced Logo language that commanded a graphic turtle. These were the first advances in the field of educational robotics. Many environments were created in this theme; however, most programming environments are highly graphical, so they do not provide accessible interfaces for visually impaired users. Thus, our research presents challenges and recommendations in terms of usability and accessibility in designing a robot programming environment for people who are visually impaired. We conjectured that by using a programming language to guide a robot in a virtual environment, the person who is visually impaired could better understand orientation and mobility skills. Hence, we created the GoDonnie programming language based on the Logo language. GoDonnie runs in a programming environment called Donnie. We show all the design process of Donnie, that was based on interactive design. Participates in this study, people who are visually impaired and sighted programming professors. Results indicate that GoDonnie and Donnie have good usability, supports the development of orientation and mobility in visually impaired people, and meets the expectations regarding the programming environment. Finally, we created a set of design guidelines for developing robot programming environments for people who are visually impaired.

Keywords: Robotic education · Accessibility · Usability · Blind programmer · Visually impaired · Orientation and mobility

1 Introduction

Robotics emerges in education as a way to make learning more meaningful, promoting, through its pedagogical use, different types of knowledge and skills [1]. Educational robotics can promote, among others, research, the development of logical reasoning, group work, and the dialogue between fields of knowledge [2].

© Springer Nature Switzerland AG 2020
M. Antona and C. Stephanidis (Eds.): HCII 2020, LNCS 12188, pp. 445–464, 2020.
https://doi.org/10.1007/978-3-030-49282-3_32

The first advances in this area came with Seymour Papert in the 1960s. Papert developed the Logo programming language, which, through commands, controlled a graphic turtle. This programming environment was easy to assimilate and encouraged children to learn unconventionally by using playful means [3]. Logo has characteristics that make it easy to assimilate as the exploration of space activities, easy terminology, and the ability to create new terms or procedures [4]. However, this environment is not accessible to people who are visually impaired (PVI).

Moreover, there is a proliferation of programming environments based on graphical interfaces that have brought difficulties for PVI that want to learn to program, or experienced programmers [5,6]. These difficulties are due to use of visual-based metaphors, lack of corresponding sound for graphical information, use of inappropriate soundtracks, incompatibility with assistive technology features [7,8], lack of users autonomy in compiling their program [9,10], and problems in identifying programming blocks [7,8].

Hence, we developed a robot programming environment based on Logo accessible to PVI. Our research presents challenges and recommendations in terms of usability and accessibility in designing this robot programming environment for PVI. Our strategy is based on teaching programming and the exercise of orientation and mobility (O&M) skills to PVI, which are used to construct representative cognitive maps of different scenarios. O&M skills are necessary for achieving autonomy by PVI and, consequently, for their independence in different spaces in society [11]. Our research follows the proposal of building systems that allow PVI to explore an environment before being in that space, in accordance with [12–15]. Thus, we have developed a robot programming environment, in which cognitive maps are constructed as the user explores familiar and unfamiliar scenarios through commands that are executed by the robot.

Our choice of building an educational programming environment is due to the importance that teaching computing has to the 21st-century education [16], and teaching and learning how to code will play a significant role in that. Therefore, research that may lead to a better understanding of teaching programming to PVI will contribute towards fairer educational practices and opportunities [17].

The main contributions for this paper are: (I) method for design usable and accessible robot programming systems, and (II) design guidelines can be used by designers that decide to develop robot programming languages for PVI.

2   Related Work

The systematic literature review is a technique that seeks to identify and organize reliable literature sources in a field of study, and then synthesize the evidence available to researchers [18]. In the context of this study, we conducted two systematic reviews on the use of robotics in the teaching of programming to PVI. For both surveys the same research protocol was applied.

The first review on the 2016 year [19] analyzed and discussed nine studies, of which we highlight the projects of Kakehashi et al. [10] and Ludi et al. [7,20].

Kakehashi et al. [10] developed P-CUBE, an educational prototype made up of cubic blocks that are used in mobile robot programming. Each programming block with motion or control functions has radio frequency identification (RFID) tags that identify its type. Programming is performed on a mat that allows sequential programming and line tracking programming. The system is also equipped with tactile information to enable its use by PVI. However, the users' assessment of P-CUBE did not include visually impaired representatives, although it shows that P-CUBE can assist in the development of computational thinking and programming learning. Also, P-CUBE commands are limited.

The design and evaluation of a programming environment for blind people was handled by Ludi et al. [7,20]. Using Lego Mindstorms NXT, a LEGO toy line for technology education, the authors sought to develop an environment that is easy to learn and easy to use, and accessible to screen readers. Generally, standard programming software available from Lego uses icons to represent commands and is not accessible to screen readers. Studies have shown that it is possible to design an Accessible Lego environment, with BricxCC and the NXC language, however, the authors created an update called JBrick [21].

Aiming at updating the education robotic theme, given the current progress of technology, we conducted a second literature review that comprised six studies published between 2016 and 2019. The study demonstrated that the methodologies prioritized by the researchers are still programming and robotics workshops, with group activities. To understand the target audience and assessments of learning and user interaction, they used data collection techniques with interviews and questionnaires. In addition to use of low-cost robots built by the researchers, the use of Arduino and Lego Mindstorm NXT was again mentioned. The difference was the mention of new robots with more modern technologies, such as Tortoise robot [22], CardBot2 [23], Turtlebot [24], and more consolidated programming languages in the developer community. Also mentioned was the use of mobile applications [23]. There was also focus on the application of more practical activities, focused on the needs of PVI users in their daily lives.

3   Method

We create a method for design usable and accessible robot programming systems based on interactive design [25]. The interactive design focuses on the user, where the user is involved in the system development process and has four stages: identify needs/establishing requirements, create design alternatives, prototyping, and evaluate [25]. These stages complement each other and repeat themselves. Figure 1 shows the interaction design with our executed activities in each stage.

3.1   Identify Needs/Establish Requirements

In this phase, we conducted extensive research about robotics education, programming teaching, educational programming language, orientation and mobility for blind people, and Human-computer interaction (HCI) methods to evaluate programming languages. Our goal was to create an understanding of end-users who are visually impaired.

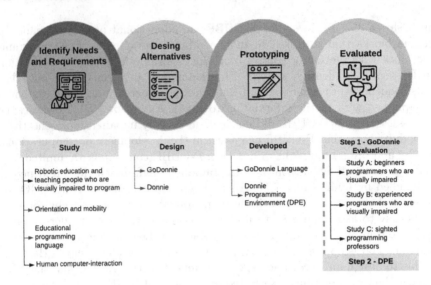

Fig. 1. Method for design usable and accessible robot programming systems.

Robotics Education and Teaching PVI to Program. We conducted a systematic literature review [19] to understand how robotics is used in teaching programming to people who are visually impaired. We found methodologies for teaching robot programming to PVI, characteristics of the programming environments, examples of good practices for teaching robot programming, and difficulties/limitations in the use of robotics as support to the teaching of programming. Some findings:

- Methodologies: use of workshops with individual or group activities; tutorials to present new programming concepts and language syntax; concrete materials constructed with Ethylene Vinyl Acetate (EVA) to delimit the environment for the robot to navigate.
- Characteristics of the programming environments: most of studies used LEGO Mindstorm NXT or own robots using the Arduino board. Among the languages were used P-CUBE programming blocks or BricxCC's basic programming commands.
- Good practices for teaching robot programming: We identify 34 recommendations and grouped in the following categories: workshop preparation (13), content and activities (12), work dynamics (4), and data acquisition and instruments (5).
- Difficulties/limitations: the process of transferring the program to the robot due to lack of accessibility of environment; the students to distinguish the start of blocks (IF, LOOP) and the end of blocks (IF, LOOP); and software was not compatible with the screen reader.

O&M. We start by study how to enable the construction of cognitive maps by PVI. Jacobson [26] defines orientation as the ability to utilize the remaining senses (hearing, touch, smell, and kinesthesia) to understand its location in the environment. While mobility is defined as the ability to move easily in an environment. Thus, creating cognitive maps of environments is essential for the efficient development of O&M skills [27]. PVI can capture environmental information (overall structure, spatial components, milestones, dimensions, and relative positions) through other senses such as touch, smell, and hearing. Having possession of the cognitive maps of the environment, it is possible to efficiently perform orientation and mobility in a space [28].

The orientation process has three basic principles, "Where am I?", "Where do I want to go?", and "How will I get to the desired location?" For this process to take place, some phases are undertaken to understand and move around the environment. They are (i) perception of the environment, (ii) analysis of what has identified, (iii) selection of the information that is needed for that moment or situation, (iv) planning of actions to accomplish the goal, which is to move, and (v) enforcement, which refers to mobility itself [29].

We thought in how consider the orientation and mobility in a program. Thus, based on the orientation phases, we believe that in order to enable blind people to develop O&M skills, these phases must be implemented in the development of a program:

- Perception: relate to the strategies used by the user, so that they can capture the information about the robot and the scenario where they is;
- Analysis: check if the user could understand the environment and where the robot is;
- Selection: check the commands that would be necessary for the robot to perform the task;
- Planning: elaborate on the program that will gather the commands so that the robot can move;
- Execution: execute the program and see if the robot has reached the previously defined goal.

To achieve these phases, it is important that the programming environment supports these phases, i.e., commands that allow the user to explore the environment.

Educational Programming Language. For us to understand programming teaching, it was important to understand how computational thinking is established. Wing [30] defines computational thinking as a set of intellectual and reasoning skills that indicate how people interact and learn to think through computational language. For Aho [31], it is the thought process involved in formulating problems so that their solutions can be represented as algorithm steps. As much as computational thinking is about understanding algorithms and learning how to think through a computational language, this ability is not restricted to computer scientists alone, it is a core competency for everyone [30].

There are five main skills of computational thinking [30,32–34]: conditional logic, algorithm building, debugging, simulation, and socialization.

In our research these questions are relevant for the elaboration of the methodology of use of the robot programming environment. These skills should be used as follows.

- Conditional logic: students identify the problem, for example, how the robot can move forward n steps without hitting objects. And check which commands they can use to solve the problem.
- Algorithm building: students build code to solve the problem and this code can be used later for similar problems.
- Debugging: students receive sound feedback. If the robot encounters any obstacles not foreseen by the student in the created code, this feedback will be given to the student by audio. This will allow you to proceed with the correction. The idea is also the student, by touch, identify the space.
- Simulation: students can test the codes created by running them with other variables to check for other situations in which their solution works.
- Socialization: group activities of visually impaired people are foreseen for problem solving and strategy development.

Human-Computer Interaction. In this phase, we seek to understand the usability-related HCI criteria that are important in PVI programming teaching environments. Programming is defined as the process of turning a mental plane into one that is compatible with the computer [35]. Programming language is the way this transformation is expressed, and the smaller the transformation, the easier it is to program [36]. In this sense, usability is an important feature for programming languages, and user evaluations can provide valuable feedback on language design [37]. Thus, the programming language that has good usability makes it easier for users to program.

In addition to the usability goals (effectiveness, efficiency, and user satisfaction), we considered in our programming language: readability, writability and expressiveness, among other criteria. Readability is the easiness that programs can be read and understood in the context of the problem domain, in our case, educational robotics for PVI. It is related to overall simplicity, i.e., the number of basic constructs of the language. The syntax and semantics of the language have a significant effect on the readability of programs and have been the focus of discussions with robotics experts, programming professors, and PVI. Writability is a measure of how easily a language can be used to create programs for a chosen problem domain. Therefore, through the created programming language, the user must be able to write programs to command a robot, to explore an environment and to identify objects in the scenario through sound information. The easier a program is to write, the more likely it is to be correct. The expressiveness of the language was also considered, i.e., programmers should express their algorithm as naturally as possible.

3.2   Create Design Alternatives

The design of the programming environment was defined by a multidisciplinary team with expertise in Engineering, Human-computer interaction, and Computer science. We chose Papert's fundamentals to design the language and environment. For this, we based our language on Logo approach [3], for the creation of commands, and the way of executing them. Logo has no audible messages to users. In this sense, we define that our language will have audible messages during execution so that users who are visually impaired can understand the simulation. Thus, students can use our language to simulate a robot's behavior in a virtual environment; the behavior is described to the user through audible messages. We named the robot Donnie, and the language GoDonnie. We chose to build the language with top of the Player/Stage robotic framework [38], running on the Linux operating system, because it is Open source. The environment was called Donnie programming environment.

GoDonnie has commands in Portuguese and English. The user can choose the version they want to work with. For the memorization facility, GoDonnie is not case-sensitive. In this way, it interprets lowercase and uppercase letters in the same way. Other design decisions are that it is not necessary to indent the code. It is also possible to write the code on the same line, without using the ENTER key. The commands can be written with or without accentuation (where used in Portuguese), and GoDonnie avoids the use of symbols that require the use of more than one key (e.g., the SHIFT key). In this version of GoDonnie, due to implementation constraints, the SHIFT key is kept for the multiplication and addition of mathematical operations, and double quotation marks for transmitting text to Text-To-Speech (TTS).

We chose to work only with the integer data type. Thus, it is not possible for the robot to walk 1 and a half steps, for example. We adopted this alternative to make it simpler for the user to understand the displacement of the robot. Then, when there is a situation that results in a Float data, the system discards (truncates) what comes after the comma, leaving only the entire part of the data.

3.3   Prototyping

In this stage, based on previous phases we create prototypes of the system.

GoDonnie. The environment are available to download[1] and all specification of language are also available[2]. Among GoDonnie's creation, Logo's main contribution was the use of natural language to move an object in an environment. We inserted commands to move the robot forward (FW) and backward (BW) and to turn it to the right (TR) and the left (TL). GoDonnie also has the selection (IF), loop (REPEAT, WHILE, FOR), procedure (PROCEDURE), and assignment commands (VAR) that are common to general-purpose programming languages.

---

[1] https://github.com/lsa-pucrs/donnie-assistive-robot-sw.

[2] https://donnie-user-manual.readthedocs.io/en/latest/docs/godonnie/index.html.

However, despite the similarities of these commands to other available languages, these languages did not serve the purpose of this research, aimed to PVI. They lacked a better integration with software screen readers, commands that avoided the use of simultaneous keys, and commands to allow the user to understand the environment; how the robot interacts with the environment. That is commands to allow the user to better understand the environment and the robot's point of view, developing O&M activities through programming.

Hence, we defined specific commands for the end-users. The SCAN command provides information about the location and color of objects in the environment, and the distance in steps between these objects and the robot. The POSITION or just POS command indicates the position of the robot in the environment, by means of the coordinates X and/or Y and/or angle A, to which the robot is directed. The STATE command brings the information from the POS command and informs the user of the last command for moving and rotation performed by the robot. The SPEAK command allows text messages, variable contents or information related to the robot and the environment to be expressed in audio. The DISTANCE command tells the user the number of steps between the robot and some object in front of the user, to the right-hand side, to the left, or behind the user. In this way, it allows the user to check if there is any possible collision. The COLOR command informs the number of objects of a given color (red, blue or green). The color characteristic is used to identify different objects in the environment, expanding the range of activities that can be performed in the environment. The HISTORY returns the number of lines of the program, and the user can navigate in the code by typing the line number or using the keys P to move to the next line, A for the previous line, and ESC to exit the history.

Also, we made some changes in the syntax of existing commands in Logo. For instance, in LOGOWritter, SuperLogo, NetLogo, and Lego-LOGO, the IF conditional command and the REPEAT loop have brackets to delimit the start and the end of blocks. Screen readers read the symbols { and } as "open braces" and "close braces", and the relation between the command block and the command to which it refers is not explained. In GoDonnie, the IF command, the begin and end delimiters are, respectively, the words THEN and END IF. For the REPEAT command, we chose to include the word TIMES, which, when indicating the number of times a block should be repeated, also indicates that the command is about to start, and END REPEAT to indicate the end of that block. Stefik and Siebert's [39] recommend the use of the term "Repeat x times" for inexperienced programmers. In the case of GoDonnie, this choice also makes the REPEAT command more intuitive when using screen readers, avoiding the use of symbols that require more than one key (e.g., the shift key).

The procedure command in GoDonnie is defined as PROCEDURE. The word END is used together with the command to which it refers; in this case, END PROCEDURE. In this version of GoDonnie, due to implementation constraints, the *SHIFT* key is kept for the multiplication and addition mathematical operations, and double quotation marks for transmitting text to TTS using the SPEAK command. Listing 1.1 introduces an example of GoDonnie code.

Listing 1.1. Running example of GoDonnie code

```
— Program that simulates a geometric shape, a square.
repeat 4 times
fw 3
tr 90
end repeat
```

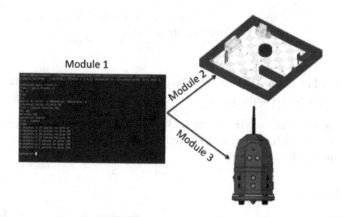

Fig. 2. Donnie programming environment.

Donnie Programming Environment (DPE). The environment consists of 3 modules, as shown in Fig. 2. Module 1 corresponds to the GoDonnie programming language, along with the development environment that supports this language. Module 2 refers to the 2D graphical simulator where the user can see the execution of the commands, i.e., the virtual robot moving in the scenario. Moreover, Module 3 corresponds to the Donnie robot and the real scenario. The use of Module 1 is mandatory and can be used with Module 2 or Module 3, i.e., it cannot be used with Module 2 and Module 3 at the same time.

The development environment includes a client interpreter, an editor, and a 2D simulator. The environment has two types of feedbacks: spoken messages played using Google's TTS feature and iconic sounds (footsteps, turns, and collisions), which are mp3 files automatically loaded into the system. Some commands combine spoken message feedbacks and iconic sounds, and others only have spoken messages (e.g., Table 1). Besides, we use the Orca screen reader that is native to the Linux operating system. This screen reader is used for users can type the language commands autonomously, so Orca reproduces what the user types in the terminal.

The 2D graphics simulator (Module 2) works in conjunction with Module 1. This graphic is configurable, i.e., the user can add new objects and change the

Table 1. An example of system sound feedbacks

Command	Iconic sound	Spoken message
FW 5 or BW 5	Footsteps sound	I walked 5 steps forward/backward
TR 90 or TL 90	Turning sound	I turned 90° to the right/left
SCAN	Turning sound	At 40° to the left: 1 green object 2 steps away. At 90° to the right: 1 red object 4 steps away
STATE	–	Command 1 was FW 3, walked 2, collided, position [2,0,0]

arrangement of objects. At this time, the user can only use objects with the colors blue, green, and red. Among the objectives for the creation of Module 2 are:

- allows the use of the environment without a physical robot and real scenario.
- allows people with low vision or sighted to follow the thinking of who is programming the robot.

3.4   Evaluated

We evaluated the Donnie programming environment in two steps. In *Step 1*, which lasted five months, we evaluated the programming language GoDonnie without the environment, the tutorial, and concrete materials developed for the study. Novices and programming experts visually impaired people, and Programming professors participated. This step included teaching the programming language and performing programming activities with increasing levels of difficulty. In *Step 2*, which lasted two weeks, we evaluated the programming language editor (Module 1) and the 2D simulator (Module 2). It also included performing programming activities and answered a questionnaire.

Step 1 - GoDonnie Evaluation. The evaluation was performed in three studies (Study A, Study B, and Study C). The main objective is to assess whether the language would be easy to learn by beginners (Study A) and experienced programmers (Study B), as well as whether the tactile materials used for teaching are easy to understand. In Study C, the language was evaluated by sighted programming professors with the goal of verifying the usability of the language. These studies occurred only using GoDonnie programming language; it is necessary to isolate problems related to the programming language from its environment (DPE).

Study A. We conducted an evaluation with a participant who is blind referred to as (P1). The participant is male, 23 years old, and a student at a Psychology graduate school. P1 has no previous programming or robotics experience. We created activities with different levels of difficulty to evaluate the GoDonnie without the environment, so that the commands of the language could be validated. We published this study on [40]. We use a small object to represent the robot, as well as a tactile map, produced in EVA material. From these resources, programming and robotics concepts were introduced. GoDonnie language evaluation occurred in 4 meetings and 3 through assignments.

Results. The user found GoDonnie easy to learn and remember. The tactile map were adapted to make more easier to understand. In this study, the COLORS command was replaced by COLOR since it only indicates the existence of objects of a given colour.

Study B. We have intentionally invited two people who are visually impaired to participate in this experiment; one who is low vision (P2) and the other who has acquired blindness (P3). P2 was 44 years old and P3 was 39 years old during the period of the experiments. Both participants were male. Considering the programming experience, P2 has an intermediate level of knowledge in C, C++, Python, Java, Pascal, and Delphi programming languages; P3 has a basic level of knowledge in Java and C programming languages. Although both participants have programming skills, they did not develop code frequently. This evaluation is also published on [40]. For these experiments we use meetings and assignments. We created five guided activities for the meeting session. These activities are direct, application-oriented, and problem-oriented with different levels of difficulty. After each activity, there was a discussion about it. In the following we introduce an example of guided activity.

For the assignment, sent by email, we created a list of 19 programming questions, which were organized into blocks of commands. After each block, we asked questions related to the usability of the programming language and the user's satisfaction, like as: ease of learning, ease of use, and appropriateness of the command to its syntax and action. The assignment goal was to review and reinforce the commands so the participants could solve problems without the presence of the examiners. We delivered to each participant a copy of the language guide, and we explained for each task of the activities where, in the guide, the users could find information about the required command. The meeting session process was the same for P2 and P3; each one done individually. We conducted two evaluations with P2, a meeting, and an assignment sent by email. Related to P3, we conducted only one meeting, since no response for the assessment was given by email. During the meeting session, we explained GoDonnie commands using the tactile map and the robot simulator object.

Results. Both participants agreed that GoDonnie was easy to understand. They think the programming language is robust and it does not miss any other commands. They also considered the proposed activities appropriate. At this stage, they had no suggestions about the activities and the language guide. P2 considered most of the commands easy to learn, to use, and appropriate to the action performed. The COLOR command was considered partially easy to learn because initially P2 did not use the parameters of this command. Then consider this command easy to use and appropriate. Mathematical operators were considered unsuitable, although they were considered easy to learn and use. The suggestion of P2 was that one could include precedence among these operators. Another issue highlighted by P2 is that of procedure blocks could be

Table 2. Profile of professors

Id	Age	Time teaches programming	Language teaching	Languages you've already teaching	Knowledge in programming teaching using robotics	Programming disciplines with PVI
Prof1	41–50	20 years	Java	C	No	No
Prof2	41–50	15 years	C, Java, Visual Basic	Logo	No	Yes
Prof3	61–70	27 years	Prolog, C++, Alice	Java, C, Basic	No	Yes
Prof4	41–50	26 years	C	C, Pascal, Java, C++, Assembly, Cobol	1 year	No (*)
Prof5	41–50	20 years	Java	C, Logo, Basic, Visual basic	No	No
Prof6	41–50	16 years	Java	Assembly, Visual basic, Basic, Logo, Quick basic	No	No
Prof7	41–50	17 years	C, Java, Python	Assembly	10 years	No (*)

(*) These professors taught other subjects to PVI

signaled with the terms DO and END, as in the WHILE and FOR commands. At this stage of the evaluation, the procedure creation command PROCEDURE was defined with BEGIN and END, and the other commands (FOR, WHILE, REPEAT) already used the terms DO and END. At the moment PROCEDURE follows the pattern of these commands.

Study C. We intentionally invite 16 programming professors from Pontifical Catholic University of Rio Grande do Sul, 7 professors accepted the invitation. Table 2 shows the profile of professors. Professors have 15 to 27 years of experience teaching programming. In addition, 2 professors have taught programming courses for PVI, and another 2 have taught other subjects. Among 7 professors, 3 have experience in language teaching Logo and 2 have taught programming using robotics.

We conduct in-person interviews with each professor. The interviews had, on average, the duration of 45 min, in which the GoDonnie commands were presented and the questionnaire on language in the form of an interview was applied. The questionnaire contained questions related to Usability (Consistency - 2 questions, Ease of use - 9 questions, Match between system and the real world - 3 questions, and Help and Documentation - 4 questions) and Ease of programming (4 questions). The 5-point Likert scale was used. The professors were instructed to choose an item from the scale and make comments about it. In addition, the questionnaire contained 2 questions about GoDonnie's design decisions and an open question for general comments about language. To assist data analysis, interviews were recorded using audio.

In the questions related to Usability, in the category of Consistency, we tried to verify if the language was consistent in the sense of coherence between the commands and what they do. In the Ease of Use category, we sought to verify if the language was simple, easy and concise. In the Match between system and the real world category, we examined whether the language is clear, understandable and whether there is a match between the commands of GoDonnie with similar languages or with terms in Portuguese. In the Help and Documentation category, we tried to verify if the GoDonnie guide can be used to learn it, if it is easy to read and has a logical order in the presentation of the commands. In the category of Ease of programming, we looked for to verify if the GoDonnie is suitable for the teaching of programming and of robot programming. In the questions of design decisions, we tried to identify the importance of adding new data types or entries in the language. And in the matter of general comments about language, it was sought to identify some case that during the evaluation had not been covered.

We analyze the information obtained in the interviews qualitatively using content analysis, carried out in two ways: a vertical analysis and then horizontal [41]. In the vertical analysis, we analyzed what each professor expressed in his interview, selecting the contents that stood out for each question. In the horizontal analysis, we analyzed separately each question of the interview, considering all professors interviewed, reviewing each item and highlighting each professor. The following is a summary of what was obtained in the interviews for each question.

Results. Programming professors found GoDonnie consistent, easy-to-use commands, that the language has correspondence with the real world, easy-to-program, and suitable for programming teaching. The professors suggested a new organization and presentation for the GoDonnie language guide. Also, they suggested including new data types such as float, alphabetic, and alphanumeric. They also indicated the need to include commands to enable data entry via the keyboard (input). We will go considered these issues in the next version of GoDonnie.

Step 2 - Donnie Programming Environment. We performed an evaluation of Module 1 and 2, with P1 (Study A) and P2 (Study B), individually [42]. The evaluation was performed through use observation and questionnaire. We designed 6 programming activities, 1 activity to evaluate the GoDonnie guide, and a questionnaire for this experiment. The questionnaire contained questions related to the following criteria: ease of use, utility, error prevention, sound interface, O&M, programming, help and documentation, and satisfaction. In total, we had 48 closed questions.

Results. The results of the evaluations have confirmed many of the design decisions for usability and accessibility, as well as identifying improvements to the programming language and user guide.

4 Design Guidelines

We synthesized the findings from our method to produce a set of design guidelines for developing robot programming environments to people who are visually impaired. We grouped the guidelines into two categories: the programming language and environment, orientation and mobility, and general. We demonstrated how we applied these guidelines to the development of the DPE.

4.1 Programming Language and Environment

1. Help the user understand **where** the program error occurs: syntax errors should be clearly reported. Where the error occurs should be clearly indicated. Example at DPE: when the user makes a syntax error, the system tells the user the line and the column error, the column corresponds to the number of letters. So if the user types fw3 the system issues error on "line 1 and column 3, check the fw3 command".

2. Allow use of screen reader: the blind person who is a computer user already uses accessibility features to convert textual information into sound information. Thus, the programming language environment should allow assistive technology features to continue to be used without requiring others to be installed. Also, this resource is set according to user preferences in terms of reading speed, punctuation, language, etc. Example at DPE: as already mentioned, DPE allows the use of Orca screen reader.

3. Help the user to understand command syntax: try to use natural language, or as close as possible to the functionality it performs. Example at DPE: We use GoDonnie commands that refer to what they execute, e.g., STATE, COLOR, POSITION, SCAN.

4. Progressive execution: the system must be able to execute commands as they are entered and by command blocks. Example at DPE: in the system the user can compile each line as they types it and can also compile a command blocks.

5. Short syntax commands: the language should have simple and short syntax commands that are easy to remember. Example at DPE: We try to use a short syntax and more simple possible, e.g., in Java language, the print is written: System.out.println(''hello world'');, while in GoDonnie is SPEAK ''hello world''.

6. Language flexibility: there should be no restricted, predefined areas for entering commands. This way, the user enters commands according to the desired execution order. Example at DPE: in GoDonnie the user to declare variables as they are needed without having to declare them at the beginning of the program.

7. Consistency: similar commands should mean similar things. Example at DPE: in GoDonnie the commands follow this idea, so for example the commands STATE, COLOR, POSITION, SCAN all show the user the robot's point of view about the environment.

8. Audio Feedback: the system should provide feedback on the execution of commands via audio. Example at DPE: as mentioned, in DPE we have two types of feedbacks, spoken messages and iconic sounds. Users liked both feedbacks.

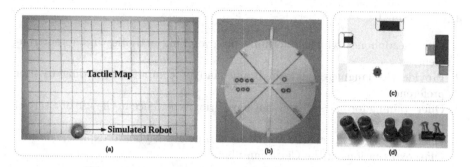

Fig. 3. (a) Tactile map in EVA and object representing the robot Donnie, (b) angle concept, (c) virtual environment objects, and (d) parts that represent the objects in the environment, from left to right: blue objects, red objects, and green objects. (Colour figure online)

4.2 Orientation and Mobility

1. Perception of environment: the language must be commands to capture information about the robot and scenario through commands such as SCAN, POSITION, DISTANCE, and COLOR. From these, the user can create a plan of action to go to the desired place using commands of movement (FW and BW) and rotation (TR and TL).
2. Tactile materials to explain programming, robot concepts, and O&M (Fig. 3):
   - Use a tactile map with an easy-to-touch material, such as EVA, and mark this material as a "matrix" where each square represents a step of the robot. This is interesting for the initial concepts of programming and execution of the commands to be taught, and for the participant to better understand the environment (See Fig. 3a).
   - Use an instrument to check angles. This is interesting in case the participants are not familiar with the use of degrees (See Fig. 3b).
   - Use objects with different shapes on the tactile map to represent different virtual environment objects (See Fig. 3d).
   - Use objects with different shapes in the virtual environment to represent different objects (See Fig. 3c).
   - Represent different objects with different colors in the virtual environment (See Fig. 3c).
   - Create the virtual environment where objects are not overlapping (See Fig. 3c).
   - Represent the robot by taking a step (frame) on the tactile map.
   - Place a palpable marking to identify the front of the physical robot (See Fig. 3a).
   - Use objects in which the person can grope without taking them out of place on the tactile map (See Fig. 3d).

4.3 General

1. Offer headphones while performing programming activities in the environment.
2. Provide the language guide in braille and/or computer according to user preference.
3. Offer training for users who do not have prior experience in the use of a screen reader.
4. Offer training for users who do not have previous keyboard experience.
5. Offer explanations of the Cartesian plane.
6. Suggest using the user own body to simulate the robot's actions.

5 Discussion and Conclusion

We believe we have demonstrated a method for building a robot programming environment with usability and accessibility for visually impaired people. From this method based on interactive design [25], we define a programming language called GoDonnie, based on the Logo language. The language runs in the Donnie programming environment, which contains a virtual robot (Module 2). It also has a physical robot (Module 3), but we have not evaluated it yet.

GoDonnie has commands that allow the user to solve logical problems and O&M. Thus, there are commands to understand where the robot is (POS, STATE), for object location (SCAN), to identify the number of objects per color (COLOR), and to check the distance between the objects and the robot (DISTANCE). Thus, the user can create an action plan to go to the desired location using motion (FW and BW) and rotation (TR and TL) commands. There are also commands common to other languages that allow the user to solve more complex problems, such as VAR, IF, REPEAT, WHILE, FOR, and PROCEDURE. All commands provide audible feedback for the user to understand the execution. There is also the SPEAK command for use in combination with the other commands already mentioned to express audible information.

We evaluated GoDonnie in two steps, with and without the Donnie programming environment. In the first step, we performed three studies (Study A, Study B, and Study C). Study A was conducted with a blind person with no programming knowledge (P1), who found that the language is easy for novice programmers to learn and, according to the participants' suggestions, the concrete materials were adapted to become even easier to understand. Study B was conducted with two participants who are visually impaired with programming experience (P2 and P3). They found GoDonnie can be used as a problem-solving resource in the area of robot programming. Study C was conducted with seven programming professors, they found GoDonnie commands practical and easy to use to programming. They suggested some modifications in the guide, such as inserting GoDonnie context and navigation links, and better organization of commands. Also, they suggested to include float, alphabetic, and alphanumeric data types. Another suggestion was support for keyboard input.

In step two, we evaluated GoDonnie with the environment. We perform with the blind user without programming knowledge (P1) and with a low vision user with programming knowledge (P2). They found GoDonnie commands ease of use, good usability, with prevention and error handling, and they were happy with their use. Also, they found that GoDonnie has an excellent sound interface. They also found that using GoDonnie aids in the development of O&M. In this way, participants were able to make a mind map of the environment and related objects. This map was externalized using a tactile map in which participants distributed objects representing the virtual environment.

Thus, we suggest that a process of evaluating a programming language that manipulates a robot, virtual or physical, includes: concrete materials to explain programming and robot concepts; guided programming tasks, and also with difficulty levels such as easy, intermediate, and hard; language guide/tutorial with navigation links. Also, we believe it is interesting to apply questionnaires about the use, as proposed in this study. As seen earlier, O&M skills are related to five phases. In the Donnie programming environment, they can be summarized as follows:

- Perception: it was shown that users were able to capture information about the robot and the scenario using commands such as SCAN, POS, DISTANCE, and COLOR.
- Analysis: We verify that the user could understand the scenario and where the robot is with the creation of the tactile map (Step 2).
- Selection: Users were able to identify which commands would be required to perform programming activities (Step 1 and Step 2).
- Planning: users were able to design the program by code the commands so that the robot could move (Step 1 - study A and B- and Step 2).
- Execution: users were able to execute the program and understand if the robot reached the previously defined goal (Step 1 - study A and B- and Step 2).

This research contributed to define a programming language with usability and accessibility to PVI. Besides, we have proposed a method for designing programming environments using robot for O&M. We also summarize our findings with guidelines for developing robot programming environments for people who are visually impaired.

Our future work includes making new assessments with visually impaired people using Module 3. Also, we intend to create a realistic environment (like a classroom) in the virtual environment (Module 2) and, after use, check if the user can move in the real environment. GoDonnie will be enhanced for keyboard input and float, alphabetic, and alphanumeric data types. The COLOR command will review functionality and attributes, as suggested by users.

References

1. de Almeida, L.C.F., da Silva, J.S.D.M., do Amaral, H.J.C.: Robótica educacional: Uma possibilidade para o ensino e aprendizagem. Revista da Escola Regional de Informática, 2(2), 178–184, November 2013

2. Júnior, N.M.F., Vasques, C.K., Francisco, T.H.A.: Robótica educacional e a produção científica na base de dados da capes. Revista Electrónica de Investigación y Docencia (REID), 35–53, July 2010

3. Solomon, C.J., Papert, S.: A case study of a young child doing turtle graphics in logo. In: National Computer Conference and Exposition, AFIPS 1976, pp. 1049–1056. ACM, New York (1976)

4. Valente, J.A.: Diferentes usos do computador na educação. Em aberto 12(57), 1–14 (2008)

5. Kane, S.K., Bigham, J.P.: Tracking stemxcomet: teaching programming to blind students via 3D printing, crisis management, and Twitter. In: ACM Technical Symposium on Computer Science Education, pp. 247–252 (2014)

6. Mealin, S., Murphy-Hill, E.: An exploratory study of blind software developers. In: IEEE Symposium on Visual Languages and Human-Centric Computing, pp. 71–74. IEEE (2012)

7. Ludi, S.A., Reichlmayr, T.: Developing inclusive outreach activities for students with visual impairments. In: 39th SIGCSE Technical Symposium on Computer Science Education, pp. 439–443. ACM (2008)

8. Ludi, S., Reichlmayr, T.: The use of robotics to promote computing to pre-college students with visual impairments. Trans. Comput. Educ. 11(3), 20:1–20:20 (2011)

9. Kakehashi, S., Motoyoshi, T., Koyanagi, K., Oshima, T., Masuta, H., Kawakami, H.: Improvement of p-cube: algorithm education tool for visually impaired persons. In: IEEE Symposium on Robotic Intelligence in Informationally Structured Space, pp. 1–6. IEEE (2014)

10. Kakehashi, S., Motoyoshi, T., Koyanagi, K., Oshima, T., Kawakami, H.: P-cube: block type programming tool for visual impairments. In: Conference on Technologies and Applications of Artificial Intelligence, pp. 294–299. IEEE Computer Society, December 2013

11. Dutra, C.P.: Orientação e Mobilidade: Conhecimentos básicos para a inclusão do deficiente visual. MEC/SEESP (2003)

12. de Borba Campos, M., Sánchez, J., Cardoso Martins, A., Schneider Santana, R., Espinoza, M.: Mobile navigation through a science museum for users who are blind. In: Stephanidis, C., Antona, M. (eds.) UAHCI 2014. LNCS, vol. 8515, pp. 717–728. Springer, Cham (2014). https://doi.org/10.1007/978-3-319-07446-7_68

13. de Borba Campos, M., Sánchez, J., Damasio, J., Inácio, T.: Usability evaluation of a mobile navigation application for blind users. In: Antona, M., Stephanidis, C. (eds.) UAHCI 2015. LNCS, vol. 9178, pp. 117–128. Springer, Cham (2015). https://doi.org/10.1007/978-3-319-20687-5_12

14. Connors, E.C., Yazzolino, L.A., Sánchez, J., Merabet, L.B.: Development of an audio-based virtual gaming environment to assist with navigation skills in the blind. JoVE (Journal of Visualized Experiments), 73, e50272 (2013)

15. Lahav, O., Schloerb, D.W., Kumar, S., Srinivasan, M.A.: Blindaid: a learning environment for enabling people who are blind to explore and navigate through unknown real spaces. In: 2008 Virtual Rehabilitation, pp. 193–197. IEEE (2008)

16. Balanskat, A., Engelhardt, K.: Computing our future: computer programming and coding-Priorities, school curricula and initiatives across Europe. European Schoolnet (2014)

17. De Oliveira, C.C.: Designing educational programming tools for the blind: mitigating the inequality of coding in schools (2017)

18. Kitchenham, B.: Procedures for performing systematic reviews. Keele, UK, Keele University 33(2004), 1–26 (2004)

19. Damasio Oliveira, J., de Borba Campos, M., de Morais Amory, A., Manssour, I.H.: Teaching robot programming activities for visually impaired students: a systematic review. In: Antona, M., Stephanidis, C. (eds.) UAHCI 2017. LNCS, vol. 10279, pp. 155–167. Springer, Cham (2017). https://doi.org/10.1007/978-3-319-58700-4_14
20. Ludi, S.L., Ellis, L., Jordan, S.: An accessible robotics programming environment for visually impaired users. In: 16th International ACM SIGACCESS Conference on Computers and Accessibility, pp. 237–238. ACM (2014)
21. Ludi, S., Abadi, M., Fujiki, Y., Sankaran, P., Herzberg, S.: Jbrick: accessible lego mindstorm programming tool for users who are visually impaired. In: Proceedings of the 12th International ACM SIGACCESS Conference on Computers and Accessibility, pp. 271–272. ACM (2010)
22. Molins-Ruano, P., Gonzalez-Sacristan, C., Garcia-Saura, C.: Phogo: a low cost, free and "maker" revisit to logo. Comput. Human Behav. 80, 428–440 (2018)
23. Barros, R.P., Burlamaqui, A.M.F., Azevedo, S.O., Sá, S.T., Gonçalves, L.M.G., Burlamaqui, A.A.R.S.: Cardbot-assistive technology for visually impaired in educational robotics: experiments and results. IEEE Latin America Trans. 15(3), 517–527 (2017)
24. Paramasivam, V., Huang, J., Elliott, S., Cakmak, M.: Computer science outreach with end-user robot-programming tools. In: ACM Technical Symposium on Computer Science Education, pp. 447–452 (2017)
25. Yvonne, R., Helen, S., Jennifer, P.: Design de interação: além da interação humano-computador. Bookman (2013)
26. Jacobson, W.H.: The art and science of teaching orientation and mobility to persons with visual impairments. American Foundation for the Blind (1993)
27. Orly, L., David, M.: A blind person's cognitive mapping of new spaces using a haptic virtual environment. J. Res. Special Educ. Needs 3(3), 172–177 (2003)
28. Lahav, O., Schloerb, D.W., Kumar, S., Srinivasan, M.A.: Blindaid: a learning environment for enabling people who are blind to explore and navigate through unknown real spaces. In: Virtual Rehabilitation, pp. 193–197 (2008)
29. Mazzaro, J.L., et al: Orientação e mobilidade: conhecimentos básicos para a inclusão do deficiente visual. MEC, SEESP, Brasília (2003)
30. Jeannette, M.: Wing. Computat. Think. 49(3), 33–35 (2006)
31. Aho, A.V.: Ubiquity symposium: computation and computational thinking. Ubiquity 2011, 1–8 (2011)
32. Berland, M., Lee, V.R.: Collaborative strategic board games as a site for distributed computational thinking. Int. J. Game-Based Learn. 1(2), 65–81 (2011)
33. Kazimoglu, C., Kiernan, M., Bacon, L., Mackinnon, L.: A serious game for developing computational thinking and learning introductory computer programming. Procedia-Soc. Behav. Sci. 47, 1991–1999 (2012)
34. Mary, K., Cagin, K., Liz, B., Lachlan, M.: Developing an educational game to support cognitive learning. J. Learn.Teach. 5(9), (2014)
35. Hoc, J.-M., Nguyen-Xuan, A.: Chapter 2.3 - language semantics, mental models and analogy. In: Psychology of Programming, pp. 139–156. Academic Press (1990)
36. Green, T.R.G.: Cognitive dimensions of notations. In: V People and Computers, pp. 443–460 (1989)
37. Sadowski, C., Kurniawan, S.: Heuristic evaluation of programming language features: two parallel programming case studies. In: ACM Workshop on Evaluation and Usability of Programming Languages and Tools, pp. 9–14 (2011)
38. Augusto, C.P., et al.: Donnie robot: towards an accessible and educational robot for visually impaired people. In: Latin American Robotics Symposium (LARS) (2017)

39. Stefik, A., Siebert, S.: An empirical investigation into programming language syntax. ACM Trans. Comput. Educ. **13**(4), 19 (2013)
40. Damasio, J., de Borba Campos, M., Amory, A., Bordini, R.H.: Godonnie: a robot programming language for teaching people who are visually impaired. In: Brazilian Symposium on Computers in Education (Simpósio Brasileiro de Informática na Educação-SBIE), vol. 30, p. 1181 (2019)
41. Engers, M.E.A.: O professor alfabetizador eficaz: análise de fatores influentes da eficácia do ensino. Ph.D. thesis, Universidade Federal do Rio Grande do Sul (1987)
42. Oliveira, J.D., de Borba Campos, M., Amory, A., Bordini, R.H.: GoDonnie: a robot programming language to improve orientation and mobility skills in people who are visually impaired. In: The 21st International ACM SIGACCESS Conference on Computers and Accessibility, ASSETS 2019, pp. 679–681. ACM, New York (2019)

Lego Robots in Puppet Play for Children with Cerebral Palsy

Hsieh-Chun Hsieh[1]([⊠]) [ID], Chun-Kai Liu[2], and Peter Kuan-Hao Chen[1]

[1] National Tsing Hua University, Hsinchu, Taiwan, R.O.C.
hchsieh@mx.nthu.edu.tw
[2] Industrial Technology Research Institute, Hsinchu, Taiwan, R.O.C.

Abstract. Objectives: The purpose of this study was to improve hand performance while playing with Chinese puppets modified with Lego robots.

Participants: Forty-two children with cerebral palsy were randomly assigned to either the intervention or control group (n = 21 each).

Design: The experimental group underwent 12 weeks of rehabilitation involving playing puppets with the Lego robot, whereas the control group played traditional Chinese puppets.

Interventions: A modified puppet therapy was designed in accordance with the motor requirements for hand control.

Main Outcome Measures: The Siliconcoach® Pro 7 software, finger tapping test (FTT), and Jamar® hydraulic pinch gauge were used to measure the kinematics and functional performance of the hand.

Results: Varying effects on motor performance between playing with commercial Chinese puppetry and adaptive Chinese puppets with Lego robots were observed. There was a significant improvement in the intervention group only according to the ANCOVA results.

Conclusion: The modified puppet therapy improved range of motion, FTT scores, and finger pressing speed after the modified puppet therapy. Further studies with modified puppets with Lego robots to provide practice in terms of hand control are needed.

Keywords: Lego robot · Cerebral palsy · Chinese puppet

1 Introduction

Impaired hand function is often a disabling symptom observed in children with CP. Almost 50% of children with CP present an arm-hand dysfunction and children with unilateral spastic CP seldom use their paretic hand spontaneously in daily activities [1]. The spastic muscle is usually active; however, voluntary movements are often impaired by co-contraction, e.g., contraction of the extensors during finger flexion [2]. Previous studies also have focused on using assistive devices such as robots to improve postural control [3, 4] and adaptive toys to facilitate fine motor control [5, 6] in children with CP. Some have established early interventions on hand motor control to improve hand function in children with CP, such as thumb opposition and finger pressing to actively tap a surface through the finger [7, 8]. Play materials should reflect

© Springer Nature Switzerland AG 2020
M. Antona and C. Stephanidis (Eds.): HCII 2020, LNCS 12188, pp. 465–476, 2020.
https://doi.org/10.1007/978-3-030-49282-3_33

the culture and social environment of an individual. Using Chinese puppets can influence Chinese children to perform exaggerated actions with well-known stories as the play becomes more interesting and meaningful. Previous studies highlight the role of toys in hand control and support the use of modified toys to promote fine motor control through repetitive practice in children with CP. Some have established early interventions on hand motor control to improve hand function in children with CP, such as thumb opposition and finger pressing. In recent years, increased attention has been given to modifying puppets in pretend play for children with CP [8]. The traditional Chinese puppet is controlled by the hand that occupies the interior of the puppet; it is more difficult to use than common puppets. It may be helpful to include some modifications in Chinese puppets and facilitate playing in situations that have similarities with life experiences.

This modified puppet therapy included the use of attractive Chinese puppets and task-specific repetitive treatment concepts with the Lego switches (e.g., finger pressing and releasing); the Lego technology allowed children to practice movements through playing with modified puppets. By adding brilliant colors, assorted textures, and exaggerated physical characteristics to the Chinese puppets, enhanced interest and attention were given to the interaction with the puppets. Therefore, the research questions in this study were as follows: "Do hand control and finger movements improve more with additional modified puppet therapy by using Lego switches as compared to that with standard puppet play alone for children with cerebral palsy?"

2 Methods

2.1 Sample

A total of 64 eligible participants from preschools of special education in Taiwan were screened by a research assistant; among them, 22 children with CP were excluded (18 children did not meet the inclusion criteria, and four had other medical conditions). Forty-two children (please see Table 1) with cerebral palsy were randomly assigned to either the experimental or control group (n = 31 each). Block randomization was accomplished after choosing the amount of groups under one block (blocked randomization by GMFCS level). The protocol for this trial followed the CONSORT 2010 guidelines [9]. The inclusion criteria were as follows: clinical diagnosis of CP, with Gross Motor Function.

The inclusion criteria were as follows: clinical diagnosis of CP, with Gross Motor Function Classification System (GMFCS) levels II–IV or Manual Ability Classification System (MACS) levels I–III; ability to follow simple commands and participate in the task; ability to perform finger pressing; and no additional significant medical problems. Children with CP classified under MACS levels II–III were selected, since they handle objects slowly and require assistance or set-up for activities; the Lego switches helped participants with sensorimotor deficits to control their fingers better.

Table 1. Demographics of participants.

	Experimental group	Control group
	N = 21	N = 21
Age(SD)	5.12 (1.05)	5.27 (1.02)
Gender		
Male	14 (66.7%)	15 (71.4%)
Female	7 (33.3%)	6 (28.6%)
CP subtype		
Spastic quadriplegia	10 (47.6%)	11 (52.4%)
Spastic diplegic	6 (28.6%)	7 (33.3%)
Athetoid	3 (14.3%)	2 (9.5%)
Ataxic	2 (9.5%)	1 (4.8%)
GMFCS level of UE		
Level II	12 (57.2%)	11 (52.4%)
Level III	5 (23.8%)	6 (28.6%)
Level IV	4 (19.0%)	4 (19.0%)

NOTE. The five levels of classification, representing meaningful distinctions in motor function, are based on self-initiated movement. In this study, participants' gross motor function varied from GMFCS level II to level IV. Level I represents the ability to walk, but experiencing difficulties in uneven terrains or in crowded or confined spaces, while Level IV represents mobility requiring physical assistance or use of the wheelchair (GMFCS; Palisano et al. 2008).

2.2 Procedures

Pre-test and post-tests were conducted to determine whether the modified puppet therapy improved the fine motor performance of the participants over a 12-week period. To ensure consistency across sessions, a specific puppet set was utilized. Distinct puppets were used in each group: (a) the experimental group used puppets modified with Lego robots (Fig. 1), while (b) the control group used Chinese puppets not modified with Lego robots. The puppet therapy for both groups (modified puppet vs. regular puppet) was provided by a qualified occupational therapist with 8 years of experience in pediatric rehabilitation. All testing sessions were conducted by one physiotherapist and one graduated student of special education. One research assistant was in charge of the randomization and recruitment processes. The well-known Chinese story, Romantic of Three Kingdoms (https://www.youtube.com/watch?v=NvZ6vTX2WAM), was used to allow the children to manipulate the puppet to role-play in the story. Both groups underwent puppets sessions once per day in a study hall in addition to regular school-based occupational therapy once per week (30 min per session). The experimental procedures were approved by the Ethics Committee at National Tsing Hua University for human research, and the parents of each participant provided informed consent.

Fig. 1. Modified puppet therapy

(a) Chinese puppet.
(b) A participant pressed the touch sensors with a poor posture in the pre-test.
(c) Skeleton created using the Lego bricks.
(d) Three switches: two touch sensors and one ultrasonic light sensor.
(e) Assessment of the range of motion in the wrist, MP, PIP, and DIP joints (MP, metacarpophalangeal; PIP, proximal interphalangeal; DIP, distal interphalangeal).
(f) The programming of the modified puppet was written in Robolab 3.

2.3   Training Instrumentation

The Lego Mindstorms NXT #9797 (The LEGO Group, Denmark) was used in this study to model and program the Chinese puppet robot. This set included the programmable NXT Brick, providing on-brick programming and data logging, three interactive servo motors, three sensors, and connecting cables. The robot was designed with movements, such as rotation of the arms, to gain the children's attention. The children with CP could manipulate the Chinese puppets through three Lego sensors attached to the robot. Three interactive servo motors were used in this robot (one ultrasonic sensor for its leg and two touch sensors for its arms), as shown in Fig. 1. The robot was designed with movements, such as rotation of the arms to gain the children's attention. Moreover, it was designed to fit within a Chinese puppet to motivate the children with CP to operate the robot. The children with CP could manipulate the Chinese puppets through three Lego sensors attached to the robot. Three interactive servo motors were used in this robot (one ultrasonic sensor for its leg and two touch sensors for its arms). As shown in Fig. 1, two servo motors were placed at the very bottom of the robot. The robot's legs were attached to one interactive servo motor. The robot was built upwards, and its arms were attached to the sides. The Lego software Robolab 3.1 was used to program the puppet's movements, and its grammar was built on an assembly of graphical "programming blocks" (Fig. 1).

2.4   Outcome Measures

The data collection instruments used were a kinematical analysis software, finger press force, and the finger tapping test (FTT). A Sony DVR (HSC-100R, Sony Ltd, Minato Tokyo) was positioned at 5 m from the participants at a height of 120 cm for the kinematical analysis. The Siliconcoach® Pro 7 software (Siliconcoach Ltd, Dunedin, New Zealand) was used for the kinematical analysis of hand control on the switch, assessing the range of motion (ROM) and movement speed of finger action, finger pressing, and wrist angle. In Bain's et al. study, the functional ROMs were $19°$–$71°$, $23°$–$87°$, and $10°$–$64°$ at the MP, proximal interphalangeal, and distal interphalangeal joints, respectively performed during 90% of daily life activities [10].

The Jamar® hydraulic pinch gauge was used to measure finger strength and pinch capabilities. The Jamar® dynamometer appears to have a good potential as a clinically useful and reliable instrument for measuring handgrip strength in children with CP [11].

The FTT involves a single-finger-tapping task used to assess the integrity of the neuromuscular system and examine motor control. Each participant was asked to tap their right index finger on the numeric "1" key and their left index finger on the "Z" key in the keyboard. The participants were also instructed to hit the key as many times as possible for 10 s and seated with their forearms resting on a tabletop in front of a computer keyboard during the FTT. The FTT procedure used has been previously described and employed in the finger control literature [12]. Memisevic et al. [13] performed the FTT in 111 preschool children (59 boys and 52 girls), aged 3 to 6 years (mean, 4.6; SD, 0.9) and found average FTT scores (mean, 31.7; SD, 8.2 for boys; mean, 32.3; SD, 6.9 for girls). In other previous studies, it was used to measure the relationship between the Wechsler Intelligence test and FTT findings in children with CP and hemiplegia aged 6 to 12 years [14] and the effects of short-term piano training in adult patients with CP [15].

2.5   Data Analysis

The datasets were collected in the pre-test and post-test phases: ROM of the hand, finger press performance, and FTT findings. Multivariate analysis of variance (MANOVA) was used, since there were two groups (experimental and control groups) and seven dependent variables (kinematics data and test results). Then, the analysis of covariance (ANCOVA) was used to identify patients who had benefited the most from the treatment, with pretreatment scores serving as covariates. The ANCOVA allowed adjustment for initial differences between the control and experimental groups for some of the prognostic factors, as well as for the identification of differences between the 2 study groups after the therapeutic intervention had started. The software program SPSS (SPSS Inc., Chicago IL, USA) for Windows was used to perform statistical analysis. In the MANOVA, Wilks's Lambda (Λ) was used as the multivariate statistical value. The partial eta squared ($\eta 2$) values were used as the effect size for significant findings. The reporting of point estimates of the effect size is useful in indicating whether the non-significant findings could be due to inadequate sample size. The power analysis results are listed in Table 2 to provide the readers a visible representation of the probability of rejecting the null hypothesis when incorrect.

3   Results

All children on the experimental group completed their intervention play Chinese puppets with Lego robots. The demographic and clinical features of the two groups were similar and summarized in Table 1. As shown in Table 2, the post-test ROM improved the hand position [Metacarphalangeal (MP) joint flexion improved from 34° to 41°; proximal interphalangeal (PIP) joint flexion improved from 31° to 20°; distal interphalangeal (DIP) joint flexion improved from 21° to 15°] compared with the pre-test ROM. The experimental group showed improvements in the movement speed and ROM after the modified puppet therapy.

The test results and bar charts are shown in Table 2 and Fig. 2, respectively. The bar charts provide a visual presentation of the test scores between the intervention group and the control group. The effectiveness of the intervention was explained in the bar chart, indicating that the modified puppet therapy can improve finger ROM, press velocity, and FTT performance (rectangular bars were used for the comparison between the two groups). The intervention was evaluated using a randomized controlled trial, and the participants were allocated to the modified puppet therapy or standard puppet conditions in a 1:1 ratio. Box's M test of equality of covariance in the SPSS software was used to determine the homogeneity of variance-covariance matrices. As shown in Table 3, the MANOVA results indicated a significant interaction between the child group and time of assessment. Therefore, a simple main effects analysis (ANCOVA) was performed later to test if there was any between-group difference over time in the finger kinematics.

Table 2. Pretest and posttest scores for each group

	Experimental Group (n = 21)				Control Group (n = 21)			
	Pre-test		Post-test		Pre-test		Post-test	
Range of motion	$\overline{X}$	SD	$\overline{X}$	SD	$\overline{X}$	SD	$\overline{X}$	SD
Wrist ROM (degree)[a]	−34.52	22.35	4.14	28.07	−36.19	24.33	−17.80	26.33
MP ROM (degree)[b]	34.61	13.96	41.57	5.09	33.42	13.64	33.14	13.49
PIP ROM (degree)[c]	31.38	14.68	20.52	6.52	33.61	14.77	28.85	12.15
DIP ROM (degree)[d]	21.61	13.41	15.19	7.09	16.42	10.67	14.33	8.47
Pressing performance								
Pressing velocity (times/5 min)[e]	22.23	4.02	27.76	6.94	21.42	4.52	21.57	4.71
Pressing force (lb)[f]	1.95	0.87	2.42	0.66	1.85	0.72	1.90	0.88
FTT (score)[g]	14.85	4.73	16.76	2.90	12.42	4.21	15.14	3.20

NOTE: [a]Max angle of wrist flexion (negative number: wrist palmar flexion: positive number: wrist dorsiflexion)
[b]Max angle of Metacarpophalangeal joint (MP) flexion
[c]Max angle of Proximal Interphalangeal joint (PIP) flexion
[d]Max angle of Distal Interphalangeal joint (DIP) flexion
[e]The speed of index finger pressing on the Lego switch
[f]Finger pressing force
[g]Finger Tapping Test (FTT)

3.1 Difference Between the Intervention and Control Groups

All children on the experimental group completed their intervention play Chinese puppets with Lego robots. The demographic and clinical features of the two groups were similar and summarized in Table 1. As shown in Table 2, the post-test ROM improved the hand position [Metacarphalangeal (MP) joint flexion improved from 34° to 41°; proximal interphalangeal (PIP) joint flexion improved from 31° to 20°; distal interphalangeal (DIP) joint flexion improved from 21° to 15°] compared with the pre-test ROM. The experimental group showed improvements in the movement speed and ROM after the modified puppet therapy.

The MANOVA and ANCOVA results (Table 3) of the test performance identified the subgroups of children that benefited the most from the therapeutic intervention. In Table 3, the post-test of the experimental group showed significantly better performance with improved hand kinematics (ROM) and significantly better results in functional hand performance (FTT and pressing velocity) than that of the control group. The MANOVA results in ROM (F = 4.088, p = .002, Λ = .502) were significant. The later ANCOVA tests were performed in Wrist ROM (F = 9.098, p = .004), MP ROM (F = 7.523, p = .009), and PIP ROM (F = 7.558, p = .009). The analyses showed that the modified puppet therapy seemed to have influenced the performance; however, there was no significant change in the DIP ROM between the 2 groups (F = .376, p = .543).

The MANOVA results in hand performance (F = 3.679, p = .006, Λ = .613) was significant. The later ANCOVA tests were performed in pressing velocity (F = 11.558, p = .002), pressing force (F = 4.978, p = .031), and FTT (F = 9.474, p = .004). The results revealed that the experimental puppet with Lego robots could improve

ROM, pressing performance, and finger tapping test more effectively than traditional Chinese puppet.

Table 3. Multivariate Analysis (MANOVE) and Analysis of Covariance (ANCOVA) Summary for finger control performance

Variable	Multivariate				Univariate (ANCOVA)			
	Λ	F	p		F	p	η^2	POWER
Range of Motion (ROM)	.502	4.088*	.002	ROM wrist	9.098*	.004	.189	.837
				ROM MP	7.523*	.009	.161	.763
				ROM PIP	7.558*	.009	.162	.765
				ROM DIP	.376	.543	.010	.092
Pressing performance	.613	3.679*	.006	Pressing velocity	11.558*	.002	.229	.912
				Pressing force	4.978*	.031	.113	.586
				FTT	9.474*	.004	.195	.851

NOTE: *$p < .05$

3.2   Parent Interview Results

The intervention group thought that the Chinese puppet was useful and attractive. The parents had equally positive perceptions on the modified puppet therapy exercises, stating "he has more motivation and interest in playing with puppets" and "she has better motivation to use her fingers." The modified puppet therapy allowed the participants to take the initiative and gain control over the games instead of just passively watching them. The switch design simplified all the steps necessary to perform the puppets' movements. Moreover, the switches allowed the participants to engage in the repetitive practice of puppet play.

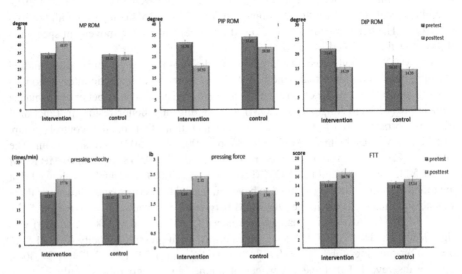

Fig. 2. Bar chart of test scores (pretest and posttest) in the intervention and control groups

4 Discussion

When completing the modified puppet therapy activities, the participants had to perform finger tapping to generate an action. If eye-hand coordination training is performed systematically with the modified puppet therapy, more functional hand control may be achieved in children with CP. The findings demonstrate that using switches to activate a robot puppet can provide practice with eye-hand coordination and targeted movement of finger control, which is stable over time; this supports the findings that toy adaptation can enhance participation during play activities [6] and pretend play performance [16]. The changes in the hand performance were significant after the modified puppet therapy. One potential explanation for this is that the intervention group exerted more effort in their actions that target movement training. The switch control allowed the participants to meet some daily functional activity needs (e.g., using handheld devices). This is because adaptation provides practice in terms of hand control for individuals when pressing or tapping. These findings are also in agreement with those of previous studies and indicate that targeted and simple movement training has a stronger effect on motor control for children with moderate to severe motor disabilities [6, 17, 18].

The functional position of the hand described in the literature is as follows: wrist in $20°$ to $30°$ of extension and slight ulnar deviation and fingers in $45°$ of MP joint flexion and $15°$ of PIP and DIP joint flexion [1, 2]. The hand position after the modified puppet therapy (MP joint flexion at $41°$; PIP joint flexion at $20°$; DIP joint flexion at $15°$) improved in relation to that in the literature on functional position. When manipulating the traditional puppets, they had problems holding the puppets' postures and generating the puppets' movements without the functional position of the hands. During the 12 weeks of intervention, the puppet was observed to be highly flexible in what it does given the same movements by the children; the children's movements can be weaved into a story or just a simple movement, such as dancing. The puppet can be moved in different ways; however, the children's motor movement was the same for all of the movements of the puppets' arms and/or legs. The use of the robot and Lego "skeleton" accomplished simple repetitive movements, while also making the result of the movements inherently interesting for and repeatable by the children. As suggested by a prior study, maintaining a child's motivation during treatment is an important rehabilitation strategy [19], and it is most likely to improve the outcome of rehabilitation.

Puppets are often used to encourage free expression, increase interaction, and provide children with special needs opportunities to participate in play [20, 21]. They can comfort children with anxiety because the presence of toys increases their familiarity with the situation. The use of puppets also provides children the opportunity to bring their stories out and onto a stage. The children with CP felt safe and comfortable while using the Lego robot to express themselves; thus, future studies may use this modified puppet therapy to project children's feelings and thoughts on puppets. A child's engagement in puppet play may positively impact the child's development [7, 21]. Puppets not only have positive effects in enhancing children's interest and engagement but can also be combined with therapeutic strategies when teaching developmentally relevant skills to children with special needs [22, 23]. For children with communication disorders or children with attention problems, modified puppets may be an effective modality to facilitate appropriate oral or play behaviors [16, 24]. There is a continuing need for an adequate theoretical basis for the practical application of modified puppet therapies.

4.1 Limitations

The study has several limitations, which should be considered when interpreting the findings. Longitudinal studies may be needed to explore cause-and-effect relationships and confirm whether the modified puppet therapy enhances finger control as indicated above. As the sample in this study was not randomly selected, there is a risk of selection bias. The techniques of building a Lego robot for Chinese puppets may present difficulties in some researchers; using other robot systems, which are familiar, may overcome this technical limitation. This study focused only on 21 children with CP who were able to manipulate the Chinese puppet through the Lego switches. Future studies regarding modified puppet therapies may focus on establishing fine motor training in larger clinical populations and the use of different outcome measures associated with optimal transfer to real-world functions.

4.2 Conclusion

In conclusion, the primary finding is that highly motivating repeatable motor actions build motor skills in children with CP. The present study provides preliminary research information on modified puppet therapy and its relevance to adaptive play materials, which are important when providing therapy services. A major finding is that simplifying movements and manipulation of puppets through Lego switches promote finger control and functional hand use. By using a Chinese puppet with Lego bricks as play materials, therapists may be able to allow children with CP to overcome resistance using their affected hands.

Acknowledgements. Our thanks to Ministry of Science and Technology in Taiwan for the research funding.

Funding. This research received specific grant from Ministry of Science and Technology in Taiwan (Grant number: MOST 108-2314-B-007-005).

References

1. Fedrizzi, E., Pagliano, E., Andreucci, E.: Hand function in children with hemiplegic cerebral palsy: prospective follow-up and functional outcome in adolescence. Dev. Med. Child Neurol. **45**, 85–91 (2003)
2. Arnould, C., Bleyenheuft, Y., Thonnard, J.L.: Hand functioning in children with cerebral palsy. Front Neurol. **5**, 48 (2014). https://doi.org/10.3389/fneur.2014.00048

3. Bayon, C., Raya, R., Sergio, L.L., et al.: Robotic therapies for children with cerebral palsy: a systematic review. Transl. Biomed. **7**, 1–20 (2016). https://doi.org/10.21767/2172-0479. 100044

4. Meyer-Heim, A., et al.: Improvement of walking abilities after robotic assisted locomotion training in children with cerebral palsy. Arch. Dis. Child. **94**, 615–620 (2009). https://doi. org/10.1136/adc.2008.145458

5. Gilliaux, M., Renders, A., Dispa, D., et al.: Upper limb robot-assisted therapy in cerebral palsy: a single-blind randomized controlled trial. Neurorehabil. Neural Repair **29**(2), 183–192 (2015). https://doi.org/10.1177/1545968314541172

6. Hsieh, H.C.: Effects of ordinary and adaptive toys on pre-school children with developmental disabilities. Res. Dev. Disabil. **28**, 459–466 (2008)

7. Basu, A.P., Pearse, J., Kelly, S., Wisher, V., Kisler, J.: Early intervention to improve hand function in hemiplegic cerebral palsy. Front. Neurol. **5**, 281 (2014). https://doi.org/10.3389/fneur.2014.00281

8. Kao, S.C., Landreth, G.L.: Play therapy with Chinese children: needed modification. In: Landreth, G.L. (ed.) Innovation in Play Therapy: Issues, Process, and Special Populations, pp. 44–49. Brunner-Routledge, Philadephia (2001)

9. Schulz, K., Altman, D.G., Moher, D., et al.: CONSORT 2010 statement: updated guidelines for reporting parallel group randomized trials. Ann. Intern. Med. **152**(11), 726–732 (2010)

10. Bain, G.I., Polites, N., Higgs, B.G., Heptinstall, R.J., McGrath, A.M.: The functional range of motion of the finger joints. J. Hand Surg. Eur. **41**, 386–391 (2014)

11. Dekkers, K.J.F.M., Rameckers, E.A.A., Smeets, R.J.E.M., Janssen-Potten, Y.J.M.: Upper extremity strength measurement for children with cerebral palsy: a system review of available instruments. Phys. Ther. **94**(5), 609–622 (2014)

12. Barut, C., Kiiltan, E., Gelir, E., Köktürk, F.: Advanced analysis of Finger-Tapping Test. Balkan Med. J. **30**, 167–171 (2013)

13. Memisevic, H., Mahmutovic, I., Pasalic, A., Biscevic, I.I.: The effects of age and gender on finger tapping speed in preschool children. Acta Neuropsychologica **15**, 55–62 (2017)

14. Lewandowski, L.L., De Rienzo, P.J.: WISC-R and K-ABC performances of hemiplegic children. J. Psychoeduc. Assess. **3**(3), 215–221 (1985)

15. Alves-Pinto, A., Ehrlich, S., Cheng, G., Turova, V., Blumenstein, T., Lampe, R.: Effects of short-term piano training on measures of finger tapping, somatosensory perception and motor-related brain activity in patients with cerebral palsy. Neuropsychiatr. Dis. Treat. **13**, 2705–2718 (2017)

16. Hsieh, H.C.: Effectiveness of adaptive pretend play on affective expression and imagination of children with cerebral palsy. Res. Dev. Disabil. **33**, 1975–1983 (2012)

17. Hsieh, H.C., Lin, H.Y., Chiu, W.H., Meng, L.F., Liu, C.K.: Upper-limb rehabilitation with adaptive video games for preschool children with developmental disabilities. Am. J. Occup. Therapy **69**, 6904290020p1–6904290020p5 (2015). https://doi.org/10.5014/ajot. 2015.014480

18. Muratori, L.M., Lamberg, E.M., Quinn, L., Duff, S.V.: Applying principles of motor learning and control to upper extremity rehabilitation. J. Hand Ther. **26**(2), 94–103 (2013)

19. Bartlett, D.J., Palisano, R.: Physical therapist's perceptions of factors influencing the acquisition of motor abilities of children with cerebral palsy: implications for clinical reasoning. Phys. Ther. **82**, 237–248 (2002)

20. Snart, F., Maguire, T.: Using puppets to increase children's knowledge and acceptance of handicapped peers. Can. J. Except. Child. **3**, 57–59 (1986)

21. Turner, T.N.: Puppets to put the whole world in their hands. Int. J. Soc. Educ. **18**(1), 35–45 (2003)

22. Caputo, R.A.: Using puppets with students with emotional and behavioral disorders. Interv. Sch. Clin. **29**(1), 26–30 (1993)
23. Salmon, M.D., Sainato, D.M.: Beyond pinocchio: puppets as teaching tools in inclusive early childhood classrooms. Young Except. Child. **8**(3), 12–19 (2005)
24. Beckung, E., Hagberg, G.: Neuroimpairments, activity limitations, and participation restrictions in children with cerebral palsy. Dev. Med. Child Neurol. **55**, 309–316 (2002)

Being Aware of One's Self
in the Auto-generated Chat
with a Communication Robot

Shu Matsuura[1]($^{(\boxtimes)}$) and Reika Omokawa[2]

[1] Faculty of Education, Tokyo Gakugei University,
4-1-1 Nukuikita, Koganei, Tokyo 184-8501, Japan
shumats0@gmail.com
[2] Setagaya Elementary School Attached to Tokyo Gakugei University,
4-10-1 Fukasawa, Setagaya, Tokyo 158-0081, Japan

Abstract. We consider a friendly robot set in the elementary school classroom. The robot should work as an extra existence in the classroom. The robot chat was generated by a recurrent neural network that learned a resource of the students' written sentences. Since the learned data were small, response speeches were imperfect, but some of the students noticed that the robot's words were about the students' activities. Many of the students remarked that they want to have a friendship with the robot, feeling the robot's self through its attitudes of talk and the word resources of students' activities. Chatting with the classroom robot and grow it might be a new way to reflect on students' activities.

Keywords: Communication robot · Chatbot · RNN

1 Introduction

In Japanese elementary schools, the homeroom teacher usually puts up their students' compositions, drawings, works, students' self-profiles, reports from students on duty, various comment cards, together with the posters of learning materials and learning progress. These posters form a classroom environment for learning and living visually and express students' classroom slogan, activities, achievements, hopes, relationships, and values. Students are interested, praise, and encourage each other by watching these presentations. They usually function as positive visual feedback for students.

Recently, using verbal assistance is attracting interest in using smart assistance devices [1, 2]. Smart assistance can work with an online learning system [3]. The assistance system's unifying voice and face detections, speech, and graphics generations and connection to the learning history data are successful for personalized virtual learning assistance [4].

On the other hand, applying communication robots to education is also a rapidly growing area [5]. Usually, the communication robot in a classroom works as an existence conveying its personality for the students. The elementary students have been observed to conclude a robot's life that is different from the life of humans and empathy between robots and humans [6].

© Springer Nature Switzerland AG 2020
M. Antona and C. Stephanidis (Eds.): HCII 2020, LNCS 12188, pp. 477–488, 2020.
https://doi.org/10.1007/978-3-030-49282-3_34

Visual feedback on the learning activities from the classroom environment is without personality based on subjectivity. A customized virtual assistant will convey personality and talk to students as a specific character. As a child talks to a teacher, or as a self-taught scholar asks himself, in-depth learning support shall be continuous dialogs between subjectivity.

This paper is a pilot study of elementary school middle grade students talking with a communication robot, Sota, with a chatbot generated from small resources of students' writings. This study aims to observe if the students have a positive and sympathetic feeling in the dialog with the robot. We expect students to have empathy with the robot that talks with the words that were collected from the corpus of what the students have done and felt. Students' thinking is surveyed from the classroom discussion, robot chat log, and a paper questionnaire.

2   Method

2.1   Classroom and Humanoid Robot

Eighteen male and seventeen female third grade students in a classroom participated in this study. Before this practice, a chatbot with a Google home smart speaker was introduced to the students. This chatbot, named as "Dr. Buddy," is an application of the Actions on Google, created by Matsui [7] as a virtual attendant for the students. The students can call Dr. Buddy in break time via the Google home device and get some drills or questions for fun. Also, Dr. Buddy helped the students to create picture-story shows in a lesson. The students expressed the animal metamorphoses in the picture-story shows. Dr. Buddy provided some hints to the student groups of the form of metamorphoses. In this way, the students participating in this study became more or less familiar with the existence of an invisible speaker in the classroom.

The subject of the entire series of classes in this study was to have a buddy. It aims to help to find oneself by considering the existences that are beneficial for one. When they are asked what they want for their buddies, they replied, "I want a buddy who can play piano" or "I want a pretty one." Then, the teacher asked the students why they want such buddies. The teacher tried to induce the students' metacognition on how they think.

The practice of this study was to talk with a buddy Artificial Intelligence (AI) robot. In contrast to Dr. Buddy, the AI robot is visible and has a cute appearance. The robot is more objectified than the Google speech system. In previous studies, we noticed that many of the participants are interested in the mechanical nature of the robot at an early stage. Through the successive sessions of discussing the robot, the students gradually feel empathy on it.

The communication robot used in this study as the talking partner was Sota ver. 1.26.1 (Social Talker, Vstone Co., Ltd.) [8] developer version with Intel Edison. In this version, an intelligent mic effective in collecting human voices in a noisy environment was equipped. The development environment used was VstoneMagic ver. 1.0.6390.17171. Sota was a table-top size of $280\,(H) \times 140\,(W) \times 160\,(D)$ mm with nine motions. Speech recognition was conducted in a cloud server in which speech-to-text and text-to-speech translation were provided. In the class, Sota was first introduced in front of the students, and later, it was set at a rear corner of the classroom for students to talk to it freely.

2.2   Speech Generation

A set of dialog corpus data was collected from students' written texts to generate words that were related to the students. Since the sizes of the corpus texts were small, as shown in Table 1, they were not enough to reproduce perfect sentences. This study, however, restricted the dialog corpus in the range of the students' writings to remind the students of themselves.

Table 1. Sizes of the students' texts used as the corpus of the chatbot

Contents	Num. of characters	Num. of sentences	Num. of words
Individual study projects during summer vacation (1)	5 510	239	3 400
Individual study projects during summer vacation (2)	4 916	279	2 881
Which buddies the students want	1 456	70	870
Students' reflections on school life in the spring	5 936	302	3 523
Students' scenarios of picture-paper shows	3 370	198	2 157
Various things about Sota	3 318	168	1 926
Students' short essays on rain	4 420	196	2 749
Total	28 926	1 452	17 506

Besides, since most of the sentences of writings were monologs, the generated responses to the human utterances often appeared to not make sense to the questions. Generated words, as a whole, however, expressed students' interests, feelings, works, and activities.

Chinese characters of students' writings were first changed to hiragana and kata-kana, the cursive syllabaries to produce responses to any questions that were not directly concerned with the contents of the corpus. The maximum number of characters for text analysis was 50. The library used for the recurrent neural network, RNN, was Keras with a batch size of 20, and with 128 neurons in the middle layer. The number of epochs calculated was around 100. The EarlyStopping Seq2Seq model was used for learning.

The chatbot application was implemented in a flask server. Sota sends a URL request to a web server, and the server transmits with the flask chatbot server to get a response phrase. Then, the response phrase is sent back to Sota.

2.3 Classroom Practices and Data Acquisition

One of the authors led the classroom as the class teacher as follows.

(L1) Before the robot sessions, the teacher asked what type of buddy the students wish to have.

(L2) The teacher introduced robot Sota as an example of the form of a future buddy for individuals or families. In the first session, the teacher set Sota on the front desk, and ten students asked questions to Sota. Then, the teacher asked the students questions about Sota's type of personality. Students only paid attention if Sota directly answered what the student asked.

(L3) In a second session with Sota, the teacher urged students to pay attention to what Sota responded. Then, one of the students in the groups talked to Sota and those who could follow what Sota said raised their hands and repeated what it said. Finally, the students discussed what Sota wanted to express. After this session, the teacher set Sota in a corner of the classroom for students to talk to.

(L4) The teacher administered a questionnaire survey to the students on the origin of Sota's talk and what Sota's speech expressed. The questions were as follows:

1. Sota eats electricity to drive the mechanic and its computer. Also, it eats words to talk. Whose words do you think Sota eats? Why do you think so?

2. What kind of feeling do Sota's words express? Can you explain why you think so?

3. If you have something to tell Sota, please write down.

Question 1, 2 examine whether the students noticed that their words were the basis of Sota's speech, and it reflected students' activities and wishes. Question 3 intends to let students encourage themselves unintentionally.

3 Results and Discussion

3.1 What Students Wish from Their Buddies

The title of this series of classroom sessions was "Have your buddy." Students imagined what their buddies would be. At the beginning of the series of these sessions, the teacher asked students what they want from their buddies.

Table 2 categorizes the students' wishes. The number of students who expected practical functionalities (35) was a little less than the students who expected psychological supports (38). Many of the practical convenience they claimed were more or less unrealistic, such as "It buys anything I want," or "It brings me anywhere I like." Thus, they simply consider themselves and do not care about empathy for the buddy. The buddies that help students' learning, enjoy hobbies with students, and provide wisdom, however, were a conscious existence.

Table 2. Types of abilities the students want from their buddies. The numbers in the right column show the numbers of students' descriptions. Many of the students wrote more than one description.

Super-category	Sub-category	Num. of comments
Practical and specific roles	It fulfills any of the students' wishes conveniently	20
	It helps students' learning	5
	The students can share their hobbies with their buddies	3
	Students can be free if their buddies work instead	3
	It provides the right knowledge and judgment	2
Psychological and abstract roles	It provides psychological support; it is an affectionate target	28
	It is strong enough to protect a student from difficulties	6
	It is so cute and portable	4

Psychological support includes "I want a brother/sister," and "I feel sad when there is no one who plays with me." Students expected that their probable buddies should make up for loneliness, should support kindness and joy, and encourage them. They required a being that stayed close and always cared about their emotional requirements. In these cases, the students had some images of the relationship between them and their buddies.

3.2 Talk with Sota

In the first talking session, L2, the students made about 14 utterances. Correct speech recognition was obtained in five (5) out of 14 utterances. This low recognition rate is attributable to the students' unclear pronunciations, the distances between the robot and the students' sitting positions, and environmental noise.

Although it is natural for a first-time talk, the students uttered question-and-answer type dialogs, such as "Are you fine?" "What do you like?" "What is your favorite play?" "Do you like the principal?" or "What do you hate?" The students, therefore, expected direct answers to these questions. The resultant dialogs, however, were, for example:

Human: "What do you like?" Sota: "It was beginning (insect) collection."
Human: "Do you like the principal?" Sota: "I thought, I was thinking it was."

In the cases misrecognition was severe, the response phrases were vaguer. Still, the students responded livelily in response to Sota's utterances, and again Sota responded accordingly.

After having a dialog with Sota, the teacher asked the students to talk about what type of robot Sota was. Table 3 summarizes the students' comments. The students seemed impressed by Sota's responses to their utterances. This impression raised positive images of Sota, as shown in the second column of the table. At the same time, the students interpreted Sota's responses as immature in verbal skills and attitudes toward humans.

These images are the personification of the robot, although the appearance of Sota is not so human-like. The students interpreted the speech skills of Sota as in a developmental process. Some of the students also asked Sota's age.

Then, the teacher asked the students why they regarded Sota as a human child. The students looked instantaneously illuminated by this question and tried to understand why they think that. A student summarized that he thought of Sota as human because he heard Sota's words were those he usually used. Using common words was found essential to have empathy.

Table 3. Discussions on "What kind of child is Sota?"

Questions	Students' descriptions (positive side)	Students' descriptions (negative side)
What kind of child is Sota?	It likes to talk	It does not understand what it means
	It responds well	We hardly understand what it wants to say It says incomprehensible words
	It is active	It is naughty It says anything it wants to say It is a little child It is immature, just like beginning to talk
Can we consider it the same as a human?	Because it talks and it has hands	Because the teacher asked us what kind of child it was
Why do we regard Sota as a human?	Because I am a human, and it says the words I usually use	

The students are interested in Sota's talk. In the 20 min break after session L2, about ten students came to chat with and touch Sota. When they could contact the robot, many of them looked interested, specifically in the mechanical aspect of the robot.

Twelve days after session L2, the students had a second talking session L3 with Sota. In the previous session, L2, many of the students were observed to not follow what Sota said. Instead, students were keen on whether Sota responded directly to the students' questions. Some students seemed to give up listening to what Sota said once they found Sota's response did not engage with their questions.

Then, the teacher asked the students to pay specific attention to Sota's words and to repeat after Sota. They tracked 25 responses out of 30 dialogs. The average tracked number of characters (using kanji and kana) was 11 ± 3 characters. The average number of characters (using kanji and kana) was 17 ± 6.

After clarifying what the students heard, the teacher asked them what Sota tried to say. Table 4 summarizes the students' comments from the surface to the depth, from top to bottom of the table. The students positively assume Sota's attitude and intent and then guessed the skills required to achieve it. Furthermore, as seen in the bottom row, at least one student noticed that what Sota said related to what the students in the classroom have done or written before. Students tried to understand Sota favorably and noticed that many of Sota's words related to what the students had written before.

Table 4. Students' impressions and remarks on Sota's talk

Category	Students' comments
State of words	It replies things different from what was questioned
Attitude to respond	It even tries to begin talking before humans finish questioning
	It accepts human questioning
	It listens to human questioning roughly
	It tries to talk about what it knows
	It says what it wants to say just now
Ability to respond	It forms a phrase by connecting the words that it knows
	Since it does not know enough variety of words, it repeats the same words
	It must be comprehending (what human wants to say), but it still cannot arrange words to respond appropriately
Content of response	It talks about what we (humans) have done before

Figure 1 shows the frequency order of the verbs, nouns, and adjectives in the response phrases of Sota. The most frequent noun was *self (I)*, with frequent verbs such as *be, think, say*, and *consider*. Also, the noun of *involvement* is notable. This implies Sota's frequent referral to subjectivity. Then, the words *play, meet, talk*, or *go* express activities of students' writings in the original corpus texts. These words might reactivate the student's memory.

Figure 2 shows the frequency order of the verbs and nouns in the original corpus text. Again *self (I)* is the third frequent noun. The noun words frequent in the Sota's response phrases were different from the norms frequent in the corpus. The frequent norms represent the contents of subtexts, as shown in Table 1, in other words, how human utterances affect the extraction of words from the corpus.

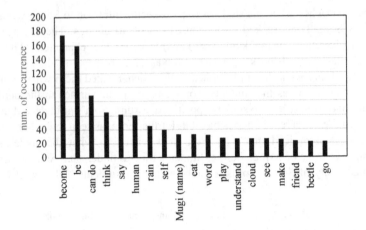

Fig. 1. Frequencies of words generated in the response phrases. a) Frequency of verb b) Noun and adjective

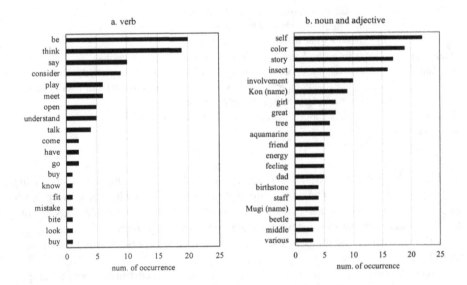

Fig. 2. Frequencies of words in the original corpus texts

3.3 Questionnaire Survey

One week after the second talking session, L3, a questionnaire survey, L4, described in Sect. 2.3, was conducted in the classroom. To recall Sota's talk, the questionnaire paper provided the following summary as "the words used repeatedly: self, make, for this, story, play, time, and be" and "the words used almost once: aquamarine, mineral, birthstone, aluminum, beetle, school lunch, and Mugi (name)."

Figure 3 shows the categorized answer distributions. In the figure, the principal means the person who programed Sota's application used was the principal of the school. As shown in Fig. 3a, 48% of the students answered that it was the principal's words and did not pursue the characteristics of the contents any further.

"Unspecified people" in Fig. 3b means that instead of considering a specific person and his/her role, 36% of the students identified a person whose words might have been used. Examples of personality were kind, gentle, and important. Also, this category includes those who speak clearly and those repeat specific words.

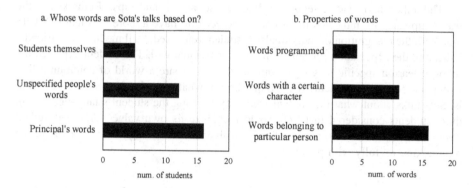

Fig. 3. How students perceived the source of Sota's talks. a) The number of the categorized answers for the question on whose words Sota's talks are based b) The number of students' descriptions on the corpus texts categorized into three types

The remaining 15% of the students described that Sota might absorb the words heard from the students themselves. A student wrote that since the words were repeated, they were valuable. The students do not know the mechanism of the chatbot system. As Sota's responses were, in many cases, imperfect, the students naturally considered that Sota's ability to generate sentences was in the process of growing. Then, many of the students felt that Sota was trying to say what they tried to say. This attitude coincided with what they wanted to express or respond to and transformed what they conceive into the words. The students projected this fundamental desire on the robot.

Figure 3b categorizes the characteristics of Sota's words that the students describe. Fifty-two percent (52%) described words as belonging to a specific person such as the principal or students themselves. Thirty-five percent (35%) described words with some characteristics such as "funny person's words," "talkative person's words," "good person's words," "if it absorbs a good person's words, Sota's talk will be polite and useful in various situations," "important person's words," "Sota will listen to the persons who are important for it," "friendly person's words," and "if it learns the words of unfriendly person, it will hurt everyone."

Question 2 asked what Sota's words mean. Of the students, 87% described what Sota might feel, and 13% described students' feelings as the source of Sota's talk, as follows: what we want to do, what we consider valuable, feelings to praise people, and the desire to make friends with everyone and tell them about myself. Being able to think in terms of the students' language can allow them to use their imaginations beyond inferencing from superficial attitudes.

Question 3 asked students to say anything to Sota. The students wrote one or more things to tell Sota. Table 5 categorized the students' remarks to the question. Half of them focused on the language function of Sota, and the other half had sympathetic remarks to Sota. In the students' expression, the requests to raise Sota's language function were, in most cases, written as if advice from elders. There were no rude expressions.

The other half was categorized into praise and friendships. Remarks in the friendship category indicated that students expected to have a more personal talk with Sota with the recognition of individuals. A student remarked, "tell me to be my friend," indicating the expectation for Sota to have an individual will. The student expected the robot to learn a specific language from him/her and share a world of communication with the robot. Three students wrote a question of what and who the robot values. That is, Sota talks about what the student values by learning the student's language. Then, these students considered that Sota could recognize its own values. Another student wrote a promise to Sota to become friends with anyone. He might be impressed to see Sota talking joyfully with people.

Table 5. What the students want to tell Sota. The numbers in the parentheses in the 1st and 2nd columns indicate the number of students.

Category	Student attitude	Students' remarks	Num. of students
Function (18)	Request (18)	Learn how to speak	8
		Learn more words	7
		Learn meanings of words	3
Relationship (19)	Praise (8)	You talk well, do your best	6
		We enjoy, thank you	1
		You are cute	1
	Friendship (11)	Please be a friend	7
		What do you value? Who do you value?	3
		I *promise* that I'll be a friend with anyone	1

Thus, despite the generation of responses being quite imperfect and many of the students are unaware that the responses come from their words, many of them expect to have a relationship with the robot and expect it to grow. The students expected psychological support from their imagined buddy. The corpus for the chat generation is a combination of the students' writings that consisted of positive, hopeful, and praising words. For students, Sota's talks were interpreted as Sota's concern with itself since the frequency of the word *self* in Sota's responses was high, as seen in Fig. 1b. Sota passionately talked about what it knew with the words that came initially from the students. This situation is interpreted as the students observing and talking to themselves, and that they have positive feelings for their relationship with Sota.

Also, as a student remarked, *what we value* conversation resources are class-based, even though the dialog is one-on-one. The feedback effect of crowd psychology by collecting strong crowd membership indicates that if an individual receives a message from a crowdsource the individual will be excessively adaptive to the crowd. If the feedback comes from an individual resource, it might cause excessive adaptation to oneself. In the Japanese elementary schools, students' drawings, works, and compositions are posted indoors and outdoors. This is a visual method for growing and accepting students as a class membership. Classroom dialog in this study is an exploration of the classroom member language activities. This method requires students to talk with the robot to extract and relate words, and in this process, they might positively recognize the robot as an existence having a subjectivity.

4 Concluding Remarks

This paper presented a pilot study of an elementary school classroom session of talking with a communication robot Sota. Sota's talk was formed from the written compositions of the classroom students as the corpus. Through two-session practices, the students talked and listened to Sota's responses. Although Sota's responses were not exact answers to the students' questions, 15% of the students noticed that Sota's talk might come from classroom member activities. In the messages to Sota, half of the students encouraged Sota's language to be more accurate, and the other half referred to having a friendship with Sota. The students experienced the robot's self through its attitude of talk and the word resources of students' activities. Talking with the classroom robot and to grow it is a new way to reflect the contexts of class member activities.

Acknowledgments. The authors thank Kyohei Matsui for developing an application of a digital assistance that stimulated students' interests prior to this study. The authors also thank Enago for English corrections. This work was partly funded by a Grant-in-Aid for Scientific Research (C) 19K02806 from the Ministry of Education, Culture, Sports, Science and Technology.

References

1. Pearl, C.: Designing Voice User Interface. O'Reilly Media (2017)
2. Dousay, T.A., Hall, C.: Alexa, tell me about using a Virtual Assistant in the Classroom. EdMedia + Innovate Learning, 2018, pp. 1413–1419 (2018)
3. Kita, T., Nagaoka, C., Hiraoka, N., Dougiamas, M.: Implementation of voice user interfaces to enhance users' activities on Moodle. In: 4th International Conference on Information Technology (InCIT), Bangkok, pp. 104–107 (2019)
4. Iannizzotto, G., Bello, L.L., Nucita, A., Grasso, G.M.: A vision and speech enabled customizable, virtual assistant for smart environments. In: 2018 11th International Conference on Human System Interaction (HSI), pp. 50–56 (2018)

5. He, B., Xia, M., Yu, X., Jian, P., Meng, H., Chen, Z.: An educational robot system of visual question answering for preschoolers. In: 2017 2nd International Conference on Robotics and Automation Engineering (ICRAE), pp. 441–445 (2017)
6. Omokawa, R., Matsuura, S.: Development of thought using a humanoid robot in an elementary school classroom. LNCS Univ. Access in Hum.-Comput. Interaction **10908**, 541–552 (2018)
7. Matsui, K., Matsuura, S. (2020, unpublished)
8. Vstone Co., Ltd., https://www.vstone.co.jp/products/sota/. Accessed 20 Feb 2020

Voice User Interfaces for Service Robots: Design Principles and Methodology

Pepi Stavropoulou[1], Dimitris Spiliotopoulos[2],
and Georgios Kouroupetroglou[1(✉)]

[1] National and Kapodistrian University of Athens, Athens, Greece
{pepis,koupe}@di.uoa.gr
[2] University of the Peloponnese, Tripoli, Greece
dspiliot@uop.gr

Abstract. This work presents the concerns, prerequisites, and methods for building interaction interfaces for service robots. It mainly deals with Voice User Interfaces - VUI (also called Spoken Dialogue Interfaces - SDIs) but also includes issues on multimodal interfaces, involving speech and other modalities. Human-machine interaction in the area of robotics raises certain challenges that respective interface design for other domains ignores. Robots, and more importantly, service robots, execute actual tasks based on plans and scenarios that, in effect, layout their usage. The completion requirements, as well as the workflow needed for those tasks, form a very significant set of rules that affect and sometimes govern the interaction between the user and the machine. Those rules are embedded to the design of the interaction system and, together with the communicated context, provide the sets and constraints that the system is based upon. These constraints can be realized in the form of specific dialogue management design, dialogue flow, belief states models, verification, disambiguation, and grounding techniques as well as more subtly use of specific speech and dialogue acts – all the above affect all stages of the lifecycle. Moreover, significant merit goes to usability, and the techniques for its evaluation, issues that are of the utmost importance when any user-machine interface is designed and assessed.

Keywords: Voice User Interfaces · Service robots · Spoken dialogue interaction · Usability evaluation · Computer-mediated communication

1 Introduction

In the recent years, the technology has allowed the idea of robotic assistants and services to become feasible for certain domains (health-related assistance, disability, help for the elderly, office assistants, etc.), where they are used for a variety of tasks by a variety of non-expert users. Nowadays, service robots have been developed to assist people at their homes and workplaces, performing household chores, delivering objects and responding to inquiries about the weather or the TV program among others. In this sense, it has become increasingly important that robots are designed to become part of the lives of ordinary people, enabling a more natural, intuitive, and effective mode of communication. To address this requirement, a considerable amount of research has

© Springer Nature Switzerland AG 2020
M. Antona and C. Stephanidis (Eds.): HCII 2020, LNCS 12188, pp. 489–505, 2020.
https://doi.org/10.1007/978-3-030-49282-3_35

been dedicated to the development of Spoken Dialogue Interfaces (SDIs) as a cornerstone aspect of Human-Robot Interaction (HRI). This trend has become more obvious now as a key area of research, spanning from mobile devices to robotics.

Voice User Interfaces utilize spoken language as the most natural and powerful means of human communication to maximize the usability of human-machine interfaces. Depending on the particular type of SDIs, different levels of flexibility and robustness in handling spoken input and output are allowed. Thus, Spoken Dialogue Systems (SDSs) may range from simple finite-state systems that handle a limited number of commands, to more advanced systems capable of inference and planning as part of a more collaborative view of interaction.

While in general-purpose SDSs, such as call routing or ticketing, the term VUI has mostly been reserved for systems that use open-ended prompts, large vocabularies, and flexible dialogue structure, for HRI in particular, the term has sometimes been used to describe systems that employ speech in the simple form of a command language as opposed or in addition to other less intuitive modalities such as GUIs and buttons. Such systems, however, are far from resembling natural human-human conversation, and their deviation from the user's natural discourse patterns often places a considerable load on cognition and hinders learnability On the other hand, the collaborative and socially-oriented nature of a service robot's tasks has led to the development of architectures that can incorporate advanced natural language processing techniques involving inference, dialogue act identification and anaphora resolution among others; more advanced practical systems have started to emerge, which – even though they make limited use of understood vocabulary and syntax – are an important first step towards truly natural HRI.

In the following sections, we will first present the basic implications, advantages, and disadvantages, as well as motivation for building SDIs for service robots. Next we will elaborate on the communicative principles that are especially important for the development of usable systems and as such map outline the requirements for the interface design. Sections 4 and 5 discuss design and evaluation methodologies for service robots. Finally, Sect. 6 touches upon more advanced subjects such as social skills, emotions, autonomy, and adaptation in robotic systems.

2   Motivation for Spoken Dialogue Interfaces

Simply put, SDI is the means of communication that the majority of people are inherently equipped and familiarized with since birth. It is the most intuitive, natural, and powerful tool in human communication. As such, it constitutes the most promising means of interaction in the emerging field of service robots, in which nonexpert users need not just to operate the robot but work with it in order to accomplish specific tasks. This is particularly important if one considers that a significant application area for service robots is helping the elderly, who are most often "technology-unaware" and have difficulties interacting in ways they are not familiar with [1, 2]. In this respect, spoken language interfaces that can only handle a limited set of commands with a fixed set of arguments, rigid preconditions, and task completion requirements (cf. points on "under-specification" in the following section) are similarly ineffective and unfriendly, as the user needs to memorize these commands adjusting to the interface contrary to a more user-centered approach in which the interface adapts to the user. Likewise, companion robots – robots that engage in conversations in a socially acceptable manner, often displaying personality traits and emotions – constitute systems that, by definition, go beyond the realm of simple command and control interfaces.

Furthermore, as service robots evolve, the variety and number of tasks they can perform increases, while at the same time, they are involved in a constantly changing, dynamic situation setting, which makes it difficult to pre-specify tasks at hand and model them in the form of stand-alone commands. The latter necessitates the use of spoken language for the development of an easier to use interface that compensates for the complexity of tasks implemented in the task manager, by providing a more flexible dialogue structure, loosening requirements on user input, handling under-specification, reference, feedback, and grounding. In addition, VUIs allows users to teach the robot contributing to an increase in robot's adaptation, learning ability and autonomy [3, 4]. In general, there is a tendency that service robots are no longer considered as simple tools, means to an end but as collaborative partners with specific social and communicative skills [5]. This view is served better through spoken language and is often intensified by the physical embodiment of the robot itself. Humanoid appearance especially triggers certain expectations on the part of the users that are, in turn, more likely to apply human-human communication principles for HRI compared to ordinary human-computer interfaces.

Finally, the use of speech ensures a design-for-all approach to robotic system design. Universal Design and accessibility denote that an application is designed in such way so that it may be used by people "with different abilities, requirements and preferences in a variety of contexts of use" [6]. Apart from providing an alternative means of interaction to users such as the elderly or people with limited dexterity, speech is also best suited for hands/eyes busy situations and multitasking. The latter is common for home or office users that may be engaged in other tasks while addressing the service robot. In the same manner, multimodality is important, enabling robust communication in situations where speech is not optimal (e.g., high noise levels, workgroup settings, teleoperation). After all, natural human conversation is not restricted to speech but is accompanied by other means such as gestures, facial expressions or posture that also convey attitudes and meaning.

The above claims are corroborated by surveys conducted to assess users' preference of modalities, in which users demonstrated a preference for spoken language as a means of interaction. Torta et al. [7] report a clear user preference for natural spoken language, followed by touch screen, gestures and command language, when interacting with a household service robot [7]. Still, overall results indicated that users favor the availability of more than one, complementary means of interaction, opting for multimodality, where available. It is still the case that for specific service robot interfaces, the detection of the presence of the user as well as the activity can be recognized and modeled in such ways as to trigger multimodality [5].

On the other hand, there are certain drawbacks in using VUIs, which – if not taken into account – may deprive the system of any practical use. First of all, speech recognition conditions in real-life settings may involve high levels of noise-causing degradation of the recognizer's performance. To address automatic speech recognition

(ASR) limitations, most robotic systems use a limited vocabulary set reaching a few hundred words at most [1, 8]. By limiting the recognizer's search space, they could achieve over 90% recognition success rate under lab test, normal/low noise conditions [9]. As a drawback the out of vocabulary rate (OOV) in users' utterances addressed to the system may increase especially in non-controlled, real-life conditions with little or no user training. Other issues concern the difficulty of long-distance (far-field) speech recognition, identification of the voice source, and identification of commands addressed to the robot in workgroup environments.

Finally, another important parameter that should be taken into account is the degree of computational efficiency affected by the use of sophisticated and computationally costly speech processing algorithms. It should be noted that even without SDI capabilities, service robots can be very complex, comprised of several modules working in parallel (e.g., navigation, visual object identification, task planning) that must respond efficiently in real-time. This necessitates VUI techniques that are easy to specify and maintain and lead to robust and fast input processing.

3 Related Work

A typical spoken dialogue system embedded in a service robot consists of the following components:

- The Speech Recognizer that converts the user's spoken input into a text string. Typical speech recognizers for service robots handle only a limited in- domain vocabulary. Hand-written, context-free rule-based grammars are used that determine the recognizer's space based on the developer's expectations of what users are likely to say [10]. Alternatively, some works have utilized real use corpora collected through Wizard of Oz settings and user testing [1] or handwritten utterances based on usage scenarios [8], in order to train statistical language models for recognition.
- The Natural Language Understanding (NLU) module that semantically interprets the string passed by the speech recognizer. A commonly used method for semantic analysis is based on semantic augmentations attached to grammar and lexicon rules to fill in dedicated slot values or construct predicate-like meaning representations relative to the task at hand for service robots [11].
- The Dialogue Manager (DM) that evaluates and reassess the NLU input with regards to dialogue history, conversation principles, specific task, domain and user knowledge, in order to decide upon the next dialogue step and fulfill a specific strategy.
- The Natural Language Generation (NLG) component produces an appropriate concrete language response based on the DMs abstract input. Simple NLG techniques that are most commonly used involve template filling methods, in which system utterances are, to a large extent, predefined. Otherwise, more advanced methods involving discourse planning and surface realization of utterances may be used [12]. Also, some NLG components add prosodic annotations to the word string, providing an enriched input to Concept-to-Speech synthesizers [13, 14].

- The Speech Synthesizer that converts NLG text input to speech. Typically, off the shelf speech synthesizers are used that are naive to discourse structure and context properties. Concept to Speech synthesizers, on the other hand, are more advanced systems that may utilize contextual information passed from the NLG module for producing appropriate, context-aware utterance intonation [15, 16].

Depending on the technology used and the specifics of the dialogue management component, in particular, there are three main types of spoken dialogue systems [12, 17]: state-based, frame-based, and more advanced information state architectures. State-based and frame-based systems have been the most commonly used so far due to their ease in development and low computational cost.

State-based systems represent dialogue as a predefined series of states, whereas the user is expected to provide specific input in a particular order. This makes the user's utterances easier to predict, leading to faster development and more robust recognition and interpretation at the expense of limited flexibility in the structure of the dialogues. Their limited flexibility, however, often renders them less appropriate for complex tasks. Frame-based systems represent dialogue as a list of slots each slot corresponding to pieces of information that the system needs to acquire to perform a task. They offer a higher level of flexibility compared to state-based models, as the dialogue is not completely pre-determined, and a limited level of mixed-initiative is allowed. That is, the system formulates questions to fill in particular slots that remain empty, but the user may take the initiative in the dialogue and provide more information than asked. This additional information is used to fill in more slots, saving the user from having to answer subsequent questions, and leading to more efficient dialogues compared to state-based approaches [9, 18–20]. Some of these approaches are combined with more advanced features such as pronoun resolution or basic speech act identification, increasing the system's robustness while minimizing computational cost [10].

Information state systems, on the other hand, make use of sophisticated discourse models in order to represent and update dialogue context, interpret and generate dialogue acts, identify, form, and execute conversational goals and plans. Such systems are equipped with advanced inference, reference resolution, speech act interpretation and grounding capabilities. As such, they can accommodate a greater degree of flexibility and mixed-initiative and are suitable for complex, collaborative tasks where the series of actions that need to be performed and the particular pieces of information required are hard to predict in advance. Their implementation and maintenance, however, is far more complex and computationally expensive compared to state or frame-based systems. Wilske and Kruijff (2006) presented an example of a service robot that incorporates a more advanced, information state architecture [11]. The system uses a BDI (Belief, Desire, Intention) module to mediate between subsystems for different modalities. It exploits knowledge about the preceding discourse, the situational context, and the task in order to referentially and rhetorically resolve the current utterance's linguistic context, infer user goals through indirect speech act identification, take initiative, ask for help and clarifications when necessary, and learn about the environment it operates in through the understanding and production of natural language.

4 Service Robot HRI: Communication and Design Principles

Service robots situated in people's everyday lives aiming to co-operatively accomplish specific tasks, often serving as human companions, need to interact with people on a more social level. It is, in fact, this elevated, enriched form of interaction with people in natural, unstructured, everyday environments that fundamentally differentiates them from traditional industrial robots. Though limitations of current technology render a truly natural, human-like HRI an issue of a not so near future, HRI design could benefit from incorporating knowledge of human communication principles. Taking into account people's well known tendency to attribute human-like characteristics to machines [21] it is reasonable to expect that people will be inclined to apply human-like conversation principles especially when interacting with a robot whose physical stature may encourage such behaviour. In fact, it is no wonder that people unconsciously apply conversational behavior that is implicitly learned and used from a very young age even when they are advised against it. Hüttenrauch et al. (2003) reported that people used gestures to navigate a service robot even though they were told beforehand that the robot was incapable of understanding such input [22].

At the heart of each dialogue, determining conversational behavior is the communicative situation itself. The "who", "when", "where", "why" and "what about" of communication determine the form and the content of the message. An example application of this principle is user modeling. Robots designed as museum tour guides, for instance, utilize knowledge of the humans that they will interact with (adults, children, experts, artists), in order to properly adjust their personality, behavior, and roles.

Most importantly, though, understanding of the situational context is a prerequisite for effective interaction and successful task fulfillment. A crucial difference between service robots employing spoken natural language and other spoken dialogue systems is the importance of the situational – including the visual – context for the former. Human-robot dialogue is a principally situated dialogue, "a spatially embedded interaction" [23, 24] in the sense that robots need to identify and perform actions on elements of a shared environment having established a correspondence between the human and the robot's perception of the environment's spatial organization. To do that, robots need to make and resolve reference to temporal and spatial aspects of the interaction, interpret pronouns, ellipsis and so forth. Such requirements lead to the adoption of more advanced dialogue management techniques and discourse models that make use of rich dialogue history and context representation, as well as sophisticated inference mechanisms based on task knowledge, knowledge of conversation principles, and current information state in general. Seemingly simple commands such as "Turn right here" or "Bring it to me" involve the not so trivial task of resolving anaphoric expressions such as "here" and "it" to salient discourse referents.

Furthermore, as users cannot be expected to unambiguously provide all information required for the robot to perform an action, robotic systems further need to address under-specification, incomplete user input, which does not fulfill the robot's knowledge preconditions. The omission of some detail is almost inevitable in all human communication. In an experiment examining spatial, direction tasks using a wheelchair robot, Tenbrink and Hui (2007) reported that users were often vague in their descriptions as well as unaware or uncertain about the level of detail that is required for the robot to unambiguously establish a spatial goal [23]. Therefore, advanced dialogue modeling techniques were required in order to either infer missing information based on discourse context or explicitly ask for it through clarifications and info requests. With regard to the latter, Tenbrink and Hui [23] point out that clarifications should depend on discourse history and be formulated based on previous user input and grounded knowledge rather than being generic clarifications [23]. This way user's and robot's perceptions are better matched, and confusion and uncertainty are reduced.

Another pertinent and most significant aspect of communication is grounding [25, 26]. Grounding is the establishment of common ground among the interlocutors. The term refers to the goal and process of achieving mutual understanding within the dialogue and acknowledging this understanding, thus making the other participant confident of the progress made to fulfill the dialogue's goal. The establishment and communication of shared understanding are primarily achieved through feedback. There are several means for providing feedback, both verbal and non-verbal. Examples of the former are relative next turns, verbatim repetition or paraphrasing of the interlocutor's previous utterance, backchannels such "uh-huh" and "hmm," explicit acknowledgments such as "I see," use of discourse markers such as "well" or even emotional prosody providing feedback on speaker's attitude. Non-verbal means for production of feedback, demonstration of attention and awareness are eye-gaze and face/object tracking mechanisms, as well as simple gestures such as nodding or pointing. Even a blinking indicator light on the robot may provide feedback that the system is on and hearing. Building on Clark and Schaefer (1989) [26], Brennan and Hulteen (1995) proposed a multimodal model of eight levels of feedback associated with specific system states, ranging from pointing out that the system is attending or not to notifications regarding intent and initialization of task execution, and reporting on task execution outcome [27]. This model was partly implemented in the development of Cero, a mobile service robot for object delivery [5].

A widely used strategy for achieving common ground, providing feedback and addressing potential problems in understanding is confirmations and clarifications. Confirmations may be explicit or implicit. In the former case, the system directly assesses the correctness of its understanding by asking a targeted yes/no question. In the case of implicit confirmation, the system combines what has been understood with a question for a missing argument in a theme-rheme informational organization of the produced utterance [23, 28, 29]. Note that, again, verbal confirmation may be accompanied and reinforced by appropriate gestures. The confirmation strategy followed – explicit or implicit – depends on various parameters: ASR confidence scores and error cost estimation are most commonly used [30], while robotic systems may also use task knowledge and dialogue history to identify inconsistent commands or plan execution failure and decide upon the subsequent dialogue act (e.g., confirmation, elaboration, clarification etc.). For example, when a robot recognizes that it cannot fulfill a request (e.g. the user asks the robot to fetch an object that is not part of the shared spatial organization), it may ask for confirmation or clarification.

Studies with service robots have demonstrated the importance of feedback for the quality and efficiency of the interaction [31]. Observations have been reported with regards to users of standard SDSs who are often confused when the system does not explicitly acknowledge shared understanding [32]. In general, grounding and feedback are especially important for HRI, also given the limitations of current ASR and NLU systems as well as users' proclaimed skepticism and occasional lack of trust towards new generation robotic systems.

Another aspect of communication that is often exploited by current robotic systems is the notion of speech dialogue acts. There are three types of speech acts [33]: (a) locutionary acts, that is the utterance that is produced and its literal meaning, (b) illocutionary, the acts that the speaker performs when producing this utterance, e.g., asking, asserting, requesting, etc. and (c) perlocutionary acts, the result of the utterance upon the hearer's beliefs, actions and so forth. A robotic system should be able to identify and reason about speech acts, in order to identify the user's intentions and plan its course of actions accordingly. However, identification of speech acts is not a trivial task, as they are based on the speaker's cognitive state, and there is no one to one correspondence between surface syntactic structure and illocutionary act type. For example, a sentence such as "Can you bring me a cup of coffee?" could in principle be a yes/no question or a request. Therefore, systems that merely make use of syntactic mood to identify speech acts risk misinterpreting users' intentions even for small domains. For an example of a more advanced BDI model that infers illocutionary and perlocutionary acts based on plan recognition techniques, interested readers may refer to Allen (1995) [34]. Wilske and Kruijff (2006) also present a more sophisticated approach to indirect speech act identification for service robots; that is identification of illocutionary acts that are produced with a syntactic form other than the one they are conventionally associated with (for example an interrogative utterance that is used to perform a request instead of an imperative) [11].

5 Designing Service Robot HRI

There are five main stages in the lifecycle of a Spoken Dialogue Interface:

- Requirements specification and initial planning
- Design
- Implementation and testing. The SDI components are developed and integrated with other system components. Unit, system and user testing is performed
- Deployment. The market-ready system is released to real users
- Evaluation: data is collected from real-life use, and the system is monitored and tuned accordingly

This section focuses on the requirements specification and design steps of the methodology. During these steps, the system functionality is analyzed, and design decisions are made resulting in a complete, detailed specification of the dialogue that serves as input to the development phase. Questionnaires and user interviews, development of usage scenarios [22] are some of the tools employed at this early stage. Furthermore, WOZ simulations [35] are the dominant method for evaluating early design choices for service robots SDIs [22, 23, 36].

In order to decide on key dialogue characteristics, designers need to perform thorough analyses of the users, their goals and needs, of the tasks to be performed, as well as the particular settings, whereas the interaction takes place. The latter is specifically important for the development of service robots, which are particularly sensitive to the situational context. In fact, designers should cater not only for primary user needs but also for bystanders and secondary users that may interfere with robot's task execution [22]. Furthermore, the variability of the scenarios and the spatial organization and context constraints pertaining to a situated interaction place upmost significance on the analysis of the "abstract" communicative situation, in order to maximize system's robustness and usability. In this sense, the development lifecycle should not just be user-centred – and much less robot (system)-centred – but rather usability and situation-centred. That is, the shared world in which the interaction draws the information from, commends the parameters of the communication that are then shaped from the user requirements and the tasks that the service robot is designed to perform. As an example, robots designed as museum tour guides have different knowledge of their environment, the humans that will interact with them (adults, children, experts, artists), their services and roles, and their personality. On the other hand, robotic assistants for the elderly have different requirements, workspace (mostly homes), target users (elderly people), and roles. The requirements for multimodal interaction, noisy environment, multiple users or user groups, personalization (for types of users), and social skills are essential for the former. Robust spoken language interaction, dedicated services for specific needs, simplified interface design, and communication are essential for the latter.

In other respects, standard principles that apply to the development of usable human-machine interfaces, apply to SDIs for robotic systems as well:

- iterative testing, design and build process, whereas design choices are re-evaluated and refined at each iteration
- user involvement from the early stages of the system lifecycle as part of user-centered design
- adherence to conversation principles such as grounding, context awareness and turn-taking
- adherence to general usability principles such as clarity and consistency
- focus on error handling and dialog repair, given that there is no error-free human-machine communication or even human-human communication for that matter
- building on the "natural" mental model that first-time users bring to the interaction, i.e., their existing – and possibly expected – view of the interaction, based on their experience and understanding of how things have worked so far.

The success of an interface greatly depends on the correspondence between this "natural" mental model and the proposed model afforded by the design of the interface [35, 37]. Ideally, a system should build on the users' prior knowledge and experience, in order to create a more familiar, intuitive, easier to learn, user interface. The same principle applies not only to the robot's behavior and language characteristics but to its appearance as well. The Care-O-bot 3 robot [38], for example, contrary to its overall tecnomorphic design, uses a human-like "arm" feature to help users relate to the robot and understand its behavior (when e.g. serving drinks).

Other aspects of interest are the distribution of initiative in dialogue as well as lower-level issues such as signaling the robot's attention. Based on the dialogue initiative strategy employed, systems may range from single to mixed-initiative. In the first case only one participant (system or user) completely controls the dialogue, while in the second case both participants may initiate topics, change the dialogue flow, and adjust their plan in response to the interlocutor's input. Though many current robotic systems are user-directed systems based on a command and control language that minimizes the complexity of the recognition and interpretation process, only mixed-initiative systems can truly serve the view of HRI as collaborative interaction. The following is an example of different sub-goals being initiated by both interlocutors at each dialogue turn, which could be handled by a mixed-initiative system alone. Suppose that the robot is again ambiguously instructed to bring a box; as a result, a clarification question is initiated, such as "Should I bring the red box?". In response, the user may specify the entity at hand based on color or – if for example, the robot has misrecognized the entity's color – use a different attribute such as the object's exact location, e.g. "the box on the table". Now, based on the robot's perception of the environment, there may again be more than one entity that matches this specification. Thus, the robot could either infer the user's goal based on each object's proximity (i.e., if the user is in the kitchen, it is most likely that the referred entity is on the kitchen's table rather than in the living room) or initiate another appropriate clarification request. In general, in mixed-initiative systems, the robot often initiates conversation, goals, and sub-goals, provides suggestions, or may even ask bystanders for help.

On top of being able to address the user and initiate conversation, more significantly, a service robot needs to understand when it is being addressed. This is especially important in workgroup settings where the primary user may be interacting with other people in the robot's proximity, and so system success cannot merely rely on key phrase spotting and recognizer's robustness. Typically, dedicated commands or keywords (e.g. "hello" [10] or "robot") are used to signal the robot's attention. In Baltus et al. (2000) all utterances directed to the robot had to begin with the robot's name "Flo", in order to minimize the probability of responding to utterances not addressed to the robot itself [1]. This, however, brought redundancy to the conversation once it had been initiated. Optimally, systems should make use of other information resources such as face tracking, recognizing face and voice direction and pose, as well as dialogue state and task information in the course of interaction in conjunction with the understood spoken input. The mobile service robot described in Takiguchi et al. (2008) makes use of acoustic features in order to discriminate between commands addressed to the robot and human-human conversations [39]. Other modalities such as on/off buttons and touch screens, may also be used.

Furthermore, with regards to service robots, in particular, physical stature, personality, social and collaborative skills are all parameters that should be taken into account when designing the system, as they may affect users' perception of the system and attitude towards it along with their willingness to interact with it. According to one line of research, anthropomorphic, human-like robots promote universality, engagement, likeness, task efficiency [36, 53].

For practical systems, however, human-like appearance and behavior may trigger expectations that are not ultimately met. Unrestricted use of spoken language, mimicking emotions, humanoid appearance could elicit human-like responses that cannot be handled by current technology. Therefore, in this sense, it is important that the appearance and behaviour of the robot matches its abilities [38]. Furthermore, with regards to the robot's appearance, in particular, Butler and Agah (2001) showed that users favored smaller, "tecnomorphic" robots moving slowly, and approaching them indirectly; contrarily, large-size, humanoid robots were found to increase the level of user discomfort [40]. These results are corroborated by findings in another study according to which users disliked being directly, frontally approached by the mobile "fetch and carry" robot [41].

Also, according to Goetz et al. (2003), the successful design depends on the appropriate match between the robot's social skills/characteristics and its role in the task that it is designed for [42]. Based on their experiments, a machine-like approach was favored for more serious tasks such as security guards or lab assistants, while artistic and entertainment tasks called for a more human-like, playful, and emotional approach. According to this association, typical service robots in human-inhabited environments, such as mail delivery or floor cleaning robots, require little social skills, which could improve acceptance by the users.

Furthermore, user profiling is important for deciding upon the interaction strategy followed. Independently living elderly people, for example, maybe more interested in social interaction with a service robot given that they often live alone [1, 5] contrary to younger users who would place more significance on efficiency and task automatism. In short, social, life-like interfaces may not always be optimal interfaces, especially with regards to issues such as practical feasibility, effectiveness, and technology limitations.

Multimodality is another aspect that calls for attention [43]. For service robots, there is more to human-robot communication than verbal dialogue concerning the specification of tasks to be solved by the robot. The communication between humans and service robots can also be multimodal, incorporating verbal utterances, visual input and output, and perhaps gestures, position, and more.

All the above lead to specific approaches on the interaction (dialogue) management techniques that need to be employed, deployed, and tested in certain stages of the development.

6 Recent and Future Trends: Social Intelligence

As it has already been mentioned, the mere fact that service robots are now placed in dynamic, unstructured, and "socially oriented" environments operated by non-expert users calls for new models of interaction that build on collaborative and social skills.

According to Bartneck and Forlizzi's (2004) definition, "a social robot is an autonomous or semi-autonomous robot that interacts and communicates with humans by following the behavioral norms expected by the people with whom the robot is intended to interact" [44]. More specifically, key behavior and appearance character-istics that indicate a robot's social intelligence are [36, 44, 45]:

- Display of personality traits such as politeness, seriousness, or playfulness.
- Compliance with social norms and rules specific to each society and culture. A robot receptionist is expected to exhibit behavior accordant to the established pattern for receptionists in the particular culture in terms of social distance, politeness, use of plural form, positioning, posture, and so forth.
- Interactivity, behavior adjustment according to the specific user and interaction setting, in response to external stimuli and contextual factors in general.
- Intelligent and intentional behavior, learning skills, decision making capability and autonomy, causal and collaborative behavior, awareness of human communication principles (e.g., turn-taking protocol, Grice's (1975) co-operative principle [46]).
- Employment of natural communication modalities such as spoken language and gesturing, facial expressions, eye contact, gazing, sensing touch.
- Posture adjustments, human-like movement (for example body part movement with varying velocity [36], appropriate positioning, talk and lip synchronization.
- Physical embodiment, based on the assumption that "life and intelligence only, develops inside a body" [47].
- Gender attribution, reference in the first person (e.g. "I'll get the coffee now" as opposed to "Getting the coffee…").
- Display and understanding of emotions, empathy.

In a study conducted by de Ruyter et al. (2005), social intelligence was shown to have a positive effect on user's perception and acceptance of the robot [36]. Human-like behavior was also shown to induce more social and collaborative behavior on the user's part. With regards to the latter, however, there is a certain degree of caution and reserve, as the underlying technology has not reached adequate maturity levels, and users may overestimate and over challenge robot's abilities, which would result in a decrease in efficiency and user satisfaction as user expectations are not met [38, 48]. In this line of thought, users are claimed to be more interested in practical characteristics as opposed to human-like characteristics. Nevertheless, interfaces that make use of at least some level of social skills and intelligence have been shown to be more enjoyable, trustworthy, usable, natural, engaging, and efficient [49–52].

Similarly, robotic systems exhibiting human-like emotive behavior as a particular aspect of social intelligence can increase user engagement and compliance, improve system acceptance, and facilitate decision making and learning processes, among others [21, 53]. In this respect, they are particularly appropriate as companions for the elderly, "game partners" or in areas such as e-learning and autism therapy. Emotions may be conveyed through facial expressions, eye-gaze and head movements, gesture and posture, touch, language/utterance content, appropriate prosody manipulation, and emotive vocalizations. Ultimately, robots should also be able to evaluate the emotional state of the user, indicated through any of the above modalities – as well as any other physiological signs such as heart rate [54] – and adjust their behavior accordingly [55, 56].

With regards to the speech modality, in particular, appropriate prosody manipulation is critical not only for affective, emotive interaction but also for displaying and communicating context-awareness. It is generally acknowledged that prosody is associated with the organization of information in an utterance, indicating how an utterance relates to the situational context [57]. For example, speakers may place pitch accents on different elements of the utterance in order to distinguish between new and given information (i.e., information that is already part of the common ground) or acknowledge the existence of alternative referents relevant to the entity under discussion (intonational contrast). Violation of intonation related grammar principles may lead to an ungrammatical, confusing, and unnatural spoken output. A model for the production of context-aware intonation in human-robot situated dialogue that is sensitive to such principles has been developed within the CogX project. The model assigns appropriate intonation patterns to convey properties such as contrast, theme-rheme distinction, uncertainty, and commitment [29] and, in this manner, support adaptation, and transparency in HRI.

7 Conclusion

This paper presented basic design principles and methodologies for the development of Spoken Dialogue Interfaces for service robots. Even more than traditional computer applications, the use of intelligent robots encourages the view of the machine as a partner in communication rather than as a tool. This suggests that people can be expected to apply more naturalness in the form of modalities and richness of interaction than in ordinary human-computer interfaces. As a result, SDIs that allow for voice as primary means of interaction have become central for the development of usable systems, especially taking into account that service robots are now typically operated by non-expert users to perform a variety of tasks in unstructured, dynamic environments.

Furthermore, contrary to on-screen, software agents or telephony-based spoken dialogue systems, mobile service robots must also reason about the spatial environment they operate in; the environment in which the robots act and the users live, the shared space between them, the location and the objects available shape the shared sub-world that the communication knowledge is drawn upon and complex use scenarios are formed. This situated form of human-robot interaction crucially affects standard design and usability evaluation methodologies, which must be adjusted to comply with these particular aspects of HRI. In this respect, design methodology should not be merely user-centered but situation and usability centered.

Similarly, usability evaluation approaches and metrics should be adjusted to appropriately address interface aspects important for HRI, such as physical embodiment, mobility, social relationships, collaboration, anthropomorphism, personalized communication, and multi-user interaction.

Acknowledgments. This work has been co-financed by the National and Kapodistrian University of Athens, Special Account for Research Grants.

References

1. Baltus, G., et al.: Towards personal service robots for the elderly. In: Workshop Interactive Robots and Entertainment (WIRE 2000) (2000). https://doi.org/10.1007/s12369-014-0232-4
2. Granata, C., Chetouani, M., Tapus, A., Bidaud, P., Dupourqué, V.: Voice and graphical-based interfaces for interaction with a robot dedicated to elderly and people with cognitive disorders. In: Proceedings of the IEEE International Workshop on Robot and Human Interactive Communication (2010). https://doi.org/10.1109/ROMAN.2010.5598698
3. Fang, H., et al.: From captions to visual concepts and back. In: Proceedings of the IEEE Computer Society Conference on Computer Vision and Pattern Recognition (2015). https://doi.org/10.1109/CVPR.2015.7298754
4. Kruijff, G.J.M., Zender, H., Jensfelt, P., Christensen, H.I.: Situated dialogue and understanding spatial organization: knowing what is where and what you can do there. In: Proceedings of the IEEE International Workshop on Robot and Human Interactive Communication (2006). https://doi.org/10.1109/ROMAN.2006.314438
5. Severinson-Eklundh, K., Green, A., Hüttenrauch, H.: Social and collaborative aspects of interaction with a service robot. Robot. Auton. Syst. (2003). https://doi.org/10.1016/S0921-8890(02)00377-9
6. Stephanidis, C., Akoumianakis, D., Sfyrakis, M., Paramythis, A.: Universal accessibility in HCI : process-oriented design guidelines and tool requirements. In: 4th ERCIM Workshop User Interfaces All (1998)
7. Torta, E., Oberzaucher, J., Werner, F., Cuijpers, R.H., Juola, J.F.: Attitudes towards socially assistive robots in intelligent homes: results from laboratory studies and field trials. J. Hum.-Robot Interact. (2013). https://doi.org/10.5898/jhri.1.2.torta
8. Zobel, M., et al.: MOBSY: integration of vision and dialogue in service robots. In: Schiele, B., Sagerer, G. (eds.) ICVS 2001. LNCS, vol. 2095, pp. 50–62. Springer, Heidelberg (2001). https://doi.org/10.1007/3-540-48222-9_4
9. Tao, Y., Wei, H., Wang, T.: A speech interaction system based on finite state machine for service robot. In: Proceedings of the International Conference on Computer Science and Software Engineering, CSSE 2008 (2008). https://doi.org/10.1109/CSSE.2008.627
10. Matsui, T., et al.: Integrated natural spoken dialogue system of Jijo-2 mobile robot for office services. In: Proceedings of the National Conference on Artificial Intelligence (1999)
11. Wilske, S., Kruijff, G.J.: Service robots dealing with indirect speech acts. In: IEEE International Conference on Intelligent Robots and Systems (2006). https://doi.org/10.1109/IROS.2006.282259
12. Martin. D.J., Jurasky, D.: Speech and language processing: an introduction to natural language processing. In: SPEECH Language Processing An Introduction to Natural Language Processing Computational Linguistic Speech Recognition (2001)
13. Xydas, G., Spiliotopoulos, D., Kouroupetroglou, G.: Modeling prosodic structures in linguistically enriched environments. In: Sojka, P., Kopeček, I., Pala, K. (eds.) TSD 2004. LNCS (LNAI), vol. 3206, pp. 521–528. Springer, Heidelberg (2004). https://doi.org/10.1007/978-3-540-30120-2_66
14. Spiliotopoulos, D., Xydas, G., Kouroupetroglou, G.: Diction based prosody modeling in table-to-speech synthesis. In: Matoušek, V., Mautner, P., Pavelka, T. (eds.) TSD 2005. LNCS (LNAI), vol. 3658, pp. 294–301. Springer, Heidelberg (2005). https://doi.org/10.1007/11551874_38

15. Spiliotopoulos, D., Androutsopoulos, I., Spyropoulos, C.D.: Human-robot interaction based on spoken natural language dialogue. In: Proceedings of the European Workshop on Service and Humanoid Robots, pp. 25–27 (2001)
16. Xydas, G., Spiliotopoulos, D., Kouroupetroglou, G.: Modeling emphatic events from non-speech aware documents in speech based user interfaces. In: Proceedings of Human Computer Interaction, pp. 806–810 (2003)
17. McTear, M.F.: Spoken dialogue technology: enabling the conversational user interface. ACM Comput. Surv. (2002). https://doi.org/10.1145/505282.505285
18. Burgard, W., et al.: Experiences with an interactive museum tour-guide robot. Artif. Intell. (1999). https://doi.org/10.1016/s0004-3702(99)00070-3
19. Siegwart, R., et al.: Robox at expo.02: a large-scale installation of personal robots. Robot. Auton. Syst. (2003). https://doi.org/10.1016/S0921-8890(02)00376-7
20. Dominey, P.F., Mallet, A., Yoshida, E.: Progress in programming the HRP-2 humanoid using spoken language. In: Proceedings of the IEEE International Conference on Robotics and Automation (2007). https://doi.org/10.1109/ROBOT.2007.363642
21. Picard, R.W.: Affective computing: challenges. Int. J. Hum Comput Stud. (2003). https://doi.org/10.1016/S1071-5819(03)00052-1
22. Hüttenrauch, H., Green, A., Norman, M., Oestreicher, L., Eklundh, K.S.: Involving users in the design of a mobile office robot. IEEE Trans. Syst. Man Cybern. Part C Appl. Rev. (2004). https://doi.org/10.1109/TSMCC.2004.826281
23. Tenbrink, T., Hui, S.: Negotiating spatial goals with a wheelchair. In: Proceedings of the 8th SIGdial Workshop on Discourse and Dialogue (2007)
24. Kruijff, G.J.M., Zender, H., Jensfelt, P., Christensen, H.I.: Situated dialogue and spatial organization: what, where... and why? Int. J. Adv. Robot. Syst. (2007). https://doi.org/10.5772/5701
25. Leech, G.: Principles of Pragmatics (2016). https://doi.org/10.4324/9781315835976
26. Clark, H.H., Schaefer, E.F.: Contributing to discourse. Cogn. Sci. (1989). https://doi.org/10.1016/0364-0213(89)90008-6
27. Brennan, S.E., Hulteen, E.A.: Interaction and feedback in a spoken language system: a theoretical framework. Knowl.-Based Syst. (1995). https://doi.org/10.1016/0950-7051(95)98376-H
28. Steedman, M.: Information structure and the syntax-phonology interface. Linguist. Inq. (2000). https://doi.org/10.1162/002438900554505
29. Kruijff-Korbayová, I., Meena, R., Pyykkönen, P.: Perception of visual scene and intonation patterns of robot utterances. In: HRI 2011 - Proceedings of the 6th ACM/IEEE International Conference on Human-Robot Interaction (2011). https://doi.org/10.1145/1957656.1957717
30. Cohen, M.H., Giangola, J.P., Balogh, J.: Introduction to voice user interfaces (2004)
31. Blandford, A.: Semi-structured qualitative studies. In: Encyclopedia Human-Computer Interaction (2013)
32. Yankelovich, N., Levow, G.A., Marx, M.: Designing speechActs: issues in speech user interfaces. In: Proceedings of the Conference on Human Factors in Computing Systems (1995)
33. Austin, J.L.: How to Do Things with Words. Harvard University Press, Cambridge (1975)
34. Allen, J.: Natural Language Understanding. Pearson, New Delhi (1995)
35. Fraser, N.M., Gilbert, G.N.: Simulating speech systems. Comput. Speech Lang. (1991). https://doi.org/10.1016/0885-2308(91)90019-M
36. De Ruyter, B., Saini, P., Markopoulos, P., Van Breemen, A.: Assessing the effects of building social intelligence in a robotic interface for the home. Interact. Comput. (2005). https://doi.org/10.1016/j.intcom.2005.03.003

37. Weinschenk, S., Barker, D.: Designing Effective Speech Interfaces. Wiley, Hoboken (2000)
38. Parlitz, C., Häagele, M., Klein, P., Seifert, J., Dautenhahn, K.: Care-O-bot 3 - rationale for human-robot interaction design. In: 39th International Symposium on Robotics, ISR 2008 (2008)
39. Takiguchi, T., Sako, A., Revaud, J., Yamagata, T., Miyake, N., Ariki, Y.: Human-robot interface using system request utterance detection based on acoustic features. In: Proceedings of the 2008 International Conference on Multimedia and Ubiquitous Engineering, MUE 2008 (2008). https://doi.org/10.1109/MUE.2008.87
40. Butler, J.T., Agah, A.: Psychological effects of behavior patterns of a mobile personal robot. Auton. Robots (2001). https://doi.org/10.1023/A:1008986004181
41. Dautenhahn, K., et al.: How may I serve you? A robot companion approaching a seated person in a helping context. In: HRI 2006: Proceedings of the 2006 ACM Conference on Human-Robot Interaction (2006)
42. Goetz, J., Kiesler, S., Powers, A.: Matching robot appearance and behavior to tasks to improve human-robot cooperation. In: Proceedings of the IEEE International Workshop on Robot and Human Interactive Communication (2003). https://doi.org/10.1109/ROMAN.2003.1251796
43. Alexandersson, J., et al.: Metalogue: A multiperspective multimodal dialogue system with metacognitive abilities for highly adaptive and flexible dialogue management. In: Proceedings of the 2014 International Conference on Intelligent Environments, IE 2014, pp. 365–368 (2014). https://doi.org/10.1109/IE.2014.67
44. Bartneck, C., Forlizzi, J.: A design-centred framework for social human-robot interaction. In: Proceedings of the IEEE International Workshop on Robot and Human Interactive Communication (2004). https://doi.org/10.1109/roman.2004.1374827
45. Fong, T., Nourbakhsh, I., Dautenhahn, K.: A survey of socially interactive robots. Robot. Auton. Syst. (2003). https://doi.org/10.1016/S0921-8890(02)00372-X
46. Grice, H.P.: Logic and conversation. In: Syntax and Semantics. Speech Arts, vol. 3 (1975)
47. Dautenhahn, K.: Embodiment and interaction in socially intelligent life-like agents. In: Nehaniv, C.L. (ed.) CMAA 1998. LNCS (LNAI), vol. 1562, pp. 102–141. Springer, Heidelberg (1999). https://doi.org/10.1007/3-540-48834-0_7
48. Pearson, J., Hu, J., Branigan, H.P., Pickering, M.J., Nass, C.I.: Adaptive language behavior in HCI: how expectations and beliefs about a system affect users' word choice. In: Proceedings of the Conference on Human Factors in Computing Systems (2006)
49. Bickmore, T., Cassell, J.: Relational agents: a model and implementation of building user trust. In: Proceedings of the Conference on Human Factors in Computing Systems (2001)
50. Heylen, D., Es, I., Nijholt, A., Dijk, E.: Experimenting with the gaze of a conversational agent. In: Proceedings of the International CLASS Workshop Natural Intelligent and Effective Interaction Multimodal Dialogue Systems (2002)
51. Bartneck, C.: Interacting with an embodied emotional character. In: Proceedings of the International Conference on Designing Pleasurable Products and Interfaces (2003). https://doi.org/10.1145/782910.782911
52. Bruce, A., Nourbakhsh, I., Simmons, R.: The role of expressiveness and attention in human-robot interaction. In: Proceedings of the IEEE International Conference on Robotics and Automation (2002). https://doi.org/10.1109/robot.2002.1014396
53. Breazeal, C.: Affective interaction between humans and robots. In: Kelemen, J., Sosík, P. (eds.) ECAL 2001. LNCS (LNAI), vol. 2159, pp. 582–591. Springer, Heidelberg (2001). https://doi.org/10.1007/3-540-44811-X_66
54. Kulíc, D., Croft, E.: Affective state estimation for human-robot interaction. In: IEEE Trans. Robot. (2007). https://doi.org/10.1109/TRO.2007.904899

55. Breazeal, C.: Designing sociable robots. In: Designing Sociable Robots (2018). https://doi.org/10.7551/mitpress/2376.003.0007
56. Dautenhahn, K.: Socially intelligent agents - the human in the loop (2001). https://doi.org/10.1109/TSMCA.2001.952709
57. Spiliotopoulos, D., Xydas, G., Kouroupetroglou, G., Argyropoulos, V., Ikospentaki, K.: Auditory universal accessibility of data tables using naturally derived prosody specification. Univ. Access Inf. Soc. 9 (2010). https://doi.org/10.1007/s10209-009-0165-0

Robotic Cane for the Visually Impaired

José Varela-Aldás[1]([⊠]) [ID], John Guamán[1] [ID], Belén Paredes[1] [ID],
and Fernando A. Chicaiza[2] [ID]

[1] SISAu Research Group, Universidad Tecnológica Indoamérica,
180103 Ambato, Ecuador
josevarela@uti.edu.ec, davidguaman6@gmail.com,
balupards@gmail.com
[2] Instituto de Automática, Universidad Nacional de San Juan,
5400 San Juan, Argentina
fachicaiza@inaut.unsj.edu.ar

Abstract. Currently, there is a growing public interest in improving the quality of life of people with disabilities, being the visual limitation one of them, where different research projects have been developed. Assistance robotics is a branch dedicated to the support in mobility and rehabilitation of people with visual disabilities and other limitations. This work describes the construction and use of a robotic cane to assist people with visual problems. The robot structure is generated by 3D printing, and the electronic system has been designed based on Arduino technology. The robot features include a sensor distance to detect possible collisions, a GPS to track its movements, and two DC motors in caterpillar-like configuration for cane mobility. In addition, the robot has connectivity with mobile devices through Bluetooth communication, where the mobile application coordinates the movements of the robot in two ways, manual and autonomous, allowing to reach the desired location and sending the user's location to the web. This proposal is tested in a structured environment so that patients cast their perspective through a usability test and their characteristics are examined through the analysis of an expert.

Keywords: Robotic cane · Visual impairment · Mobile robot · App

1 Introduction

The interaction of a living being with its surroundings is carried out through the use of the senses, being the vision one of the fundamental ones that allow both the manipulation of objects and the displacement in spaces, whether they are structured or unstructured [1]. However, a condition in the visual sense greatly limits an individual in the way he/she interacts with his environment. In fact, until 2010 approximately 285 million people with visual disabilities were reported in the world, of which 39 million are blind and 246 million have a low vision [2]. To mitigate this problem and provide opportunities for inclusion to people with these limitations, appropriate languages, methods, and techniques have been developed for people to use other senses such as touch and hearing to compensate for visual impairment [3]. Mainly, independent displacement is a challenge for people with vision problems, particularly in unstructured

M. Antona and C. Stephanidis (Eds.): HCII 2020, LNCS 12188, pp. 506–517, 2020.
https://doi.org/10.1007/978-3-030-49282-3_36

or unknown environments. In this case, other people or guide dogs are required to support the blind, however, the first solution involves costs that often are not in the possibilities of the disabled, while guide dogs can help evade obstacles but being red-green color blind and unable to interpret street signs could present problems for guiding [4]. From another perspective, navigation assistance technologies try to provide additional support to users by increasing recognition of their environment or serving as a guide in places that have adequate infrastructure for blind people, but precise solutions are not yet widely available in cases where cities are not adapted for this type of people, especially in developing countries [5]. For its part, assistance robotics seeks to provide a greater benefit for people with visual disabilities through robots that can be customized according to the blind, considering characteristics such as their level of blindness, age, height, and so on [6], this with the objective of providing greater opportunities for disabled people, giving them independence and improving their inclusion in society [7].

Apart from the solutions given for the industry, robotics has evolved to support society. Assistance robotics tries to provide support in daily tasks that are developed by people who commonly do not have any type of disability. In this context, in recent years assistance robots have given significant support to people suffering from some type of disability, either to improve their lifestyle at the time of performing domestic work or improving rehabilitation techniques that speed up a patient's recovery [8]. On the other hand, the use of robotics for the assistance of people with visual disabilities has had an important contribution in recent years, whether through camera arrangements, presence sensors or some type of robotic stick, the same that can have some kind of feedback, either sound or through forces.

The proposals that support blind people in the field of robotics are diverse. In this regard, in the case where blind people have to interact in buildings such as hotels and shops, solutions such as the one shown in [9] are presented, where the implemented robot is focused on welcoming the user, showing three forms of assistance (sighted guide, escort, and Information Kiosk), in addition to receiving infrastructure information from the robot. With the condition that the robotic mechanism knows the building's layout, the mechanism can provide assistance that does not depend on third parties to facilitate the location of the affected person within a highly traveled area. Likewise, some works have focused on the latest technology lenses to support people with visual limitations. [10] raises the use of intelligent Smart glass for visually impaired using Deep learning machine vision techniques and ROS (Robot Operating System). The work presents the fusion of GPS devices, head-phones, ultrasonic, and an information processor (Raspberry Pi Zero) to provide visual support for the recognition of objects present in the path of a user with visual limitations. A work of similar characteristics is presented by [11], where the arrangement of wireless sensors connected to a main camera and a speaker allows detecting obstacles through the recognition of spaces where the user walks. Solutions based on robots that move on the ground to detect obstacles in the area on which users walk are other forms of support for blind users. Indeed, a system that can equip the traditional canes with sensors that detect obstacles beyond the reach of the patient's hands can foresee dangers when traveling over unknown spaces. In this case, [12–14] propose a cane-type robot as a guide in semi-structured interior spaces. Unlike navigation with guide dogs, users of this type of proposals claim that it increases their confidence, sense of security, and confidence with this type of robots that are shown as the solution to free mobility and sense of independence for blind people, especially for places which don't have the necessary infrastructure to guide these types of people.

The present work shows the design of an intelligent cane which serves as a support for the user to overcome obstacles positioned along the path of his walk. In order to achieve mobilization in unfamiliar areas, the designed cane has an ultrasonic sensor, a GPS module, sound notification devices, vibration devices, and a structure based on two engines with a caterpillar-type traction system. This document is divided into 6 sections. In the first section, the introduction and state of the art are presented. The second section mentions the formulation of the problem, while the fourth shows the development of the proposal. The fifth section indicates the results obtained and finally, the sixth section presents the Discussions and Conclusions.

2   Problem Formulation

The purpose of the robotic cane is to facilitate the mobility of people with visual disabilities, for which it is important to design the robot based on the requirements of the visually impaired. Figure 1 shows the components of the proposed robot, presenting an Arduino Nano as a system information processor. The components required in the robot are an ultrasonic sensor for the evasion of obstacles, a GPS module for localization, a Bluetooth module for external connectivity, a motor driver and 2 DC motors for mobility, and a vibration motor to alert potential shocks.

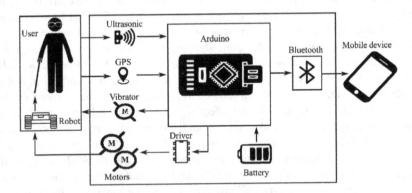

Fig. 1. General diagram of the proposed robotic cane.

Regarding connectivity, it is intended to link the robot to a mobile device via a wireless connection that allows bidirectional communication. The application of the mobile device controls the actions of the robot according to the mobility needs of the cane, for this, the app uses the basic motion equations of the mobile robot. In addition, the App takes GPS data to record and share data, so that the users' supervisory can access the information collected on the robot through the web.

3 Proposal Development

3.1 Motion Equations

The movements of the robot are executed by means of a unicycle-type mobile located at the end of the cane, so that it pulls the user in the desired direction. To improve traction on uneven terrain, the mobile robot is designed using caterpillars, although this proposal focuses on structured work spaces. Figure 2 shows the parameters for the movements of the mobile robot.

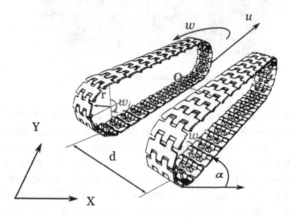

Fig. 2. Parameters of motion equations.

The movements allowed in a mobile unicycle type robot are: linear speed (1), which moves the robot forward and backward; and, angular speed (2), which allows the robot to rotate on its own axis. The equations of motion are a function of the angular velocity of the right motor ω_d, the angular velocity of the left motor ω_i, the radius of the caterpillar r, and the distance between caterpillar d.

$$u = (\omega_d + \omega_i)\, r/2 \tag{1}$$

$$\omega = (\omega_d - \omega_i) r/d \tag{2}$$

3.2 Hardware

The physical components of the robot are designed in a way that optimizes space and reduces weight to facilitate movement. Figure 3 shows the 3D model made in Tinkercad; in the front part the spaces to locate the distance sensor are observed, in the sides the driving gears and support gears are located to install the caterpillar, in the upper part each space for the electrical elements is distinguished; At the rear, the perforation is observed to insert the cane tube. All these components are generated by 3D printing with polyacid lactic (PLA).

Fig. 3. 3D design of mobile robot.

Another of the hardware-related systems is the electronic circuit, the components used are low cost (60–80 USD). In Fig. 4, the proposed circuit implemented in the Fritzing software can be seen, all the input and output elements are connected to the Arduino Nano. A 9 V battery provides the power supply for the operation of the sensors, actuators, and controllers; two motors of continuous current and a driver TB6612NG that allows to control the speed and the direction of rotation; a Bluetooth module (HC-06) connects directly to the serial communication pins; the vibration motor is controlled using a BJT transistor, with a 1 K resistor connected to the transistor base; distance (HC-SR04) and positioning (GPS) sensors use digital pins for data reading.

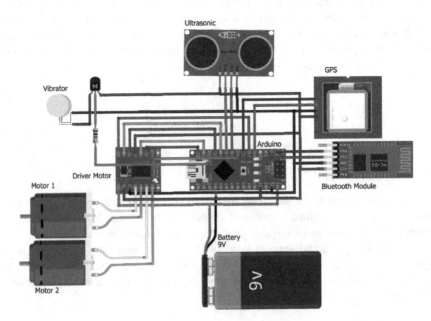

Fig. 4. Electronic circuit of the mobile robot.

3.3   Software

The robotic cane works with two programs, the main program installed in the Arduino software, and the user interface developed in a mobile application. Figure 5 presents the main program algorithm. At startup, the configuration of the robot's outputs and inputs is made; the sensors then read data and send the robot's position to the mobile device via Bluetooth; the robot receives the App's orders according to the movements required to move to the desired location. In case of possible collision, the robot sends an alert to the user through shaking actions and corrects the movement by rotation.

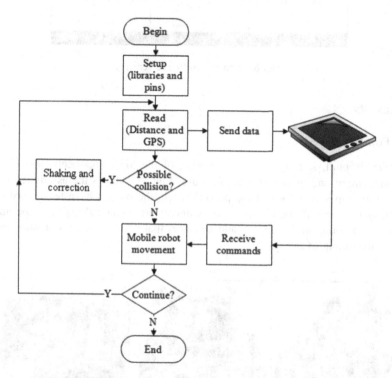

Fig. 5. Flowchart of the main program.

The mobile application is developed in App Inventor 2, with support for mobile devices with Android operating system. Figure 6 shows the screens that make up the user interface of the App; in the start window the user selects the type of control to be performed. Manual control allows to command the robot movements by pressing buttons, this option is for the caregiver, allowing the user to be guided as required; and autonomous control (tracking) allows you to choose a location on the map, in this case the application sends the movement orders to move to the destination. In addition, the mobile application graphs all robot positions and records them in a non-SQL database (Firebase), which is accessed from a web browser connected to the Internet.

Fig. 6. App user interface screens.

4 Results

4.1 Functional Tests

The robot is built, starting from the printing of the 3D components, installing the electronic circuit and running the applications. Figure 7 shows the assembled mobile robot, in the top part is located the power switch, the motors have been fixed to the traction system, and all the electronic components are contained inside. Experimental tests are carried out on the sensors and actuators that make up the robot, showing the correct functioning of the system.

Fig. 7. Mobile robot built for the robotic cane.

Evaluating the control of the movement in a structured environment (the consistency of the ground and the obstacles to evade is known) a destination is set in the mobile application and this sends the orders to the robotic cane. The route traveled by the robot is observed in Fig. 8, the application screen shows the path followed by the robot to reach the desired position with the instructions generated, where obstacles are avoided as they appear, so, the data sent to the database is displayed on the web using latitude and longitude coordinates.

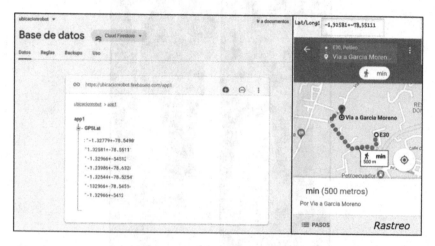

Fig. 8. Robotic cane positions presented in the mobile application and web address.

4.2 Participants

To study the proposal from the user's point of view, tests were carried out on 4 patients with visual impairment who belong to the "Association of blind workers of Ambato", who were interested in the possibility of being assisted daily by this technology, but other members of the association refused to participate in the tests due to fear of accident. Figure 9 shows the participants using the robotic stick in the experiments performed.

4.3 Usability Test

Once the experiments have been carried out on the patients, the System Usability Scale SUS is applied, which allows measuring the level of compliance of the users with the benefits of the proposal. Table 1 shows the results of the usability test with a score of 68.125/100 of usability, this implies a certain disagreement with the characteristics of the robotic cane, especially regarding the frequent use and safety provided by the robot, this is because the users have no control of the movements and this creates fear and insecurity, according to the patients.

4.4 Medical Perspective

To analyze this proposal from a medical perspective, an optometrist doctor is interviewed, who witnessed the experiments, the analysis is carried out based on four topics detailed below:

Fig. 9. Participants of the experiments carried out with the robotic cane.

Table 1. Results of system usability scale.

Question	Score N = 4	Operation
I think I would like to use this system frequently	2	1
I find this system unnecessarily complex	**1**	**4**
I think the system is easy to use	4.5	3.5
I think you would need technical support to make use of the system	**1.75**	**3.25**
I find the various functions of the system quite well integrated	**4.5**	**3.5**
I have found too much inconsistency in this system	2	3
I think most people would learn to make use of the system quickly	**4**	**3**
I found the system quite uncomfortable to use	2	3
I have felt very safe using the system	**1.5**	**0.5**
I would need to learn a lot of things before I can manage the system	2.5	2.5
Total		27.25 × 2.5 = 68.125

- *Design of the robotic cane.* The system only detects a frontal point of depth, this is not favorable because the obstacles have irregular shapes and generate several levels of depth that must be considered in evasion. In addition, users of conventional canes are not used to being dragged and prefer to have control of their movements. However, the proposal can be useful in patients in the training stage, who could get used to this mobility method.
- *Needs of the patient.* This proposal has useful components to cover the needs of patients with visual impairment, but user comfort must be considered when directing it to the desired destination, so that it must support its mobility instead of making it independent.
- *Technology built into the cane.* The world is experiencing a technological era and the assistance teams must have the greatest amount of technologies incorporated. Specifically, this robot has a good advance when using a mobile device as a support tool, but requires connectivity with more external components that help in the mobility of the person with visual impairment.
- *Improvement.* The system should fully scan the surrounding environment, including soil characteristics, and then determine the best movements to reach the destination. In addition, the user should have control of the robot's speed, this could be done manually on the handle of the cane. Finally, obstacle feedback should be subtler, so that the patient does not panic in case of possible collisions.

5 Discussions and Conclusions

Assistive technologies are constantly developing, so new products are continuously implemented to improve the quality of life of people with disabilities. Patients with visual impairment require daily mobility aids, these devices can be incorporated into the conventional cane and improve the assistance characteristics. In this work a robotic cane is built based on a caterpillar mobile robot, so that it moves the patient to their destination, for this an obstacle sensor and a GPS have been incorporated. The robot is controlled by a mobile application that provides the tools to direct the movements manually or autonomously, the robot's position is always sent to a database of a web server. Experiments in real patients show that the cane meets the objectives set, and the usability test indicates some dissatisfaction with some characteristics of the robot, specifically with the insecurity caused by the actions of the cane, because the user is unaware of the movements the robot will perform. Finally, a specialist doctor recognizes the positive aspects of the proposal and criticizes the shortcomings, highlighting the lack of environment data and a movement speed control for the user.

The revised bibliography describes works with sensors and actuators similar to this proposal, displacing robots in structured and semi-structured environments, marking the main difference with this work in the use of a mobile device as a support element to control and direct the movements of the robot, including the database that continuously reports the position of the robot. In addition, this work is carried out using low-cost devices, unlike the laboratory robots used in others research, this allows the prototype to be replicated if necessary. Finally, the criticisms stated in the proposal serve as a starting point for new products and future work.

References

1. Krishna, S., Panchanathan, S.: Assistive technologies as effective mediators in interpersonal social interactions for persons with visual disability. In: Miesenberger, K., Klaus, J., Zagler, W., Karshmer, A. (eds.) ICCHP 2010. LNCS, vol. 6180, pp. 316–323. Springer, Heidelberg (2010). https://doi.org/10.1007/978-3-642-14100-3_47
2. Pascolini, D., Mariotti, S.: Global data on visual impairments. Br. J. Ophthalmol. (2010). https://doi.org/10.1136/bjophthalmol-2011-300539
3. Rajapandian, B., Harini, V., Raksha, D., Sangeetha, V.: A novel approach as an AID for blind, deaf and dumb people. In: Proceedings of 2017 3rd IEEE International Conference on Sensing, Signal Processing and Security, ICSSS 2017, pp. 403–408. Institute of Electrical and Electronics Engineers Inc. (2017). https://doi.org/10.1109/SSPS.2017.8071628
4. Park, D., et al.: Active robot-assisted feeding with a general-purpose mobile manipulator: design, evaluation, and lessons learned. Robot. Auton. Syst. **124** (2020). https://doi.org/10.1016/j.robot.2019.103344
5. Herrera, D., Roberti, F., Carelli, R., Andaluz, V., Varela, J., Ortiz, J.: Modeling and path-following control of a wheelchair in human-shared environments. Int. J. Humanoid Robot. **15**, 1–33 (2018). https://doi.org/10.1142/S021984361850010X
6. Guerreiro, J., Sato, D., Ahmetovic, D., Ohn-Bar, E., Kitani, K.M., Asakawa, C.: Virtual navigation for blind people: Transferring route knowledge to the real-World. Int. J. Hum. Comput. Stud. **135** (2020). https://doi.org/10.1016/j.ijhcs.2019.102369
7. Bolotnikova, A., Courtois, S., Kheddar, A.: Multi-contact planning on humans for physical assistance by humanoid. IEEE Robot. Autom. Lett., 1–8 (2019). https://doi.org/10.1109/lra.2019.2947907
8. Bonani, M., Oliveira, R., Correia, Filipa Rodrigues, A., Guerreiro, T., Paiva, A.: What my eyes can't see, a robot can show me: exploring the collaboration between blind people and robots. In: The 20th International ACM SIGACCESS Conference, pp. 15–27 (2018). https://doi.org/10.1145/3234695.3239330
9. Mohammed, S., Park, H.W., Park, C.H., Amirat, Y., Argall, B.: Special issue on assistive and rehabilitation robotics. Auton. Robots, 513–517 (2017). https://doi.org/10.1007/s10514-017-9627-z
10. Azenkot, S., Feng, C., Cakmak, M.: Enabling building service robots to guide blind people a participatory design approach. In: 11th ACM/IEEE International Conference on Human-Robot Interaction (HRI). IEEE (2016). https://doi.org/10.1109/HRI.2016.7451727
11. Suresh, A., Arora, C., Laha, D., Gaba, D., Bhambri, S.: Intelligent smart glass for visually impaired using deep learning machine vision techniques and Robot Operating System (ROS). In: Kim, J.-H., et al. (eds.) RiTA 2017. AISC, vol. 751, pp. 99–112. Springer, Cham (2019). https://doi.org/10.1007/978-3-319-78452-6_10
12. Vera, D., Marcillo, D., Pereira, A.: Blind guide: anytime, anywhere solution for guiding blind people. In: Rocha, Á., Correia, A.M., Adeli, H., Reis, L.P., Costanzo, S. (eds.) WorldCIST 2017. AISC, vol. 570, pp. 353–363. Springer, Cham (2017). https://doi.org/10.1007/978-3-319-56538-5_36

13. Guerreiro, J., Sato, D., Asakawa, S., Dong, H., Kitani, K.M., Asakawa, C.: CaBot: designing and evaluating an autonomous. In: ASSETS 2019: The 21st International ACM SIGACCESS Conference on Computers and Accessibility, pp. 68–82 (2019). https://doi.org/10.1145/3308561.3353771
14. Megalingam, R.K., Vishnu, S., Sasikumar, V., Sreekumar, S.: autonomous path guiding robot for visually impaired people. In: Mallick, P.K., Balas, V.E., Bhoi, A.K., Zobaa, Ahmed F. (eds.) Cognitive Informatics and Soft Computing. AISC, vol. 768, pp. 257–266. Springer, Singapore (2019). https://doi.org/10.1007/978-981-13-0617-4_25
15. Noman, A.T., Chowdhury, M.A.M., Rashid, H., Rahman Faisal, S.M.S., Ahmed, I.U., Reza, S.M.T.: Design and implementation of microcontroller based assistive robot for person with blind autism and visual impairment. In: 20th International Conference of Computer and Information Technology (ICCIT). IEEE (2017). https://doi.org/10.1109/ICCITECHN.2017.8281806

Author Index

Printed in the United States
By Bookmasters